An Introduction To the Law of Business Organizations

CASES, NOTES AND QUESTIONS

Third Edition

■ ■ ■

By

Stephen B. Presser

Raoul Berger Professor of Legal History
Northwestern University School of Law
Professor of Business Law
Kellogg School of Management
Northwestern University

AMERICAN CASEBOOK SERIES®

WEST®

A Thomson Reuters business

Mat #40903566

American Casebook Series is a trademark registered in the U.S. Patent and Trademark Office.

© West, a Thomson business, 2005, 2008
© 2010 Thomson Reuters
    610 Opperman Drive
    St. Paul, MN 55123
    1–800–313–9378
Printed in the United States of America

ISBN: 978–0–314–91243–5

To David, Elisabeth,
Joseph and Eastman

PREFACE TO THE THIRD EDITION

Law school casebooks are works in progress, and this third edition seeks to make the book even more accessible to its dual primary audiences of law students and management school students. To that end, the glossary has been supplemented, the longest and increasingly less influential case, *Omnicare*, has been eliminated and two shorter cases substituted (*Paramount v. Time*, and *Paramount v. QVC*); notes on current developments, particularly those regarding the duty to monitor, have been added; and materials have been augmented by consideration of two wonderful introductory guides to the law of corporations, Jonathan R. Macey, Ed., The Iconic Cases in Corporate Law (2008) and J. Mark Ramseyer, Ed., Corporate Law Stories (2009), either of which would be a fine addition to the library of any aspiring lawyer or manager.

I want to express my continuing gratitude to Louis Higgins and Bonnie Karlen of Thomson/Reuters, who have encouraged my work for more than a decade, and to my assistant Tim Jacobs, without whose aid I would be paralyzed. Northwestern's Dean David Van Zandt, and its Associate Deans for Research, David Dana and Kimberly Yuracko, have been similarly supportive. Finally, my law student research assistants for the summer of 2009, Kirt Gallatin, Andrew Neustein, Corey Walker, Andrew Zures, and my undergraduate intern, Daniel Innamorati, gave me the delightful feeling that I was a senior partner in a small boutique law firm, rather than a harried pedagogue. As I have requested in the past, any suggestions for future revisions from students, faculty, or other readers would be gratefully received.

STEPHEN B. PRESSER
s-presser@law.northwestern.edu

Chicago, Illinois
December, 2009

PREFACE TO THE SECOND EDITION

This second edition is designed even further to facilitate the use of this introductory text by both business school and law students. The major alteration is the addition of a glossary, which appears at the end of the book. Words highlighted in light gray in the text are briefly defined in that appendix. Much fuller definitions can generally be obtained on the web, or in a first-class law dictionary, such as Black's Law Dictionary, which is recommended as an indispensible reference for any one working with the law, as, alas, managers these days must. Two other substantive changes are also included, a note on the requirement of "good faith" in Delaware law discussing the recent Disney case, and a note on the recent rejection by the SEC of a "shareholder access" proposal, which would have required publicly-listed corporations to permit shareholders to put forth nominations for Boards of Directors. Let me once again express my gratitude to my assistant, Tim Jacobs for help in the preparation of the manuscript, and to David Van Zandt, Northwestern University School of Law's Dean, and David Dana, the Associate Dean for Faculty and Research, who provided summer support which made possible the first and second editions. As before, any suggestions from faculty or students with regard to subjects in need of omission, alteration, or expansion are invited.

STEPHEN B. PRESSER
s-presser@law.northwestern.edu

Chicago, Illinois
February, 2008

Summary of Contents

TABLE OF CONTENTS

TABLE OF CASES

The principal cases are in bold type. Cases cited or discussed in the text are in roman type. References are to pages. Cases cited in principal cases and within other quoted materials are not included.

TABLE OF AUTHORITIES

References are to pages.

AN INTRODUCTION TO THE LAW OF BUSINESS ORGANIZATIONS
CASES, NOTES AND QUESTIONS

Third Edition

CHAPTER 1

INTRODUCTION TO LAW

■ ■ ■

A. PROPERTY

PIERSON v. POST

Supreme Court of New York.
3 Cai. R. 175, 2 Am. Dec. 264 (1805).

* * *

This was an action of trespass on the case commenced in a justice's court, by the present defendant against the now plaintiff.

The declaration stated that *Post,* being in possession of certain dogs and hounds under his command, did, "upon a certain wild and uninhabited, unpossessed and waste land, called the beach, find and start one of those noxious beasts called a fox," and whilst there hunting, chasing and pursuing the same with his dogs and hounds, and when in view thereof, *Pierson,* well knowing the fox was so hunted and pursued, did, in the sight of *Post,* to prevent his catching the same, kill and carry it off. A verdict having been rendered for the plaintiff below, the defendant there sued out a *certiorari* [petition for an appeal], and now assigned for error, that the declaration and the matters therein contained were not sufficient in law to maintain an action.

TOMPKINS, J. delivered the opinion of the court.

* * *

The question submitted by the counsel in this cause for our determination is, whether *Lodowick Post,* by the pursuit with his hounds in the manner alleged in his declaration, acquired such a right to, or property in, the fox, as will sustain an action against *Pierson* for killing and taking him away?

The cause * * * presents for our decision a novel and nice question. It is admitted that a fox is an animal *ferae naturae* ["of a wild nature"], and that property in such animals is acquired by occupancy only. These admissions narrow the discussion to the simple question of what acts amount to occupancy, applied to acquiring right to wild animals?

1

If we have recourse to the ancient writers upon general principles of law, the judgment below is obviously erroneous. *Justinian's Institutes,* lib. 2. tit. 1. s. 13. and *Fleta,* lib. 3. c. 2. p. 175. adopt the principle, that pursuit alone vests no property or right in the huntsman; and that even pursuit, accompanied with wounding, is equally ineffectual for that purpose, unless the animal be actually taken. The same principle is recognised by *Bracton,* lib. 2. c. 1. p. 8.

Puffendorf, lib. 4. c. 6. s. 2. and 10. defines occupancy of beasts *ferae naturae,* to be the actual corporal possession of them, and *Bynkershoek* is cited as coinciding in this definition. It is indeed with hesitation that *Puffendorf* affirms that a wild beast mortally wounded, or greatly maimed, cannot be fairly intercepted by another, whilst the pursuit of the person inflicting the wound continues. The foregoing authorities are decisive to show that mere pursuit gave *Post* no legal right to the fox, but that he became the property of *Pierson,* who intercepted and killed him.

It therefore only remains to inquire whether there are any contrary principles, or authorities, to be found in other books, which ought to induce a different decision. Most of the cases which have occurred in *England,* relating to property in wild animals, have either been discussed and decided upon the principles of their positive statute regulations, or have arisen between the huntsman and the owner of the land upon which beasts *ferae naturae* have been apprehended * * *. Little satisfactory aid can, therefore, be derived from the *English* reporters.

Barbeyrac, in his notes on *Puffendorf,* does not accede to the definition of occupancy by the latter, but, on the contrary, affirms, that actual bodily seizure is not, in all cases, necessary to constitute possession of wild animals. He does not, however, *describe* the acts which, according to his ideas, will amount to an appropriation of such animals to private use, so as to exclude the claims of all other persons, by title of occupancy, to the same animals; and he is far from averring that pursuit alone is sufficient for that purpose. To a certain extent, and as far as *Barbeyrac* appears to me to go, his objections to *Puffendorf's* definition of occupancy are reasonable and correct. That is to say, that actual bodily seizure is not indispensable to acquire right to, or possession of, wild beasts; but that, on the contrary, the mortal wounding of such beasts, by one not abandoning his pursuit, may, with the utmost propriety, be deemed possession of him; since, thereby, the pursuer manifests an unequivocal intention of appropriating the animal to his individual use, has deprived him of his natural liberty, and brought him within his certain control. So also, encompassing and securing such animals with nets and toils, or otherwise intercepting them in such a manner as to deprive them of their natural liberty, and render escape impossible, may justly be deemed to give possession of them to those persons who, by their industry and labour, have used such means of apprehending them. * * * The case now under consideration is one of mere pursuit, and presents no circumstances or acts which can bring it within the definition of occupancy by [the great treatise writers on the subject.]

The case cited from 11 *Mod.* 74–130. I think clearly distinguishable from the present; inasmuch as there the action was for maliciously hindering and disturbing the plaintiff in the exercise and enjoyment of a private franchise; and in the report of the same case, 3 *Salk.* 9. *Holt,* Ch. J. states, that the ducks were in the plaintiff's decoy pond, and *so in his possession,* from which it is obvious the court laid much stress in their opinion upon the plaintiff's possession of the ducks, *ratione soli* ["by reason of the soil" that is, because he owned the land.]

We are the more readily inclined to confine possession or occupancy of beasts *ferae naturae,* within the limits prescribed by the learned authors above cited, for the sake of certainty, and preserving peace and order in society. If the first seeing, starting, or pursuing such animals, without having so wounded, circumvented or ensnared them, so as to deprive them of their natural liberty, and subject them to the control of their pursuer, should afford the basis of actions against others for intercepting and killing them, it would prove a fertile source of quarrels and litigation.

However uncourteous or unkind the conduct of *Pierson* towards *Post,* in this instance, may have been, yet his act was productive of no injury or damage for which a legal remedy can be applied. We are of opinion the judgment below was erroneous, and ought to be reversed.

Livingston, J., my opinion differs from that of the court.

Of six exceptions, taken to the proceedings below, all are abandoned except the third, which reduces the controversy to a single question.

Whether a person who, with his own hounds, starts and hunts a fox on waste and uninhabited ground, and is on the point of seizing his prey, acquires such an interest in the animal, as to have a right of action against another, who in view of the huntsman and his dogs in full pursuit, and with knowledge of the chase, shall kill and carry him away?

This is a knotty point, and should have been submitted to the arbitration of sportsmen, without poring over *Justinian, Fleta, Bracton, Puffendorf, Locke, Barbeyrac,* or *Blackstone,* all of whom have been cited; they would have had no difficulty in coming to a prompt and correct conclusion. In a court thus constituted, the skin and carcass of poor *reynard* would have been properly disposed of, and a precedent set, interfering with no usage or custom which the experience of ages has sanctioned, and which must be so well known to every votary of *Diana.* But the parties have referred the question to our judgment, and we must dispose of it as well as we can, from the partial lights we possess, leaving to a higher tribunal, the correction of any mistake which we may be so unfortunate as to make. By the pleadings it is admitted that a fox is a "wild and noxious beast." Both parties have regarded him, as the law of nations does a pirate, "*hostem humani generis,*" ["enemy of the human race"] and although "*de mortuis nil nisi bonum,*" ["of the dead we should speak only good"] be a maxim of our profession, the memory of the deceased has not been spared. His depredations on farmers and on barn yards, have not been forgotten; and to put him to death wherever found, is allowed to be meritorious, and of public benefit. Hence it follows, that our decision should have in view the greatest possible encouragement to the destruction of an animal, so cunning and ruthless in his career. But who would keep a pack of hounds; or what gentleman, at the sound of the horn, and at peep of day, would mount his steed, and for hours together, "*sub jove frigido,*" ["under a cold sky," or "in bad weather,"] or a vertical sun, pursue the windings of this wily quadruped, if, just as night came on, and his stratagems and strength were nearly exhausted, a saucy intruder, who had not shared in the honours or labours of the chase, were permitted to come in at the death, and bear away in triumph the object of pursuit? Whatever *Justinian* may have thought of the matter, it must be recollected that his code was compiled many hundred years ago, and it would be very hard indeed, at the distance of so many centuries, not to have a right to establish a rule for ourselves. In his day, we read of no order of men who made it a business, in the language of the declaration in this cause, "with hounds and dogs to find, start, pursue, hunt, and chase," these animals, and that, too, without any other motive than the preservation of *Roman* poultry; if this diversion had been then in fashion, the lawyers who composed his institutes, would have taken care not to pass it by, without suitable encouragement. If any thing, therefore, in the digests or pandects shall appear to militate against the defendant in error, who, on this occasion, was the foxhunter, we have only to say *tempora mutantur* ["times change"]; and if men themselves change with the times, why should not laws also undergo an alteration?

* * * Writers on general law, who have favoured us with their speculations on these points, differ on them all; but, great as is the diversity of sentiment among them, some conclusion must be adopted on the question immediately before us. After mature deliberation, I embrace that of *Barbeyrac,* as the most rational, and least liable to objection. If at liberty, we might imitate the courtesy of a certain emperor, who, to avoid giving offence to the advocates of any of these different doctrines, adopted a middle course, and by ingenious distinctions, rendered it difficult to say (as often happens after a fierce and angry contest) to whom the palm of victory belonged. He ordained, that if a beast be followed with *large dogs and hounds,* he shall belong to the hunter, not to the chance occupant; and in like manner, if he be killed or wounded with a lance or sword; but if chased with *beagles only,* then he passed to the captor, not to the first pursuer. If slain with a dart, a sling, or a bow, he fell to the hunter, if still in chase, and not to him who might afterwards find and seize him.

Now, as we are without any municipal regulations of our own, and the pursuit here, for aught that appears on the case, being with dogs and hounds of *imperial stature,* we are at liberty to adopt one of the provisions just cited, which comports also with the learned conclusion of *Barbeyrac,* that property in animals *ferae naturae* may be acquired without bodily touch or manucaption ["physical control"], provided the pursuer be within reach, or have a *reasonable* prospect (which certainly existed here) of taking, what he has *thus* discovered an intention of converting to his own use.

When we reflect also that the interest of our husbandmen, the most useful of men in any community, will be advanced by the destruction of a beast so pernicious and incorrigible, we cannot greatly err, in saying, that a pursuit like the present, through waste and unoccupied lands, and which must inevitably and speedily have terminated in corporal possession, or bodily *seisin* ["physical ownership of the propery"], confers such a right to the object of it, as to make any one a wrongdoer, who shall interfere and shoulder the spoil. The *justice's* judgment ought, therefore, in my opinion, to be affirmed. * * *

NOTES AND QUESTIONS

1. This first case is concerned with private property, the basis of most of our law. Volumes have been written for and against the institution of private property, but from at least John Locke on, the central idea has been that private property is a means of securing the fruits of one's labors, and that property is the most important body of doctrine in the law. See generally James W. Ely, The Guardian of Every Other Right: A Constitutional History of Property Rights (3rd ed., 2008). Does the majority decision in *Pierson* do what it should? If Post invested a large amount of labor in pursuing the fox, should his effort be rewarded? Is Pierson a "saucy intruder" who took something that doesn't rightfully belong to him? How should we determine who "owns" a piece of property?

2. This case will serve as an introduction to the "common law" system of judicial decision-making for those of you who are just beginning your study of law. In some areas of law, most prominently the criminal law, offenses are carefully defined, and the rules are set forth in statutes. With regard to the "common law," however, which includes many matters of the law of property, torts, contracts, and even corporations, the governing rules are developed on a case-by-case basis, with judges using prior judicial *precedents* or even the writing of experts on the law ("treatises") dealing with the same or similar issues to guide their decisions. In such a system, so the theory goes, reliance on prior decisions will ensure that the law develops objectively, rather than becoming something subject to the whims of individual judges or juries. Thus both the majority opinion of Judge Tomkins, writing for the court, and the dissenting opinion by Judge Livingston, rely on the discussions of legal theories advanced by prior judges and by the great treatise writers such as Hugo Grotius (Dutch, 1583–1645), Samuel Puffendorf (German, 1632–94), Jean Barbeyrac (French, 1674–1744), and William Blackstone (English, 1723–1780). Because New York itself had no prior cases on the issue, cases from other jurisdictions and the opinions of the treatise writers were the only source for the decision. Note that the authorities cited go all the way back to the time of the Romans, and note the liberal use of Latin in the opinion. Are you comfortable with this reliance on ancient and foreign authority? Is this a

means of allowing the living to be ruled by the dead? Is Judge Livingston, in his dissenting opinion, correct that "the distance of so many centuries" means that thinkers like Puffendorf and Barbeyrac are no longer relevant? Do you agree that "men themselves change with the times" and that the laws should change as well? When is it appropriate for a judge to disregard precedent or ancient custom?

3.   What do you suppose the goals of the law of property should be? We have touched on one goal, the rewarding of labor. Are there others? Is stability and certainty of expectations one of them? Surely, stability encourages the development of property and the production of wealth, and even if this is done to favor ownership interests in individuals, doesn't society in general benefit from such development? Is the court considering this issue? Can you think of an English or American maxim, dealing with fractions and possession that might explain the case? Does Pierson win the case because of the difficulty of administering a rule of the kind that Post presumably contends for? Which opinion, that of the dissent which presumably seeks to reward productive effort, or that of the majority, which seeks to find a certain easily-administered rule, do you favor?

4.   Another policy concern in this case, as in most cases, is reducing excessive litigation. Judge Tompkins writes that if the majority decides the case for Post, and gives ownership rights to the pursuer, the decision will "provide a fertile source of quarrels and litigation." Given the uncertainty inherent in determining whether an animal is being pursued at a particular point in time, did Judge Tompkins correctly analyze the policy concern of reducing future litigation? Do you agree that reducing litigation is a worthwhile goal, or should judges base their decisions solely on notions of fairness? Many Americans, and some of them even lawyers, have concluded that ours is a society that encourages too much litigation. It has been estimated that because of our litigiousness, we have in effect, a "litigation tax" on products that raises prices to consumers by several hundred billions of dollars a year. Large amounts of litigation can also tie up the court system and require substantial expenditure of public funds to administer. On the other hand, it may be fundamentally unfair to deny legal protection simply because it costs too much or takes too long. Those who believe that it is wise to encourage litigation usually claim that recourse to the courts is necessary to secure justice on the part of individuals confronted with the power of great wealth or giant corporations. Does that make sense to you?

5.   This point about justice underscores that whatever the policies of the law of property with regard to encouraging productive investment and securing certainty and stability, another important policy concern is achieving fairness. Is the holding in *Pierson* fair? Why? Keep the question of whether the most desirable result is a fair result in mind as you read the next two cases. For comments on the iconic status of *Pierson v. Post*, and for what its history reveals about the post-revolutionary social situation in Long Island, New York (the case turns out not only to be a dispute about a fox, but also a dispute about whether old patrician proprietors or the *nouveau riche* would have more influence in the community), see the historical treatment of the case in

Bethany R. Berger, "It's Not About the Fox: The Untold Story of *Pierson v. Post*," 55 Duke L. J. 1029 (2006).

B. CONTRACTS

WILLIAMS ET AL. v. WALKER–THOMAS FURNITURE CO.

United States Court of Appeals for the District of Columbia Circuit.
350 F.2d 445, 18 A.L.R.3d 1297, 121 U.S.App.D.C. 315, 2 UCC Rep.Serv. 955 (1965).

J. Skelly Wright, Circuit Judge:

Appellee, Walker–Thomas Furniture Company, operates a retail furniture store in the District of Columbia. During the period from 1957 to 1962 each appellant in these cases purchased a number of household items from Walker–Thomas, for which payment was to be made in installments. The terms of each purchase were contained in a printed form contract which set forth the value of the purchased item and purported to lease the item to appellant for a stipulated monthly rent payment. The contract then provided, in substance, that title would remain in Walker–Thomas until the total of all the monthly payments made equaled the stated value of the item, at which time appellants could take title. In the event of a default in the payment of any monthly installment, Walker–Thomas could repossess the item.

The contract further provided that 'the amount of each periodical installment payment to be made by (purchaser) to the Company under this present lease shall be inclusive of and not in addition to the amount of each installment payment to be made by (purchaser) under such prior leases, bills or accounts; and all payments now and hereafter made by (purchaser) shall be credited pro rata on all outstanding leases, bills and accounts due the Company by (purchaser) at the time each such payment is made.' The effect of this rather obscure provision was to keep a balance due on every item purchased until the balance due on all items, whenever purchased, was liquidated. As a result, the debt incurred at the time of purchase of each item was secured by the right to repossess all the items previously purchased by the same purchaser, and each new item purchased automatically became subject to a security interest arising out of the previous dealings.

On May 12, 1962, appellant Thorne purchased an item described as a Daveno, three tables, and two lamps, having total stated value of $391.10. Shortly thereafter, he defaulted on his monthly payments and appellee sought to replevy ["take possession of for non-payment"] all the items purchased since the first transaction in 1958. Similarly, on April 17, 1962, appellant Williams bought a stereo set of stated value of $514.95.[1] She too

---

1. At the time of this purchase her account showed a balance of $164 still owing from her prior purchases. The total of all the purchases made over the years in question came to $1,800. The total payments amounted to $1,400.

defaulted shortly thereafter, and appellee sought to replevy all the items purchased since December, 1957. The Court of General Sessions granted judgment for appellee. The District of Columbia Court of Appeals affirmed, and we granted appellants' motion for leave to appeal to this court.

Appellants' principal contention, rejected by both the trial and the appellate courts below, is that these contracts, or at least some of them, are unconscionable and, hence, not enforceable. In its opinion in Williams v. Walker–Thomas Furniture Company, 198 A.2d 914, 916 (1964), the District of Columbia Court of Appeals explained its rejection of this contention as follows:

> 'Appellant's second argument presents a more serious question. The record reveals that prior to the last purchase appellant had reduced the balance in her account to $164. The last purchase, a stereo set, raised the balance due to $678. Significantly, at the time of this and the preceding purchases, appellee was aware of appellant's financial position. The reverse side of the stereo contract listed the name of appellant's social worker and her $218 monthly stipend from the government. Nevertheless, with full knowledge that appellant had to feed, clothe and support both herself and seven children on this amount, appellee sold her a $514 stereo set.

> 'We cannot condemn too strongly appellee's conduct. It raises serious questions of sharp practice and irresponsible business dealings. A review of the legislation in the District of Columbia affecting retail sales and the pertinent decisions of the highest court in this jurisdiction disclose, however, no ground upon which this court can declare the contracts in question contrary to public policy. We note that were the Maryland Retail Installment Sales Act, Art. 83 §§ 128–153, or its equivalent, in force in the District of Columbia, we could grant appellant appropriate relief. We think Congress should consider corrective legislation to protect the public from such exploitive contracts as were utilized in the case at bar.'

We do not agree that the court lacked the power to refuse enforcement to contracts found to be unconscionable. In other jurisdictions, it has been held as a matter of common law that unconscionable contracts are not enforceable. * * * While no decision of this court so holding has been found, the notion that an unconscionable bargain should not be given full enforcement is by no means novel. In Scott v. United States, 79 U.S. (12 Wall.) 443, 445, 20 L.Ed. 438 (1870), the Supreme Court stated:

> '* * * If a contract be unreasonable and unconscionable, but not void for fraud, a court of law will give to the party who sues for its breach damages, not according to its letter, but only such as he is equitably entitled to. * * *'

Since we have never adopted or rejected such a rule, * * * the question here presented is actually one of first impression.

Congress has recently enacted the Uniform Commercial Code, which specifically provides that the court may refuse to enforce a contract which it finds to be unconscionable at the time it was made. 28 D.C.CODE § 2–302 (Supp. IV 1965). The enactment of this section, which occurred subsequent to the contracts here in suit, does not mean that the common law of the District of Columbia was otherwise at the time of enactment, nor does it preclude the court from adopting a similar rule in the exercise of its powers to develop the common law for the District of Columbia. In fact, in view of the absence of prior authority on the point, we consider the congressional adoption of § 2–302 persuasive authority for following the rationale of the cases from which the section is explicitly derived. * * * Accordingly, we hold that where the element of unconscionability is present at the time a contract is made, the contract should not be enforced.

Unconscionability has generally been recognized to include an absence of meaningful choice on the part of one of the parties together with contract terms which are unreasonably favorable to the other party. Whether a meaningful choice is present in a particular case can only be determined by consideration of all the circumstances surrounding the transaction. In many cases the meaningfulness of the choice is negated by a gross inequality of bargaining power. The manner in which the contract was entered is also relevant to this consideration. Did each party to the contract, considering his obvious education or lack of it, have a reasonable opportunity to understand the terms of the contract, or were the important terms hidden in a maze of fine print and minimized by deceptive sales practices? Ordinarily, one who signs an agreement without full knowledge of its terms might be held to assume the risk that he has entered a one-sided bargain. But when a party of little bargaining power, and hence little real choice, signs a commercially unreasonable contract with little or no knowledge of its terms, it is hardly likely that his consent, or even an objective manifestation of his consent, was ever given to all the terms. In such a case the usual rule that the terms of the agreement are not to be questioned should be abandoned and the court should consider whether the terms of the contract are so unfair that enforcement should be withheld. * * *

In determining reasonableness or fairness, the primary concern must be with the terms of the contract considered in light of the circumstances existing when the contract was made. The test is not simple, nor can it be mechanically applied. The terms are to be considered 'in the light of the general commercial background and the commercial needs of the particular trade or case.' [Comment, Uniform Commercial Code § 2–307.] Corbin suggests the test as being whether the terms are 'so extreme as to appear unconscionable according to the mores and business practices of the time and place.' 1 [Arthur] CORBIN, [CONTRACTS § 128 (1963).] We think this formulation correctly states the test to be applied in those cases where no meaningful choice was exercised upon entering the contract.

Because the trial court and the appellate court did not feel that enforcement could be refused, no findings were made on the possible unconscionability of the contracts in these cases. Since the record is not sufficient for our deciding the issue as a matter of law, the cases must be remanded to the trial court for further proceedings. * * *

DANAHER, Circuit Judge (dissenting):

The District of Columbia Court of Appeals obviously was as unhappy about the situation here presented as any of us can possibly be. Its opinion in the Williams case, quoted in the majority text, concludes: 'We think Congress should consider corrective legislation to protect the public from such exploitive contracts as were utilized in the case at bar.'

My view is thus summed up by an able court which made no finding that there had actually been sharp practice. Rather the appellant seems to have known precisely where she stood.

There are many aspects of public policy here involved. What is a luxury to some may seem an outright necessity to others. Is public oversight to be required of the expenditures of relief funds? A washing machine, e.g., in the hands of a relief client might become a fruitful source of income. Many relief clients may well need credit, and certain business establishments will take long chances on the sale of items, expecting their pricing policies will afford a degree of protection commensurate with the risk. * * *

I mention such matters only to emphasize the desirability of a cautious approach to any such problem, particularly since the law for so long has allowed parties such great latitude in making their own contracts. I dare say there must annually be thousands upon thousands of installment credit transactions in this jurisdiction, and one can only speculate as to the effect the decision in these cases will have. * * *

NOTES AND QUESTIONS

1. The law of contracts is perhaps second only in importance to the law of property, and one could conceptualize the law of contracts simply as that body of doctrine which governs voluntary transfers of property. The right to enter into agreements and to have a legal remedy if those agreements are breached is of such importance that the Framers explicitly prohibited the states from passing any "law impairing the obligation of contracts" in Article 1, § 10 cl. 1 of the United States Constitution. Like property, the law of contracts attempts to guarantee certainty. If A contracts with B to build B's house, A can be certain that if he completes B's house, B will either pay him voluntarily or the courts will require B to pay. The law of contracts encourages development by reducing the uncertainty associated with transactions. Still, contract law embodies more than simple business interests. Contract law is also about personal liberty and personal choice and perhaps even political equality. These are also basic constitutional concerns, but are there limits to their exercise? Is this case about such limits?

2. Another similarity between contract law and property law in America is that both bodies of law developed from British common law. However, as we saw in *Pierson*, relying entirely on the common law can often lead to confusion, as judges struggle to determine which precedents are relevant and which are simply left over remnants of a time long passed. In order to reduce this uncertainty, a group of lawyers, academics and judges drafted the Uniform Commercial Code (UCC) in hopes of providing more uniformity in an area of vital business concern to the laws of the states. The UCC is an attempt to codify, to set down in the form of a statute, the basic principles of the common law of contracts. The idea was for each state to pass the code as part of its legislation, and forty-nine of the states did, in very short order. The last holdout was Louisiana, where the civil law (a code system introduced by Napoleon) was already in effect. An intriguing difficulty in Judge J. Skelly Wright's opinion for the majority is that he is adopting the rule of the UCC, but applying it to a transaction that took place before the effective date of adoption of the UCC by Congress, which was functioning as if it were the state legislature for the District of Columbia. Does what the judge did in this regard make sense?

3. You'll remember that it was hinted at the end of the *Pierson* notes and questions that legal rules might be circumscribed by other principles or concerns. Is the doctrine of *unconscionability*, involved in *Williams v. Walker–Thomas*, an example of such circumscription? What do you understand that doctrine to provide? Interpreted literally, the doctrine provides that an agreement between private parties should not be enforced if it "shocks the conscience." Was the agreement between Mrs. Williams and Walker–Thomas something that ought to "shock the conscience?" Did Judge Wright so hold?

4. How does Judge Wright define "unconscionability?" Do you agree with this definition? Note that just as the judges in *Pierson* consulted the work of great treatise writers such as Puffendorf and Blackstone, Judge Wright relies on the writings of one of the great modern contracts scholars—Arthur Corbin. It is from Corbin, actually, that Wright derives the notion that there are two elements to unconscionability—lack of meaningful choice on the part of one party and commercially unreasonable terms that favor the other. Corbin did not write that these were the only possible tests, and, in fact described different fact patterns which would support a proper refusal to enforce a contract based on unconscionability. After Judge Wright's opinion, however, subsequent courts held that *both* elements Wright marked out must be present in order to find an agreement unconscionable. Given that Judge Wright's decision actually limited the number of cases in which unconscionability could be applied, do you feel the case was correctly decided?

5. Are you sympathetic to Mrs. Williams? To many readers of this case, it seems patently unfair for a business to capitalize on the misfortunes of the poor. Part of Judge Wright's reasoning for his opinion is that parties need to take into account "obvious education or lack of it." Is this appropriate protectionism or improper paternalism? Is it appropriate for the courts to step in and render such deals void? Do you think the court would have reached the same decision if the plaintiff in *Walker–Thomas* was wealthy?

6.   Judge Danaher in his dissent points out that Ms. Williams "seems to have known precisely where she stood," and he implicitly suggests that perhaps her agreement with Walker–Thomas should not be set aside. He continues "relief clients may well need credit, and certain business establishments will take long chances on the sale of items, expecting their pricing policies will afford a degree of protection commensurate with the risk." Could it be said that Judge Danaher is seeking to help people of modest means? How can both judges have the same policy concern, yet reach opposite results? Who got it right?

7.   As America entered the second half of the twentieth century, there was a feeling that active entrepreneurs may need more supervision than 19th century law was willing to provide, and cases like *Walker–Thomas* resulted. There is still room for freedom of contract, but it is also clear that the courts have a tendency to seek to police private dealings, especially where there is an inequality of bargaining power, but in many other instances as well. Consider the next case, one involving a different set of doctrines, and ask yourself whether the courts may be going too far. For further reading on what happened to the law of contract in the twentieth century, see, e.g., Grant Gilmore, The Death of Contract (2nd ed. 1995, Ronald K.L. Collins, ed.)

C.   TORTS

LOVELACE v. ASTRA TRADING CORP.
United States District Court, S.D. Mississippi.
439 F.Supp. 753 (1977).

DAN M. RUSSELL, Jr., Chief Judge.

* * *

During November or December of 1973, Edwina Lovelace, the plaintiff's wife, purchased a compact styled hair dryer (mini-dryer). The hair dryer in question was purchased at the Howard Brothers store on I–55 North in Jackson, Mississippi. It appears that the mini-dryer was purchased for the plaintiff's son, Terry Lovelace, at his request. * * * The record shows that the mini-dryer was exclusively used by Terry Lovelace, with the possible exception of a male boarder in the Lovelace home. * * *

The mini-dryer apparently functioned properly until February 10, 1974. On that date, while the plaintiff and his family were at church, the family residence was severely damaged by fire. The plaintiff alleges, and seeks to prove, that the fire resulted as a direct and proximate result of the defective nature of the mini hair dryer. The dryer was left plugged in, though not in use at the time of the fire. Some 18 days after the fire in question, plaintiff was diagnosed as having extremely high blood pressure. This led to open heart surgery and a coronary bypass, resulting in plaintiff's total and permanent disability. Plaintiff alleges that this condition was brought about as a direct result of the fire. Defendant Astra disputes this allegation, claiming that plaintiff's surgery was necessitated by a pre-existing heart condition.

Defendant Astra is an importer of merchandise, importing various items primarily from the Far East. It appears to be conceded that Astra did not manufacture the mini-dryer in issue. Astra imported and distributed approximately 48,000 mini-dryers. The record also shows that some of these mini-dryers were purchased from Astra by the Howard Brothers chain.

Astra's agent in the Far East was, for the transaction in question, the Chaun Ching Co., defendant herein. Chaun Ching is an exporter and manufacturer of sundry goods. The affidavit of Frank Friedheim, Astra's president, and board chairman, states that the dryers were actually manufactured by the Wan Nien Electric Appliance Company of Taiwan. The record also reveals that defendant Astra furnished Chaun Ching with the design and specifications for the hair dryer it desired to import. Production samples were returned to Astra, and the two defendants reached an agreement for the products' importation into the United States.

The mini-dryers were shipped to this country in individual boxes, with each box containing one dryer enclosed in a plastic bag. The boxes containing the individual dryers prominently bore the notation "Stellar". Stellar is a registered trademark of the defendant Astra.

* * * [U]pon receiving shipments, Astra would run random sample checks. This entailed a cursory visual inspection and an actual testing of the product for a period of time thought sufficient to disclose any malfunctions. Other than these samples, the dryers were shipped to retailers in the same boxes in which Astra received them. The product was in no way altered or enhanced by Astra. * * *

The plaintiff's suit sounds in the ever growing theory of products liability. Liability is asserted against Chaun Ching for negligence in the design and manufacture of the mini-dryer. Astra is also charged with negligence in the selection, testing and distribution of the hair dryers. Finally, plaintiff asserts that both defendants are strictly liable in tort for the property damage and personal injuries suffered by the plaintiff herein. * * *

Defendant Astra's motion for partial summary judgment [for failure to state a valid claim] raises two separate legal issues. First, it is asserted that since the plaintiff was neither a user nor a consumer of the product, that he is thereby barred from suing under a strict liability in tort theory. Secondly, Astra seeks a declaration limiting damages, if any, to the claims for damages to personal property. Astra maintains that the plaintiff's claim for personal injury is, under the facts of this case, noncompensable.

[This case calls for the application of the law of Mississippi, where the damage occurred, but a] problem presented herein is that the Mississippi Supreme Court has not yet addressed the issue of whether recovery under a strict liability in tort theory should be extended to those denominated as "bystanders".

*   *   *

* * * [T]his Court must take the "role of a prophet" and seek to forecast how this issue will ultimately be resolved by the state courts. * * *Absent definitive guidance from Mississippi decisional or statutory law, this Court may therefore look to other available resources, i.e., decisions in other states, by other federal courts "... and the general weight and trend of authority." Julander v. Ford Motor Co., 488 F.2d 839 (10th Cir. 1973).

Defendant Astra, in its brief and during oral argument, has stressed the point that it did not manufacture the mini-dryer that is the alleged cause of the plaintiff's damages. Defendant states that as a wholesaler, it was under no duty to inspect for latent defects, and under the authority of Shainberg v. Barlow, 258 So.2d 242 (Miss.1972), is absolved from liability herein.

In Shainberg, the plaintiff sued the wholesaler and the retailer when the heel of her shoe suddenly dislodged, thereby causing her bodily injury. The manufacturer was not joined as a party-defendant. The court stated the applicable rule thusly:

> "Where the wholesaler or distributor purchases an article from a reputable and reliable manufacturer, sells it to a retailer in its original condition, and the retailer in turn sells the article—exactly as it came from the manufacturer—to a customer in the regular course of business, no duty devolves on the wholesaler or retailer to inspect and discover a latent defect." 258 So.2d at 244 * * *.

The court concluded that the co-defendants could not be held accountable, reasoning that a contrary holding would make "... each retail merchant an insurer or guarantor ..." of articles sold in its capacity as a mere sales conduit. Id. at 246.

However, certain factors take the case *sub judice* ["before this court"] out of the purview of Shainberg. First, on this motion for partial summary judgment, this Court is unwilling to take judicial notice and assume that Astra did in fact deal with a "reputable and reliable manufacturer". Secondly, plaintiff has raised serious factual issues as to Astra's knowledge of the defective nature and propensities of the mini-dryers. Plaintiff claims that such knowledge preceded the fire in issue here. If established, Shainberg would be, by its facts, inapplicable here. The defendants in Shainberg had no advance notice that the heels on a certain brand of shoes were prone to collapse. Plaintiff's assertion here is pertinent:

> "The seller of a product has a duty to test or inspect it to determine whether it is dangerous where he has knowledge of defects in the product, or where he is otherwise put on notice of such defects (by receiving complaints regarding the injury-causing product....)" Hursh 1 American Law of Products Liability 2d § 245 at 261.

Additional facts mitigate in favor of plaintiff's position here. The record so far reveals that Astra was not a stereotypical wholesaler or retailer. On the contrary, Astra selected the design for the hair dryers and approved the prototype before full scale manufacturing began. Therefore, defendants' conduct goes far beyond that of a mere "sales conduit".

Finally, the boxes containing the individual mini-dryers were distinctively emblazoned "Stellar", defendant Astra's trademark. ** *

Therefore, the markings on the individual boxes would indicate, to the average consumer, that they were purchasing a "Stellar" manufactured product. Legal support for this proposition is found in the Restatement (Second) of Torts § 400 (1965), which provides that one "putting out" a product as his own is subject to a manufacturer's liability even though the product in question was in fact manufactured by another. * * * The foregoing principal is soundly based in logic, and serves to meet the reasonable expectations of the consuming public. Therefore, Shainberg's applicability to the instant case fades into oblivion, as defendant Astra's status shifts to that of a manufacturer.

Just as motorists on the Gulf Coast soon learn that all roads lead to Vancleave, any discussion of products liability law in Mississippi will have its roots in the seminal decision of State Stove Mfg. Co. v. Hodges, 189 So.2d 113 (Miss.1966) * * *. In State Stove, the plaintiff homeowner sued the manufacturer of a water heater and the builder-contractor who installed it, when after installation, it subsequently exploded to plaintiff's chagrin. * * *

The court in State Stove explicitly adopted § 402A of the Restatement (Second) of Torts, "... insofar as it applies to a manufacturer of a product and to a contractor who builds and sells a house with the product in it." 189 So.2d at 118. Later cases disclose, however, that the theory of strict products liability as set forth in § 402A has not been limited to those cases falling within a factual analogue to State Stove. * * *

As set forth in State Stove, Section 402A, provides:

"(1) One who sells any product in a defective condition unreasonably dangerous to the user or consumer or to his property is subject to liability for physical harm thereby caused to the ultimate user or consumer, or to his property, if (a) the seller is engaged in the business of selling such a product, and (b) it is expected to and does reach the user or consumer without substantial change in the condition in which it is sold. (2) The rule stated in Subsection (1) applies although (a) the seller has exercised all possible care in the preparation and sale of his product, and (b) the user or consumer has not bought the product from or entered into any contractual relation with the seller." * * *

It is readily apparent that the rule, by its very terms, extends liability to users and consumers. The hair dryer in question was kept in the plaintiff's house, however, only by a strained construction could plaintiff be construed as either a user or consumer. Therefore, for purposes of this motion, Mr. Lovelace will be deemed a "bystander". And, it should be noted that the Institute, by caveat, expressed no opinion on the issue of extending § 402A liability to bystanders.

As mentioned earlier, Mississippi courts have not addressed this issue yet. However, certain intimations do appear. State Stove expressly abrogated the requirement of privity in a suit by a consumer against a manufacturer, and stated that since liability sounds in tort, warranty concepts are irrelevant. Plaintiff's brief directs the Court to Miss.Code Ann. § 75–2–318 (1972) [The Mississippi version of the Uniform Commerical Code ("UCC")]. Section 2–318 of the U.C.C. delineates the scope of warranty protection under the code, with liability extending to include members of the purchaser's household, or guests therein. However, this Court does not perceive that plaintiff advances any warranty theory of liability. Accordingly, since strict liability in tort and breach of warranty are two different breeds of cat, this Court does not feel that the adoption of U.C.C. § 2–318 necessarily implies any legislative, or judicial, intent to extend liability to bystanders in all circumstances and under all causes of action.

More on point is the quotation from Greenman v. Yuba Power Products, Inc., 59 Cal.2d 57, 27 Cal.Rptr. 697, 377 P.2d 897 (1963), wherein the plaintiff recovered from the manufacturer for injuries from a power tool purchased by the plaintiff's wife.

> "A manufacturer is strictly liable in tort when an article he places on the market, knowing that it is to be used without inspection for defects, proves to have a defect that causes injury to a human being...." Quoted in State Stove, 189 So.2d at 119.

The Mississippi Supreme Court also quoted with approval Dean Prosser's summary of the [law regarding negligence in the manufacture of a product]:

> "The conclusion is clear that the duty extends to any one who may reasonably be expected to be in the vicinity of the chattel's probable use, and to be endangered if it is defective ..." Id. at 116.

This Court recognizes that Dean Prosser's statement refers to claims under a negligence theory, and not strict products liability. However, as discussed infra, negligence concepts are finding useful application in strict products liability cases, even though negligence itself need not be proven.

In Mississippi, strict liability is predicated upon three elements, to-wit:

1. Plaintiff's proof that his injury was caused by the product in question;

2. Proof that the injury resulted from a defect in the product which rendered it unreasonably dangerous; and,

3. Proof that the defect existed at the time it left the hands of the manufacturer. Early–Gary, Inc. v. Walters, 294 So.2d 181 (Miss.1974).

* * *

Negligence concepts found application in Walton v. Chrysler Motor Corp., 229 So.2d 568 (Miss.1970), where the plaintiff's car was struck from the rear and the resulting injuries were allegedly aggravated due to a defect in the plaintiff's car. In holding for the defendant, the Mississippi Supreme Court stated:

" … but this rule (strict liability) does not eliminate the requirement that, even where there is a defect in the product, that there must be some duty owed to the plaintiff with regard to the defect …" Id. at 573 * * *.

And, in Ford Motor Co. v. Cockrell, 211 So.2d 833 (Miss.1968), Dean Prosser's observations as set forth in State Stove were once again applied.

"The conclusion is clear that the duty extends to anyone who may reasonably be expected to be in the vicinity of the chattels probable use, and to be endangered if it is defective." Id. at 836.

Thus, without explicit reference, the Mississippi Supreme Court was impliedly applying concepts of foreseeability, traditionally an element of a count in negligence, to a strict liability case. * * * Finally, as pointed out infra, other courts have used the concept of foreseeability in determining whether the umbrella of strict liability also shields bystanders.

Absent more definitive guidance from the Mississippi cases, this Court now turns to the decisional law of other jurisdictions * * *

As noted earlier, the American Law Institute, * * * refused to express an opinion as to whether the theory of strict liability in tort would inure to the benefit of those who are neither users nor consumers. However, Comment C thereto sets forth the general policies underlying the strict liability concept. Seriatim, and in brief, § 402A is premised upon the assumptions that a seller assumes a special responsibility to the public; that the public has a right to expect reputable sellers to stand behind their products; that public policy demands the cost of injuries due to defective products be placed on those who market them; and, such injuries are properly treated as a cost of production and insurable risks by those in the best position to seek such protection. If the general policies and the intent of the drafters are taken as stated, it is apparent to this Court that third-party bystanders are properly protected by § 402A. Decisions of other courts, and the trend of recent authority, supports this conclusion.

In Elmore v. American Motors, 70 Cal.2d 578, 75 Cal.Rptr. 652, 451 P.2d 84, 33 A.L.R.3d 406 (1969), the plaintiff's car malfunctioned. The plaintiff lost control, crossed the roadway and struck a second plaintiff's (Waters) car. The lower court sustained nonsuits on behalf of the manufacturer and retailer. The California Supreme Court reversed, basing its holding on the general policy grounds that manufacturers should bear the cost of injuries caused by their defective products. For purposes of application to the present controversy, the Court in Elmore stated:

"If anything, bystanders should be entitled to greater protection than the consumer or user where injury to bystanders from the defect is reasonably foreseeable. Consumers and users, at least, have the opportunity to inspect for defects and to limit their purchases to articles manufactured by reputable manufacturers and sold by reputable retailers, whereas the bystander ordinarily has no such opportunities. In short, the bystander is in greater need of protection from defective products which are dangerous, and if any distinction should be made between bystanders and users, it should be made, contrary to the position of defendants, to extend greater liability in favor of the bystanders." * * *

Similarly, Chrysler Corp. v. Alumbaugh, 342 N.E.2d 908 (Ind.App.1976), limits bystander recovery "to those whom the manufacturer or supplier should reasonably foresee as being subject to the harm caused by the defect." Defendant relies upon Winnett v. Winnett, 57 Ill.2d 7, 310 N.E.2d 1 (1974), in support of its position. In Winnett, the four year old plaintiff was injured when she put her fingers in the moving screen of a farm forage wagon. The Supreme Court of Illinois denied recovery against the manufacturer on a strict products liability theory. In so doing, that court stated:

> "In our judgment the liability of a manufacturer properly encompasses only those individuals to whom injuries from a defective product may reasonably be foreseen and only those situations where the product is being used for the purpose for which it was intended or for which it is reasonably foreseeable that it may be used." * * *

The manufacturer was therefore absolved from liability because it could not reasonably foresee that a four-year-old child would be allowed to put her fingers in the forage screen. However, the emphasis of the court in Winnett was on foreseeability, and only under the facts of that case was the plaintiff-bystander denied recovery. Therefore, the Winnett case is reconcilable with those allowing recovery by bystanders.

The issue has been addressed and resolved by other courts also. [The court proceeds to discuss decisions holding that manufacturers are strictly liable for damage to bystanders in New York, Louisiana, Kentucky, and Oklahoma, which discussion is here omitted.]

The Missouri Supreme Court also extended strict liability recovery to bystanders in Giberson v. Ford Motor Co., 504 S.W.2d 8 (Mo.1974), wherein the court, quoting from Tucson Indus., Inc. v. Schwartz, 108 Ariz. 464, 501 P.2d 936, 939–40 (1972), gave the basic justification for extending liability.

> "Strict liability is a public policy device to spread the risk from one to whom a defective product may be a catastrophe, to those who marketed the product, profit from its sale, and have the know-how to remove its defects before placing it in the chain of distribution."

Mississippi courts are generally in accord with the policy judgment that manufacturers should shoulder the costs of injuries resulting from their defective products. * * * The general consensus therefore appears to favor extension of the strict liability doctrine to provide relief to bystanders. * * *

One final case is worth noting. In West v. Caterpillar Tractor Co., Inc., 336 So.2d 80 (Fla.1976), the plaintiff was crossing the street to board a bus when she was run over by a Caterpillar tractor driven by a contractor's employee. The Fifth Circuit Court of Appeals certified the issue of bystander recovery to the Florida Supreme Court. The Florida court noted that no adequate rationale or theoretical explanation existed to deny strict liability to bystanders. That court also summed up the situation well * * *:

> "All states which have adopted the theory of strict tort liability have extended the theory to the bystander when called upon to do so ..." * * *

Part of the basis for the Florida court's holding is the notion that any restriction of the doctrine to users or consumers only "... would have to rest on the vestige of the disappearing privity requirement." Id. at 89. As mentioned earlier, the Mississippi Supreme Court in State Stove abandoned the privity requirement in suits by a consumer against a manufacturer. The court thereupon concluded:

> "The obligation of the manufacturer must become what in justice it ought to be—an enterprise liability ... The cost of injuries or damages, either to persons or property, resulting from defective products, should be borne by the makers of the products who put them into the channels of trade ... This doctrine of strict liability applies when harm befalls a foreseeable bystander who comes within range of the danger." * * *

Based upon the foregoing, this Court holds that the plaintiff herein may avail himself of the strict liability doctrine enunciated in § 402A of the Restatement, and as adopted and construed by the Mississippi Supreme Court. Defendants' motion for partial summary judgment on this ground is therefore denied.

* * *

* * * 31 states have adopted § 402A in one form or another, with two federal court "predictions" in Utah and Vermont. Even a cursory perusal of the cited cases discloses that Mississippi was in the forefront in adopting § 402A. This Court has no reason to believe that the state supreme court, given the appropriate case, would not extend strict liability concepts to include "bystanders". The Mississippi court's willingness to be among judicial innovators in this area indicates a concern for consumers in general; and a sensitivity to the delicate interplay among responsible social policy, enterprise liability and the reasonable expectations of the consuming public.

Defendants' second contention, that plaintiff may not recover for his personal injuries, may be dealt with in a more summary manner. First,

§ 402A by its very terms speaks to both property damage and personal injuries arising from the use of a defective product. Secondly, defendants' case authority is distinguishable in its application to the case sub judice. In Aldridge v. Johnson, 318 So.2d 870 (Miss.1975), the plaintiff was denied recovery for her mental anguish where her family doctor testified that there was no causal relationship between the accident in issue and plaintiff's resultant nervous condition. Defendant herein has presented materials indicating that plaintiff may have had a pre-existing heart condition. However, the record also discloses that the plaintiff is prepared to prove, by expert testimony, that his personal injuries were a direct result of the fire allegedly caused by defendants' defective mini-dryer. * * *

Thirdly, the cases disclose that foreseeability is at the heart of a strict liability case. Foreseeability is a matter for the trier of fact, and the plaintiff should be allowed to prove his case. * * * [Accordingly, defendant's motion for partial summary judgment is denied.]

NOTES AND QUESTIONS

1.   As is true for the law of contracts and property, much of Tort law derives from common-law precedents rather than statutes. Contracts is all about private agreements, but torts is all about what happens when one stranger causes injury to another. Familiar torts include such matters as assault, battery, intentional infliction of mental distress, trespass, and negligence. In his classroom lectures, one noted authority, Northwestern University Law Professor Marshall Shapo, condenses the law of torts into a single question "what should society do when party A injures party B, and A could have avoided it?" The law of torts is concerned with compensation, but also with deterrence. If a doctor knows he must compensate a patient if he operates when inebriated, for example, the doctor will be unlikely to engage in such conduct. Is that what the *Astra* decision is all about?

2.   Do you think the corporation which sold and marketed the "mini-dryer" should compensate Mr. Lovelace for his house that burned down? What about the pain and suffering and medical costs of his heart condition? Until recently, the standard that used to apply in the case of harm caused by manufactured items was "negligence," that is, whether the person or corporation causing harm failed to manufacture a product using "due care," or the care a reasonably prudent person would use under the same circumstances. Is this an appropriate standard?

3.   Whether or not negligence is an appropriate standard in products liability cases, this is no longer the rule. Beginning in the 1960's, led by courts in California, the rule applied in products liability came to be the "strict liability" rule, which is referred to in *Astra* as the rule codified in Restatement 402A. "Restatements" are summaries of the applicable law prepared by the American Law Institute, a scholarly group of lawyers, law professors, and judges. The restatements, which summarize and, to a certain extent, clarify decisions of courts, are then referred to and applied by courts in subsequent cases, although generally they have not been enacted as statutes. Does this seem wise to you? What do you understand to be the policy basis for the

"strict liability" rule? Does it seem consistent with the contract and property cases you have read? Does Restatement 402A protect the common man from some sort of corporate leviathan, or does the rule work an injury to American industry?

4. Is it accurate to suggest, as the court in *Astra* does, that the defendant corporation is in a better position either to prevent the injury through inspection, or to pass on the costs to consumers? This latter concept, called "loss spreading", treats injuries as a cost of production and passes that cost onto consumers through higher prices. Since Astra is in the best position to understand the risks and their consequences and the precautions that should be taken, so the theory goes, Astra can buy products liability insurance, and the cost of the insurance will be incorporated into the price of all the hairdryers. The economic burden will not, then, be borne by Astra, but rather all consumers of Astra's products. Does this strike you as a desirable social goal? Keeping in mind that it is all consumers who eventually pay in a strict liability case, do you find yourself more or less sympathetic to the Lovelaces? What, in particular, do you make of the fact that in Astra the damage for which compensation is sought is damage not to the buyer of the hairdryer or even the user of the hairdryer, but rather to a "bystander?" Should this make a difference? There used to be a general requirement in a torts suit that there be "privity," that is, a direct legal connection formed by the law of contract or some similar doctrine such as warranty, before there could be compensation. Was it a good idea to abandon that "privity" doctrine in cases such as *Astra*?

5. As you will soon learn, one of the fundamental principles of American law is that those who invest in corporations are not normally liable for the contracts the corporations make or for the torts that they cause. Limiting the liability of corporate shareholders, so the argument goes, encourages investment and economic development. At the turn of the twentieth century, the President of Columbia University said "the limited liability corporation is the greatest single discovery of modern times.... It substitutes cooperation on a large scale for individual, cut-throat, parochial competition. It makes possible huge economy in production and trading...." Given that corporations serve a social good, and that limiting the liability of corporations is a positive advancement, do cases of strict products liability threaten to restrain economic progress? Or is it possible that strict liability for products actually helps the market place? Are you more or less likely to purchase a product when you know that its manufacturer is, in effect, guaranteeing its safety?

6. As we move away from the basics we have been exploring in this introductory chapter, try to remember the policy concerns explored in these three cases, and see if they do not show up in the more specialized doctrines of agency, partnership, and corporations, which, you may discover, are actually complex applications and variations of the rules of property, contracts, and torts.

CHAPTER 2

AGENCY, PARTNERSHIP, AND THE LIMITED LIABILITY COMPANY

■ ■ ■

A. AGENCY

CROISANT v. WATRUD

Supreme Court of Oregon.
248 Ore. 234, 432 P.2d 799 (1967).

*   *   *

[O'CONNELL, Justice, for the court] This is a suit in equity for an accounting brought against co-partners in a firm of certified public accountants and the executrix of a deceased partner, LaVern Watrud. Plaintiff appeals from a decree in favor of defendants.

We shall refer to the deceased partner, Watrud, as one of the defendants. The defendants engaged in the accounting practice with their principal office in Klamath Falls and their branch office in Medford. Watrud was in charge of the Medford office.

Plaintiff was the owner of a sawmill, timberlands, and other property over which she exercised general control, delegating the details of management of the business to others.

In 1955 plaintiff employed the defendant partnership to advise her on tax matters and to prepare income tax returns for her business enterprises. All of these services were performed by Watrud * * *.

In 1956 plaintiff sold her sawmill. Thereafter her business activities consisted almost entirely of making collections under the contract for the sale of the mill, collections on the sale of timber, collections of rents, and various disbursements from the moneys so collected.

In 1957 plaintiff moved to California. She made arrangements with Watrud to make the collections referred to above, to make certain disbursements, to keep her financial books and records, and to prepare her financial statements and tax returns. The moneys collected by Watrud were deposited in the account of the Lloyd Timber Company (plaintiff's business name in Oregon) in a Grants Pass bank.

In 1957 plaintiff learned that her husband, Glenn Lloyd, had induced Watrud to make unauthorized payments out of the Lloyd Timber Company account to him. Plaintiff instructed Watrud not to make any further payments to her husband, but Watrud violated her instructions. Plaintiff was informed of these subsequent misappropriations by Watrud on behalf of Glenn Lloyd in 1958. She also learned that her husband was unfaithful to her. Plaintiff again excused Watrud's breach of trust and her husband's infidelity. After their reconciliation, plaintiff and her husband took a trip to Europe. When they returned, plaintiff discovered that her husband had forged checks on her California bank account and had also forged her signature upon a $75,000 note and negotiated it. Plaintiff also became aware of the fact that Watrud had continued to pay money to Glenn Lloyd out of plaintiff's Oregon account. In addition, she learned that Watrud, without authorization, had drawn a check payable to himself. When Watrud was confronted with this evidence he finally acknowledged his abuse of his trust. Soon thereafter Watrud died from gunshot wounds while hunting. Plaintiff then filed this suit for an accounting against the surviving partners.

*   *   *

It is undisputed that plaintiff's initial business arrangements for tax advice and the preparation of tax returns were with the partnership and not simply with Watrud individually. After the partnership was employed, Watrud individually performed all of the services sought by plaintiff. As time went on plaintiff called upon Watrud to perform additional services in connection with her business including the collection and disbursements of funds. The initial question is whether these subsequent services performed by Watrud are to be regarded as having been performed as a part of the partnership business or under a separate arrangement calling only for the services of Watrud personally.

The record suggests that plaintiff, Watrud, and defendants considered all of Watrud's services to the plaintiff as services performed by a member of a partnership on behalf of that firm. The partnership received a check each month for all of Watrud's services including the services involved in handling plaintiff's business affairs. Had the parties viewed the services in making collections and disbursements for plaintiff as independent activities separate compensation would have been in order. Although the partnership's Medford office was geographically separated from the Klamath Falls office, both operations constituted one autonomous business enterprise and consequently defendants cannot insulate themselves from liability on the ground that the Medford office was a separate business operation. Defendants are liable, therefore, if Watrud can be regarded as the agent of the partnership in performing the fund-handling services for plaintiff.

It is clear that Watrud had no express authority from defendants to perform these services. And there was no evidence from which an authority implied in fact could be derived. If it were common knowledge that accountants frequently act as trustees in the collection and disbursement of funds, we would be in a position to take judicial notice of the common practice and thus find an implied authority or an apparent authority. But we have no basis for saying that accountants commonly or frequently perform fund-handling services. Thus we conclude that liability cannot be rested upon a manifestation by defendants that they assented to be bound for such services. However, an agent can impose liability upon his principal even where there is no actual or apparent authority or estoppel. An agent may have an "inherent agency power" to bind his principal. Such power is defined in *Restatement (Second), Agency § 8A* as "the power of an agent which is derived not from authority, apparent authority or estoppel, but solely from the agency relation and exists for the protection of persons harmed by or dealing with a servant or other agent." When an agent has acted improperly in entering into a contract the inherent agency power "is based neither upon the consent of the principal nor upon his manifestations." * * * The scope of the principal's liability under an inherent agency power is stated in Section 161:

"A general agent for a disclosed or partially disclosed principal subjects his principal to liability for acts done on his account which usually accompany or are incidental to transactions which the agent is authorized to conduct if, although they are forbidden by the principal, the other party reasonably believes that the agent is authorized to do them and has no notice that he is not so authorized." *Restatement (Second), Agency § 161*, p. 378 (1958).

It will be noted that Section 161 states that the principal is liable only for his agent's acts "which *usually accompany* or are *incidental* to transactions which the agent is authorized to conduct * * *." (Emphasis added.) As we have previously observed, we have neither evidence nor judicial knowledge of the practice of accountancy from which to decide whether the collection and disbursement of accounts is commonly undertaken by accountants. We cannot say, therefore, that the fund-handling services performed by Watrud in this case were the type which "usually accompany" the transactions which accountants ordinarily conduct viewed from the standpoint of those engaged in accountancy. Upon similar reasoning we are unable to say that the services here were "incidental" to the transactions Watrud was authorized to conduct.

But this does not conclude the matter. Assuming that accountants do not regard the collection and disbursement of funds as a part of the services usually offered by members of their profession, what significance should this have if, in the particular circumstances, a person dealing with a member of an accounting partnership reasonably believes that accountants perform the kind of service which he seeks to have performed? If the phrase "acts * * * which usually accompany * * * transactions which the agent is authorized to conduct" is to be tested solely from the viewpoint of accountants in describing the kind of services they usually perform then, of course, *Section 161 of the Restatement (Second) of Agency* would not be applicable even though a client of an accounting firm mistakenly but reasonably believed that the services he requested were not alien to the work of accountants. The basis for the principal's liability under these circumstances is best explained by the comments appended to Section 8A and related sections of the Restatement; whether the theory is categorized as one of apparent authority (treating the circumstances as a manifestation of authority by principal), or as arising out of an inherent agency power is immaterial. The rationale begins with the idea that:

> "The principles of agency have made it possible for persons to utilize the services of others in accomplishing far more than could be done by their unaided efforts. * * * [The] primary function in modern life is to make possible the commercial enterprises which could not exist otherwise. * * * Partnerships and corporations, through which most of the work of the world is done today, depend for their existence upon agency principles. The rules designed to promote the interests of these enterprises are necessarily accompanied by rules to police them. It is inevitable that in doing their work, either through negligence or excess of zeal, agents will harm third persons or will deal with them in unauthorized ways. It would be unfair for an enterprise to have the benefit of the work of its agents without making it responsible to some extent for their excesses and failures to act carefully. The answer of the common law has been the creation of special agency powers or, to phrase it otherwise, the imposition of liability upon the principal because of unauthorized or negligent acts of his servants and other agents. * * * " *Restatement (Second) Agency, § 8A*, comment *a* (1958).

The basis for principal's liability under this section is further explained in the comment as follows:

> "* * * His liability exists solely because of his relation to the agent. It is based primarily upon the theory that, if one appoints an agent to conduct a series of transactions over a period of time, it is fair that he should bear losses which are incurred when such an agent, although without authority to do so, does something which is usually done in connection with the transactions he is employed to conduct. Such agents can properly be regarded as part of the principal's organization in much the same way as a servant is normally part of the master's business enterprise. In fact most general agents are also servants, such as managers and other persons continuously employed and subject to physical supervision by the employer. The basis of the extended liability stated in this Section is comparable to the liability of a master for the torts of his servant. * * * In the case of the master, it is thought fair that one who benefits from the enterprise and has a right to control the physical activities of those who make the enterprise profitable, should pay for the physical harm resulting from the errors and derelictions of the servants while doing the kind of

thing which makes the enterprise successful. The rules imposing liability upon the principal for some of the contracts and conveyances of a general agent, whether or not a servant, which he is neither authorized nor apparently authorized to make, are based upon a similar public policy. Commercial convenience requires that the principal should not escape liability where there have been deviations from the usually granted authority by persons who are such essential parts of his business enterprise. In the long run it is of advantage to business, and hence to employers as a class, that third persons should not be required to scrutinize too carefully the mandates of permanent or semi-permanent agents who do no more than what is usually done by agents in similar positions." *Restatement (Second), Agency § 161* at p. 379–380.

If a third person reasonably believes that the services he has requested of a member of an accounting partnership is undertaken as a part of the partnership business, the partnership should be bound for a breach of trust incident to that employment even though those engaged in the practice of accountancy would regard as unusual the performance of such service by an accounting firm.

The reasonableness of a third person's belief in assuming that a partner is acting within the scope of the partnership should not be tested by the profession's own description of the function of its members. Those who seek accounting services may not understand the refinements made by accountants in defining the services they offer to the public. Whether a third person's belief is reasonable in assuming that the service he seeks is within the domain of the profession is a question which must be answered upon the basis of the facts in the particular case.

We are of the opinion that the facts in the present case are sufficient to establish a reasonable belief on the part of plaintiff that Watrud had undertaken all of the work assigned to him by plaintiff as a continuation of the original employment of the partnership firm. The initial work for which defendants were engaged was the preparation of income tax returns. Thereafter plaintiff sought Watrud's advice on tax matters and continued to have him prepare income tax returns for her business ventures. Watrud did not do the actual bookkeeping for plaintiff's business activities when the partnership was first employed, but eventually he prepared and kept in his own custody the financial books and records of plaintiff's enterprises. This service was assumed by Watrud when plaintiff decided to move to California permanently. When plaintiff left Grants Pass she also arranged with Watrud to have him receive all the income from her Oregon and California properties and to make disbursements from the money so collected. Before she employed him to handle her funds she asked him if he was bonded and he assured her that he was. We think it is important to note that the increased responsibilities directed to Watrud coincided with plaintiff's departure for California. Thereafter, Watrud was the only person who drew checks on the account set up pursuant to the arrangement with plaintiff, although the bank signature card included the names of plaintiff and others. Watrud handled a very substantial amount of plaintiff's money during the course of his employment, drawing as many as 1500 checks per year. The bank statements and cancelled checks were sent directly to Watrud; he collected her business mail at her post office box in Grants Pass and in other respects acted in her behalf after her departure for California. As we have already mentioned, the partnership received compensation for these services at the rate of $800 per month.

As plaintiff testified, nothing was ever said or done by Watrud which might have indicated to her that he was acting on his account as distinguished from acting for the partnership. It was reasonable for plaintiff to assume that the added assignment of collecting and disbursing funds delegated to Watrud was an integral part of the function of one employed to keep the accounts reflecting the income and disbursement of those funds. This assumption, we think, is even more likely in circumstances such as we have here where there is trust and confidence reposed in the person employed. * * * This is not a case in which a person deals with an ordinary commercial partnership. Accountants stand in a fiduciary relation to their clients and out of that relationship there is generated a trust and confidence which invites the client to rely upon the advice and guidance of the one she employs. * * * The fiduciary character of the relationship in these circumstances is clearly explained in *Cafritz v. Corporation Audit Co., 60 F. Supp. 627* (D.C. Dist., 1945). In that case the defendant, an accounting firm, was employed by the plaintiff to maintain and audit the records of his enterprises. The defendant was authorized to perform a variety of services for plaintiff including the preparation of checks for plaintiff's signature and the deposit of checks to the plaintiff's account. * * * Defendant's general manager misappropriated some of the checks deposited with defendant and the plaintiff brought suit for an accounting. In holding the defendant liable for the defalcation the court emphasized the fiduciary relation which arose between the plaintiff and the defendant accounting firm. The court said:

> "It is well established that when the defendant is an accounting party, and stands as one occupying a fiduciary relation toward the plaintiff, because of money or property intrusted to him, the burden is upon him to show that he has performed his trust and the manner of its performance. He owes this duty because of the confidential relation he bears to his principal, and because he is presumed to know how he has performed his duty. * * * The burden of proof is on the accountant after he has admitted the relation and the receipt of a certain sum, to prove that he had disposed properly of the amount for which he is accountable, and to show what that amount is." * * *

In the present case defendants owed a similar duty for the defalcation of Watrud.

* * *

NOTES AND QUESTIONS

1.   This case serves many purposes for us, but perhaps the primary one is to introduce you to the doctrines of agency and partnership. To begin with the basics, an *agent* is someone who acts on behalf of and subject to the control of another, known as the *principal*. While acting on behalf of a principal, an agent possesses a *fiduciary duty* to the principal, which means that he or she must place the principal's financial interests above the agent's own. As this case makes clear, enunciating another basic principle of agency, the principal is bound by the acts of the agent, that is the principal is liable to third parties as a result of obligations created by the agent's interaction with the third party, if the agent was acting according to the directions of the principal, within the scope of his employment, or, as the law puts it, if the agent acted pursuant to sufficient *authority* given by the principal.

As you will have discerned from the case, there are several different kinds of authority the principal can grant the agent. These include, among others, *actual* authority, *apparent* authority, agency by *estoppel*, and, finally, the elusive kind of authority discussed in the *Croisant* case, "inherent" authority. Can you understand from the case when a court ought to find such authority present? A principal is also liable for the acts of his or her agent even if no authority was present when the acts purportedly binding the principal were done, if the principal later *ratifies* the acts of the agent, that is, agrees to accept liability for them. As agency is an important body of doctrines for both partnerships and corporations, it is worth going into a bit more detail about the agent's authority. Consider the following types of authority and the situations in which they apply. Do these rules make sense to you?

2.   *Actual Authority*: An agent exercises *actual authority* if the agent reasonably believes from the principal's conduct or words that the principal has authorized him to act. Even when the principal's subjective intention may have been otherwise, if an agent reasonably understands that the principal intended to confer authority, then the agent has actual authority and the principal will be liable for the acts of the agent. Actual authority can be either *express,* when a principal specifies exactly what the agent is to do or not do, or *implied*, when a principal specifies what an agent is to do, but the power to choose the method or other acts incidental to the specified act can be reasonably inferred by the agent. A common type of implied actual authority is *incidental authority* in which the agent is authorized to do acts reasonably or usually necessary to accomplish the principal's desired objectives. Note that the determination of whether an agent has actual authority is done with reference to what the *agent* reasonably believed, and does not turn on what the third party knew regarding the agent's authority. Unless otherwise specified, actual authority terminates when either the agent or the principal provides notice to the other of his wish to terminate their relationship.

Example: P leaves a note on the desk of a stockbroker, A, saying, "I authorize you to purchase 100 shares of Intel for me today." When A acts on P's behalf in accordance with the note, A has *actual* authority to serve as a stockbroker for P, *express* authority to purchase the shares, perhaps *implied* authority to wait until the price drops in the afternoon before buying, and *incidental* authority to pay the transactional fees for purchasing the shares. Would A have been acting within a grant of authority from P if he sold the shares mid-day and repurchased them when the price dropped again? What if A used the profits from that transaction to purchase additional shares of Intel?

3. *Apparent Authority*: An agent acts with *apparent authority* if the principal's manifestations led the involved third party reasonably to conclude that the principal had authorized the agent to act in a specified manner. Here it is not the understanding of the agent that is at issue, but the understanding of the *third party*. Nevertheless, you can probably understand why apparent authority often coincides with actual authority. Note that apparent authority can be present even if a principal does not intend to authorize the agent to act, in a manner similar to how actual authority can be found. Frequently an officer's position within a corporation provides apparent authority, if a third party reasonably believes the agent's authority to be consistent with his position. This is termed *authority by position*.

Example: A is the President and Chairman of the Board, the Chief Executive Officer (CEO) of XYZ, Inc. In his position, A is the agent of corporation. T, a third party who signs a contract with A, could reasonably believe from the corporation's Board of Directors (which body selects the officers) appointing of A to a high position within the corporation that the Board had implicitly or expressly authorized A to sign contracts on behalf of XYZ, especially if that is the usual practice for executives in his position. In this situation, A would have apparent authority to sign a contract with T, and XYZ, Inc. would be liable for A's actions, even if no one else involved in the corporation had wished for A to sign a contract with T.

4. *Agency by estoppel*: A would-be principal can be *estopped* [prevented by the law] from denying an agency relationship and become liable to a third party if the third party relied to his detriment on his belief in an agent's authority. The third party's belief must have been caused either by intentional or careless behavior of the would-be principal, or a failure of the principal to take reasonable steps to notify the third party of the error of such belief. (Restatement (3rd) of Agency § 2.05). Although agency by estoppel usually involves false representations by an actor purporting to be an agent, a would-be principal will still be found liable because it was his acts or his failure reasonably to act to deny authority which enabled the purported agent to misrepresent his or her authority to third parties.

Agency by estoppel, like apparent authority, rests on the *third party's* understanding. Unlike apparent authority, in order to be invoked, agency by estoppel requires detrimental reliance on the part of the third party.

Example: T enters a store called "P's Stereos" and is approached by A, wearing a "P's Stereos" shirt and otherwise acting like a salesman. Although T doesn't know it, A had found the shirt and a P's Stereos receipt book on the sidewalk, where P had negligently left them the day before. A induces T to purchase a stereo, and, in exchange for cash, gives T an official-looking receipt and explains that the stereo will be delivered later in the day. T never receives his stereo, nor does P ever receive the cash from the transaction. A is neither an agent nor employee of P, and does not have actual or apparent authority to sell from P's inventory. Even so, P may be liable for T's detrimental reliance through the creation of agency by estoppel because P's carelessness with identifying materials and lack of surveillance over the store's sales force facilitated T's reasonable belief that A was authorized as an agent of P.

5.   *Authority by Ratification*: An agent who acts on behalf of a principal, but without actual or apparent authority, can still bind the principal to third parties if the principal, who later acquires knowledge of the material facts regarding the agent's dealings with the third party, either objectively manifests his consent to being liable for the agent's conduct, or behaves in such a way that consent can be inferred. The legal consequence of the principal's *ratification* is that the agency relationship is treated as if the agent possessed *actual authority* at the time of the relevant acts.

6.   *Inherent Authority*: According to Restatement (Second) of Agency and, as demonstrated in *Croisant v. Watrud*, even when an agent acts without actual authority or apparent authority, a principal can still be liable through *inherent authority*. Somewhat similar to apparent authority, inherent authority turns on the beliefs of the involved third party. The difference between apparent and inherent authority has not always been easy for courts or commentators to discern. Inherent authority exists when a third party has an actual and reasonable belief that the agent possesses authority to act in a specified manner, even if his belief is not based on particular manifestations by the principal (as is true for apparent authority). Inherent authority arises solely from the agency relationship itself, and, as the *Croisant* court indicates, is based on the theory that if a principal appoints an agent to conduct a series of transactions, it is only fair that the principal should bear losses that are incurred when the agent, although not authorized to do so, does something that is closely connected with the transactions he is employed to conduct. As in *Croisant*, a principal is liable for his agent's actions that "usually accompany or are incidental to transactions which the agent is authorized to conduct," even if no authority is given or implied. Because inherent agency imposes liability on a principal in an indefinite variety of circumstances, potentially beyond those when actual or apparent authority are present, the existence of the doctrine purportedly encourages principals to exercise more caution in selecting agents, thereby minimizing their potential liability and perhaps avoiding harm to third persons.

7.   Don't worry if you're having trouble figuring out exactly what inherent authority is and how it differs from apparent authority. *Inherent authority* has recently been eliminated in drafts of the Restatement (Third) of Agency. The drafters of this Third Restatement (as the law develops, the Restatements have gone through subsequent drafts) removed the distinction between inherent authority and apparent authority by expanding the definition of principal's manifestations to include situations without verbal communications by the principal, such as appointments of agents to certain positions. The confusion between apparent and inherent authority explains the suggestion in *Croisant* that "whether the theory is characterized as one of apparent authority ... or as arising out of an inherent agency power is immaterial." In the reporter's notes for the Third Restatement, the authors argue that as the Restatements are designed to simplify the law and create a more

unified, concise statement of the law of the states, elimination of inherent agency is needed.

In a recent law review article, one critic of the Third Restatement's elimination of inherent authority argues that apparent authority ought to be conceptualized as only a small subset of inherent authority, and thus it should not be expanded to replace inherent authority. This critic explains the distinction between the two kinds of authority by suggesting that inherent authority requires only that the third party's belief be actual and reasonable, whereas apparent authority requires that the third party's belief be actual, reasonable, and based on the principal's manifestations. Inherent authority thus becomes the most useful in cases, such as *Croisant*, where the third party's beliefs are reasonable but cannot be traced to manifestations by the principal. Because of this narrow but useful difference between inherent authority and actual authority, it is suggested that elimination of inherent authority breaks with precedent cases like *Croisant* and constitutes an inappropriate substantive change of the law. Matthew P. Ward, Note: A Restatement or a Redefinition: Elimination of Inherent Agency in the Tentative Draft of the Restatement (Third) of Agency, 59 Wash & Lee L. Rev. 1585, 1626 (2002). Remember that Restatements are not supposed to change the law, just to reflect it. Having read a case in which apparent authority and inherent authority both play a large role, do you agree with the new Restatement's elimination of inherent authority? Do you think this change potentially makes the law clearer or does the new Restatement increase confusion?

8. Why all this fuss about different kinds of authority in the first place? Does having multiple types of authority benefit business? Does it further fairness? Do you think it adds certainty and predictability? Is there an economic benefit to allowing agents to act on behalf of principals, and bind the principals (whether individuals, partnerships (as in *Croisant*), or corporations) without requiring more formal, explicit grants of authority? What would happen if courts required a showing of express actual authority before they would allow a principal to be bound by an agent's acts?

9. What difference does it make, if any, that the purported principal in Croisant is a *partnership*? What can you infer about the nature of partnerships from the case? See if your inferences are born out by the consideration of partnership law which follows this section on Agency.

TARNOWSKI v. RESOP

Supreme Court of Minnesota.
236 Minn. 33, 51 N.W.2d 801 (1952).

* * *

[KNUTSON, J.] Plaintiff * * * engaged defendant as his agent to investigate and negotiate for the purchase of a route of coin-operated music machines. On June 2, 1947, relying upon the advice of defendant * * * plaintiff purchased such a business from Phillip Loechler and Lyle Mayer of Rochester, Minnesota, who will be referred to hereinafter as the sellers.

The business was located at La Crosse, Wisconsin, and throughout the surrounding territory. Plaintiff alleges that defendant represented to him that he had made a thorough investigation of the route; that it had 75 locations in operation; that one or more machines were at each location; that the equipment at each location was not more than six months old; and that the gross income from all locations amounted to more than $3,000 per month. As a matter of fact, defendant had made only a superficial investigation and had investigated only five of the locations. Other than that, he had adopted false representations of the sellers as to the other locations and had passed them on to plaintiff as his own. Plaintiff was to pay $30,620 for the business. He paid $11,000 down. About six weeks after the purchase, plaintiff discovered that the representations made to him by defendant were false, in that there were not more than 47 locations; that at some of the locations there were no machines and at others there were machines more than six months old, some of them being seven years old; and that the gross income was far less than $3,000 per month. Upon discovering the falsity of defendant's representations and those of the sellers, plaintiff rescinded the sale. He offered to return what he had received, and he demanded the return of his money. The sellers refused to comply, and he brought suit against them in the district court of Olmsted county. The action was tried, resulting in a verdict of $10,000 for plaintiff. Thereafter, the sellers paid plaintiff $9,500, after which the action was dismissed with prejudice pursuant to a stipulation of the parties.

In this action, brought in Hennepin county, plaintiff alleges that defendant, while acting as agent for him, collected a secret commission from the sellers for consummating the sale, which plaintiff seeks to recover under his first cause of action. In his second cause of action, he seeks to recover damages [besides the side-payment to the agent, incidental to the case.] The case was tried to a jury, and plaintiff recovered a verdict of $5,200. This appeal is from the judgment entered pursuant thereto.

Defendant contends that after recovery of a verdict by plaintiff in his action for rescission against the sellers he cannot maintain this action against defendant. Principally, defendant argues that recovery in the action against the sellers is a bar to this action * * *.

1.   With respect to plaintiff's first cause of action, the principle that all profits made by an agent in the course of an agency belong to the principal, whether they are the fruits of performance or the violation of an agent's duty, is firmly established and universally recognized. * * *

It matters not that the principal has suffered no damage or even that the transaction has been profitable to him. * * *

The rule and the basis therefor are well stated in *Lum v. McEwen, 56 Minn. 278, 282, 57 N.W. 662,* where, speaking through Mr. Justice Mitchell, we said:

> "Actual injury is not the principle the law proceeds on, in holding such transactions void. Fidelity in the agent is what is aimed at, and,

as a means of securing it, the law will not permit him to place himself in a position in which he may be tempted by his own private interests to disregard those of his principal. * * * It is not material that no actual injury to the company [principal] resulted, or that the policy recommended may have been for its best interest. Courts will not inquire into these matters. It is enough to know that the agent in fact placed himself in such relations that he might be tempted by his own interests to disregard those of his principal.

"The transaction was nothing more or less than the acceptance by the agent of a bribe to perform his duties in the manner desired by the person who gave the bribe. Such a contract is void.

"This doctrine rests on such plain principles of law, as well as common business honesty, that the citation of authorities is unnecessary."

The right to recover profits made by the agent in the course of the agency is not affected by the fact that the principal, upon discovering a fraud, has rescinded the contract and recovered that with which he parted. Restatement, Agency, § 407(2). *Comment e on Subsection* (2) reads:

"If an agent has violated a duty of loyalty to the principal so that the principal is entitled to profits which the agent has thereby made, the fact that the principal has brought an action against a third person and has been made whole by such action does not prevent the principal from recovering from the agent the profits which the agent has made. Thus, if the other contracting party has given a bribe to the agent to make a contract with him on behalf of the principal, the principal can rescind the transaction, recovering from the other party anything received by him, or he can maintain an action for damages against him; in either event the principal may recover from the agent the amount of the bribe."

It follows that, insofar as the secret commission of $2,000 received by the agent is concerned, plaintiff had an absolute right thereto, irrespective of any recovery resulting from the action against the sellers for rescission.

2. Plaintiff's second cause of action is brought to recover damages for (1) losses suffered in the operation of the business prior to rescission; (2) loss of time devoted to operation; (3) expenses in connection with rescission of the sale and investigation therewith; (4) nontaxable expenses in connection with the prosecution of the suit against the sellers; and (5) attorneys' fees in connection with the suit.

* * * Our inquiry is limited to a consideration of the question whether a principal may recover of an agent who has breached his trust the items of damage mentioned after a successful prosecution of an action for rescission against the third parties with whom the agent dealt for his principal.

The general rule is stated in Restatement, Agency, § 407(1), as follows:

"If an agent has received a benefit as a result of violating his duty of loyalty, the principal is entitled to recover from him what he has so received, its value, or its proceeds, and also the amount of damage thereby caused, except that if the violation consists of the wrongful disposal of the principal's property, the principal cannot recover its value and also what the agent received in exchange therefor."

In *Comment a on Subsection* (1) we find the following:

" * * * In either event, whether or not the principal elects to get back the thing improperly dealt with or to recover from the agent its value or the amount of benefit which the agent has improperly received, he is, in addition, entitled to be indemnified by the agent for any loss which has been caused to his interests by the improper transaction. Thus, if the purchasing agent for a restaurant purchases with the principal's money defective food, receiving a bonus therefor, and the use of the food in the restaurant damages the business, the principal can recover from the agent the amount of money improperly expended by him, the bonus which the agent received, and the amount which will compensate for the injury to the business."

The general rule with respect to damages for a tortious act is that—

"The wrong-doer is answerable for all the injurious consequences of his tortious act which, according to the usual course of events and general experience, were likely to ensue and which, therefore, when the act was committed, he may reasonably be supposed to have foreseen and anticipated." 1 Sutherland, Damages (4 ed.) § 45 * * *.

The general rule is given in Restatement, Torts, § 910, as follows:

"A person injured by the tort of another is entitled to recover damages from him for all harm, past, present and prospective, legally caused by the tort."

Bergquist v. Kreidler, 158 Minn. 127, 196 N.W. 964, involved an action to recover attorneys' fees expended by plaintiffs in an action seeking to enforce and protect their right to the possession of real estate. Defendant, acting as the owner's agent, had falsely represented to plaintiffs that they could have possession on August 1, 1920. It developed after plaintiffs had purchased the premises that a tenant had a lease running to August 1, 1922, on a rental much lower than the actual value of the premises. Defendant (the agent) conceded that plaintiffs were entitled to recover the loss in rent, but contended that attorneys' fees and disbursements expended by plaintiffs in testing the validity of the tenant's lease were not recoverable. In affirming plaintiffs' right to recover we said *(158 Minn. 132, 196 N.W. 966):*

" * * * the litigation in which plaintiffs became involved was the direct, legitimate and a to-be-expected result of appellant's misrepresentation. The loss sustained by plaintiffs in conducting that litigation 'is plainly traceable' to appellant's wrong and he should make compensation accordingly."

So far as the right to recover attorneys' fees is concerned, the same may be said in this case. Plaintiff sought to return what had been received and demanded a return of his down payment. The sellers refused. He thereupon sued to accomplish this purpose, as he had a right to do, and was successful. His attorneys' fees and expenses of suit were directly traceable to the harm caused by defendant's wrongful act. As such, they are recoverable.

* * *

The same is true of the other elements of damage involved. See, generally, 15 Am. Jur., Damages, § 138.

3. Defendant contends that plaintiff had an election of remedies and, having elected to proceed against the sellers to recover what he had paid, is now barred from proceeding against defendant. It is true that upon discovery of the fraud plaintiff had an election of remedies against the sellers. It is not true, however, that, having elected to sue for recovery of that with which he had parted, he is barred from proceeding against his agent to recover damages for [the agent's] tortious conduct. While some of the allegations in plaintiff's complaint against the sellers are similar to or identical with those in his complaint in this case, insofar as the fraud is concerned, the right of recovery here against the agent goes much further than the action against the sellers. Many of the elements of damage against the agent are not available to plaintiff against the sellers. For instance, he has no right to recover attorneys' fees and expenses of the litigation against the sellers. He has that right against the agent. * * * Losses directly flowing from the agent's tortious conduct are not recoverable against the sellers in an action for rescission, but they may be recovered against the agent, whose breach of faith has caused such losses.

4. Nor is the settlement and dismissal of the action against the sellers a bar to an action against the agent, for the same reasons as stated above. The sellers and agent are not joint tortfeasors in the sense that their wrongful conduct necessarily grows out of the same wrong. Their individual torts may have been based on the same fraud, but their liabilities to plaintiff do not have the same limitations. In simple terms, the causes of action are not the same.

* * *

NOTES AND QUESTIONS

1. So far you have learned that agents are authorized to conduct business for a principal and can enter into contracts which bind the principal, if they act with sufficient authority. The *Tarnowski* case is your introduction to an equally important aspect of agency law, the *fiduciary responsibility* of the

agent to the principal. As indicated, the essence of this fiduciary responsibility is that the agent is required to put the principal's interests ahead of his own. Why should this be so? Because many business entities, particularly corporations, can only act through agents (can you understand why this is the case?) regulating their behavior is tremendously important. Can you understand why the fiduciary principle is necessary given the enormous discretion that agents may have not only to make binding contracts for their principals, but also to negotiate and execute them?

2.   Given human nature, one will want to look out for one's own interests ahead of those of others. Agency law must come to grips with the fact that the inevitable agency relationship will require some mechanisms so that the principal can minimize the temptation of the agent to betray the principal's interests in favor of the agent's own. There is a vast economic literature on this problem, but for our purposes it is enough to note that without legal restraints on the agent, and even with them, principals will often expend "monitoring costs" to ensure that their agents act according to the principal's wishes. The principal might also require that the agent enter into some kind of security arrangement so that funds are forfeited if the agent acts in a manner contrary to the principal's interest. The costs of such an arrangement are known as "bonding costs." Finally, as we have seen in *Tarnowski*, if the agent does fail to perform according to the wishes and interests of the principal, the principal may face some loss, either of lost opportunity, or of money expended for inferior goods. This is generally referred to as "residual loss." The economic literature explains that "agency costs" the costs to all concerned of employing agents to carry out transactions, is the sum of the monitoring expenses expended by the principal, the bonding expenditures of the agent, and the residual loss faced by the principal. Can you understand how imposing a fiduciary duty on the agent serves to reduce "agency costs?"

3.   In *Tarnowski* the agent, Resop, took a bribe and bound his principal in a business deal that featured fraud on the part of the sellers (the third parties) and also the agent. The principal, Tarnowski, sued the sellers, and essentially recovered his losses from the fraudulent transaction, and then Tarnowski proceeded to bring a second lawsuit against his disloyal agent. Because he had previously been made virtually whole as a result of the favorable settlement of the lawsuit against the sellers, it might be said that Tarnowski was no longer financially harmed by his agent's taking of a bribe, yet the court rules that he is still entitled to the side payment made by the sellers to the agent. Why? The court writes in its decision, "all profits made by an agent in the course of an agency belong to the principal, whether they are the fruits of performance or the violation of an agent's duty." The court continues "it matters not that the principal has suffered no damage or even that the transaction has been profitable to him." How can this be? Is it wise policy? If side-payments from third parties to agents can be recovered by principals will this result in principals taking less care to hire trustworthy agents?

4.   As you may know, Courts rarely and reluctantly award attorney's fees, particularly in private disputes, unless such remedy is set forth in a statute. In this case, the court awarded attorneys fees expended by Tarnowski. In the logic of the court, "the attorneys' fees and expenses of suit were

directly traceable to the harm caused by defendant's wrongful act." Does this decision seem fair to you, given the usual reluctance to award attorney's fees? Note that the court reaches this decision after consulting authorities regarding the law of torts. Is this a torts case or a contracts case? Should it make a difference? For further thoughts on the fiduciary duty as it applies to agents in a variety of contexts, see Victor Brudney, Contract and Fiduciary Duty in Corporate Law, 38 B.C.L. Rev. 595 (1997), and, for an analysis of the problem of agency from a literary perspective, see Allen D. Boyer, Agents, Lovers, and Institutions: John Le Carre as Legal Critic, 65 Notre Dame L. Rev. 78 (1989).

B. PARTNERSHIP

(1) WHEN IS THERE A PARTNERSHIP?

MARTIN v. PEYTON

Court of Appeals of New York.
246 N.Y. 213, 158 N.E. 77 (1927).

[ANDREWS, J.] * * * Partnership results from contract, express or implied. If denied it may be proved by the production of some written instrument; by testimony as to some conversation; by circumstantial evidence. If nothing else appears the receipt by the defendant of a share of the profits of the business is enough. * * *

Assuming some written contract between the parties the question may arise whether it creates a partnership. If it be complete; if it expresses in good faith the full understanding and obligation of the parties, then it is for the court to say whether a partnership exists. It may, however, be a mere sham intended to hide the real relationship. Then other results follow. In passing upon it effect is to be given to each provision. Mere words will not blind us to realities. Statements that no partnership is intended are not conclusive. If as a whole a contract contemplates an association of two or more persons to carry on as co-owners a business for profit a partnership there is. * * * On the other hand, if it be less than this no partnership exists. Passing on the contract as a whole, an arrangement for sharing profits is to be considered. It is to be given its due weight. But it is to be weighed in connection with all the rest. It is not decisive. It may be merely the method adopted to pay a debt or wages, as interest on a loan or for other reasons.

*   *   *

In the case before us the claim that the defendants became partners in the firm of Knauth, Nachod & Kuhne, doing business as bankers and brokers, depends upon the interpretation of certain instruments. * * * "The plaintiff's position is not," we are told, "that the agreements of June 4, 1921, were a false expression or incomplete expression of the intention of the parties. We say that they express defendants' intention and that that intention was to create a relationship which as a matter of law constitutes a partnership." Nor may the claim of the plaintiff be rested on any question of estoppel. "The plaintiff's claim," he stipulates, "is a claim of actual partnership, not of partnership by estoppel * * *."

Remitted then, as we are, to the documents themselves, we refer to circumstances surrounding their execution only so far as is necessary to make them intelligible. And we are to remember that although the intention of the parties to avoid liability as partners is clear, although in language precise and definite they deny any design to then join the firm of K. N. & K.; although they say their interests in profits should be construed merely as a measure of compensation for loans, not an interest in profits as such; although they provide that they shall not be liable for any losses or treated as partners, the question still remains whether in fact they agree to so associate themselves with the firm as to "carry on as co-owners a business for profit."

In the spring of 1921 the firm of K. N. & K. found itself in financial difficulties. John R. Hall was one of the partners. He was a friend of Mr. Peyton. From him he obtained the loan of almost $500,000 of Liberty bonds, which K. N. & K. might use as collateral to secure bank advances. This, however, was not sufficient. The firm and its members had engaged in unwise speculations, and it was deeply involved. Mr. Hall was also intimately acquainted with George W. Perkins, Jr., and with Edward W. Freeman. He also knew Mrs. Peyton and Mrs. Perkins and Mrs. Freeman. All were anxious to help him. He, therefore, representing K. N. & K., entered into negotiations with them. While they were pending a proposition was made that Mr. Peyton, Mr. Perkins and Mr. Freeman or some of them should become partners. It met a decided refusal. Finally an agreement was reached. It is expressed in three documents, executed on the same day, all a part of the one transaction. * * * We shall refer to them as "the agreement," "the indenture" and "the option."

We have no doubt as to their general purpose. The respondents were to loan K. N. & K. $2,500,000 worth of liquid securities, which were to be returned to them on or before April 15, 1923. The firm might hypothecate them to secure loans totalling $2,000,000, using the proceeds as its business necessities required. To insure respondents against loss K. N. & K. were to turn over to them a large number of their own securities which may have been valuable, but which were of so speculative a nature that they could not be used as collateral for bank loans. In compensation for the loan the respondents were to receive 40 per cent of the profits of the firm until the return was made, not exceeding, however, $500,000 and not less than $100,000. Merely because the transaction involved the transfer of securities and not of cash does not prevent its being a loan * * *. The respondents also were given an option to join the firm if they or any of them expressed a desire to do so before June 4, 1923.

Many other detailed agreements are contained in the papers. Are they such as may be properly inserted to protect the lenders? Or do they go further? Whatever their purpose, did they in truth associate the respondents with the firm so that they and it together thereafter carried on as co-owners a business for profit? * * *

As representing the lenders, Mr. Peyton and Mr. Freeman are called "trustees." The loaned securities when used as collateral are not to be mingled with other securities of K. N. & K., and the trustees at all times are to be kept informed of all transactions affecting them. To them shall be paid all dividends and income accruing therefrom. They may also substitute for any of the securities loaned securities of equal value. With their consent the firm may sell any of its securities held by the respondents, the proceeds to go, however, to the trustees. In other similar ways the trustees may deal with these same securities, but the securities loaned shall always be sufficient in value to permit of their hypothecation for $2,000,000. If they rise in price the excess may be withdrawn by the defendants. If they fall they shall make good the deficiency.

So far there is no hint that the transaction is not a loan of securities with a provision for compensation. Later a somewhat closer connection with the firm appears. Until the securities are returned the directing management of the firm is to be in the hands of John R. Hall, and his life is to be insured for $1,000,000, and the policies are to be assigned as further collateral security to the trustees. These requirements are not unnatural. Hall was the one known and trusted by the defendants. Their acquaintance with the other members of the firm was of the slightest. These others had brought an old and established business to the verge of bankruptcy. As the respondents knew, they also had engaged in unsafe speculation. The respondents were about to loan $2,500,000 of good securities. As collateral they were to receive others of problematical value. What they required seems but ordinary caution. Nor does it imply an association in the business.

The trustees are to be kept advised as to the conduct of the business and consulted as to important matters. They may inspect the firm books and are entitled to any information they think important. Finally they may veto any business they think highly speculative or injurious. Again we hold this but a proper precaution to safeguard the loan. The trustees may not initiate any transaction as a partner may do. They may not bind the firm by any action of their own. Under the circumstances the safety of the loan depended upon the business success of K. N. & K. This success was likely to be compromised by the inclination of its members to engage in speculation. * * * The trustees, therefore, might prohibit it, and that their prohibition might be effective, information was to be furnished them. Not dissimilar agreements have been held proper to guard the interests of the lender.

As further security each member of K. N. & K. is to assign to the trustees their interest in the firm. No loan by the firm to any member is permitted and the amount each may draw is fixed. No other distribution of profits is to be made. So that realized profits may be calculated the existing capital is stated to be $700,000, and profits are to be realized as promptly as good business practice will permit. In case the trustees think this is not done, the question is left to them and to Mr. Hall, and if they differ then to an arbitrator. There is no obligation that the firm shall continue the business. It may dissolve at any time. Again we conclude there is nothing here not properly adapted to secure the interest of the respondents as lenders. If their compensation is dependent on a percentage of the profits still provision must be made to define what these profits shall be.

The "indenture" is substantially a mortgage of the collateral delivered by K. N. & K. to the trustees to secure the performance of the "agreement." It certainly does not strengthen the claim that the respondents were partners.

Finally we have the "option." It permits the respondents or any of them or their assignees or nominees to enter the firm at a later date if they desire to do so by buying 50 per cent or less of the interests therein of all or any of the members at a stated price. Or a corporation may, if the respondents and the members agree, be formed in place of the firm. Meanwhile, apparently with the design of protecting the firm business against improper or ill-judged action which might render the option valueless, each member of the firm is to place his resignation in the hands of Mr. Hall. If at any time he and the trustees agree that such resignation should be accepted, that member shall then retire, receiving the value of his interest calculated as of the date of such retirement.

This last provision is somewhat unusual, yet it is not enough in itself to show that on June 4, 1921, a present partnership was created nor taking these various papers as a whole do we reach such a result. It is quite true that even if one or two or three like provisions contained in such a contract do not require this conclusion, yet it is also true that when taken together a point may come where stipulations immaterial separately cover so wide a field that we should hold a partnership exists. As in other branches of the law a question of degree is often the determining factor. Here that point has not been reached. * * *

NOTES AND QUESTIONS

1. The partnership is one of the oldest and simplest ways for multiple parties to organize a business. Partnerships were originally part of the common law, but are now more commonly regulated by the Uniform Partnership Act (UPA), drafted in 1914, and passed in many jurisdictions. The UPA was itself recently revised in 1994, and is now denominated as the Revised Uniform Partnership Act (RUPA). The UPA and the RUPA provide the basic definitions and governing rules for partnerships, but for our purposes the UPA, and the RUPA can be understood as simply restating the basic principles of the common law of partnership. Note, in particular, as indicated in the opening paragraphs of *Martin v. Peyton*, that partnership is primarily regarded as a creature of contract. Because partners are personally jointly and severally

liable for the debts of the partnership, it is important that all parties understand what they are doing, and understand the consequences of creating a partnership. Still, as ought to be the clear implication from *Martin v. Peyton*, just as agency (another creature of contract) can be determined to be present even if it was not the intention of the parties involved, a partnership will exist whenever a court determines that it has before it "An association of two or more persons to carry on, as co-owners, a business for profit." UPA Sec. 6(1). This will be true whatever may have been the expressed intention of the putative partners. When do you suppose a court will determine that a partnership exists (and impose liability on partners to third persons) in spite of clear expressions to the contrary by those associated in the business?

2.   In *Martin*, the distinction between creditor and partner is of crucial importance. The bargain between Hall and his friends is an elaborate one, featuring three different documents, the "agreement," the "indenture," and the "option." Do you understand the purposes of each of them? If you had to come up with a single purpose or set of purposes of the three, what would it be? Do these six friends of Mr. Hall strike you as having more control over the workings of the K,N, & K firm than your average creditor? Do you agree with Judge Andrews's opinion that the six friends were only creditors and not partners?

In a recent excellent treatment of *Martin v. Peyton*, longtime UCLA Law Professor William Klein, a distinguished practitioner of law and economics analysis, argues that when one examines "each of the deal points—most notably, modified profit share (40 Percent of profit, with a minimum of $100,000 and a maximum of $500,000) and control (designation of the managing partner (Hall), veto, and resignations)–with an effort to determine whether each element pointed more to partnership or to debt" then the case "could have gone either way." William A. Klein, "The Story of *Martin v. Peyton*: Rich Investors, Risky Investment, and the Line Between Lenders and Undisclosed Partners," in J. Mark Ramseyer, Ed., Corporate Law Stories 77, 91 (2009). Which way do you think the case should have gone, and why? Is the outcome of the case explainable in part because of the extraordinary social prominence of the Hall, Peyton, Perkins, and Freeman families? Which result in the case, imposing partnership liability on those families, or treating them as creditors, is most consonant with economic efficiency? Which with fairness? On these points generally, consult Klein, *supra*.

3.   Why do you suppose we impose unlimited personal liability on partners? Why not on creditors? Based on what you know of the law of agency, for example, is it likely that there is a real possibility of harm to innocent third parties? Consider the situation where A and B agree to go into business together. A, who is very wealthy, provides all the capital, while B provides industry know-how and contacts, but has no personal net worth to speak of. A and B agree to share the profits of their business equally (which, by the way, is the default rule for partnerships). If C, a third party, is injured by a product produced by the partnership of A and B, C could go after the assets of both partners. If, however, A, having read *Martin v. Peyton*, had set up the business agreement to look as though he loaned the money to B, C is left with only the assets of the business and the meager personal assets of B to com-

pensate him for any injury. You can see that those who can afford to hire attorneys to draft sophisticated agreements such as those in *Martin v. Peyton* may be able to exercise a great deal of control over the business while still facing no personal financial risks other than losing their initial investment. Does this seem fair to you?

4.   Other forms of partnership have arisen to combat the shortcomings and potential liability issues in general partnerships. One alternative is a *limited partnership*, in which one or more general partners are active in managing the business and are personally liable for the partnership's debts and obligations. The limited partner or partners have limited liability, that is, under normal circumstances their liability is limited to their investment in the firm, and, in turn, the limited partners have no right to control the day-to-day operations of the partnership, and usually cannot act as agents of the partnership. Most states also offer *limited liability partnerships* (LLP's) which are general partnerships, in terms of management, but give limited liability protection to all partners. Generally speaking, there are filing and other requirements (such as the provision of indemnification to at least some extent for third parties who deal with these entities) for limited partnerships or LLP's. LLP's are popular with law and accounting firms, but not widely used in commercial business. The newest and most generally successful business form to emerge is the *limited liability company* (LLC) which, in the space of a very few years, became accepted in virtually all the states. We will have more to say about LLC's soon, but for now we need only remark that an LLC provides limited liability for all participants, whether or not they are active in the management of the business. Given the availability of Limited Partnerships, LLP's, and LLC's, why would any firm now choose the partnership form? Do the following cases provide any clues?

(2) WHAT IS THE NATURE OF PARTNERSHIP GOVERNANCE?

NATIONAL BISCUIT CO., INC. v. STROUD

Supreme Court of North Carolina.
249 N.C. 467, 106 S.E.2d 692 (1959).

[PARKER, J.] C. N. Stroud and Earl Freeman entered into a general partnership to sell groceries under the firm name of Stroud's Food Center. There is nothing in the agreed statement of facts to indicate or suggest that Freeman's power and authority as a general partner were in any way restricted or limited by the articles of partnership in respect to the ordinary and legitimate business of the partnership. Certainly, the purchase and sale of bread were ordinary and legitimate business of Stroud's Food Center during its continuance as a going concern.

Several months prior to February 1956 Stroud advised plaintiff that he personally would not be responsible for any additional bread sold by plaintiff to Stroud's Food Center. After such notice to plaintiff, it from 6 February 1956 to 25 February 1956, at the request of Freeman, sold and delivered bread in the amount of $171.04 to Stroud's Food Center.

In *Johnson v. Bernheim, 76 N.C. 139,* this Court said: "A and B are general partners to do some given business; the partnership is, by operation of law, a power to each to bind the partnership in any manner legitimate to the business. If one partner go to a third person to buy an article on time for the partnership, the other partner cannot prevent it by writing to the third person not to sell to him on time; or, if one party attempt to buy for cash, the other has no right to require that it shall be on time. And what is true in regard to buying is true in regard to selling. What either partner does with a third person is binding on the partnership. It is otherwise where the partnership is not general, but is upon special terms, as that purchases and sales must be with and for cash. There the power to each is special, in regard to all dealings with third persons at least who have notice of the terms." * * *

The General Assembly of North Carolina in 1941 enacted a Uniform Partnership Act, which became effective 15 March 1941. G.S. Ch. 59, Partnership, Art. 2.

G.S. 59–39 is entitled PARTNER AGENT OF PARTNERSHIP AS TO PARTNERSHIP BUSINESS, and subsection (1) reads: "Every partner is an agent of the partnership for the purpose of its business, and the act of every partner, including the execution in the partnership name of any instrument, for apparently carrying on in the usual way the business of the partnership of which he is a member binds the partnership, unless the partner so acting has in fact no authority to act for the partnership in the particular matter, and the person with whom he is dealing has knowledge of the fact that he has no such authority." *G.S. 59–39(4)* states: "No act of a partner in contravention of a restriction on authority shall bind the partnership to persons having knowledge of the restriction."

G.S. 59–45 provides that "all partners are jointly and severally liable for the acts and obligations of the partnership."

G.S. 59–48 is captioned RULES DETERMINING RIGHTS AND DUTIES OF PARTNERS. Subsection (e) thereof reads: "All partners have equal rights in the management and conduct of the partnership business." Subsection (h) thereof is as follows: "Any difference arising as to ordinary matters connected with the partnership business may be decided by a majority of the partners; but no act in contravention of any agreement between the partners may be done rightfully without the consent of all the partners."

Freeman as a general partner with Stroud, with no restrictions on his authority to act within the scope of the partnership business so far as the agreed statement of facts shows, had under the Uniform Partnership Act "equal rights in the management and conduct of the partnership business." Under *G.S. 59–48(h)* Stroud, his co-partner, could not restrict the power and authority of Freeman to buy bread for the partnership as a going concern, for such a purchase was an "ordinary matter connected with the partnership business," for the purpose of its business and within its scope, because in the very nature of things Stroud was not, and could not be, a majority of the partners. Therefore, Freeman's purchases of bread from plaintiff for Stroud's Food Center as a going concern bound the partnership and his co-partner Stroud. * * *

In Crane on Partnership, 2nd Ed., p. 277, it is said: "In cases of an even division of the partners as to whether or not an act within the scope of the business should be done, of which disagreement a third person has knowledge, it seems that logically no restriction can be placed upon the power to act. The partnership being a going concern, activities within the scope of the business should not be limited, save by the expressed will of the majority deciding a disputed question; half of the members are not a majority."

Sladen v. Lance, 151 N.C. 492, 66 S.E. 449, is distinguishable. That was a case where the terms of the partnership imposed special restrictions on the power of the partner who made the contract.

At the close of business on 25 February 1956 Stroud and Freeman by agreement dissolved the partnership. By their dissolution agreement all of the partnership assets, including cash on hand, bank deposits and all accounts receivable, with a few exceptions, were assigned to Stroud, who bound himself by such written dissolution agreement to liquidate the firm's assets and discharge its liabilities. It would seem a fair inference from the agreed statement of facts that the partnership got the benefit of the bread sold and delivered by plaintiff to Stroud's Food Center, at Freeman's request, from 6 February 1956 to 25 February 1956. See *Guano Co. v. Ball, 201 N.C. 534, 160 S.E. 769*. But whether it did or not, Freeman's acts, as stated above, bound the partnership and Stroud.

* * *

NOTES AND QUESTIONS

1. Generally, every partner has an equal share in the partnership, including decision making power, profit sharing and liability for the partnership's debts. Should partners wish to create a different set-up, including unequal divisions of authority, profits and liability, or even requirements for super-majorities, they must specify any variations in a *partnership agreement* when forming their original partnership, or unanimously modify the agreement at a later date. Contracts explicitly detailing the management of the partnership will then govern future disputes. Can you think of situations in which adjusting partners' liability and power is beneficial to the partnership? What about situations in which requiring unanimity of partners is more desirable than requiring a simple majority of partners?

2. The rule applied in *National Biscuit Company, Inc. v. Stroud* is that although neither partner in two-person partnership constitutes a majority, absent previous agreement to the contrary, "no restriction can be placed on the power" of one partner to act. Does this make sense to you? Who is pro-

tected by such a rule? The result in *National Biscuit Company* would not occur in some jurisdictions, at least with matters of hiring employees. In another leading case, *Summers v. Dooley*, 94 Idaho 87, 481 P.2d 318 (1971), the Supreme Court of Idaho held that where there are only two partners, and one objects to the hiring of an employee, since the will of the majority ought to govern, and one party does not constitute a majority when partners are equally divided, the party who forbids a change must have his way. Would you have applied this rule under the facts of *National Biscuit Company?* There is a hint, at the end of *National Biscuit*, that a relevant question might be if one partner acted contrary to the wishes of the other, and still the partnership benefited, the dissenting partner might not be able to escape liability for the action taken. Is this the kind of an argument you have seen before? Does it make sense? * * *

3.   One of the worst dilemmas of partnership law is what to do when the partners are divided, especially where there are only two partners. You will have noticed that the partnership in question in *National Biscuit Company, Inc. v. Stroud* ended in dissolution. Generally speaking, and absent contrary agreement, any partner may dissolve the partnership at will, and the assets of the partnership are then divided, usually with one partner buying out the other. Is this any way to run a business? Another feature of the common law of partnership (and also the default position of the UPA) is that absent contrary agreement, the profits of the partnership are divided equally among the members, and, as you have already understood, each partner is jointly and severally liable for the debts of the partnership. Do you understand why it is one of the oldest old saws of business that partnership is the "worst ship?" Why does the form persist? One reason is the tax treatment of partnerships, where income and losses are annually allocated directly to the partners, thus avoiding the so-called "double-taxation" of the corporate form, where revenues are first taxed to the corporation, and then, when profits are distributed as dividends, taxed to the individual shareholders receiving the dividends. Are there other reasons for favoring the partnership form, or for embracing the message being partners suggests? Consider the implications of the next case, not, strictly speaking, a partnership case, but one that is frequently cited in the partnership context.

(3) THE FIDUCIARY DUTY OF PARTNERS (AND "COADVENTURERS")

MEINHARD v. SALMON

Court of Appeals of New York.
249 N.Y. 458, 164 N.E. 545, 62 A.L.R. 1 (1928).

[CARDOZO, Ch. J.] On April 10, 1902, Louisa M. Gerry leased to the defendant Walter J. Salmon the premises known as the Hotel Bristol at the northwest corner of Forty-second street and Fifth avenue in the city of New York. The lease was for a term of twenty years, commencing May 1, 1902, and ending April 30, 1922. The lessee undertook to change the hotel building for use as shops and offices at a cost of $200,000. * * *

Salmon, while in course of treaty with the lessor as to the execution of the lease, was in course of treaty with Meinhard, the plaintiff, for the necessary funds. The result was a joint venture with terms embodied in a writing. Meinhard was to pay to Salmon half of the moneys requisite to reconstruct, alter, manage and operate the property. Salmon was to pay to Meinhard 40 per cent of the net profits for the first five years of the lease and 50 per cent for the years thereafter. If there were losses, each party was to bear them equally. Salmon, however, was to have sole power to "manage, lease, underlet and operate" the building. * * *

The two were coadventurers, subject to fiduciary duties akin to those of partners * * *. As to this we are all agreed. The heavier weight of duty rested, however, upon Salmon. He was a coadventurer with Meinhard, but he was manager as well. During the early years of the enterprise, the building, reconstructed, was operated at a loss. If the relation had then ended, Meinhard as well as Salmon would have carried a heavy burden. Later the profits became large with the result that for each of the investors there came a rich return. For each, the venture had its phases of fair weather and of foul. The two were in it jointly, for better or for worse.

When the lease was near its end, Elbridge T. Gerry had become the owner * * *. He owned much other property in the neighborhood, one lot adjoining the Bristol Building on Fifth avenue and four lots on Forty-second street. He had a plan to lease the entire tract for a long term to some one who would destroy the buildings then existing, and put up another in their place. In the latter part of 1921, he submitted such a project to several capitalists and dealers. He was unable to carry it through with any of them. Then, in January, 1922, with less than four months of the lease to run, he approached the defendant Salmon. The result was a new lease to the Midpoint Realty Company, which is owned and controlled by Salmon, a lease covering the whole tract, and involving a huge outlay. The term is to be twenty years, but successive covenants for renewal will extend it to a maximum of eighty years at the will of either party. The existing buildings may remain unchanged for seven years. They are then to be torn down, and a new building to cost $3,000,000 is to be placed upon the site. The rental, which under the Bristol lease was only $55,000, is to be from $350,000 to $475,000 for the properties so combined. Salmon personally guaranteed the performance by the lessee of the covenants of the new lease until such time as the new building had been completed and fully paid for.

The lease between Gerry and the Midpoint Realty Company was signed and delivered on January 25, 1922. Salmon had not told Meinhard anything about it. * * * The first that he knew of it was in February when the lease was an accomplished fact. He then made demand on the defendants that the lease be held in trust as an asset of the venture, making offer upon the trial to share the personal obligations incidental to the guaranty. The demand was followed by refusal, and later by this suit. A referee gave judgment for the plaintiff, limiting the plaintiff's interest in the lease, however, to 25 percent. The limitation was on the theory that the plaintiff's equity was to be restricted to one-half of so much of the value of the lease as was contributed or represented by the occupation of the Bristol site. Upon cross-appeals to the Appellate Division, the judgment was modified so as to enlarge the equitable interest to one-half of the whole lease. With this enlargement of plaintiff's interest, there went, of course, a corresponding enlargement of his attendant obligations. The case is now here on an appeal by the defendants.

Joint adventurers, like copartners, owe to one another, while the enterprise continues, the duty of the finest loyalty. Many forms of conduct permissible in a workaday world for those acting at arm's length, are forbidden to those bound by fiduciary ties. A trustee is held to something stricter than the morals of the market place. Not honesty alone, but the punctilio of an honor the most sensitive, is then the standard of behavior. As to this there has developed a tradition that is unbending and inveterate. Uncompromising rigidity has been the attitude of courts of equity when petitioned to undermine the rule of undivided loyalty by the "disintegrating erosion" of particular exceptions * * *. Only thus has the level of conduct for fiduciaries been kept at a level higher than that trodden by the crowd. It will not consciously be lowered by any judgment of this court.

The owner * * *, Mr. Gerry, had vainly striven to find a tenant who would favor his ambitious scheme of demolition and construction. Baffled in the search, he turned to the defendant Salmon in possession of the Bristol, the keystone of the project. He figured to himself beyond a doubt that the man in possession would prove a likely customer. To the eye of an observer, Salmon held the lease as owner in his own right, for himself and no one else. In fact he held it as a fiduciary, for himself and another, sharers in a common venture. If this fact had been proclaimed, if the lease by its terms had run in favor of a partnership, Mr. Gerry, we may fairly assume, would have laid before the partners, and not merely before one of them, his plan of reconstruction. The pre-emptive privilege, or, better, the pre-emptive opportunity, that was thus an incident of the enterprise, Salmon appropriated to himself in secrecy and silence. He might have warned Meinhard that the plan had been submitted, and that either would be free to compete for the award. If he had done this, we do not need to say whether he would have been under a duty, if successful in the competition, to hold the lease so acquired for the benefit of a venture then about to end, and thus prolong by indirection its responsibilities and duties. The trouble about his conduct is that he excluded his coadventurer from any chance to compete, from any chance to enjoy the opportunity for benefit that had come to him alone by virtue of his agency. This chance, if nothing more, he was under a duty to concede. The price of its denial is an extension of the trust at the option and for the benefit of the one whom he excluded.

No answer is it to say that the chance would have been of little value even if seasonably offered. Such a calculus of probabilities is beyond the science of the chancery. Salmon, the real estate operator, might have been preferred to Meinhard, the woolen merchant. On the other hand, Meinhard might have offered better terms, or reinforced his offer by alliance with the wealth of others. Perhaps he might even have persuaded the lessor to renew the Bristol lease alone, postponing for a time, in return for higher rentals, the improvement of adjoining lots. We know that even under the lease as made the time for the enlargement of the building was delayed for seven years. All these opportunities were cut away from him through another's intervention. He knew that Salmon was the manager. As the time drew near for the expiration of the lease, he would naturally assume from silence, if from nothing else, that the lessor was willing to extend it for a term of years, or at least to let it stand as a lease from year to year. Not impossibly the lessor would have done so, whatever his protestations of unwillingness, if Salmon had not given assent to a project more attractive. At all events, notice of termination, even if not necessary, might seem, not unreasonably, to be something to be looked for, if the business was over and another tenant was to enter. In the absence of such notice, the matter of an extension was one that would naturally be attended to by the manager of the enterprise and not neglected altogether. At least, there was nothing in the situation to give warning to any one that while the lease was still in being, there had come to the manager an offer of extension which he had locked within his breast to be utilized by himself alone. The very fact that Salmon was in control with exclusive powers of direction charged him the more obviously with the duty of disclosure, since only through disclosure could opportunity be equalized. If he might cut off renewal by a purchase for his own benefit when four months were to pass before the lease would have an end, he might do so with equal right while there remained as many years * * *. He might steal a march on his comrade under cover of the darkness, and then hold the captured ground. Loyalty and comradeship are not so easily abjured.

Little profit will come from a dissection of the precedents. None precisely similar is cited in the briefs of counsel. What is similar in many, or so it seems to us, is the animating principle. Authority is, of course, abundant that one partner may not appropriate to his own use a renewal of a lease, though its term is to begin at the expiration of the partnership (*Mitchell v. Reed, 61 N. Y. 123; 84 N. Y. 556*). The lease at hand with its many changes is not strictly a renewal. Even so, the standard of loyalty for those in trust relations is without the fixed divisions of a graduated scale. There is indeed a dictum in one of our decisions that a partner, though he may not renew a lease, may purchase [the property itself] if he acts openly and fairly (*Anderson v. Lemon, 8 N. Y. 236 * * *). It is a dictum, and no more, for on the ground that he had acted slyly he was charged as a trustee. The holding is thus in favor of the conclusion that a purchase as well as a lease will succumb to the infection of secrecy and silence. Against the dictum in that case, moreover, may be set the opinion of Dwight, C., in *Mitchell* v. *Read*, where there is a dictum to the contrary

(61 N. Y. at p. 143). To say that a partner is free without restriction to buy * * * the [leased] property where the business is conducted is to say in effect that he may strip the good will of its chief element of value, since good will is largely dependent upon continuity of possession * * * Equity refuses to confine within the bounds of classified transactions its precept of a loyalty that is undivided and unselfish. Certain at least it is that a "man obtaining his *locus standi* [literally "place of standing"], and his opportunity for making such arrangements, by the position he occupies as a partner, is bound by his obligation to his co-partners in such dealings not to separate his interest from theirs, but, if he acquires any benefit, to communicate it to them" * * *

We have no thought to hold that Salmon was guilty of a conscious purpose to defraud. Very likely he assumed in all good faith that with the approaching end of the venture he might ignore his coadventurer and take the extension for himself. He had given to the enterprise time and labor as well as money. He had made it a success. Meinhard, who had given money, but neither time nor labor, had already been richly paid. There might seem to be something grasping in his insistence upon more. Such recriminations are not unusual when coadventurers fall out. They are not without their force if conduct is to be judged by the common standards of competitors. That is not to say that they have pertinency here. Salmon had put himself in a position in which thought of self was to be renounced, however hard the abnegation. He was much more than a coadventurer. He was a managing coadventurer * * * For him and for those like him, the rule of undivided loyalty is relentless and supreme * * *. A different question would be here if there were lacking any nexus of relation between the business conducted by the manager and the opportunity brought to him as an incident of management.* * * For this problem, as for most, there are distinctions of degree. If Salmon had received from Gerry a proposition to lease a building at a location far removed, he might have held for himself the privilege thus acquired, or so we shall assume. Here the subject-matter of the new lease was an extension and enlargement of the subject-matter of the old one. A managing coadventurer appropriating the benefit of such a lease without warning to his partner might fairly expect to be reproached with conduct that was underhand, or lacking, to say the least, in reasonable candor, if the partner were to surprise him in the act of signing the new instrument. Conduct subject to that reproach does not receive from equity a healing benediction

A question remains as to the form and extent of the equitable interest to be allotted to the plaintiff. The trust as declared has been held to attach to the lease which was in the name of the defendant corporation. We think it ought to attach at the option of the defendant Salmon to the shares of stock which were owned by him or were under his control. The difference may be important if the lessee shall wish to execute an assignment of the lease, as it ought to be free to do with the consent of the lessor. On the other hand, an equal division of the shares might lead to other hardships.

It might take away from Salmon the power of control and management which under the plan of the joint venture he was to have from first to last. The number of shares to be allotted to the plaintiff should, therefore, be reduced to such an extent as may be necessary to preserve to the defendant Salmon the expected measure of dominion. To that end an extra share should be added to his half.

Subject to this adjustment, we agree with the Appellate Division that the plaintiff's equitable interest is to be measured by the value of half of the entire lease, and not merely by half of some undivided part. A single building covers the whole area. Physical division is impracticable along the lines of the Bristol site, the keystone of the whole. Division of interests and burdens is equally impracticable. Salmon, as tenant under the new lease, or as guarantor of the performance of the tenant's obligations, might well protest if Meinhard, claiming an equitable interest, had offered to assume a liability not equal to Salmon's, but only half as great. He might justly insist that the lease must be accepted by his coadventurer in such form as it had been given, and not constructively divided into imaginary fragments. What must be yielded to the one may be demanded by the other. The lease as it has been executed is single and entire. If confusion has resulted from the union of adjoining parcels, the trustee who consented to the union must bear the inconvenience * * *.

* * *

ANDREWS, J. (dissenting). * * *

* * * Fair dealing and a scrupulous regard for honesty is required. But nothing more. It may be stated generally that a partner may not for his own benefit secretly take a renewal of a firm lease to himself. * * * Yet under very exceptional circumstances this may not be wholly true. * * *

Where the trustee, or the partner or the tenant in common, takes no new lease but buys the [property] in good faith a somewhat different question arises. Here is no direct appropriation of the expectancy of renewal. Here is no offshoot of the original lease. We so held in *Anderson v. Lemon (8 N.Y. 236)* * * * The issue then is whether actual fraud, dishonesty, unfairness is present in the transaction. If so, the purchaser may well be held as a trustee. * * *

With this view of the law I am of the opinion that the issue here is simple. Was the transaction in view of all the circumstances surrounding it unfair and inequitable? I reach this conclusion for two reasons. There was no general partnership, merely a joint venture for a limited object, to end at a fixed time. The new lease, covering additional property, containing many new and unusual terms and conditions, with a possible duration of eighty years, was more nearly the purchase of the [property] than the ordinary [lease] renewal with which the authorities are concerned.

The findings of the referee are to the effect that before 1902, Mrs. Louisa M. Gerry was the owner of a plot on the corner of Fifth avenue and

Forty-second street, New York, containing 9,312 square feet. On it had been built the old Bristol Hotel. Walter J. Salmon was in the real estate business, renting, managing and operating buildings. On April 10th of that year Mrs. Gerry leased the property to him for a term extending from May 1, 1902, to April 30, 1922. The property was to be used for offices and business, and the design was that the lessee should so remodel the hotel at his own expense as to fit it for such purposes, all alterations and additions, however, at once to become the property of the lessor. The lease might not be assigned without written consent.

Morton H. Meinhard was a woolen merchant. At some period during the negotiations between Mr. Salmon and Mrs. Gerry, so far as the findings show without the latter's knowledge, he became interested in the transaction. Before the lease was executed he advanced $5,000 toward the cost of the proposed alterations. Finally, on May 19th he and Salmon entered into a written agreement. "During the period of twenty years from the 1st day of May, 1902," the parties agree to share equally in the expense needed "to reconstruct, alter, manage and operate the Bristol Hotel property;" and in all payments required by the lease, and in all losses incurred "during the full term of the lease, *i.e.*, from the first day of May, 1902, to the 1st day of May, 1922." During the same term net profits are to be divided. Mr. Salmon has sole power to "manage, lease, underlet and operate" the premises. If he dies, Mr. Meinhard shall be consulted before any disposition is made of the lease, and if Mr. Salmon's representatives decide to dispose of it, and the decision is theirs, Mr. Meinhard is to be given the first chance to take the unexpired term upon the same conditions they could obtain from others.

The referee [the person employed to determine the facts of the case and render an initial judgment] finds that this arrangement did not create a partnership between Mr. Salmon and Mr. Meinhard. In this he is clearly right. He is equally right in holding that while no general partnership existed the two men had entered into a joint adventure and that while the legal title to the lease was in Mr. Salmon, Mr. Meinhard had some sort of an equitable interest therein. Mr. Salmon was to manage the property for their joint benefit. He was bound to use good faith. He could not willfully destroy the lease, the object of the adventure, to the detriment of Mr. Meinhard.

Mr. Salmon went into possession and control of the property. The alterations were made. At first came losses. Then large profits which were duly distributed. At all times Mr. Salmon has acted as manager.

Some time before 1922 Mr. Elbridge T. Gerry became the owner of the reversion. He was already the owner of an adjoining lot on Fifth avenue and of four lots adjoining on Forty-second street, in all 11,587 square feet, covered by five separate buildings. Obviously all this property together was more valuable than the sum of the value of the separate parcels. Some plan to develop the property as a whole seems to have occurred to

Mr. Gerry. He arranged that all leases on his five lots should expire on the same day as the Bristol Hotel lease. Then in 1921 he negotiated with various persons and corporations seeking to obtain a desirable tenant who would put up a building to cover the entire tract, for this was the policy he had adopted. These negotiations lasted for some months. They failed. About January 1, 1922, Mr. Gerry's agent approached Mr. Salmon and began to negotiate with him for the lease of the entire tract. Upon this he insisted as he did upon the erection of a new and expensive building covering the whole. He would not consent to the renewal of the Bristol lease on any terms. This effort resulted in a lease to the Midpoint Realty Company, a corporation entirely owned and controlled by Mr. Salmon. For our purposes the paper may be treated as if the agreement was made with Mr. Salmon himself.

In many respects, besides the increase in the land demised, the new lease differs from the old. Instead of an annual rent of $55,000 it is now from $350,000 to $475,000. Instead of a fixed term of twenty years it may now be, at the lessee's option, eighty. Instead of alterations in an existing structure costing about $200,000 a new building is contemplated costing $3,000,000. Of this sum $1,500,000 is to be advanced by the lessor to the lessee, "but not to its successors or assigns," and is to be repaid in installments. Again no assignment or sale of the lease may be made without the consent of the lessor.

This lease is valuable. In making it Mr. Gerry acted in good faith without any collusion with Mr. Salmon and with no purpose to deprive Mr. Meinhard of any equities he might have. But as to the negotiations leading to it or as to the execution of the lease itself Mr. Meinhard knew nothing. Mr. Salmon acted for himself to acquire the lease for his own benefit.

Under these circumstances the referee has found and the Appellate Division agrees with him, that Mr. Meinhard is entitled to an interest in the second lease, he having promptly elected to assume his share of the liabilities imposed thereby. This conclusion is based upon the proposition that under the original contract between the two men "the enterprise was a joint venture, the relation between the parties was fiduciary and governed by principles applicable to partnerships," therefore, as the new lease is a graft upon the old, Mr. Salmon might not acquire its benefits for himself alone.

Were this a general partnership between Mr. Salmon and Mr. Meinhard I should have little doubt as to the correctness of this result assuming the new lease to be an offshoot of the old. * * *

We have here a different situation governed by less drastic principles. I assume that where parties engage in a joint enterprise each owes to the other the duty of the utmost good faith in all that relates to their common venture. Within its scope they stand in a fiduciary relationship. I assume *prima facie* that even as between joint adventurers one may not secretly obtain a renewal of the lease of property actually used in the joint adventure where the possibility of renewal is expressly or impliedly involved in the enterprise. I assume also that Mr. Meinhard had an equitable interest in the Bristol Hotel lease. Further, that an expectancy of renewal inhered in that lease. Two questions then arise. Under his contract did he share in that expectancy? And if so, did that expectancy mature into a graft of the original lease? To both questions my answer is "no."

The one complaint made is that Mr. Salmon obtained the new lease without informing Mr. Meinhard of his intention. Nothing else. There is no claim of actual fraud. No claim of misrepresentation to any one. Here was no movable property to be acquired by a new tenant at a sacrifice to its owners. No good will, largely dependent on location, built up by the joint efforts of two men. Here was a refusal of the landlord to renew the Bristol lease on any terms; a proposal made by him, not sought by Mr. Salmon, and a choice by him and by the original lessor of the person with whom they wished to deal shown by the covenants against assignment or underletting, and by their ignorance of the arrangement with Mr. Meinhard.

What then was the scope of the adventure into which the two men entered? It is to be remembered that before their contract was signed Mr. Salmon had obtained the lease of the Bristol property. Very likely the matter had been earlier discussed between them. The $5,000 advance by Mr. Meinhard indicates that fact. But it has been held that the written contract defines their rights and duties.

Having the lease Mr. Salmon assigns no interest in it to Mr. Meinhard. He is to manage the property. It is for him to decide what alterations shall be made and to fix the rents. But for twenty years from May 1, 1902, Salmon is to make all advances from his own funds and Meinhard is to pay him personally on demand one-half of all expenses incurred and all losses sustained "during the full term of said lease," and during the same period Salmon is to pay him a part of the net profits. There was no joint capital provided.

It seems to me that the venture so inaugurated had in view a limited object and was to end at a limited time. There was no intent to expand it into a far greater undertaking lasting for many years. The design was to exploit a particular lease. Doubtless in it Mr. Meinhard had an equitable interest, but in it alone. This interest terminated when the joint adventure terminated. There was no intent that for the benefit of both any advantage should be taken of the chance of renewal—that the adventure should be continued beyond that date. Mr. Salmon has done all he promised to do in return for Mr. Meinhard's undertaking when he distributed profits up to May 1, 1922. Suppose this lease, non-assignable without the consent of the lessor, had contained a renewal option. Could Mr. Meinhard have exercised it? Could he have insisted that Mr. Salmon do so? Had Mr. Salmon done so could he insist that the agreement to share losses still existed or could Mr. Meinhard have claimed that the joint adventure was still to continue for twenty or eighty years? I do not think so. The adventure by its express terms ended on May 1, 1922. The contract by its language and by its whole import excluded the idea that the tenant's expectancy was to subsist for the benefit of the plaintiff. On that date whatever there was left of value in the lease reverted to Mr. Salmon, as it would had the lease been for thirty years instead of twenty. Any equity which Mr. Meinhard possessed was in the particular lease itself, not in any possibility of renewal. There was nothing unfair in Mr. Salmon's conduct.

I might go further were it necessary. Under the circumstances here presented had the lease run to both the parties I doubt whether the taking by one of a renewal without the knowledge of the other would cause interference by a court of equity. An illustration may clarify my thought. A and B enter into a joint venture to resurface a highway between Albany and Schenectady. They rent a parcel of land for the storage of materials. A, unknown to B, agrees with the lessor to rent that parcel and one adjoining it after the venture is finished, for an iron foundry. Is the act unfair? Would any general statements, scattered here and there through opinions dealing with other circumstance, be thought applicable? In other words, the mere fact that the joint venturers rent property together does not call for the strict rule that applies to general partners. Many things may excuse what is there forbidden. Nor here does any possibility of renewal exist as part of the venture. The nature of the undertaking excludes such an idea.

So far I have treated the new lease as if it were a renewal of the old. As already indicated, I do not take that view. Such a renewal could not be obtained. Any expectancy that it might be had vanished. What Mr. Salmon obtained was not a graft springing from the Bristol lease, but something distinct and different—as distinct as if for a building across Fifth avenue. I think also that in the absence of some fraudulent or unfair act the secret purchase of the reversion even by one partner is rightful. Substantially this is such a purchase. Because of the mere label of a transaction we do not place it on one side of the line or the other. Here is involved the possession of a large and most valuable unit of property for eighty years, the destruction of all existing structures and the erection of a new and expensive building covering the whole. No fraud, no deceit, no calculated secrecy is found. Simply that the arrangement was made without the knowledge of Mr. Meinhard. I think this not enough. * * *

NOTES AND QUESTIONS

1. This is a case that turns on its facts, but it has also come to be accepted as the leading case on fiduciary responsibility, widely applicable to the duty not only of joint adventurers and partners, but also to corporate officers and directors. Do you understand what is meant by "fiduciary" responsibility, as Cardozo outlines it? It is also a case involving "equity," which for our purposes we can define as the power of the court to remake the legal relationship between parties when one of them has engaged in conduct which is found to be unfair or unethical. A court exercising equitable powers,

for example, can set aside a contract for fraud. Generally speaking, as law students know, remedies in equity are exceptional, and may only be granted where legal remedies (e.g. monetary remedies for breach of contract) are inadequate. Do you understand why an equitable remedy might be appropriate in *Meinhard v. Salmon*?

2. The principal technical legal issue in *Meinhard v. Salmon,* or at least the one that seems to divide the majority from the dissenters, is the legal effect of the distinction between a joint venture and a partnership. A joint venture can involve individuals, as in *Meinhard v. Salmon*, or it can involve giant corporations. This joint venture case is of interest to us not only to read two opinions from two of the greatest New York common law judges, but also to understand the precise nature of the fiduciary duty of partners, since, as both Cardozo and Andrews make clear, while the joint venture is ongoing, and with regard to the specific task of the joint venture, the parties owe each other the same fiduciary duty as that owed by partners to each other. Judge Andrews's opinion is particularly good at laying out the differences between joint ventures and partnerships. Why does he dissent from Cardozo's opinion, which opinion, by the way, is the one that has gained lasting fame? Is this fame deserved? Who got it right, Cardozo or Andrews?

3. Robert B. Thompson, a law professor at Vanderbilt, and one of the country's leading experts on fiduciary duties, has formulated an intriguing hypothetical in connection with *Meinhard v. Salmon.* Suppose, he suggests, that Salmon, before making his agreement with Gerry, had said to Meinhard, "I know we haven't talked in a long time, but I wanted you to know that Mr. Gerry is looking to develop a large new building on the Bristol property plus some additional land he owns at 5th Avenue and 42nd and I am talking to him about a[n] eighty-year lease for the construction of a new skyscraper. You are welcome to pursue the opportunity on your own, but as for us, I have done the lion's share of the work for twenty years and I am not interested in entering into a similar relationship going forward. I am tired of carrying you." If Solomon had said that to Meinhard, would Cardozo have decided the case differently? Would you? See generally, for this hypothetical and an informative study of the background of the case, Robert B. Thompson, "The Story of *Meinhard v. Salmon*: Fiduciary Duty's Punctilio," in J. Mark Ramseyer, Ed., Corporate Law Stories 105, 126–127 (2009).

4. What happened in *Meinhard v. Salmon* can perhaps be a bit better appreciated if one knows a bit more about Judge Benjamin Cardozo. Apart from being widely regarded as one of the greatest legal minds in American history both from his distinguished service on the Court of Appeals of New York and later the US Supreme Court, Cardozo is considered one of our greatest legal writers. Several of Cardozo's decisions are a staple part of the law school canon, and are regularly included in casebooks. Because of his stature in the pantheon of American jurisprudence, Cardozo's life has increasingly become a subject of scholarly interest. Harvard Law Professor Andrew L. Kaufman, a Cardozo clerk, and the author of the leading Cardozo biography, *Cardozo* (1998), examines Cardozo's early life, in particular Cardozo's relationship with his father, Albert. Albert Cardozo was a New York state judge with strong ties to the notoriously corrupt Democratic political organization,

Tammany Hall. Albert conducted his court in a highly unorthodox manner, including occasionally meeting with only one side's counsel before issuing a decision. He eventually faced five impeachment charges, among them for refusing to block an order which denied alimony to the wife of a New York State Senator, Thomas C. Fields. Id., at 17. Albert Cardozo eventually resigned rather than face removal by the state senate. Professor Kaufman examines how Cardozo's father's misconduct led Benjamin Cardozo to pursue a career in the law. Kaufman reports that according to E.R.A. Seligman, a Columbia University professor and close family friend, Cardozo "felt that he had to clear up the disgrace to his family name and could do this only as a lawyer." Similarly, according to Judge Abram Elkus, a friend and brief colleague on the Court of Appeals, "Cardozo once mentioned to him a desire to 'work away' his father's disgrace." Id., at 40. Given Judge Cardozo's family background, does it make sense that his decision in *Meinhard* places such a heavy weight on the "punctilio of honor most sensitive"?

5. Professor Kaufman also points out that critics have often disagreed as to the level of candor in Judge Cardozo's decisions. While some critics praise Cardozo for his honesty and seemingly morally driven decisions, others have called him a master of deception. Kaufman writes "Cardozo was fundamentally honest in his opinions. He said what he meant, and he meant what he said." Id., at 445. Kaufman goes on to write "sometimes ... he left out some facts that now seem important to a full understanding of the problem, especially from the perspective of the losing party. This situation did not happen often, and I see no evidence that Cardozo was being manipulative. Either his literary bent may have led him astray, or he may simply have made a mistake in assuming that he had stated everything he needed for the reader to understand the case." Ibid. Reading *Meinhard*, did you find Cardozo's opinion completely candid with the facts, especially compared to the account given by Judge Andrews? Do you agree with Kaufman, that Cardozo was essentially honest, although his literary style sometimes got the better of him?

6. Professor Kaufman and many other legal scholars generally praise what we might describe as the delightfully florid prose of Judge Cardozo, but one other prominent liberal legal theorist, United States Court of Appeals Judge Jerome Frank, published an anonymous scathing critique of Cardozo's decisions shortly after Cardozo died. Beginning with a biographical interpretation and relying on psychoanalysis, Frank writes of a Cardozo "[d]eeply hurt, in his youth" who "retreat[ed] from 20th Century living" and "re-entered it disguised as an 18th Century scholar and gentleman." Frank goes on to describe Cardozo's writing as having "an alien grace." Anon Y. Mous [Jerome Frank]. "The Speech of Judges: A Dissenting Opinion." 29 Va. L. Rev. 625, 630 (1942–1943). Said Frank, Cardozo's writing style is "an unmitigated nuisance to the lawyer who must, in a work-a-day world, make use of his judicial opinions. They sometimes obscure where there is need for clarity." Id, at 637–638. Frank indicates that he prefers the writing style of Justices Black, Douglas, and Jackson, because "[t]hey write much as they talk, as their fellow Americans talk." Id., at 639. Given all this fuss about Cardozo's style, what importance do you give to the manner in which a judge explains the reasoning behind a decision? Is it more important to be clear and concise? Do judges

have to persuade as well as explain, and is style important for that purpose? Judge Frank was a notoriously scrappy individual. Is he barking up the wrong tree here?

7. Situated somewhere between the many members in the legal academy of the Cardozo fan club and more dyspeptic scholars like Jerome Frank is Judge Richard Posner, formerly chief judge of the United States Court of Appeals for the Seventh Circuit, and formerly a law professor at the University of Chicago. Posner, the most famous practitioner of the law and economics school, now a leading legal pragmatist, wrote in his book *Cardozo: A Study in Reputation* (1990), that Cardozo's decision in *Meinhard* is "the most famous of Cardozo's moralistic opinions." Id., at 104. Referring to the punctilio passage, Posner writes "it is possible to object that these are just words, and florid ones at that. But they are memorable words, and they set a tone. They make the difference between an arm's length relationship and a fiduciary relationship vivid, unforgettable." Id., at 105. Posner continues, "a more informative description of the concept would be that, while normally a party to a contract is entitled, with certain exceptions, to take advantage of the other party's ignorance, a fiduciary is not; he must treat the other party's interests as if they were his own. But this is awfully dry." Ibid. Posner argues that there is a "halo effect" surrounding Cardozo's opinion, and concludes that it is "the power of the vivid statement" that lifts Cardozo's opinions "out of the swarm of humdrum, often numbing, judicial opinions, rivets attention, crystallizes relevant concerns and considerations, [and] provokes thoughts." Id., at 136. For Posner, the success of Judge Cardozo's opinions comes as much from his rhetoric as it does from his logic. Does all this scholarly attention to the rhetorical skills, and psychological underpinnings of Cardozo's decision make sense to you? After reading about Cardozo, do you have more or less faith in the wisdom of *Meinhard v. Salmon*?

8. There was a time when whole courses in agency and whole courses in partnership were required parts of the law school curriculum, but for a short course in business associations, where our concentration is on the form of entity that will most probably concern most of you, the corporation, we can limit our consideration of agency and partnership to the fundamental principles of authority, equality, and fiduciary duty that the cases you have so far studied have explored. Before going on to study corporations, and to contrast them with other legal entities, we should pause to recognize an increasingly popular hybrid form, the limited liability company, or LLC.

C. THE LIMITED LIABILITY COMPANY

ELF ATOCHEM NORTH AMERICA, INC. v. JAFFARI AND MALEK, LLC

Supreme Court of Delaware.
727 A.2d 286, 79 A.L.R.5th 803 (1999).

VEASEY, Chief Justice:

This is a case of first impression before this Court involving the Delaware Limited Liability Company Act (the "Act"). The limited liability company ("LLC") is a relatively new entity that has emerged in recent years as an attractive vehicle to facilitate business relationships and transactions. The wording and architecture of the Act is somewhat complicated, but it is designed to achieve what is seemingly a simple concept—to permit persons or entities ("members") to join together in an environment of private ordering to form and operate the enterprise under an LLC agreement with tax benefits akin to a partnership and limited liability akin to the corporate form.

*   *   *

FACTS

Plaintiff below-appellant Elf Atochem North America, Inc., a Pennsylvania Corporation ("Elf"), manufactures and distributes solvent-based maskants to the aerospace and aviation industries throughout the world. * * * Defendant below-appellee Cyrus A. Jaffari is the president of Malek, Inc., a California Corporation. Jaffari had developed an innovative, environmentally friendly alternative to the solvent-based maskants that presently dominate the market.

For decades, the aerospace and aviation industries have used solvent-based maskants in the chemical milling process. [Manufacturers of airplanes and missiles use maskants in the process of chemical milling in order to reduce the weight of their products. Chemical milling is a process where a caustic substance is placed on metal parts in order to dissolve the metal with which it comes into contact. Maskants are used to protect those areas of metal intended to be preserved.] Recently, however, the Environmental Protection Agency ("EPA") classified solvent-based maskants as hazardous chemicals and air contaminants. To avoid conflict with EPA regulations, Elf considered developing or distributing a maskant less harmful to the environment.

In the mid-nineties, Elf approached Jaffari and proposed investing in his product and assisting in its marketing. Jaffari found the proposal attractive since his company, Malek, Inc., possessed limited resources and little international sales expertise. Elf and Jaffari agreed to undertake a joint venture that was to be carried out using a limited liability company as the vehicle.

On October 29, 1996, Malek, Inc. caused to be filed a Certificate of Formation with the Delaware Secretary of State, thus forming Malek LLC, a Delaware limited liability company under the Act. The certificate of formation is a relatively brief and formal document that is the first statutory step in creating the LLC as a separate legal entity. * * * The certificate does not contain a comprehensive agreement among the parties, and the statute contemplates that the certificate of formation is to be complemented by the terms of the Agreement.[1]

Next, Elf, Jaffari and Malek, Inc. entered into a series of agreements providing for the governance and operation of the joint venture. Of particular importance to this litigation, Elf, Malek, Inc., and Jaffari entered into the Agreement,[2] a comprehensive and integrated document of 38 single-spaced pages setting forth detailed provisions for the governance of Malek LLC, which is not itself a signatory to the Agreement. Elf and Malek LLC entered into an Exclusive Distributorship Agreement in which Elf would be the exclusive, worldwide distributor for Malek LLC. The Agreement provides that Jaffari will be the manager of Malek LLC. Jaffari and Malek LLC entered into an employment agreement providing for Jaffari's employment as chief executive officer of Malek LLC.

The Agreement is the operative document for purposes of this Opinion, however. Under the Agreement, Elf contributed $1 million in exchange for a 30 percent interest in Malek LLC. Malek, Inc. contributed its rights to the water-based maskant in exchange for a 70 percent interest in Malek LLC.

The Agreement contains an arbitration clause covering all disputes. The clause, Section 13.8, provides that "any controversy or dispute arising out of this Agreement, the interpretation of any of the provisions hereof, or the action or inaction of any Member or Manager hereunder shall be submitted to arbitration in San Francisco, California...." Section 13.8 further provides: "No action ... based upon any claim arising out of or related to this Agreement shall be instituted in any court by any Member except (a) an action to compel arbitration ... or (b) an action to enforce an award obtained in an arbitration proceeding...." The Agreement also contains a forum selection clause, Section 13.7, providing that all members consent to: "exclusive jurisdiction of the state and federal courts sitting in California in any action on a claim arising out of, under or in connection with this Agreement or the transactions contemplated by this Agreement, provided such claim is not required to be arbitrated pursuant to Section 13.8"; and personal jurisdiction in California. The Distribution Agreement contains no forum selection or arbitration clause.

ELF'S SUIT IN THE COURT OF CHANCERY

On April 27, 1998, Elf sued Jaffari and Malek LLC individually and derivatively[3] on behalf of Malek LLC, in the Delaware Court of Chancery,

---

1. *See* 6 Del. C. § 18–201(d), which provides:

A limited liability company agreement may be entered into either before, after, or at the time of the filing of a certificate of formation and, whether entered into before, after or at the time of such filing, may be made effective as of the formation of the limited liability company or at such other time or date as provided in the limited liability company agreement.

2. *See* the definition section of the statute, 6 *Del. C.* § 18–101(7), defining the term "limited liability company agreement" as "any agreement ... of the ... members as to the affairs of a limited liability company and the conduct of its business," and setting forth a nonexclusive list of what it may provide.

3. A "derivative" lawsuit is one brought by a shareholder in order to pursue a cause of action seeking equitable remedies. Among other claims, Elf alleged that Jaffari breached his fiduciary duty to Malek LLC, pushed Malek LLC to the brink of insolvency by withdrawing funds for personal use, interfered with business opportunities, failed to make disclosures to Elf, and threatened to make poor quality maskant and to violate environmental regulations. Elf also alleged breach of contract, tortious interference with prospective business relations, and (solely as to Jaffari) fraud.

The Court of Chancery granted defendants' motion to dismiss based on lack of subject matter jurisdiction. * * * The court held that Elf's claims arose under the Agreement, or the transactions contemplated by the agreement, and were directly related to Jaffari's actions * * * as manager of Malek LLC. * * * Therefore, the court found that the Agreement governed the question of jurisdiction and that only a court of law or arbitrator in California is empowered to decide these claims. * * * Elf now appeals the order of the Court of Chancery dismissing the complaint.

CONTENTIONS OF THE PARTIES

Elf claims that the Court of Chancery erred in holding that the arbitration and forum selection clauses in the Agreement governed, and thus deprived that court of jurisdiction to adjudicate all of Elf's claims, including its derivative claims made on behalf of Malek LLC. Elf contends that, since Malek LLC is not a party to the Agreement, it is not bound by the forum selection provisions. Elf also argues that the court erred in failing to classify its claim as derivative on behalf of Malek LLC against Jaffari as manager. Therefore, Elf claims that the Court of Chancery should have adjudicated the dispute. Finally, Elf argues that the dispute resolution clauses of the Agreement are invalid under Section 109(d) of the Act, which, it alleges, prohibits the parties from vesting exclusive jurisdiction in a forum outside of Delaware. * * *

Defendants claim that Elf contracted with Malek, Inc. and Jaffari that all disputes that arise out of, under, or in connection with the Agreement must be resolved exclusively in California by arbitration or court proceedings. Defendants allege that the characterization of Elf's claim as direct or derivative is irrelevant, as the Agreement provides that the members would not institute "any" action at law or equity except one to compel arbitration, and that any such action must be brought in California. Defendants also argue that, in reality, Elf's claims are direct, not derivative, claims against its fellow LLC members, Malek, Inc. and Jaffari.

---

that belongs to the shareholder's corporation, or, in this case, the LLC of which the plaintiff is a member. If there is any recovery in the derivative action the recovery (after attorneys fees are deducted) goes to the entity to whom the action belongs, and not to the plaintiff. In this case, you will have noticed there are both individual and derivative causes of action, so that, in other words, Elf is claiming that not only was there damage caused to it by the defendant's alleged misconduct, but there was also damage caused to the LLC. The opinion of the court is primarily concerned with the derivative action, that is the one that alleges wrong to the LLC, and it treats that action as if it were brought by the LLC itself, thus necessitating examination of the question whether the LLC itself is bound by the agreement to arbitrate disputes and to sue only in the courts of California.—ED.

With regard to the validity of Section 13.7, defendants argue that Section 18–109(d) of the Act is a permissive statute and does not prohibit the parties from vesting exclusive jurisdiction outside of Delaware. Thus, defendants assert that the Court of Chancery correctly held that the dispute resolution provisions of the Agreement are valid and apply to bar Elf from seeking relief in Delaware.

GENERAL SUMMARY OF BACKGROUND OF THE ACT

The phenomenon of business arrangements using "alternative entities" has been developing rapidly over the past several years. Long gone are the days when business planners were confined to corporate or partnership structures.

Limited partnerships date back to the 19th Century. They became an important and popular vehicle with the adoption of the Uniform Limited Partnership Act in 1916. Sixty years later, in 1976, the National Conference of Commissioners on Uniform State Laws approved and recommended to the states a Revised Uniform Limited Partnership Act ("RULPA"), many provisions of which were modeled after the innovative 1973 Delaware Limited Partnership (LP) Act. Difficulties with the workability of the 1976 RULPA prompted the Commissioners to amend RULPA in 1985. * * *

To date, 48 states and the District of Columbia have adopted the RULPA in either its 1976 or 1985 form. * * * Delaware adopted the RULPA with innovations designed to improve upon the Commissioners' product. * * * Since 1983, the General Assembly has amended the LP Act eleven times, with a view to continuing Delaware's status as an innovative leader in the field of limited partnerships.

The Delaware Act [regarding LLC's] was adopted in October 1992. * * * To date, the Act has been amended six times with a view to modernization. The LLC is an attractive form of business entity because it combines corporate-type limited liability with partnership-type flexibility and tax advantages.[4] The Act can be characterized as a "flexible statute" because it generally permits members to engage in private ordering with substantial freedom of contract to govern their relationship, provided they do not contravene any mandatory provisions of the Act. * * * Indeed, the LLC has been characterized as the "best of both worlds."[5]

The Delaware [LLC] Act has been modeled on the popular Delaware LP Act. * * * In fact, its architecture and much of its wording is almost identical to that of the Delaware LP Act. * * * Under the Act, a member of an LLC is treated much like a limited partner under the LP Act. * * *

---

4. *See* 1 Larry E. Ribstein & Robert R. Keatinge, *Ribstein and Keatinge on Limited Liability Companies,* § 2.02, at 2 (1998); Martin I. Lubaroff & Paul M. Altman, *Delaware Limited Liability Companies, in Delaware Law of Corporations & Business Organizations,* § 20.1 (R. Franklin Balotti & Jesse A. Finkelstein eds., 1998).

5. Lubaroff & Altman, supra, note [4] at § 20.1.

The policy of freedom of contract underlies both the Act and the LP Act. * * *

In August 1994, nearly two years after the enactment of the Delaware LLC Act, the Uniform Law Commissioners promulgated the Uniform Limited Liability Company Act (ULLCA). * * * To coordinate with later developments in federal tax guidelines regarding manager-managed LLCs, the Commissioners adopted minor changes in 1995. * * * The Commissioners further amended the ULLCA in 1996. Despite its purpose to promote uniformity and consistency, the ULLCA has not been widely popular. In fact, only seven jurisdictions have adopted the ULLCA since its creation in 1994. * * * A notable commentator on LLCs has argued that legislatures should look to either the Delaware Act or the Prototype Act created by the ABA when drafting state statutes.[6]

POLICY OF THE DELAWARE ACT

The basic approach of the Delaware Act is to provide members with broad discretion in drafting the Agreement and to furnish default provisions when the members' agreement is silent. * * * The Act is replete with fundamental provisions made subject to modification in the Agreement (*e.g.,* "unless otherwise provided in a limited liability company agreement....").[7]

* * *

FREEDOM OF CONTRACT

Section 18–1101(b) of the Act, like the essentially identical Section 17–1101(c) of the LP Act, provides that "it is the policy of [the Act] to give the maximum effect to the principle of freedom of contract and to the enforceability of limited liability company agreements." * * *

In general * * * only where the agreement is inconsistent with mandatory statutory provisions will the members' agreement be invalidated. * * * Such statutory provisions are likely to be those intended to protect third parties * * * not necessarily the contracting members. As a framework for decision, we apply that principle to the issues before us, without expressing any views more broadly. * * *

THE ARBITRATION AND FORUM SELECTION CLAUSES IN THE AGREEMENT ARE A BAR TO JURISDICTION IN THE COURT OF CHANCERY

In vesting the Court of Chancery with jurisdiction, the Act accomplished at least three purposes: (1) it assured that the Court of Chancery

---

6. See Larry B. Ribstein, A Critique of the Uniform Limited Liability Company Act, 25 Stetson L. Rev. 311, 329 (1995).

7. * * * For example, members are free to contract among themselves concerning management of the LLC, including who is to manage the LLC, the establishment of classes of members, voting, procedures for holding meetings of members, or considering matters without a meeting.* * *

has jurisdiction it might not otherwise have because it is a court of limited jurisdiction that requires traditional equitable relief or specific legislation to act; * * * (2) it established the Court of Chancery as the default forum in the event the members did not provide another choice of forum or dispute resolution mechanism; and (3) it tends to center interpretive litigation in Delaware courts with the expectation of uniformity. Nevertheless, the arbitration provision of the Agreement in this case fosters the Delaware policy favoring alternate dispute resolution mechanisms, including arbitration. Such mechanisms are an important goal of Delaware legislation, * * * court rules,* * * and jurisprudence.[8]

MALEK LLC's FAILURE TO SIGN THE AGREEMENT DOES NOT AFFECT THE MEMBERS' AGREEMENT GOVERNING DISPUTE RESOLUTION

Elf argues that because Malek LLC, on whose behalf Elf allegedly brings these claims, is not a party to the Agreement, the derivative claims it brought on behalf of Malek LLC are not governed by the arbitration and forum selection clauses of the Agreement.

Elf argues that Malek LLC came into existence on October 29, 1996, when the parties filed its Certificate of Formation with the Delaware Secretary of State. The parties did not sign the Agreement until November 4, 1996. Elf contends that Malek LLC existed as an LLC as of October 29, 1996, but never agreed to the Agreement because it did not sign it. Because Malek LLC never expressly assented to the arbitration and forum selection clauses within the Agreement, Elf argues it can sue derivatively on behalf of Malek LLC pursuant to 6 *Del. C.* § 18–1001.[9]

We are not persuaded by this argument. Section 18–101(7) defines the limited liability company agreement as "any agreement, written or oral, *of the member or members* as to the affairs of a limited liability company and the conduct of its business." * * * Here, Malek, Inc. and Elf, the members of Malek LLC, executed the Agreement to carry out the affairs and business of Malek LLC and to provide for arbitration and forum selection.

Notwithstanding Malek LLC's failure to sign the Agreement, Elf's claims are subject to the arbitration and forum selection clauses of the Agreement. The Act is a statute designed to permit members maximum flexibility in entering into an agreement to govern their relationship. * * * It is the members who are the real parties in interest. The LLC is simply their joint business vehicle. This is the contemplation of the statute in prescribing the outlines of a limited liability company agreement. * * *

---

8. *See SBC Interactive, Inc. v. Corporate Media Partners, Del. Supr., 714 A.2d 758, 761 (1998)* (holding that public policy of Delaware favors arbitration and doubt as to arbitrability is to be resolved in favor of arbitration). * * *

9. 6 Del. C. § 18–1001 provides: "Right to bring action. A member may ... bring an action in the Court of Chancery in the right of a limited liability company to recover a judgment in its favor if managers or members with authority to do so have refused to bring the action or if an effort to cause those managers or members to bring the action is not likely to succeed."

CLASSIFICATION BY ELF OF ITS CLAIMS AS DERIVATIVE IS IRRELEVANT

Elf argues that the Court of Chancery erred in failing to classify its claims against Malek LLC as derivative. Elf contends that, had the court properly characterized its claims as derivative instead of direct, the arbitration and forum selection clauses would not have applied to bar adjudication in Delaware.

In the corporate context, "the derivative form of action permits an individual shareholder to bring 'suit to enforce a corporate cause of action against officers, directors and third parties.' "[10] The derivative suit is a corporate concept grafted onto the limited liability company form.[11] The Act expressly allows for a derivative suit, providing that "a member … may bring an action in the Court of Chancery in the right of a limited liability company to recover a judgment in its favor if managers or members with authority to do so have refused to bring the action or if an effort to cause those managers or members to bring the action is not likely to succeed." [6 *Del. C.* § 18–1001.]

Notwithstanding the Agreement to the contrary, Elf argues that Section 18–1001 permits the assertion of derivative claims of Malek LLC against Malek LLC's manager, Jaffari.

Although Elf correctly points out that Delaware law allows for derivative suits against management of an LLC, Elf contracted away its right to bring such an action in Delaware and agreed instead to dispute resolution in California. That is, Section 13.8 of the Agreement specifically provides that the parties (*i.e.,* Elf) agree to institute "no action at law or in equity based upon *any* claim arising out of or related to this Agreement" except an action to compel arbitration or to enforce an arbitration award. * * * Furthermore, under Section 13.7 of the Agreement, each member (*i.e.,* Elf) "consented to the exclusive jurisdiction of the state and federal courts sitting in California in *any* action on a claim arising out of, under or in connection with this Agreement or the transactions contemplated by this Agreement." * * *

Sections 13.7 and 13.8 of the Agreement do not distinguish between direct and derivative claims. They simply state that the members may not initiate *any* claims outside of California. Elf initiated this action in the Court of Chancery in contravention of its own contractual agreement. As a result, the Court of Chancery correctly held that all claims, whether derivative or direct, arose under, out of or in connection with the Agree-

---

10. Kamen v. Kemper Fin. Serv., 500 U.S. 90, 95, 114 L. Ed. 2d 152, 111 S. Ct. 1711 (1991) (citation omitted). See also Schleiff v. Baltimore & Ohio R.R. Co., Del. Ch., 36 Del. Ch. 342, 130 A.2d 321, 327 (1955) (in derivative action, shareholder "stands in the shoes" of the corporation).

11. See 6 Del. C. § 18–1001 (member of LLC may bring derivative action); Gotham Partners, L.P. v. Hallwood Realty Partners, L.P., 1998 WL 832631 (Nov. 10, 1998), Steele, V.C. (Nov. 10, 1998), (stating that derivative suit is a corporate action grafted onto the limited partnership form); see also Litman v. Prudential–Bache Properties, Inc., Del. Ch., 611 A.2d 12, 15 (1992) (holding "the determination of whether a fiduciary duty lawsuit is derivative or direct in nature is substantially the same for corporate cases as it is for limited partnership cases").

ment, and thus are covered by the arbitration and forum selection clauses.

This prohibition is so broad that it is dispositive of Elf's claims * * * that purport to be under the Distributorship Agreement that has no choice of forum provision. Notwithstanding the fact that the Distributorship Agreement is a separate document, in reality these counts are all subsumed under the rubric of the Agreement's forum selection clause for any claim "arising out of" and those that are "in connection with" the Agreement or transactions "contemplated by" or "related to" that Agreement under Sections 13.7 and 13.8. We agree with the Court of Chancery's decision that:

> plaintiffs's claims arise under the LLC Agreement or the transactions contemplated by the Agreement, and are directly related to Jaffari's "action or inaction" in connection with his role as the manager of Malek. Plainly, all of plaintiff's claims revolve around Jaffari's conduct (or misconduct) as Malek's manager. Virtually all the remedies that plaintiff seeks bear directly on Jaffari's duties and obligations under the LLC Agreement. Plaintiff's complaint that "Jaffari ... has totally disregarded his obligations under the *LLC Agreement* also lends support to my conclusion." * * *

The Court of Chancery was correct in holding that Elf's claims bear directly on Jaffari's duties and obligations under the Agreement. Thus, we decline to disturb its holding.

The Argument that Chancery Has "Special" Jurisdiction for Derivative Claims Must Fail

Elf claims that *6 Del. C.* §§ 18–110(a), 18–111 and 18–1001 vest the Court of Chancery with subject matter jurisdiction over this dispute. According to Elf, the Act grants the Court of Chancery subject matter jurisdiction over its claims for breach of fiduciary duty and removal of Jaffari, even though the parties contracted to arbitrate all such claims in California. In effect, Elf argues that the Act affords the Court of Chancery "special" jurisdiction to adjudicate its claims, notwithstanding a clear contractual agreement to the contrary.

Again, we are not persuaded by Elf's argument. Elf is correct that 6 *Del. C.* §§ 18–110(a) and 18–111 vest jurisdiction with the Court of Chancery in actions involving removal of managers and interpreting, applying or enforcing LLC agreements respectively. As noted above, Section 18–1001 provides that a party may bring derivative actions in the Court of Chancery. * * * Nevertheless, for the purpose of designating a more convenient forum, we find no reason why the members cannot alter the default jurisdictional provisions of the statute and contract away their right to file suit in Delaware.

For example, Elf argues that Section 18–110(a), which grants the Court of Chancery jurisdiction to hear claims involving the election or removal of a manager of an LLC, applies to the case at bar because Elf is seeking removal of Jaffari. * * * While Elf is correct on the substance of

Section 18–110(a), Elf is unable to convince this Court that the parties may not contract to avoid the applicability of Section 18–110(a). We hold that, because the policy of the Act is to give the maximum effect to the principle of freedom of contract and to the enforceability of LLC agreements, the parties may contract to avoid the applicability of Sections 18–110(a), 18–111, and 18–1001. * * * Here, the parties contracted as clearly as practicable when they relegated to California in Section 13.7 "any" dispute "arising out of, under or in connection with [the] Agreement or the transactions contemplated by [the] Agreement...." * * * Likewise, in Section 13.8: "*no action* at law or in equity based upon *any claim arising out of or related to*" * * * the Agreement may be brought, except in California, and then only to enforce arbitration in California.

Our conclusion is bolstered by the fact that Delaware recognizes a strong public policy in favor of arbitration. * * * Normally, doubts on the issue of whether a particular issue is arbitrable will be resolved in favor of arbitration. * * * In the case at bar, we do not believe there is any doubt of the parties' intention to agree to arbitrate *all* disputed matters in California. If we were to hold otherwise, arbitration clauses in existing LLC agreements could be rendered meaningless. By resorting to the alleged "special" jurisdiction * * * of the Court of Chancery, future plaintiffs could avoid their own arbitration agreements simply by couching their claims as derivative. Such a result could adversely affect many arbitration agreements already in existence in Delaware.

VALIDITY OF SECTION 13.7 OF THE AGREEMENT UNDER 6 DEL. C. § 18–109(D)

Elf argues that Section 13.7 of the Agreement, which provides that each member of Malek LLC "consents to the exclusive jurisdiction of the state and federal courts sitting in California in any action on a claim arising out of, under or in connection with this Agreement or the transactions contemplated by this Agreement ..." is invalid under Delaware law. Elf argues that Section 13.7 is invalid because it violates 6 *Del. C.* § 18–109(d).

Subsection 18–109(d) is part of Section 18–109 relating to "Service of process on managers and liquidating trustee." It provides:

> In a written limited liability company agreement or other writing, a manager or member *may* consent to be subject to the nonexclusive jurisdiction of the courts of, or arbitration in, a specified jurisdiction, or the exclusive jurisdiction of the courts of the State of Delaware, or the exclusivity of arbitration in a specified jurisdiction or the State of Delaware.... * * *

Section 18–109(d) does not expressly state that the parties are prohibited from agreeing to the *exclusive* subject matter jurisdiction of the courts or arbitration fora of a foreign jurisdiction. Thus, Elf contends that Section 18–109(d) prohibits vesting exclusive jurisdiction in a court outside of Delaware, which the parties have done in Section 13.7.

We decline to adopt such a strict reading of the statute. * * * Section 109(d) * * * is permissive in that it provides that the parties "may" agree to the non-exclusive jurisdiction of the courts of a foreign jurisdiction or to submit to the exclusive jurisdiction of Delaware. * * * In general, the legislature's use of "may" connotes the voluntary, not mandatory or exclusive, set of options.[12] The permissive nature of Section 18–109(d) complements the overall policy of the Act to give maximum effect to the parties' freedom of contract. * * * Although Section 18–109(d) fails to mention that the parties may agree to the *exclusive* jurisdiction of a foreign jurisdiction, the Act clearly does not state that the parties must agree to either one of the delineated options for subject matter jurisdiction. Had the General Assembly intended to prohibit the parties from vesting exclusive jurisdiction in arbitration or court proceedings in another state, it could have proscribed such an option. The Court of Chancery did not err in declining to strike down the validity of Section 13.7 or Section 13.8 of the Agreement.

CONCLUSION

We affirm the judgment of the Court of Chancery dismissing Elf Atochem's amended complaint for lack of subject matter jurisdiction.

NOTES AND QUESTIONS

1. This is a complex case, involving as it does obscure questions about subject matter jurisdiction, arbitration, derivative lawsuits, and the nature of the Limited Liability Corporation (LLC). You are not expected, on first reading, to be able to grasp all of these subtleties, but the case serves as an interesting introduction to the LLC and its nature, as well as an example of the careful approach of the Delaware Supreme Court, which you will be encountering in many of the cases which follow.

2. Note the notion that the LLC combines the "best of both worlds" referring to the purported advantages of the partnership and corporate forms. Do you understand how this might be true? Are you convinced? The LLC, insofar as it combines the limited liability of the corporation and the pass-through taxation features of the partnership was a form that existed in other countries, but was not widely permitted in the United States until close to the end of the twentieth century. Its planting and flourishing in this country was apparently the result of an oil company that had used the form advantageously abroad, and sought to create a similar entity here. For that story, see Susan Pace Hamill, The Origins Behind the Limited Liability Company, 59 Ohio St. L.J. 1459 (1998). If the LLC is so terrific, why do we still have corporations? Does the underlying dispute in the *Elf Atochem* case give you any clues? Keep this problem in mind as you are introduced to corporations in the next chapter.

---

12. See Delaware Citizens for Clean Air v. Water and Air Resources Comm'n, Del. Super., 303 A.2d 666, 667, aff'd, Del. Supr., 310 A.2d 128 (1973) ("While the words 'shall' and 'may' do not always by themselves determine the mandatory or permissive character of a statute, it is generally presumed that the word 'shall' indicates a mandatory requirement.")

3. If you were asked to explain what the primary characteristic of LLC's (apart from tax and liability issues), based on your reading of the *Elf Atochem* case, what would it be? Note that the Delaware court is so impressed with this purpose it is even willing to forgo jurisdiction over the dispute between the parties ("subject matter jurisdiction"). Why does the Court do this, and would you have construed the relevant Delaware statutes any differently?

4. What do you make of the so-called "derivative" claims? Consider the authorization of such claims by the Delaware statute, and the Delaware Supreme Court's refusal to hear them in this case. Did the court do the right thing? Perhaps the Court may have wished to avoid the somewhat tricky task of figuring out what precisely are the fiduciary duties of the parties to an LLC. This is an area of some controversy, and courts are not yet certain whether the fiduciary duties should be those of partners, as expressed, for example in *Meinhard v. Solomon*, or whether the standards should be those of corporate law, giving, perhaps, more discretion to act to members of an LLC than is available in a partnership. See, e.g., J. William Callison, Blind Men and Elephants: Fiduciary Duties Under the Revised Uniform Partnership Act, and Beyond, 1 Jnl. Small and Emerging Business Law, 109, 163–4 (1997). There is also some doubt about just how extended the limited liability protection in LLC's is, and whether it is as broad as that for corporations. On this question and others relating to LLC's, see, e.g., Robert W. Hamilton & Jonathan R. Macey, Cases and Materials on Corporations Including Partnerships and Limited Liability Companies 201–206 (8th ed. 2003), and sources there cited.

5. Do you understand the reasons for choosing sole proprietorships, partnerships, LLC's, or corporations as business vehicles? Do you see why the LLC, though increasingly popular, is still not as popular a choice as the corporation? Consider the discussion of the advantages and disadvantages of these forms which begins the next chapter.

CHAPTER 3

BASICS OF THE CORPORATION

■ ■ ■

A. CHOICE OF ENTITY

Although most of our time in this chapter will be spent studying aspects of the corporation, it is still important to understand the basics of the other business associations, how they differ from corporations, and why a business might choose one form over another. Although each state has authorized different forms of business associations, the same types of organizations exist throughout the nation, and the laws governing them are similar. Three basic business forms were widely used in Britain and pre-Revolutionary America—the general partnership, the limited partnership, and the corporation.[1] The other business forms available to modern enterprises include a variety of hybrid forms in which some benefits of partnerships are combined with some characteristics of corporations. The following is an outline of the currently most-popular business organizations.

Sole Proprietorship

A *sole proprietorship*, the simplest business organization to start and maintain, is an unincorporated business owned by one individual. There is no separate existence of the business apart from the owner, so all liabilities of the proprietorship are personal liabilities, and all income or expenses of the business must be included on the owner's personal tax return.

Advantages of the sole proprietorship include ease of creation and termination—states do not require any organizational documents to be filed—and operational flexibility, as the business is operated entirely at the discretion of the owner, without required formalities such as shareholder meetings. The principal disadvantage is the unlimited liability that results because there is no separate existence of the business apart from the owner.[2]

---

1. Robert W. Hamilton, *Entity Proliferation*, 37 Suffolk U. L. Rev. 859, 862 (2004).

2. Small Business Opportunity Clinic, Northwestern University School of Law. "Comparison of Business Entities Overview," (privately distributed paper prepared by David Gaffin, used by permission of the author).

General Partnership

A *general partnership*, which is the type of partnership you have studied, for example, in the *Croisant* and *National Biscuit Company* cases, is the simplest business organization for two or more people jointly carrying on a trade or business. General partnerships can be formed by nothing more than a verbal agreement among the partners that each party will contribute and expects to share in the profits and losses of the business. Frequently, however, written agreements and contracts will be drafted by lawyers to ensure that the organization is precisely as the partners want it. Until very recently, in most jurisdictions, a partnership was not actually a legally separate entity, so the partnership could not hold property, sue or be sued, and (as is still true) was not taxed as a separate entity.

Advantages of general partnerships include the ease of formation and, as indicated earlier, avoidance of the "double tax" corporations and their shareholders must pay. Income and expenses of the partnership are taxed only once, on individual partners' personal tax returns. The disadvantages of partnerships include joint and several liability on the part of individual partners for the entirety of the partnership's obligations and the fact that each partner is potentially an agent of the partnership able to bind all the others. In addition, ownership of a partnership is generally not transferable and partnerships are not perpetual, dissolving when one partner dies or withdraws from the business.[3]

Limited Partnership

While the general partnership emerged from the common law, the *limited partnership* is a creature of statute. Still, a limited partnership is in many respects similar to a general partnership, the primary difference being that a limited partnership involves limited liability for one or more of the partners. A limited partnership must have at least one *general partner*, which general partner will be personally liable for the limited partnership's debts and obligations and will actively manage the business. This general partner can be an individual or a corporation. The other partners, called, not surprisingly, *limited partners*, are not liable for partnership obligations, do not control the day-to-day operations of the partnership, and are not authorized to act as agents of the limited partnership. When limited partners withdraw or transfer their interest in the business, the limited partnership does not dissolve.

As in general partnerships, the partner's share of the income and expenses of the limited partnership are reported on each partner's personal tax returns. Another advantage of limited partnerships is that the law of limited partnerships is well established and well settled, unlike that of other more recently-developed business associations. The law governing limited partnerships is more complex than that of general partnerships, however, and several state and federal requirements must be ful-

---

3. Id.

filled to set up this type of partnership. Another disadvantage of limited partnership is the fragility of a limited partner's liability shield. In the past, a limited partner could be personally liable for the partnership's debts if he participated in the control and management of the business. This "control rule" was eliminated in the Uniform Limited Partnership Act of 2001, which made it easier for a limited partner to participate in business as a limited partner, and allowed for a limited partner to become a general partner with the implied consent of the other partners, instead of requiring written consent.[4]

Limited Liability Partnership (LLP)

A *limited liability partnership* is organized as a general partnership but allows for all partners to avoid personal liability for firm obligations, whether or not they are active in the management of the business. This is a relatively new business form, authorized first in Texas in the late 1980s, and now adopted in virtually all states.[5] LLPs are popular business organizations for law and accounting firms, but not widely used in commercial businesses. LLPs are essentially hybrids of the general partnership and corporate forms, including the tax and control advantages of a partnership and the limited liability advantage of a corporation. One disadvantage of the LLP is that, as in a partnership, ownership is not transferable. Another disadvantage of the LLP form is increased formalities—LLPs must register with the permitting state, and many states require that a minimum amount of liability insurance be carried by the firm or that the firm segregate client funds from its own.

Limited Liability Limited Partnership (LLLP)

A *limited liability limited partnership* is permitted by statute in something less than half of the states. This business organization applies the limited liability partnership concept of limited personal liability to the limited partnership concept of general and limited partners. In an LLLP, there is still a distinction between general and limited partners' roles in the organization, as in a limited partnership, but all general partners have the protection of an LLP—no personal liability. Because the name serves as a beacon to third parties that they may not rely upon the credit and personal liability of any partner in the firm, this organization theoretically eliminates liability through estoppel against partners, as may have been a problem in limited partnerships.[6] As with all other partnerships, the business is not a separate legal entity, and individual partners must report their share of the firm's expenses and income on their personal tax returns.

---

4. Carter G. Bishop, *The New Limited Partner Liability Shield: Has the Vanquished Control Rule Unwittingly Resurrected Lingering Limited Partner Estoppel Liability as well as Full General Partner Liability?,* 37 Suffolk U. L. Rev. 667, 668 (2004).

5. Hamilton, 37 Suffolk U. L. Rev. at 863.

6. Bishop, supra, 37 Suffolk U. L. Rev. at 716.

Corporation

The most significant features of a *corporation* include (1) limited liability for shareholders, (2) free transferability of ownership interest, (3) perpetual existence, (4) separation of ownership and management ("centralized control"), and (5) legal status of the corporation as a separate entity ("artificial personality"). As a legally separate entity, a corporation can sue and be sued, can own property, and can generally exercise rights as a person would, including enjoying the benefits of some Constitutional protections. A corporation must generally pay income taxes as a separate entity, and shareholders must pay taxes on the dividends or distributions they receive from their corporations (this is the so-called "double taxation" applicable to corporations and their shareholders).

Corporations were originally permitted only if the King granted a charter, and after American independence the state legislatures took the place of the King in making the decision whether corporations would be permitted to exist. During the course of the Nineteenth century, instead of requiring a separate legislative act, incorporation became routinely available if certain state requirements were met and certain information was filed with a state official, usually the Secretary of State. Each of the fifty states has its own separate corporations code, though there are increasing similarities. Generally speaking, corporations are statutorily required to have a three-tiered structure, including shareholders, directors and officers.

Shareholders are the owners of the corporation, but they have limited managerial control. Their primary power is to elect and remove directors, although they must also vote on major decisions of the corporation, such as the amendment of the corporate charter, mergers, or sale of substantially all of the assets of the corporation.

Directors have general management power, and depending on the size of the corporation, the directors either monitor the management or act as managers themselves. Large corporations often have professional managers to conduct the day-to-day business operations, and the Board of Directors, who are legally required to meet at least once a year, are responsible for voting on major decisions, and for conducting votes by shareholders when those are required. Directors may be paid for their services, or may be compensated by stock or stock options in the corporation. Directors, like partners, are fiduciaries, who must place the interests of the corporation above their own. Directors are agents of the *corporation*, not of its shareholders. More, as has been held in some cases, they are bound to exercise their independent judgment and cannot simply take orders from shareholders.

Officers of the corporation are selected and terminated by the board of directors. Typical officers might include a Chairman of the Board, a President, a Secretary, a Treasurer, a Comptroller, and assorted Vice Presidents. Generally officers and their responsibilities are not spelled out in statutes, but will vary with the individual corporate charter or bylaws. The precise nature of the officers' duties and powers will thus vary across corporations, but an officer's position may carry with it certain generally understood powers, giving rise to apparent or inherent authority. For example, Presidents can usually enter into contracts on behalf of the corporation, treasurers and comptrollers have broad power to monitor the financial activity of the corporation, and secretaries will have custody over the shareholder lists and the books and records of the corporation. In theory, at least, the officers carry out the directors' decisions, rather than setting policy for the corporation.

There are two main types of corporations we will be considering. One is the "publicly-held" corporation, so-called because share ownership is widely dispersed among members of the public. A second is the "closely-held" or "close" corporation, the most notable feature of which is that ownership is in a smaller number of shareholders. In close corporations, the divisions between shareholders, directors, and officers may not be as distinct as in larger, publicly traded, publicly held corporations, and some states, most notably Delaware, permit close corporations entirely to dispense with the three-tiered structure of publicly-held corporations, and have shareholders manage the corporation as if they were partners. When they choose to do so, they assume a fiduciary liability akin to that of partners. In all the states, close corporations generally are operated more informally, although they must still meet some formal statutory requirements. Other significant characteristics of close corporations are that they are often family-run businesses, there is generally not a significant public market for their shares, and the transferability of those shares is often limited by shareholders' agreements. A third type of corporation, the charitable corporation, is not, strictly speaking, a business organization, and is beyond the scope of this course.

Corporations are similarly divided into two types under the United States Internal Revenue Code, called subchapter "S" and subchapter "C" corporations.

In Subchapter "S" corporations (sometimes called "S-corps") the shareholders are treated like partners for tax purposes, and profits or losses of the S-corp are taxed directly to shareholders. Small corporations may elect subchapter S status only if they meet certain requirements: the corporation must have no more than 75 shareholders, only one class of stock is permitted, all shareholders must be US residents, and all shareholders must be individuals and not other corporate entities. The number of shareholders allowed in an S corporation changed from 35 to 75 in 1996.[7] The basic advantage of S corporation election is to avoid double taxation. An S corporation is generally exempt from federal income tax, so shareholders include on their personal tax returns their share of the corporation's income, deductions and losses.

---

7. 26 USCS § 1361 (2004).

A "C corporation," on the other hand, is any corporation which does not meet the criteria for S corporation election or has not chosen to become an S corporation. A C corporation can have an unlimited number of shareholders, non-US resident shareholders, and can be owned by S or C corporations or any other business form. A C corporation, is, of course, subject to "double" taxation.

It is likely that the primary advantage of the corporate form is shareholder limited liability. A corporation is also the entity through which shares can most easily be marketed to the public (except for close corporations), which market availability is often essential for raising large amounts of capital. Other advantages of the corporate form include free transferability of interest, and potentially perpetual existence. This is to be contrasted with the partnership form, where ownership interests cannot change hands without the agreement of all the partners, and where the business ends if any partner wishes to end it.[8]

The process of incorporation is also more formalized, regulated and expensive than the process required of partnerships or sole practitioners, where normally nothing must be filed with the state. All states require a filing procedure for corporations, require a filing fee that may amount to several hundred dollars or more, and often require regular reports as well as the filing of corporate tax returns. An important feature of corporate law is that the internal affairs of the corporation (the relationship among officers, directors, and shareholders) will be governed by the state of incorporation, and one can choose to incorporate in any state, even if corporate headquarters will be in another state, and business will be conducted in still other states. Some states require that any corporations operating in their jurisdiction must make certain filings or pay certain fees, but all states recognize that when they deal with corporations it is the law of the state of incorporation that governs internal matters, the so-called "internal affairs" doctrine.

A closely held corporation will generally choose to incorporate in the state in which it expects to do business. As a corporation must pay taxes on both its income and a franchise tax to the state for the privilege of conducting business in the state, limiting the number of states in which a small corporation must pay taxes is seen as an advantage. For larger, publicly held corporations, on the other hand, state taxes and filings are frequently inconsequential compared to overall revenues. Considerations for choosing where to incorporate publicly-held companies often include how state laws affect business organization or shareholder voting. States generally wish to encourage incorporation, because of the revenue from filing fees, and some states have crafted their corporate law governing internal affairs to encourage such incorporation. As we will see, of all the states, Delaware has been so successful in crafting its corporate law, that

---

8. Comparison of Business Entities Overview, Small Business Opportunity Clinic, Northwestern University School of Law.

most large publicly-held United States corporations now choose to incorporate in Delaware.

After choosing a state of incorporation, a corporation must file a "certificate of incorporation," "articles of incorporation" or a "charter" with the state (the three terms refer to the same document), which charter contains provisions meeting statutory requirements. The certificate of incorporation designates the classes of stock and the number of shares that the corporation is authorized to issue, as well as other important corporate specifications, including such matters as the number of Board Members, the kinds of officers, the corporation's purpose, and the location of its headquarters. The "bylaws" of the corporation, which specify the manner in which the corporation will conduct its ongoing operations, including such matters as how vacancies in the board are to be filled, how many members of the board constitute a quorum, which officers can perform which functions, etc., must generally also be filed with the state of incorporation.

Limited Liability Company (LLC)

A *limited liability company*, as we have seen in the preceding case, is a relatively new business form, developed since the late 1970s, which provides the limited liability and tax benefits of an S corporation, commonly called "partnership-tax status," without the restrictions placed on S corporation ownership.[9] Like a corporation and unlike a partnership, an LLC is treated as a legally separate entity, distinct from its members. As such, the LLC members are shielded from personal liability for the business's obligations, whether or not they are active in management. Another benefit of an LLC is the breadth of flexibility in management—it can be managed as if it were a sole proprietorship, partnership or corporation. The manner in which the LLC will be managed will be set out in a "Members Agreement" which might be regarded as analogous to the Corporate Charter, or the Partnership Agreement. Members can also transfer their interest in an LLC without causing dissolution, an advantage over partnerships and LLPs.

LLCs are becoming the most popular form for new small businesses; over 697,000 were formed in 2002, as compared to 63,000 partnerships.[10] LLCs are primarily replacing general and limited partnerships, although they provide a good alternative to closely-held corporations as well. The law governing LLCs is not yet well established, and can vary greatly between states. In Florida and Texas, for example, LLCs are taxed as corporations for purposes of the state corporate franchise tax, eliminating some incentive for forming this type of organization in those states. In Illinois and some other states LLCs are more expensive to form than cor-

---

9. Hamilton, supra, 37 Suffolk U. L. Rev. at 863

10. 2002 Report of International Association of Commercial Administrators (IACA), www.iaca.org, as cited by Daniel S. Kleinberger, *A User's Guide to the New Uniform Limited Partnership Act*, 37 Suffolk U. L. Rev. 583, 588 n31–32. (Fall, 2004).

porations due to higher initial filing fees and annual report filing fees.[11] We will occasionally refer to the LLC in what follows, but, again, our primary interest is in the corporation. While LLC caselaw is still in its infancy, it does appear that for many matters, most prominently shareholder liability for entity debts when shareholders abuse their power to the detriment of third parties ("piercing the corporate veil"), the law of LLC's tracks that of corporations.

B. A SHORT HISTORY OF THE CORPORATION

As we will soon see, there is now and has been for some time considerable debate about the social responsibility of American corporations. At one time it might have been said that there was a burden of proof that incorporators had to meet before the monarch, or the legislature, as a matter of discretion, would confer what was then regarded as the *privilege* of incorporation. That privilege was only to be granted if incorporation served the public good, and that notion is not completely absent from the law even today. Still, it is more common to view incorporation as a ministerial act, one to which any incorporators meeting simple and formal registration requirements can claim a right. The view of incorporation as a privilege granted to serve the public interest, however, was central to corporate existence through many centuries, and a full understanding of the law of corporations and the policies it seeks to implement is impossible without some consideration of this history.

The corporate form dates back to the early Roman Empire, but its use for private commercial enterprise is considerably more recent. Blackstone attributed the idea for the corporate form to Numa Pompilius, a Roman who helped the warring factions of Sabines and Romans incorporate as separate municipal entities, believing that if the groups could govern and view themselves as independent, it would reduce bloodshed.[12]

The life of the corporation as a creature of English law began in England during the twelfth and thirteenth centuries, as towns sought independence from feudal and ecclesiastical control and were incorporated as self-governing municipalities. During the same era, general merchant or crafts guilds were the most important form of commercial organization, and in exchange for substantial fees to the crown, enjoyed a monopoly of their trade within a city's walls.[13] These merchant guilds were perhaps more like trade unions than modern corporations, as they were principally concerned with supervising apprenticeships, determining who ought to be admitted to the trade, and taking other steps to protect guild members'

---

11. Small Business Opportunity Clinic, Northwestern University School of Law. "Comparison of Business Entities Overview," supra note 2.

12. Douglas Arner, *Article in Tribute: Development of the American Law of Corporations to 1832*, 55 SMU L. Rev. 23, 25 (2002).

13. John Micklethwait & Adrian Wooldridge, *The Company: A Short History of a Revolutionary Idea* 23 (Weidenfeld and Nicolson 2003).

interests and their exclusive right to carry on trade. In the manner in which they functioned, however, the guilds can properly be viewed as prototypical corporate forms. The Guilds were governed by a council, similar to the modern corporate board of directors, and as early as 1437, the guilds had to be registered with and approved by the town where they were established.[14] Beginning in the fifteenth century, the crafts guild and the municipal borough were viewed as distinct in function, with the municipal corporation acting as a governing body while the crafts guild served as an economic tool only for its members, although the corporate forms of the two types of entities were identical and both ensured survival of the institutions themselves, even though the governing persons and the individual members would eventually pass on. Both types of corporations could include either natural members or "bodies incorporate and political," indicating that corporations could be part of other corporations.[15]

Nineteenth century American legal scholars Joseph K. Angell and Samuel Ames and English economist Adam Smith divided early economic corporations into two classes: regulated companies and joint stock companies.[16] Regulated companies were state-chartered monopolies authorized to pursue interests beneficial to the state and were dependent on the state for their continued power and success. The most successful of the regulated companies was the Staple of London, founded in 1248 to control wool exports and granted power in 1357 to collect taxes on wool exports in return for helping finance Edward III's French wars.[17] Joint stock companies, which emerged during the sixteenth and seventeenth centuries, more closely resemble the modern business corporation, as they involved owners who left the management of the business entirely to a body of directors.[18] Joint stock companies did not invent the selling of shares on the open market—an idea that dates back to at least the thirteenth century when shares in mines and ships were commonly sold—but they did substantially advance the technique of selling shares as a means of raising large amounts of corporate capital.[19]

Shareholders in joint stock companies also enjoyed some limited liability, enhanced by the fact that the company itself usually held substantial assets in land, and exposure to tort liability during this period was rare. Generally, shareholders would agree to be responsible for the contribution of a certain amount of total capital, even though they would customarily not pay the entire amount as an initial investment. The result was that even though the shareholder could be liable for more than his initial investment, his liability was capped at that agreed-upon

---

14. Arner, *supra* n. 12 at 26

15. *Id.* at 29–30, citing Coke 5. Co. Rep. 23, 29b (1526–1616).

16. *Id.* at 26 and 38.

17. Mickelthwait and Wooldridge, *supra* n. 13 at 24.

18. Arner, *supra* n. 12 at 26, citing Joseph K. Angell and Samuel Ames, *Treatise on the Law of Private Corporations Aggregate* 32 (reprint N.Y. Arno Press 1972) (1832).

19. Mickelthwait and Wooldridge, *supra* n. 13 at 26.

amount.[20] Joint stock companies appear to have gradually developed due to the activities of wealthy merchants, property owners, and successful tradesmen who combined their resources to undertake ventures beyond their individual means or tolerance for risk, and utilizing the now available corporate form in a manner very different from that of the early incorporated towns and guilds. This development reflects the general expansion of markets and private capital investment, which became as important to commerce as the specialized skills of merchant craftsmen had been earlier.[21]

In the first two decades of the seventeenth century, forty joint stock "colonizing" companies were granted charters and trading monopolies in exchange for the crown's rights to the land discovered or settled by the corporations. The trade monopolies granted to these corporations encouraged shareholders to invest in these high risk ventures, even though their liability was not fully limited.[22] In addition, the shares held in these corporations were not fully protected as an individual property right, since the monarch retained the prerogative to refuse to renew or to withdraw the corporate charter. Nevertheless, interests in those corporations were widely traded on a stock exchange, much in the manner they are now.[23] As with earlier regulated corporations, the division between those that ought to be regarded as purely private and those that might be classified as "public" was often difficult to determine—directors of the British East India Company, for example, a concern that made many of its individual investors wealthy men, reported that "the Company traded more for the benefit of the nation [England] than for itself."[24]

The English "Bubble Act" of 1720 marks a definitive point in the history of modern business corporations. When the South Sea Company took over the British national debt in an attempt to retire it by selling shares on the open market to individuals, other corporations fought to participate in this emerging public debt market. The South Sea Company lobbied for the Bubble Act to be passed, in an attempt to restrict competing enterprises. The act, among other things, made it clearly illegal for any joint stock company to operate without a charter from parliament or the king.[25] As formalized charters were relatively difficult to obtain for most businesses, the act essentially cut off the growth of the private corporation in England until the nineteenth century, leaving contract-formed partnerships to emerge as the preferred vehicle of business in England.[26] The

---

20. Arner, *supra* n. 12 at 39.

21. *Id.* at 27.

22. Janet McLean, *The Transnational Corporation in History: Lessons for Today?*, 79 Ind. L.J. 363, 365–66 (2004).

23. *Id.* at 370 n.43

24. *Id.* at 369 n, 33, citing K.N Chaudhuri, *The Trading World of Asia and the English East India Company, 1660–1760* 121 (1978).

25. Mickelthwait and Wooldridge, *supra* n. 13 at 40–41.

26. Arner, *supra* n. 12 at 33–34.

Bubble Act was extended to the colonies in 1741 and, along with the general political unrest that characterized the colonies in the eighteenth century, slowed the development of the corporation there. To circumvent the Bubble Act, many colonial businesses were formed according to private articles of agreement, and although legally partnerships, these businesses were able to approximate the joint stock form.[27]

After the American Revolution, it was commonly understood that the power to grant corporate charters, which in England had eventually come to be shared by the king and parliament, was possessed in America solely by the state legislatures.[28] Colonial legislatures had made frequent use of the corporate form to organize religious congregations and units of local government, and general incorporation statutes for creating these organizations were passed in many states shortly after the Revolution.[29] Forming a private business corporation, however, required more formalities. State legislatures had to pass a special act of incorporation for each new entity, which was required first to demonstrate that its operation would confer a public benefit. A charter might then be granted, which gave legal standing to the corporation and might also confer special franchise rights such as monopolies. As a result, the majority of early American corporations might be characterized as close to "public utilities," and included banks, insurance companies, universities, and companies engaged in constructing turnpikes, bridges and canals.[30] These early American corporations were usually limited to 5 to 30-year terms, with perpetual duration of corporations remaining rare until after the Civil War.[31]

In the nineteenth century, four important developments in American business and politics combined to produce changes that led to the form of business corporation we have today, which entity does, perhaps, represent American law's greatest contribution to world commerce.

The first important event was a clarification of the Constitutional status of the American corporation, through one of the most important decisions ever rendered by the United States Supreme Court. In *Dartmouth College v. Woodward*, 17 U.S. (4 Wheat.) 518, 4 L.Ed. 629 (1819), the Court held that the charter of Dartmouth College (organized as a corporation) was a contract conferring private rights on the incorporators and their successors. The charter, then, was understood to be the valuable private property of the corporation, rather than property held in trust for the state, as had previously been the more commonly accepted view. Prior to *Dartmouth College*, it was understood that the granting of a corporate

---

27. *Id.* at 43, citing Shaw Livermore, Unlimited Liability in Early American Corporations, 43 J. of Pol. Econ. 674, 674 n.2 (1935).

28. E. Dodd, *American Business Corporations Until 1860* 196 (1954).

29. Ronald E. Seavoy, *The Origins of the American Business Corporation, 1784–1855: Broadening the Concept of Public Service During Industrialization* 4–5 (1982).

30. James Willard Hurst, *The Legitimacy of the Business Corporation in the Law of the United States 1780–1970* 18 (U. Press of Va. 1970).

31. Lawrence Friedman, *A History of American Law* 188–192 (2d ed. 1985).

charter by a state legislature was no different from any other legislative act, and that as was true for any other law, the grant of a charter might be amended or repealed if the operation of the corporation was deemed by the legislature no longer to be in the public interest.[32] Because the corporate charter was held to be a contract in *Dartmouth College*, this brought into play Article I, Section 10, clause 1 of the United States Constitution, which provides in pertinent part that "No State [legislature] shall ... pass any ... Law impairing the Obligation of Contracts." This meant, then, that no state legislature could alter any corporate charter unless it had reserved the right to do so in the original grant. Writing for the Court in *Dartmouth College*, Chief Justice John Marshall observed that private colleges were essential in America, and that no one would ever found or invest in a college or other corporation while "believing that it is immediately to be deemed a public institution, whose funds are to be governed and applied, not by the will of the donor, but by the will of the legislature."[33] Justice Story, in his concurrence in the case, suggested that private colleges were like privately-funded banks, and that while both performed functions that were beneficial to the public, neither should be regarded as "public corporations," but rather as private entities, the private property of which required insulation from legislative interference. As Story put it, "the mere act of incorporation will not change the charity from a private to a public one."[34]

The second important development was the rise of the railroads, the first national-scale businesses. Administering these enterprises required the creation of a complex hierarchy of managers who, although they did not own the businesses with which they were involved, came to stake their professional careers on enabling enterprise to grow and prosper. This separation of management and ownership also further accelerated the development of large-scale public markets for the sale of shares, since it was now possible for investors passively to reap the rewards of investment in corporations without participating in management. By 1898, railroads accounted for over 60% of the publicly-issued stock in the US.[35]

The third development was the formation of large-scale manufacturing, mining and other industrial concerns which created a rapid increase in the number of charters granted to businesses that did not directly perform a public benefit. As requests for such charters became more frequent and were granted, the understanding that corporate charters were a privilege granted only to those who served the public began to erode. As corporations became more common and legislators became more familiar with the corporation as an instrument of private business, political, legal and structural changes followed. In what, as you will see, has been character-

---

32. See, for the leading case expressing this view, Currie's Administrators v. The Mutual Assurance Society, 14 Va. 315 (1809).

33. 17 U.S. (4 Wheat.) at 647.

34. *Id.* at 671.

35. Mickelthwait and Wooldridge, *supra* n. 13 at 66.

ized as a "race to the bottom" that began in the 1820s and purportedly continues today, states began to loosen their regulation of corporations and to make it easier to incorporate. This occurred not only because the economic operations of corporations might be beneficial to the state of incorporation, but also because incorporators began to understand that they had some choice in determining in which state they might incorporate, and states found that incorporation and franchise fees could be an important source of state income.[36]

These changes led to the the passage of general incorporation laws that removed the requirement of the legislature's individual approval for each entity and, eventually, evolved into a system that made incorporation an option for almost any enterprise. The standard general incorporation acts of the 1880s made corporate status available through simple administrative procedures, but required very strict compliance with limits on capitalization, corporate organization and share structure.[37] By the1930s, a more liberalized type of general incorporation had been put in place throughout the country, providing a standard corporate structure but allowing variations as the drafters of individual corporate bylaws desired.[38] Throughout the twentieth century, general incorporation statutes came to grant expansive power for incorporators to vary, through contracts, charter or bylaws, the terms that the law might otherwise impose for corporate organization and governance.[39]

Finally, in what may have been the most important of these developments, limited shareholder liability became commonplace during the nineteenth century. Some firms chartered in the eighteenth and early nineteenth centuries were granted a form of limited liability, perhaps in exchange for the firms' building of public improvements without the expenditure of public funds.[40] Although limited liability was thus not unknown in the eighteenth century, there is at least one instance of a corporate charter's dictating that shareholders had *unlimited* liability for the enterprise's debts.[41] Unlimited liability became even more common in the first part of the nineteenth century, as a legislative policy of protecting corporate creditors took hold in many American jurisdictions.[42] This policy was based, at least in part, on the belief that corporations could more easily amass the necessary capital from creditors' loans if creditors knew that there was recourse against the individuals involved. Making capital more easily available from creditors, so the argument ran, would itself benefit fledgling entrepreneurs, and this would ultimately benefit the public. By

---

36. Hurst, *supra* n. 30 at 18.

37. *Id.* at 69.

38. *Id.* at 70.

39. *Id.* at 120.

40. Seavoy, *supra* n. 29 at 257–58.

41. Dodd, *supra* n. 28 at 227.

42. *E.g.,* Handlin and Handlin, *Origins of the American Business Corporation*, 5 J. Econ. Hist. 1, 10 (1945).

1840, however, perhaps as private equity investment became a preferred means of raising capital, many states' legislators amended their corporate laws to provide for limited shareholder liability. This legislative change was supported not only by the economic argument that lowering liability would lead to additional investment in the state's businesses, but also by the notion that by removing the threat of unlimited liability, shareholders of modest means would be able to invest in corporations, thus democratizing corporate ownership.[43]

One of most recent and most important developments in the operations of private corporations, one that has led to an explosion of corporate development in the twentieth and on into the twenty-first century, is the increasing prevalence of subsidiary and affiliated corporations. These are corporations owned by each other, or sister corporations for whom ownership is identical, often in another corporation. Giant global business entities, many incorporated in the state of Delaware, now function all over the world through separately-incorporated subsidiaries and affiliates. As we will see in Chapter Four, it is now universally accepted that absent an abuse of the corporate form, a corporate shareholder has the same limited liability for the debts of its subsidiaries and affiliates as does an individual investing in a corporation. The rise of operation through subsidiaries and affiliates appears to have come about in tandem with the wide dispersal of passive shareholder investors, and the rise of professional managers. The number of individuals owning shares in corporations rose from two million in 1920 to over ten million in 1930. Current estimates suggest that approximately sixty percent of American households can be regarded as investors in corporations, and, during the 2004 Presidential election, some commentators suggested that "investor interests" were important in the reelection of the Republican candidate, George W. Bush.

In the 1960s, diversified conglomerate corporate entities emerged and grew to be a powerful economic force by taking over divisions of other corporations, either through friendly negotiated buyouts or hostile "takeovers." By 1973, fifteen of the top 200 American manufacturing corporations were conglomerates, but by then this particular wave of mergers and acquisitions was ending, as the conglomerates failed to deliver expected returns and the stock value of these huge businesses declined.[44]

Even so, the urge to merge grew again as financing became more generally available in the 1980s. Large corporations grew even larger and more diverse through the "merger boom" of the 1980s, but all was not well.[45] From 1970 to 1990, the rate at which large American companies left the Fortune 500 increased four times, and many large conglomerates found it more profitable to slim down and focus on core businesses.[46] The

---

43. Seavoy, *supra* n. 29 at 115.

44. *Id.* at 120.

45. *Id.* at 138.

46. *Id.* at 125.

business of many American corporations also changed radically toward the turn of the Century. By 1999, the most valuable American export was probably intellectual capital, as old-style manufacturing gave way to the "information age" and the "service economy" and new groups of entrepreneurs found success in small, flexible upstart corporations.[47]

By the end of the twentieth century, there seemed to be a discernable trend for state and national governments to set the corporation free by deregulating markets, simplifying general incorporation procedures, and loosening trade barriers. At the same time, however, and somewhat paradoxically, the state legislatures and Congress increasingly regulated the ongoing operations of corporations through laws governing accounting procedures, the health and safety of workers, the environment, affirmative action, and the protection of employee, consumer and even investor rights.[48] Although general incorporation statutes had been simplified and streamlined such that the act of incorporation seemed little more than a formality, modern corporations still needed some form of government authorization to exist, and the corporate laws and other regulatory measures of particular states continued to have great influence on where businesses chose to incorporate. In 1999, most of the largest American companies were incorporated in Delaware, a state whose laws favored the discretion of managers and majority shareholders over the purported corporate governance rights of minority shareholders.

We will explore several of the implications of this brief history of corporations, but this whistle-stop tour should give you enough information to reach some preliminary conclusions. Are you comfortable with the ubiquity of the corporation (and other similar business vehicles such as the limited liability company (LLC))? Is the history of the development of the corporation, and the emergence of the modern American business corporation (the model for the rest of the world) an unqualifiedly noble human achievement? How should the corporation be regulated in the public interest? Consider the implications of *Ford v. Dodge* and *Smith v. Barlow*, which follow.

C.   THE PURPOSE OF THE CORPORATION

DODGE v. FORD MOTOR CO.

Supreme Court of Michigan.
204 Mich. 459, 170 N.W. 668, 3 A.L.R. 413 (1919).

OSTRANDER, J. *(after stating the facts)*. The authorized capital stock of the defendant company is $2,000,000. Its capital, in July, 1916, invested in some form of property, including accounts receivable, was $78,278,418.65, and, less liabilities other than capital stock, was more

---

47. *Id.* at 139.

48. *Id.* at 146.

than $60,000,000. Besides this, it had and was using as capital nearly $54,000,000 in cash or the equivalent of cash.

*   *   *

* * * [T]he case for plaintiffs must rest upon the claim, and the proof in support of it, that the proposed expansion of the business of the corporation, involving the further use of profits as capital, ought to be enjoined because inimical to the best interests of the company and its shareholders, and upon the further claim that in any event the withholding of the special dividend asked for by plaintiffs is arbitrary action of the directors requiring judicial interference.

The rule which will govern courts in deciding these questions is not in dispute. It is, of course, differently phrased by judges and by authors, and, as the phrasing in a particular instance may seem to lean for or against the exercise of the right of judicial interference with the actions of corporate directors, the context, or the facts before the court, must be considered. This court, in *Hunter v. Roberts, Throp & Co., 83 Mich. 63, 71,* recognized the rule in the following language:

> "It is a well-recognized principle of law that the directors of a corporation, and they alone, have the power to declare a dividend of the earnings of the corporation, and to determine its amount. * * * Courts of equity will not interfere in the management of the directors unless it is clearly made to appear that they are guilty of fraud or misappropriation of the corporate funds, or refuse to declare a dividend when the corporation has a surplus of net profits which it can, without detriment to its business, divide among its stockholders, and when a refusal to do so would amount to such an abuse of discretion as would constitute a fraud, or breach of that good faith which they are bound to exercise towards the stockholders."

In 2 Cook on Corporations (7th Ed.), § 545, it is expressed as follows:

> "The board of directors declare the dividends, and it is for the directors, and not the stockholders, to determine whether or not a dividend shall be declared.

> "When, therefore, the directors have exercised this discretion and refused to declare a dividend, there will be no interference by the courts with their decision, unless they are guilty of a willful abuse of their discretionary powers, or of bad faith or of a neglect of duty. It requires a very strong case to induce a court of equity to order the directors to declare a dividend, inasmuch as equity has no jurisdiction, unless fraud or a breach of trust is involved. There have been many attempts to sustain such a suit, yet, although the courts do not disclaim jurisdiction, they have quite uniformly refused to interfere. The discretion of the directors will not be interfered with by the courts, unless there has been bad faith, willful neglect, or abuse of discretion.

"Accordingly, the directors may, in the fair exercise of their discretion, invest profits to extend and develop the business, and a reasonable use of the profits to provide additional facilities for the business cannot be objected to or enjoined by the stockholders."

In 1 Morawetz on Corporations (2d Ed.), § 447, it is stated:

"Profits earned by a corporation may be divided among its shareholders; but it is not a violation of the charter if they are allowed to accumulate and remain invested in the company's business. The managing agents of a corporation are impliedly invested with a discretionary power with regard to the time and manner of distributing its profits. They may apply profits in payment of floating or funded debts, or in development of the company's business; and so long as they do not abuse their discretionary powers, or violate the company's charter, the courts cannot interfere.

"But it is clear that the agents of a corporation, and even the majority, cannot arbitrarily withhold profits earned by the company, or apply them to any use which is not authorized by the company's charter. The nominal capital of a company does not necessarily limit the scope of its operations; a corporation may borrow money for the purpose of enlarging its business, and in many instances it may use profits for the same purpose. But the amount of the capital contributed by the shareholders is an important element in determining the limit beyond which the company's business cannot be extended by the investment of profits. If a corporation is formed with a capital of $100,000 in order to carry on a certain business, no one would hesitate to say that it would be a departure from the intention of the founders to withhold profits, in order to develop the company's business, until the sum of $500,000 had been amassed, unless the company was formed mainly for the purpose of accumulating the profits from year to year. The question in each case depends upon the use to which the capital is put, and the meaning of the company's charter. If a majority of the shareholders or the directors of a corporation wrongfully refuse to declare a dividend and distribute profits earned by the company, any shareholder feeling aggrieved may obtain relief in a court of equity.

"It may often be reasonable to withhold part of the earnings of a corporation in order to increase its surplus fund, when it would not be reasonable to withhold all the earnings for that purpose. The shareholders forming an ordinary business corporation expect to obtain the profits of their investment in the form of regular dividends. To withhold the entire profits merely to enlarge the capacity of the company's business would defeat their just expectations. After the business of a corporation has been brought to a prosperous condition, and necessary provision has been made for future prosperity, a reasonable share of the profits should be applied in the payment of regular dividends, though a part may be reserved to increase the surplus and enlarge the business itself."

One other statement may be given from *Park v. Grant Locomotive Works, 40 N.J. Eq. 114 (3 Atl. 162, 45 N.J. Eq. 244, 19 Atl. 621):*

> "In cases where the power of the directors of a corporation is without limitation, and free from restraint, they are at liberty to exercise a very liberal discretion as to what disposition shall be made of the gains of the business of the corporation. Their power over them is absolute as long as they act in the exercise of their honest judgment. They may reserve of them whatever their judgment approves as necessary or judicious for repairs or improvements, and to meet contingencies, both present and prospective. And their determination in respect of these matters, if made in good faith and for honest ends, though the result may show that it was injudicious, is final, and not subject to judicial revision."

It is not necessary to multiply statements of the rule.

*   *   *

When plaintiffs made their complaint and demand for further dividends the Ford Motor Company had concluded its most prosperous year of business. The demand for its cars at the price of the preceding year continued. It could make and could market in the year beginning August 1, 1916, more than 500,000 cars. Sales of parts and repairs would necessarily increase. The cost of materials was likely to advance, and perhaps the price of labor, but it reasonably might have expected a profit for the year of upwards of $60,000,000. It had assets of more than $132,000,000, a surplus of almost $112,000,000, and its cash on hand and municipal bonds were nearly $54,000,000. Its total liabilities, including capital stock, was a little over $20,000,000. It had declared no special dividend during the business year except the October, 1915, dividend. It had been the practice, under similar circumstances, to declare larger dividends. Considering only these facts, a refusal to declare and pay further dividends appears to be not an exercise of discretion on the part of the directors, but an arbitrary refusal to do what the circumstances required to be done. These facts and others call upon the directors to justify their action, or failure or refusal to act. In justification, the defendants have offered testimony tending to prove, and which does prove, the following facts. It had been the policy of the corporation for a considerable time to annually reduce the selling price of cars, while keeping up, or improving, their quality. As early as in June, 1915, a general plan for the expansion of the productive capacity of the concern by a practical duplication of its plant had been talked over by the executive officers and directors and agreed upon, not all of the details having been settled and no formal action of directors having been taken. The erection of a smelter was considered, and engineering and other data in connection therewith secured. In consequence, it was determined not to reduce the selling price of cars for the year beginning August 1, 1915, but to maintain the price and to accumulate a large surplus to pay for the proposed expansion of plant and equipment, and perhaps to build a plant for smelting ore. It is hoped, by Mr. Ford, that eventually 1,000,000 cars will be annually produced. The contemplated changes will permit the increased output.

The plan, as affecting the profits of the business for the year beginning August 1, 1916, and thereafter, calls for a reduction in the selling price of the cars. It is true that this price might be at any time increased, but the plan called for the reduction in price of $80 a car. The capacity of the plant, without the additions thereto voted to be made (without a part of them at least), would produce more than 600,000 cars annually. This number, and more, could have been sold for $440 instead of $360, a difference in the return for capital, labor and materials employed of at least $48,000,000. In short, the plan does not call for and is not intended to produce immediately a more profitable business but a less profitable one; not only less profitable than formerly but less profitable than it is admitted it might be made. The apparent immediate effect will be to diminish the value of shares and the returns to shareholders.

It is the contention of plaintiffs that the apparent effect of the plan is intended to be the continued and continuing effect of it and that it is deliberately proposed, not of record and not by official corporate declaration, but nevertheless proposed, to continue the corporation henceforth as a semi-eleemosynary institution and not as a business institution. In support of this contention they point to the attitude and to the expressions of Mr. Henry Ford.

Mr. Henry Ford is the dominant force in the business of the Ford Motor Company. No plan of operations could be adopted unless he consented, and no board of directors can be elected whom he does not favor. One of the directors of the company has no stock. One share was assigned to him to qualify him for the position, but it is not claimed that he owns it. A business, one of the largest in the world, and one of the most profitable, has been built up. It employs many men, at good pay.

"My ambition," said Mr. Ford, "is to employ still more men, to spread the benefits of this industrial system to the greatest possible number, to help them build up their lives and their homes. To do this we are putting the greatest share of our profits back in the business."

"With regard to dividends, the company paid sixty per cent. on its capitalization of two million dollars, or $1,200,000, leaving $58,000,000 to reinvest for the growth of the company. This is Mr. Ford's policy at present, and it is understood that the other stockholders cheerfully accede to this plan."

He had made up his mind in the summer of 1916 that no dividends other than the regular dividends should be paid, "for the present."

"Q. For how long? Had you fixed in your mind any time in the future, when you were going to pay—

"A. No.

"Q. That was indefinite in the future?

"A. That was indefinite, yes, sir."

The record, and especially the testimony of Mr. Ford, convinces that he has to some extent the attitude towards shareholders of one who has dispensed and distributed to them large gains and that they should be content to take what he chooses to give. His testimony creates the impression, also, that he thinks the Ford Motor Company has made too much money, has had too large profits, and that although large profits might be still earned, a sharing of them with the public, by reducing the price of the output of the company, ought to be undertaken. We have no doubt that certain sentiments, philanthropic and altruistic, creditable to Mr. Ford, had large influence in determining the policy to be pursued by the Ford Motor Company—the policy which has been herein referred to.

It is said by his counsel that—

"Although a manufacturing corporation cannot engage in humanitarian works as its principal business, the fact that it is organized for profit does not prevent the existence of implied powers to carry on with humanitarian motives such charitable works as are incidental to the main business of the corporation."

And again:

"As the expenditures complained of are being made in an expansion of the business which the company is organized to carry on, and for purposes within the powers of the corporation as hereinbefore shown, the question is as to whether such expenditures are rendered illegal because influenced to some extent by humanitarian motives and purposes on the part of the members of the board of directors."

[The decision in this case, as in other similar cases, must] turn finally upon * * * whether it appears that the directors were not acting for the best interests of the corporation. We do not draw in question, nor do counsel for the plaintiffs do so, the validity of the general propositions stated by counsel nor the soundness of the opinions delivered in the cases cited [by them, which uphold expenditures of some corporate funds for charitable purposes which benefit employees]. The case presented here is not like any of them. The difference between an incidental humanitarian expenditure of corporate funds for the benefit of the employees, like the building of a hospital for their use and the employment of agencies for the betterment of their condition, and a general purpose and plan to benefit mankind at the expense of others, is obvious. There should be no confusion (of which there is evidence) of the duties which Mr. Ford conceives that he and the stockholders owe to the general public and the duties which in law he and his codirectors owe to protesting, minority stockholders. A business corporation is organized and carried on primarily for the profit of the stockholders. The powers of the directors are to be employed for that end. The discretion of directors is to be exercised in the choice of means to attain that end and does not extend to a change in the end itself, to the reduction of profits or to the nondistribution of profits among stockholders in order to devote them to other purposes.

There is committed to the discretion of directors, a discretion to be exercised in good faith, the infinite details of business, including the wages which shall be paid to employees, the number of hours they shall work, the conditions under which labor shall be carried on, and the prices for which products shall be offered to the public. It is said by appellants that the motives of the board members are not material and will not be inquired into by the court so long as their acts are within their lawful powers. As we have pointed out, and the proposition does not require argument to sustain it, it is not within the lawful powers of a board of directors to shape and conduct the affairs of a corporation for the merely incidental benefit of shareholders and for the primary purpose of benefiting others, and no one will contend that if the avowed purpose of the defendant directors was to sacrifice the interests of shareholders it would not be the duty of the courts to interfere.

We are not, however, persuaded that we should interfere with the proposed expansion of the business of the Ford Motor Company. In view of the fact that the selling price of products may be increased at any time, the ultimate results of the larger business cannot be certainly estimated. The judges are not business experts. It is recognized that plans must often be made for a long future, for expected competition, for a continuing as well as an immediately profitable venture. The experience of the Ford Motor Company is evidence of capable management of its affairs. It may be noticed, incidentally, that it took from the public the money required for the execution of its plan and that the very considerable salaries paid to Mr. Ford and to certain executive officers and employees were not diminished. We are not satisfied that the alleged motives of the directors, in so far as they are reflected in the conduct of the business, menace the interests of shareholders. It is enough to say, perhaps, that the court of equity is at all times open to complaining shareholders having a just grievance.

Assuming the general plan and policy of expansion and the details of it to have been sufficiently, formally, approved at the October and November, 1917, meetings of directors, and assuming further that the plan and policy and the details agreed upon were for the best ultimate interest of the company and therefore of its shareholders, what does it amount to in justification of a refusal to declare and pay a special dividend, or dividends? The Ford Motor Company was able to estimate with nicety its income and profit. It could sell more cars than it could make. Having ascertained what it would cost to produce a car and to sell it, the profit upon each car depended upon the selling price. That being fixed, the yearly income and profit was determinable, and, within slight variations, was certain.

There was appropriated-voted-for the smelter $11,325,000. As to the remainder voted there is no available way for determining how much had been paid before the action of directors was taken and how much was paid thereafter, but assuming that the plans required an expenditure sooner or later of $9,895,000 for duplication of the plant, and for land and other expenditures $3,000,000, the total is $24,220,000. The company was continuing business, at a profit—a cash business. If the total cost of proposed expenditures had been immediately withdrawn in cash from the cash surplus (money and bonds) on hand August 1, 1916, there would have remained nearly $30,000,000.

Defendants say, and it is true, that a considerable cash balance must be at all times carried by such a concern. But, as has been stated, there was a large daily, weekly, monthly, receipt of cash. The output was practically continuous and was continuously, and within a few days, turned into cash. Moreover, the contemplated expenditures were not to be immediately made. The large sum appropriated for the smelter plant was payable over a considerable period of time. So that, without going further, it would appear that, accepting and approving the plan of the directors, it was their duty to distribute on or near the first of August, 1916, a very large sum of money to stockholders.

In reaching this conclusion, we do not ignore, but recognize, the validity of the proposition that plaintiffs have from the beginning profited by, if they have not lately, officially, participated in, the general policy of expansion pursued by this corporation. We do not lose sight of the fact that it had been, upon an occasion, agreeable to the plaintiffs to increase the capital stock to $100,000,000 by a stock dividend of $98,000,000. These things go only to answer other contentions now made by plaintiffs and do not and cannot operate to estop them to demand proper dividends upon the stock they own. It is obvious that an annual dividend of sixty per cent. upon $2,000,000, or $1,200,000, is the equivalent of a very small dividend upon $100,000,000, or more.

The decree of the court below fixing and determining the specific amount to be distributed to stockholders is affirmed. * * * Plaintiffs will recover interest at five per cent. per annum upon their proportional share of said dividend from the date of the decree of the lower court. * * *

NOTES AND QUESTIONS

1. *Dodge v. Ford Motor Corp.* is presented as a means of studying why we allow corporations, and what their purpose ought to be. What is the view of the court, and what was the view of Mr. Henry Ford on this question? Which do you find most congenial? By the way, are the Court's assumptions about what shareholders are looking for consistent with how you understand the expectations of shareholders today? Consider the facts of the case. *Ford v. Dodge* centers on the fiduciary duties of corporate managers and whether such duties allow for the consideration of the interests of non-shareholders, such as workers or consumers. By 1919, when the case arose, Henry Ford had

become the Bill Gates of his era; he was a phenomenally-successful business-man, and as the Court observes, he had increased the wealth of his investors, including the plaintiffs in this case, the Dodge brothers (is that name famil-iar to you?), many times over. What do you understand to be the nature of the debate between Ford and the Dodge brothers? The dispute is over how the profits of the company should be distributed. Ford wants to reinvest in the company, lower the production price of his cars, and ultimately pass the sav-ings on to the buyers of Fords. The Dodge brothers believe the amount of money Ford is reinvesting is excessive and that the money should be distrib-uted to the investors in the form of a special dividend. To whom do you think Ford owes the greater duty, the consumers whose expenditures have allowed him to build his fortune, and increase the wealth of the corporation, or the investors who have originally financed his enterprise? The court rules in favor of the Dodge brothers, holding that Ford should distribute the earnings in the form of a special dividend. One reason is that "[t]he purpose of any [corporate] organization under the law is earnings." Should corporations be guided by anything other than making profits for their investors? If so, what outside concerns should be considered? Is the Court's view of the limited purposes of corporations persuasive?

2.   We will return to this particular theme later in the course, but con-sider, for a moment, how the court views its role in intervening in a dispute between corporate directors and their President on the one hand, and share-holders on the other. Note that the court begins by indicating the rule of the common law that it is inappropriate to interfere with directors' discretion to declare a dividend "unless they are guilty of a willful abuse of their discretion-ary powers, or of bad faith or of a neglect of duty." Furthermore there must be "a very strong case to induce a court of equity to order the directors to declare a dividend." In your view, was *Dodge v. Ford* such a case? If the same factual situation arose today, would it be appropriate for a court to intervene? Are there any other remedies for shareholders in such a situation of refusal to pay dividends besides a lawsuit to compel their payment? To determine whether this situation merits intervention, the court looks to the profit history of the company. Ford had been making large profits and was in the habit of declar-ing large dividends. Furthermore, Ford's business plan which would ulti-mately reduce production costs had the immediate effect of "diminish[ing] the value of shares and the returns to shareholders." Is it fair to help non-shareholders at the expense of corporate investors? If you are an investor, do you want Ford as a CEO? If you are a CEO, should you consider non-shareholder interests at all?

3.   The court ultimately views the testimony of Henry Ford as evincing "the attitude towards shareholders of one who has dispensed and distributed to them large gains and that they should be content to take what he chooses to give." Should a corporate officer or director have this attitude? Do you agree that Ford's desire to reduce the cost of cars to consumers, presumably enabling more people to purchase the company's product, is the arbitrary action of a wealthy tycoon who feels insufficient concern for his investors? Could it be dangerous for a corporate director to distribute profits as he or she sees fit? On the other hand, the Dodge brothers have been given large returns

on their initial investment. If the corporate directors and shareholders have already made large amounts of money, do they have less of a claim on future profits? Should the amount of money already distributed affect a corporation's duties to non-shareholders?

4. In his testimony, Ford says his ambition "is to employ still more men, to spread the benefits of this industrial system to the greatest possible number, to help them build up their lives and their homes." In 1918, Ford's workers were paid $6 for an eight hour day, which at the time was quite a substantial wage, one almost unheard of for laborers. Ford also allowed his employees to enter into an innovative profit-sharing program. Is there an extra-legal obligation among managers to enable more people than shareholders to reap the benefits of the industrial system? Even if there is not an implicit obligation, should the courts allow or encourage this type of benefit sharing? Did the court's decision help or harm capitalism?

5. The court's decision does not prevent corporations from undertaking philanthropic endeavors. However, as we will see in the next case, such philanthropic undertakings must be connected to the interests of the corporation. In *Dodge v. Ford*, the court holds "[t]he difference between an incidental humanitarian expenditure of corporate funds for the benefit of the employees, like the building of a hospital for their use and the employment of agencies for the betterment of their condition, and a general purpose and plan to benefit mankind at the expense of others, is obvious." Does it make sense that a corporation can use some of its profits to help its workers, but not reduce its profits to benefit non-shareholders in general? How closely related does the use of corporate funds need to be to the interests of the corporation?

6. The court is ultimately persuaded that it should interfere in the management of Ford's corporate assets. The judges recognize the capability of Ford Motor Company to manage its own affairs, yet still feel compelled to second-guess the board's decision on dividend policy. Although the court's members are "not business experts" they cite the fact that "the very considerable salaries paid to Mr. Ford and to certain executive officers and employees were not diminished" as evidence of wrongdoing to support their intervention. Is it generally appropriate for judges, based on their assessment of what is good for the business or the business community, to overrule the business decision of a board selected by shareholders? Should judges substitute their knowledge for the knowledge of business experts? Given that Mr. Ford's own earnings were not reduced, do you agree that this is a case where judicial intervention was warranted?

7. Professor Stephen M. Bainbridge writes in the *Northwestern Law Review* that "*Dodge's* theory of shareholder wealth maximization has widely been accepted by the courts." Professor Bainbridge continues "shareholder wealth maximization is not only the law, but also is a basic feature of corporate ideology."[49] Is this an ideology to which you subscribe? Is there an alternative? Given that such a high percentage of Americans have portions of their earnings, or retirement or pension funds invested in the stock market, either

---

49. Stephen M. Bainbridge, Director Primacy: The Means and Ends of Corporate Governance, 97 Nw. U.L. Rev. 547, 575–576 (2003).

directly through their purchase of stocks or mutual funds, or indirectly through the purchase of insurance underwritten by entities invested in the market, or through their participation as students attending endowed universities, is the *Dodge* theory of shareholder primacy with regards to the distribution of corporate assets the fairest method to the largest group of people? To what extent should corporate officers and directors be able to act on the basis of the interests of other constituencies or stakeholders such as creditors, employees, workers, consumers or the community generally? As the economy is increasingly global, do American corporations owe any obligations to their overseas workers? Do corporations have a duty to be ambassadors for capitalism? Should American corporations be more considerate of how Americans will be perceived in the era of a war on terrorism? Remember these issues as you read through the next case.

8.   In a very provocative piece, law Professor Lynn A. Stout, Professor Bainbridge's colleague at UCLA, has argued that it is a mistake to continue to teach *Dodge v. Ford Motor Co.*, because, she asserts, it is now no longer true (if it ever was) that the legally-sanctioned purpose of corporations is to make money for shareholders. Lynn A. Stout, "Why We Should Stop Teaching *Dodge v. Ford*," Chapter 1 of Jonathan R. Macey, ed., The Iconic Cases in Corporate Law 1 (2008). Is this correct? Bear this question in mind as you continue to work your way through this course. If making money for shareholders is not the *raison d'etre* of corporations, what is? For further background on *Dodge v. Ford Motor Co.*, including biographical information on Henry Ford and the Dodge brothers, and for the suggestion that what happened in that case foreshadowed current battles for corporate control and shareholder influence on corporate boards, see M. Todd Henderson, "The Story of *Dodge v. Ford Motor Company*: Everything Old is New Again," in J. Mark Ramseyer, Ed., Corporate Law Stories 37 (2009). Professor Henderson argues, among other things, that the case would be decided differently today, and that, in particular, a court would be more likely to defer to Ford's decision to reinvest, to pay his workers more, and to sell more cars, instead of using revenues to pay dividends. Do you agree?

9.   When is it appropriate for a corporation to issue dividends? Corporate dividends and distributions are matters that we will not explore in any detail in this course, leaving these and other such issues for you to explore, should you choose to do so, on your own, or in a future course in corporate finance. Even so, a few brief sentences on the topic may help put *Dodge v. Ford* in further perspective.

The decision about whether or not to issue dividends, or to use corporate funds for other corporate purposes, for example to expand the productive capacity of the corporation, as you may have been able to discern from *Dodge v. Ford*, is normally a matter of the "business judgment" of directors, and, absent obvious conflicts of interest, as seems to have been found in that case, the courts will leave the matter to the decision of the directors. Still, there are some legal limits that state legislatures have placed on the situations in which dividends may be declared. These statutes are currently in a state of flux, but all share a common perspective that dividends should not be permitted where they would unduly endanger the continuing operations of the corporation.

Thus, in many states, dividends may not be declared unless the corporation's Balance Sheet (the accountants' report on the financial health of the corporation) reveals that the corporation's capital accounts (which reflect initial investment in the corporation) are undiminished, and that there is a capital surplus (a condition where accrued earnings result in an amount over and above the amount initially invested). Because the Balance Sheet is based on initial valuations of assets, and because some assets (for example accounts receivable), may not be reliable indicators of positive value, this "Balance Sheet" test for declaration of dividends has been replaced in some states by newer means of evaluating the financial health of the corporation. These include, for example, requirements that corporate assets be valued at their present worth, and that this value be higher (sometimes by a specified ratio) than the liabilities of the corporation after any proposed dividends are paid, or simply that dividends may not be paid if the corporation will be rendered incapable of meeting its expected debts as they mature.

For further reading on the law and economics of dividend payments see, e.g., Stephen M. Bainbridge, Corporation Law and Economics 768–796 (2002), William A. Klein, and John C. Coffee, Jr., Business Organization and Finance: Legal and Economic Principles 218–220 (8th ed. 2002), Jeffrey J. Haas, Corporate Finance in a Nutshell, 331–358 (2004). These three paperback volumes contain a wealth of information relevant to all economic issues we will consider, and are worthy additions to the library of any student seriously interested in economic analysis of the law of business organizations.

A.P. SMITH MANUFACTURING CO. v. BARLOW

Supreme Court of New Jersey.
13 N.J. 145, 98 A.2d 581 (1953).

[JACOBS, J.] The Chancery Division * * * determined that a donation by the plaintiff The A.P. Smith Manufacturing Company to Princeton University was *intra vires* ["within the powers of the corporation"]. Because of the public importance of the issues presented, the appeal duly taken to the Appellate Division has been certified directly to this court * * *.

The company was incorporated in 1896 and is engaged in the manufacture and sale of valves, fire hydrants and special equipment, mainly for water and gas industries. Its plant is located in East Orange and Bloomfield and it has approximately 300 employees. Over the years the company has contributed regularly to the local community chest and on occasions to Upsala College in East Orange and Newark University, now part of Rutgers, the State University. On July 24, 1951 the board of directors adopted a resolution which set forth that it was in the corporation's best interests to join with others in the 1951 Annual Giving to Princeton University, and appropriated the sum of $1,500 to be transferred by the corporation's treasurer to the university as a contribution towards its maintenance. * * *

Mr. Hubert F. O'Brien, the president of the company, testified that he considered the contribution to be a sound investment, that the public expects corporations to aid philanthropic and benevolent institutions, that they obtain good will in the community by so doing, and that their charitable donations create favorable environment for their business operations. In addition, he expressed the thought that in contributing to liberal arts institutions, corporations were furthering their self-interest in assuring the free flow of properly trained personnel for administrative and other corporate employment. Mr. Frank W. Abrams, chairman of the board of the Standard Oil Company of New Jersey, testified that corporations are expected to acknowledge their public responsibilities in support of the essential elements of our free enterprise system. He indicated that it was not "good business" to disappoint "this reasonable and justified public expectation," nor was it good business for corporations "to take substantial benefits from their membership in the economic community while avoiding the normally accepted obligations of citizenship in the social community." Mr. Irving S. Olds, former chairman of the board of the United States Steel Corporation, pointed out that corporations have a self-interest in the maintenance of liberal education as the bulwark of good government. He stated that "Capitalism and free enterprise owe their survival in no small degree to the existence of our private, independent universities" and that if American business does not aid in their maintenance it is not "properly protecting the long-range interest of its stockholders, its employees and its customers." Similarly, Dr. Harold W. Dodds, President of Princeton University, suggested that if private institutions of higher learning were replaced by governmental institutions our society would be vastly different and private enterprise in other fields would fade out rather promptly. Further on he stated that "democratic society will not long endure if it does not nourish within itself strong centers of non-governmental fountains of knowledge, opinions of all sorts not governmentally or politically originated. If the time comes when all these centers are absorbed into government, then freedom as we know it, I submit, is at an end."

The objecting stockholders have not disputed any of the foregoing testimony nor the showing of great need by Princeton and other private institutions of higher learning and the important public service being rendered by them for democratic government and industry alike. Similarly, they have acknowledged that for over two decades there has been state legislation on our books which expresses a strong public policy in favor of corporate contributions such as that being questioned by them. Nevertheless, they have taken the position that (1) the plaintiff's certificate of incorporation does not expressly authorize the contribution and under common-law principles the company does not possess any implied or incidental power to make it, and (2) the New Jersey statutes which expressly authorize the contribution may not constitutionally be applied to the plaintiff, a corporation created long before their enactment. * * *

In his discussion of the early history of business corporations Professor Williston refers to a 1702 publication where the author stated flatly that "The general intent and end of all civil incorporations is for better government." And he points out that the early corporate charters, particularly their recitals, furnish additional support for the notion that the corporate object was the public one of managing and ordering the trade as well as the private one of profit for the members. See 3 *Select Essays on Anglo-American Legal History* 201 (1909); 1 *Fletcher, Corporations (rev. ed.* 1931), 6. See also *Currie's Administrators v. The Mutual Assurance Society, 4 Hen. & M. 315, 347 (Va. Sup. Ct. App. 1809),* where Judge Roane referred to the English corporate charters and expressed the view that acts of incorporation ought never to be passed "but in consideration of services to be rendered to the public." However, with later economic and social developments and the free availability of the corporate device for all trades, the end of private profit became generally accepted as the controlling one in all businesses other than those classed broadly as public utilities. *Cf. Dodd, For Whom Are Corporate Managers Trustees?, 45 Harv. L. Rev. 1145, 1148 (1932).* As a concomitant the common-law rule developed that those who managed the corporation could not disburse any corporate funds for philanthropic or other worthy public cause unless the expenditure would benefit the corporation. *Hutton v. West Cork Railway Company, 23 Ch. D. 654 (1883); Dodge v. Ford Motor Co., 204 Mich. 459, 170 N.W. 668, 3 A.L.R. 413 (Sup. Ct. 1919). Ballantine, Corporations (rev. ed.* 1946), 228; 6A *Fletcher, supra,* 667. During the 19th Century when corporations were relatively few and small and did not dominate the country's wealth, the common-law rule did not significantly interfere with the public interest. But the 20th Century has presented a different climate. *Berle and Means, The Modern Corporation and Private Property* (1948). Control of economic wealth has passed largely from individual entrepreneurs to dominating corporations, and calls upon the corporations for reasonable philanthropic donations have come to be made with increased public support. In many instances such contributions have been sustained by the courts within the common-law doctrine upon liberal findings that the donations tended reasonably to promote the corporate objectives. * * *

Thus, in the leading case of *Evans v. Brunner, Mond & Company, Ltd. [1921] 1 Ch. 359,* the court held that it was within the incidental power of a chemical company to grant $100,000 to universities or other scientific institutions selected by the directors "for the furtherance of scientific education and research." The testimony indicated that the company desired to encourage and assist men who would devote their time and abilities to scientific study and research generally, a class of men for whom the company was constantly on the lookout. This benefit was not considered by the court to be so remote as to bring it outside the common-law rule. Similarly, in *Armstrong Cork Co. v. H.A. Meldrum Co., 285 F. 58 (D.C.W.D.N.Y. 1922),* the court sustained contributions made by the corporation to the University of Buffalo and Canisius College. In the course of its opinion the court quoted the familiar comment from *Steinway v. Stein-*

way & Sons, 17 Misc. 43, 40 N.Y.S. 718 (Sup. Ct. 1896), to the effect that as industrial conditions change business methods must change with them and acts become permissible which theretofore were considered beyond the corporate powers; and on the issue as to whether the corporation had received any corporate benefit it said:

> "It was also considered, in making the subscriptions or donations, that the company would receive advertisement of substantial value, including the good will of many influential citizens and of its patrons, who were interested in the success of the development of these branches of education, and, on the other hand, suffer a loss of prestige if the contributions were not made, in view of the fact that business competitors had donated and shown a commendable public spirit in that relation. In the circumstances the rule of law that may fairly be applied is that the action of the officers of the company was not *ultra vires* ["outside the powers of the corporation"], but was in fact within their corporate powers, since it tended to promote the welfare of the business in which the corporation was engaged."

In *American Rolling Mill Co. v. Commissioner of Internal Revenue, 41 F. 2d* 314 *(C.C.A. 6 1930),* the corporation had joined with other local industries in the creation of a civic improvement fund to be distributed amongst community enterprises including the Boy Scouts and Girl Scouts, the Y.M.C.A., the Hospital, etc. The court readily sustained the contribution as an ordinary and necessary expense of the business within the Revenue Act. And in *Greene County Nat. Farm Loan Ass'n v. Federal Land Bank of Louisville, 57 F. Supp. 783, 789 (D.C.W.D. Ky. 1944),* affirmed *152 F. 2d* 215 *(6th Cir. 1945),* 328 U.S. 834, 66 S. Ct. 978, 90 L. Ed. 1610 (1946), the court in dealing with a comparable problem said:

> "But it is equally well established that corporations are permitted to make substantial contributions which have the outward form of gifts where the activity being promoted by the so-called gift tends reasonably to promote the goodwill of the business of the contributing corporation. Courts recognize in such cases that although there is no dollar and cent supporting consideration, yet there is often substantial indirect benefit accruing to the corporation which supports such action. So-called contributions by corporations to churches, schools, hospitals, and civic improvement funds, and the establishment of bonus and pension plans with the payment of large sums flowing therefrom have been upheld many times as reasonable business expenditures rather than being classified as charitable gifts. * * *"

The foregoing authorities illustrate how courts, while adhering to the terms of the common-law rule, have applied it very broadly to enable worthy corporate donations with indirect benefits to the corporations. In *State ex rel. Sorensen v. Chicago B. & Q.R. Co., 112 Neb. 248, 199 N.W. 534, 537 (1924),* the Supreme Court of Nebraska, through Justice Letton, went even further and without referring to any limitation based on economic benefits to the corporation said that it saw "no reason why if a railroad company desires to foster, encourage and contribute to a charitable enterprise, or to one designed for the public weal and welfare, it may not do so" * * *. Similarly, the court in *Carey v. Corporation Commission of Oklahoma, 168 Okla. 487, 33 P. 2d* 788, 794 (*Sup. Ct.* 1934), while holding that a public service company was not entitled to an increase in its rates because of its reasonable charitable donations, broadly recognized that corporations, like individuals, have power to make them. * * * In the course of his opinion for the court in the *Carey* case Justice Bayless said:

> "Next is the question of dues, donations, and philanthropies of the Company. It is a matter for the discretion of corporate management in making donations and paying dues. In that respect a corporation does not occupy a status far different from an individual. An individual determines the propriety of joining organizations, and contributing to their support by paying dues, and all contribution to public charities, etc., according to his means. He does not make such contributions above his means with the hope that his employer will increase his compensation accordingly. A corporation likewise should not do so. Its ultimate purpose, from its own standpoint, is to earn and pay dividends. If, as a matter of judgment, it desires to take part of its earnings, just as would an individual, and contribute them to a worthy public cause, it may do so; but we do not feel that it should be allowed to increase its earnings to take care thereof."

Over 20 years ago Professor Dodd, *supra, 45 Harv. L. Rev., at 1159, 1160,* cited the views of Justice Letton in *State ex rel. Sorensen v. Chicago B. & Q.R. Co., supra,* with seeming approval and suggested the doctrine that corporations may properly support charities which are important to the welfare of the communities where they do business as soundly representative of the public attitude and actual corporate practice. Developments since he wrote leave no doubts on this score.

When the wealth of the nation was primarily in the hands of individuals they discharged their responsibilities as citizens by donating freely for charitable purposes. With the transfer of most of the wealth to corporate hands and the imposition of heavy burdens of individual taxation, they have been unable to keep pace with increased philanthropic needs. They have therefore, with justification, turned to corporations to assume the modern obligations of good citizenship in the same manner as humans do. Congress and state legislatures have enacted laws which encourage corporate contributions, and much has recently been written to indicate the crying need and adequate legal basis therefor. * * * In actual practice corporate giving has correspondingly increased. Thus, it is estimated that annual corporate contributions throughout the nation aggregate over 300 million dollars with over 60 million dollars thereof going to universities and other educational institutions. Similarly, it is estimated that local community chests receive well over 40% of their contributions from corporations; these contributions and those made by corporations to the American Red Cross, to Boy Scouts and Girl Scouts, to 4–H Clubs and similar organizations have almost invariably been unquestioned.

During the first world war corporations loaned their personnel and contributed substantial corporate funds in order to insure survival; during the depression of the '30s they made contributions to alleviate the desperate hardships of the millions of unemployed; and during the second world war they again contributed to insure survival. They now recognize that we are faced with other, though nonetheless vicious, threats from abroad which must be withstood without impairing the vigor of our democratic institutions at home and that otherwise victory will be pyrrhic indeed. More and more they have come to recognize that their salvation rests upon sound economic and social environment which in turn rests in no insignificant part upon free and vigorous non-governmental institutions of learning. It seems to us that just as the conditions prevailing when corporations were originally created required that they serve public as well as private interests, modern conditions require that corporations acknowledge and discharge social as well as private responsibilities as members of the communities within which they operate. Within this broad concept there is no difficulty in sustaining, as incidental to their proper objects and in aid of the public welfare, the power of corporations to contribute corporate funds within reasonable limits in support of academic institutions. But even if we confine ourselves to the terms of the common-law rule in its application to current conditions, such expenditures may likewise readily be justified as being for the benefit of the corporation; indeed, if need be the matter may be viewed strictly in terms of actual survival of the corporation in a free enterprise system. The genius of our common law has been its capacity for growth and its adaptability to the needs of the times. Generally courts have accomplished the desired result indirectly through the molding of old forms. Occasionally they have done it directly through frank rejection of the old and recognition of the new. But whichever path the common law has taken it has not been found wanting as the proper tool for the advancement of the general good. *Cf. Holmes, The Common Law*, 1, 5 (1951); *Cardozo, Paradoxes of Legal Science, Hall, Selected Writings*, 253 (1947).

In 1930 a statute was enacted in our State which expressly provided that any corporation could cooperate with other corporations and natural persons in the creation and maintenance of community funds and charitable, philanthropic or benevolent instrumentalities conducive to public welfare, and could for such purposes expend such corporate sums as the directors "deem expedient and as in their judgment will contribute to the protection of the corporate interests." *L.* 1930, *c.* 105; *L.* 1931, *c.* 290; *R.S. 14:3–13*. * * * Under the terms of the statute donations in excess of 1% of the capital stock required 10 days' notice to stockholders and approval at a stockholders' meeting if written objections were made by the holders of more than 25% of the stock; in 1949 the statute was amended to increase the limitation to 1% of capital and surplus. * * * In 1950 a more comprehensive statute was enacted. *L.* 1950, *c.* 220; *N.J.S.A. 14:3–13.1 et seq.* In this enactment the Legislature declared that it shall be the public policy of our State and in furtherance of the public interest and welfare that encouragement be given to the creation and maintenance of institutions engaged in community fund, hospital, charitable, philanthropic, educational, scientific or benevolent activities or patriotic or civic activities conducive to the betterment of social and economic conditions; and it expressly empowered corporations acting singly or with others to contribute reasonable sums to such institutions, provided, however, that the contribution shall not be permissible if the donee institution owns more than 10% of the voting stock of the donor and provided, further, that the contribution shall not exceed 1% of capital and surplus unless the excess is authorized by the stockholders at a regular or special meeting. To insure that the grant of express power in the 1950 statute would not displace preexisting power at common law or otherwise, the Legislature provided that the "act shall not be construed as directly or indirectly minimizing or interpreting the rights and powers of corporations, as heretofore existing, with reference to appropriations, expenditures or contributions of the nature above specified." *N.J.S.A. 14:3–13.3.* It may be noted that statutes relating to charitable contributions by corporations have now been passed in 29 states. * * *

The appellants contend that the foregoing New Jersey statutes may not be applied to corporations created before their passage. Fifty years before the incorporation of The A.P. Smith Manufacturing Company our Legislature provided that every corporate charter thereafter granted "shall be subject to alteration, suspension and repeal, in the discretion of the legislature." *L.* 1846, *p.* 16; *R.S. 14:2–9.* A similar reserved power was placed into our State Constitution in 1875 (*Art.* IV, *Sec.* VII, *par.* 11), and is found in our present Constitution. *Art.* IV, *Sec.* VII, *par.* 9. In the early case of *Zabriskie v. Hackensack and New York Railroad Company, 18 N.J. Eq. 178 (Ch. 1867),* the court was called upon to determine whether a railroad could extend its line, above objection by a stockholder, under a legislative enactment passed under the reserve power after the incorporation of the railroad. Notwithstanding the breadth of the statutory language and persuasive authority elsewhere * * *, it was held that the proposed extension of the company's line constituted a vital change of its corporate object which could not be accomplished without unanimous consent. See *Lattin, A Primer on Fundamental Corporate Changes, 1 West. Res. L. Rev. 3, 7 (1949).* The court announced the now familiar New Jersey doctrine that although the reserved power permits alterations in the public interest of the contract between the state and the corporation, it has no effect on the contractual rights between the corporation and its stockholders and between stockholders * * *. Unfortunately, the court did not consider whether it was not contrary to the public interest to permit the single minority stockholder before it to restrain the railroad's normal corporate growth and development as authorized by the Legislature and approved, reasonably and in good faith, by the corporation's managing directors and majority stockholders. Although the later cases in New Jersey have not disavowed the doctrine of the *Zabriskie* case, it is noteworthy that they have repeatedly recognized that where justified by the advancement of the public interest the reserved power may be invoked to sustain later charter alterations even though they affect contractual rights between the corporation and its stockholders and between stockholders * * *. See *Berger v. United States Steel Corporation, 63 N.J. Eq. 809, 824 (E. & A. 1902); Murray v. Beattie Manufacturing Co., 79 N.J. Eq. 604, 609 (E. & A. 1912); Grausman v. Porto Rican–American Tobacco Co., 95 N.J. Eq. 155 (Ch. 1923)* * * * *Bingham v. Savings Investment & Trust Co., 101 N.J. Eq. 413, 415 (Ch. 1927),* affirmed *102 N.J. Eq. 302 (E. & A. 1928); In re Collins–Doan Co., 3 N.J. 382, 391 (1949). Cf. State v. Miller, 30 N.J.L. 368, 373 (Sup. Ct. 1863),* affirmed *31 N.J.L. 521 (E. & A. 1864); Montclair v. New York & Greenwood Lake Railway Co., 45 N.J. Eq 436, 444 (Ch. 1889),* * * * *Moore v. Conover, 123 N.J. Eq. 61, 74 (Ch. 1937).*

Thus, in the *Berger* case the Court of Errors and Appeals sustained the applicability under the reserved power of provisions relating to corporate borrowing and the purchase of corporate stock, and in considering the doctrine of the *Zabriskie* case noted that the rights of the stockholders * * * may not be impaired "except in so far as impairment may result from an alteration required by the public interest." And later in its opinion the court, referring to the provision in the Corporation Act of 1896 that the act and all amendments shall be a part of the charter of every corporation formed theretofore or thereafter, said: "It is difficult to perceive how any substantial force can be accorded to it, unless some amendment may be made which may affect the rights of stockholders *inter sese* ['among themselves'] to some extent." In the *Murray* case the court sustained a statute substituting a discretionary power to pay dividends for a pre-existing duty; in the course of his opinion Justice Swayze indicated that even apart from stockholders' consent the statutory alteration could be sustained since it was "a matter of state concern that a corporation should be permitted to accumulate a sufficient fund to secure its credit and make permanent its successful operation." And in the *Bingham* case the court sustained a bank merger under the authority of legislation enacted after the incorporation of the bank, with Vice-Chancellor Backes pointing out that the office of the reserve power in our organic and statutory law "is to safeguard the public interests in corporate grants."

This court had recent occasion to deal with the problem in *In re Collins-Doan Co., supra.* There it appeared that the board of directors was hopelessly deadlocked and application was duly made under *L.* 1938, *c.* 303 (*N.J.S.A. 14:13–15*) by the plaintiffs, representing half the directors and stockholders, for dissolution of the corporation. The defendants representing the other half resisted the application, contending that since the corporation was formed in 1916 it could not be dissolved except with the consent of two-thirds of the stockholders. This court, while recognizing that the later enactment did affect the rights between the corporation and its stockholders and between the stockholders *inter se* ["among them-

selves"], nevertheless held that it was applicable to the pre-existing corporation as a proper exercise of the reserved power. In the course of his
opinion for the court Justice Heher pointed out that "the contractual
rights of the stockholders *inter se* are not proof against 'alteration
required by the public interest.' " It may be noted that the later enactment
not only affected the relations between the corporation and stockholders
and the stockholders *inter se,* but also enabled complete termination of the
original corporate objectives; yet this court found little difficulty in subor-
dinating these considerations to the paramount public interest in avoiding
the indefinite continuance of a corporation which could not function with
propriety because of the "stalemate in corporate management." * * * The
legislative function recognized here may be considered somewhat akin to
that under the police power generally where private interests frequently
are called upon to give way to the paramount public interest. See * * *
*Lakewood Express Service, Inc. v. Board of Public Utility Commissioners,
1 N.J. 45, 50 (1948),* where Justice Oliphant, in discussing the police
power, said:

> "This power extends to all great public needs and the constitu-
> tional interdictions as to due process and the protection of property
> rights does not prevent a state from exercising such powers as are
> vested in it for the promotion of the common weal or are necessary for
> the general good of the public even though property or contract rights
> are affected. * * * "

State legislation adopted in the public interest and applied to pre-
existing corporations under the reserved power has repeatedly been sustained by the United States Supreme Court above the contention that it
impairs the rights of stockholders and violates constitutional guarantees
under the Federal Constitution. Thus, in *Looker v. Maynard, 179 U.S. 46,
21 S. Ct. 21, 45 L. Ed. 79 (1900),* the court sustained the application to
pre-existing corporations of later legislation designed to secure minority
representation on boards of directors by permitting cumulative voting by
stockholders; in *Polk v. Mutual Reserve Fund Life Association of New
York, 207 U.S. 310, 28 S. Ct. 65, 52 L. Ed. 222 (1907),* the court sustained
state legislation which permitted reorganizations of existing corporations
involving changes in their corporate purposes * * * and in *Sutton v. New
Jersey, 244 U.S. 258, 37 S. Ct. 508, 61 L. Ed. 1117 (1917),* a New Jersey
statute which required pre-existing street railway corporations to carry
police officers without charge was upheld as a proper exercise of the
reserve power. * * *

It seems clear to us that the public policy supporting the statutory
enactments under consideration is far greater and the alteration of pre-
existing rights of stockholders much lesser than in the cited cases sustaining various exercises of the reserve power. In encouraging and expressly
authorizing reasonable charitable contributions by corporations, our State
has not only joined with other states in advancing the national interest
but has also specially furthered the interests of its own people who must

bear the burdens of taxation resulting from increased state and federal aid upon default in voluntary giving. It is significant that in its enactments the State had not in anywise sought to impose any compulsory obligations or alter the corporate objectives. And since in our view the corporate power to make reasonable charitable contributions exists under modern conditions, even apart from express statutory provision, its enactments simply constitute helpful and confirmatory declarations of such power, accompanied by limiting safeguards.

In the light of all of the foregoing we have no hesitancy in sustaining the validity of the donation by the plaintiff. There is no suggestion that it was made indiscriminately or to a pet charity of the corporate directors in furtherance of personal rather than corporate ends. On the contrary, it was made to a preeminent institution of higher learning, was modest in amount and well within the limitations imposed by the statutory enactments, and was voluntarily made in the reasonable belief that it would aid the public welfare and advance the interests of the plaintiff as a private corporation and as part of the community in which it operates. We find that it was a lawful exercise of the corporation's implied and incidental powers under common-law principles and that it came within the express authority of the pertinent state legislation. As has been indicated, there is now widespread belief throughout the nation that free and vigorous nongovernmental institutions of learning are vital to our democracy and the system of free enterprise and that withdrawal of corporate authority to make such contributions within reasonable limits would seriously threaten their continuance. Corporations have come to recognize this and with their enlightenment have sought in varying measures, as has the plaintiff by its contribution, to insure and strengthen the society which gives them existence and the means of aiding themselves and their fellow citizens. Clearly then, the appellants, as individual stockholders whose private interests rest entirely upon the well-being of the plaintiff corporation, ought not be permitted to close their eyes to present-day realities and thwart the long-visioned corporate action in recognizing and voluntarily discharging its high obligations as a constituent of our modern social structure.

*   *   *

NOTES AND QUESTIONS

1. At issue in *Smith v. Barlow* is a $1500 donation to Princeton University that plaintiffs argue the corporate charter does not grant the directors the power to authorize. The defendant corporation argues that such philanthropic donations obtain good-will from the community, create a "favorable environment for their business," and further the corporation's "self-interest in assuring the free flow of properly trained personnel for … corporate employment." To resolve the dispute the court looks to the common law rule that corporations cannot "disburse any corporate funds for philanthropic or other worthy public cause[s] unless the expenditure would benefit the corporation."

The court holds that a contribution to Princeton does benefit the corporation. Do you agree? Where would you draw the line? If a contribution to a university benefits the corporation, what kind of contributions would not? Even if you think the judges applied the rule correctly, does it make sense that corporations can only act in their own self-interest?

2. To support the claim that corporations should be allowed to make public donations, the defendants offer testimony from various industry leaders such as the chairmen of Standard Oil and U.S. Steel. The President of Princeton University goes so far as to suggest that "democratic society will not long endure" if corporations cannot make charitable contributions. Is this correct? The court observes that "we are faced with other ... threats from abroad which must be withstood without impairing the vigor of our democratic institutions at home." The court continues, indicating that corporate "survival rests upon [a] sound economic and social environment which in turn rests in no insignificant part upon free and vigorous non-governmental institutions of learning." What threats do you suppose the court had in mind? Do they continue? Have other "threats" taken their place? Is protecting a $1500 donation to Princeton really saving the democratic cause? On the other hand, after the collapse of the Berlin Wall and the demise of Soviet-style communism, do you think decisions like *Barlow* did in fact help promote and protect capitalism?

3. What do you make of the Court's analysis and exposition of the manner of operation of the common law? You will have noted that the Court, citing, *inter alia*, Holmes and Cardozo, suggests that it is part of the task of the common law judge to mold the common law to fit the needs of the times. Is this what judges are supposed to do? From an historical perspective, the Supreme Court of New Jersey seems to have decided the case correctly. They accurately note that the common-law rule has been applied "very broadly to enable worthy corporate donations with indirect benefits to the corporations." The court observes that early 19th century corporations would most likely not have been allowed to make such a contribution to Princeton, but the court suggests that changes in wealth patterns should alter the common-law rule. The court points out that "[c]ontrol of economic wealth has passed largely from individual entrepreneurs to dominating corporations, and calls upon the corporation for reasonable philanthropic donations have come to be made with increased public support." Because wealth was no longer held by a limited number of individuals who, under the old rule, could distribute their income to any source they desired, but instead by a limited number of corporations who cannot donate under the old rule, the court believed that the rule had already been relaxed according to widespread public interest and desire. The court is correct in its analysis of wealth distribution. Still, if some of the profits of a corporation that might have been used for charitable contributions are distributed to its shareholders, as dividends, is it clear that they would only use those funds for personal purposes, or might the individuals donate to the charities of their choice, possibly not including Princeton? If there really are social problems that require public donations to private institutions to ameliorate, would shareholders not also be sensitive to these needs and wish to contribute as individuals? If the court holds true to the principle of

shareholder primacy, does that really spell doom for charities and public institutions, or would it enable a more democratic selection of charitable donations, in which individuals may select which charities and causes they wish to support? Is the *Smith v. Barlow* case undemocratic?

4.   As we saw in *Ford v. Dodge*, the issue of the social responsibilities and duties of corporations is a complicated one. Debates over to whom corporations owe obligations have no doubt existed since the first corporation, but one important debate in American legal circles, alluded to by the court in *Smith v. Barlow*, took place in the pages of the *Harvard Law Review* between A.A. Berle and E. Merrick Dodd in 1932.

Writing in 2002, Professor C.A. Harwell Wells[50] argued that all subsequent debates over corporate responsibility "shar[e] conceptual foundations" with the debate between Berle and Dodd.[51] Professor Wells indicates that like the controversy between Berle and Dodd, all subsequent controversies share four characteristic premises. The first is that corporate "social responsibility is about big business" and that legal scholars writing about corporate responsibility always "really mean the responsibility of giant corporations." The second premise is that the goal is "to reform corporate power, not eliminate it," and because of this goal, no "proponents of corporate social responsibility were genuinely radical." Third, the general form of the debate, regardless of the period when it took place, always remains "duty to owners alone versus duties to many constituencies." The final premise, according to Wells, is that "each decade supplies its own reason why corporations should assume greater responsibility," which Wells calls "an unchanging solution to an ever-new problem."[52]

The publication of E. Merrick Dodd's "For Whom Are Corporate Managers Trustees?"[53] helped to begin the still-ongoing modern debate regarding corporate social responsibility. Dodd saw the 1920s, before the crash of 1929, as "a moment in time when corporations had finally begun to take responsibility for their employees and communities."[54] Both Dodd and his principal adversary, A.A. Berle, were responding to the fact, noted earlier, that by the first third of the twentieth century, at least with regard to large publicly-held corporations, there had come to be an increasing separation between ownership and management, as corporations were controlled by their officers and directors, and shareholders had become, essentially, passive investors.

A.A. Berle saw this separation as something that should be reflected by changes in the law, that the law had formerly given too much deference to corporate owners, and that since they were now removed from control, managers should be regulated, to make them act more like responsible owners, and, in particular, to get them to assume responsibility not just to line the

---

50.   C.A. Harwell Wells, "The Cycles of Corporate Social Responsibility: An Historical Retrospective for the Twenty-first century," 51 Kan L.Rev. 77 (2002).

51.   Id., at 79.

52.   Id., at 80–81.

53.   E. Merrick Dodd, Jr., For Whom Are Corporate Managers Trustees?, 45 Harv. L. Rev. 1145 (1932).

54.   Wells, supra note 50, at 92.

pockets of their passive shareholders, but also to assume some of the social burdens of the time.[55] Dodd, while sympathizing somewhat with Berle's desire for social responsibility, saw Berle's solution—increased regulation—as too radical.

Dodd argued that appropriate rules were already in place, and that added regulation would probably halt or, at best, slow economic progress. Dodd wanted managers, instead of being subject to regulation, to have the flexibility to respond to the times as they saw fit. He wrote "many conservatives ... believe that capitalism is worth saving but that it can not permanently survive under modern conditions unless it treats the economic security of the worker as one of its obligations and is intelligently directed so as to attain that object."[56] Dodd argued, however, that regulations passed in the interests of employees and consumers "may increasingly limit the methods which managers of incorporated business enterprises may employ in seeking profits for their stockholders without in any way affecting the proposition that the sole function of such managers is to work for the best interests of the stockholders."

Dodd saw business as "a profession of public service, not primarily because the law had made it such but because a public opinion shared by business men themselves had brought about a professional attitude."[57] Dodd believed that if corporate managers were to be left to their own devices, they would come up with solutions to problems more efficiently than if government regulations mandated charitable contributions or safe workplaces—that public outcry would direct the actions of those at the top of corporations more efficiently than federal regulation. Dodd wrote "power over the lives of others tends to create on the part of those most worthy to exercise it a sense of responsibility."[58] Do you agree? Are those in charge often those most "worthy"?

A.A. Berle was much less sanguine. As did many American academics, he believed that the Great Depression and the stock market crash came about because of widespread misconduct. He saw the 1920s as a time rife with corporate wrongdoing and stock market fraud. Writing in response to Dodd, Berle suggested that leaving management unfettered by outside regulation "might be unsafe" and was "an invitation not to law or orderly government, but to a process of economic civil war."[59] Berle believed that corporate management had accomplished a "seizure of power without recognition of responsibility-ambition without courage."[60] According to Professor Wells, Berle's "problem with Dodd's proposal was not that it replaced shareholder primacy with broader responsibilities, but that it replaced shareholder primacy with nothing at all."[61] Does *Smith v. Barlow* follow the principle of "shareholder primacy," or does it replace it with something else?

---

55. This argument was most fully elaborated in A.A. Berle and Gardner Means, The Corporation and Private Property (1932), a modern classic.

56. Dodd, "For Whom Are Corporate Managers Trustees?" 45 Harv. L. Rev 1145.

57. Dodd, supra note 56, at 1154.

58. Id., at 1157.

59. A.A. Berle, Jr., For Whom Corporate Managers Are Trustees: A Note, 45 Harv. L. Rev. 1365, 1369 (1932).

60. Ibid.

61. Wells, supra, note 50, at 95.

6. Professor Cynthia A. Williams nicely suggests that what Dodd and Berle were arguing about was "the extent to which the corporation should be thought of primarily as an economic entity, versus the extent to which it should be thought of primarily as a social entity."[62] Professor Williams argues that globalization "undermines sovereigns' power to regulate corporate activity ... companies can, and do, move their productive processes to different countries or 'outsource' to independent producers in other countries to take advantage of competitive opportunities."[63] Williams wonders whether the principle of shareholder primacy with its attendant lack of regulation in the interest of non-shareholder constituencies is appropriate for our age of globalization. She suggests that we should require greater "transparency" in the international activities of our corporations, primarily through mandating increased disclosure of corporate activities. One could, of course, go further, and suggests that American courts, realizing the problem of there being no appropriate international body to regulate corporations, should, once they shake off the purportedly archaic notions of shareholder primacy, offer themselves as a forum to aid non-shareholder plaintiffs from all over the world in getting corporations to operate in their interests. Would this sort of a change in the common law be appropriate? Would the judges in *Smith v. Barlow* have approved? Is the notion of "shareholder primacy" archaic, or is there still much to be said for it? And what of Delaware, the state that has done more than any other to facilitate the operation of and the investment in the management-run modern American corporation?

D.   A NOTE ON DELAWARE INCORPORATION

Over 50% of all publicly-traded American corporations and 58% of Fortune 500 corporations are incorporated in Delaware. According to the state's webpage, "[b]usinesses choose Delaware because we provide a complete package of incorporation services including modern and flexible corporate laws, our highly-respected Court of Chancery, a business-friendly State Government, and the customer service oriented Staff of the Delaware Division of Corporations."

At first blush, it seems surprising that a tiny state on the Eastern Seaboard should be the nominal home to so many great American corporations. How did this come about? As already indicated, towards the end of the 19th century, many states began to relax their general incorporation laws in an attempt to attract more corporations and acquire more revenue from franchise taxes and fees associated with incorporation. Initially, it was Delaware's neighbor, New Jersey, which won this battle. In 1896, New Jersey enacted the most liberal general incorporation law in the nation. Soon, however, Woodrow Wilson, then governor of New Jersey,

---

62.   Cynthia A. Williams "Symposium: Corporations Theory and Corporate Governance Law: Corporate Social Responsibility in an Era of Economic Globalization." 35 U.C. Davis L. Rev. 705. 707 (2002).

63.   Id. at 726.

spearheaded an effort to change the policies of the state, and New Jersey passed the "Seven Sisters Act" in 1913, effectively outlawing trusts (a device by which a very small number of persons could control a large number of corporations) and holding companies (corporations that owned other corporations). Soon after, Delaware, which still permitted such devices, found itself the nation's leading haven for incorporation.

After the stock market crash of 1929, and the passage of significant federal legislation to regulate the issuance and trading in the stock of corporations, the wave of incorporations in Delaware subsided somewhat, and after the close of World War II, many states revised their laws to compete more effectively with Delaware. In 1967 the Delaware Bar Association, with the aid of many leading corporate law experts, substantially revised Delaware's General Corporation Law in order once again to make the state the most attractive for incorporation. One of the most important changes to come out of that revision is a speedy amendment process for the Delaware Corporations statutes, which "allows the Delaware General Assembly to keep ahead of legal developments, fix ambiguities in the law, and correct problems noted by judicial decisions."

Delaware's Corporate legislation, and the process whereby the state seeks to be the premier site for incorporation, are not without their critics. Over the years, many scholars, politicians and even some judges have blasted Delaware and other states that have purportedly loosened restrictions on corporations. One of the most famous such critiques came from Supreme Court Associate Justice Louis Brandeis writing in dissent in *Louis K. Liggett Co. v. Lee*. Said the great Justice and former prototype of the public interest lawyer,

> "[t]he removal by the leading industrial states of the limitations upon the size and powers of business corporations appears to have been due, not to their conviction that maintenance of the restrictions was undesirable in itself, but to the conviction that it was futile to insist upon them; because local restriction would be circumvented by foreign incorporation. Indeed, local restriction seemed worse than futile. Lesser states, eager for the revenue derived from the traffic in charters, had removed safeguards from their own incorporation laws. Companies were early formed to provide charters for corporations in states where the cost was lowest and the laws least restrictive. The states joined in advertising their wares. *The race was one not of diligence but of laxity.* Incorporation under such laws was possible; and the great industrial States yielded in order not to lose wholly the prospect of the revenue and the control incident to domestic incorporation." [Emphasis supplied][64]

Brandeis thus regarded Delaware's attempts to liberalize corporate law as a cynical ploy by the state to raise and protect revenue associated

---

64. Louis K. Liggett Co. v. Lee, 288 U.S. 517, 557–560, 53 S.Ct. 481, 77 L.Ed. 929 (1933).

with incorporation. Was Brandeis correct, or are there more benign explanations for Delaware's success as a haven for incorporation?

In a manner similar to the assertions of BRANDEIS, after the 1967 revisions of Delaware's Corporations Law, in a seminal piece for the Yale Law Journal,[65] Professor William L. Cary stated that "Delaware is both the sponsor and the victim of a system contributing to the deterioration of corporation standards." Professor Cary argued that the competition among the states to attract incorporation was "a race to the bottom," in which the states tried to outdo each other in creating the most lenient business laws, to attract incorporations in order to raise funds through fees, while failing to protect shareholders, workers and consumers.

Professor Cary did not level all of his fire on Delaware for the race to the bottom phenomenon, noting that "other states would have joined in to attract the lucrative business of incorporating." Still, Cary challenged Delaware's claim to be acting in the best interests of its corporations, as he observed that at the time his article was published, Delaware derived approximately a quarter of its state revenue from incorporations and franchise taxes. In Delaware, Cary stated, "both the courts and the legislature may be said to lack the neutrality and detachment 'to hold the balance nice, clear, and true' required in passing upon the complaints of shareholders." Cary thought that Delaware's corporate law unduly favored management and thus posed a danger to shareholders. He thought it wrong that one tiny state should possess such power to "set social policy in the corporate field." His solution was to advocate federal chartering of corporations, with more stringent regulatory standards.

Consider Professor Cary's thesis. Do you think that because Delaware raises large amounts of revenue through incorporations that the state has lost its impartiality, and cannot be trusted to come up with a system that is fair to shareholders, managers, and the rest of the corporate constituencies or stakeholders? Do you think if Delaware's laws were dangerous to shareholders that shareholders would invest in Delaware corporations, instead of corporations incorporated in states with laws that may be more favorable? Professor Cary argues that management decisions "should be disclosed and monitored by outside groups" to protect investors. Cary favors a federally supervised plan requiring frequent shareholder approval of corporate transactions, the abolition of nonvoting shares and federal fiduciary standards. Do you agree with Professor Cary as to the extent of the threat states like Delaware pose to shareholders' rights? Do you think that increased federal regulation would better protect shareholders' rights? As we will soon see, ever since Cary's piece there has been substantial federal intervention further to regulate corporations, on the theory that state law does not adequately protect shareholders. The solution endorsed by many critics of the current system of corporate management continues to be to give shareholders more explicitly-protected rights

---

65. William L. Cary, Federalism and Corporate Law: Reflections upon Delaware, 83 Yale LJ. 663 (1974).

and more opportunities for corporate control. Do you think investors desire this level of involvement or do more investors prefer a passive role in the management of corporate affairs? Would changes such as those Cary advocates (changes, by the way, that seem to be the thrust of modern federal legislation) solve the problem that Berle perceived because of the separation of corporate ownership from management?

Professor Cary's "race to the bottom" thesis was attacked by equally passionate defenders of Delaware. They argued that Delaware and other states were engaged not in a "race to the bottom," but rather in a "race to the top" to find the optimal form of corporate regulation. According to this view Delaware's success in attracting incorporators is the result of Delaware's success in crafting legislation which permitted more profitable corporate operation, thus benefiting shareholders, who otherwise would not stand for incorporation or reincorporation (moving one's state of incorporation) in Delaware. The fact that the traffic in reincorporation seemed to run virtually only one way (into Delaware) is often cited as evidence of Delaware's positive achievement, as is the fact that the stock market prices shares higher once corporations reincorporate in Delaware. Nevertheless, although no general federal incorporation statute, along the lines advocated by Cary was ever passed, his "race to the bottom thesis" still survives, especially in some parts of the legal academy. Professor John C. Coffee, Jr. wrote in a response to critics of Cary that Cary's article, among other effects, "embarrassed and infuriated the Delaware bench and bar, may have been responsible for a surprising string of pro-shareholder decisions in Delaware over the next decade, provoked the then adolescent 'law and economics' movement to argue that the race was to the top, not the bottom, and motivated Ralph Nader and similar corporate reformers to join Cary in recommending federal chartering of corporations."[66]

Catherine Holst has pointed out that "the American debate over the 'race to the bottom' thesis assumes as a starting point that regulatory competition has beneficial effects."[67] Holst believes that federal minimum standards could be designed to place limits on the extent to which states could favor management over shareholders. Holst concludes that while Professor Cary's article has advanced the debate over the nature of competition for corporate charters, "his conclusions are arguably not self-evident and indeed, his call for federal regulatory intervention has gone unheeded in the U.S." See if you agree with Ms. Holst after considering the federal law to which will soon turn.

It may still be true, however, that state law is still the primary regulator of corporations. Why do you suppose, then, that Cary's call for fed-

---

66. John C. Coffee, Jr., Commentary on William L. Cary, Federalism and Corporate Law: Reflections Upon Delaware, 83 YALE L.J. 663 (1974), 100 Yale L.J. 1449 (1991) (Part of commentary on the most-cited law review articles from the Yale Law Journal. Cary's article was number fourteen).

67. Catherine Holst, European Company Law after Centros: Is the EU on the Road to Delaware?, 8 Colum. J. Eur. L. 323 (2002).

eral regulation has been unsuccessful? Who gets it right, Cary or his critics? Cary singled out several purportedly pernicious provisions of the Delaware Corporate law, some of which we will return to later, but which might be quickly summarized.

(1) Cary observed that it was easier to accomplish organic change (mergers, sale of substantially all of the assets, amending of the corporate charter, etc.) in Delaware than in any other state, since all that was required was a vote of the majority of the board followed by a vote of the majority of the shareholders. Other states often required super-majority votes to accomplish such matters. (2) Cary suggested that it was easier to declare dividends in Delaware than in any other state, and (3) Cary observed that Delaware did not require cumulative voting for shareholders (which procedure made it easier for shareholder minorities to be represented on the Board), that (4) Delaware did not require that all members of the Board be subject to election each year, that (5) Delaware did not require pre-emptive rights (allowing shareholders the first option of purchasing an aliquot share of new issues of corporate stock), and that (6) Delaware went further than any other state in allowing corporations to hold officers and directors harmless for action taken in good faith, but which later proved deleterious to the corporation. Looking at all of this, in a famous metaphor, Cary stated that Delaware "waters down the rights of shareholders to a thin gruel." Do you agree?

One way of trying to understand whether Delaware law is good or bad for shareholders is to try to discern how Delaware law orders the relationship among shareholders, directors, and officers. A fine vehicle for seeking to achieve this understanding is the great case of *Campbell v. Loews*, which follows. Would you say that the opinion of Judge SEITZ in that case seeks admirably to protect shareholders or not?

E. THE PLAYERS IN THE CORPORATION: SHAREHOLDERS, DIRECTORS, AND OFFICERS

CAMPBELL v. LOEW'S INC.

Court of Chancery of Delaware, New Castle County.
36 Del.Ch. 563, 134 A.2d 852 (1957).

SEITZ, Chancellor: This is the decision on plaintiff's request for a preliminary injunction to restrain the holding of a stockholders' meeting or alternatively to prevent the meeting from considering certain matters or to prevent the voting of certain proxies. * * *

The corporate defendant appeared and resisted the motion. * * *

Some background is in order if the many difficult and novel issues are to be understood. Two factions have been fighting for control of Loew's. One faction is headed by Joseph Tomlinson (hereafter "Tomlinson faction") while the other is headed by the President of Loew's, Joseph Vogel (hereafter "Vogel faction"). At the annual meeting of stockholders last February a compromise was reached by which each nominated six directors and they in turn nominated a thirteenth or neutral director. But the battle had only begun. Passing by much of the controversy, we come to the July 17–18 period of this year when two of the six Vogel directors and the thirteenth or neutral director resigned. A quorum is seven.

On the 19th of July the Tomlinson faction asked that a directors' meeting be called for July 30 to consider, *inter alia*, the problem of filling director vacancies. On the eve of this meeting one of the Tomlinson directors resigned. This left five Tomlinson directors and four Vogel directors in office. Only the five Tomlinson directors attended the July 30 meeting. They purported to fill two of the director vacancies and to take other action. This Court has now ruled that for want of a quorum the two directors were not validly elected and the subsequent action taken at that meeting was invalid. See *Tomlinson v. Loew's Inc.* [36 Del.Ch. 516, 134 A.2d 518 (1957)].

On July 29, the day before the noticed directors' meeting, Vogel, as president, sent out a notice calling a stockholders' meeting for September 12 for the following purposes:

1. to fill director vacancies.

2. to amend the by-laws to increase the number of the board from 13 to 19; to increase the quorum from 7 to 10 and to elect six additional directors.

3. to remove Stanley Meyer and Joseph Tomlinson as directors and to fill such vacancies.

Still later, another notice for a September 12 stockholders' meeting as well as a proxy statement went out over the signature of Joseph R. Vogel, as president. It was accompanied by a letter from Mr. Vogel dated August 9, 1957, soliciting stockholder support for the matters noticed in the call of the meeting, and particularly seeking to fill the vacancies and newly created directorships with "his" nominees. Promptly thereafter, plaintiff began this action. An order was entered requiring that the stockholders' meeting be adjourned until October 15, to give the Court more time to decide the serious and novel issues raised. * * *

* * *

Plaintiff contends that the president had no authority in fact to call a special meeting of stockholders to act upon policy matters which have not been defined by the board of directors. Defendant says that the by-laws specifically authorize the action taken.

It is helpful to have in mind the pertinent by-law provisions:

Section 7 of *Article* I provides:

> "Special meetings of the stockholders for any purpose or purposes, other than those regulated by statute, may be called by the President * * * *"

Section 2 of *Article* IV reads:

"The President * * * shall have power to call special meetings of the stockholders * * * for any purpose or purposes * * *"

It is true that *Section* 8(11) of *Article* II [of the bylaws] also provides that the board of directors may call a special meeting of stockholders for any purpose. But, in view of the explicit language of the by-laws above quoted, can this Court say that the president was without authority to call this meeting for the purposes stated? I think not. I agree that the purposes for which the president called the meeting were not in furtherance of the routine business of the corporation. Nevertheless, I think the stockholders, by permitting the quoted by-laws to stand, have given the president the power to state these broad purposes in his call. Moreover, it may be noted that at least one other by-law (*Article* V, § 2) makes certain action of the president subject to board approval. The absence of such language in connection with the call [of a shareholders' meeting] provision, while not conclusive, is some evidence that it was intended that the call provision should not be so circumscribed.

The plaintiff argues that if this by-law purports to give the president the power to call special stockholders' meetings for the purposes here stated, then it is contrary to *8 Del.C. § 141(a)*, which provides:

> "The business of every corporation organized under the provisions of this chapter shall be managed by a board of directors, except as hereinafter or in its certificate of incorporation otherwise provided."

I do not believe the call of a stockholders' meeting for the purposes mentioned is action of the character which would impinge upon the power given the directors by the statute. I say this because I believe a by-law giving the president the power to submit matters for stockholder action presumably only embraces matters which are appropriate for stockholder action. So construed the by-laws do not impinge upon the statutory right and duty of the board to manage the business of the corporation. Plaintiff does not suggest that the matters noticed are inappropriate for stockholder consideration. And, of course, the Court is not concerned with the wisdom of the grant of such power to the president.

Plaintiff's next argument is that the president has no authority, without board approval, to propose an amendment of the by-laws to enlarge the board of directors. Admittedly this would be a most radical change in this corporate management. Indeed, it may well involve the determination of control. However, as I have already indicated, I believe the wording of the by-laws authorizes such action.

Plaintiff next argues that the president had no power to call a stockholders' meeting to fill vacancies on the board. As I understand plaintiff's argument it is that the existence of *Article* V, § 2 of the by-laws, which provides that the stockholders or the remaining directors may fill vacancies, by implication, precludes the president from calling a stockholders' meeting for that purpose, that provision being intended for stockholder use only at the initiative of the stockholders. First of all, the by-laws permit the president to call a meeting for any purpose. This is broad and all-embracing language and I think it must include the power to call a meeting to fill vacancies. The fact that the stockholders may on their initiative have the right to call a meeting for that purpose does not seem to be a sufficient reason for implying that the president is thereby deprived of such power.

Plaintiff points to the "extraordinary state of affairs" which the recognition of such power in the president would create. Obviously it gives the president power which may place him in conflict with the members of the board. But such consequences inhere in a situation where those adopting the by-laws grant such broad and concurrent power to the board and to the president. The validity but not the wisdom of the grant of power is before the Court. I conclude that under the by-laws the president has the power to call a meeting to fill vacancies on the board.

Plaintiff next argues that the president's action in calling a stockholders' meeting to fill vacancies was unlawful because it was in conflict with the previously scheduled action by the board on the same subject. It should be noted that the proxy statement sent out by the president states that the stockholders would only fill the two vacancies purportedly filled by the board, if their election by the board was held to be invalid. To this extent then the call was not in conflict with this aspect of the board's action. But in any event I have now ruled that the board did not legally fill the vacancies and so the matter would seem to be moot. * * *

* * *

I therefore conclude that the president had the power to call the meeting for the purposes noticed. * * *

Plaintiff next argues that the stockholders have no power between annual meetings to elect directors to fill newly created directorships.

Plaintiff argues in effect that since the Loew's by-laws provide that the stockholders may fill "vacancies", and since our Courts have construed "vacancy" not to embrace "newly created directorships" (*Automatic Steel Products v. Johnston, 31 Del. Ch. 469, 64 A.2d 416, 6 A.L.R.2d 170*), the attempted call by the president for the purpose of filling newly created directorships was invalid.

Conceding that "vacancy" as used in the by-laws does not embrace "newly created directorships", that does not resolve this problem. I say this because in *Moon v. Moon Motor Car Co., 17 Del. Ch. 176, 151 A. 298*, it was held that the stockholders had the inherent right between annual meetings to fill newly created directorships. See also *Automatic Steel Products v. Johnston*, above. There is no basis to distinguish the *Moon* case unless it be because the statute has since been amended to provide that not only vacancies but newly created directorships "may be filled by a majority of the directors then in office * * * unless it is otherwise provided in the certificate of incorporation or the by-laws * * * ". *8 Del.C. § 223*. Obviously, the amendment to include new directors is not worded so as to make the statute exclusive. It does not prevent the stockholders from filling the new directorships.

Is there any reason to consider the absence of a reference in the by-laws to new directorships to be significant? I think not. The by-law relied upon by plaintiff was adopted long before the statutory amendment and it does not purport to be exclusive in its operation. It would take a strong by-law language to warrant the conclusion that those adopting the by-laws intended to prohibit the stockholders from filling new director-ships between annual meetings. No such strong language appears here and I do not think the implication is warranted in view of the subject matter.

I therefore conclude that the stockholders of Loew's do have the right between annual meetings to elect directors to fill newly created director-ships.

Plaintiff next argues that the shareholders of a Delaware corporation have no power to remove directors from office even for cause and thus the call for that purpose is invalid. * * *

While there are some cases suggesting the contrary, I believe that the stockholders have the power to remove a director for cause. * * * This power must be implied when we consider that otherwise a director who is guilty of the worst sort of violation of his duty could nevertheless remain on the board. It is hardly to be believed that a director who is disclosing the corporation's trade secrets to a competitor would be immune from removal by the stockholders. Other examples, such as embezzlement of corporate funds, etc., come readily to mind.

But plaintiff correctly states that there is no provision in our statu-tory law providing for the removal of directors by stockholder action. In contrast he calls attention to § 142 of 8 *Del.C.*, dealing with officers, which specifically refers to the possibility of a vacancy in an office by removal. He also notes that the Loew's by-laws provide for the removal of officers and employees but not directors. From these facts he argues that it was intended that directors not be removed even for cause. I believe the statute and by-law are of course some evidence to support plaintiff's con-tention. But when we seek to exclude the existence of a power by implica-tion, I think it is pertinent to consider whether the absence of the power can be said to subject the corporation to the possibility of real damage. I say this because we seek intention and such a factor would be relevant to that issue. Considering the damage a director might be able to inflict upon his corporation, I believe the doubt must be resolved by construing the statutes and by-laws as leaving untouched the question of director removal for cause. This being so, the Court is free to conclude on reason that the stockholders have such inherent power.

* * *

Plaintiff next argues that the removal of Tomlinson and Meyer as directors would violate the right of minority shareholders to representation on the board and would be contrary to the policy of the Delaware law regarding cumulative voting. Plaintiff contends that where there is cumulative voting, as provided by the Loew's certificate, a director cannot be removed by the stockholders even for cause.

It is true that the Chancellor noted in [an earlier case] that the provision for cumulative voting in the Delaware law was one reason why directors should not be considered to have the power to remove a fellow director even for cause. And it is certainly evident that if not carefully supervised the existence of a power in the stockholders to remove a director even for cause could be abused and used to defeat cumulative voting. * * *

Does this mean that there can be no removal of a director by the stockholders for cause in any case where cumulative voting exists? The conflicting considerations involved make the answer to this question far from easy. Some states have passed statutes dealing with this problem but Delaware has not. The possibility of stockholder removal action designed to circumvent the effect of cumulative voting is evident. This is particularly true where the removal vote is, as here, by mere majority vote. On the other hand, if we assume a case where a director's presence or action is clearly damaging the corporation and its stockholders in a substantial way, it is difficult to see why that director should be free to continue such damage merely because he was elected under a cumulative voting provision.

On balance, I conclude that the stockholders have the power to remove a director for cause even where there is a provision for cumulative voting. I think adequate protection is afforded not only by the legal safeguards announced in this opinion but by the existence of a remedy to test the validity of any such action, if taken.

The foregoing points constitute all of the arguments advanced by plaintiff which go to the validity of the call of the meeting for the purposes stated. It follows from my various conclusions that the meeting was validly called by the president to consider the matters noticed.

I turn next to plaintiff's charges relating to procedural defects and to irregularities in proxy solicitation by the Vogel group.

Plaintiff's first point is that the stockholders can vote to remove a director for cause only after such director has been given adequate notice of charges of grave impropriety and afforded an opportunity to be heard.

Defendant raises a preliminary point that plaintiff, being only a stockholder, has no standing to make the contention that the foregoing requirements have not been met. * * * [O]n reason, there would seem no basis for telling a stockholder, particularly where cumulative voting is involved, that he has no right to challenge the legal propriety of action proposed to be taken to remove a member of the board of directors. After all, the board is managing the corporation for all the stockholders and while a director may have sufficient standing to attack the action himself, I cannot believe that a stockholder is lacking a sufficient interest to warrant legal recognition.

I am inclined to agree that if the proceedings preliminary to submitting the matter of removal for cause to the stockholders appear to be legal and if the charges are legally sufficient on their face, the Court should ordinarily not intervene. The sufficiency of the evidence would be a matter for evaluation in later proceedings. But where the procedure adopted to remove a director for cause is invalid on its face, a stockholder can attack such matters before the meeting. This conclusion is dictated both by the desirability of avoiding unnecessary and expensive action and by the importance of settling internal disputes, where reasonably possible, at the earliest moment. * * * Otherwise a director could be removed and his successor could be appointed and participate in important board action before the illegality of the removal was judicially established. This seems undesirable where the illegality is clear on the face of the proceedings.

* * *

Turning now to plaintiff's contentions, it is certainly true that when the shareholders attempt to remove a director for cause, " * * * there must be the service of specific charges, adequate notice and full opportunity of meeting the accusation * * * ". See *Auer v. Dressel [306 N.Y. 427, 118 N.E.2d 590]*. While it involved an invalid attempt by directors to remove a fellow director for cause, nevertheless, this same general standard was recognized in *Bruch v. National Guarantee Credit Corp. [13 Del. Ch. 180, 116 A. 738]*. The Chancellor said that the power of removal could not "be exercised in an arbitrary manner. The accused director would be entitled to be heard in his own defense".

Plaintiff asserts that no specific charges have been served upon the two directors sought to be ousted; that the notice of the special meeting fails to contain a specific statement of the charges; that the proxy statement which accompanied the notice also failed to notify the stockholders of the specific charges; and that it does not inform the stockholders that the accused must be afforded an opportunity to meet the accusations before a vote is taken.

Matters for stockholder consideration need not be conducted with the same formality as judicial proceedings. The proxy statement specifically recites that the two directors are sought to be removed for the reasons stated in the president's accompanying letter. Both directors involved received copies of the letter. Under the circumstances I think it must be said that the two directors involved were served with notice of the charges against them. It is true, as plaintiff says, that the notice and the proxy statement failed to contain a specific statement of charges. But as indicated, I believe the accompanying letter was sufficient compliance with the notice requirement.

* * *

I next consider plaintiff's contention that the charges against the two directors do not constitute "cause" as a matter of law. It would take too much space to narrate in detail the contents of the president's letter. I must therefore give my summary of its charges. First of all, it charges that the two directors (Tomlinson and Meyer) failed to cooperate with Vogel in his announced program for rebuilding the company; that their purpose has been to put themselves in control; that they made baseless accusations against him and other management personnel and attempted to divert him from his normal duties as president by bombarding him with correspondence containing unfounded charges and other similar acts; that they moved into the company's building, accompanied by lawyers and accountants, and immediately proceeded upon a planned scheme of harassment. They called for many records, some going back twenty years, and were rude to the personnel. Tomlinson sent daily letters to the directors making serious charges directly and by means of innuendos and misinterpretations.

Are the foregoing charges, if proved, legally sufficient to justify the ouster of the two directors by the stockholders? I am satisfied that a charge that the directors desired to take over control of the corporation is not a reason for their ouster. Standing alone, it is a perfectly legitimate objective which is a part of the very fabric of corporate existence. Nor is a charge of lack of cooperation a legally sufficient basis for removal for cause.

The next charge is that these directors, in effect, engaged in a calculated plan of harassment to the detriment of the corporation. Certainly a director may examine books, ask questions, etc., in the discharge of his duty, but a point can be reached when his actions exceed the call of duty and become deliberately obstructive. In such a situation, if his actions constitute a real burden on the corporation then the stockholders are entitled to relief. The charges in this area made by the Vogel letter are legally sufficient to justify the stockholders in voting to remove such directors. * * * In so concluding I of course express no opinion as to the truth of the charges.

I therefore conclude that the charge of "a planned scheme of harassment" as detailed in the letter constitutes a justifiable legal basis for removing a director.

I next consider whether the directors sought to be removed have been given a reasonable opportunity to be heard by the stockholders on the charges made.

The corporate defendant freely admits that it has flatly refused to give the five Tomlinson directors or the plaintiff a stockholders' list. Any doubt about the matter was removed by the statement of defendant's counsel in open court at the argument that no such list would be supplied. The Vogel faction has physical control of the corporate offices and facilities. By this action the corporation through the Vogel group has deliberately refused to afford the directors in question an adequate opportunity to be heard by the stockholders on the charges made. This is contrary to the legal requirements which must be met before a director can be removed for cause.

At the oral argument the defendant's attorney offered to mail any material which might be presented by the Tomlinson faction. This falls far short of meeting the requirements of the law when directors are sought to be ousted for cause. Nor does the granting of the statutory right to inspect and copy some 26,000 names fulfill the requirement that a director sought to be removed for cause must be afforded an opportunity to present his case to the stockholders before they vote.

When Vogel as president caused the notice of meeting to be sent, he accompanied it with a letter requesting proxies granting authority to vote for the removal of the two named directors. It is true that the proxy form also provided a space for the stockholder to vote against such removal. However, only the Vogel accusations accompanied the request for a proxy. Thus, while the stockholder could vote for or against removal, he would be voting with only one view-point presented. This violates every sense of equity and fair play in a removal for cause situation.

While the directors involved or some other group could mail a letter to the stockholders and ask for a proxy which would revoke the earlier proxy, this procedure does not comport with the legal requirement that the directors in question must be afforded an opportunity to be heard before the shareholders vote. This is not an ordinary proxy contest case and a much more stringent standard must be invoked, at least at the initial stage, where it is sought to remove a director for cause. This is so for several reasons. Under our statute the directors manage the corporation and each has a somewhat independent status during his term of office. This right could be greatly impaired if substantial safeguards were not afforded a director whose removal for cause is sought. The possibility of abuse is evident. Also, as the Chancellor pointed out in the *Bruch* case, the power of removal can be a threat to cumulative voting rights. This is particularly true where, as here, the removal is by mere majority vote.

There seems to be an absence of cases detailing the appropriate procedure for submitting a question of director removal for cause for stockholder consideration. I am satisfied, however, that to the extent the matter is to be voted upon by the use of proxies, such proxies may be solicited only after the accused directors are afforded an opportunity to present their case to the stockholders. This means, in my opinion, that an opportunity must be provided such directors to present their defense to the stockholders by a statement which must accompany or precede the initial solicitation of proxies seeking authority to vote for the removal of such director for cause. If not provided then such proxies may not be voted for removal. And the corporation has a duty to see that this opportunity is given the directors at its expense. Admittedly, no such opportunity was given the two directors involved. Indeed, the corporation admittedly refused to supply them with a stockholders' list.

To require anything less than the foregoing is to deprive the stockholders of the opportunity to consider the case made by both sides before voting and would make a mockery of the requirement that a director sought to be removed for cause is entitled to an opportunity to be heard before the stockholders vote. * * *

I therefore conclude that the procedural sequence here adopted for soliciting proxies seeking authority to vote on the removal of the two directors is contrary to law. The result is that the proxy solicited by the Vogel group, which is based upon unilateral presentation of the facts by those in control of the corporate facilities, must be declared invalid insofar as they purport to give authority to vote for the removal of the directors for cause.

A preliminary injunction will issue restraining the corporation from recognizing or counting any proxies held by the Vogel group and others insofar as such proxies purport to grant authority to vote for the removal of Tomlinson and Meyer as directors of the corporation.

* * *

Plaintiff seeks a preliminary injunction restraining the defendant from using the corporate funds, employees and facilities for the solicitation of proxies for the Vogel group and from voting proxies so solicited. Plaintiff bases this request upon the contention that Vogel and his group, by calling the meeting and by using corporate funds and facilities, are usurping the authority of the board of directors. Plaintiff says that the president in effect is using his corporate authority and the corporate resources to deny the will of the board of directors and to maintain himself in office.

This brings the Court to an analysis of this most unusual aspect of this most unusual case. The by-laws provide for thirteen directors. Seven is a quorum. Due to four resignations there are now nine directors in office. Five of the nine are of the Tomlinson faction while the remaining four are of the Vogel faction. Since the Vogel faction will not attend directors' meetings, or at least will not attend directors meetings at which matters may possibly be considered which they do not desire to have considered, it follows that the Tomlinson faction is unable to muster a quorum of the board and thus is unable to take action on behalf of the board. See *Tomlinson v. Loew's Inc., supra p.* 516, 134 A.2d 518. In this setting, where a special stockholders' meeting for the election of directors is pending, it becomes necessary to determine the status of each faction in order to resolve the issues posed. And it must be kept in mind that this election can determine which faction will control the corporation.

We start with the basic proposition that the board of directors acting as a board must be recognized as the only group authorized to speak for "management" in the sense that under the statute they are responsible for the management of the corporation. *8 Del.C. § 141(a).* In substance that was the holding of the Court in *Empire Southern Gas Co. v. Gray, 29 Del. Ch. 95, 46 A.2d 741.* However, we are not here confronted with the situation in the *Gray* case because Loew's board as such cannot act for want of a quorum. Thus, there is no board policy as such with respect to the matters noticed for stockholder consideration. I am nevertheless persuaded that at least where a quorum of directors is in office the majority thereof are not "outsiders" merely because they cannot procure the attendance of a quorum at a meeting. By this I mean that they are not like the customary opposition which is seeking to take control of corporate management. To hold otherwise would be to set a most undesirable legal precedent in connection with the allocation of corporate powers.

Since the Vogel group, being in physical possession of the records and facilities of the corporation, treated the request of the directors for a stockholders' list as though it were to be judged by standards applicable to a mere stockholder's request, I think they violated the duty owed such directors as directors. I need not decide how far the rights of such directors go but I am satisfied that they are not less than the rights of the four "in" directors insofar as the right to have a stockholders' list is concerned. The fact that Vogel, as president, had the power to call a stockholders' meeting to elect directors, and is, so to speak, in physical control of the corporation, cannot obscure the fact that the possible proxy fight is between two sets of directors. Vogel, as president, has no legal standing to make "his" faction the exclusive voice of Loew's in the forthcoming election.

On balance, I believe the conclusion on this point should not result in the absolute nullification of all proxies submitted by the Vogel group. However, I believe it does require that their use be made subject to terms. I say this because they should not be permitted to benefit merely because they have physical control of the corporate facilities when they represent less than a majority of the directors in office.

I conclude that the Vogel group should be enjoined from voting any proxies unless and until the Tomlinson board members are given a reasonable period to solicit proxies after a stockholders' list is made available to them without expense by the corporation.

* * *

I next consider how these two groups should be classified for purposes of determining the rights of the Vogel group in connection with the use of corporate money and facilities for proxy solicitation at a stockholders' meeting duly called by the president. Basically, the stockholders are being asked whether they approve of a record made by one group and perhaps opposed by another. While the Tomlinson faction has five of the nine directors, it would be most misleading to have them represent to the stockholders that they are "management" in the sense that they have been responsible for the corporate policy and administration up to this stage. Resignations of directors have created the unusual situation now presented.

Viewing the situation in the light of what has just been said, it is apparent that the Vogel group is entitled to solicit proxies, not as representing a majority of the board, but as representing those who have been and are now responsible for corporate policy and administration. Whereas, the Tomlinson group, while not management in the sense that it is able on its own to take effective director action, is representative of the majority of the incumbent directors and is entitled to so represent to the stockholders if it decides to solicit proxies.

Since the stockholders will, in the event of a proxy fight, be asked to determine which group should run the corporation in the future, the Vogel faction, because it symbolizes existing policy, has sufficient status to justify the reasonable use of corporate funds to present its position to the stockholders. I am not called upon to decide whether the Tomlinson board members would also be entitled to have the corporation pay its reasonable charges for proxy solicitation.

* * *

I next consider whether the Vogel faction is entitled to use corporate facilities and employees in connection with its solicitation. Because such action would carry the intra-corporate strife even deeper within the corporation and because there is no practical way, if there is a proxy contest, to assure equal treatment for both factions in this area when only one is in physical control of such facilities and personnel, I conclude that the defendant should be preliminarily enjoined from using corporate facilities and personnel in soliciting proxies. I emphasize that this conclusion is based upon the corporate status of the two factions herein involved.

Plaintiff next claims that the Vogel group should be enjoined from voting any proxies obtained as a result of the material sent out by Vogel. He argues that Vogel's letter to the stockholders, the proxy statement and the form of proxy deceived and misled the stockholders into believing that the matters noticed for consideration by the stockholders were proposed by the company or its management, whereas the Vogel group is not authorized to speak as "management".

I should say preliminarily that I believe the proxy statement would have been more accurately informative had it contained a concise statement showing the factual situation which created the present status of the two groups. * * *

I turn now to the various factors which, according to plaintiff, show that the Vogel faction represented, contrary to fact, that it was soliciting proxies as management.

1. The letter of Mr. Vogel to the shareholders is reproduced on the letterhead of Loew's, Incorporated and comes from the "Office of the President".

I have already pointed out that this is not the case of a working majority of the board versus the president. Indeed, in this case Vogel's administration as president symbolizes one choice in the policy dispute. This dispute is evident from a reading of the material in its entirety. I therefore conclude that by sending the letter on Loew's stationery from the office of the president, Vogel, was not misleading the stockholders.

2.   The notice of the special meeting is reproduced on the letterhead of Loew's, Incorporated, signed, by order of the president, by Irving H. Greenfield, Secretary.

The fact is that there was no misrepresentation when the notice of the special meeting was reproduced on Loew's letterhead and signed by the order of the president. I say this because the president was authorized as president to call such a meeting.

3.   I assume that plaintiff had now abandoned this point which deals with the power to close the transfer books.

4.   The proxy statement recites that "it is considered to be in the best interest of Loew's and the stockholders to remove * * * [Mr. Meyer and Mr. Thomlinson] as a director".

This is nothing more than a statement of belief of Vogel and his group. I cannot see how it is misleading.

5.   The proxy material states that Loew's will bear all costs in connection with the solicitation of proxies; that Loew's will reimburse the brokerage houses for expenses incident to the solicitation of proxies; that Loew's has entered into contracts with certain firms to solicit proxies and has agreed to pay them a fee for their services, and that the costs to be paid by Loew's for proxy solicitation will be approximately $100,000.

Plaintiff is here saying in effect that Vogel's group was representing to the stockholders that the corporation would pay for the expenses of proxy solicitation for the Vogel group and thus leading the reader to believe that it was a management solicitation. First of all, such was the intention of the Vogel group and thus it did not constitute a misrepresentation as to their intention. But, in any event, I have now held that reasonable expenses of such solicitation are properly chargeable to the corporation and so no factual misrepresentation was involved. In any event, since the Vogel group was synonymous with management in the policy sense, I cannot see how a stockholder would be misled.

6.   The proxy material states that the officers and employees of Loew's will solicit and request the return of proxies.

This is not a misrepresentation in the sense that it was contrary to the intention of the Vogel group. The Court has now determined that the officers and employees in such capacity, cannot solicit proxies. This does not mean that the representation is so material that it can be said to influence stockholders to the extent that the proxies should be voided.

7.   The proxy statement is signed by Joseph R. Vogel, as president.

There is no merit to this contention. Vogel as president was certainly authorized to sign the statement in view of the fact that he had the authority to call the meeting.

8.   The business reply envelope included with the proxy has on it that postage will be paid by the secretary of Loew's Inc., and is addressed to him in his official capacity. The permit on the envelope is Loew's permit.

The foregoing facts are true but I do not believe that they are so misleading as to void the proxies. After all, the Vogel group is soliciting proxies on the basis of its record in administering the corporation.

Plaintiff contends that in any event the cumulative effect of the various statements mentioned is to lead the ordinary reader to believe that the solicitation is by management.

Plaintiff recognizes that the proxy statement and the form of proxy both recite that "this proxy is solicited by the President and George L. Killion [of the Vogel group] who are members of the executive committee of Loew's, Inc., and in view of the circumstances, not by the management". However, he argues that the import of this statement is lost in the overall impact of the material. Since the meeting was validly called by the president, there was nothing misleading in the creation of the impression that the meeting and material were initiated by the company. I think the whole impact of the proxy material conveyed to the average reader the impression that there is a bitter fight between the president and his faction and another faction on the board.

While I have no doubt that it would have been better for the material to have contained a more explicit factual narrative of the status of the board personnel at the time of the proxy solicitation, I cannot believe that the overall result is so misleading as to justify this Court in concluding that the proxies may not be used for any purpose. * * * This is particularly so in view of the statement made that it was not solicited by management. Indeed, I think the statement * * * may have been somewhat misleading in the sense that it may have suggested to the reader that the Vogel group was not responsible for the corporate policy up to that date. To this extent, it was more prejudicial to the Vogel group than the Tomlinson group, if a stockholder desired to vote for "management" in the policy sense.

* * * This disposes of the issues raised in connection with the stockholders' meeting.

Plaintiff next seeks a mandatory injunction to compel the individual defendants (four Vogel directors) to attend directors' meetings. He argues that Vogel and his associates acted unlawfully in attempting to cause the absence of a quorum at meetings of the board of directors for the purpose of preventing the board from exercising its powers.

While a concerted plan to abstain from attending directors' meetings may be improper under some circumstances, I cannot find that the fact that the so-called Vogel directors did not attend directors' meetings called to take action which would give an opposing faction an absolute majority of the board—solely because of director resignations—is such a breach of their fiduciary duty that they should be judicially compelled to attend board meetings. This is particularly so where stockholder action is in the offing to fill the board.

* * *

I should add that the prolix factual presentation was put before the Court in such a fashion that it has been at times difficult for the Court to determine whether or not the facts relied upon here are all of record. If I have taken liberties with the record I will expect counsel to promptly so inform me in detail.

* * *

1. No preliminary injunction will issue to enjoin the holding of the meeting, now fixed for October 15, 1957.

2. The corporation will be preliminarily enjoined from recognizing and counting any proxies held by the individual defendants unless the corporation supplies the Tomlinson board members the stockholders' list as herein provided.

3. Without regard to the action taken by the defendant under Point 2, the corporation will be preliminarily enjoined from recognizing or counting any proxies held by the Vogel group or others to the extent that such proxies purport to grant authority to vote for the removal of Tomlinson and Meyer as directors.

4. No preliminary injunction will issue to restrain the corporation from paying reasonable sums incurred by the Vogel group in soliciting proxies.

5. A preliminary injunction will issue restraining the corporation from permitting the use of its personnel and facilities for the solicitation of proxies by the Vogel group.

6. No mandatory preliminary injunction will issue to compel the individual defendants to attend directors' meetings.

* * *

NOTES AND QUESTIONS

1. *Campbell v. Loew's* was part of the fall-out of a titanic struggle for control of Loews, Inc. the owner of MGM, the once-peerless great American movie studio. In particular, it involved an attempt by the recently-resigned movie mogul, Louis B. Mayer, to take back the company he had originally built. The story is wonderfully (if not particularly objectively) told in the autobiography of Louis B. Nizer, My Life in Court 427–524 (1961). Nizer was the lawyer hired by Joseph Vogel, Loew's President, and his book does a

splendid job of illuminating the legal issues and explaining how a brilliant corporate counsel can also work as a corporate strategist. Our use of the case is a bit more prosaic, however, and our principal concerns are with the respective roles of shareholders, directors, and officers, and, in particular, how they share and exercise power in the corporation. We are also concerned with the role of formalities and bylaws in the operation of the corporation.

2. On the point of the corporate bylaws, consider an earlier stage in the litigation, cited by the court, Tomlinson v. Loew's Inc., 134 A.2d 518 (Del.Ch.1957). As the court in *Campbell v. Loew's* notes, there was a struggle among Board factions, which emerged after the creation of a thirteen-member Board of Directors, six of whom were chosen by the "Tomlinson faction," six of whom were chosen by the "Vogel faction," and one of whom was a "neutral," acceptable to both sides. Following ceaseless bickering between the factions over the competence of Vogel as President, and whether he ought to be replaced by Louis B. Mayer, two of the Vogel-friendly directors, and the neutral director, Reid, resigned. Shortly thereafter one of the Tomlinson-friendly directors also resigned. This left four vacancies on the Board of Directors. The Vogel faction (then at 4 directors) wanted to call a special shareholders' meeting to fill the vacancies, but the Tomlinson faction (then at 5 directors), since it held a one-vote majority, wanted to fill the vacancies by a vote of the remaining Board members, not the shareholders. Accordingly it scheduled a Board meeting to fill the vacancies. As you might be able to infer from your reading of the case, the Vogel faction decided not to attend that Board meeting, which meant that the Tomlinson faction was deprived of a quorum, which the bylaws provided was to be 7 directors. Nevertheless the 5 Tomlinson directors met, and, taking advantage of a Delaware statute, 8 Del. C. § 223, which stated in pertinent part that "Unless otherwise provided in the certificate of incorporation or bylaws, when 1 or more directors shall resign from the board, effective at a future date, a majority of the directors then in office.... shall have power to fill such vacancy or vacancies ..." they filled two of the vacancies, giving themselves a quorum to act on other matters. The Vogel faction challenged this action.

The question for the Delaware court to decide then became whether Loew's bylaws "otherwise provided" that what the Tomlinson faction had done was impermissible. In the relevant portions of the bylaws, one stated that "seven (7) of the directors shall constitute a quorum for the transaction of business, and the act of a majority of directors present at a meeting in the presence of a quorum, shall constitute the act of the Board of Directors ..." while another enumerated "some 14 specified powers granted 'the directors' and number (14) grants power to the directors 'to fill vacancies in the Board of Directors.'" (Quoting from the court's opinion in Tomlinson v. Loews, 134 A.2d, at 522). Would that mean that only a quorum of the Board of Directors could fill vacancies? There was one more bylaw dealing with the problem. That bylaw provided, in pertinent part, that "A vacancy in the Board of Directors may be filled by the stockholders or by the directors in office (although less than a quorum)." Should the presence of that bylaw mean that what the Tomlinson faction did (filling the vacancies through a vote of only the five of them) was permissible? The Delaware Chancellor concluded that this last bylaw referred to was not applicable (do you understand why?) and he nulli-fied the election of the two new directors, leaving the matter for Loew's share-holders to decide. Who can do a better job filling vacancies on the Board, the shareholders or the remaining directors? Was it legitimate for the 4 directors from the Vogel faction to refuse to attend Board meetings? One of the reasons the Vogel faction wanted to deprive the Tomlinson faction of a quorum was to prevent it from firing Vogel. The Board has the power to hire and fire officers, and what the Vogel faction did deprived the Board of this power, and every other power of the Board. Was this appropriate? What does Chancellor Seitz say on this issue? Do you agree?

3.   With this background, let's further consider the actual issues raised in the *Campbell v. Loew's* case. We should note, at the outset, the key statu-tory provision Delaware § 141, which provides that "The business of every corporation organized under the provisions of this chapter shall be managed by a board of directors, except as hereinafter or in its certificate of incorpora-tion otherwise provided." How, exactly, should Directors charged with the management of the corporation carry out their task? Tomlinson, one of the directors, as you may have discerned, believed that it was his job to ferret out information as to how the corporation was being run, and, in his efforts to gather data (which he hoped would demonstrate the incompetence of Vogel and that he ought to be replaced by Mayer) he brought the operations of the corporation to a virtual standstill. Was this an abuse of his powers as direc-tor? Chancellor Seitz suggested that there is nothing wrong with a Director seeking to take over control, or being unwilling to cooperate with other direc-tors on the Board. Do you agree? What should be the role of corporate offic-ers, as distinguished from those of Directors? Is it wise for corporate officers to be members of the Board of Directors? This last is a sorely-contended mod-ern point of dispute among corporate scholars, by the way.

4.   Note that considering the possibility of abuses by directors such as those suggested in the last question, Chancellor Seitz decides, without benefit of relevant statute, that "the Court is free to conclude on reason that the stockholders have … [an] inherent power" to remove directors for cause. What does he mean by "on reason?" Do you agree with his conclusion?

5.   We have earlier alluded to the fact that Delaware law does not require cumulative voting, and that some critics of Delaware's corporate law believe that this provides insufficient protection to shareholders. Delaware law does permit a corporation to institute cumulative voting if it so desires, however, and Loew's, Inc., at the time of this case, did provide for cumulative voting in its Articles of Incorporation. Note that this presents a difficulty for Chancellor Seitz, because he sees some inconsistency between the provision of cumulative voting and permitting shareholders, by majority vote, to remove a director elected through cumulative voting. Do you understand why this is a problem? Cumulative voting is not a particularly easy procedure to grasp, but, for our purposes, it can be considered to be a form of proportional representa-tion, more easily permitting minorities among the shareholders to be repre-sented on the Board. Without wishing to get too bogged down in numbers (law students, unlike management students, tend to be frightened by matters of calculation), where there is no cumulative voting (the default position in Dela-

ware), sometimes referred to as a "straight voting" regime, each share of stock may cast one vote for each open position on the Board of Directors. So that if one owns 100 shares, for example, and there are nine open slots on the Board, one may cast 100 votes for one's favored candidate for each of the nine slots. A little reflection should allow even law students to understand how in a "straight voting" regime, if one owns a majority of the shares, one can dictate the entire composition of the Board of Directors.

Where there is cumulative voting, however, a shareholder with 100 shares is not restricted to casting only 100 votes for each Board vacancy, but can multiply his or her number of shares by seats up for election on the Board of Directors, and "cumulate" or aggregate votes for any one or more seats on the Board. So that, if there are nine seats on the board up for election, our holder of 100 shares will have 900 votes to cast in any manner he or she sees fit. 900 may be cast for one seat on the board, 450 may be cast for each of two seats, 300 may be cast for each of three seats, or 100 may be cast for each of nine seats, and so on. While this point is a little tougher to grasp, you may be able to understand how this allows a shareholder with less than a majority of shares to obtain representation on the Board. If your brain has not yet seized up, you may realize that there are mathematical formulae that will yield how many shares must be owned in order to fill any particular number of seats on the Board.

One formula for determining the minimum number of shares needed to elect a particular number of directors, where X is the minimum number of shares needed, S is the total number of shares that will be voted at a shareholders' meeting, N is the number of directors one desires to elect, and D is the total number of directors to be elected is:

$$X = (S \times N)/(D + 1) + 1$$

So that, for example, if there are 900 total shares that will be voted, one desires to elect only 1 director, and there are 9 directors up for election, the number of shares that one will need is $(900 \times 1)/(9 + 1) + 1$ or $900/10 + 1$ or 91 shares. Can you understand Seitz's concern better? Do you favor cumulative voting or not? After the controversy that resulted in *Campbell v. Loew's*, Loew's shareholders voted to amend Loew's charter to eliminate cumulative voting. Can you understand why? If this is a subject you'd like to pursue further see Randall S. Thomas & Catherine T. Dixon's Aranow & Einhorn, Proxy Contests for Corporate Control 10.04[B] (3d ed. 1998), quoted from and discussed in Melvin Aron Eisenberg, Corporations and Other Business Organizations 159–162 (8th concise ed. 2000).

6. There are several other interesting procedural and substantive issues raised in *Campbell v. Loew's*. The first is a problem lawyers call "standing," the legal requirement that someone attempting to bring a lawsuit have a sufficient interest in the outcome of the case for the court to be certain that it will have all the facts brought before it, and that it will be dealing with a real legal problem. Here the "standing" question was whether a shareholder has standing to bring a lawsuit complaining about procedural irregularities in an attempt to remove a director for cause, specifically that the director had not received adequate notice of charges and an adequate opportunity to be heard in his defense. This would seem, at first blush anyway, to be a cause of action

that belongs to the Director, not the shareholder. Why does Chancellor Seitz rule that the shareholder-plaintiff has standing? What exactly is the nature of the relationship between Directors and Shareholders? Are Directors the agents of shareholders? It is clear that Directors have a fiduciary responsibility to the shareholders, or at least to the corporation, but it does appear that the weight of authority on this issue, as indicated earlier, is that the Directors are agents of the corporation and not exactly agents of the shareholders. In a leading case on the subject the New York Court of Appeals stated that the directors "hold such office charged with the duty to act for the corporation according to their best judgment, and in so doing they cannot be controlled [by the shareholders] in the reasonable exercise and performance of such duty.... The relation of the directors to the stockholders is essentially that of trustee and *cestui que trust* ['the beneficiary for whom the trustee acts'] ... The corporation is the owner of the property, but the directors in the performance of their duty possess it, and act in every way as if they owned it." People ex rel. Manice v. Powell, 201 N.Y. 194, 200–01, 94 N.E. 634, 637 (1911). Would you want to be a corporate director?

7. Much of *Campbell v. Loew's* is concerned with the proxy vote. We will explore this in a bit more detail later, when we consider the federal regulation of proxy voting, but for now we can observe that large publicly-held corporations, that is those whose shares are dispersed among hundreds, thousands, or even millions of stockholders, can only have their shareholders vote by deputizing corporate officials to vote for them. Conducting such voting, or asking for the votes of shareholders, is called *soliciting proxies*, and at issue in *Campbell v. Loew's* is whether proxies to remove Tomlinson as a director were properly solicited. What does the Court decide on this issue? Note that the court observes that there is a difference between corporate proceedings and judicial proceedings, but precisely how much of a difference is there? In any event, you will have observed that Chancellor Seitz does say that whatever the difference, there is still a need to make sure that proxy battles are conducted pursuant to notions of equity and fair play. Did the Vogel faction so conduct itself? You will have noticed that Seitz states that the Vogel faction refused to supply a shareholder list to the Tomlinson faction, that it initially refused to mail out a statement from Tomlinson, and that the Vogel faction sought to use corporate funds and corporate personnel to wage a proxy battle against the Tomlinson faction. Was this appropriate?

You will have observed that, in the end, Seitz did rule that it was appropriate for the Vogel faction to make use of the corporation's funds. Was this decision correct? Is it appropriate for a corporate officer to use the funds of the corporation to solicit proxies to remove one of the directors when that director is seeking to fire that officer? The issue wasn't before Judge Seitz, but should the Tomlinson faction have been permitted to use the corporation's funds to solicit proxies against the removal of Tomlinson as director? Officers are hired and fired by the Board. Does that mean that officers owe a fiduciary duty to the Board or to the corporation? If the duty is to the corporation, is such a duty different from a duty owed to the shareholders? If you were a shareholder of Loew's, would you have been happy with the decision in this case? It appears to be a strong rule of Delaware law that a Board which seeks to prevent a shareholder vote bears a heavy burden of demonstrating a compelling justification for such action, and that it is rare that the Delaware courts will sustain such Board action. While the Board (with the aid of the officers it appoints) is supposed to manage the corporation, the Board may not deliberately frustrate the exercise of the shareholders' right ultimately to control. Was the Vogel faction or the Tomlinson faction seeking to do that? For important Delaware cases addressing this frustration of shareholder control issue, see Schnell v. Chris–Craft Industries, Inc., 285 A.2d 437 (Del. 1971), Blasius Industries, Inc. v. Atlas Corp., 564 A.2d 651 (Del.Ch. 1988), and Stroud v. Grace, 606 A.2d 75 (Del. 1992).

We have now learned a little bit about the interaction among officers, directors, and shareholders, and we have sought to begin to understand who is recognized as ultimately in control of the corporation. We next turn to some instances of the manner that such control can be abused, and the consequences to the abuser.

CHAPTER 4

PIERCING THE CORPORATE VEIL

■ ■ ■

A. STATE LAW

MINNIE B. BERKEY v. THIRD AVENUE RAILWAY COMPANY
Court of Appeals of New York.
244 N.Y. 84, 155 N.E. 58, 50 A.L.R. 599 (1926).

[Opinion by CARDOZO, J.] The plaintiff boarded a street car at Fort Lee Ferry and One Hundred and Twenty-fifth street on October 4, 1916, in order to go east on One Hundred and Twenty-fifth street to Broadway, and thence south on Broadway to Columbia University at One Hundred and Seventeenth street. She was hurt in getting out of the car through the negligence of the motorman in charge of it. The franchise to operate a street railroad along the route traveled by the plaintiff belongs to the Forty-second Street, Manhattanville and Saint Nicholas Avenue Railway Company (described for convenience as the Forty-second Street Company) and no one else. Substantially all the stock of that company is owned by the Third Avenue Railway Company, the defendant, which has its own franchise along other streets and avenues. Stock ownership alone would be insufficient to charge the dominant company with liability for the torts of the subsidiary * * *. The theory of the action is that under the screen of this subsidiary and others, the defendant does in truth operate for itself the entire system of connected roads, and is thus liable for the torts of the consolidated enterprise * * *.

We are unable to satisfy ourselves that such dominion was exerted. The Forty-second Street Company deposits in its own bank account the fares collected on its route. It pays out of that account and no other the wages of the motormen and conductors engaged in the operation of its cars. It was not organized by the defendant as a decoy or a blind. It was not organized, so far as the record shows, by the defendant at all. There is no evidence that at the time of its formation the defendant had any interest in it as shareholder or otherwise. Its franchise goes back to the year 1884, and through all the intervening years it has preserved its corporate organization with property adequate to the maintenance of life. Its balance sheet for the year ending July, 1917, shows assets of $12,456,847.86. The values there stated are much in excess of the debts and liabilities, including in the reckoning of liabilities the outstanding capital stock. In no possible view * * * are they unsubstantial or nominal. True the subsidiary lost money that year, but so also did its parent. The fact remains that it was functioning as a corporation continuously and actively. It was so functioning at the trial in 1924. There is no evidence or suggestion that it has ceased to function since.

The question is whether other circumstances yet to be noted neutralize these indicia of separate life and operation. The defendant, as we have seen, was the owner in 1916 of substantially all the stock of the subsidiary corporation. Its president in reporting to the stockholders the financial situation at the end of the fiscal year informed them that to make the picture accurate, the statement must exhibit the consolidated income, and this was obviously true. Other ties must be shown in addition to the one resulting from ownership of shares. The members of the two boards of directors were nearly, though not quite the same. Each road had the same executive officers, *i.e.*, the same president, treasurer, general manager, paymaster and counsel. The parent has made loans to the subsidiary from time to time, sometimes for construction, sometimes for operating expenses. The loan for construction expenses ($6,415,152.92) is represented by a demand note. * * * The parent is also the holder of the second mortgage bonds, $1,487,000, the first mortgage bonds, however ($1,200,000), being issued to the public. The operating loans are temporary advances for electric power, for materials or supplies and for the salaries of executive officers. As a matter of convenience these are made in the first instance out of the treasury of the parent company. They are then charged to the account of the subsidiary, and repaid generally the following month, and not later than the following year. Repayment is inconsistent with an understanding that the parent in making the advances was operating on its own account the cars of a connecting line. The charges are more than book entries, mere devices of an accountant. Drafts are drawn upon the subsidiary and paid with its own money. The unpaid advances for operation in July, 1917, were only $253,029.37, and this at the end of a poor year. We are not to confuse the salaries of the executive officers with the wages of motormen and conductors. The latter, as already pointed out, were paid in the first instance as well as ultimately by the subsidiary itself. So were many other expenses for maintenance and repair. So were the many judgments for personal injuries recovered in the past.

One other circumstance or group of circumstances is the subject of much emphasis in the arguments of counsel. The defendant was the dominant stockholder, not only in this subsidiary, but also in many others. The routes when connected cover an area from the lower part of Manhattan at the south to Yonkers and other points in Westchester at the north. All the cars, wherever used, are marked "Third Avenue System." On the other hand, the transfer slips bear the name in each instance of the company that issues them. The cars, when new ones become necessary, are bought by the defendant, and then leased to the subsidiaries, including, of course, the Forty-second Street Company, for a daily rental which is paid. The cars leased to one road do not continue along the routes [of] others. The motormen and conductors do not travel beyond their respective lines. With the approval of the Public Service Commission, transfer slips are issued between one route and another, but transfers could have been required by the Commission if not voluntarily allowed * * *.

Upon these facts we are to say whether the parent corporation, the owner of a franchise to operate a street railroad on Third avenue and the Bowery and a few connected streets, has in truth operated another railroad on Broadway and Forty-second street, and this in violation of the statutes of the State. The plaintiff's theory of the action requires us to assume the existence of a contract between the defendant on the one side and the Forty-second Street Company on the other. The several circumstances relied upon—community of interest and in a sense community of management—are important only in so far as they are evidence from which the existence of a contract may fairly be inferred. The contract in the plaintiff's view was one between the two corporations by which the defendant was to use and operate the other's franchise as its own. If such a contract was made, it was not only *ultra vires*, but illegal, because prohibited by statute. By Public Service Commissions Law (§ 54), "no franchise nor any right to or under any franchise, to own or operate a railroad or street railroad shall be assigned, transferred or leased, nor shall any contract or agreement with reference to or affecting any such franchise or right be valid or of any force or effect whatsoever, unless the assignment, transfer, lease, contract or agreement shall have been approved by the proper commission." By section 56 any violation of the provisions of the statute exposes the offending corporation to continuing fines of large amounts, and its officers and agents to prosecution and punishment as guilty of a misdemeanor. If a written contract had been made for the operation by the defendant of the subsidiary's line no one would doubt that such contract would fall within the condemnation of section 54 of the act. The contract is not the less illegal because made by word of mouth.

We cannot bring ourselves to believe that an agreement, criminal in conception and effect, may be inferred from conduct or circumstances so indefinite and equivocal. Community of interest there must obviously be between a subsidiary corporation and a parent corporation, the owner of its stock. This community of interest would prompt the parent, not unnaturally, to make advances for operating expenses to the subsidiary when convenience would be thus promoted. The advances so made have for the most part been repaid, and in so far as they remain unpaid have been carried as a debt. During all this time the cars have been manned by the subsidiary's servants, who are paid for their work out of the subsidiary's fares. We do not stop to inquire whether the inference of unified operation would be legitimate in a case where a contract for such an extension of the area of activity would be permitted by the law. We feel assured that no such inference is to be drawn from acts so uncertain in their suggestions where the inference is also one of the commission of a crime.

The law prohibits a contract for operation by the parent of a franchise other than its own without the consent of the appropriate commission. It does not prohibit stock ownership, or at least did not, so far as the record shows, when the defendant bought the shares. We are now asked to draw from conduct appropriate to the ownership of stock, and fairly explicable thereby, the inference of a contract prohibited by law. We do not obviate the difficulty when we say that the stockholders by acquiescence have ratified any departure from the restrictions of the charter. They could do this so as to wipe out the transgression of their officers if the act constituting the transgression were *ultra vires* only. They could not do so where the act was one prohibited by law * * *. The statute is aimed at more than the protection of the stockholders. It protects the creditors also, and beyond the creditors the public. Creditors are to be guarded against an increase of liabilities and an impairment of assets by an extension of corporate activities not approved by the Public Service Commission, the representative of the State. The public is to be guarded against like consequences, for the public which rides upon the cars has an interest, not to be ignored, in cheap, continuous and efficient operation. These benefits cannot be enjoyed if a road has been plunged into insolvency by improvident extensions. "The business of a railroad [*i.e.*, a street railroad] is to run its own lines. The law does not permit it at its pleasure to run the lines of others" (*Doran v. N. Y. City Int. Ry. Co., 239 N. Y. 448*).

We do not mean that a corporation which has sent its cars with its own men over the route of another corporation may take advantage of the fact that its conduct in so doing is illegal to escape liability for the misconduct of its servant * * *. There is no room for varying constructions when operation results from acts so direct and unequivocal. A defendant in such circumstances is liable for the tort, however illegitimate the business, just as much as it would be if its board of directors were to order a motorman to run a traveler down. We do mean, however, that an intention to operate a route in violation of a penal statute is not to be inferred from acts which reasonably interpreted are as compatible with innocence as with guilt * * *. Such, it seems to us, whether viewed distributively or together, are the acts relied on here to establish an agreement between two corporations that the business of one shall be the business of the other. Many arrangements for economy of expense and for convenience of administration may be made between carriers without subjecting them to liability as partners or as coadventurers "either *inter sese* or as to third persons" (*Ins. Co. v. Railroad Co., 104 U.S. 146, 158*). For like reasons such arrangements may be made without establishing a relation of principal and agent. Where the coadventure or the agency, if created, carries consequences along with it that are offensive to public policy, the law will not readily imply the relation it condemns. The basis for the implication must be either intention or estoppel. We perceive no evidence sufficient to support a finding of estoppel. Intention is presumed, unless the inference of innocence is belied with reasonable certainty, to be conformable to law.

* * *

* * * [I]n *Davis v. Alexander [269 U.S. 114]* the case was submitted to the jury upon the theory that the proceeds of operation over the two routes were commingled in a single fund. Not only that, but engines and cars were used indiscriminately, and so also were the crews. The jury were told that all these facts must be found to coexist before the wrong of the subsidiary could be charged against the parent. The Supreme Court in its opinion does not catalogue the circumstances supporting the inference of unity of control. The opinion is confined to the statement that "the shippers introduced substantial evidence in support of their allegations." The facts are disclosed when we examine the record on appeal. So in *Wichita Falls Ry. Co. v. Puckett [53 Okla. 463]* the same employees worked on the entire route, and a common treasury received the proceeds of the system. Between such cases and the one before us there exists a distinction plain upon the surface. * * * Liability of the parent has never been adjudged when the subsidiary has maintained so consistently and in so many ways as here the separate organization that is the mark of a separate existence, and when the implication of a contract for unity of operation would be the implication of a contract for the commission of a crime.

The whole problem of the relation between parent and subsidiary corporations is one that is still enveloped in the mists of metaphor. Metaphors in law are to be narrowly watched, for starting as devices to liberate thought, they end often by enslaving it. We say at times that the corporate entity will be ignored when the parent corporation operates a business through a subsidiary which is characterized as an "alias" or a "dummy." All this is well enough if the picturesqueness of the epithets does not lead us to forget that the essential term to be defined is the act of operation. Dominion may be so complete, interference so obtrusive, that by the general rules of agency the parent will be a principal and the subsidiary an agent. Where control is less than this, we are remitted to the tests of honesty and justice (Ballantine, Parent & Subsidiary Corporations, *14 Calif. Law Review, 12, 18, 19, 20).* The logical consistency of a juridical conception will indeed be sacrificed at times when the sacrifice is essential to the end that some accepted public policy may be defended or upheld. This is so, for illustration, though agency in any proper sense is lacking, where the attempted separation between parent and subsidiary will work a fraud upon the law *(Chicago, etc., Ry. Co. v. Minn. Civic Assn., 247 U.S. 490; United States v. Reading Company, 253 U.S. 26, 61, 63).* At such times unity is ascribed to parts which, at least for many purposes, retain an independent life, for the reason that only thus can we overcome a perversion of the privilege to do business in a corporate form. We find in the case at hand neither agency on the one hand, nor on the other abuse to be corrected by the implication of a merger. On the contrary, merger might beget more abuses than it stifled. Statutes carefully framed for the protection, not merely of creditors, but of all who travel upon railroads, forbid the confusion of liabilities by extending operation over one route to operation on another. In such circumstances, we thwart the public policy of the State instead of defending or upholding it, when we ignore the separation between subsidiary and parent, and treat the two as one.

* * *

CRANE, J. (dissenting). The United States Supreme Court in *Davis v. Alexander (269 U.S. 114)* said: "Where one railroad company actually controls another and operates both as a single system, the dominant company will be liable for injuries due to the negligence of the subsidiary company." This court decided in *Stone v. Cleveland, C., C. & St. L. Ry. Co. (202 N.Y. 352)* "that the ownership of a majority of the stock of a corporation, while it gives a certain control of the corporation, does not give that control of corporate transactions which makes the holder of the stock responsible for the latter."

These two decisions are not inconsistent. Each depends upon the particular facts and the nature and extent of the control by the dominant company of the subsidiary. It is largely a question of degree. This was recognized in the opinion in the *Stone* case when referring to the Federal authorities. We there said (p. 361) that the facts in those cases were stronger for the plaintiff than in the *Stone* action.

* * *

The plaintiff was injured on the evening of October 4, 1916, by stepping into an unlighted excavation in the street, while alighting from a car at the corner of Broadway and One Hundred and Seventeenth street. The proof of negligence for this appeal is unquestioned and need not be further mentioned, so that we may turn our attention at once to the corporation responsible.

The Forty-second Street Railway Company is a street railroad corporation having a franchise to operate passenger cars through Broadway at the point in question. Its authorized capital stock is $2,500,000, of which $2,494,900 is outstanding, and of this the Third Avenue Railway Company owns $2,471,300. The Third Avenue Railway Company is also a duly authorized and chartered railroad, operating surface lines in the city of New York connecting with and transferring to the cars running on the Forty-second Street line. Its system, which includes the Third Avenue and Amsterdam line, the One Hundred and Twenty-fifth Street Crosstown line, Broadway-Kingsbridge line as well as the branches of the Forty-second Street Railway, was termed and called "The Third Avenue Railway System." The car from which the plaintiff fell had on it the words, "Third Avenue Railway System."

The report of the president to the stockholders for the year ending June 30, 1917, stated:

"The Third Avenue Railway System is composed of the Third Avenue Railway Company and the following subsidiary companies."

The Forty-second Street Railway Company was one of these named subsidiary companies.

"The Third Avenue Railway Company," says the report, "controls all the above companies through ownership of stock and to arrive at the result of the operations it is necessary to consolidate the income accounts and the balance sheets of all the corporations and eliminate the inter-company transactions so that all duplications may be avoided. This explanation is made in order that there may be no misunderstanding in considering the statements appearing in this report."

The outstanding second mortgage bonds, amounting to $1,487,000, were entirely owned by the Third Avenue Railway Company. This second mortgage was past due. $6,415,152.98 was due for construction. It was represented by a note of the Forty-second Street Railway Company given years ago to the Third Avenue Railway Company. It is a demand note.

The officers for both companies were the same. Edward A. Maher, Jr., was the assistant manager of the Third Avenue Railway Company and of the Forty-second Street Railway Company. His father, Edward A. Maher, was the general manager of both. Each railway company had the same president, treasurer, secretary and the same board of directors with some slight variation. "They were practically all the same directors." The following question was asked of Edward A. Maher, Jr.: "Q. Take the Third Avenue Railroad Company and the Forty-second Street and Manhattan-ville Railroad Company, were they identical? A. They were."

The general auditor, Walter Farrington, was asked:

"Q. I notice on page 6 of this report this statement: The Employees Association—the statement is as follows: 'The Association on June 30th, 1917, had a membership of 3,412, and had to its credit on that date New York City bonds valued at $79,833.30, and cash on deposit amounting to $13,285.51, the total of $93,116.81.' These employees were employees of the entire system? A. Yes.

"Q. The next item to which I would call your attention is on page 6: 'It is most gratifying to contrast the attitude of some of the employees of the company with the strikes, was the response of the men to the company's invitation to subscribe to the Liberty Loan of 1917 within two weeks of the announcement of the company's partial payment plan of 3,265 subscriptions which have been received from 73%, and investment of bonds to the value of $200,000.' That refers to the employees of the subsidiary companies as well as of the others; as well as of the Third Avenue? A. May I see what you are reading from?

"Q. Yes. 'Subscription to Liberty Loan Bonds.' A. It does.

"Q. They are all treated as employees of the Third Avenue, with reference to that loan? A. Employees of all the companies."

The company referred to, of which these men were the employees, was the Third Avenue Railway Company. In its report the company did not discriminate.

Again, the Third Avenue Railway Company had a printing plant, referred to as follows:

"Q. I find on page 9 of this report this expression: 'The economical effect to the operation of its own printing plant has continued during the past year. All of the company's printing has been done in its own plant.' That refers to the printing plant which was used for printing matter of not only the Third Avenue Railway Company, but of the subsidiary Companies? A. It does, yes."

As to pensions for employees, the report of the president said: "Under this plan, any employees who have reached the age of seventy years after at least twenty years service with the company, or who have reached the age of sixty-five and have been incapacitated are eligible for pensions," etc. That the company referred to was the Third Avenue Railway Company appears from this testimony:

"Q. You had a system of pensions for the employees, didn't you? A. Yes.

"Q. That was entirely under the control of the Third Avenue Railway Company, wasn't it? A. Yes.

"Q. Which handled that entirely; is that right? A. Yes."

The executive officers, above referred to, were paid by the checks of the Third Avenue Railway Company; the general manager of the entire system had charge of the superintendents of operation, who in turn had control of the conductors and motormen, all of whom reported to a central school for instruction; repairs and construction were operated from a single department; the cars of both the Third Avenue Railway Company and the Forty-second Street Railway Company were marked "Third Avenue Railway System;" the Third Avenue Railway Company contracted and paid for the electricity to be used in the system; there was one common purchasing agent, and it is conceded that the Third Avenue Railway Company in the first instance paid the bills for all general and miscellaneous expenses, including salaries of claim agents and expenses for services and for material purchased. The Third Avenue Company owned all the cars which were operated over the lines of the system. One paymaster for the entire system, with assistants, paid the motormen and conductors of the Forty-second Street Railway Company with cash obtained at the bank by checks drawn by Mr. Sage, who was the treasurer of the Third Avenue Railway Company and the Forty-second Street Railway Company. The testimony of this point is as follows:

"Q. How many paymasters were there for the whole system? A. I think there was one so-called paymaster, possibly two assistants.

"Q. And they were employees of the Third Avenue Railway Company? A. They were paid out of the Third Avenue Railway Company's general fund.

"Q. Was there any such department in the Forty-second Street and Manhattan Railway Company pay department? A. No. * * * They were employees just as much of the 42nd Street company as they were of the Third Avenue. * * *

"Q. Who pays that paymaster and his subordinates? A. The paymaster was paid out of the Third Avenue Company's fund."

The legal department for the adjustment and settlement of claims and the claims themselves were paid by the Third Avenue Railway Company. So, too, the accounting department was for the entire system paid by the Third Avenue Railway Company. Walter Farrington, the general auditor, testified as to the advertising:

"Q. Do you know where the money for that advertising came from, from the various advertisements? A. Yes.

"Q. Who was it paid to? A. It was paid to the Third Avenue Railway."

Ely M. T. Ryder, engineer of the Forty-second Street Railway Company, swore that the annual report of that company states that the road was held in joint title by the Third Avenue Railway Company and the Forty-second Street Railway Company.

"Q. What does that mean, joint title? A. That is the title to the ownership of the road, which has nothing to do with maintenance.

"Q. Then the ownership of the road is jointly in the two companies; is that right? A. It is so stated.

"Q. Will you go a little further and read the next section, 'Operated jointly with,' and say whether the same statement is not made there? A. It states, 'Operated jointly with.'

"Q. That means the joint operation of the two, does it not? A. Yes.

"Q. Do you still adhere to your former statement that it was operated alone by the Forty-second Street and Manhattanville Railway Company? A. I did not say that it was operated alone, but it was maintained by the Forty-second Street.

"Q. You admit that it is jointly owned, jointly operated, but that you say that it is jointly—it is maintained solely by the one road? A. Correct."

These being the facts regarding the maintenance and operation of the Third Avenue Railway System, what is our conclusion? Is it that the Forty-second Street Railway Company maintained a separate and distinct existence as a corporation operating its railroad as a corporate entity under the guidance and control of its own officers and board of directors? Such to my mind would be an absurd conclusion, especially in the face of

the declarations of the Third Avenue Railway Company through its officers. They certainly know the facts, and it is the facts, and the facts alone
which the law seizes upon to form and to justify its conclusion. These facts
are that the Third Avenue Railway Company owned and controlled the
Forty-second Street Railway. It dominated its entire existence. It not only
owned the majority of the stock; it owned nearly all of its bonded and
floating indebtedness. It officered it with its own officers; it executed the
work and the service by its own executives; it paid the employees, including motormen and conductors, by and through its own paymaster; it
bought and paid for all materials, supplies and operating facilities. Every
activity as an operating railroad was dominated, controlled and executed
by the Third Avenue Railway Company, its officers and employees. Ryder,
the engineer, had it right when he said that both railroads jointly owned
and operated this branch of the system.

These are the facts which cannot be changed by mere bookkeeping
entries. It is true that the Forty-second Street Railway Company made
out separate reports required by law; that it existed as a corporation; that
it owned the street franchise; that upon the books of the Third Avenue
Company charges were made for the various services and expenses to the
Forty-second Street Railway Company as though it were in reality an
independent, vital organism. But all these things cannot hide the reality
or cover up the fact that the Third Avenue Railway Company in operation,
in control, in dominance, in execution and in the furnishing of service to
the city of New York was the Forty-second Street Railway Company.

No facts could exist which would justify the application of the statement in the *Davis Case* (*supra*), if these facts did not. "Where one railroad
company actually controls another and operates both as a single system,
the dominant company will be liable for injuries due to the negligence of
the subsidiary company." Such was the rule with which I commenced this
opinion, as laid down in *Davis* v. *Alexander* by the United States Supreme
Court, and such is the law which must be applied to the Third Avenue
Railway Company in this case. Its activities fit it exactly. * * * A quotation may not be inapt at this point.

"Much emphasis is laid upon statements made in various decisions of this court that ownership, alone, of capital stock in one corporation by another, does not create an identity of corporate interest
between the two companies, or render the stockholding company the
owner of the property of the other, or create the relation of principal
and agent or representative between the two. * * *

"While the statements of the law thus relied upon are satisfactory
in the connection in which they were used, they have been plainly and
repeatedly held not applicable where stock ownership has been
resorted to, not for the purpose of participating in the affairs of a corporation in the normal and usual manner, but for the purpose, as in
this case, of controlling a subsidiary company so that it may be used
as a mere agency or instrumentality of the owning company or com-

panies." [Chicago, M. & S. P. R. Co. v. Minneapolis Civic & Commerce Ass'n, 247 U.S. 490, 500–501 (1918)].

The attorney for the appellant, with his customary fairness and frankness, admits that some * * * authorities are directly against his contention, and he relies upon our ruling in *Stone v. Cleveland, C., C. & St. L. Ry. Co. (202 N. Y. 352); Elenkrieg v. Siebrecht (238 N. Y. 254),* and *Doran v. N. Y. City Interborough Ry. Co. (239 N. Y. 448)* as supporting his view, and as conflicting with these [other] authorities. The *Stone* case I have already referred to. It follows *Peterson v. Chicago, Rock Island & Pac. Ry. Co. (205 U.S. 364)* in holding that mere stock ownership and control is not sufficient to make the one company liable for the other, its subsidiary. The facts in this case go much further than the facts in the *Stone* case, as I have already explained. *Elenkrieg v. Siebrecht (238 N. Y. 254)* dealt with real property owned by a corporation. It was there shown that the corporation and not the stockholder was liable for the care and maintenance of the real property. The corporation was in actual control as much as any corporation can be and had engaged its authorized real estate agent to look after the property. We held that the fact that the principal stockholder had previously owned the real property which he conveyed indirectly to the corporation did not make him liable for the neglect of this agent. Here also was a question regarding control or dominance, a question of degree. * * *

BARTLE v. HOME OWNERS COOPERATIVE, INC.

Court of Appeals of New York.
309 N.Y. 103, 127 N.E.2d 832 (1955).

FROESSEL, J. Plaintiff, as trustee in bankruptcy of Westerlea Builders, Inc., has by means of this litigation attempted to hold defendant liable for the contract debts of Westerlea, defendant's wholly owned subsidiary. Defendant, as a co-operative corporation composed mostly of veterans, was organized in July, 1947, for the purpose of providing low-cost housing for its members. Unable to secure a contractor to undertake construction of the housing planned, Westerlea was organized for that purpose on June 5, 1948. With building costs running considerably higher than anticipated, Westerlea, as it proceeded with construction on some 26 houses, found itself in a difficult financial situation. On January 24, 1949, the creditors, pursuant to an extension agreement, took over the construction responsibilities. Nearly four years later, in October, 1952, Westerlea was adjudicated a bankrupt. Meanwhile, defendant had contributed to Westerlea not only its original capital of $25,000 but additional sums amounting to $25,639.38.

Plaintiff's principal contention on this appeal is that the courts below erred in refusing to "pierce the corporate veil" of Westerlea's corporate existence; as subordinate grounds for recovery he urged that the defendant equitably pledged its assets toward the satisfaction of the debts of the bankrupt's creditors, and that the doctrine of unjust enrichment should apply.

The trial court made detailed findings of fact which have been unanimously affirmed by the Appellate Division, which are clearly supported by the evidence, and by which we are bound. It found that while the defendant, as owner of the stock of Westerlea, controlled its affairs, the outward indicia of these two separate corporations were at all times maintained during the period in which the creditors extended credit; that the creditors were in no wise misled; that there was no fraud; and that the defendant performed no act causing injury to the creditors of Westerlea by depletion of assets or otherwise. The trial court also held that the creditors were estopped by the extension agreement from disputing the separate corporate identities.

We agree with the courts below. The law permits the incorporation of a business for the very purpose of escaping personal liability * * * Generally speaking, the doctrine of "piercing the corporate veil" is invoked "to prevent fraud or to achieve equity" (*International Aircraft Trading Co. v. Manufacturers Trust Co., 297 N.Y. 285, 292)* * * * But in the instant case there has been neither fraud, misrepresentation nor illegality. Defendant's purpose in placing its construction operation into a separate corporation was clearly within the limits of our public policy.

The judgment appealed from should be affirmed, without costs.

* * *

VAN VOORHIS, J. (dissenting). The judgment of the Appellate Division should be reversed on the law, as it seems to me, and plaintiff should have judgment declaring defendant to be liable for the debts of the bankrupt, Westerlea Builders, Inc., and that defendant holds its real property subject to the claims of creditors of Westerlea. Not only is Westerlea a wholly owned subsidiary of defendant Home Owners, having the same directors and management, but also and of primary importance, business was done on such a basis that Westerlea could not make a profit. Home Owners owned a residential subdivision; Westerlea was organized as a building corporation to erect homes for stockholders of Home Owners upon lots in this tract. Home Owners arranged with Westerlea for the construction of houses and then would sell the lots on which such houses had been erected to Home Owners' stockholders—at prices fixed by Home Owners' price policy committee in such amounts as to make no allowance for profit by Westerlea. The object was to benefit Home Owners' stockholders by enabling them to obtain their houses at cost, with no builder's profit.

The consequence is that described by Latty, Subsidiaries and Affiliated Corporations at pages 138–139: "The subsidiaries had, to begin with, nothing, made nothing, and could only end up with nothing. It is not surprising that the parent was held liable in each case." And again: "This set-up is often, though not necessarily, found in combination with a scheme whereby the corporation cannot possibly make profits (or can at the most make only nominal profits), and whereby all the net income in the course of the corporation's business is drained off as operating charges of one sort or another. The presence of this additional factor should remove any doubt that may remain as to the right of the creditor of the corporation not to be limited to the corporate assets for the satisfaction of his debt."

In the present instance, Westerlea was organized with a small capital supplied by Home Owners, which soon became exhausted. Thereafter, it had no funds and could acquire none over and beyond the actual cost of the houses which it was building for stockholders of Home Owners. Those stockholders obtained the entire benefit of Westerlea's operations by obtaining these houses at cost. Not only was Westerlea allowed no opportunity to make money, but it was placed in a position such that if its business were successful and times remained good, it would break even, otherwise it would inevitably become insolvent. The stockholders of Home Owners became the beneficiaries of its insolvency. This benefit to the stockholders of Home Owners was analogous to dividends, at least it was something of value which was obtained by them from Home Owners by virtue of their stock ownership. Under the circumstances, this benefit to its stockholders was a benefit to Home Owners as a corporation.

It follows that Westerlea was merely an agent of Home Owners to construct houses at cost for Home Owners' stockholders, and therefore Home Owners is rendered liable for Westerlea's indebtedness.

WALKOVSZKY v. CARLTON

Court of Appeals of New York.
18 N.Y.2d 414, 223 N.E.2d 6, 276 N.Y.S.2d 585 (1966).

* * *

[FULD, J.] This case involves what appears to be a rather common practice in the taxicab industry of vesting the ownership of a taxi fleet in many corporations, each owning only one or two cabs.

The complaint alleges that the plaintiff was severely injured four years ago in New York City when he was run down by a taxicab owned by the defendant Seon Cab Corporation and negligently operated at the time by the defendant Marchese. The individual defendant, Carlton, is claimed to be a stockholder of 10 corporations, including Seon, each of which has but two cabs registered in its name, and it is implied that only the minimum automobile liability insurance required by law (in the amount of $10,000) is carried on any one cab. Although seemingly independent of one another, these corporations are alleged to be "operated * * * as a single entity, unit and enterprise" with regard to financing, supplies, repairs, employees and garaging, and all are named as defendants. * * * The plaintiff asserts that he is also entitled to hold their stockholders personally liable for the damages sought because the multiple corporate structure constitutes an unlawful attempt "to defraud members of the general public" who might be injured by the cabs.

The defendant Carlton has moved * * * to dismiss the complaint on the ground that as to him it "fails to state a cause of action". The court at Special Term granted the motion but the Appellate Division, by a divided vote, reversed, holding that a valid cause of action was sufficiently stated. The defendant Carlton appeals to us * * *.

The law permits the incorporation of a business for the very purpose of enabling its proprietors to escape personal liability (see, e.g., *Bartle v. Home Owners Co-op., 309 N. Y. 103, 106)* but, manifestly, the privilege is not without its limits. Broadly speaking, the courts will disregard the corporate form, or, to use accepted terminology, "pierce the corporate veil", whenever necessary "to prevent fraud or to achieve equity". *(International Aircraft Trading Co. v. Manufacturers Trust Co., 297 N. Y. 285, 292.)* In determining whether liability should be extended to reach assets beyond those belonging to the corporation, we are guided, as Judge Cardozo noted, by "general rules of agency". *(Berkey v. Third Ave. Ry. Co., 244 N. Y. 84, 95.)* In other words, whenever anyone uses control of the corporation to further his own rather than the corporation's business, he will be liable for the corporation's acts "upon the principle of *respondeat superior* applicable even where the agent is a natural person". *(Rapid Tr. Subway Constr. Co. v. City of New York, 259 N. Y. 472, 488.)* Such liability, moreover, extends not only to the corporation's commercial dealings * * * but to its negligent acts as well. * * *

In the *Mangan* case *([Mangan v. Terminal Transp. System], 247 App. Div. 853,* mot. for lv. to app. den. *272 N. Y. 676),* the plaintiff was injured as a result of the negligent operation of a cab owned and operated by one of four corporations affiliated with the defendant Terminal. Although the defendant was not a stockholder of any of the operating companies, both the defendant and the operating companies were owned, for the most part, by the same parties. The defendant's name (Terminal) was conspicuously displayed on the sides of all of the taxis used in the enterprise and, in point of fact, the defendant actually serviced, inspected, repaired and dispatched them. These facts were deemed to provide sufficient cause for piercing the corporate veil of the operating company—the nominal owner of the cab which injured the plaintiff—and holding the defendant liable. The operating companies were simply instrumentalities for carrying on the business of the defendant without imposing upon it financial and other liabilities incident to the actual ownership and operation of the cabs. * * *

In the case before us, the plaintiff has explicitly alleged that none of the corporations "had a separate existence of their own" and, as indicated above, all are named as defendants. However, it is one thing to assert that a corporation is a fragment of a larger corporate combine which actually conducts the business. (See Berle, The Theory of Enterprise Entity, *47 Col. L. Rev. 343, 348–350.)* It is quite another to claim that the corporation is a "dummy" for its individual stockholders who are in reality carrying on the business in their personal capacities for purely personal rather than corporate ends. * * * Either circumstance would justify treating the corporation as an agent and piercing the corporate veil to reach the principal but a different result would follow in each case. In the first, only a larger *corporate* entity would be held financially responsible * * * while, in the other, the stockholder would be personally liable. * * * Either the stockholder is conducting the business in his individual capacity or he is not. If he is, he will be liable; if he is not, then, it does not matter—insofar as his personal liability is concerned—that the enterprise is actually being carried on by a larger "enterprise entity". * * *

At this stage in the present litigation, we are concerned only with the pleadings and, since [our law] permits causes of action to be stated "alternatively or hypothetically", it is possible for the plaintiff to allege both theories as the basis for his demand for judgment. In ascertaining whether he has done so, we must consider the entire pleading, reducing therefrom " 'whatever can be implied from its statements by fair and reasonable intendment.' " (*Condon v. Associated Hosp. Serv., 287 N. Y. 411, 414 * * *). Reading the complaint in this case most favorably and liberally, we do not believe that there can be gathered from its averments the allegations required to spell out a valid cause of action against the defendant Carlton.

The individual defendant is charged with having "organized, managed, dominated and controlled" a fragmented corporate entity but there are no allegations that he was conducting business in his individual capacity. Had the taxicab fleet been owned by a single corporation, it would be readily apparent that the plaintiff would face formidable barriers in attempting to establish personal liability on the part of the corporation's stockholders. The fact that the fleet ownership has been deliberately split up among many corporations does not ease the plaintiff's burden in that respect. The corporate form may not be disregarded merely because the assets of the corporation, together with the mandatory insurance coverage of the vehicle which struck the plaintiff, are insufficient to assure him the recovery sought. If Carlton were to be held individually liable on those facts alone, the decision would apply equally to the thousands of cabs which are owned by their individual drivers who conduct their businesses through corporations organized pursuant to * * * the Business Corporation Law and carry the minimum insurance required by subdivision 1 (par. [a]) of *section 370* of the Vehicle and Traffic Law. These taxi owner-operators are entitled to form such corporations * * * and we agree with the court at Special Term that, if the insurance coverage required by statute "is inadequate for the protection of the public, the remedy lies not with the courts but with the Legislature." It may very well be sound policy to require that certain corporations must take out liability insurance which will afford adequate compensation to their potential tort victims. However, the responsibility for imposing conditions on the privilege of incorporation has been committed by the Constitution to the Legislature (N. Y. Const., art. X, § 1) and it may not be fairly implied, from any statute, that the Legislature intended, without the slightest discussion or debate, to require of taxi corporations that they carry automobile liability insurance over and above that mandated by the Vehicle and Traffic Law

This is not to say that it is impossible for the plaintiff to state a valid cause of action against the defendant Carlton. However, the simple fact is that the plaintiff has just not done so here. While the complaint alleges that the separate corporations were undercapitalized and that their assets have been intermingled, it is barren of any "sufficiently [particularized] statements" * * * that the defendant Carlton and his associates are actually doing business in their individual capacities, shuttling their personal funds in and out of the corporations "without regard to formality and to suit their immediate convenience." (*Weisser v. Mursam Shoe Corp., 127 F. 2d 344, 345, supra.*) Such a "perversion of the privilege to do business in a corporate form" (*Berkey v. Third Ave. Ry. Co., 244 N. Y. 84, 95, supra*) would justify imposing personal liability on the individual stockholders. * * * Nothing of the sort has in fact been charged, and it cannot reasonably or logically be inferred from the happenstance that the business of Seon Cab Corporation may actually be carried on by a larger corporate entity composed of many corporations which, under general principles of agency, would be liable to each other's creditors in contract and in tort. * * *

In point of fact, the principle relied upon in the complaint to sustain the imposition of personal liability is not agency but fraud. Such a cause of action cannot withstand analysis. If it is not fraudulent for the owner-operator of a single cab corporation to take out only the minimum required liability insurance, the enterprise does not become either illicit or fraudulent merely because it consists of many such corporations. The plaintiff's injuries are the same regardless of whether the cab which strikes him is owned by a single corporation or part of a fleet with ownership fragmented among many corporations. Whatever rights he may be able to assert against parties other than the registered owner of the vehicle come into being not because he has been defrauded but because, under the principle of *respondeat superior*, he is entitled to hold the whole enterprise responsible for the acts of its agents.

In sum, then, the complaint falls short of adequately stating a cause of action against the defendant Carlton in his individual capacity. * * *

*   *   *

KEATING, J. (dissenting). The defendant Carlton, the shareholder here sought to be held for the negligence of the driver of a taxicab, was a principal shareholder and organizer of the defendant corporation which owned the taxicab. The corporation was one of 10 organized by the defendant, each containing two cabs and each cab having the "minimum liability" insurance coverage mandated by *section 370* of the Vehicle and Traffic Law. The sole assets of these operating corporations are the vehicles themselves and they are apparently subject to mortgages. [It appears that the [taxicab] medallions, which are of considerable value, are judgment proof. (Administrative Code of City of New York, § 436–2.0.)]

From their inception these corporations were intentionally undercapitalized for the purpose of avoiding responsibility for acts which were bound to arise as a result of the operation of a large taxi fleet having cars out on the street 24 hours a day and engaged in public transportation. And during the course of the corporations' existence all income was continually drained out of the corporations for the same purpose.

The issue presented by this action is whether the policy of this State, which affords those desiring to engage in a business enterprise the privilege of limited liability through the use of the corporate device, is so strong that it will permit that privilege to continue no matter how much it is abused, no matter how irresponsibly the corporation is operated, no matter what the cost to the public. I do not believe that it is.

Under the circumstances of this case the shareholders should all be held individually liable to this plaintiff for the injuries he suffered. * * *

"If a corporation is organized and carries on business without substantial capital in such a way that the corporation is likely to have no sufficient assets available to meet its debts, it is inequitable that shareholders should set up such a flimsy organization to escape personal liability. The attempt to do corporate business without providing any sufficient basis of financial responsibility to creditors is an abuse of the separate entity and will be ineffectual to exempt the shareholders from corporate debts. It is coming to be recognized as the policy of law that shareholders should in good faith put at the risk of the business unincumbered capital reasonably adequate for its prospective liabilities. If capital is illusory or trifling compared with the business to be done and the risks of loss, this is a ground for denying the separate entity privilege." (Ballantine, Corporations [rev. ed., 1946], § 129, pp. 302–303.)

In *Minton v. Cavaney (56 Cal. 2d 576)* the Supreme Court of California had occasion to discuss this problem in a negligence case. The corporation of which the defendant was an organizer, director and officer operated a public swimming pool. One afternoon the plaintiffs' daughter drowned in the pool as a result of the alleged negligence of the corporation.

Justice ROGER TRAYNOR, speaking for the court, outlined the applicable law in this area. "The figurative terminology 'alter ego' and 'disregard of the corporate entity' ", he wrote, "is generally used to refer to the various situations that are an abuse of the corporate privilege * * * The equitable owners of a corporation, for example, are personally liable when they treat the assets of the corporation as their own and add or withdraw capital from the corporation at will * * *; when they hold themselves out as being personally liable for the debts of the corporation * * *; *or when they provide inadequate capitalization and actively participate in the conduct of corporate affairs". (56 Cal. 2d, p. 579;* italics supplied.)

Examining the facts of the case in light of the legal principles just enumerated, he found that "[it was] undisputed that there was no attempt to provide adequate capitalization. [The corporation] never had any substantial assets. It leased the pool that it operated, and the lease was forfeited for failure to pay the rent. Its capital was 'trifling compared with the business to be done and the risks of loss' ". *(56 Cal. 2d, p. 580.)*

It seems obvious that one of "the risks of loss" referred to was the possibility of drownings due to the negligence of the corporation. And the defendant's failure to provide such assets or any fund for recovery resulted in his being held personally liable.

In *Anderson v. Abbott (321 U.S. 349)* the defendant shareholders had organized a holding company and transferred to that company shares which they held in various national banks in return for shares in the holding company. The holding company did not have sufficient assets to meet the double liability requirements of the governing Federal statutes which provided that the owners of shares in national banks were personally liable for corporate obligations "to the extent of the amount of their stock therein, at the par value thereof, in addition to the amount invested in such shares" (U. S. Code, tit. 12, former § 63).

The court had found that these transfers were made in good faith, that other defendant shareholders who had purchased shares in the holding company had done so in good faith and that the organization of such a holding company was entirely legal. Despite this finding, the Supreme Court, speaking through Mr. Justice Douglas, pierced the corporate veil of the holding company and held all the shareholders, even those who had no part in the organization of the corporation, individually responsible for the corporate obligations as mandated by the statute.

"Limited liability", he wrote, "is the rule, not the exception; and on that assumption large undertakings are rested, vast enterprises are launched, and huge sums of capital attracted. But there are occasions when the limited liability sought to be obtained through the corporation will be qualified or denied. Mr. Justice Cardozo stated that a surrender of that principle of limited liability would be made 'when the sacrifice is essential to the end that some accepted public policy may be defended or upheld.' * * * The cases of fraud make up part of that exception * * * But they do not exhaust it. *An obvious inadequacy of capital, measured by the nature and magnitude of the corporate undertaking, has frequently been an important factor in cases denying stockholders their defense of limited liability * * * That rule has been invoked even in absence of a legislative policy which undercapitalization would defeat.* It becomes more important in a case such as the present one where the statutory policy of double liability will be defeated if impecunious bank-stock holding companies are allowed to be interposed as non-conductors of liability. *It has often been held that the interposition of a corporation will not be allowed to defeat a legislative policy, whether that was the aim or only the result of the arrangement* * * * 'the courts will not permit themselves to be blinded or deceived by mere forms of law' but will deal 'with the substance of the transaction involved as if the corporate agency did not exist and as the justice of the case may require.' " *(321 U.S., pp. 362–363;* emphasis added.)

The policy of this State has always been to provide and facilitate recovery for those injured through the negligence of others. The automobile, by its very nature, is capable of causing severe and costly injuries when not operated in a proper manner. The great increase in the number of automobile accidents combined with the frequent financial irresponsibility of the individual driving the car led to the adoption of *section 388* of the Vehicle and Traffic Law which had the effect of imposing upon the owner of the vehicle the responsibility for its negligent operation. It is upon this very statute that the cause of action against both the corporation and the individual defendant is predicated.

In addition the Legislature, still concerned with the financial irresponsibility of those who owned and operated motor vehicles, enacted a statute requiring minimum liability coverage for all owners of automobiles. The important public policy represented by both these statutes is outlined in *section 310* of the Vehicle and Traffic Law. That section provides that: "The legislature is concerned over the rising toll of motor vehicle accidents and the suffering and loss thereby inflicted. The legislature determines that it is a matter of grave concern that motorists shall be financially able to respond in damages for their negligent acts, so that innocent victims of motor vehicle accidents may be recompensed for the injury and financial loss inflicted upon them."

The defendant Carlton claims that, because the minimum amount of insurance required by the statute was obtained, the corporate veil cannot and should not be pierced despite the fact that the assets of the corporation which owned the cab were "trifling compared with the business to be done and the risks of loss" which were certain to be encountered. I do not agree.

The Legislature in requiring minimum liability insurance of $10,000, no doubt, intended to provide at least some small fund for recovery against those individuals and corporations who just did not have and were not able to raise or accumulate assets sufficient to satisfy the claims of those who were injured as a result of their negligence. It certainly could not have intended to shield those individuals who organized corporations, with the specific intent of avoiding responsibility to the public, where the operation of the corporate enterprise yielded profits sufficient to purchase additional insurance. Moreover, it is reasonable to assume that the Legislature believed that those individuals and corporations having substantial assets would take out insurance far in excess of the minimum in order to protect those assets from depletion. Given the costs of hospital care and treatment and the nature of injuries sustained in auto collisions, it would be unreasonable to assume that the Legislature believed that the minimum provided in the statute would in and of itself be sufficient to recompense "innocent victims of motor vehicle accidents * * * for the injury and financial loss inflicted upon them".

The defendant, however, argues that the failure of the Legislature to increase the minimum insurance requirements indicates legislative acquiescence in this scheme to avoid liability and responsibility to the public. In the absence of a clear legislative statement, approval of a scheme having such serious consequences is not to be so lightly inferred.

The defendant contends that the court will be encroaching upon the legislative domain by ignoring the corporate veil and holding the individual shareholder. This argument was answered by Mr. Justice Douglas in *Anderson v. Abbot (supra, pp. 366–367)* where he wrote that: "In the field in which we are presently concerned, judicial power hardly oversteps the bounds when it refuses to lend its aid to a promotional project which would circumvent or undermine a legislative policy. To deny it that function would be to make it impotent in situations where historically it has made some of its most notable contributions. If the judicial power is helpless to protect a legislative program from schemes for easy avoidance, then indeed it has become a handy implement of high finance. *Judicial interference to cripple or defeat a legislative policy is one thing; judicial interference with the plans of those whose corporate or other devices would circumvent that policy is quite another*. Once the purpose or effect of the scheme is clear, once the legislative policy is plain, we would indeed forsake a great tradition to say we were helpless to fashion the instruments for appropriate relief." (Emphasis added.)

The defendant contends that a decision holding him personally liable would discourage people from engaging in corporate enterprise.

What I would merely hold is that a participating shareholder of a corporation vested with a public interest, organized with capital insufficient to meet liabilities which are certain to arise in the ordinary course of the corporation's business, may be held personally responsible for such liabilities. Where corporate income is not sufficient to cover the cost of insurance premiums above the statutory minimum or where initially adequate finances dwindle under the pressure of competition, bad times or extraordinary and unexpected liability, obviously the shareholder will not be held liable. * * *

The only types of corporate enterprises that will be discouraged as a result of a decision allowing the individual shareholder to be sued will be those such as the one in question, designed solely to abuse the corporate privilege at the expense of the public interest.

* * *

MORRIS v. NEW YORK STATE DEPARTMENT OF TAXATION AND FINANCE

Court of Appeals of New York.
82 N.Y.2d 135, 623 N.E.2d 1157, 603 N.Y.S.2d 807 (1993).

HANCOCK, JR., J.

Petitioner, a New Jersey resident who maintained a rented apartment in New York, was the president of Sunshine Developers, Inc. (Sunshine), a closely held corporation owned entirely by his brother and his nephew. Respondent New York State Department of Taxation and Finance (the Department) assessed a compensating use tax against petitioner for two cabin cruisers purchased by the corporation outside of New York and allegedly used by him on his individual business in State waters. Although owning no stock in Sunshine, petitioner assertedly controlled the corporation and his responsibility for the tax has been upheld by disregarding the separate corporate entity under the doctrine of piercing the corporate veil. Because of his leasing a New York apartment, it has been held that petitioner, although a New Jersey resident, could not claim the nonresident's exemption from the tax *(see, Tax Law § 1118* [2]). On his appeal, the decisive question is whether the Tax Appeals Tribunal and Appellate Division properly sustained the assessment against petitioner on the theory of piercing the corporate veil. For reasons to be explained, we conclude that, on the facts in this record, that theory should not have been applied. We, therefore, reverse.

I

* * * Sunshine was a company with offices in New Jersey incorporated in Delaware in 1977 for the purpose of purchasing, owning, operating and leasing boats. Petitioner's brother, Robert Morris, was the majority shareholder and acted as Sunshine's secretary-treasurer; petitioner's nephew Drew, 14 years old at the time of incorporation, was the other shareholder. Robert Morris knew little about the assets or business activities of the corporation and did not participate in business decisions. As the sole board member, petitioner acted as chair and board secretary and made all corporate decisions. Petitioner had been a resident of New Jersey since 1980; from 1977 until 1984 he rented an apartment in New York City for the rare occasion when he stayed in New York overnight for business reasons.

In 1977 and in 1978 Sunshine purchased, owned, and operated at different times its primary assets, two boats ("the 1977 boat" and "the 1978 boat"), which it leased for the purpose of business entertainment to other companies owned by petitioner and Robert Morris. In October 1982, the Department assessed sales and use taxes against Sunshine for the purchase and use of these boats * * *. On appeal, an Administrative Law Judge (ALJ), finding delivery of the boats to have occurred outside of New York, cancelled all sales tax assessments as well as the use tax on the

1977 boat, which had been used only infrequently in New York. The ALJ sustained the use tax on the 1978 boat, however. The Appellate Division upheld the tax, concluding that the 1978 boat "was seasonally moored, and therefore used, in New York. These facts support [the Department's] further conclusion that petitioners [including Sunshine] were engaged in carrying on a business in this State and, thus, not entitled to the exemption for nonresidents" * * * The use tax assessed on the 1978 boat was paid to the Department.

The corporation subsequently sold these assets, and from June 1981 through August 1984 it purchased, owned and operated at different times two other boats ("the 1981 boat" and "the 1984 boat"). The corporation bought them following special board meetings at which petitioner, sitting as sole board member, authorized the purchases. Both boats were picked up by petitioner in North Carolina. And both boats were moored during the summer months at Montauk, New York.

In April 1985, the Department sent a notice of determination of sales and use taxes due on the 1981 and 1984 boats in the amount of $76,390, plus interest and penalties, to petitioner, Robert Morris and Sunshine. The Department's action was based upon the mooring of the 1981 and 1984 boats at Montauk as well as on the allegation that Sunshine was a corporate resident of New York. On appeal, it was claimed that no sales tax was due as Sunshine was exempt from the use tax as a nonresident corporation. In May 1990, an ALJ concluded: (1) that Sunshine was entitled to the nonresident exemption pursuant to *Tax Law § 1118(2)*; and (2) that, notwithstanding the Department's contentions, the corporate veil should not be pierced to impose personal liability for the taxes upon either petitioner or Robert Morris. In 1988, the sales and use tax on the 1981 boat was paid to the New Jersey Department of the Treasury.

The Department appealed to respondent Tax Appeals Tribunal (the Tribunal). In May 1991, the Tribunal sustained the ALJ's determination of no imposition of sales or use taxes upon Sunshine, concluding that Sunshine was a nonresident corporation, which did no business in New York; it also sustained the determination pertaining to Robert Morris that he had insufficient control of Sunshine to justify piercing the corporate veil. But the Tribunal reversed as to petitioner Joseph Morris and pierced the corporate veil, concluding that he was the equitable owner and controlling principal of Sunshine and therefore personally liable for the tax. The Tribunal also held that petitioner Joseph Morris did not qualify for the nonresident tax exemption due to his rental of a New York City apartment when the 1981 and 1984 boats were purchased. The Tribunal modified the total amount of tax assessed against him to reflect a credit for the sales and use tax paid to the State of New Jersey on the 1981 boat.

Petitioner commenced a CPLR article 78 proceeding in the Appellate Division to review the Tribunal's determination. * * * We granted petitioner leave to appeal and now reverse.

II

In *Walkovszky v Carlton (18 N.Y.2d 414, 276 N.Y.S.2d 585, 223 N.E.2d 6)*, we stated the general rule that:

"Broadly speaking, the courts will disregard the corporate form, or, to use accepted terminology, 'pierce the corporate veil', whenever necessary 'to prevent fraud or to achieve equity.' " * * *

The concept of piercing the corporate veil is a limitation on the accepted principles that a corporation exists independently of its owners, as a separate legal entity, that the owners are normally not liable for the debts of the corporation, and that it is perfectly legal to incorporate for the express purpose of limiting the liability of the corporate owners *(see, Bartle v. Home Owners Coop., 309 N.Y. 103, 106, 127 N.E.2d 832;* * * * Presser, Piercing the Corporate Veil § 1.01, at 1–4—1–5).

The doctrine of piercing the corporate veil is typically employed by a third party seeking to go behind the corporate existence in order to circumvent the limited liability of the owners and to hold them liable for some underlying corporate obligation *(see, e.g,* * * * *Walkovszky v Carlton, supra; Bartle v Home Owners Coop., supra).* The concept is equitable in nature and assumes that the corporation itself is liable for the obligation sought to be imposed *(see,* 1 Fletcher, Cyclopedia of Private Corporations § 41, at 603 [perm ed]). Thus, an attempt of a third party to pierce the corporate veil does not constitute a cause of action independent of that against the corporation; rather it is an assertion of facts and circumstances which will persuade the court to impose the corporate obligation on its owners * * *.

Because a decision whether to pierce the corporate veil in a given instance will necessarily depend on the attendant facts and equities, the New York cases may not be reduced to definitive rules governing the varying circumstances when the power may be exercised *(see,* Presser, Piercing the Corporate Veil § 2.33 [1], at 2–291—2–293). * * * Generally, however, piercing the corporate veil requires a showing that: (1) the owners exercised complete domination of the corporation in respect to the transaction attacked; and (2) that such domination was used to commit a fraud or wrong against the plaintiff which resulted in plaintiff's injury *(see,* * * * *Lowendahl v Baltimore & Ohio R. R. Co., 247 A.D. 144, 157, 287 N.Y.S. 62, affd 272 N.Y. 360, 6 N.E.2d 56; American Protein Corp. v AB Volvo, 844 F.2d 56, 60* [2d Cir. 1988] [analyzing New York law and citing *Lowendahl (supra)];* * * * see generally, Presser, Piercing the Corporate Veil § 2.33 [3], at 2–304—2–313).

While complete domination of the corporation is the key to piercing the corporate veil, especially when the owners use the corporation as a mere device to further their personal rather than the corporate business *(see, Walkovszky, supra, at 417),* such domination, standing alone, is not enough; some showing of a wrongful or unjust act toward plaintiff is required *(see* * * * *Passalacqua Bldrs. v. Resnick Developers S., 933 F.2d*

131, 138 [2d Cir. 1991]) [applying New York law]. * * * The party seeking to pierce the corporate veil must establish that the owners, through their domination, abused the privilege of doing business in the corporate form to perpetrate a wrong or injustice against that party such that a court in equity will intervene. * * *

III

In deciding whether respondents have established a sufficient basis for piercing the corporate veil under these general rules, we first address the element of petitioner's control of the corporation. Because petitioner was not a stockholder of Sunshine, he argues that, as a matter of law, he was not in a position to exercise the necessary domination of the corporation, * * *. Respondents contend, nevertheless, that Joseph Morris, although not a stockholder—through his status as Sunshine's president and its only director and his close relationship with his brother and nephew, the only stockholders—was in a position to and did dominate the corporation with respect to the transactions at issue * * *. The Appellate Division accepted this argument, holding: "we perceive that we should be concerned with 'reality and not form [and] with how the corporation operated and [petitioner's] relationship to that operation' [citation omitted]" i* * *

We have found no definitive authority on the issue of whether a non-shareholder could be personally liable under a theory of piercing the corporate veil * * *. It is not necessary to decide the question, however, because respondents fell far short of meeting their burden on the second critical point: that petitioner, through his domination, misused the corporate form for his personal ends so as to commit a wrong or injustice on the taxing authorities of New York State * * *. The specific finding of the ALJ that there is no indication of "fraud or wrongdoing" on the part of petitioner or the corporation, it must be noted, was not disturbed on review by either the Tax Appeals Tribunal or the Appellate Division. But, respondents maintain that *there was* wrongful conduct in any event and characterize the purchase of the boats by Sunshine as part of an illicit scheme to use the corporation to avoid New York taxes. We disagree.

There is no contention that there was anything improper in the formation of Sunshine for the stated purpose of purchasing, owning and leasing boats. Sunshine, it appears, in the early years after its incorporation, carried on its stated business; the very basis of the Department's successful 1982 assessment of the use tax against Sunshine for the 1978 boat was that the corporation *was conducting its business* within the State of New York—i.e., buying boats and chartering them to businesses for entertaining clients * * *.

Indeed, as in the 1982 assessment, the Department initially argued that Sunshine was liable for the current assessment because of its business presence in New York. However, once the ALJ and the Tribunal determined in this proceeding that Sunshine was a nonresident corporation and *not engaged in business in New York* and, therefore, entitled to the nonresident exemption on the 1981 and 1984 boats * * * respondents abandoned that course and took a different tack. They now claim that in doing no business during the period when the 1981 and 1984 boats were purchased, Sunshine must have operated solely as a sham to do the personal business of petitioner. They further argue that, because Sunshine was a sham, it existed solely for the purpose of avoiding taxes due on its asset.

However, there is no evidence of an intent to defraud by using the corporation as a tax shield. The corporation, not petitioner, purchased and owned the boats. There is no suggestion that any obligations of the corporation remained unpaid, including use taxes found to be due in New York. There is no reason to believe that if respondents had succeeded in their current assessment against the corporation on the 1984 boat, as they had in their 1982 assessment, Sunshine would not have paid the tax. That the Tribunal sustained the nonresident tax exemption for Sunshine on the 1984 purchase and declined to sustain it as to petitioner does not give rise to a claim of fraud or wrongdoing by petitioner.

Finally, there is a fundamental problem with respondents' claim that petitioner has somehow perverted the protective benefits of the corporate privilege to commit a wrong against respondents. This is not the usual case where a third party seeks to impose a corporate obligation on a controlling owner by penetrating the shield of limited liability. Quite the contrary. Here, there was no corporate obligation for respondents to impose. Sunshine, it has been determined, *was entitled to the nonresident exemption* for the 1984 boat and owes nothing. Thus, the claim against petitioner cannot be for what the corporation owed. Respondents, nevertheless, seek to collect the tax directly from petitioner because, unlike Sunshine, he maintained a rental apartment in New York and assertedly was deprived of his nonresident exemption. But, to pursue petitioner under the doctrine of piercing the corporate veil presupposes that "the corporation is liable" (1 Fletcher, Cyclopedia of Private Corporations § 41, at 603 [perm ed] * * *). To hold petitioner liable by piercing the corporate veil for a debt Sunshine does not owe, we think, would be inconsistent with the essential theory of the doctrine.

We are not persuaded by respondents' argument that we should disregard the corporate entity and sustain the tax against petitioner under the theory articulated in Federal tax cases * * * In general, in matters relating to revenue a corporation will be recognized as having a separate taxable identity unless it is shown to have had no legitimate business purpose either in its formation or its subsequent existence or that it was a sham or set up for tax avoidance * * *. First, of course, we are dealing here not with Federal law but with New York decisional law and a New York sales and use tax * * *. But, even applying the rule of the Federal cases the result would be the same, for it appears that Sunshine *had a legitimate business purpose* in its formation and carried on its business of owning and chartering boats thereafter. There is no showing that it was set up as a sham or for the purpose of tax avoidance.

*   *   *

The judgment of the Appellate Division should be reversed, with costs * * *

NOTES AND QUESTIONS[1]

1. It is now accepted as one of the first principles of American law that those who own shares in corporations, whether such shareholders are individuals or are themselves corporations, normally are not liable for the debts of their corporations.[2] As you noted in the *Bartle* case above, it is further accepted as perfectly legal to incorporate for the express purpose of limiting the liability of the corporation's owners.

Indeed, there has been an almost romantic aspect about American law when some scholars have considered the doctrine of shareholder limited liability. This view is rarely expressed today, but when one consults an early twentieth century treatise on the corporate entity one can find it said that "This attribute of limited liability is regarded by most persons as the greatest advantage of incorporation. Indeed many immigrants doubtless possess full knowledge of this fact before coming within hailing distance of the Statute of Liberty."[3] As indicated earlier, in the early part of the twentieth century the then President of Columbia University declared that:

> [T]he limited liability corporation is the greatest single discovery of modern times [and that] even steam and electricity are far less important than the limited liability corporation, and they would be reduced to comparative impotence without it.... It substitutes co-operation on a large scale for individual, cut-throat, parochial competition. It makes possible huge economy in production and in trading ... it means the only possible engine for carrying on international trade on a scale commensurate with modern needs and opportunities.[4]

---

1. Most of the material in notes 1–4 has been taken from Stephen B. Presser, Piercing the Corporate Veil § 1:1 (Thomson/West originally published 1991, updated annually).

2. For the evolution of the acceptance of this "first principle," see, e.g., Dodd, "The Evolution of Limited Liability in American Industry: Massachusetts," 61 Harv. L. Rev. 1351 (1948).

For some typical examples of statutory treatment see Delaware General Corporate Law Section 102(b)(6), which provides that the certificate of incorporation may contain "A provision imposing personal liability for the debts of the corporation on its stockholders or members to a specified extent and upon specified conditions; *otherwise, the stockholders or members of a corporation shall not be personally liable for the payment of the corporation's debts except as they may be liable by reason of their own conduct or acts.*" (emphasis supplied), or the Revised Model Business Corporation Act, § 6.22(b), which states that "Unless otherwise provided in the articles of incorporation *a shareholder of a corporation is not personally liable for the acts or debts of the corporation except that he may become personally liable by reason of his own acts or conduct.*" (Emphasis supplied).

3. M. Wormser, Disregard of the Corporate Fiction and Allied Corporation Problems 14 (New York: Baker, Voorhis and Co. 1927). See also Barber, "Piercing the Corporate Veil," 17 Willamette L. Rev. 371–372 (1981): "This incentive to business investment has been called the most important legal development of the nineteenth century."

4. Quoted by M. Wormser, Disregard of the Corporate Fiction and Allied Corporation Problems

Would you agree with these sentiments? Do these four New York cases lead you to believe that limited shareholder liability is a good idea? Why or why not?

2. You should understand, though, that even in jurisdictions where this "first principle" of shareholder limited liability exists, there are exceptions to the rule of no liability of shareholders for corporate debts. For example, it is commonly true that shareholders will be liable to the corporation or to its creditors if they fail to pay the full consideration for their shares.[5] Some states impose liability on shareholders of small corporations for certain debts to corporate employees.[6] There is also criminal or civil liability for shareholders or officers who commit crimes or torts on behalf of their corporations, where they personally possess the requisite intent to cause harm.

We are now concerned with still another exception to the rule absolving shareholders from liability for the debts of their corporations. This exception, known as the "piercing the veil" doctrine, has long been a rule, equitable in nature, applied by American and foreign courts to fasten liability on shareholders of corporations of varying size and character for corporate debts of all kinds.

3. The "veil" of the "corporate fiction," or the "artificial personality" of the corporation, is "pierced," and the individual or corporate shareholder exposed to personal or corporate liability, as the case may be, when a court determines that the debt in question *is not really a debt of the corporation,* but ought, in fairness, *to be viewed as a debt of the individual or corporate shareholder or shareholders.* While it can probably be stated that what is involved in veil-piercing is a paradigm case of a judgment call on the part of judge or jury,[7] the articulation of the doctrine is usually in terms that suggest that more than mere equitable discretion is involved.

The most commonly quoted general rule is probably that stated by Judge SANBORN in *United States v. Milwaukee Refrigerator Transit Co.*:

> [A] corporation will be looked upon as a legal entity as a general rule, and until sufficient reason to the contrary appears; but, when the notion of legal entity is used to defeat public convenience, justify wrong, protect fraud, or defend crime, the law will regard the corporation as an association of persons.

Applying this general rule, do you believe it was appropriate to pierce the corporate veil in any of the four cases you have just read? Note that there is a

---

2–3 (New York: Baker, Voorhis and Co. 1927). To strikingly similar effect see the comments from the Economist of 18 December 1926 quoted by Halpern, Trebilcock & Turnbull, "An Economic Analysis of Limited Liability in Corporation Law," 30 U. of Toronto L.J. 117, 118 (1980): "The economic historian of the future may assign to the nameless inventor of the principle of limited liability, as applied to trading corporations, a place of honor with Watt and Stephenson, and other pioneers of the Industrial Revolution."

5. See, e.g., Delaware General Corporation Law § 162, Revised Model Business Corporation Act § 6.22(a).

6. At least as of 1987 this was the situation in New York and Wisconsin. See P. Blumberg, The Law of Corporate Groups: Tort, Contract, and Other Common Law Problems in the Substantive Law of Parent and Subsidiary Corporations 50 (1987).

7. *United States v. Milwaukee Refrigerator Transit Co.*, 142 F. 247, 255 (C.C.E.D. Wis. 1905).

majority and dissenting opinion in the first three of these cases, which should give you some sense of the difficulty of the area. Who gets it right in each of those cases, the majority or the dissent?

4. Until about the last two decades of the twentieth century there was relatively little theoretical or scholarly work done on the issue of "piercing the veil," considering that any brief perusal of the state or federal reporters is likely to show as many corporation law cases on piercing the veil as those devoted to any other issue, and occasionally more than the other various issues combined. The explanation for the reluctance of scholars to tackle the issue is probably to be found in the doctrine's frustrating fluidity, of which you have already had a glimpse. As the general language of Judge Sanborn suggests, there has been a real reluctance on the part of courts clearly to define piercing the veil standards.

Scholars who have examined the piercing the veil doctrine have seemed almost in despair, remarking that the rationales for piercing the veil are "vague and illusory," and that the jurisprudence of veil-piercing is a "legal quagmire."[8] As it was stated in a relatively recent attempt to impose order on the field, the law of piercing the veil "like lightning ... is rare, severe, and unprincipled. There is a consensus that the whole area of limited liability, and conversely of piercing the corporate veil, is among the most confusing in corporate law."[9] One leading scholar of corporations, taking all of this into consideration has simply thrown up his hands and declared that we should do away with the piercing the veil doctrine altogether, at least in the case of individual shareholder liability for corporate debts.[10]

Veil-piercing is a doctrine that often incorporates and bears a strong resemblance to fraud, and thus it is not too difficult to understand why courts have been reluctant, just as they have been in fraud cases, to enunciate hard and fast rules, lest the ingenuity of man (or woman) find a way to pervert the spirit while sticking to the letter of the law.[11] Piercing the veil has thus remained one of the great tightly-held possessions of what one of the first commentators called "Our lady of the common law."[12] It is a doctrine applied

---

8. Ballantine on "Parent and Subsidiary Corporations," 14 Cal. L. Rev., at 15 (1925). Ballantine on Private Corporations, p. 34, quoted in Frederick J. Powell, Parent and Subsidiary Corporations: Liability of a Parent Corporation for the Obligations of Its Subsidiary (Chicago, Callaghan and Co. 1931), at iv.

9. Easterbrook & Fischel, "Limited Liability and the Corporation," 52 U. Chi. L. Rev. 89 (1985). Easterbrook and Fischel's arguments have been reprinted in their book, The Economic Structure of Corporate Law 40–62 (1991).

10. Stephen M. Bainbridge, "Abolishing Veil Piercing," 26 Journal of Corporation Law 479 (2001).

11. Cf. Krendl & Krendl, "Piercing the Corporate Veil: Focusing the Inquiry," 55 Denver L. J. 1, 22 (1978) ("In this equitable area [of piercing the corporate veil] involving as wide a variety of situations as foolishness or deviousness can contrive, there appears to be no single determinative factor."), and Thompson, "Piercing the Corporate Veil: An Empirical Study," 76 Cornell L. Rev. 1043 (1991) ("As with insider trading and much of the law of directors' fiduciary duties, additional specification may not be possible without inviting greater abuse, as investors and their lawyers plan transactions to avoid specific terms of the law." (footnotes omitted)).

12. M. Wormser, Disregard of the Corporate Fiction and Allied Corporation Problems (New York: Baker, Voorhis and Co. 1927). For an examination of that common-law ethos, as practiced by some leading common lawyers, see R. Cosgrove, Our Lady The Common Law: An Anglo–American Legal Community, 1870–1930 (1987).

by courts in an extremely discretionary manner, in accordance with the individual consciences of judges. In an age dominated by statutes, piercing the veil remains a vital and robust common-law doctrine. Do you see evidence of this vitality or robustness in these four cases?

5. The first three cases, *Berkey*, *Bartle*, and *Walkovsky* are some of the most important cases decided by the highest New York Court, the Court of Appeals (New York's "Supreme Court," somewhat paradoxically, unlike the situation in many states, is an intermediate appellate court. Go figure.). New York, as the commercial capital of the country, has had more than its share of veil-piercing cases, and it could probably be characterized as the leading jurisdiction for veil-piercing law. When you add in the fourth case, *Morris*, would you characterize New York as a jurisdiction in which it is difficult or easy to pierce the corporate veil? Note that the majority opinion in *Berkey* is by Judge CARDOZO, whom you encountered earlier in *Meinhard v. Solomon*. Does this seem like the work of the same judge? Why or why not? Note CARDOZO's caution that when we are thinking about whether it is proper to pierce the corporate veil of a subsidiary corporation to reach a parent we should be careful lest our way be obscured by the "mists of metaphor." What do you suppose that means? Note that Cardozo is reluctant to apply agency doctrine to find the controlling parent liable for the acts of the subsidiary. Is this reluctance justified? Why doesn't the dissent go along? *Berkey* and *Bartle* are cases involving attempts to pierce the corporate veil of subsidiaries to reach parents, while *Walkovsky* and *Morris* are attempts to fasten liability on an individual shareholder in one case and a controlling individual in the other. Should there be a difference in the manner of treatment between corporations and individuals when veil-piercing is at issue? Generally speaking the law says "no." Do you agree?

6. *Berkey* and *Walkovsky* are cases in which plaintiffs seek to recover for torts committed by the agents of defendant corporations, and to impute these torts to the shareholders through the principle of *respondeat superior* (literally "let the master answer," a broad principle in the law of torts which provides that the employer is liable for the acts of employees under his or her direction, or, if you like, that the principal is responsible for the torts committed by his or her agent). *Bartle* is a case of a plaintiff suing in breach of contract. Which plaintiffs should be entitled to easier piercing of the veil—voluntary creditors who agree to enter into agreement with corporations, or involuntary creditors injured by the acts of agents of corporations? Most courts suggest that it should be easier for tort creditors to recover. Do you understand why? It is not clear, however, that as far as actual cases are concerned, it is easier to pierce for tort creditors than it is for contract creditors. The leading empirical study reached a contrary conclusion, but this may be because the vast majority of cases settle before they can be tried.[13] *Morris* is a case of a governmental entity seeking to pierce the corporate veil to collect

---

13. For that empirical study see Robert Thompson, "Piercing the Corporate Veil: An Empirical Study," 76 Cornell L. Rev. 1036 (1991). See also, for further data, Robert Thompson, The Limits of Liability in the New Limited Liability Entities, 32 Wake Forest L. Rev. 1–29 (1997), where Professor Thompson reports that with regard to individual shareholders piercing the corporate veil has never occurred in a corporation with more than nine shareholders and usually occurs as to shareholders who are also managers of the entity. Would you have expected this?

taxes from an individual, accusing that individual of incorporating to avoid such taxation. Should we be more or less reluctant to permit piercing in such cases?

While there was relatively little scholarly interest in the piercing issue until recently, it is now a red-hot topic in the law reviews. The thrust of such scholarship seems to be the suggestion that we should eliminate the protection of limited liability for parent corporations in the case of torts committed by their subsidiaries. Would you agree? Henry Hansmann and Reinier Kraakman fired the opening shot in the now more than decade-old academic war over limited liability in their article "Toward Unlimited Shareholder Liability for Corporate Torts," 100 Yale L.J. 1879 (1991). Professor Kraakman's casebook with William T. Allen, Allen & Kraakman, Commentaries and Cases of the Law of Business Organization 169 (2003), identifies the following articles as providing "subsequent and related contributions to the debate": Janet Alexander, Unlimited Shareholder Liability Through a Procedural Lens, 106 Harv. L. Rev. 387 (1992); Peter Z. Grossman, The Market for Shares of Companies with Unlimited Liability, 24 J. Leg. Stud. 63 (1995); Joseph Grundfest, The Limited Future of Unlimited Liability 102 Yale L. Rev. 387 (1992); Hansmann & Kraakman, A Procedural Focus on Unlimited Liability, 106 Harv. L. Rev. 446 (1992); Hansmann & Kraakman, Do the Capital Markets Compel Limited Liability? A Response to Professor Grundfest, 102 Yale L. Rev. 427 (1992); David Leebron, Limited Liability, Tort Victims, and Creditors, 91 Colum. L. Rev. 1565 (1991); Jonathan R. Macey & Geoffrey P. Miller, Double Liability of Bank Shareholders: History and Implications, 27 Wake Forest L.Rev. 31 (1992); Note, In Defense of Limited Liability: A Reply to Hansmann & Kraakman, 1 Geo. Mason U.L.Rev. 59 (1994); and Stephen B. Presser, Thwarting the Killing of the Corporation: Limited Liability, Democracy and Economics, 87 Nw. U. L. Rev. 148 (1992). See also Stephen M. Bainbridge, Abolishing Veil Piercing, 26 Iowa J. Corp. L. 479 (2001); Richard A. Booth, Limited Liability and the Efficient Allocation of Resources, 89 Nw. U. L. Rev. 140 (1994); Rebecca J. Huss, Revamping Veil-Piercing for all Limited Liability Entities: Forcing the Common Law Doctrine into the Statutory Age, 70 U. Cinn. L. Rev. 95 (2001); Lynn M. LoPucki, The Death of Liability, 106 Yale L.J. 1 (1996); Nina A. Mendelson, A Control-Based Approach to Shareholder Liability for Corporate Torts, 102 Colum. L. Rev. 1203 (2002); and Robert B. Thompson, Unpacking Limited Liability: Direct and Vicarious Liability of Corporate Participants for Torts of the Enterprise, 47 Vand. L. Rev. 1 (1994).

Is limited liability for torts likely to be abolished, as many of these scholars suggest? Consider the opinion of the United States Supreme Court, which follows.

B. FEDERAL LAW

UNITED STATES v. BESTFOODS ET AL.
Supreme Court of the United States.
524 U.S. 51, 118 S.Ct. 1876, 141 L.Ed.2d 43 (1998).

JUSTICE SOUTER delivered the opinion of [a unanimous] Court.

The United States brought this action for the costs of cleaning up industrial waste generated by a chemical plant. The issue before us, under the Comprehensive Environmental Response, Compensation, and Liability Act of 1980 (CERCLA), 94 Stat. 2767, as amended, *42 U.S.C. § 9601 et seq.*, is whether a parent corporation that actively participated in, and exercised control over, the operations of a subsidiary may, without more, be held liable as an operator of a polluting facility owned or operated by the subsidiary. We answer no, unless the corporate veil may be pierced. But a corporate parent that actively participated in, and exercised control over, the operations of the facility itself may be held directly liable in its own right as an operator of the facility.

I

In 1980, CERCLA was enacted in response to the serious environmental and health risks posed by industrial pollution. * * * "As its name implies, CERCLA is a comprehensive statute that grants the President broad power to command government agencies and private parties to clean up hazardous waste sites." * * * If it satisfies certain statutory conditions, the United States may, for instance, use the "Hazardous Substance Superfund" to finance cleanup efforts, see *42 U.S.C. § § 9601*(11), 9604; *26 U.S.C. § 9507,* which it may then replenish by suits brought under § 107 of the Act against, among others, "any person who at the time of disposal of any hazardous substance owned or operated any facility." *42 U.S.C. § 9607*(a)(2). So, those actually "responsible for any damage, environmental harm, or injury from chemical poisons [may be tagged with] the cost of their actions," S. Rep. No. 96–848, p. 13 (1980). * * * The term "person" is defined in CERCLA to include corporations and other business organizations, see *42 U.S.C. § 9601*(21), and the term "facility" enjoys a broad and detailed definition as well, see § 9601(9).[14] The phrase "owner or operator" is defined only by tautology, however, as "any person owning or operating" a facility, § 9601(20)(A)(ii), and it is this bit of circularity that prompts our review. Cf. *Exxon Corp. v. Hunt, supra, at 363* (CERCLA, "unfortunately, is not a model of legislative draftsmanship").

II

In 1957, Ott Chemical Co. (Ott I) began manufacturing chemicals at a plant near Muskegon, Michigan, and its intentional and unintentional dumping of hazardous substances significantly polluted the soil and ground water at the site. In 1965, respondent CPC International Inc. [CPC has recently changed its name to Bestfoods. Consistently with the briefs and the opinions below, we use the name CPC herein.] incorporated a wholly owned subsidiary to buy Ott I's assets in exchange for CPC stock.

---

14. "The term 'facility' means (A) any building, structure, installation, equipment, pipe or pipeline (including any pipe into a sewer or publicly owned treatment works), well, pit, pond, lagoon, impoundment, ditch, landfill, storage container, motor vehicle, rolling stock, or aircraft, or (B) any site or area where a hazardous substance has been deposited, stored, disposed of, or placed, or otherwise come to be located; but does not include any consumer product in consumer use or any vessel."

The new company, also dubbed Ott Chemical Co. (Ott II), continued chemical manufacturing at the site, and continued to pollute its surroundings. CPC kept the managers of Ott I, including its founder, president, and principal shareholder, Arnold Ott, on board as officers of Ott II. Arnold Ott and several other Ott II officers and directors were also given positions at CPC, and they performed duties for both corporations.

In 1972, CPC sold Ott II to Story Chemical Company, which operated the Muskegon plant until its bankruptcy in 1977. Shortly thereafter, when respondent Michigan Department of Natural Resources (MDNR) * * * examined the site for environmental damage, it found the land littered with thousands of leaking and even exploding drums of waste, and the soil and water saturated with noxious chemicals. MDNR sought a buyer for the property who would be willing to contribute toward its cleanup, and after extensive negotiations, respondent Aerojet-General Corp. arranged for transfer of the site from the Story bankruptcy trustee in 1977. Aerojet created a wholly owned California subsidiary, Cordova Chemical Company (Cordova/California), to purchase the property, and Cordova/California in turn created a wholly owned Michigan subsidiary, Cordova Chemical Company of Michigan (Cordova/Michigan), which manufactured chemicals at the site until 1986. * * *

By 1981, the federal Environmental Protection Agency had undertaken to see the site cleaned up, and its long-term remedial plan called for expenditures well into the tens of millions of dollars. To recover some of that money, the United States filed this action * * * in 1989, naming five defendants as responsible parties: CPC, Aerojet, Cordova/California, Cordova/Michigan, and Arnold Ott.[15] (By that time, Ott I and Ott II were defunct.) After the parties (and MDNR) had launched a flurry of contribution claims, counterclaims, and cross-claims, the District Court consolidated the cases for trial * * * [and] in 1991, the District Court held a 15-day bench trial on the issue of liability. * * * [T]he trial focused on the issues of whether CPC and Aerojet, as the parent corporations of Ott II and the Cordova companies, had "owned or operated" the facility within the meaning of § 107(a)(2).

The District Court said that operator liability may attach to a parent corporation both directly, when the parent itself operates the facility, and indirectly, when the corporate veil can be pierced under state law. See *CPC Int'l, Inc. v. Aerojet–General Corp., 777 F. Supp. 549, 572 (W.D. Mich. 1991).* The court explained that, while CERCLA imposes direct liability in situations in which the corporate veil cannot be pierced under traditional concepts of corporate law, "the statute and its legislative history do not suggest that CERCLA rejects entirely the crucial limits to liability that are inherent to corporate law." *Id., at 573.* As the District Court put it,

> "a parent corporation is directly liable under section 107(a)(2) as an operator only when it has exerted power or influence over its sub-

---

15.   Arnold Ott settled out of court with the Government on the eve of trial.

sidiary by actively participating in and exercising control over the subsidiary's business during a period of disposal of hazardous waste. A parent's actual participation in and control over a subsidiary's functions and decision-making creates 'operator' liability under CERCLA; a parent's mere oversight of a subsidiary's business in a manner appropriate and consistent with the investment relationship between a parent and its wholly owned subsidiary does not." *Ibid.*

Applying that test to the facts of this case, the District Court held both CPC and Aerojet liable under § 107(a)(2) as operators. As to CPC, the court found it particularly telling that CPC selected Ott II's board of directors and populated its executive ranks with CPC officials, and that a CPC official, G.R.D. Williams, played a significant role in shaping Ott II's environmental compliance policy.

After a divided panel of the Court of Appeals for the Sixth Circuit reversed in part, *United States v. Cordova/Michigan, 59 F.3d 584,* that court granted rehearing en banc and vacated the panel decision, *67 F.3d 586 (1995).* This time, 7 judges to 6, the court again reversed the District Court in *part. 113 F.3d 572 (1997).* The majority remarked on the possibility that a parent company might be held directly liable as an operator of a facility owned by its subsidiary: "At least conceivably, a parent might independently operate the facility in the stead of its subsidiary; or, as a sort of joint venturer, actually operate the facility alongside its subsidiary." *Id., at 579.* But the court refused to go any further and rejected the District Court's analysis with the explanation:

> "Where a parent corporation is sought to be held liable as an operator * * * based upon the extent of its control of its subsidiary which owns the facility, the parent will be liable only when the requirements necessary to pierce the corporate veil [under state law] are met. In other words, ... whether the parent will be liable as an operator depends upon whether the degree to which it controls its subsidiary and the extent and manner of its involvement with the facility, amount to the abuse of the corporate form that will warrant piercing the corporate veil and disregarding the separate corporate entities of the parent and subsidiary." *Id., at 580.*

Applying Michigan veil-piercing law, the Court of Appeals decided that neither CPC nor Aerojet * * * was liable for controlling the actions of its subsidiaries, since the parent and subsidiary corporations maintained separate personalities and the parents did not utilize the subsidiary corporate form to perpetrate fraud or subvert justice.

We granted certiorari * * * to resolve a conflict among the Circuits over the extent to which parent corporations may be held liable under CERCLA for operating facilities ostensibly under the control of their subsidiaries. * * * We now vacate and remand.

III

It is a general principle of corporate law deeply "ingrained in our economic and legal systems" that a parent corporation (so-called because of control through ownership of another corporation's stock) is not liable for the acts of its subsidiaries. Douglas & Shanks, Insulation from Liability Through Subsidiary Corporations, *39 Yale L. J. 193 (1929)* (hereinafter Douglas); * * * cf. *Anderson v. Abbott, 321 U.S. 349, 362, 88 L. Ed. 793, 64 S. Ct. 531 (1944)* ("Limited liability is the rule, not the exception"); *Burnet v. Clark, 287 U.S. 410, 415, 77 L. Ed. 397, 53 S. Ct. 207 (1932)* ("A corporation and its stockholders are generally to be treated as separate entities"). Thus it is hornbook law that "the exercise of the 'control' which stock ownership gives to the stockholders … will not create liability beyond the assets of the subsidiary. That 'control' includes the election of directors, the making of by-laws … and the doing of all other acts incident to the legal status of stockholders. Nor will a duplication of some or all of the directors or executive officers be fatal." Douglas 196 (footnotes omitted). Although this respect for corporate distinctions when the subsidiary is a polluter has been severely criticized in the literature, see, *e.g.*, Note, Liability of Parent Corporations for Hazardous Waste Cleanup and Damages, *99 Harv. L. Rev. 986 (1986),* nothing in CERCLA purports to reject this bedrock principle, and against this venerable common-law backdrop, the congressional silence is audible. Cf. *Edmonds v. Compagnie Generale Transatlantique, 443 U.S. 256, 266–267, 61 L. Ed. 2d 521, 99 S. Ct. 2753 (1979)* ("silence is most eloquent, for such reticence while contemplating an important and controversial change in existing law is unlikely"). The Government has indeed made no claim that a corporate parent is liable as an owner or an operator under § 107 simply because its subsidiary is subject to liability for owning or operating a polluting facility.

But there is an equally fundamental principle of corporate law, applicable to the parent-subsidiary relationship as well as generally, that the corporate veil may be pierced and the shareholder held liable for the corporation's conduct when, *inter alia*, the corporate form would otherwise be misused to accomplish certain wrongful purposes, most notably fraud, on the shareholder's behalf. See, *e.g.*, *Anderson v. Abbott, supra, at 362* ("there are occasions when the limited liability sought to be obtained through the corporation will be qualified or denied"); *Chicago, M. & St. P. R. Co. v. Minneapolis Civic and Commerce Assn., 247 U.S. 490, 501, 62 L. Ed. 1229, 38 S. Ct. 553 (1918)* (principles of corporate separateness "have been plainly and repeatedly held not applicable where stock ownership has been resorted to, not for the purpose of participating in the affairs of a corporation in the normal and usual manner, but for the purpose … of controlling a subsidiary company so that it may be used as a mere agency or instrumentality of the owning company") * * *. Nothing in CERCLA purports to rewrite this well-settled rule, either. CERCLA is thus like many another congressional enactment in giving no indication "that the entire corpus of state corporation law is to be replaced simply because a plaintiff's cause of action is based upon a federal statute," *Burks v. Lasker, 441 U.S. 471, 478, 60 L. Ed. 2d 404, 99 S. Ct. 1831 (1979)*, and the failure of the statute to speak to a matter as fundamental as the liability implications of corporate ownership demands application of the rule that "in order to abrogate a common-law principle, the statute must speak directly to the question addressed by the common law," *United States v. Texas, 507 U.S. 529, 534, 123 L. Ed. 2d 245, 113 S. Ct. 1631 (1993)* (internal quotation marks omitted). The Court of Appeals was accordingly correct in holding that when (but only when) the corporate veil may be pierced,[16] may a parent corporation be charged with derivative CERCLA liability for its subsidiary's actions. * * *

IV

A

If the act rested liability entirely on ownership of a polluting facility, this opinion might end here; but CERCLA liability may turn on operation as well as ownership, and nothing in the statute's terms bars a parent corporation from direct liability for its own actions in operating a facility owned by its subsidiary. As Justice (then-Professor) Douglas noted almost 70 years ago, derivative liability cases are to be distinguished from those in which "the alleged wrong can seemingly be traced to the parent through the conduit of its own personnel and management" and "the parent is directly a participant in the wrong complained of." Douglas 207, 208. * * * In such instances, the parent is directly liable for its own actions. See H. Henn & J. Alexander, Laws of Corporations 347 (3d ed. 1983) (hereinafter Henn & Alexander) ("Apart from corporation law principles, a shareholder, whether a natural person or a corporation, may be liable on the ground that such shareholder's activity resulted in the liability"). The fact that a corporate subsidiary happens to own a polluting facility operated by its parent does nothing, then, to displace the rule that the parent "corporation is [itself] responsible for the wrongs committed by its agents in the course of its business," *Mine Workers v. Coronado Coal Co., 259 U.S. 344, 395, 66 L. Ed. 975, 42 S. Ct. 570 (1922)*, and whereas

---

16. There is significant disagreement among courts and commentators over whether, in enforcing CERCLA's indirect liability, courts should borrow state law, or instead apply a federal common law of veil piercing. Compare, *e.g.,* * * * *Lansford–Coaldale Joint Water Auth. v. Tonolli Corp., 4 F.3d at 1225* ("given the federal interest in uniformity in the application of CERCLA, it is federal common law, and not state law, which governs when corporate veil-piercing is justified under CERCLA") * * * with, *e.g.,* Dennis, Liability of Officers, Directors and Stockholders under CERCLA: The Case for Adopting State Law, *36 Vill. L. Rev. 1367 (1991)* (arguing that state law should apply). Cf. *In re Acushnet River & New Bedford Harbor Proceedings, 675 F. Supp. 22, 33 (Mass. 1987)* (noting that, since "federal common law draws upon state law for guidance, ... the choice between state and federal [veil-piercing law] may in many cases present questions of academic interest, but little practical significance"). But cf. Note, Piercing the Corporate Law Veil: The Alter Ego Doctrine Under Federal Common Law, *95 Harv. L. Rev. 853 (1982)* (arguing that federal common law need not mirror state law, because "federal common law should look to federal statutory policy rather than to state corporate law when deciding whether to pierce the corporate veil"). Since none of the parties challenges the Sixth Circuit's holding that CPC and Aerojet incurred no derivative liability, the question is not presented in this case, and we do not address it further.

the rules of veil-piercing limit derivative liability for the actions of another corporation, CERCLA's "operator" provision is concerned primarily with direct liability for one's own actions. * * *

Under the plain language of the statute, any person who operates a polluting facility is directly liable for the costs of cleaning up the pollution. See *42 U.S.C. § 9607*(a)(2). This is so regardless of whether that person is the facility's owner, the owner's parent corporation or business partner, or even a saboteur who sneaks into the facility at night to discharge its poisons out of malice. If any such act of operating a corporate subsidiary's facility is done on behalf of a parent corporation, the existence of the parent-subsidiary relationship under state corporate law is simply irrelevant to the issue of direct liability. See *Riverside Market Dev. Corp. v. International Bldg. Prods., Inc., 931 F.2d 327, 330* (CA5) ("CERCLA prevents individuals from hiding behind the corporate shield when, as 'operators,' they themselves actually participate in the wrongful conduct prohibited by the Act") * * * *United States v. Kayser-Roth Corp., 910 F.2d 24, 26 (CA1 1990)* ("a person who is an operator of a facility is not protected from liability by the legal structure of ownership").[17]

This much is easy to say; the difficulty comes in defining actions sufficient to constitute direct parental "operation." Here of course we may again rue the uselessness of CERCLA's definition of a facility's "operator" as "any person … operating" the facility, *42 U.S.C. § 9601*(20)(A)(ii), which leaves us to do the best we can to give the term its "ordinary or natural meaning." * * * In a mechanical sense, to "operate" ordinarily means "to control the functioning of; run: *operate a sewing machine*." American Heritage Dictionary 1268 (3d ed. 1992); see also Webster's New International Dictionary 1707 (2d ed. 1958) ("to work; as, to *operate* a machine"). And in the organizational sense more obviously intended by CERCLA, the word ordinarily means "to conduct the affairs of; manage: *operate a business*." American Heritage Dictionary, *supra,* at 1268; see also Webster's New International Dictionary, *supra,* at 1707 ("to manage"). So, under CERCLA, an operator is simply someone who directs the workings of, manages, or conducts the affairs of a facility. To sharpen the definition for purposes of CERCLA's concern with environmental contamination, an operator must manage, direct, or conduct operations specifically related to pollution, that is, operations having to do with the leakage or disposal of hazardous waste, or decisions about compliance with environmental regulations.

---

17. See Oswald, Bifurcation of the Owner and Operator Analysis under CERCLA, *72 Wash. U. L. Q. 223, 257 (1994)* ("There are … instances … in which the parent has not sufficiently overstepped the bounds of corporate separateness to warrant piercing, yet is involved enough in the facility's activities that it should be held liable as an operator. Imagine, for example, a parent who strictly observed corporate formalities, avoided intertwining officers and directors, and adequately capitalized its subsidiary, yet provided active, daily supervision and control over hazardous waste disposal activities of the subsidiary. Such a parent should not escape liability just because its activities do not justify a piercing of the subsidiary's veil").

B

With this understanding, we are satisfied that the Court of Appeals correctly rejected the District Court's analysis of direct liability. But we also think that the appeals court erred in limiting direct liability under the statute to a parent's sole or joint venture operation, so as to eliminate any possible finding that CPC is liable as an operator on the facts of this case.

1

By emphasizing that "CPC is directly liable under section 107(a)(2) as an operator because CPC actively participated in and exerted significant control over Ott II's business and decision-making," *777 F. Supp. at 574*, the District Court applied the "actual control" test of whether the parent "actually operated the business of its subsidiary," *id., at 573*, as several Circuits have employed it * * *.

The well-taken objection to the actual control test, however, is its fusion of direct and indirect liability; the test is administered by asking a question about the relationship between the two corporations (an issue going to indirect liability) instead of a question about the parent's interaction with the subsidiary's facility (the source of any direct liability). If, however, direct liability for the parent's operation of the *facility* is to be kept distinct from derivative liability for the *subsidiary's own operation*, the focus of the enquiry must necessarily be different under the two tests. [emphasis supplied.] "The question is not whether the parent operates the subsidiary, but rather whether it operates the facility, and that operation is evidenced by participation in the activities of the facility, not the subsidiary. Control of the subsidiary, if extensive enough, gives rise to indirect liability under piercing doctrine, not direct liability under the statutory language." Oswald 269 * * *. The District Court was therefore mistaken to rest its analysis on CPC's relationship with Ott II, premising liability on little more than "CPC's 100-percent ownership of Ott II" and "CPC's active participation in, and at times majority control over, Ott II's board of directors." *777 F. Supp. at 575*. The analysis should instead have rested on the relationship between CPC and the Muskegon facility itself.

In addition to (and perhaps as a reflection of) the erroneous focus on the relationship between CPC and Ott II, even those findings of the District Court that might be taken to speak to the extent of CPC's activity at the facility itself are flawed, for the District Court wrongly assumed that the actions of the joint officers and directors are necessarily attributable to CPC. The District Court emphasized the facts that CPC placed its own high-level officials on Ott II's board of directors and in key management positions at Ott II, and that those individuals made major policy decisions and conducted day-to-day operations at the facility: "Although Ott II corporate officers set the day-to-day operating policies for the company without any need to obtain formal approval from CPC, CPC actively participated in this decision-making because high-ranking CPC officers served in Ott II management positions." *Id., at 559;* see also *id., at 575* (relying on "CPC's involvement in major decision-making and day-to-day operations through CPC officials who served within Ott II management, including the positions of president and chief executive officer," and on "the conduct of CPC officials with respect to Ott II affairs, particularly Arnold Ott"); *id., at 558* ("CPC actively participated in, and at times controlled, the policy-making decisions of its subsidiary thorough its representation on the Ott II board of directors"); *id., at 559* ("CPC also actively participated in and exercised control over day-to-day decision-making at Ott II through representation in the highest levels of the subsidiary's management").

In imposing direct liability on these grounds, the District Court failed to recognize that "it is entirely appropriate for directors of a parent corporation to serve as directors of its subsidiary, and that fact alone may not serve to expose the parent corporation to liability for its subsidiary's acts." *American Protein Corp. v. AB Volvo, 844 F.2d 56, 57* (CA2)* * * see also *Kingston Dry Dock Co. v. Lake Champlain Transp. Co., 31 F.2d 265, 267 (CA2 1929)* (L. Hand, J.) ("Control through the ownership of shares does not fuse the corporations, even when the directors are common to each"); Henn & Alexander 355 (noting that it is "normal" for a parent and subsidiary to "have identical directors and officers").

This recognition that the corporate personalities remain distinct has its corollary in the "well established principle [of corporate law] that directors and officers holding positions with a parent and its subsidiary can and do 'change hats' to represent the two corporations separately, despite their common ownership." *Lusk v. Foxmeyer Health Corp., 129 F.3d 773, 779 (CA5 1997)* * * * Since courts generally presume "that the directors are wearing their 'subsidiary hats' and not their 'parent hats' when acting for the subsidiary," P. Blumberg, Law of Corporate Groups: Procedural Problems in the Law of Parent and Subsidiary Corporations § 1.02.1, at 12 (1983) * * * it cannot be enough to establish liability here that dual officers and directors made policy decisions and supervised activities at the facility. The Government would have to show that, despite the general presumption to the contrary, the officers and directors were acting in their capacities as CPC officers and directors, and not as Ott II officers and directors, when they committed those acts.[18] The District Court made no such enquiry here, however, disregarding entirely this time-honored common law rule.

In sum, the District Court's focus on the relationship between parent and subsidiary (rather than parent and facility), combined with its automatic attribution of the actions of dual officers and directors to the corpo-

---

18.   We do not attempt to recite the ways in which the Government could show that dual officers or directors were in fact acting on behalf of the parent. Here, it is prudent to say only that the presumption that an act is taken on behalf of the corporation for whom the officer claims to act is strongest when the act is perfectly consistent with the norms of corporate behavior, but wanes as the distance from those accepted norms approaches the point of action by a dual officer plainly contrary to the interests of the subsidiary yet nonetheless advantageous to the parent.

rate parent, erroneously, even if unintentionally, treated CERCLA as though it displaced or fundamentally altered common law standards of limited liability. Indeed, if the evidence of common corporate personnel acting at management and directorial levels were enough to support a finding of a parent corporation's direct operator liability under CERCLA, then the possibility of resort to veil piercing to establish indirect, derivative liability for the subsidiary's violations would be academic. There would in essence be a relaxed, CERCLA-specific rule of derivative liability that would banish traditional standards and expectations from the law of CERCLA liability. But, as we have said, such a rule does not arise from congressional silence, and CERCLA's silence is dispositive.

2

We accordingly agree with the Court of Appeals that a participation-and-control test looking to the parent's supervision over the subsidiary, especially one that assumes that dual officers always act on behalf of the parent, cannot be used to identify operation of a facility resulting in direct parental liability. Nonetheless, a return to the ordinary meaning of the word "operate" in the organizational sense will indicate why we think that the Sixth Circuit stopped short when it confined its examples of direct parental operation to exclusive or joint ventures, and declined to find at least the possibility of direct operation by CPC in this case.

In our enquiry into the meaning Congress presumably had in mind when it used the verb "to operate," we recognized that the statute obviously meant something more than mere mechanical activation of pumps and valves, and must be read to contemplate "operation" as including the exercise of direction over the facility's activities. * * * The Court of Appeals recognized this by indicating that a parent can be held directly liable when the parent operates the facility in the stead of its subsidiary or alongside the subsidiary in some sort of a joint venture. * * * We anticipated a further possibility above, however, when we observed that a dual officer or director might depart so far from the norms of parental influence exercised through dual officeholding as to serve the parent, even when ostensibly acting on behalf of the subsidiary in operating the facility. See n. [18], *supra*. Yet another possibility, suggested by the facts of this case, is that an agent of the parent with no hat to wear but the parent's hat might manage or direct activities at the facility.

Identifying such an occurrence calls for line drawing yet again, since the acts of direct operation that give rise to parental liability must necessarily be distinguished from the interference that stems from the normal relationship between parent and subsidiary. Again norms of corporate behavior (undisturbed by any CERCLA provision) are crucial reference points. Just as we may look to such norms in identifying the limits of the presumption that a dual officeholder acts in his ostensible capacity, so here we may refer to them in distinguishing a parental officer's oversight of a subsidiary from such an officer's control over the operation of the subsidiary's facility. "Activities that involve the facility but which are consistent with the parent's investor status, such as monitoring of the subsidiary's performance, supervision of the subsidiary's finance and capital budget decisions, and articulation of general policies and procedures, should not give rise to direct liability." Oswald 282. The critical question is whether, in degree and detail, actions directed to the facility by an agent of the parent alone are eccentric under accepted norms of parental oversight of a subsidiary's facility.

There is, in fact, some evidence that CPC engaged in just this type and degree of activity at the Muskegon plant. The District Court's opinion speaks of an agent of CPC alone who played a conspicuous part in dealing with the toxic risks emanating from the operation of the plant. G.R.D. Williams worked only for CPC; he was not an employee, officer, or director of Ott II, see Tr. of Oral Arg. 7, and thus, his actions were of necessity taken only on behalf of CPC. The District Court found that "CPC became directly involved in environmental and regulatory matters through the work of ... Williams, CPC's governmental and environmental affairs director. Williams ... became heavily involved in environmental issues at Ott II." *777 F. Supp. at 561* He "actively participated in and exerted control over a variety of Ott II environmental matters," *ibid.*, and he "issued directives regarding Ott II's responses to regulatory inquiries," *id., at 575.*

We think that these findings are enough to raise an issue of CPC's operation of the facility through Williams's actions, though we would draw no ultimate conclusion from these findings at this point. Not only would we be deciding in the first instance an issue on which the trial and appellate courts did not focus, but the very fact that the District Court did not see the case as we do suggests that there may be still more to be known about Williams's activities. Indeed, even as the factual findings stand, the trial court offered little in the way of concrete detail for its conclusions about Williams's role in Ott II's environmental affairs, and the parties vigorously dispute the extent of Williams's involvement. Prudence thus counsels us to remand, on the theory of direct operation set out here, for reevaluation of Williams's role, and of the role of any other CPC agent who might be said to have had a part in operating the Muskegon facility. * * *

* * *

NOTES AND QUESTIONS

1. *U.S. v. Bestfoods* offers an opportunity to consider whether the rules for piercing the corporate veil should be different for federal law and state law. Should they? Note that the position of the United States Supreme court, clearly articulated in the *Bestfoods* case, is that if Congress wants to remove the traditional corporate law protection for limited liability it needs to do so in clear unequivocal language, and that courts should not otherwise place federal goals ahead of the traditional limited liability for shareholders. Do you agree with this perspective? Should there be different treatment accorded in the case of individual or corporate shareholders?

2. Most of the cases that we have considered have been those involving corporate shareholders, that is, the case of parent and subsidiary corporations. Probably there has been more scholarly writing on this topic than that of the topic of piercing the corporate veil to reach individual shareholders, and it remains true, as Professor Thompson noted in his earlier-cited empirical study, that there does not seem to be a single example of individual shareholders being held liable in a veil-piercing action concerning a large publicly-held corporation. This is not the case, however, with shareholders in small, closely-held corporations, such as those involved in the *Walkovszky v. Carlton* case, *supra*. Another excellent example of a court specifying what is required before a corporate veil can be pierced to reach an individual shareholder is Sea–Land Services, Inc. v. Pepper Source, 993 F.2d 1309 (7th Cir. 1993), where the federal court, applying Illinois law, observed that it was appropriate to fasten liability on an individual shareholder where he treated as "playthings" corporations he controlled, including manipulating and diverting funds among them so that debtor entities were left with insufficient funds to pay their creditors, and where he used corporate funds to pay his personal expenses rendering corporations in question unable to pay their monetary obligations to vendors, creditors, and federal and state tax authorities.

3. As you have already seen, there are a variety of formulations of the test for piercing the corporate veil, although all seem to involve, as the *Best-foods* Court indicates, an "abuse" of the corporate form in order to favor the controlling shareholder at the expense of creditors or the government. Put slightly differently:

> Although some courts do not require actual fraud, the language they use suggests that something close to common-law fraud is required. See, e.g., Hystro Prods. v. MPN Corp., 18 F.3d 1384, 1390 (7th Cir. 1994) (noting that the [element in addition to showing control, the] "promote injustice" test requires something less than an affirmative showing of fraud, but it requires something more than the mere prospect of an unsatisfied judgment); Sea–Land Servs., Inc. v. Pepper Source, 941 F.2d 519, 523 (7th Cir. 1991) ("Some element of unfairness, something akin to fraud or deception or the existence of a compelling public interest must be present in order to disregard the corporate fiction." (internal quotation marks omitted)); Associated Vendors, Inc. v. Oakland Meat Co., 26 Cal.Rptr. 806, 813 (Ct. App. 1963) ("While the doctrine does not depend on the presence of actual fraud, it is designed to prevent what would be fraud or injustice if accomplished. Accordingly, bad faith in one form or another is an underlying consideration and will be found ... in those cases wherein the trial court was justified in disregarding the corporate entity.").

Timothy P. Glynn, Beyond "Unlimiting" Shareholder Liability: Vicarious Tort Liability for Corporate Officers, 57 Vand. L. Rev. 329, n.84 (2004).

Just what such an "abuse" is, or what constitutes such "bad faith" is a bit elusive. Faced with the problem, some courts have sought to provide extensive laundry lists of what may constitute abuse, with a notable one appearing in Associated Vendors, Inc. v. Oakland Meat Co., 26 Cal.Rptr. at 814–815 (Ct. App. 1963):

[1]   Commingling of funds and other assets, [2] failure to segregate funds of the separate entities, and [3]the unauthorized diversion of corporate funds or assets to other than corporate uses * * * [4] the treatment by an individual of the assets of the corporation as his own * * *; [5] the failure to obtain authority to issue stock or to subscribe to or issue the same * * *; [6] the holding out by an individual that he is personally liable for the debts of the corporation * * *; [7] the failure to maintain minutes or adequate corporate records, and [8] the confusion of the records of the separate entities * * *; [9] the identical equitable ownership in the two entities; [10] the identification of the equitable owners thereof with the domination and control of the two entities; [11] identification of the directors and officers of the two entities in the responsible supervision and management; [12] sole ownership of all of the stock in a corporation by one individual or the members of a family * * *; [13] the use of the same office or business location; [14] the employment of the same employees and/or attorney * * *; [15] the failure to adequately capitalize a corporation; [16] the total absence of corporate assets and undercapitalization [17] the use of a corporation as a mere shell, instrumentality or conduit for a single venture or the business of an individual or another corporation * * *; [18] the concealment and misrepresentation of the identity of the responsible ownership, management and financial interest, or [19] concealment of personal business activities * * *; [20] the disregard of legal formalities and [21] the failure to maintain arm's length relationships among related entities * * *; [22] the use of the corporate entity to procure labor, services or merchandise for another person or entity * * *; [23] the diversion of assets from a corporation by or to a stockholder or other person or entity, to the detriment of creditors, or [24] the manipulation of assets and liabilities between entities so as to concentrate the assets in one and the liabilities in another * * * [25] the contracting with another with intent to avoid performance by use of a corporate entity as a shield against personal liability, or [26] the use of a corporation as a subterfuge of illegal transactions * * *; and [27] the formation and use of a corporation to transfer to it the existing liability of another person or entity * * *. A perusal of these cases [for which citations were omitted here] reveals that in all instances several of the factors mentioned were present. It is particularly significant that while it was held, in each instance, that the trial court was warranted in disregarding the corporate entity, the factors considered by it were not deemed to be conclusive upon the trier of fact but were found to be supported by substantial evidence.

How many of these *Associated Vendors, Inc.* factors strike you as serious instances of "abuse" of the corporate form, and how many do not? Which ones have you already encountered, and how seriously have they been treated? By now you will understand that the question of whether or not to pierce the corporate veil in any given situation is heavily dependent on the facts, on the discretion of the individual judge, or on the sympathies of particular juries (there is not even universal agreement over whether the question of piercing the corporate veil ought to be one for the judge or for the jury). Do you understand why some commentators would like to do away with the doctrine altogether and others regard "piercing the corporate veil," as "unprincipled" or capricious as lightning?

4. As you have learned, the various veil-piercing tests are designed to ensure that shareholders do not shift corporate resources to themselves in a manner that unfairly cheats creditors, although the motive for incorporation of limiting shareholder liability is always and everywhere recognized as appropriate. Limiting liability, in other words, is perfectly appropriate, but manipulating corporations to avoid liability is something else again. Similar doctrines in corporate law seek to achieve the same effect of fastening liability on those who manipulate corporations for their own advantage, including for example, *fraudulent conveyance*, where assets of an insolvent corporation are wrongly transferred to shareholders or others, see generally Robert C. Clark, The Duties of the Corporate Debtor to Its Creditors, 90 Harv. L. Rev. 505 (1977), or *equitable subordination*, where corporate debts to shareholders of insolvent corporations are to be paid only out of assets remaining after non-affiliated creditors are paid. See, e.g., Taylor v. Standard Gas & Electric Co., 306 U.S. 307, 59 S.Ct. 543, 83 L.Ed. 669 (1939).

5. We have concentrated, in our review of piercing the corporate veil, on the corporation. You should understand that, generally speaking, the same sort of analysis applies in the case of the limited liability company (LLC), when creditors seek to impose liability for LLC debts on individual members of the LLC, although, generally speaking, LLC's are not expected to adhere to the same degree of formalities as are corporations so that a lack of corporate formalities may not be as much of a risk factor for veil-piercing in the case of an LLC as it is in a corporation. See, e.g., David L. Cohen, Theories of the Corporation and the Limited Liability Company: How Should Courts and Legislatures Articulate Rules for Piercing the Veil, Fiduciary Responsibility and Securities Regulation for the Limited Liability Company?, 51 Okla. L. Rev. 427, 429 (1998), Eric Fox, Piercing the Veil of Limited Liability Companies, 62 Geo. Wash. L. Rev. 1143 (1994), and Emily A. Lackey, COMMENT: Piercing the Veil of Limited Liability in the Non-Corporate Setting, 55 Ark. L. Rev. 553 (2002).

6. In this brief Chapter we have been concerned with the problem of shareholders abusing the corporation to the detriment of third parties, including contract, tort, and governmental creditors. We return in the next chapter to our principal issue, regulating the conduct of those controlling the corporation to protect the owners of the corporation.

CHAPTER 5

STATE LAW ON FIDUCIARY DUTY OF DIRECTORS AND OFFICERS

■ ■ ■

A. NONFEASANCE

FRANCIS v. UNITED JERSEY BANK
Supreme Court of New Jersey.
87 N.J. 15, 432 A.2d 814 (1981).

[POLLOCK, J.] The primary issue on this appeal is whether a corporate director is personally liable in negligence for the failure to prevent the misappropriation of trust funds by other directors who were also officers and shareholders of the corporation.

Plaintiffs are trustees in bankruptcy of Pritchard & Baird Intermediaries Corp. (Pritchard & Baird), a reinsurance broker or intermediary. Defendant Lillian P. Overcash is the daughter of Lillian G. Pritchard and the executrix of her estate. At the time of her death, Mrs. Pritchard was a director and the largest single shareholder of Pritchard & Baird. Because Mrs. Pritchard died after the institution of suit but before trial, her executrix was substituted as a defendant. United Jersey Bank is joined as the administrator of the estate of Charles Pritchard, Sr., who had been president, director and majority shareholder of Pritchard & Baird.

This litigation focuses on payments made by Pritchard & Baird to Charles Pritchard, Jr. and William Pritchard, who were sons of Mr. and Mrs. Charles Pritchard, Sr., as well as officers, directors and shareholders of the corporation. Claims against Charles, Jr. and William are being pursued in bankruptcy proceedings against them.

The trial court, sitting without a jury, characterized the payments as fraudulent conveyances within *N.J.S.A.* 25:2–10 and entered judgment of $10,355,736.91 plus interest against the estate of Mrs. Pritchard. * * * The judgment includes damages from her negligence in permitting payments from the corporation [styled as "shareholder loans"] of $4,391,133.21 to Charles, Jr. and $5,483,799.02 to William. * * *

174

The Appellate Division affirmed, but found that the payments were a conversion of trust funds, rather than fraudulent conveyances of the assets of the corporation. * * * We granted certification limited to the issue of the liability of Lillian Pritchard as a director. * * *

* * * [T]he initial question is whether Mrs. Pritchard was negligent in not noticing and trying to prevent the misappropriation of funds held by the corporation in an implied trust. A further question is whether her negligence was the proximate cause of the plaintiffs' losses. * * *

I

The matrix for our decision is the customs and practices of the reinsurance industry and the role of Pritchard & Baird as a reinsurance broker. Reinsurance involves a contract under which one insurer agrees to indemnify another for loss sustained under the latter's policy of insurance. Insurance companies that insure against losses arising out of fire or other casualty seek at times to minimize their exposure by sharing risks with other insurance companies. Thus, when the face amount of a policy is comparatively large, the company may enlist one or more insurers to participate in that risk. Similarly, an insurance company's loss potential and overall exposure may be reduced by reinsuring a part of an entire class of policies * * *. The selling insurance company is known as a ceding company. The entity that assumes the obligation is designated as the reinsurer.

The reinsurance broker arranges the contract between the ceding company and the reinsurer. In accordance with industry custom before the Pritchard & Baird bankruptcy, the reinsurance contract or treaty did not specify the rights and duties of the broker. Typically, the ceding company communicates to the broker the details concerning the risk. The broker negotiates the sale of portions of the risk to the reinsurers. In most instances, the ceding company and the reinsurer do not communicate with each other, but rely upon the reinsurance broker. The ceding company pays premiums due a reinsurer to the broker, who deducts his commission and transmits the balance to the appropriate reinsurer. When a loss occurs, a reinsurer pays money due a ceding company to the broker, who then transmits it to the ceding company.

The reinsurance business was described by an expert at trial as having "a magic aura around it of dignity and quality and integrity." A telephone call which might be confirmed by a handwritten memorandum is sufficient to create a reinsurance obligation. Though separate bank accounts are not maintained for each treaty, the industry practice is to segregate the insurance funds from the broker's general accounts. * * *

* * * The proofs supporting the judgment relate only to one corporation, Pritchard & Baird Intermediaries Corp. (Pritchard & Baird) * * *. [From] June 1964 * * * the corporation operated as a close family corporation with Mr. and Mrs. Pritchard and their two sons [Charles, Jr. and

William] as the only directors. After the death of Charles, Sr. in 1973, only the remaining three directors continued to operate as the board. Lillian Pritchard inherited 72 of her husband's 120 shares in Pritchard & Baird, thereby becoming the largest shareholder in the corporation with 48% of the stock.

The corporate minute books reflect only perfunctory activities by the directors, related almost exclusively to the election of officers and adoption of banking resolutions and a retirement plan. None of the minutes for any of the meetings contain a discussion of the loans to Charles, Jr. and William or of the financial condition of the corporation. Moreover, upon instructions of Charles, Jr. that financial statements were not to be circulated to anyone else, the company's statements for the fiscal years beginning February 1, 1970, were delivered only to him.

Charles Pritchard, Sr. was the chief executive and controlled the business [from 1964 to 1966]. Beginning in 1966, he gradually relinquished control over the operations of the corporation. In 1968, Charles, Jr. became president and William became executive vice president. Charles, Sr. apparently became ill in 1971 and during the last year and a half of his life was not involved in the affairs of the business. He continued, however, to serve as a director until his death on December 10, 1973. Notwithstanding the presence of Charles, Sr. on the board until his death in 1973, Charles, Jr. dominated the management of the corporation and the board from 1968 until the bankruptcy in 1975.

Contrary to the industry custom of segregating funds, Pritchard & Baird commingled the funds of reinsurers and ceding companies with its own funds. All monies (including commissions, premiums and loss monies) were deposited in a single account. Charles, Sr. began the practice of withdrawing funds from the commingled account in transactions identified on the corporate books as "loans." As long as Charles, Sr. controlled the corporation, the "loans" correlated with corporate profits and were repaid at the end of each year. Starting in 1970, however, Charles, Jr. and William begin to siphon ever-increasing sums from the corporation under the guise of loans. As of January 31, 1970, the "loans" to Charles, Jr. were $230,932 and to William were $207,329. At least by January 31, 1973, the annual increase in the loans exceeded annual corporate revenues. By October 1975, the year of bankruptcy, the "shareholders' loans" had metastasized to a total of $12,333,514.47.

The trial court rejected the characterization of the payments as "loans." * * * No corporate resolution authorized the "loans," and no note or other instrument evidenced the debt. Charles, Jr. and William paid no interest on the amounts received. The "loans" were not repaid or reduced from one year to the next; rather, they increased annually.

The designation of "shareholders' loans" on the balance sheet was an entry to account for the distribution of the premium and loss money to Charles, Sr., Charles, Jr. and William. As the trial court found, the entry was part of a "woefully inadequate and highly dangerous bookkeeping system." * * *.

The "loans" to Charles, Jr. and William far exceeded their salaries and financial resources. If the payments to Charles, Jr. and William had been treated as dividends or compensation, then the balance sheets would have shown an excess of liabilities over assets. If the "loans" had been eliminated, the balance sheets would have depicted a corporation not only with a working capital deficit, but also with assets having a fair market value less than its liabilities. The balance sheets for 1970–1975, however, showed an excess of assets over liabilities. This result was achieved by designating the misappropriated funds as "shareholders' loans" and listing them as assets offsetting the deficits. Although the withdrawal of the funds resulted in an obligation of repayment to Pritchard & Baird, the more significant consideration is that the "loans" represented a massive misappropriation of money belonging to the clients of the corporation.

The "loans" were reflected on financial statements that were prepared annually as of January 31, the end of the corporate fiscal year. Although an outside certified public accountant prepared the 1970 financial statement, the corporation prepared only internal financial statements from 1971–1975. In all instances, the statements were simple documents, consisting of three or four 8 1/2 X 11 inch sheets.

[The] financial statements showed working capital deficits increasing annually in tandem with the amounts that Charles, Jr. and William withdrew as "shareholders' loans." In the last complete year of business (January 31, 1974, to January 31, 1975), "shareholders' loans" and the correlative working capital deficit increased by approximately $3,200,000.

The funding of the "loans" left the corporation with insufficient money to operate. Pritchard & Baird could defer payment on accounts payable because its clients allowed a grace period, generally 30 to 90 days, before the payment was due. During this period, Pritchard & Baird used the funds entrusted to it as a "float" to pay current accounts payable. By recourse to the funds of its clients, Pritchard & Baird not only paid its trade debts, but also funded the payments to Charles, Jr. and William. Thus, Pritchard & Baird was able to meet its obligations as they came due only through the use of clients' funds.

The pattern that emerges * * * is the substantial increase in the monies appropriated by Charles Pritchard, Jr. and William Pritchard after their father's withdrawal from the business and the sharp decline in the profitability of the operation after his death. This led ultimately to the filing in December, 1975, of an involuntary petition in bankruptcy and the appointments of the plaintiffs as trustees in bankruptcy of Pritchard & Baird.

Mrs. Pritchard was not active in the business of Pritchard & Baird and knew virtually nothing of its corporate affairs. She briefly visited the corporate offices in Morristown on only one occasion, and she never read or obtained the annual financial statements. She was unfamiliar with the rudiments of reinsurance and made no effort to assure that the policies and practices of the corporation, particularly pertaining to the withdrawal of funds, complied with industry custom or relevant law. Although her husband had warned her that Charles, Jr. would "take the shirt off my back," Mrs. Pritchard did not pay any attention to her duties as a director or to the affairs of the corporation. * * *

After her husband died in December 1973, Mrs. Pritchard became incapacitated and was bedridden for a six-month period. She became listless at this time and started to drink rather heavily. Her physical condition deteriorated, and in 1978 she died. The trial court rejected testimony seeking to exonerate her because she "was old, was grief-stricken at the loss of her husband, sometimes consumed too much alcohol and was psychologically overborne by her sons." * * * That court found that she was competent to act and that the reason Mrs. Pritchard never knew what her sons "were doing was because she never made the slightest effort to discharge any of her responsibilities as a director of Pritchard & Baird." * * *

II

* * * Although many of the creditors are located outside the state, all had contacts with Pritchard & Baird in New Jersey. Consequently, the trial court applied New Jersey law. * * * The parties agree that New Jersey law should apply. We are in accord.

III

Individual liability of a corporate director for acts of the corporation is a prickly problem. Generally directors are accorded broad immunity and are not insurers of corporate activities. The problem is particularly nettlesome when a third party asserts that a director, because of nonfeasance, is liable for losses caused by acts of insiders, who in this case were officers, directors and shareholders. Determination of the liability of Mrs. Pritchard requires findings that she had a duty to the clients of Pritchard & Baird, that she breached that duty and that her breach was a proximate cause of their losses.

The New Jersey Business Corporation Act, which took effect on January 1, 1969, was a comprehensive revision of the statutes relating to business corporations. One section, *N.J.S.A. 14A:6–14*, concerning a director's general obligation had no counterpart in the old Act. That section makes it incumbent upon directors to discharge their duties in good faith and with that degree of diligence, care and skill which ordinarily prudent men would exercise under similar circumstances in like positions. [*N.J.S.A. 14A:6–14*]

This provision was based primarily on section 43 of the Model Business Corporation Act and is derived also from section 717 of the New York

Business Corporation Law * * * Before the enactment of *N.J.S.A. 14A:6–14*, there was no express statutory authority requiring directors to act as ordinarily prudent persons under similar circumstances in like positions. Nonetheless, the requirement had been expressed in New Jersey judicial decisions.

A leading New Jersey opinion is *Campbell v. Watson, 62 N.J.Eq. 396 (Ch.1901),* which, like many early decisions on director liability, involved directors of a bank that had become insolvent. A receiver of the bank charged the directors with negligence that allegedly led to insolvency. In the opinion, Vice Chancellor Pitney explained that bank depositors have a right to rely upon the character of the directors and officers [and upon the representation] that they will perform their sworn duty to manage the affairs of the bank according to law and devote to its affairs the same diligent attention which ordinary, prudent, diligent men pay to their own affairs; and … such diligence and attention as experience has shown it is proper and necessary that bank directors should give to that business in order to reasonably protect the bank and its creditors against loss. [*Id. at 406]*

Because *N.J.S.A. 14A:6–14* is modeled in part upon section 717 of the New York statute, *N.Y.Bus.Corp. Law § 717* (McKinney), we consider also the law of New York in interpreting the New Jersey statute. * * *

Prior to the enactment of section 717, the New York courts, like those of New Jersey, had espoused the principle that directors owed that degree of care that a businessman of ordinary prudence would exercise in the management of his own affairs. * * * In addition to requiring that directors act honestly and in good faith, the New York courts recognized that the nature and extent of reasonable care depended upon the type of corporation, its size and financial resources. Thus, a bank director was held to stricter accountability than the director of an ordinary business. * * *

In determining the limits of a director's duty, section 717 continued to recognize the individual characteristics of the corporation involved as well as the particular circumstances and corporate role of the director. * * *

This approach was consonant with the desire to formulate a standard that could be applied to both publicly and closely held entities. * * *

Underlying the pronouncements in section 717, *Campbell v. Watson, supra,* and *N.J.S.A. 14A:6–14* is the principle that directors must discharge their duties in good faith and act as ordinarily prudent persons would under similar circumstances in like positions. Although specific duties in a given case can be determined only after consideration of all of the circumstances, the standard of ordinary care is the wellspring from which those more specific duties flow.

As a general rule, a director should acquire at least a rudimentary understanding of the business of the corporation. Accordingly, a director should become familiar with the fundamentals of the business in which the corporation is engaged. * * * Because directors are bound to exercise ordinary care, they cannot set up as a defense lack of the knowledge needed to exercise the requisite degree of care. If one "feels that he has not had sufficient business experience to qualify him to perform the duties of a director, he should either acquire the knowledge by inquiry, or refuse to act." * * *

Directors are under a continuing obligation to keep informed about the activities of the corporation. Otherwise, they may not be able to participate in the overall management of corporate affairs. * * * Directors may not shut their eyes to corporate misconduct and then claim that because they did not see the misconduct, they did not have a duty to look. The sentinel asleep at his post contributes nothing to the enterprise he is charged to protect. * * *

Directorial management does not require a detailed inspection of day-to-day activities, but rather a general monitoring of corporate affairs and policies. * * * Accordingly, a director is well advised to attend board meetings regularly. Indeed, a director who is absent from a board meeting is presumed to concur in action taken on a corporate matter, unless he files a "dissent with the secretary of the corporation within a reasonable time after learning of such action." *N.J.S.A. 14A:6–13* (Supp.1981–1982). Regular attendance does not mean that directors must attend every meeting, but that directors should attend meetings as a matter of practice. A director of a publicly held corporation might be expected to attend regular monthly meetings, but a director of a small, family corporation might be asked to attend only an annual meeting. The point is that one of the responsibilities of a director is to attend meetings of the board of which he or she is a member. That burden is lightened by *N.J.S.A.* 14A:6–7(2) (Supp.1981–1982), which permits board action without a meeting if all members of the board consent in writing.

While directors are not required to audit corporate books, they should maintain familiarity with the financial status of the corporation by a regular review of financial statements. * * * In some circumstances, directors may be charged with assuring that bookkeeping methods conform to industry custom and usage. * * * The extent of review, as well as the nature and frequency of financial statements, depends not only on the customs of the industry, but also on the nature of the corporation and the business in which it is engaged. Financial statements of some small corporations may be prepared internally and only on an annual basis; in a large publicly held corporation, the statements may be produced monthly or at some other regular interval. Adequate financial review normally would be more informal in a private corporation than in a publicly held corporation.

Of some relevance in this case is the circumstance that the financial records disclose the "shareholders' loans". Generally directors are immune from liability if, in good faith, they rely upon the opinion of counsel for the corporation or upon written reports setting forth financial data concerning the corporation and prepared by an independent public accountant or certified public accountant or firm of such accountants or upon financial statements, books of account or reports of the corporation represented to them to be correct by the president, the officer of the corporation having charge of its books of account, or the person presiding at a meeting of the board. [*N.J.S.A. 14A:6–14*]

The review of financial statements, however, may give rise to a duty to inquire further into matters revealed by those statements. * * * Upon discovery of an illegal course of action, a director has a duty to object and, if the corporation does not correct the conduct, to resign. * * *

In certain circumstances, the fulfillment of the duty of a director may call for more than mere objection and resignation. Sometimes a director may be required to seek the advice of counsel. * * * One New Jersey case recognized the duty of a bank director to seek counsel where doubt existed about the meaning of the bank charter. *Williams v. McKay, supra, 46 N.J.Eq. at 60.* The duty to seek the assistance of counsel can extend to areas other than the interpretation of corporation instruments. Modern corporate practice recognizes that on occasion a director should seek outside advice. A director may require legal advice concerning the propriety of his or her own conduct, the conduct of other officers and directors or the conduct of the corporation. * * * Sometimes the duty of a director may require more than consulting with outside counsel. A director may have a duty to take reasonable means to prevent illegal conduct by co-directors; in an appropriate case, this may include threat of suit. * * *.

A director is not an ornament, but an essential component of corporate governance. Consequently, a director cannot protect himself behind a paper shield bearing the motto, "dummy director." * * * The New Jersey Business Corporation Act, in imposing a standard of ordinary care on all directors, confirms that dummy, figurehead and accommodation directors are anachronisms with no place in New Jersey law. Similarly, in interpreting section 717, the New York courts have not exonerated a director who acts as an "accommodation." *Barr v. Wackman, 36 N.Y.2d 371, 381, 329 N.E.2d 180, 188, 368 N.Y.S.2d 497, 507 (Ct.App.1975)* (director "does not exempt himself from liability by failing to do more than passively rubberstamp the decisions of the active managers"). *See Kavanaugh v. Gould, 223 N.Y. at 111–117, 119 N.E. at 240–241* (the fact that bank director never attended board meetings or acquainted himself with bank's business or methods held to be no defense, as a matter of law, to responsibility for speculative loans made by the president and acquiesced in by other directors). Thus, all directors are responsible for managing the business and affairs of the corporation. * * *

* * *

A director's duty of care does not exist in the abstract, but must be considered in relation to specific obligees. In general, the relationship of a corporate director to the corporation and its stockholders is that of a fiduciary. * * * Shareholders have a right to expect that directors will exercise reasonable supervision and control over the policies and practices of a corporation. The institutional integrity of a corporation depends upon the proper discharge by directors of those duties.

While directors may owe a fiduciary duty to creditors also, that obligation generally has not been recognized in the absence of insolvency. * * * With certain corporations, however, directors are deemed to owe a duty to creditors and other third parties even when the corporation is solvent. Although depositors of a bank are considered in some respects to be creditors, courts have recognized that directors may owe them a fiduciary duty. * * * Directors of nonbanking corporations may owe a similar duty when the corporation holds funds of others in trust. * * *

In three cases originating in New Jersey, directors who did not participate actively in the conversion of trust funds were found not liable. In each instance, the facts did not support the conclusion that the director knew or could have known of the wrongdoing even if properly attentive. * * * To the extent that the cases support the proposition that directors are not liable unless they actively participate in the conversion of trust funds, they are disapproved.

Courts in other states have imposed liability on directors of nonbanking corporations for the conversion of trust funds, even though those directors did not participate in or know of the conversion. *Preston-Thomas Constr. Inc. v. Central Leasing Corp., 518 P.2d 1125 (Okl.Ct.App.1973)* (director liable for conversion of funds entrusted to corporation for acquisition of stock in another corporation); *Vujacich v. Southern Commercial Co., 21 Cal.App. 439, 132 P. 80 (Dist.Ct.App.1913)* (director of wholesale grocery business personally liable for conversion by corporation of worker's funds deposited for safekeeping). The distinguishing circumstances in regard to banks and other corporations holding trust funds is that the depositor or beneficiary can reasonably expect the director to act with ordinary prudence concerning the funds held in a fiduciary capacity. Thus, recognition of a duty of a director to those for whom a corporation holds funds in trust may be viewed as another application of the general rule that a director's duty is that of an ordinary prudent person under the circumstances.

The most striking circumstances affecting Mrs. Pritchard's duty as a director are the character of the reinsurance industry, the nature of the misappropriated funds and the financial condition of Pritchard & Baird. The hallmark of the reinsurance industry has been the unqualified trust and confidence reposed by ceding companies and reinsurers in reinsurance brokers. Those companies entrust money to reinsurance intermediaries with the justifiable expectation that the funds will be transmitted to the appropriate parties. Consequently, the companies could have assumed rightfully that Mrs. Pritchard, as a director of a reinsurance brokerage corporation, would not sanction the commingling and the conversion of loss and premium funds for the personal use of the principals of Pritchard & Baird.

As a reinsurance broker, Pritchard & Baird received annually as a fiduciary millions of dollars of clients' money which it was under a duty to segregate.[1] To this extent, it resembled a bank rather than a small family business. Accordingly, Mrs. Pritchard's relationship to the clientele of Pritchard & Baird was akin to that of a director of a bank to its depositors. All parties agree that Pritchard & Baird held the misappropriated funds in an implied trust. That trust relationship gave rise to a fiduciary duty to guard the funds with fidelity and good faith. * * *

As a director of a substantial reinsurance brokerage corporation, she should have known that it received annually millions of dollars of loss and premium funds which it held in trust for ceding and reinsurance companies. Mrs. Pritchard should have obtained and read the annual statements of financial condition of Pritchard & Baird. Although she had a right to rely upon financial statements prepared in accordance with *N.J.S.A. 14A:6–14*, such reliance would not excuse her conduct. The reason is that those statements disclosed on their face the misappropriation of trust funds.

From those statements, she should have realized that, as of January 31, 1970, her sons were withdrawing substantial trust funds under the guise of "Shareholders' Loans." The financial statements for each fiscal year commencing with that of January 31, 1970, disclosed that the working capital deficits and the "loans" were escalating in tandem. Detecting a misappropriation of funds would not have required special expertise or extraordinary diligence; a cursory reading of the financial statements would have revealed the pillage. Thus, if Mrs. Pritchard had read the financial statements, she would have known that her sons were converting trust funds. When financial statements demonstrate that insiders are bleeding a corporation to death, a director should notice and try to stanch the flow of blood.

In summary, Mrs. Pritchard was charged with the obligation of basic knowledge and supervision of the business of Pritchard & Baird. Under the circumstances, this obligation included reading and understanding financial statements, and making reasonable attempts at detection and prevention of the illegal conduct of other officers and directors. She had a duty to protect the clients of Pritchard & Baird against policies and practices that would result in the misappropriation of money they had entrusted to the corporation. She breached that duty.

IV

Nonetheless, the negligence of Mrs. Pritchard does not result in liability unless it is a proximate cause of the loss. *Kulas v. Public Serv. Elec. and Gas Co., 41 N.J. 311, 317 (1964).* Analysis of proximate cause requires

---

1. Following the Pritchard & Baird bankruptcy, New York, a reinsurance center, adopted legislation regulating reinsurance intermediaries. One statute codified the industry standard by prohibiting reinsurance intermediaries from commingling their funds with funds of their principals. *N.Y. Ins. Law* § 122–a(9) (McKinney Supp. 1980–1981).

an initial determination of cause-in-fact. Causation-in-fact calls for a finding that the defendant's act or omission was a necessary antecedent of the loss, *i.e.*, that if the defendant had observed his or her duty of care, the loss would not have occurred. * * * Further, the plaintiff has the burden of establishing the amount of the loss or damages caused by the negligence of the defendant. * * * Thus, the plaintiff must establish not only a breach of duty, "but in addition that the performance by the director of his duty would have avoided loss, and the amount of the resulting loss." * * *

Cases involving nonfeasance present a much more difficult causation question than those in which the director has committed an affirmative act of negligence leading to the loss. Analysis in cases of negligent omissions calls for determination of the reasonable steps a director should have taken and whether that course of action would have averted the loss.

Usually a director can absolve himself from liability by informing the other directors of the impropriety and voting for a proper course of action. * * * Conversely, a director who votes for or concurs in certain actions may be "liable to the corporation for the benefit of its creditors or shareholders, to the extent of any injuries suffered by such persons, respectively, as a result of any such action." *N.J.S.A. 14A:6–12* (Supp.1981– 1982). A director who is present at a board meeting is presumed to concur in corporate action taken at the meeting unless his dissent is entered in the minutes of the meeting or filed promptly after adjournment. *N.J.S.A. 14A:6–13*. In many, if not most, instances an objecting director whose dissent is noted in accordance with *N.J.S.A. 14A:6–13* would be absolved after attempting to persuade fellow directors to follow a different course of action. * * *

Even accepting the hypothesis that Mrs. Pritchard might not be liable if she had objected and resigned, there are two significant reasons for holding her liable. First, she did not resign until just before the bankruptcy. Consequently, there is no factual basis for the speculation that the losses would have occurred even if she had objected and resigned. Indeed, the trial court reached the opposite conclusion: "The actions of the sons were so blatantly wrongful that it is hard to see how they could have resisted any moderately firm objection to what they were doing." * * * Second, the nature of the reinsurance business distinguishes it from most other commercial activities in that reinsurance brokers are encumbered by fiduciary duties owed to third parties. In other corporations, a director's duty normally does not extend beyond the shareholders to third parties.

In this case, the scope of Mrs. Pritchard's duties was determined by the precarious financial condition of Pritchard & Baird, its fiduciary relationship to its clients and the implied trust in which it held their funds. Thus viewed, the scope of her duties encompassed all reasonable action to stop the continuing conversion. Her duties extended beyond mere objection and resignation to reasonable attempts to prevent the misappropriation of the trust funds. * * *

A leading case discussing causation where the director's liability is predicated upon a negligent failure to act is *Barnes v. Andrews, 298 F. 614 (S.D.N.Y.1924)*. In that case the court exonerated a figurehead director who served for eight months on a board that held one meeting after his election, a meeting he was forced to miss because of the death of his mother. Writing for the court, Judge Learned Hand distinguished a director who fails to prevent general mismanagement from one such as Mrs. Pritchard who failed to stop an illegal "loan":

> When the corporate funds have been illegally lent, it is a fair inference that a protest would have stopped the loan, and that the director's neglect caused the loss. But when a business fails from general mismanagement, business incapacity, or bad judgment, how is it possible to say that a single director could have made the company successful, or how much in dollars he could have saved? [*Id. at 616–617*]

* * *

Other courts have refused to impose personal liability on negligent directors when the plaintiffs have been unable to prove that diligent execution of the directors' duties would have precluded the losses. [See, e.g.] *Briggs v. Spaulding, 141 U.S. 132, 11 S.Ct. 924, 35 L.Ed. 662 (1891)* (no causal relationship because discovery of defalcations could have resulted only from examination of books beyond duty of director); * * * *Sternberg v. Blaine, 179 Ark. 448, 17 S.W.2d 286 (Sup.Ct.1929)* ("[n]o ordinary examination usually made by directors of a country bank, however careful, would have discovered" misappropriations); * * * *Allied Freightways, Inc. v. Cholfin, 325 Mass. 630, 91 N.E.2d 765 (Sup.Jud.Ct.1950)* (director not liable where losses resulted from general mismanagement and director, in the reasonable exercise of her duties, could not have discovered illegal payments from examination of corporate books) * * *.

Other courts have held directors liable for losses actively perpetrated by others because the negligent omissions of the directors were considered a necessary antecedent to the defalcations. [See, e.g.] *Ringeon v. Albinson, 35 F.2d 753 (D.Minn.1929)* (negligent director not excused from liability for losses that could have been prevented by supervision and prompt action); *Heit v. Bixby, 276 F.Supp. 217, 231 (E.D.Mo.1967)* (directors liable for 40% commissions taken by co-directors because directors' "lackadaisical attitude" proximately caused the loss); *Ford v. Taylor, 176 Ark. 843, 4 S.W.2d 938 (1928)* (bank directors liable for losses due to misappropriations of cashier who "felt free to pursue [misconduct] without fear of detection by the directors through their failure to discharge the functions of their office"); * * * *Neese v. Brown, 218 Tenn. 686, 405 S.W.2d 577 (Sup.Ct.1964)* (directors who abdicate control liable for losses caused by breach of trust by those left in control if due care on part of inactive directors could have avoided loss).

In assessing whether Mrs. Pritchard's conduct was a legal or proximate cause of the conversion, "[l]egal responsibility must be limited to those causes which are so closely connected with the result and of such significance that the law is justified in imposing liability." *Prosser on Torts*, § 41 at 237. Such a judicial determination involves not only considerations of causation-in-fact and matters of policy, but also common sense and logic. * * * The act or the failure to act must be a substantial factor in producing the harm. *Prosser, supra*, § 41 at 240 * * *.

Within Pritchard & Baird, several factors contributed to the loss of the funds: commingling of corporate and client monies, conversion of funds by Charles, Jr. and William and dereliction of her duties by Mrs. Pritchard. The wrongdoing of her sons, although the immediate cause of the loss, should not excuse Mrs. Pritchard from her negligence which also was a substantial factor contributing to the loss. * * * Her sons knew that she, the only other director, was not reviewing their conduct; they spawned their fraud in the backwater of her neglect. Her neglect of duty contributed to the climate of corruption; her failure to act contributed to the continuation of that corruption. Consequently, her conduct was a substantial factor contributing to the loss.

Analysis of proximate cause is especially difficult in a corporate context where the allegation is that nonfeasance of a director is a proximate cause of damage to a third party. Where a case involves nonfeasance, no one can say "with absolute certainty what would have occurred if the defendant had acted otherwise." *Prosser, supra*, § 41 at 242. Nonetheless, where it is reasonable to conclude that the failure to act would produce a particular result and that result has followed, causation may be inferred. *Ibid.* We conclude that even if Mrs. Pritchard's mere objection had not stopped the depredations of her sons, her consultation with an attorney and the threat of suit would have deterred them. That conclusion flows as a matter of common sense and logic from the record. Whether in other situations a director has a duty to do more than protest and resign is best left to case-by-case determinations. In this case, we are satisfied that there was a duty to do more than object and resign. Consequently, we find that Mrs. Pritchard's negligence was a proximate cause of the misappropriations.

To conclude, by virtue of her office, Mrs. Pritchard had the power to prevent the losses sustained by the clients of Pritchard & Baird. With power comes responsibility. She had a duty to deter the depredation of the other insiders, her sons. She breached that duty and caused plaintiffs to sustain damages.

* * *

B.   THE BUSINESS JUDGMENT RULE

NURSING HOME BUILDING CORPORATION v. DEHART

Court of Appeals of Washington, Division One.
13 Wn. App. 489, 535 P.2d 137 (1975).

[SWANSON, J.] Nursing Home Building Corporation, doing business as Arden Nursing Home (hereinafter referred to as "the corporation"), appeals from a judgment which awarded it only $9,914.85 of its $121,865 claim based upon alleged fraudulent misappropriation of corporate funds by Richard L. and Phoebe DeHart, the former sole shareholders of the corporation. * * *

The factual context in which this appeal arose is as follows: Two Seattle doctors, Dr. H. P. Clausing and Dr. G. E. Deer, were the sole owners of the corporation which in turn owned and operated the Arden Nursing Home located on Aurora Avenue in the city of Seattle. On January 20, 1970, the two doctors sold all of the outstanding stock (3,000 shares) of the corporation to the DeHarts on an installment contract for $700,000. The DeHarts made an initial down payment of $80,000 from their own resources and made subsequent payments on the stock purchase contract by checks totaling $34,089.64 drawn on the corporation checking account. In addition, as required by the terms of the stock purchase agreement, they transferred to Clausing and Deer a $29,099 account receivable asset of the corporation known as the "Southside Receivable." The payments from the corporate bank account and the transfer of the account receivable to Clausing and Deer were reflected in a loan account known as "Owner's Receivable." This account had a $45,563.45 loan balance due the corporation when the DeHarts were dispossessed of the nursing home in May 1971.

During the 15–month period of the DeHarts' management of the corporation, it had serious cash flow problems so that by March 1971, the corporation was unable to pay its creditors and keep current the payments on the building mortgage due the Bank of California as required by the sales contract. The DeHarts' breach of the mortgage obligation resulted in an action by Clausing and Deer to forfeit [that is, nullify] the stock purchase contract. * * *

On August 6, 1971, Robert Thompson, who was named receiver [by the court] to manage the nursing home and to maintain the forfeiture action, sued the DeHarts to recover $121,865 in corporate funds he alleged were "fraudulently misappropriated" and diverted to the DeHarts' personal use and benefit. At the outset of this litigation, the receiver obtained a writ of attachment * * * to secure his claimed creditor's lien on the DeHarts' real estate. * * * The receiver Thompson was discharged prior to the trial of this action but the corporation, which was once again owned by the original owners Clausing and Deer, remained as a party plaintiff. After a trial to the court in which the DeHarts conceded an obligation to reimburse the corporation for $9,914.85 of corporate funds used for personal purposes unrelated to any corporate benefit, judgment was entered in that amount, but the court denied the corporation's claim for additional funds allegedly "fraudulently misappropriated" as is reflected in the following conclusions of law:

> The business expenses, salary, fringe benefits and reimbursed expenses were reasonable and proper exercises of business judgment by the DeHarts except as set forth in Finding of Fact VII. [Finding of fact No. 7 contains the $9,914.85 item upon which judgment was rendered.]

Conclusion of law No. 2.

> The payments to Drs. Clausing and Deer were authorized by all shareholders and, in addition, Drs. Clausing, Deer and the corporation ratified and accepted the payments. The corporation is not entitled to recover these payments from the DeHarts.

Conclusion of law No. 3.

> The transfer of the Southside Receivable was pursuant to a contract which the corporation approved when Drs. Clausing and Deer controlled the corporation. In addition, the transfer was approved by the sole shareholders of the corporation at the time the transfer took place and was ratified and accepted by the present shareholders, Drs. Clausing and Deer. The corporation is not entitled to recover the value of the [Southside Receivable] from the DeHarts.

Conclusion of law No. 4.

On appeal, the corporation contends the trial court erred in failing to enter judgment for $92,996.61 in additional funds which it contends were misappropriated by the DeHarts. The corporation assigns error to the quoted conclusions of law and to these findings of fact:

> All other disbursements presented to the Court were proper business expenses.

Finding of fact No. 12.

> The funds which would have been used for taxes were applied to other business expenses, such as staff salaries and trade accounts necessary to keep the nursing home open and provide patient care.

Finding of fact No. 14, in part. The corporation's assignments of error focus primarily upon three categories of alleged misappropriation of funds: (1) Loans by the corporation to the DeHarts as reflected by the $45,563.45 balance shown in the Owner's Receivable; (2) corporate funds totaling $21,000 used in the management of the corporation; and (3) corporate funds totaling $26,433.16 which the corporation claims should have been used by the DeHarts to pay federal taxes.

In considering the first category, we note that the $45,563.45 loan balance item primarily consists of two items, (1) the corporate funds used to make the installment payments to Clausing and Deer on the stock purchase contract, and (2) the transfer to Clausing and Deer pursuant to the stock purchase contract of the Southside Receivable. The corporation asserts that such payments from corporate funds or by transfer of corporate assets amounts to money borrowed from the corporation for a personal obligation which must be repaid. As to the first item, the court found in an unchallenged finding that the obligation to make the installment payments was the personal obligation of the DeHarts but also found that

> [i]t was understood by all parties at the time the contract was signed that payments would probably come from the earnings of the business distributed to DeHarts if possible.

Finding of fact No. 9, in part. In addition, the court entered the following significant findings to which no error is assigned:

> Payments were made to Drs. Clausing and Deer by checks dated April 16, 1970, of $5,000.00 each, drawn on the account of Arden Nursing Home at The Bank of California; and checks dated January 20, 1971, of $7,500.00 each, February 8, 1971, of $2,272.41 each, and March 3, 1971, of $4,544.82 total, all drawn on the account of Nursing Home Building Corporation, d/b/a Arden Nursing Home at Pacific National Bank, Everett Banking Center. Drs. Clausing and Deer received and cashed all such checks. On March 30, 1971, Dr. Clausing wrote [the] DeHarts formally demanding that all future payments be paid by [the] DeHarts from their personal funds.

Finding of fact No. 10.

> All existing shareholders of the corporation, being the DeHarts, approved and ratified the payment of the above amounts to Drs. Clausing and Deer from corporate funds.

Finding of fact No. 11. The trial court concluded that because all shareholders of the corporation approved the payments and Clausing and Deer ratified and accepted them, there can be no recovery by the corporation. We agree.

The corporation argues that the receipt by Clausing and Deer of these payments could not operate as an estoppel against it because they had no control over it but were merely creditors of the DeHarts with a pledgee's interest in the corporate stock. * * * Thus, it is the corporation's theory of recovery that despite the facts that the DeHarts were the sole owners of the corporation when the payments were made and that Clausing and Deer, the recipients of the funds, had regained sole ownership of the corporation at the time of trial, the corporation's identity remained separate and apart from that of the individual stockholders and therefore it could recover the payments from the DeHarts through its right to an accounting and repayment of loans. In support of this argument, the corporation cites the following rule governing the conduct of corporate officers:

As a general rule, the corporate officers or agents have no right or authority to use, divert, or appropriate corporate funds or property for their own individual interests or purposes, and they are responsible for the wrongful use or diversion of the corporate property and are accountable for any profits made thereby. Thus, it is generally held that a corporate officer has no authority to use corporate funds for payment of his own debts....

(Footnotes omitted.) *19 Am. Jur. 2d Corporations § 1235* (1965).

Further, the corporation contends that ownership by a borrower of all the shares of stock in a corporation does not prevent the corporation from recovering the balance due on a loan to the corporation. * * *

Although it cannot be doubted that a corporation's separate legal identity is not lost merely because all of its stock is held by the members of a single family or by one person and thus the fact of sole ownership does not *of itself* immunize a sole shareholder from liability to the corporation, it is just as firmly established that the corporate entity will be disregarded when justice so requires. * * *

Here, as previously noted, the trial court found that all parties understood at the time the contract for the purchase of stock was signed that the payments probably would come from the earnings of the business distributed to the DeHarts. * * * Moreover, it is undisputed that at the time the contract was executed Clausing and Deer were the sole owners of the corporate stock. It is also unchallenged that after execution of the contract the payments from corporate funds were approved and ratified by all of the shareholders of the corporation, namely, the DeHarts. We are of the opinion that to permit the corporation to recover the amount of such payments from the DeHarts on the theory of misappropriation of corporate funds would be to require us to close our eyes to the realities of the situation. An award in favor of the corporation in the amount of the corporate funds previously paid to Clausing and Deer, who are now the present owners of the corporation, would amount to a double recovery. A corporation's separate identity cannot be preserved at the expense of fostering an obvious injustice; however, in this case, it is not necessary to disregard the corporate entity in order to uphold the trial court because the record reveals that the trial court's findings are supported by substantial evidence.

The court below properly found that the disbursements of corporate assets to Clausing and Deer were ratified by all of the shareholders and therefore the challenged transactions are governed by the general rule that limitations on corporate action can be waived by informed and unanimous consent by corporate shareholders. * * * As is stated in W. Fletcher [Private Corporations] § 1104 at page 725 [(perm. ed. 1974) (hereinafter cited as "W. Fletcher")]:

If all the stockholders of a corporation consent, and it is not detrimental to creditors, officers may appropriate corporate assets. It follows that if there are no stockholders except the directors and officers, the latter may, of course, by unanimous consent, give away corporate property, where the rights of creditors are not impaired.

(Footnotes omitted.) * * * In the case at bar, there is no showing or claim that the rights of any creditors of the corporation were impaired. * * * Clausing and Deer, who make no argument that the corporation's identity ought to be disregarded were only creditors of the DeHarts individually and not of the corporation. The rule governing the management of solely-owned corporations which we apply here is stated as follows in W. Fletcher at page 724:

> If an officer is the owner of all the stock of a corporation, it seems that he may use the corporate assets as he sees fit, and there can be no misappropriation of corporate assets by him; but if there is even one share of stock outstanding he cannot use the corporate assets to pay his individual debts without the consent of the holder of such one share of stock.

(Footnotes omitted.) * * *

We conclude that the trial court did not err in declining to hold the DeHarts liable to the corporation for installment payments made with corporate assets to Clausing and Deer. Similarly, as to the claim that the DeHarts are liable for the transfer of the Southside Receivable, the trial court's unchallenged finding of fact No. 8 states:

> The contract for the sale of stock was executed by all parties to this action, including Nursing Home Building Corporation. It provided that an asset of the corporation, known as the Southside Receivable and worth approximately $29,099.00 would be assigned to Drs. Clausing and Deer and not later than January 1971, and earlier if the corporation was dissolved. The corporation approved this contract at a time when Drs. Clausing and Deer were the sole shareholders and were a majority of the Board of Directors. The contract was assigned in April 1970. All parties consented to and ratified that assignment by their execution of the contract and by their subsequent acts in assigning or accepting assignment of the receivable.

The trial court properly concluded that the ratification of this transaction by all parties in accordance with the stock purchase contract is binding on the corporation.

Directing our attention to the second category of alleged "fraudulent misappropriation," the corporation asserts that such expenditures as management fees to the DeHarts, leased automobiles, and miscellaneous fringe benefits amounted to a waste of corporate assets and that the DeHarts failed to sustain the burden of proving that the expenditures were made in good faith. We disagree. Courts are reluctant to interfere with the internal management of corporations and generally refuse to substitute their judgment for that of the directors. *See Sanders v. E–Z Park, Inc., 57 Wn.2d 474, 358 P.2d 138 (1960).* The "business judgment rule" immunizes management from liability in a corporate transaction undertaken within both the power of the corporation and the authority of management where there is a reasonable basis to indicate that the transaction was made in good faith. An excellent statement of the "business judgment rule" is found in W. Fletcher § 1039 at pages 621–25:

> It is too well settled to admit of controversy that ordinarily neither the directors nor the other officers of a corporation are liable for mere mistake or errors of judgment, either of law or fact. In other words, directors of a commercial corporation may take chances, the same kind of chances that a man would take in his own business. Because they are given this wide latitude, the law will not hold directors liable for honest errors, for mistakes of judgment, when they act without corrupt motive and in good faith, that is, for mistakes which may properly be classified under the head of honest mistakes. And that is true even though the errors may be so gross that they may demonstrate the unfitness of the directors to manage the corporate affairs. This rule is commonly referred to as the "business judgment rule."

(Footnotes omitted.) * * *

In this connection, the trial court entered detailed findings of fact which are not disputed and state as follows:

> Mr. and Mrs. DeHart were experienced in the operation of businesses of various types, including nursing home. Both were involved in the day-to-day management of Arden Nursing Home on a full-time or greater than full-time basis; most of the time they were in possession of Arden Nursing Home. Each was licensed by the State of Washington as nursing home administrators. Each performed a variety of duties and responsibilities in addition to the day-to-day management.

Finding of fact No. 5.

> Mr. and Mrs. DeHart each received a management fee of $1,000.00 a month, plus certain fringe benefits such as a leased car, car operation expenses and key man life insurance. The cars were used predominantly for corporate purposes. The DeHarts used credit cards for such items as lunch conferences with staff, for entertainment of doctors and nurses who might refer patients to Arden. While some of these expenses may not have been necessary or wise in retrospect, all of these expenses were reasonable expenditures for proper business purposes.

Finding of fact No. 6. As we have noted previously, finding of fact No. 12 states:

> All other disbursements presented to the Court were proper business expenses.

This finding, though disputed, is properly supported by substantial evidence and must be upheld. The quoted findings support the trial court's conclusion of law that the challenged expenditures were made by the DeHarts within the scope of the proper exercise of their business judgment. This is especially so in view of the unchallenged finding of fact No. 16 which states:

> There is no evidence of any fraud or conspiracy to remove corporate assets wrongfully.

The corporation's third major argument centers upon the DeHarts' failure to pay federal withholding taxes and social security contributions which had accumulated to a sum in excess of $20,000 by the time the DeHarts' ownership of the corporation was forfeited. Again, the "business judgment rule" is controlling. Phoebe DeHart explained why the taxes were not paid in her testimony at trial, stating in part:

> We did not have the funds to pay them. We were using the money for food and heat and light, for patient care.

The trial court specifically found:

> The funds which would have been used for taxes were applied to other business expenses, such as staff salaries and trade accounts necessary to keep the nursing home open and provide patient care.

Finding of fact No. 14, in part. This finding of fact, though challenged, is supported by substantial evidence and therefore must be sustained. Thus, the trial court was entitled to conclude that the use of corporate funds for the payment of expenses other than taxes constituted a valid exercise of business judgment with which the courts will not interfere in the absence of bad faith or fraud. There was no error.

* * *

Judgment affirmed.

NOTES AND QUESTIONS

1. You have just read two cases which involve "shareholder loans." Why do they result in liability for a defendant in one case, and not in the other? Consider *Francis v. United Jersey Bank*. This case has recently been called "[t]he paradigm case of director liability for breach of the fiduciary duty of care in the oversight context." Andrew D. Shaffer, The Fiduciary Relationship Your Corporate Law Professor (Should Have) Warned You About, 8 Am. Bankr. Inst. L. Rev. 479, 501 (2000). Until relatively recently, however, it was almost unheard of for a director to be held liable for losses to a corporation or to its shareholders—much less to its creditors—for director misconduct that did not involve bad faith. Why, precisely, is Lillian Pritchard found to have breached her duty as a director, and why did that breach of duty result in liability? Are you convinced that, even if Mrs. Prichard failed in her duty as a director she should have been found liable to her corporation's creditors?

If the standard of due care for a director is that of a reasonably-prudent similarly-situated person, is it reasonable to expect that, as the court suggests, she should have engaged in conduct up to and over the point of litigating with her own children? Is it significant that Mrs. Pritchard is no longer with us, and that only her estate would be liable? A typical comment in praise of this decision was that of the trial court judge whose opinion in the case was affirmed in the decision you read. That judge declared that "I wish I had had the wit, the time, and the skill to write the thorough, sophisticated, yet simple lesson on the responsibility of corporate directors contained in Justice Pollock's opinion." Reginald Stanton, Stewart G. Pollock—As Seen from the Perspective of a Lawyer and Trial Judge, 74 N.Y.U.L. Rev. 1215, 1216 (1999). Do you share Judge Stanton's views? For a powerful argument that Judge Pollock got it quite wrong in *Francis*, with information on the unsuccessful criminal trial against Charles, Jr. and William, on the social background of the Pritchards, and on the currently evolving liability of directors for failure to monitor, see Reinier Kraakman & Jay Kesten, "The Story of *Francis v. United Jersey Bank*: When A Good Story Makes Bad Law," Chapter 6 in J. Mark Ramseyer, ed. Corporate Law Stories 163 (2009).

2. *Nursing Home Building Corporation v. DeHart* is notable primarily because of the manner it which it lucidly sets forth what has come to be called the "business judgment rule." Note that the case also has something to say to us about the distinctions to be made between the owners of the corporation and the corporation itself. Is the court correct that since the "shareholder loans" in question were made with the knowledge of the once and future owners of the corporation there should be no liability to pay back the loans? Is this something like a "piercing the corporate veil" case? Do you understand why the result would have been different if there were other creditors who might suffer?

What do you understand the "business judgment rule" to be? It has been suggested from time to time that the "business judgment rule" is really not a rule of law at all, but rather ought to be viewed as "a rebuttable evidentiary presumption that business decisions are made by disinterested and independent directors * * * on an informed basis and with a good faith belief that the decision is in the best interest of the corporation and its shareholders." Shaffer, supra, 8 Am. Bankr. Inst. L. Rev., at 498. If a plaintiff can successfully demonstrate that the directors were not disinterested or independent, that they were uninformed, or that they acted in bad faith, liability may still attach to the directors if it turns out that their actions were harmful to the corporation. What is necessary to rebut the presumption?

3. Consider another famous "business judgment case," *Kamin v. American Express*, 86 Misc.2d 809, 383 N.Y.S.2d 807 (Sup. Ct. 1976), aff'd, 54 A.D.2d 654, 387 N.Y.S.2d 993 (App. Div. 1976), as described in a recent law review article:

> In 1972, American Express bought almost two million shares of Donaldson, Lufkin & Jenrette, Inc. ("DLJ") common stock for about $30 million. In 1975, when the value of that stock had declined to about $4 million, American Express announced that it would distribute the stock to its shareholders as a dividend.

> Two American Express shareholders urged the company to sell the DLJ stock, rather than distribute it as a dividend. They pointed out that if

American Express sold the DLJ stock, it could reduce otherwise taxable capital gains by an amount equal to the roughly $26 million loss it would incur on the sale of its DLJ stock and thus save approximately $8 million in federal income taxes. On the other hand, by distributing the DLJ stock as a dividend, American Express would lose this potential tax saving and would provide no significant tax benefits to its shareholders. Put differently, if the board wanted to pay a dividend to shareholders, by selling the DLJ stock it would be able to distribute $12 million (the sale price plus the tax savings) in cash, which shareholders surely would prefer to receiving DLJ stock worth $4 million.

The American Express board of directors considered the shareholders' argument and then rejected it. The board had previously been advised by American Express's CPAs that if American Express distributed the DLJ stock as a dividend, instead of selling it, American Express could account for the transaction by reducing its retained earnings by the $30 million it had paid for the DLJ stock—the value at which American Express continued to carry that stock on its books. The advantage of this treatment, from the board's point of view, was that it allowed American Express to avoid reporting a loss of $26 million on its investment in DLJ and reducing its reported earnings by a like amount. The board was concerned that reporting such a loss, and a resulting reduction in American Express's income, would have a serious negative effect on the market value of American Express stock.

Elliott J. Weiss, ACCOUNTING AND TAXATION: TEACHING ACCOUNTING AND VALUATION IN THE BASIC CORPORATION LAW COURSE, 19 Cardozo L. Rev. 679, 689–690 (1997).[2] The two shareholders later brought suit against the directors arguing that they had breached their fiduciary duty to the corporation. The court upheld the directors' decision as a proper exercise of "business judgment," and *Kamin v. American Express* is now a leading "business judgment" precedent. Was it correctly decided?

4. How, precisely, are we to determine when we are confronted with a situation where the "business judgment" rule governs, and when we are in an area where directors are liable for their misconduct, even when they are acting in good faith? Consider the next famous (or, if you like, notorious) case, *Smith v. Van Gorkom*.

C.   NONFEASANCE OR THE BUSINESS JUDGMENT RULE?

SMITH v. VAN GORKOM

Supreme Court of Delaware.
488 A.2d 858 (1985).

[HORSEY, J.] This appeal from the Court of Chancery involves a class action brought by shareholders of the defendant Trans Union Corporation

---

2. Reprinted with the kind permission of Mr. Weiss.

("Trans Union" or "the Company"), * * * against the defendant members of the Board of Directors of Trans Union * * *.

Following trial, the former Chancellor granted judgment for the defendant directors * * * based on two findings: (1) that the Board of Directors had acted in an informed manner so as to be entitled to protection of the business judgment rule in approving the cash-out merger; and (2) that the shareholder vote approving the merger should not be set aside because the stockholders had been "fairly informed" by the Board of Directors before voting thereon. The plaintiffs appeal. * * *

Speaking for the [three-person] majority of the Court, we conclude that both rulings of the Court of Chancery are clearly erroneous. * * *

I.

* * *

A

Trans Union was a publicly-traded, diversified holding company, the principal earnings of which were generated by its railcar leasing business. During the period here involved, the Company had a cash flow of hundreds of millions of dollars annually. However, the Company had difficulty in generating sufficient taxable income to offset increasingly large investment tax credits (ITCs). Accelerated depreciation deductions had decreased available taxable income against which to offset accumulating ITCs. * * *

Beginning in the late 1960s, and continuing through the 1970's, Trans Union pursued a program of acquiring small companies in order to increase available taxable income. In July 1980, Trans Union Management prepared the annual revision of the Company's Five Year Forecast. This report was presented to the Board of Directors at its July, 1980 meeting. The report projected an annual income growth of about 20%. The report also concluded that Trans Union would have about $195 million in spare cash between 1980 and 1985, "with the surplus growing rapidly from 1982 onward." The report referred to the ITC situation as a "nagging problem" * * *.

B

On August 27, 1980, [Jerome W. Van Gorkom, Trans Union's Chairman and Chief Executive Officer] met with Senior Management of Trans Union. Van Gorkom reported * * * his desire to find a solution to the tax credit problem more permanent than a continued program of acquisitions. Various alternatives were suggested and discussed preliminarily, including the sale of Trans Union to a company with a large amount of taxable income.

Donald Romans, Chief Financial Officer of Trans Union, stated that his department had done a "very brief bit of work on the possibility of a leveraged buy-out." * * * The work consisted of a "preliminary study" of the cash which could be generated by the Company if it participated in a leveraged buy-out. As Romans stated, this analysis "was very first and rough cut at seeing whether a cash flow would support what might be considered a high price for this type of transaction."

On September 5, at another Senior Management meeting which Van Gorkom attended, Romans again brought up the idea of a leveraged buy-out as a "possible strategic alternative" to the Company's acquisition program. Romans and Bruce S. Chelberg, President and Chief Operating Officer of Trans Union, had been working on the matter in preparation for the meeting. According to Romans: They did not "come up" with a price for the Company. They merely "ran the numbers" at $50 a share and at $60 a share with the "rough form" of their cash figures at the time. Their "figures indicated that $50 would be very easy to do but $60 would be very difficult to do under those figures." * * *

At this meeting, Van Gorkom stated that he would be willing to take $55 per share for his own 75,000 shares. He vetoed the suggestion of a leveraged buy-out by Management, however, as involving a potential conflict of interest for Management. Van Gorkom, a certified public accountant and lawyer, had been an officer of Trans Union for 24 years, its Chief Executive Officer for more than 17 years, and Chairman of its Board for 2 years. It is noteworthy in this connection that he was then approaching 65 years of age and mandatory retirement.

* * * Van Gorkom * * * had participated in many acquisitions as a manager and director of Trans Union and as a director of other companies. He was familiar with acquisition procedures, valuation methods, and negotiations; and he privately considered the pros and cons of whether Trans Union should seek a privately or publicly-held purchaser.

Van Gorkom decided to meet with Jay A. Pritzker, a well-known corporate takeover specialist and a social acquaintance. However, rather than approaching Pritzker simply to determine his interest in acquiring Trans Union, Van Gorkom assembled a proposed per share price for sale of the Company and a financing structure by which to accomplish the sale. Van Gorkom did so without consulting either his Board or any members of Senior Management except * * * Carl Peterson, Trans Union's Controller. Telling Peterson that he wanted no other person on his staff to know what he was doing, but without telling him why, Van Gorkom directed Peterson to calculate the feasibility of a leveraged buy-out at an assumed price per share of $55. Apart from the Company's historic stock market price,[3] and Van Gorkom's long association with Trans Union, the record is devoid of any competent evidence that $55 represented the per share intrinsic value of the Company.

---

3. * * * Over the five year period from 1975 through 1979, Trans Union's stock had traded within a range of a high of $39 1/2 and a low of $24 1/4. Its high and low range for 1980 through September 19 (the last trading day before announcement of the merger) was $38 1/4–$29 1/2.

* * *

Van Gorkom arranged a meeting with Pritzker at the latter's home on Saturday, September 13, 1980. Van Gorkom prefaced his presentation by stating to Pritzker: "Now as far as you are concerned, I can, I think, show how you can pay a substantial premium over the present stock price and pay off most of the loan in the first five years. * * * If you could pay $55 for this Company, here is a way in which I think it can be financed."

* * * Although Pritzker mentioned $50 as a more attractive figure, no other price was mentioned. However, Van Gorkom stated that to be sure that $55 was the best price obtainable, Trans Union should be free to accept any better offer. Pritzker demurred, stating that his organization would serve as a "stalking horse" for an "auction contest" only if Trans Union would permit Pritzker to buy 1,750,000 shares of Trans Union stock at market price which Pritzker could then sell to any higher bidder. After further discussion on this point, Pritzker told Van Gorkom that he would give him a more definite reaction soon.

On Monday, September 15, Pritzker advised Van Gorkom that he was interested in the $55 cash-out merger proposal and requested more information on Trans Union. Van Gorkom agreed to meet privately with Pritzker, accompanied by Peterson, Chelberg, and Michael Carpenter, Trans Union's consultant from the Boston Consulting Group. The meetings took place on September 16 and 17. Van Gorkom was "astounded that events were moving with such amazing rapidity."

On Thursday, September 18, Van Gorkom met again with Pritzker. At that time, Van Gorkom knew that Pritzker intended to make a cash-out merger offer at Van Gorkom's proposed $55 per share. Pritzker instructed his attorney, a merger and acquisition specialist, to begin drafting merger documents. There was no further discussion of the $55 price. However, the number of shares of Trans Union's treasury stock to be offered to Pritzker was negotiated down to one million shares; the price was set at $38–75 cents above the per share price at the close of the market on September 19. At this point, Pritzker insisted that the Trans Union Board act on his merger proposal within the next three days, stating to Van Gorkom: "We have to have a decision by no later than Sunday [evening, September 21] before the opening of the English stock exchange on Monday morning." Pritzker's lawyer was then instructed to draft the merger documents, to be reviewed by Van Gorkom's lawyer, "sometimes with discussion and sometimes not, in the haste to get it finished."

On Friday, September 19, Van Gorkom, Chelberg, and Pritzker consulted with Trans Union's lead bank regarding the financing of Pritzker's purchase of Trans Union. The bank indicated that it could form a syndicate of banks that would finance the transaction. On the same day, Van Gorkom retained James Brennan, Esquire, to advise Trans Union on the legal aspects of the merger. Van Gorkom did not consult with * * * Trans Union's [in-house] legal staff.

On Friday, September 19, Van Gorkom called a special meeting of the Trans Union Board for noon the following day. He also called a meeting of the Company's Senior Management to convene at 11:00 a.m.* * *. No one, except Chelberg and Peterson, was told the purpose of the meetings. Van Gorkom did not invite Trans Union's investment banker, Salomon Brothers or its Chicago-based partner, to attend.

Of those present at the Senior Management meeting on September 20, only Chelberg and Peterson had prior knowledge of Pritzker's offer. Van Gorkom disclosed the offer and described its terms, but he furnished no copies of the proposed Merger Agreement. Romans announced that his department had done a second study which showed that, for a leveraged buy-out, the price range for Trans Union stock was between $55 and $65 per share. Van Gorkom neither saw the study nor asked Romans to make it available for the Board meeting.

Senior Management's reaction to the Pritzker proposal was completely negative. No member of Management, except Chelberg and Peterson, supported the proposal. Romans objected to the price as being too low;[4] he was critical of the timing and suggested that consideration should be given to the adverse tax consequences of an all-cash deal for low-basis shareholders; and he took the position that the agreement to sell Pritzker one million newly-issued shares at market price would inhibit other offers, as would the prohibitions against soliciting bids and furnishing inside information to other bidders. Romans argued that the Pritzker proposal was a "lock up" and amounted to "an agreed merger as opposed to an offer." Nevertheless, Van Gorkom proceeded to the Board meeting as scheduled without further delay.

Ten directors served on the Trans Union Board, five inside * * * and five outside * * *. All directors were present at the meeting, except [one] who was ill. Of the outside directors, four were corporate chief executive officers and one was the former Dean of the University of Chicago Business School. None was an investment banker or trained financial analyst. All members of the Board were well informed about the Company and its operations as a going concern. They were familiar with the current financial condition of the Company * * *. * * *

Van Gorkom began the Special Meeting of the Board with a twenty-minute oral presentation. Copies of the proposed Merger Agreement were delivered too late for study before or during the meeting. * * * He reviewed the Company's ITC and depreciation problems and the efforts theretofore made to solve them. He discussed his initial meeting with Pritzker and his motivation in arranging that meeting. Van Gorkom did not disclose to the Board, however, the methodology by which he alone

---

4. Van Gorkom asked Romans to express his opinion as to the $55 price. Romans stated that he "thought the price was too low in relation to what he could derive for the company in a cash sale, particularly one which enabled us to realize the values of certain subsidiaries and independent entities."

had arrived at the $55 figure, or the fact that he first proposed the $55 price in his negotiations with Pritzker.

Van Gorkom outlined the terms of the Pritzker offer as follows: Pritzker would pay $55 in cash for all outstanding shares of Trans Union stock upon completion of which Trans Union would be merged into New T Company, a subsidiary wholly-owned by Pritzker and formed to implement the merger; for a period of 90 days, Trans Union could receive, but could not actively solicit, competing offers; the offer had to be acted on by the next evening, Sunday, September 21; Trans Union could only furnish to competing bidders published information, and not proprietary information; the offer was subject to Pritzker obtaining the necessary financing by October 10, 1980; if the financing contingency were met or waived by Pritzker, Trans Union was required to sell to Pritzker one million newly-issued shares of Trans Union at $38 per share.

Van Gorkom took the position that putting Trans Union "up for auction" through a 90–day market test would validate a decision by the Board that $55 was a fair price. He told the Board that the "free market will have an opportunity to judge whether $55 is a fair price." Van Gorkom framed the decision before the Board not as whether $55 per share was the highest price that could be obtained, but as whether the $55 price was a fair price that the stockholders should be given the opportunity to accept or reject. * * *

Attorney Brennan advised the members of the Board that they might be sued if they failed to accept the offer and that a fairness opinion was not required as a matter of law.

Romans * * * told the Board that he had not been involved in the negotiations with Pritzker and knew nothing about the merger proposal until the morning of the meeting; that his studies did not indicate either a fair price for the stock or a valuation of the Company; that he did not see his role as directly addressing the fairness issue; and that he and his people "were trying to search for ways to justify a price in connection with such a [leveraged buy-out] transaction, rather than to say what the shares are worth." * * *

Romans told the Board that, in his opinion, $55 was "in the range of a fair price," but "at the beginning of the range."

Chelberg, Trans Union's President, supported Van Gorkom's presentation and representations. * * *

* * * Based solely upon Van Gorkom's oral presentation, Chelberg's supporting representations, Romans' oral statement, Brennan's legal advice, and their knowledge of the market history of the Company's stock, * * * the directors approved the proposed Merger Agreement. However, the Board later claimed to have attached two conditions to its acceptance: (1) that Trans Union reserved the right to accept any better offer that was made during the market test period; and (2) that Trans Union could share its proprietary information with any other potential bidders. * * * [T]he Board did not reserve the right to actively solicit alternate offers.

The Merger Agreement was executed by Van Gorkom during the evening of September 20 at a formal social event that he hosted for the opening of the Chicago Lyric Opera. Neither he nor any other director read the agreement prior to its signing and delivery to Pritzker.

*   *   *

On Monday, September 22, the Company issued a press release announcing that Trans Union had entered into a "definitive" Merger Agreement with an affiliate of the Marmon Group, Inc., a Pritzker holding company. Within 10 days of the public announcement, dissent among Senior Management over the merger had become widespread. Faced with threatened resignations of key officers, Van Gorkom met with Pritzker who agreed to several modifications of the Agreement. Pritzker was willing to do so provided that Van Gorkom could persuade the dissidents to remain on the Company payroll for at least six months after consummation of the merger.

Van Gorkom reconvened the Board on October 8 and secured the directors' approval of the proposed amendments—sight unseen. The Board also authorized the employment of Salomon Brothers, its investment banker, to solicit other offers for Trans Union during the proposed "market test" period.

The next day, October 9, Trans Union issued a press release announcing: (1) that Pritzker had obtained "the financing commitments necessary to consummate" the merger with Trans Union; (2) that Pritzker had acquired one million shares of Trans Union common stock at $38 per share; (3) that Trans Union was now permitted to actively seek other offers and had retained Salomon Brothers for that purpose; and (4) that if a more favorable offer were not received before February 1, 1981, Trans Union's shareholders would thereafter meet to vote on the Pritzker proposal.

It was not until the following day, October 10, that the actual amendments to the Merger Agreement were prepared by Pritzker and delivered to Van Gorkom for execution. [T]he amendments were considerably at variance with Van Gorkom's representations of the amendments to the Board on October 8; and the amendments placed serious constraints on Trans Union's ability to negotiate a better deal and withdraw from the Pritzker agreement. Nevertheless, Van Gorkom proceeded to execute what became the October 10 amendments to the Merger Agreement without conferring further with the Board members and apparently without comprehending the actual implications of the amendments.

*   *   *

Salomon Brothers' efforts over a three-month period from October 21 to January 21 produced only one serious suitor for Trans Union-General Electric Credit Corporation ("GE Credit") * * * However, GE Credit was unwilling to make an offer for Trans Union unless Trans Union first rescinded its Merger Agreement with Pritzker. When Pritzker refused, GE Credit terminated further discussions with Trans Union in early January.

In the meantime, in early December, the investment firm of Kohlberg, Kravis, Roberts & Co. ("KKR"), the only other concern to make a firm offer for Trans Union, withdrew its offer * * *.

On December 19, this litigation was commenced * * *. On January 21, Management's Proxy Statement for the February 10 shareholder meeting was mailed to Trans Union's stockholders. On January 26, Trans Union's Board met and, after a lengthy meeting, voted to proceed with the Pritzker merger. The Board also approved for mailing, "on or about January 27," a Supplement to its Proxy Statement. The Supplement purportedly set forth all information relevant to the Pritzker Merger Agreement, which had not been divulged in the first Proxy Statement.

*   *   *

On February 10, the stockholders of Trans Union approved the Pritzker merger proposal. Of the outstanding shares, 69.9% were voted in favor of the merger; 7.25% were voted against the merger; and 22.85% were not voted.

II.

We turn to the issue of the application of the business judgment rule to the September 20 meeting of the Board. * * *

The Court of Chancery [found] that the Board's conduct over the entire period from September 20 through January 26, 1981 was not reckless or improvident, but informed. This ultimate conclusion was premised upon three subordinate findings, one explicit and two implied. The Court's explicit finding was that Trans Union's Board was "free to turn down the Pritzker proposal" not only on September 20 but also on October 8, 1980 and on January 26, 1981. The Court's implied, subordinate findings were: (1) that no legally binding agreement was reached by the parties until January 26; and (2) that if a higher offer were to be forthcoming, the market test would have produced it, * * * and Trans Union would have been contractually free to accept such higher offer. However, the Court offered no factual basis or legal support for any of these findings; and the record compels contrary conclusions.

*   *   *

The plaintiffs contend that the Court of Chancery erred as a matter of law by exonerating the defendant directors under the business judgment rule without first determining whether the rule's threshold condition of "due care and prudence" was satisfied. * * *

* * * Under Delaware law, the business judgment rule is the offspring of the fundamental principle, * * * that the business and affairs of a Delaware corporation are managed by or under its board of directors.

* * * In carrying out their managerial roles, directors are charged with an unyielding fiduciary duty to the corporation and its shareholders. * * * The business judgment rule exists to protect and promote the full and free exercise of the managerial power granted to Delaware directors. * * * The rule itself "is a presumption that in making a business decision, the directors of a corporation acted on an informed basis, in good faith and in the honest belief that the action taken was in the best interests of the company." * * * Thus, the party attacking a board decision as uninformed must rebut the presumption that its business judgment was an informed one.

* * *

Under the business judgment rule there is no protection for directors who have made "an unintelligent or unadvised judgment." * * * A director's duty to inform himself [of all material information reasonably available] in preparation for a decision derives from the fiduciary capacity in which he serves the corporation and its stockholders. * * * Such obligation does not tolerate faithlessness or self-dealing. But fulfillment of the fiduciary function requires more than the mere absence of bad faith or fraud. Representation of the financial interests of others imposes on a director an affirmative duty to protect those interests and to proceed with a critical eye in assessing information of the type and under the circumstances present here. * * *

Thus * * * a director's duty to exercise an informed business judgment is in the nature of a duty of care, as distinguished from a duty of loyalty. Here, there were no allegations of fraud, bad faith, or self-dealing, or proof thereof. Hence, it is presumed that the directors reached their business judgment in good faith * * * and considerations of motive are irrelevant to the issue before us.

* * *

* * * We think the concept of gross negligence is * * * the proper standard for determining whether a business judgment reached by a board of directors was an informed one. * * *

In the specific context of a proposed merger of domestic corporations, a director has a duty * * * along with his fellow directors, to act in an informed and deliberate manner in determining whether to approve an agreement of merger before submitting the proposal to the stockholders. Certainly in the merger context, a director may not abdicate that duty by leaving to the shareholders alone the decision to approve or disapprove the agreement. * * *

III.

The defendants argue that the determination of whether their decision to accept $55 per share for Trans Union represented an informed business judgment requires consideration, not only of that which they knew and learned on September 20, but also of that which they subsequently learned and did over the following four-month period before the shareholders met to vote on the proposal in February, 1981. * * * Thus, the defendants contend that what the directors did and learned subsequent to September 20 and through January 26, 1981, was properly taken into account by the Trial Court in determining whether the Board's judgment was an informed one. We disagree with this *post hoc* approach.

The issue of whether the directors reached an informed decision to "sell" the Company on September 20, 1980 must be determined only upon the basis of the information then reasonably available to the directors and relevant to their decision to accept the Pritzker merger proposal. * * *

A

On the record before us, we must conclude that the Board of Directors did not reach an informed business judgment on September 20, 1980 in voting to "sell" the Company for $55 per share pursuant to the Pritzker cash-out merger proposal. Our reasons, in summary, are as follows:

The directors (1) did not adequately inform themselves as to Van Gorkom's role in forcing the "sale" of the Company and in establishing the per share purchase price; (2) were uninformed as to the intrinsic value of the Company; and (3) given these circumstances, at a minimum, were grossly negligent in approving the "sale" of the Company upon two hours' consideration, without prior notice, and without the exigency of a crisis or emergency.

As has been noted, the Board based its September 20 decision to approve the cash-out merger primarily on Van Gorkom's representations. None of the directors, other than Van Gorkom and Chelberg, had any prior knowledge that the purpose of the meeting was to propose a cash-out merger of Trans Union. No members of Senior Management were present, other than Chelberg, Romans and Peterson; and the latter two had only learned of the proposed sale an hour earlier. * * *

Without any documents before them concerning the proposed transaction, the members of the Board were required to rely entirely upon Van Gorkom's 20-minute oral presentation of the proposal. No written summary of the terms of the merger was presented; the directors were given no documentation to support the adequacy of $55 price per share for sale of the Company; and the Board had before it nothing more than Van Gorkom's statement of his understanding of the substance of an agreement which he admittedly had never read, nor which any member of the Board had ever seen.

[Pursuant to the Corporations statutes in Delaware] "directors are fully protected in relying in good faith on reports made by officers." * * * The term "report" has been liberally construed to include reports of informal personal investigations by corporate officers, * * * However, there is no evidence that any "report," * * * concerning the Pritzker proposal, was presented to the Board on September 20. Van Gorkom's oral presentation of his understanding of the terms of the proposed Merger Agreement, which he had not seen, and Romans' brief oral statement of his preliminary study regarding the feasibility of a leveraged buy-out of Trans Union do not qualify as * * * "reports" for these reasons: The former lacked substance because Van Gorkom was basically uninformed as to the essential provisions of the very document about which he was talking. Romans' statement was irrelevant to the issues before the Board since it did not purport to be a valuation study. At a minimum for a report [to be something on which directors may rely] it must be pertinent to the subject matter upon which a board is called to act, and otherwise be entitled to good faith, not blind, reliance. Considering all of the surrounding circumstances—hastily calling the meeting without prior notice of its subject matter, the proposed sale of the Company without any prior consideration of the issue or necessity therefor, the urgent time constraints imposed by Pritzker, and the total absence of any documentation whatsoever—the directors were duty bound to make reasonable inquiry of Van Gorkom and Romans, and if they had done so, the inadequacy of that upon which they now claim to have relied would have been apparent.

The defendants rely on the following factors to sustain the Trial Court's finding that the Board's decision was an informed one: (1) the magnitude of the premium or spread between the $55 Pritzker offering price and Trans Union's current market price of $38 per share; (2) the amendment of the Agreement as submitted on September 20 to permit the Board to accept any better offer during the "market test" period; (3) the collective experience and expertise of the Board's "inside" and "outside" directors; and (4) their reliance on Brennan's legal advice that the directors might be sued if they rejected the Pritzker proposal. * * *

(1)

A substantial premium may provide one reason to recommend a merger, but in the absence of other sound valuation information, the fact of a premium alone does not provide an adequate basis upon which to assess the fairness of an offering price. Here, the judgment reached as to the adequacy of the premium was based on a comparison between the historically depressed Trans Union market price and the amount of the Pritzker offer. Using market price as a basis for concluding that the premium adequately reflected the true value of the Company was a clearly faulty, indeed fallacious, premise, as the defendants' own evidence demonstrates.

The record is clear that before September 20, Van Gorkom and other members of Trans Union's Board knew that the market had consistently undervalued the worth of Trans Union's stock, despite steady increases in the Company's operating income in the seven years preceding the merger. The Board related this occurrence in large part to Trans Union's inability to use its ITCs as previously noted. Van Gorkom testified that he did not believe the market price accurately reflected Trans Union's true worth;

and several of the directors testified that, as a general rule, most chief executives think that the market undervalues their companies' stock. Yet, on September 20, Trans Union's Board apparently believed that the market stock price accurately reflected the value of the Company for the purpose of determining the adequacy of the premium for its sale.

In the Proxy Statement * * * the directors * * * stated that, although the earnings prospects for Trans Union were "excellent," they found no basis for believing that this would be reflected in future stock prices. With regard to past trading, the Board stated that the prices at which the Company's common stock had traded in recent years did not reflect the "inherent" value of the Company. But having referred to the "inherent" value of Trans Union, the directors ascribed no number to it. Moreover, nowhere did they disclose that they had no basis on which to fix "inherent" worth beyond an impressionistic reaction to the premium over market and an unsubstantiated belief that the value of the assets was "significantly greater" than book value. * * *

The parties do not dispute that a publicly-traded stock price is solely a measure of the value of a minority position and, thus, market price represents only the value of a single share. * * *

* * * As of September 20, the Board had made no evaluation of the Company designed to value the entire enterprise, nor had the Board ever previously considered selling the Company or consenting to a buy-out merger. * * *

Despite the foregoing facts and circumstances, there was no call by the Board, either on September 20 or thereafter, for any valuation study or documentation of the $55 price per share as a measure of the fair value of the Company in a cash-out context. It is undisputed that the major asset of Trans Union was its cash flow. Yet, at no time did the Board call for a valuation study taking into account that highly significant element of the Company's assets.

We do not imply that an outside valuation study is essential to support an informed business judgment; nor do we state that fairness opinions by independent investment bankers are required as a matter of law. Often insiders familiar with the business of a going concern are in a better position than are outsiders to gather relevant information; and under appropriate circumstances, such directors may be fully protected in relying in good faith upon the valuation reports of their management. * * *

Here, the record establishes that the Board did not request its Chief Financial Officer, Romans, to make any valuation study or review of the proposal to determine the adequacy of $55 per share for sale of the Company. On the record before us: The Board rested on Romans' elicited response that the $55 figure was within a "fair price range" within the context of a leveraged buy-out. No director sought any further information from Romans. * * *

* * *

The record also establishes that the Board accepted without scrutiny Van Gorkom's representation as to the fairness of the $55 price per share for sale of the Company—a subject that the Board had never previously considered. The Board thereby failed to discover that Van Gorkom had suggested the $55 price to Pritzker and, most crucially, that Van Gorkom had arrived at the $55 figure based on calculations designed solely to determine the feasibility of a leveraged buy-out. * * *

We do not say that the Board of Directors was not entitled to give some credence to Van Gorkom's representation that $55 was an adequate or fair price. Under [Delaware law] the directors were entitled to rely upon their chairman's opinion of value and adequacy, provided that such opinion was reached on a sound basis. Here, the issue is whether the directors informed themselves as to all information that was reasonably available to them. Had they done so, they would have learned of the source and derivation of the $55 price and could not reasonably have relied thereupon in good faith.

None of the directors, Management or outside, were investment bankers or financial analysts. Yet the Board did not consider recessing the meeting until a later hour that day (or requesting an extension of Pritzker's Sunday evening deadline) to give it time to elicit more information as to the sufficiency of the offer, either from inside Management (in particular Romans) or from Trans Union's own investment banker, Salomon Brothers * * *.

* * *

(2)

This brings us to the post-September 20 "market test" * * *. In this connection, the directors present a two-part argument: (a) that by making a "market test" of Pritzker's $55 per share offer a condition of their September 20 decision to accept his offer, they cannot be found to have acted impulsively or in an uninformed manner on September 20; and (b) that the adequacy of the $17 premium for sale of the Company was conclusively established over the following 90 to 120 days by the most reliable evidence available—the marketplace. * * *.

Again, the facts of record do not support the defendants' argument. There is no evidence: (a) that the Merger Agreement was effectively amended to give the Board freedom to put Trans Union up for auction sale to the highest bidder; or (b) that a public auction was in fact permitted to occur. The minutes of the Board meeting make no reference to any of this. Indeed, the record compels the conclusion that the directors had no rational basis for expecting that a market test was attainable, given the terms of the Agreement as executed during the evening of September 20. * * *

The Merger Agreement, specifically identified as that originally presented to the Board on September 20, has never been produced by the defendants, notwithstanding the plaintiffs' several demands for production before as well as during trial. No acceptable explanation of this failure to produce documents has been given to either the Trial Court or this Court. * * *

Van Gorkom states that the Agreement as submitted incorporated the ingredients for a market test by authorizing Trans Union to receive competing offers over the next 90–day period. However, he concedes that the Agreement barred Trans Union from actively soliciting such offers and from furnishing to interested parties any information about the Company other than that already in the public domain. Whether the original Agreement of September 20 went so far as to authorize Trans Union to receive competitive proposals is arguable. The defendants' unexplained failure to produce and identify the original Merger Agreement permits the logical inference that the instrument would not support their assertions in this regard. * * * Van Gorkom, conceding that he never read the Agreement, stated that he was relying upon his understanding that, under corporate law, directors always have an inherent right, as well as a fiduciary duty, to accept a better offer notwithstanding an existing contractual commitment by the Board. * * *

Several of Trans Union's outside directors resolutely maintained that the Agreement as submitted was approved on the understanding that, "if we got a better deal, we had a right to take it." Director Johnson so testified; but he then added, "And if they didn't put that in the agreement, then the management did not carry out the conclusion of the Board. And I just don't know whether they did or not." The only clause in the Agreement as finally executed to which the defendants can point as "keeping the door open" is the following [italicized] statement found in subparagraph (a) of section 2.03 of the Merger Agreement as executed:

> The Board of Directors shall recommend to the stockholders of Trans Union that they approve and adopt the Merger Agreement ('the stockholders' approval') and to use its best efforts to obtain the requisite votes therefor. *GL acknowledges that Trans Union directors may have a competing fiduciary obligation to the shareholders under certain circumstances.*

Clearly, this language on its face cannot be construed as incorporating either of the two "conditions" described above: either the right to accept a better offer or the right to distribute proprietary information to third parties. * * *

The defendants attempt to downplay the significance of the prohibition against Trans Union's actively soliciting competing offers by arguing that the directors "understood that the entire financial community would know that Trans Union was for sale upon the announcement of the Pritzker offer, and anyone desiring to make a better offer was free to do so." Yet, the press release issued on September 22, with the authorization of the Board, stated that Trans Union had entered into "definitive agreements" with the Pritzkers; and the press release did not even disclose

Trans Union's limited right to receive and accept higher offers. Accompanying this press release was a further public announcement that Pritzker had been granted an option to purchase at any time one million shares of Trans Union's capital stock at 75 cents above the then-current price per share.

* * *

(3)

The directors' unfounded reliance on both the premium and the market test as the basis for accepting the Pritzker proposal undermines the defendants' remaining contention that the Board's collective experience and sophistication was a sufficient basis for finding that it reached its September 20 decision with informed, reasonable deliberation. * * *

[The court observes in a footnote that] Trans Union's five "inside" directors had backgrounds in law and accounting, 116 years of collective employment by the Company and 68 years of combined experience on its Board. Trans Union's five "outside" directors included four chief executives of major corporations and an economist who was a former dean of a major school of business and chancellor of a university. The "outside" directors had 78 years of combined experience as chief executive officers of major corporations and 50 years of cumulative experience as directors of Trans Union. Thus, defendants argue that the Board was eminently qualified to reach an informed judgment on the proposed "sale" of Trans Union notwithstanding their lack of any advance notice of the proposal, the shortness of their deliberation, and their determination not to consult with their investment banker or to obtain a fairness opinion. [But the court rejects this experience as a significant factor because of its belief that there wasn't enough information on which to base a decision.]

(4)

Part of the defense is based on a claim that the directors relied on legal advice rendered at the September 20 meeting by James Brennan, Esquire, who was present at Van Gorkom's request. Unfortunately, Brennan did not appear and testify at trial even though his firm participated in the defense of this action. There is no contemporaneous evidence of the advice given by Brennan on September 20, only the later deposition and trial testimony of certain directors as to their recollections or understanding of what was said at the meeting. Since counsel did not testify, and the advice attributed to Brennan is hearsay received by the Trial Court over the plaintiffs' objections, we consider it only in the context of the directors' present claims. In fairness to counsel, we make no findings that the advice attributed to him was in fact given. We focus solely on the efficacy of the defendants' claims, made months and years later, in an effort to extricate themselves from liability.

Several defendants testified that Brennan advised them that Delaware law did not require a fairness opinion or an outside valuation of the Company before the Board could act on the Pritzker proposal. If given, the advice was correct. However, that did not end the matter. Unless the directors had before them adequate information regarding the intrinsic value of the Company, upon which a proper exercise of business judgment could be made, mere advice of this type is meaningless; and, given this record of the defendants' failures, it constitutes no defense here. * * *

*   *   *

A second claim is that counsel advised the Board it would be subject to lawsuits if it rejected the $55 per share offer. It is, of course, a fact of corporate life that today when faced with difficult or sensitive issues, directors often are subject to suit, irrespective of the decisions they make. However, counsel's mere acknowledgement of this circumstance cannot be rationally translated into a justification for a board permitting itself to be stampeded into a patently unadvised act. While suit might result from the rejection of a merger or tender offer, Delaware law makes clear that a board acting within the ambit of the business judgment rule faces no ultimate liability. * * * Thus, we cannot conclude that the mere threat of litigation, acknowledged by counsel, constitutes either legal advice or any valid basis upon which to pursue an uninformed course.

*   *   *

B

We now examine the Board's post-September 20 conduct for the purpose of determining first, whether it was informed and not grossly negligent; and second, if informed, whether it was sufficient to legally rectify and cure the Board's derelictions of September 20

(1)

First, as to the Board meeting of October 8: Its purpose arose in the aftermath of the September 20 meeting: (1) the September 22 press release announcing that Trans Union "had entered into definitive agreements to merge with an affiliate of Marmon Group, Inc.;" and (2) Senior Management's ensuing revolt.

Trans Union's press release stated:

FOR IMMEDIATE RELEASE:

CHICAGO, IL—Trans Union Corporation announced today that it had entered into definitive agreements to merge with an affiliate of The Marmon Group, Inc. in a transaction whereby Trans Union stockholders would receive $55 per share in cash for each Trans Union share held. The Marmon Group, Inc. is controlled by the Pritzker family of Chicago.

The merger is subject to approval by the stockholders of Trans Union at a special meeting expected to be held sometime during December or early January.

Until October 10, 1980, the purchaser has the right to terminate the merger if financing that is satisfactory to the purchaser has not been obtained, but after that date there is no such right.

In a related transaction, Trans Union has agreed to sell to a designee of the purchaser one million newly-issued shares of Trans Union common stock at a cash price of $38 per share. Such shares will be issued only if the merger financing has been committed for no later than October 10, 1980, or if the purchaser elects to waive the merger financing condition. In addition, the New York Stock Exchange will be asked to approve the listing of the new shares pursuant to a listing application which Trans Union intends to file shortly.

Completing of the transaction is also subject to the preparation of a definitive proxy statement and making various filings and obtaining the approvals or consents of government agencies.

The press release made no reference to provisions allegedly reserving to the Board the rights to perform a "market test" and to withdraw from the Pritzker Agreement if Trans Union received a better offer before the shareholder meeting. The defendants also concede that Trans Union never made a subsequent public announcement stating that it had in fact reserved the right to accept alternate offers, the Agreement notwithstanding.

The public announcement of the Pritzker merger resulted in an "en masse" revolt of Trans Union's Senior Management. The head of Trans Union's tank car operations (its most profitable division) informed Van Gorkom that unless the merger were called off, fifteen key personnel would resign.

Instead of reconvening the Board, Van Gorkom again privately met with Pritzker, informed him of the developments, and sought his advice. Pritzker then made the following suggestions for overcoming Management's dissatisfaction: (1) that the Agreement be amended to permit Trans Union to solicit, as well as receive, higher offers; and (2) that the shareholder meeting be postponed from early January to February 10, 1981. In return, Pritzker asked Van Gorkom to obtain a commitment from Senior Management to remain at Trans Union for at least six months after the merger was consummated.

Van Gorkom then advised Senior Management that the Agreement would be amended to give Trans Union the right to solicit competing offers through January, 1981, if they would agree to remain with Trans Union. Senior Management was temporarily mollified; and Van Gorkom then called a special meeting of Trans Union's Board for October 8.

Thus, the primary purpose of the October 8 Board meeting was to amend the Merger Agreement, in a manner agreeable to Pritzker, to permit Trans Union to conduct a "market test." * * * Van Gorkom understood that the proposed amendments were intended to give the Company an unfettered "right to openly solicit offers down through January

31." * * * In a brief session, the directors approved Van Gorkom's oral presentation of the substance of the proposed amendments, the terms of which were not reduced to writing until October 10. But rather than waiting to review the amendments, the Board again approved them sight unseen and adjourned, giving Van Gorkom authority to execute the papers when he received them. * * *.

The next day, October 9, and before the Agreement was amended, Pritzker moved swiftly to off-set the proposed market test amendment. First, Pritzker informed Trans Union that he had completed arrangements for financing its acquisition and that the parties were thereby mutually bound to a firm purchase and sale arrangement. Second, Pritzker announced the exercise of his option to purchase one million shares of Trans Union's treasury stock at $38 per share * * *. Trans Union's Management responded the same day by issuing a press release announcing: (1) that all financing arrangements for Pritzker's acquisition of Trans Union had been completed; and (2) Pritzker's purchase of one million shares of Trans Union's treasury stock * * *.

The next day, October 10, Pritzker delivered to Trans Union the proposed amendments to the September 20 Merger Agreement. Van Gorkom promptly proceeded to countersign all the instruments on behalf of Trans Union without reviewing the instruments to determine if they were consistent with the authority previously granted him by the Board. * * * The record does not affirmatively establish that Trans Union's directors ever read the October 10 amendments.

The October 10 amendments to the Merger Agreement did authorize Trans Union to solicit competing offers, but the amendments had more far-reaching effects. The most significant change was in the definition of the third-party "offer" available to Trans Union as a possible basis for withdrawal from its Merger Agreement with Pritzker. Under the October 10 amendments, a better *offer* was no longer sufficient to permit Trans Union's withdrawal. Trans Union was now permitted to terminate the Pritzker Agreement and abandon the merger only if, prior to February 10, 1981, Trans Union had either consummated a merger (or sale of assets) with a third party or had entered into a "definitive" merger agreement more favorable than Pritzker's and for a greater consideration—subject only to stockholder approval. Further, the "extension" of the market test period to February 10, 1981 was circumscribed by other amendments which required Trans Union to file its preliminary proxy statement on the Pritzker merger proposal by December 5, 1980 and use its best efforts to mail the statement to its shareholders by January 5, 1981. Thus, the market test period was effectively reduced, not extended. * * *

In our view, the record compels the conclusion that the directors' conduct on October 8 exhibited the same deficiencies as did their conduct on September 20 * * *.

We conclude that the Board acted in a grossly negligent manner on October 8. * * *

The October 9 press release, coupled with the October 10 amendments, had the clear effect of locking Trans Union's Board into the Pritzker Agreement. Pritzker had thereby foreclosed Trans Union's Board from negotiating any better "definitive" agreement * * *.

(2)

Next, as to the "curative" effects of the Board's post-September 20 conduct, we review in more detail the reaction of Van Gorkom to the KKR proposal and the results of the Board-sponsored "market test."

The KKR proposal was the first and only offer received subsequent to the Pritzker Merger Agreement. The offer resulted primarily from the efforts of Romans and other senior officers to propose an alternative to Pritzker's acquisition of Trans Union. In late September, Romans' group contacted KKR about the possibility of a leveraged buy-out by all members of Management, except Van Gorkom. By early October, Henry R. Kravis of KKR gave Romans written notice of KKR's "interest in making an offer to purchase 100% of Trans Union's common stock."

Thereafter, and until early December, Romans' group worked with KKR to develop a proposal. It did so with Van Gorkom's knowledge and apparently grudging consent. On December 2, Kravis and Romans hand-delivered to Van Gorkom a formal letter-offer to purchase all of Trans Union's assets and to assume all of its liabilities for an aggregate cash consideration equivalent to $60 per share. The offer was contingent upon completing equity and bank financing of $650 million, which Kravis represented as 80% complete. The KKR letter made reference to discussions with major banks regarding the loan portion of the buy-out cost and stated that KKR was "confident that commitments for the bank financing * * * can be obtained within two or three weeks." The purchasing group was to include certain named key members of Trans Union's Senior Management * * * and a major Canadian company. Kravis stated that they were willing to enter into a "definitive agreement" under terms and conditions "substantially the same" as those contained in Trans Union's agreement with Pritzker. The offer was addressed to Trans Union's Board of Directors and a meeting with the Board, scheduled for that afternoon, was requested.

Van Gorkom's reaction to the KKR proposal was completely negative; he did not view the offer as being firm because of its financing condition. It was pointed out, to no avail, that Pritzker's offer had not only been similarly conditioned, but accepted on an expedited basis. Van Gorkom refused Kravis' request that Trans Union issue a press release announcing KKR's offer, on the ground that it might "chill" any other offer. * * * Romans and Kravis left with the understanding that their proposal would be presented to Trans Union's Board that afternoon.

Within a matter of hours and shortly before the scheduled Board meeting, Kravis withdrew his letter-offer. He gave as his reason a sudden decision by the Chief Officer of Trans Union's rail car leasing operation to withdraw from the KKR purchasing group. Van Gorkom had spoken to that officer about his participation in the KKR proposal immediately after his meeting with Romans and Kravis. However, Van Gorkom denied any responsibility for the officer's change of mind.

At the Board meeting later that afternoon, Van Gorkom did not inform the directors of the KKR proposal because he considered it "dead." Van Gorkom did not contact KKR again until January 20, when faced with the realities of this lawsuit, he then attempted to reopen negotiations. KKR declined due to the imminence of the February 10 stockholder meeting.

GE Credit Corporation's interest in Trans Union did not develop until November; and it made no written proposal until mid-January. Even then, its proposal was not in the form of an offer. Had there been time to do so, GE Credit was prepared to offer between $2 and $5 per share above the $55 per share price which Pritzker offered. But GE Credit needed an additional 60 to 90 days; and it was unwilling to make a formal offer without a concession from Pritzker extending the February 10 "deadline" for Trans Union's stockholder meeting. As previously stated, Pritzker refused to grant such extension; and on January 21, GE Credit terminated further negotiations with Trans Union. Its stated reasons, among others, were its "unwillingness to become involved in a bidding contest with Pritzker in the absence of the willingness of [the Pritzker interests] to terminate the proposed $55 cash merger."

*   *   *

* * * Our review of the record compels a finding that confirmation of the appropriateness of the Pritzker offer by an unfettered or free market test was virtually meaningless in the face of the terms and time limitations of Trans Union's Merger Agreement with Pritzker as amended October 10, 1980.

(3)

Finally, we turn to the Board's meeting of January 26, 1981. The defendant directors rely upon the action there taken to refute the contention that they did not reach an informed business judgment in approving the Pritzker merger. * * *

The Board's January 26 meeting was the first meeting following the filing of the plaintiffs' suit in mid-December and the last meeting before the previously-noticed shareholder meeting of February 10. All ten members of the Board and three outside attorneys attended the meeting. At that meeting the following facts, among other aspects of the Merger Agreement, were discussed:

(a) The fact that prior to September 20, 1980, no Board member or member of Senior Management, except Chelberg and Peterson, knew that

Van Gorkom had discussed a possible merger with Pritzker;

(b) The fact that the price of $55 per share had been suggested initially to Pritzker by Van Gorkom;

(c) The fact that the Board had not sought an independent fairness opinion;

(d) The fact that, at the September 20 Senior Management meeting, Romans and several members of Senior Management indicated both concern that the $55 per share price was inadequate and a belief that a higher price should and could be obtained;

(e) The fact that Romans had advised the Board at its meeting on September 20, that he and his department had prepared a study which indicated that the Company had a value in the range of $55 to $65 per share, and that he could not advise the Board that the $55 per share offer made by Pritzker was unfair.

* * * On the basis of this evidence, the defendants argue that whatever information the Board lacked to make a deliberate and informed judgment on September 20, or on October 8, was fully divulged to the entire Board on January 26. Hence, the argument goes, the Board's vote on January 26 to again "approve" the Pritzker merger must be found to have been an informed and deliberate judgment.

The Board then reviewed and discussed at great length the entire sequence of events pertaining to the proposed $55 cash merger * * *. Each of the Directors was involved in this discussion as well as counsel who had earlier joined the meeting. Following this review and discussion, such counsel advised the Directors that in light of their discussions, they could (a) continue to recommend to the stockholders that the latter vote in favor of the proposed merger, (b) recommend that the stockholders vote against the merger, or (c) take no position with respect to recommending the proposed merger and simply leave the decision to stockholders. After further discussion, it was moved, seconded, and unanimously voted that the Board of Directors continue to recommend that the stockholders vote in favor of the proposed merger * * *.

On the basis of this evidence, the defendants assert: (1) that the Trial Court was legally correct in widening the time frame for determining whether the defendants' approval of the Pritzker merger represented an informed business judgment to include the entire four-month period during which the Board considered the matter from September 20 through January 26; and (2) that, given this extensive evidence of the Board's further review and deliberations on January 26, this Court must affirm the Trial Court's conclusion that the Board's action was not reckless or improvident.

We cannot agree. We find the Trial Court to have erred, both as a matter of fact and as a matter of law, in relying on the action on January 26 to bring the defendants' conduct within the protection of the business judgment rule.

[The evidence indicates] recognition that the question of the alternative courses of action, available to the Board on January 26 with respect to the Pritzker merger, was a legal question, presenting to the Board (*after* its review of the full record developed through pre-trial discovery) *three* options: (1) to "continue to recommend" the Pritzker merger; (2) to "recommend that the stockholders vote against" the Pritzker merger; or (3) to take a noncommittal position on the merger and "simply leave the decision to [the] shareholders."

We must conclude from the foregoing that the Board was mistaken as a matter of law regarding its available courses of action on January 26, 1981. Options (2) and (3) were not viable or legally available to the Board * * *. The Board could not remain committed to the Pritzker merger and yet recommend that its stockholders vote it down; nor could it take a neutral position and delegate to the stockholders the unadvised decision as to whether to accept or reject the merger. Under § 251 (b) [of the Delaware Corporations Code], the Board had but two options: (1) to proceed with the merger and the stockholder meeting, with the Board's recommendation of approval; *or* (2) to rescind its agreement with Pritzker, withdraw its approval of the merger, and notify its stockholders that the proposed shareholder meeting was cancelled. There is no evidence that the Board gave any consideration to these * * *.

But the second course of action would have clearly involved a substantial risk—that the Board would be faced with suit by Pritzker for breach of contract based on its September 20 agreement as amended October 10. As previously noted, under the terms of the October 10 amendment, the Board's only ground for release from its agreement with Pritzker was its entry into a more favorable definitive agreement to sell the Company to a third party. Thus, in reality, the Board was not "free to turn down the Pritzker proposal" as the Trial Court found. Indeed, short of negotiating a better agreement with a third party, the Board's only basis for release from the Pritzker Agreement without liability would have been to establish fundamental wrongdoing by Pritzker. Clearly, the Board was not "free" to withdraw from its agreement with Pritzker on January 26 by simply relying on its self-induced failure to have reached an informed business judgment at the time of its original agreement. * * *

Therefore, the Trial Court's conclusion that the Board reached an informed business judgment on January 26 in determining whether to turn down the Pritzker "proposal" on that day cannot be sustained. * * *

* * *

[SECTION IV IS OMITTED]

V.

The defendants ultimately rely on the stockholder vote of February 10 for exoneration. The defendants contend that the stockholders' "overwhelming" vote approving the Pritzker Merger Agreement had the legal effect of curing any failure of the Board to reach an informed business judgment in its approval of the merger.

The parties tacitly agree that a discovered failure of the Board to reach an informed business judgment in approving the merger constitutes a voidable, rather than a void, act. Hence, the merger can be sustained, notwithstanding the infirmity of the Board's action, if its approval by majority vote of the shareholders is found to have been based on an informed electorate. * * * The disagreement between the parties arises over: (1) the Board's burden of disclosing to the shareholders all relevant and material information; and (2) the sufficiency of the evidence as to whether the Board satisfied that burden.

On this issue the Trial Court summarily concluded "that the stockholders of Trans Union were fairly informed as to the pending merger.... " The Court provided no supportive reasoning nor did the Court make any reference to the evidence of record.

The plaintiffs contend that the Court committed error by applying an erroneous disclosure standard of "adequacy" rather than "completeness" in determining the sufficiency of the Company's merger proxy materials. The plaintiffs also argue that the Board's proxy statements, both its original statement dated January 19 and its supplemental statement dated January 26, were incomplete in various material respects. * * *

The defendants deny that the Court committed legal or equitable error. On the question of the Board's burden of disclosure, the defendants state that there was no dispute at trial over the standard of disclosure required of the Board; but the defendants concede that the Board was required to disclose "all germane facts" which a reasonable shareholder would have considered important in deciding whether to approve the merger. * * *

The settled rule in Delaware is that "where a majority of fully informed stockholders ratify action of even interested directors, an attack on the ratified transaction normally must fail." * * * The question of whether shareholders have been fully informed such that their vote can be said to ratify director action, "turns on the fairness and completeness of the proxy materials submitted by the management to the ... shareholders."

[C]orporate directors owe to their stockholders a fiduciary duty to disclose all facts germane to the transaction at issue in an atmosphere of complete candor. We defined "germane" in the tender offer context as all "information such as a reasonable stockholder would consider important in deciding whether to sell or retain stock." * * * In reality, "germane" means material facts.

Applying this standard to the record before us, we find that Trans Union's stockholders were not fully informed of all facts material to their vote on the Pritzker Merger and that the Trial Court's ruling to the contrary is clearly erroneous. We list the material deficiencies in the proxy materials:

(1) The fact that the Board had no reasonably adequate information indicative of the intrinsic value of the Company, other than a concededly depressed market price, was without question material to the shareholders voting on the merger. * * *

Accordingly, the Board's lack of valuation information should have been disclosed. Instead, the directors cloaked the absence of such information in both the Proxy Statement and the Supplemental Proxy Statement. Through artful drafting, noticeably absent at the September 20 meeting, both documents create the impression that the Board knew the intrinsic worth of the Company. In particular, the Original Proxy Statement contained the following:

> although the Board of Directors regards the intrinsic value of the Company's assets to be significantly greater than their book value ..., systematic liquidation of such a large and complex entity as Trans Union is simply not regarded as a feasible method of realizing its inherent value. Therefore, a business combination such as the merger would seem to be the only practicable way in which the stockholders could realize the value of the Company.

The Proxy stated further that "in the view of the Board of Directors ... , the prices at which the Company's common stock has traded in recent years have not reflected the inherent value of the Company." What the Board failed to disclose to its stockholders was that the Board had not made any study of the intrinsic or inherent worth of the Company; nor had the Board even discussed the inherent value of the Company prior to approving the merger on September 20, or at either of the subsequent meetings on October 8 or January 26. * * *

(2) We find false and misleading the Board's characterization of the Romans report in the Supplemental Proxy Statement. The Supplemental Proxy stated:

> At the September 20, 1980 meeting of the Board of Directors of Trans Union, Mr. Romans indicated that while he could not say that $55.00 per share was an unfair price, he had prepared a preliminary report which reflected that the value of the Company was in the range of $55.00 to $65.00 per share.

Nowhere does the Board disclose that Romans stated to the Board that his calculations were made in a "search for ways to justify a price in connection with" a leveraged buy-out transaction, "rather than to say what the shares are worth," and that he stated to the Board that his conclusion thus arrived at "was not the same thing as saying that I have a valuation of the Company at X dollars." * * *

(3) We find misleading the Board's references to the "substantial" premium offered. The Board gave as their primary reason in support of the

merger the "substantial premium" shareholders would receive. But the Board did not disclose its failure to assess the premium offered in terms of other relevant valuation techniques, thereby rendering questionable its determination as to the substantiality of the premium over an admittedly depressed stock market price.

(4) We find the Board's recital in the Supplemental Proxy of certain events preceding the September 20 meeting to be incomplete and misleading. It is beyond dispute that a reasonable stockholder would have considered material the fact that Van Gorkom not only suggested the $55 price to Pritzker, but also that he chose the figure because it made feasible a leveraged buy-out. The directors disclosed that Van Gorkom suggested the $55 price to Pritzker. But the Board misled the shareholders when they described the basis of Van Gorkom's suggestion as follows:

> Such suggestion was based, at least in part, on Mr. Van Gorkom's belief that loans could be obtained from institutional lenders (together with about a $200 million equity contribution) which would justify the payment of such price, ...

Although by January 26, the directors knew the basis of the $55 figure, they did not disclose that Van Gorkom chose the $55 price because that figure would enable Pritzker to both finance the purchase of Trans Union through a leveraged buy-out and, within five years, substantially repay the loan out of the cash flow generated by the Company's operations.

(5) The Board's Supplemental Proxy Statement, mailed on or after January 27, added significant new matter, material to the proposal to be voted on February 10, which was not contained in the Original Proxy Statement. Some of this new matter was information which had only been disclosed to the Board on January 26; much was information known or reasonably available before January 21 but not revealed in the Original Proxy Statement. Yet, the stockholders were not informed of these facts. Included in the "new" matter first disclosed in the Supplemental Proxy Statement were the following:

(a) The fact that prior to September 20, 1980, no Board member or member of Senior Management, except Chelberg and Peterson, knew that Van Gorkom had discussed a possible merger with Pritzker;

(b) The fact that the sale price of $55 per share had been suggested initially to Pritzker by Van Gorkom;

(c) The fact that the Board had not sought an independent fairness opinion;

(d) The fact that Romans and several members of Senior Management had indicated concern at the September 20 Senior Management meeting that the $55 per share price was inadequate and had stated that a higher price should and could be obtained; and

(e) The fact that Romans had advised the Board at its meeting on September 20 that he and his department had prepared a study which indicated that the Company had a value in the range of $55 to $65 per share, and that he could not advise the Board that the $55 per share offer which Pritzker made was unfair.

* * *

The burden must fall on defendants who claim ratification based on shareholder vote to establish that the shareholder approval resulted from a fully informed electorate. On the record before us, it is clear that the Board failed to meet that burden. * * *.

* * *

VI.

* * *

We hold, therefore, that the Trial Court committed reversible error in applying the business judgment rule in favor of the director defendants in this case.

On remand, the Court of Chancery shall conduct an evidentiary hearing to determine the fair value of the shares represented by the plaintiffs' class, based on the intrinsic value of Trans Union on September 20, 1980. * * * Thereafter, an award of damages may be entered to the extent that the fair value of Trans Union exceeds $55 per share.

* * *

REVERSED and REMANDED for proceedings consistent herewith.

DISSENT:

McNEILLY, Justice, dissenting:

The majority opinion reads like an advocate's closing address to a hostile jury. * * * Throughout the opinion great emphasis is directed only to the negative, with nothing more than lip service granted the positive aspects of this case. In my opinion Chancellor Marvel (retired) should have been affirmed. The Chancellor's opinion was the product of well reasoned conclusions, based upon a sound deductive process, clearly supported by the evidence and entitled to deference in this appeal. Because of my diametrical opposition to all evidentiary conclusions of the majority, I respectfully dissent.

* * * The majority has spoken and has effectively said that Trans Union's Directors have been the victims of a "fast shuffle" by Van Gorkom and Pritzker. That is the beginning of the majority's comedy of errors. The first and most important error made is the majority's assessment of the directors' knowledge of the affairs of Trans Union and their combined ability to act in this situation under the protection of the business judgment rule.

* * * At the time the merger was proposed the inside five directors had collectively been employed by the Company for 116 years and had 68 years of combined experience as directors. * * * With the exception of [outside director, Dr.] Wallis, these were all chief executive officers of Chicago based corporations that were at least as large as Trans Union. The five "outside" directors had 78 years of combined experience as chief executive officers, and 53 years cumulative service as Trans Union directors.

The inside directors wear their badge of expertise in the corporate affairs of Trans Union on their sleeves. But what about the outsiders? Dr. Wallis is or was an economist and math statistician, a professor of economics at Yale University, dean of the graduate school of business at the University of Chicago, and Chancellor of the University of Rochester. Dr. Wallis had been on the Board of Trans Union since 1962. He also was on the Board of Bausch & Lomb, Kodak, Metropolitan Life Insurance Company, Standard Oil and others.

[Director] William B. Johnson is a University of Pennsylvania law graduate, President of Railway Express until 1966, Chairman and Chief Executive of I.C. Industries Holding Company, and member of Trans Union's Board since 1968.

[Director] Joseph Lanterman, a Certified Public Accountant, is or was President and Chief Executive of American Steel, on the Board of International Harvester, Peoples Energy, Illinois Bell Telephone, Harris Bank and Trust Company, Kemper Insurance Company and a director of Trans Union for four years.

[Director] Graham Morgan is a chemist, was Chairman and Chief Executive Officer of U.S. Gypsum, and in the 17 and 18 years prior to the Trans Union transaction had been involved in 31 or 32 corporate takeovers.

[Director] Robert Reneker attended University of Chicago and Harvard Business Schools. He was President and Chief Executive of Swift and Company, director of Trans Union since 1971, and member of the Boards of seven other corporations including U.S. Gypsum and the Chicago Tribune.

Directors of this caliber are not ordinarily taken in by a "fast shuffle". I submit they were not taken into this multi-million dollar corporate transaction without being fully informed and aware of the state of the art as it pertained to the entire corporate panorama of Trans Union. * * * These men knew Trans Union like the back of their hands and were more than well qualified to make on the spot informed business judgments concerning the affairs of Trans Union including a 100% sale of the corporation. Lest we forget, the corporate world of then and now operates on what is so aptly referred to as "the fast track". These men were at the time an integral part of that world, all professional business men, not intellectual figureheads.

The majority of this Court holds that the Board's decision, reached on September 20, 1980, to approve the merger was not the product of an *informed* business judgment, that the Board's subsequent efforts to amend the Merger Agreement and take other curative action were *legally and factually* ineffectual, and that the Board did *not deal with complete candor* with the stockholders by failing to disclose all material facts, which they knew or should have known, before securing the stockholders' approval of the merger. I disagree.

At the time of the September 20, 1980 meeting the Board was acutely aware of Trans Union and its prospects. The problems created by accumulated investment tax credits and accelerated depreciation were discussed repeatedly at Board meetings, and all of the directors understood the problem thoroughly. Moreover, at the July, 1980 Board meeting the directors had reviewed Trans Union's newly prepared five-year forecast, and at the August, 1980 meeting Van Gorkom presented the results of a comprehensive study of Trans Union made by The Boston Consulting Group. This study was prepared over an 18 month period and consisted of a detailed analysis of all Trans Union subsidiaries, including competitiveness, profitability, cash throw-off, cash consumption, technical competence and future prospects for contribution to Trans Union's combined net income.

At the September 20 meeting Van Gorkom reviewed all aspects of the proposed transaction and repeated the explanation of the Pritzker offer he had earlier given to senior management. Having heard Van Gorkom's explanation of the Pritzker's offer, and Brennan's explanation of the merger documents the directors discussed the matter. Out of this discussion arose an insistence on the part of the directors that two modifications to the offer be made. First, they required that any potential competing bidder be given access to the same information concerning Trans Union that had been provided to the Pritzkers. Second, the merger documents were to be modified to reflect the fact that the directors could accept a better offer and would not be required to recommend the Pritzker offer if a better offer was made. The following language was inserted into the agreement:

> "Within 30 days after the execution of this Agreement, TU shall call a meeting of its stockholders (the 'Stockholder's Meeting') for the purpose of approving and adopting the Merger Agreement. The Board of Directors shall recommend to the stockholders of TU that they approve and adopt the Merger Agreement (the 'Stockholders' Approval') and shall use its best efforts to obtain the requisite vote therefor; *provided, however, that GL and NTC acknowledge that the Board of Directors of TU may have a competing fiduciary obligation to the Stockholders under certain* circumstances." (Emphasis added)

While the language is not artfully drawn, the evidence is clear that the intention underlying that language was to make specific the right that the directors assumed they had, that is, to accept any offer that they thought was better, and not to recommend the Pritzker offer in the face of a better one. At the conclusion of the meeting, the proposed merger was approved.

At a subsequent meeting on October 8, 1981 the directors, with the consent of the Pritzkers, amended the Merger Agreement so as to establish the right of Trans Union to *solicit* as well as to receive higher bids, although the Pritzkers insisted that their merger proposal be presented to the stockholders at the same time that the proposal of any third party was presented. A second amendment, which became effective on October 10, 1981, further provided that Trans Union might unilaterally terminate the proposed merger with the Pritzker company in the event that prior to February 10, 1981 there existed a definitive agreement with a third party for a merger, consolidation, sale of assets, or purchase or exchange of Trans Union stock which was more favorable for the stockholders of Trans Union than the Pritzker offer and which was conditioned upon receipt of stockholder approval and the absence of an injunction against its consummation.

Following the October 8 board meeting of Trans Union, the investment banking firm of Salomon Brothers was retained by the corporation to search for better offers than that of the Pritzkers, Salomon Brothers being charged with the responsibility of doing "whatever possible to see if there is a superior bid in the marketplace over a bid that is on the table for Trans Union". In undertaking such project, it was agreed that Salomon Brothers would be paid the amount of $500,000 to cover its expenses as well as a fee equal to 3/8ths of 1% of the aggregate fair market value of the consideration to be received by the company in the case of a merger or the like, which meant that in the event Salomon Brothers should find a buyer willing to pay a price of $56.00 a share instead of $55.00, such firm would receive a fee of roughly $2,650,000 plus disbursements.

As the first step in proceeding to carry out its commitment, *Salomon Brothers had a brochure prepared, which set forth Trans Union's financial history, described the company's business in detail and set forth Trans Union's operating and financial projections. Salomon Brothers also prepared a list of over 150 companies which it believed might be suitable merger partners, and while four of such companies, namely, General Electric, Borg-Warner, Bendix, and Genstar, Ltd. showed some interest in such a merger, none made a firm proposal to Trans Union and only General Electric* showed a sustained interest. * * * As matters transpired, no firm offer which bettered the Pritzker offer of $55 per share was ever made.

On January 21, 1981 a proxy statement was sent to the shareholders of Trans Union advising them of a February 10, 1981 meeting in which the merger would be voted. On January 26, 1981 the directors held their regular meeting. At this meeting the Board discussed the instant merger as well as all events, including this litigation, surrounding it. At the conclusion of the meeting the Board unanimously voted to recommend to the stockholders that they approve the merger. Additionally, the directors reviewed and approved a Supplemental Proxy Statement which, among other things, advised the stockholders of what had occurred at the instant meeting and of the fact that General Electric had decided not to make an offer. On February 10, 1981 the stockholders of Trans Union met pursuant to notice and voted overwhelmingly in favor of the Pritzker merger, 89% of the votes cast being in favor of it.

I have no quarrel with the majority's analysis of the business judgment rule. It is the application of that rule to these facts which is wrong. An overview of the entire record, rather than the limited view of bits and pieces which the majority has exploded like popcorn, convinces me that the directors made an informed business judgment which was buttressed by their test of the market.

At the time of the September 20 meeting the 10 members of Trans Union's Board of Directors were highly qualified and well informed about the affairs and prospects of Trans Union. These directors were acutely aware of the historical problems facing Trans Union which were caused by the tax laws. They had discussed these problems *ad nauseam.* * * * At the September 20 meeting Van Gorkom presented the Pritzker offer, and the board then heard from James Brennan, the company's counsel in this matter, who discussed the legal documents. Following this, the Board directed that certain changes be made in the merger documents. These changes made it clear that the Board was free to accept a better offer than Pritzker's if one was made. The above facts reveal that the Board did not act in a grossly negligent manner in informing themselves of the relevant and available facts before passing on the merger. To the contrary, this record reveals that the directors acted with the utmost care in informing themselves of the relevant and available facts before passing on the merger.

The majority finds that Trans Union stockholders were not fully informed and that the directors breached their fiduciary duty of complete candor to the stockholders * * * in that the proxy materials were deficient in five areas.

Here again is exploitation of the negative by the majority without giving credit to the positive. To respond to the conclusions of the majority would merely be unnecessary prolonged argument. But briefly what did the proxy materials disclose? The proxy material informed the shareholders that projections were furnished to potential purchasers and such projections indicated that Trans Union's net income might increase to approximately $153 million in 1985. That projection, what is almost three times the net income of $58,248,000 reported by Trans Union as its net income for December 31, 1979 confirmed the statement in the proxy materials that the "Board of Directors believes that, assuming reasonably favorable economic and financial conditions, the Company's prospects for future earnings growth are excellent." This material was certainly sufficient to place the Company's stockholders on notice that there was a reasonable basis to believe that the prospects for future earnings growth were excellent, and that the value of their stock was more than the stock market value of their shares reflected.

Overall, my review of the record leads me to conclude that the proxy materials adequately complied with Delaware law in informing the shareholders about the proposed transaction and the events surrounding it.

* * *

CHRISTIE, Justice, dissenting:

I respectfully dissent.

* * * I believe that the record taken as a whole supports a conclusion that the actions of the defendants are protected by the business judgment rule. * * * I also am satisfied that the record supports a conclusion that the defendants acted with * * * complete candor * * *. * * *

NOTES AND QUESTIONS

1.   Who got it right, the majority or the dissent in *Smith v. Van Gorkom*? The consensus among corporations scholars is probably that one of their number got it right when he called this case, "one of the worst decisions in the history of corporate law." Daniel R. Fischel, The Business Judgment Rule and the Trans Union Case, 40 Bus. Law. 1437, 1455 (1985). Still, even the dissenters seem to indicate that the majority got the law right, but their application of the law to the facts seems to be the difficulty. Why, precisely, does the majority feel that the Board failed in their duty, and, why, precisely, doesn't the business judgment rule cover? In other words, is this really the same case as *Francis v. United Jersey Bank*, as the majority seems to think, or is it a case more like *Kamin v. American Express*, discussed in the last set of notes and questions? For something of a dissent to Professor Fischel's view of *Smith v. Van Gorkom*, and a fascinating study of the background and the personalities of the case, see Stephen M. Bainbridge, "The Story of *Smith v. Van Gorkom*," in J. Mark Ramseyer, ed., Corporate Law Stories 198 (2009). Professor Bainbridge observes that the Delaware Supreme Court's decision in *Smith v. Van Gorkom* "encourages inquiry, deliberation, care, and process. The decision strongly encourages boards to seek outside counsel and financial advice, which is consistent with evidence that groupthink can be prevented by outside expert advice and evaluations. [footnote omitted]" *Id.*, at 221. The implication is that the decision was a wise one. Do you agree?

2.   It is certainly of interest that shortly after the Delaware Court's decision in *Smith v. Van Gorkom* the Delaware legislature amended its corporate law to provide that the charter of a corporation in Delaware may contain

A provision eliminating or limiting the personal liability of a director to the corporation or its stockholders for monetary damages for breach of fiduciary duty as a director, provided that such provision shall not eliminate or limit the liability of a director: (i) For any breach of the director's duty of loyalty to the corporation or its stockholders; (ii) for acts or omissions not in good faith or which involve intentional misconduct or a knowing violation of law; (iii) under § 174 of this title; or (iv) for any transaction from which the director derived an improper personal benefit. * * *

Del. Corp. Code 102(b)(7). What would have been the effect on the Directors in *Smith v. Van Gorkom* if Trans Union's charter contained such a provision?

Would you have voted for the adoption of 102(b)(7)? Can you understand how it can be said that, in effect, 102(b)(7) overrules *Smith v. Van Gorkom*? Note, however, that *Smith v. Van Gorkom* is still, technically speaking, good law, and that if a Delaware corporation fails to take advantage of 102(b)(7), liability of a kind that was imposed in *Smith* is still a possibility. You will not be surprised to learn that since the passage of 102(b)(7) the great majority of Delaware corporations have amended their charters accordingly if they were in existence before 102(b)(7)'s passage, and those formed subsequently have routinely incorporated provisions authorized by 102(b)(7). Is it becoming clearer to you why Delaware is such an attractive state for incorporation?

3. What do you make of the facts (and the law) of *Smith v. Van Gorkom*? It is a lengthy case, and is offered here (even in light of Section 102(b)(7)), as a splendid opportunity to distinguish between acts of nonfeasance and what we might label acts of misfeasance, the one giving rise to liability if there is director negligence or director gross negligence, and the other covered by the business judgment rule. Again, the majority believes it is confronted with a situation involving director gross negligence, and the dissenters believe they are examining a classic business judgment rule situation. Does the analysis in the case help you sort out which is which? Chancellor ALLEN, perhaps the pre-eminent Delaware Chancellor of our era, remarked in his opinion in the case of *In re RJR Nabisco, Inc. Shareholders Litigation*, 1989 WL 7036 (Del.Ch. 1989), "that the amount of information that it is prudent to have before a decision is made is itself a business judgment of the very type that courts are institutionally poorly equipped to make." *Id.*, at *19, quoted in Bainbridge, *supra* at 217–218, n. 121. How does that suggest *Smith v. Van Gorkom* should have been decided?

Virtually every corporations casebook includes *Smith v. Van Gorkom*, but in an intriguing recent essay, Lawrence A. Hamermesh, Fiduciary Duty, Limited Liability and the Law of Delaware: Why I do not teach *Smith v. Van Gorkom*, 34 Ga. L. Rev. 477 (2000), a law professor at Widener University in Delaware argues that it is a mistake to teach the case to law students. Professor Hamermesh states that "The case is simply too involved factually, too dependent upon knowledge of complex factual and legal matters concerning mergers and acquisitions and valuation, and too light on good legal reasoning to justify an extended effort by students, especially when most students have no intention of representing business clients at all, let alone engaging in a mergers and acquisitions practice." Id., at 479. How would you respond to each of Hamermesh's points? Most important, says Hamermesh, *"Van Gorkom's* greatest vice is that it conveys the inaccurate impression that claims for money damages against corporate managers for failure of attention constitute a common and viable form of litigation. Nothing could be further from the truth. Exculpatory charter provisions adopted pursuant to statutes, almost universally enacted since *Van Gorkom*, have rendered the damages claim for breach of the duty of care essentially non-existent." *Ibid.* Do you suppose he is correct about that? Does *Francis v. United Jersey Bank* suggest otherwise? It is intriguing to observe that from 1985 to 1994, Professor Hamermesh was a partner in the leading Wilmington, Delaware law firm of Morris, Nichols, Arsht & Tunnell, which represented the corporate defendants in *Smith v. Van Gorkom*, though he had no personal role in the litigation. Would you say that fact enhances or detracts from his credibility?

4. In another line of cases the Delaware courts have also indicated that the Directors' obligations include a "duty to monitor." In key language from the most important of this line of cases, *In re Caremark International Inc. Derivative Litigation* 698 A.2d 959 (Del.Ch. 1996), the very well respected then Chancellor of Delaware, WILLIAM ALLEN, stated that "A director's obligation includes a duty to attempt in good faith to assure that a corporate information and reporting system, which the board concludes is adequate, exists, and that failure to do so under some circumstances may, in theory at least, render a director liable for losses." The duty to monitor, a duty enacted into federal law in the Sarbanes–Oxley Act of 2002, which we will encounter later, is particularly important in regulated industries, such as banks, utility companies, or, as in *Caremark* itself, the provision of health-care services.

Precisely how the duty to monitor is carried out seems to be a subject of some controversy. For example, it is a nice question whether the inside directors can be trusted effectively to monitor the conduct of the officers of the corporation. To meet this problem, in the *Caremark* case, as part of the settlement, Caremark agreed to from a "Compliance and Ethics Committee," made up of four directors, two of whom were to be outside directors. The Compliance and Ethics Committee was to "report to the Caremark board on monitoring and compliance systems." On the *Caremark* settlement, see generally Hillary A. Sale, "Good Faith's Procedure and Substance: In re Caremark International Inc., Derivative Litigation," Chapter 14 in Jonathan R. Macey, Ed., The Iconic Cases in Corporate Law 278, 282 (2008).

As Ms. Sale notes, quoting from Chancellor ALLEN's opinion, when a court is reviewing whether the board did an an adequate job performing its duty to monitor, the standard to be used is the business judgment rule, and the question to be asked is whether the board undertook a good faith effort "to be informed to exercise appropriate judgment." Id., at 283, quoting 698 A.2d, at 968. (Is this standard of "good faith" consistent with the Court's holding in *Smith v. Van Gorkom*?) An earlier case on the duty to monitor had held that "absent cause for suspicion there is no duty upon the directors to install and operate a corporate system of espionage to ferret out wrongdoing which they have no reason to suspect exists." *Graham v. Allis–Chalmers Manufacturing Co.*, 188 A.2d 125, 130 (Del. 1963), but Ms. Sale quite correctly observes that Chancellor ALLEN found this exculpatory language too broad, and that, given the requirements of the times, it was better to mandate that "directors needed to establish information and reporting systems to satisfy their good-faith obligations to be reasonably informed." Sale, supra, at 285.

For further guidance on the requirements of good faith in fulfilling directors' oversight and monitoring roles see *Stone v. Ritter*, 911 A.2d 362 (Del. 2006), discussed in Sale, *supra* at 289–292. Ms. Sale concludes that Stone "clarifies that a board that fails to either implement the appropriate [monitoring] system *or* fails to respond to red flags, is not a good-faith or loyal monitor." Id., at 293 (emphasis in original). Such "red flags" might include "problematic practices revealed in audit reports," "newspaper of other media reports of specific company problems" or "pending governmental investigations," or "general media stories of significant industry or broad-based governance or accounting issues." Id., at 293–294. Similar "red flags" might be raised by "negative government inspections of companies in a regulated industry," or "resignations of fellow directors." Id., at 293.

For another penetrating study of the duty to monitor cases, and another appreciation of the manner in which Chancellor ALLEN sought to balance the requirements for the Delaware courts to monitor director conduct with the need to allow business persons the freedom to manage their firms in a manner to serve the interests of shareholders, see Jennifer Arlen, "The Story of *Allis–Chalmers*, *Caremark*, and *Stone*: Directors' Evolving Duty to Monitor," Chapter 11 in J. Mark Ramseyer, ed., Corporate Law Stories 323 (2009).

D.   DUTY OF LOYALTY

HOLDEN v. CONSTRUCTION MACHINERY CO.
Supreme Court of Iowa.
202 N.W.2d 348 (1972).

[RAWLINGS, J.]

* * *

[Construction Machinery Co. ("CMC")] is a Waterloo-based corporation engaged primarily in the manufacture of tools and equipment for concrete and construction industries. About 1936, L.S. Holden became the sole owner of CMC. He and his first wife, now Mrs. Leona Hansen, had three children, Herle, Warren and a younger daughter, Mrs. Melva Davey. During the years pertinent to this lawsuit and until his death, July 3, 1955, L.S. Holden was married to Carmen Holden. Except for the last few months of his life L.S. Holden ran the business, but gradually accorded Warren more authority in the management area.

During his lifetime L.S. Holden made substantial gifts of CMC stock to his three children. The father also engineered a series of transactions by which Herle and Warren acquired additional stock from other family shareholders. Resultantly, at time of the father's death July 3, 1955, he possessed 544 shares, Herle and Warren each then owning 2028 shares.

Within a few days after L.S. Holden's demise the contents of his will became known. To the extent here relevant it bequeathed 25 percent of his stock in CMC to Herle, 75 percent to Warren.

Herle testified he was extremely disappointed upon learning his father's will gave majority control of CMC to Warren. There followed several months of frequent discussions between the brothers during which Herle vainly explored possible courses which would make him an equal stockholder with Warren. The latter remained firm in his resolution not to relinquish control. The problem was compounded by the fact that Carmen elected to take her statutory dower interest in the estate instead of the share provided under terms of the will. This meant, among other things, if her dower interest was to be monetarily satisfied some method must be employed which would make cash available to the estate for that purpose.

Although no comprehensive agreement between all of the interested parties was ever reduced to writing, it is evident an accord was reached. Melva received $42,510, Warren $26,924.73, and Carmen $56,060.66. Furthermore, 540 shares of CMC stock were passed by the estate to Carmen, which she then transferred to CMC in consideration of its agreement to pay her a total of $93,484.80 in five equal payments. The $26,924.73 check to Warren was apparently an adjustment for the fact that since the will left him with 272 shares more than Herle, an agreement had been reached which retired 540 shares. Consequently, Warren held 2031 shares, Herle 2029 shares.

Herle testified all of this was resolved between himself and Warren during a discussion early in 1956. That under this agreement (1) Herle consented to the arrangement giving Warren "control" of CMC (2) Herle promised to keep all of his CMC stock, fulfill his contractual commitments to Carmen and Melva, and remain in CMC's employ; (3) Warren agreed in return that both of them would have employment with CMC of equal duration, and their compensation, salaries and bonuses, would always be the same. Warren denies any discussion regarding duration of employment or equal recompense.

After the father's death Warren became president of CMC and continued as general manager. Herle remained vice-president in charge of manufacturing. From 1955 through 1963 they received equal remuneration. There appears, however, to have been a noticeable deterioration in their relationship during that period of time.

In December 1960, the board of directors had been expanded to include five key employees, along with Warren and Herle. Active monthly meetings followed for a period of time. This regularity was discontinued by Warren not long after the board out-voted him regarding expansion of research and development facilities. Abandonment of the regular board meeting program served to deprive Herle of an appropriate forum in which he could, and often did, take issue with Warren.

In early 1964, CMC engaged Batten and Associates (Batten), a management consultant organization, to effect a survey of CMC's operations. Joe McBride was then working for Batten. The first report of that study (Batten I) was submitted April 22, 1964. Based upon problems there disclosed a second study was suggested and undertaken in mid-1964 primarily to (1) evaluate management personnel by tests and interviews, and (2) propose a plan of organization. Batten II was made available August 27, 1964. One of the major recommendations there advanced was that manufacturing be placed directly under Warren rather than Herle as in the past. It also suggested Herle retain responsibility only in the areas of purchasing and design engineering. In any event, the organizational formula proposed in Batten II was never followed. Warren shortly announced a plan putting Herle in charge of engineering only, with production, purchasing, industrial engineering, research and development being under Warren's control. The result was a further deterioration of the brothers' relationship.

Near the end of 1964, Warren paid himself a supplemental bonus of $1500 which Herle did not receive. When salaries were fixed for 1965, Warren got a $50 per month increase but Herle's pay remained at the 1964 level.

The latter became aware of the bonus and salary differential sometime after the first of the year 1965, and in March or April contacted Mr. Beecher, a Waterloo attorney, seeking advice concerning violation of his claimed equal compensation agreement * * * and other related problems. Beecher realized Herle's very substantial estate was "locked" in the minority interest of a closely held family corporation. A series of meetings followed among Warren, Herle and their respective attorneys. Mr. Beecher asserted Herle's claimed violation of an equal compensation agreement. Counsels' efforts were directed, however, toward possible solution of the larger overall problems. The relationship between Warren and Herle had then seriously deteriorated and they were communicating almost entirely through their attorneys and by memos passed or placed on the other's desk.

In June 1965, Joe McBride was hired as vice-president of operations, a position comparable to that held by Herle prior to Batten II. Herle was replaced as head of engineering and given the title vice-president in charge of corporate development with no management authority. Being no longer involved in operations he was not participating in meetings and discussions relative to CMC's operations, but continued to report for work regularly and attended those board meetings irregularly held.

In the spring of 1966 Herle was relieved of all duties and advised [that] a Stock Purchase Agreement which existed between him and CMC was being cancelled, as were life insurance policies on Herle's life, owned by CMC. Although then also told his salary was being reduced, this did not actually occur until later. Upon advice of counsel Herle continued to report for work but had nothing to do.

At the annual stockholders' meeting in early 1968, Herle was reelected to the board of directors, but not made an officer. In April 1968, came a letter from Mr. Hoxie, corporation secretary, proposing Herle's early retirement. This was effectuated by board action in late May. Herle was thereby allowed retirement compensation equivalent to half the average of his highest five years pay within the last ten years. That has continued to date. After Herle's forced retirement he was required to vacate his office, and allowed only limited access to restricted corporate records. * * *

* * *

I.   Our review is de novo. Although we are not bound by trial court's fact findings they are accorded weight, especially when considering credibility of witnesses. * * *

II.   First to be considered is defendants' proposition to the effect [that the] trial court erroneously found for Herle regarding the Chamberlain [a local corporation] stock transaction. More specifically they take issue with the finding that such stock was purchased by Warren in 1959 as an investment on behalf of CMC, being thereafter held by him in constructive trust for the corporation.

The record reveals, while Warren was president of the Waterloo Chamber of Commerce in 1954, a successful Chamberlain stock subscription campaign was undertaken. Warren actively participated in that program. His election as a Chamberlain director followed.

In 1959, 2000 shares of Chamberlain stock, restricted to board members, were issued in Warren's name, but paid for by a $10,000 check from CMC. This transaction was shown on CMC books as a purchase of "Stock in Other Corporations", and so remained until 1964. Warren claims, on April 6 of that year he gave CMC his personal no-interest-note for $10,000. In any event, a journal voucher dated April 30, 1964, was then entered debiting "Secured Loans to Officers" account; crediting "Stock in Other Corporations" account for $10,000, with an explanatory memo reciting "to show transfer of 2000 shares common stock of CC (Chamberlain) to W.A. Holden. Note for $10,000 given CMC by W.A. Holden secured by 6500 shares Chamberlain Stock".

[Herle]   alleges the Chamberlain stock was at all times an asset of CMC and the transfer to Warren in 1964 was for less than its fair value, thus a fraud on CMC.

In an attempt to support their opposing position defendants, and more particularly Warren, attempted to show (a) the transaction was first mistakenly entered upon CMC books as "Stock in Other Corporations"; (b) the 1964 paper transaction was merely a correction of an original error; (c) Warren gave CMC his personal note for $10,000 when the stock was purchased in 1959, and then delivered to Mr. Ries, head of CMC accounting department, a memo directing the transaction be recorded to show the $10,000 payment as a loan to Warren, both instruments being since lost; (d) purchase of the Chamberlain stock was at all times his personal investment.

The testimony with regard thereto is so intermittently protracted and involved as to preclude any summarization. We can do no more than observe that defense counsel endeavored to explain Warren's testimonial statements as being, even to them, a belatedly revealed and self-initiated reconstruction of past events effort on Warren's part. It still remains, however, [that] Warren's testimony on the subject at hand, and that of his quasi-corroborative associate, Leonard Ries, is so replete with inconsistent, improbable and paralogistic statements as to be of no evidential weight or value. * * *

III.   But defendants argue Herle is estopped to assert his derivative complaint regarding the Chamberlain transaction, and the claim is barred by laches.

The elements of equitable estoppel are well established. There must be conduct amounting to false representation or concealment, and a party relying thereon must be thereby misled into doing or failing to do something he would not otherwise have done or omitted. A party asserting this defense has the burden to establish all essential elements thereof by clear, convincing and satisfactory proof. * * *

Also, despite defendants' claim to the contrary, one must knowingly take a position with intention it be acted upon, and that there be reliance thereon by another to his prejudice. * * *

The record discloses Herle's examination of the 1960 CMC audit led him to believe the corporation, absent board authorization, had purchased some Chamberlain stock. From the subsequent 1964 audit he assumed Warren had bought it because the amount owing by Warren to CMC went up by the same amount as the account regarding Chamberlain stock went down. But this alone revealed no actionable irregularity. Later events, however, so alerted Herle that in December 1965 or January 1966, he discussed this matter with attorney Beecher. The latter initially saw nothing wrong from an examination of the audits and suggested Herle talk to Warren, the accountants, or Mr. Lynch, a Chamberlain officer. Also, at a December 1967 CMC board meeting Warren directed that Herle talk to no one about assets of the company, Herle being at the same time ordered to get out and stay out. Moreover, Herle was unaware of any purported "correcting" 1964 voucher until just prior to the filing of this action.

It is to us apparent the factual situation here involved precludes application of estoppel as alleged by defendants. Stated otherwise, they have failed to establish by clear and convincing proof, requisite knowledge on Herle's part, deceptive or fraudulent conduct or representations by him, actual detriment to defendants, or any other essential elements of estoppel.

By the same token, we find no merit in defendants' assertion of laches which is purely an equitable doctrine based on public policy and closely related to estoppel. It pertains to delay in asserting or prosecuting a claim to the disadvantage or prejudice of another. * * *

* * *

An inspection of the record before us reveals no such unreasonable delay by Herle in asserting this derivative cause nor, for reasons set forth above, is there any such prejudice to defendants shown as will support the asserted laches defense.

It further appears defendants here endeavor to invoke estoppel and laches upon the basis of their own concealments, misleading tactics and misrepresentations. This alone defeats their attempt to fasten the consequences of any claimed delay on Herle's shoulders. * * *

* * *

IV. Furthermore, the corporate records disclose, and Herle established by a preponderance of evidence, in support of the instantly considered derivative action, [that] Warren breached his fiduciary duties as a corporate director of CMC. On that matter several well established legal principles come into full play.

"Where it appears a corporate director is dealing on behalf of the corporation with another corporation of which he is also a director he is required to make a full disclosure and obtain the consent of all concerned. When it appears he has not done so the burden is on him to establish the good faith, honesty and fairness of the transaction. *First Trust and Savings Bank v. Iowa–Wisconsin Bridge Co., 8 Cir., 98 F.2d 416, 425;* and *Des Moines Bank and Trust Co. v. George M. Bechtel and Co., 243 Iowa 1007, 1081, 51 N.W.2d 174 (1952).* We said, in *Gord v. Iowana Farms Milk Co., 245 Iowa 1, 18, 60 N.W.2d 820, 830 (1953):*

"This rule and burden should also apply in dealings between directors who are stockholders, especially in a relatively small corporation in which the stock is closely held.'

"Such director is not liable merely for failure to make full disclosure and to obtain consent but because the transaction is not in good faith, honest and fair." *Charles v. Epperson and Co., Inc., 258 Iowa 409, 414, 137 N.W.2d 605 (1965).*

And in *Gord v. Iowana Farms Milk Co., 245 Iowa at 16–17, 60 N.W.2d at 829,* this court said:

"And bearing upon the fiduciary relation of corporate directors and officers, * * * 'It is the policy of the courts to put such fiduciaries beyond the reach of temptation and the enticement of illicit profit. These principles are founded on the soundest morality and have received the clearest recognition in all courts'.

"A director is required to act in the utmost good faith and not for his own personal interest. * * *

"And in *Hoyt v. Hampe, 206 Iowa 206, 220, 214 N.W. 718, 724,* reh'g overruled, *206 Iowa 222, 220 N.W. 45* * * * this court stated:" * * * 'The policy of the law is to put fiduciaries beyond the reach of temptation, by making it unprofitable for them to yield to it. To that end an act by the fiduciary in which personal interest and duty conflict is voidable at the mere option of the beneficiary, regardless of good faith or results. The court will not inquire into its profitableness to the trustee or prejudice to the beneficiary. This rule is applicable to the acts of boards of directors [citing cases].' "

Also, because of its pertinency as an overall guiding principle, we quote this from *Des Moines Bank and Trust Co. v. Bechtel and Co., 243 Iowa at 1081, 51 N.W.2d at 216:*

"As * * * noted, the promoters, officers and directors of a corporation are the agents of and act for it, and indirectly for its stockholders, and they are the trustees or quasi trustees, at least, of the property of the corporation for the company and its stockholders. They occupy a fiduciary relation to the corporation on which relation the stockholders may rely. The corporate entity and the stockholders, in particular, may presume that these trustees will perform their duties with the diligence, honesty and the utmost good faith, inherent and implicit in their functions. They are not required to be ever on their guard and watchful lest those trustees misapply, destroy, embezzle, steal the corporate assets, or defraud them. Corporate directors and officers may under proper circumstances transact business with the corporation including the purchase or sale of property, but it must be done in the strictest good faith and with full disclosure of the facts to, and the consent of, all concerned. And the burden is upon them to establish their good faith, honesty and fairness. Such transactions are scanned by the courts with skepticism and the closest scrutiny, and may be nullified on slight grounds. It is the policy of the courts to put such fiduciaries beyond the reach of temptation and the enticement of illicit profit. These principles are founded on the soundest morality and have received the clearest recognition in all courts. * * * "

From all this flows the conclusion, officers and directors of a corporate entity, particularly management controlling directors of closely held corporations, occupy a fiduciary, or at least a quasi-fiduciary position as to the corporation and its stockholders. They are thus required to at all times act in utmost good faith, and must exercise powers held for the sole benefit of the corporation and its stockholders, never for their personal gain. Equity holds them strictly accountable as trustees. * * *

Therefore, Warren must be held strictly accountable to CMC for the Chamberlain stock or its fair market value, and for all increases, income, proceeds or dividends realized therefrom.

V.   An examination of the record reveals to us, as it did to trial court, a preponderance of the evidence supports these conclusions: (1) Warren acquired and held the Chamberlain stock in constructive trust for CMC; (2) as of April 3, 1970, he had received these cash dividends from Chamberlain:

$640.00 in July 1967

$640.00 in October 1967

$640.00 in January 1968

$640.00 in April 1968

$800.00 in July 1968

$800.00 in October 1968

$800.00 in January 1969

$800.00 in April 1969

$800.00 in July 1969

$800.00 in October 1969

$800.00 in January 1970

(3) Warren liquidated his April 6, 1964, note to CMC by payment of $2000 December 15, 1964, $2000 May 11, 1966, $6000 January 2, 1968; (4) since 1959 the 2000 shares of Chamberlain stock have been twice split, two for one, resulting in 8000 total shares.

Upon the aforesaid substantially supported holdings and conclusions, trial court decreed the 8000 shares of Chamberlain stock held in constructive trust by Warren be forthwith transferred to CMC; as of April 3, 1970, Warren had received cash dividends on Chamberlain stock which, with interest at five percent, made a total of $14,363; as of the same date Warren's liquidation of his aforesaid April 6, 1964 note, with five percent interest, totaled $11,517; the amount due CMC from Warren exceeded the refund owing to Warren by CMC and that Warren owes and shall pay the excess of $2,845.50 to CMC. To that must be added any dividends since received by Warren on the Chamberlain stock, to be accordingly determined and assessment made, on remand. * * *

* * *

Alternatively[, the] trial court held, in event Warren did not still possess the 8000 shares of stock in Chamberlain then, upon satisfactory proof thereof, judgment would be entered for CMC against Warren upon a determination of [compensatory damages] due by utilization of a $7 per share value. On remand, however, Warren shall be held accountable for all additional stock which may have been derivatively acquired by him as the result of any split of Chamberlain stock subsequent to entry of judgment in trial court from which this appeal is taken.

* * *

VI. On cross-appeal Herle contends, however, trial court erred in holding exemplary damages were not allowable against Warren by reason of (1) his intentional acts of fraud in connection with the Chamberlain stock transaction, (2) his malicious attempt to "freeze" Herle out of CMC.

* * *

Ordinarily, actual damage must be established as a condition precedent to an allowance of punitive damages. * * *

On the other hand, in a stockholder's derivative action an equity court may, in its discretion, award exemplary damages upon a showing that some legally protected right has been invaded, such as an intentional act of fraud or other wrongful conduct. * * *

Turning now to the matter of Warren's alleged fraudulent conduct, trial court was:

" * * * not sufficiently satisfied that an intentionally fraudulent act was committed in transferring the asset in April, 1964, the finding heretofore made being only that the transfer constituted a 'legal fraud' upon CMC. The fact that Warren might well have felt that he was entitled to the advantage of the CC (Chamberlain) stock transaction because his position as a board member made its original acquisition possible adds further to the Court's conclusion that exemplary damages should not be awarded for that act."

We cannot agree.

An intentional act of fraud, as the term is here used, does not mean actionable fraud or deceit. * * *

On the contrary, an intentional act of fraud in a court of equity includes all acts, omissions and concealments which involve a breach of either legal or equitable duties, trust or confidence, justly reposed, which are injurious to another or by which an undue or unconscionable advantage is taken. * * *

For reasons heretofore disclosed, we find Warren's acts and conduct embracing the entire Chamberlain transaction were dedicated to his own personal gain or advantage, to the detriment of CMC. In this regard the record reveals he, as managing president of the corporation, (1) personally engineered every phase of the Chamberlain deal, (2) appropriated to his own use all dividends issued upon the Chamberlain stock, (3) directed a falsification of corporate records and other documents when exposed by Herle's instant action, (4) aggravated the aforesaid deception by attempted use of a "reconstruction" stratagem which included the giving of his no-interest-note to CMC, absent board authorization, and (5) subsequently endeavored to impress upon the whole transaction a coloration of honesty by liquidating the no-interest-note prior to commencement of the trial of this case.

Also, as previously determined, Warren unquestionably did all in his power to isolate Herle from any rights or privileges pertaining to CMC management, even to the point of removing him from any corporate office, save as a director. This was patently a wrongful if not malicious "freeze-out".

In sum total the foregoing constituted conduct which * * * compels an assessment of exemplary damages.

We therefore reverse on this issue and direct that on remand trial court shall enter a $10,000 judgment against defendant, Warren A. Holden, in favor of defendant corporation, Construction Machinery Company.

VII. Herle also contends trial court improperly refused to appoint him or someone else as overseeing "fiscal agent" or receiver for CMC.

Any such appointment is addressed to the court's sound legal discretion. * * *

Further discussion will serve no useful purpose. We find no basis upon which to fault trial court for refusing to appoint a "fiscal agent" or receiver. * * *

VIII.   It still remains, trial court (1) enjoined CMC from lending money to its officers or stockholders except on such terms, including reasonable interest, as its board of directors may establish, (2) restrained defendants, individually and collectively, from taking any action which would have the effect of denying to Herle a reasonable opportunity to exercise his rights as a CMC stockholder and member of the board of directors.

Defendants challenge the grant of any such injunctive relief. In support of this stand they again argue absence of any "freeze-out" tactics. That issue has been heretofore resolved adverse to them.

We believe it self-evident trial court adopted the foregoing injunctive approach upon the sound premise it would be less drastic than appointment of a "fiscal agent" or receiver.

Defendants, more particularly Warren, have borrowed from CMC without board authorization, and squeezed Herle out of any effective corporate management activities. It may therefore be reasonably assumed, practices of like nature would be continued in the future if not enjoined. There is nothing in the record which can be said to indicate otherwise.

In any event, Herle established a sound premise upon which trial court acted within the ambit of its discretion in both areas denoted above. * * *

IX.   By his petition Herle individually alleges:

"In 1955, defendant Warren A. Holden, acting on behalf of defendant corporation and as controlling stockholder, made an oral agreement with plaintiff which by its terms, gave to plaintiff lifetime employment with defendant corporation. Said oral agreement further provided that the salary, bonuses and other compensation paid to plaintiff would always be equal to that paid to defendant Warren A. Holden."

Defendants, in resisting, first contend the asserted employment agreement was lacking in consideration and not sufficiently specific to permit a measure of damages, therefore invalid, unenforceable and terminable at the will of either party.

Kitchen v. Stockman National Life Insurance Co., 192 N.W.2d 796 (Iowa 1971), involved an employment contract. We there held in pertinent part, *192 N.W.2d at 801,* extrinsic evidence may be admitted for the limited purpose of interpreting any language or terms of a contract, and promise for promise creates a mutually legal duty, the breach thereof by one giving rise to a cause of action by the other.

More nearly on point is *LaFontaine v. Developers and Builders, Inc., 261 Iowa 1177, 156 N.W.2d 651 (1968).* There the parties entered into a written installment agreement for the sale and purchase of corporate stock. Plaintiff-purchaser claimed he and defendant-seller simultaneously entered into an oral agreement by which the former was to be employed by the latter for the equivalent of 25 years. As in the instant case, the oral agreement was effected on behalf of defendant corporation by its managing president. Upholding plaintiff-employee's action for breach of contract we said, *261 Iowa at 1182–1183, 156 N.W.2d at 655:*

> "The parties are entitled to the benefit of that interpretation of their evidence, and of all reasonable inferences most favorable to their case, in an effort to prove the real intent of the parties to an agreement, and if reasonable minds may differ as to the conclusions to be drawn from that evidence, a question of fact exists. 'The existence of a contract, 'meeting of the minds', intention to assume an obligation, the understanding, is to be determined not alone from words used, but in the situation, acts, and conduct of the parties, and from their situation and the attending circumstances, and by the inferences which mankind would ordinarily and reasonably draw therefrom.' (Authorities cited)."

This court also aptly stated in *LaFontaine, 261 Iowa at 1185–1186, 156 N.W.2d at 657:*

> "Equity courts will not hesitate to indulge in inferences which will avoid unfair or inequitable results. On this matter we have stated, ' * * * that an agreement will not be construed so as to give one party an unfair, oppressive or inequitable advantage over the other, that unless the terms of the contract clearly require it, an interpretation will not be given which places one party at the mercy of the other, that courts will endeavor to give the contract that interpretation most equitable to the parties, * * *.' * * *

> "Bearing this rule in mind, after careful analysis of the record, it is our considered opinion that the agreement sued upon was a partially-integrated contract and that the interpretation given the oral provisions of the agreement by the trial court was correct."

Recently, in *Stauter v. Walnut Grove Products, 188 N.W.2d 305 (Iowa 1971),* we were called upon to review a damage award for breach of an oral lifetime employment contract. Plaintiff and his associates in business were approached by defendant's representatives with an offer of purchase. Included was a verbal agreement to engage plaintiff's services at an escalating annual salary for as long as he performed efficiently. In affirming, this court said, *188 N.W.2d at 311–312:*

> "Absent any consideration beyond the employee's promise to perform, a contract for permanent or lifetime employment is construed to be for an indefinite time, terminable at the will of either party. (Authorities cited).

> "However, a different situation arises where there is consideration in addition to the promise to perform services. Where the

employee furnishes consideration in addition to his services, a contract for permanent or lifetime employment is valid and enforceable and continues to operate as long as the employer remains in business and has work for the employee once the employee performs competently. * * *.

* * *

"In the case at bar, the alleged oral employment contract was incidental to the agreement for the sale of plaintiff's property to defendant W. R. Grace and Company. It is obvious this is not a case where the employee simply promises to perform services without additional consideration involved. In *Thompson v. Miller, supra, [251 Iowa 324, 100 N.W.2d 410]* this court held plaintiff had more involved than a mere promise to perform services; that plaintiff had paid half of advertising and sales cost, and his traveling expenses, and we there held plaintiff had a capital as well as a labor investment. * * *

"In the matter before us, plaintiff gave up a competitive business to defendant, and as a part of the agreement to sell the business and its equipment, an oral agreement to employ plaintiff under the terms indicated in Division I was entered into. Thus the permanent employment contract had additional consideration to make it valid and enforceable, and not terminable at will."

We deem *Stauter, supra,* to be here applicable and controlling. * * *

As previously disclosed, L.S. Holden's will served to give Warren 75 percent and Herle 25 percent of all CMC stock held by the father at time of his death. Repeated discussions followed between Herle and Warren. The former was bent upon an equalization of stock holdings, the latter being resolutely determined to retain majority control. In other words corporate control was at stake. After several stormy months had passed an agreement was formulated by which Warren was permitted to have two more shares of stock than Herle. At the same time Herle was promised employment with CMC of the same duration and with compensation equal to that enjoyed by Warren. This agreement was amply supported by special consideration, i.e., settlement of the litigious controversy regarding the father's will and stockholding rights in CMC. * * * This means Herle had more involved than a promise for a promise.

Surely defendants cannot successfully contend the agreement between Warren and Herle, sole CMC stockholders, was not made and entered into on behalf of the corporation. Unquestionably, the rising tension between Warren and Herle posed a threat to efficient corporate operations, if not to its very existence. Thus the employment agreement was ultimately, albeit arduously, reached with the common thought that such was beneficial to CMC, a closely held corporation. * * *

The record also discloses that from 1956, date of the subject agreement, through 1963, the brothers did receive equal compensation. Under these circumstances it appears all parties here concerned accorded full recognition to the agreement until it was breached in 1964. * * *

We therefore conclude the oral contract of employment asserted by Herle (1) finds substantial support in the record, (2) is predicated upon adequate special consideration, (3) was effected for and on behalf of CMC, and (4) is binding upon that corporation.

X. Furthermore, the term or duration of Herle's promised employment was sufficiently specific to permit a measure of damages for any breach thereof. * * *

Trial court found Herle entitled to affirmative relief and judgment should be entered in his favor against CMC for the amount of variance in compensation received by Herle and Warren from 1964 to date of the decree, with interest. Trial court also found Herle had expressed a willingness to perform his part of the contract and a decree for specific performance would be appropriate. * * *

Noting, however, the deterioration in the brothers' relationship and effect thereof on the corporation, trial court directed that if either party deemed specific performance not in the best interests of CMC then such party should declare an election with the filing of proper notice. April 28, 1970, Herle filed a declaration of intent to resume working for CMC. May 26, 1970, trial court found Warren, not having filed an election as provided, necessitated an alternative remedy. June 24, 1970, the court accordingly ordered that the first of each year, commencing January 1971, and continuing for the life of the employment period, plaintiff be required to file a verified statement of earnings for personal services, including those received from CMC, and that the corporation likewise file verified statements regarding all compensation paid to Warren. If either party disputed the verified statements, request for hearing could be made. Also, in such event, if CMC contended Herle had not exercised reasonable diligence in finding other employment of the same general character it should thereupon file an appropriate pleading, the burden of proof being then on CMC to prove its contention by a preponderance of the evidence. Judgment is to be entered accordingly.

In resisting this decree defendants assert there is no precedent for same. We find that argument nonpersuasive.

"Wherever a situation exists which is contrary to the principles of equity and which can be redressed within the scope of judicial action, a court of equity will devise a remedy to meet the situation, though no similar relief has been given before." McClintock on Equity, § 29 at 76 (2d ed. 1948). * * *

Furthermore, mere difficulty in ascertaining and measuring damages does not alone constitute a cause for denial of recovery. * * *

We are satisfied trial court equitably tailored the relief accorded to the exigent circumstances peculiar to this case. * * *

XI. Countering, defendants take the position all compensatory relief is precluded because Herle's conduct was hostile to CMC's interests and was a breach of the employment agreement, all of which constituted a good cause for his discharge.

Unquestionably a corporate officer, employee or agent is required to obey all reasonable rules, orders and instructions issued by the employer and to at all times act in the best interests of the corporation. * * *

The record here discloses:

(1) In 1964 Warren breached the employment agreement;

(2) at all times prior to January 1, 1965, Herle efficiently performed all work assigned him at CMC in such manner as to give no cause for his discharge;

(3) to the extent Herle may have precipitated any disagreements or contributed to disunity between himself and Warren prior to January 1, 1965, he was acting reasonably as an officer, director and holder of a 49.98 percent interest in the corporation;

(4) Warren's violation of the equal compensation agreement in 1964 and 1965 invited and provoked any absence of work efficiency by Herle;

(5) regardless of Warren's violation of the employment agreement, Herle continued to report for work and performed acceptably until placed on early retirement and directed to vacate his office in 1968; and

(6) Warren was at all times the dominant personality, his actions were adverse to Herle's and CMC's best interests as is well demonstrated by the "freeze-out" tactics employed by Warren and his co-defendants.

The burden was on defendants to prove the alleged justification for Herle's discharge and removal from any corporate position. See *LaFontaine v. Developers and Builders, Inc., 261 Iowa at 1187, 156 N.W.2d at 658*. They failed to meet or carry that burden.

Moreover, there was no such conduct on Herle's part which justified his arbitrary removal as a CMC officer or employee.

We hereby affirm (1) trial court's judgment in favor of Herle against CMC in the sum of $86,742.38 as the amount owing for compensation due him from 1964 to April 3, 1970; (2) trial court's *in futuro* judgment with jurisdiction retained to annually determine and adjudicate the compensation owing to Herle by CMC in accord with the employment agreement and applicable standards. * * *

XII. Defendants further assert trial court erroneously awarded Herle attorneys' fees in connection with his derivative action prior to conclusion of all proceedings, the amount allowed is excessive, and not adequately supported by the record.

On cross-appeal Herle urges allowance of the aforesaid fees and expenses was timely but inadequate.

These interrelated contentions will be thus considered.

It should be inceptionally understood that where a corporation stands to suffer loss, or some detriment to stockholders' essential rights will be suffered if appropriate action is not taken, and those in authority are at fault, or fail or refuse to act, then a stockholder may proceed on behalf of the corporation or other stockholders. This is commonly referred to as a derivative action. * * * And where such stockholder's derivative action produces a discernible benefit to the corporation, or effects some protection to the stockholders as a class, monetary or otherwise, or serves to expose and redress a breach of any corporate function or duty, the corporation is liable for all attendant reasonable attorneys' fees and expenses. Explicatively, where a private stockholder pursues a derivative action which corrects or prevents an abuse of any corporate rights, duties, privileges or procedures, which has a corporate therapeutic effect, all reasonable concomitant attorneys' fees and expenses are chargeable to the involved corporate entity. * * *

Mindful of the foregoing, we now set forth the substance of trial court's findings, followed by our related conclusions regarding fees and expenses to be allowed in connection with Herle's derivative action or actions.

1. Trial court found the only aspect of this case derivative in nature was the Chamberlain transaction.

For reasons later set forth we disagree. Furthermore, the trial time monetary benefit to CMC by reason of Herle's derivative action challenging the Chamberlain stock deal resulted in a net benefit of approximately $55,000 to CMC.

2. Trial court found the injunction issue, being nonderivative, was resolved favorably to the corporation.

The court apparently here alludes to a pretrial injunction proceeding not involved in this appeal. On the other hand trial court understandably overlooked the grant of injunctive relief sought by Herle, by which CMC was qualifiedly enjoined from loaning money to defendants, and they were precluded from encroaching upon Herle's rights as a stockholder-director. For reasons heretofore stated this injunctive proceeding was patently derivative in nature.

3. Trial court found the "freeze-out" issue was so much a part of the employment contract that it inured to Herle's personal benefit.

In light of the foregoing applicable precepts that finding is not entirely correct. True, it entailed no pecuniary benefit to CMC, but as previously disclosed such is instantly of no consequence. We are also satisfied the "freeze-out" went primarily to Herle's role as a stockholder-officer, and only secondarily to his personal rights under the employment contract.

The record as a whole discloses Warren, a bare majority shareholder, was a dominant factor in the corporation. He exercised his assumed authority accordingly and usually in a manner best suited to his individual interests. Furthermore, the broad scope of "freeze-out" tactics employed included the creation of a captive board which means it had little or no power to exercise broad and independent judgment on matters of corporate policy. Closely related thereto is Warren's abandonment of regular board meetings which served, in part at least, to deprive that body of Herle's engineering experience and advice. Additionally, the "freeze-out" must certainly have had an adverse effect on all corporate personnel with an attendant negative reflection upon CMC's general business complexion.

From all this flows the conclusion that the remedial effect of trial court's findings and our holdings regarding the "freeze-out" should inure to CMC's benefit. That in turn means the "freeze-out" phase of this case was basically of a derivative nature. * * *

4. Trial court held the computation of fees and expenses should be exclusive of time devoted by counsel and others to the preparation and presentation of a claim for same.

In the absence of argument or citation of supportive authority by either plaintiff or defendants, in opposition to or support of this holding, error if any is deemed waived. * * *

5. Trial court held a tremendous amount of preparation and trial time was devoted to impeachment of Warren and his associates, which time should be allocated in part to the nonderivative portions of this case.

We cannot from this alone determine the "part" to which trial court refers. An examination of the record leads us to conclude, however, that not more than one-third of the time to which trial court referred was devoted to nonderivative matters.

Upon the basis of the foregoing we now hold plaintiff, Herle H. Holden, is entitled to judgment against defendant corporation, Construction Machinery Company, for an amount equal to two-thirds of all reasonable attorneys' fees and expenses incurred by plaintiff in connection with the trial of this case and appeal here taken.

We affirm trial court in holding reasonable attorneys' fees and expenses incurred by Herle in connection with his derivative action or actions are chargeable to CMC, but modify as to the basis upon which computation was effected and remand for further proceedings.

* * *

XIII. On cross-appeal Herle asserts trial court erred in permitting use of corporate funds to pay 75 percent of the total defense expenses.

In support thereof Herle argues he, in effect, is being unjustly required to pay 37 1/2 percent of expenses incurred (1) in resisting his action for benefit of the corporation, and (2) for defense of conduct by those who have breached their fiduciary duties and wrongfully exercised their corporate authority.

This court said in *State ex rel. Weede v. Bechtel, 244 Iowa at 835, 56 N.W.2d at 200:* "A stockholders' derivative action is one in which the corporation should take a strictly neutral part. * * * The corporation should not use its funds in behalf of those who have despoiled it." * * *

The principles enunciated in *Weede, supra,* are here applicable as to the Chamberlain transaction, breach of fiduciary duties, the "freeze-out", and need for injunctive remedy, all previously discussed.

Other phases of the case not involved in this appeal do not, however, come within the perimeter of *Weede's* preclusionary precepts. We believe a line of demarcation can and should be here drawn.

* * * Upon an examination of the whole record we find the individual defendants are entitled to be indemnified by defendant Construction Machinery Company, a corporation, in an amount equal to 25 percent of the total of all reasonable attorneys' fees and expenses incurred by said defendants in connection with the trial of this case and appeal here taken.

We affirm trial court in holding the individual defendants are entitled to indemnification from CMC for reasonable attorneys' fees and expenses incurred in defense of Herle's nonderivative action, but modify as to the basis upon which computation was effected, and remand for further proceedings.

*   *   *

XIV. Herle also here urges his pretrial motion for appointment of separate counsel to represent defendant corporation was erroneously overruled.

Viewing the situation in retrospect we are inclined to believe such an appointment would have obviated some of the problems instantly presented.

CMC is unquestionably a nominal or passive, though real, party defendant and as such it was required to adopt a neutral position with regard to this litigation. * * *

Here, however, we find neither reversible abuse of discretion by trial court nor actual prejudice to Herle.

XV. Costs attendant upon this appeal are taxed one-fourth to plaintiff, three fourths to the individual defendants. * * *

*   *   *

All Justices concur, except REES J., who takes no part.

NOTES AND QUESTIONS

1. This case is primarily offered at this point in the text for what it teaches us about what is usually referred to as the "duty of loyalty," but it raises two other issues, one of which, the nature of closely held corporations, that we will treat in a subsequent chapter, and another, the nature of deriva-

tive lawsuits, which is often a subject in corporations casebooks, and which we encountered in the Elf Atochem case, in Chapter Two.

Do you understand what a "derivative lawsuit" is? Generally speaking, it is one brought in the name of the corporation, by a shareholder, in order to recover for damages done to the corporation. Whether to allow such a lawsuit is discretionary with the court, in the exercise of its equitable powers. Usually, if there is any recovery in a derivative lawsuit it goes to the corporation, although the court has the discretion to allow attorney's fees to the plaintiff-shareholder who brings the lawsuit, and the court may, in some limited circumstances, allow "pro-rata recovery" to go directly to the plaintiff shareholder/s where there is a likelihood that if there is full recovery by the corporation wrongdoers controlling the corporation will misappropriate the funds or be wrongly rewarded for their misconduct. See, e.g., Richard A. Booth, "Derivative Suits and Pro Rata Recovery," 61 Geo. Wash. L. Rev. 1274 (1993), and Note, Individual Pro Rata Recovery in Stockholders' Derivative Suits, 69 Harv. L. Rev. 1314 (1956).

There is a disagreement among lawyers, courts, and commentators about whether the derivative lawsuit really is a useful tool to police officer, director, or majority shareholder misconduct, or whether it actually does more harm than good because it encourages "strike suits," litigation brought for the purpose of compelling a settlement favorable to plaintiff or plaintiff's lawyers, settlements that, because of indemnity provisions, may end up being paid out of the corporate treasury. There is also controversy about (1) whether shareholders should be required to make a demand on the directors or other shareholders to deal with the problem before actually bringing a derivative lawsuit (particularly in closely held corporations), (2) which shareholders can bring such suits, (3) whether incumbent managers or board members should be able to decide to intervene to seek dismissal of derivative lawsuits on the grounds that they are not brought in the best interest of the corporation, and (4) precisely what procedures ought to be followed in seeking such a dismissal. For further reading on the debate over derivative lawsuits, see, e.g., Ross v. Bernhard, 396 U.S. 531, 90 S.Ct. 733, 24 L.Ed.2d 729 (1970).

There is no doubt that the topic of shareholder derivative lawsuits is one of the most complex in corporate law, but those subtle complexities need not concern us here, other than to try and understand why the court in *Holden v. Construction Machinery Co.*, indicates that some of the plaintiff's claims are derivative in nature and some are "individual" in nature. A shareholder's claim that he or she suffers a particular injury apart from an injury done to the corporation as an entity is an "individual" claim, and, of course, requires no exercise of court discretion or demand on the directors before it may be heard. To avoid the procedural hurdles of a derivative suit, plaintiffs often try to get their claims characterized as "individual" or "direct" (which means the same thing) rather than "derivative." In 12B W. Fletcher, Cyclopedia of the Law of Private Corporations section 5911 (rev. perm. ed. 1984), a leading authority, the author indicates that a given action is a derivative one, one enforcing a corporate right, "if the gravamen of the complaint is injury to the corporation, or to the whole body of its stock or property without any severance or distribution among individual holders." "A direct action," on the other hand, "can be brought either when there is a special duty, such as a contractual duty, between the wrongdoer and the shareholder, or when the shareholder suffers injury separate and distinct from that suffered by other shareholders." Sax v. World Wide Press, Inc., 809 F.2d 610, 614 (9th Cir. 1987), citing Fletcher, supra. Do you understand which aspects of the lawsuit brought by Herle Holden are characterized as "direct" or "individual" claims, and which are characterized as "derivative?" Do you understand how Herle's lawsuit spotlights potential problems in the small, closely held corporation?

*   *   *

2.   Herle suggested that Warren breached the fiduciary duty of loyalty that Warren owed to the corporation. How exactly did Warren do so? What is the standard for evaluating a claim that a director or officer has breached his duty of loyalty because of self-dealing? The case you have just read is a common-law case, but this is a matter dealt with in many jurisdictions by statute, although the statutes tend not really to depart from the common law rules. An excellent such case of purported director/officer self-dealing is Cookies Food Products v. Lakes Warehouse, 430 N.W.2d 447 (Iowa 1988). That was a derivative action brought against a majority shareholder of Cookies Food Products, Duane "Speed" Herrig and two of his family owned corporations, Lakes Warehouse Distributing, Inc. and Speed's Automotive Co., Inc. Herrig had used his control of the board of directors of Cookies to engage in contracts with his family-owned corporations in order to store and market Cookies' principal products, barbecue and taco sauce. Herrig had turned Cookies Food Products from a failing business into an enormously profitable enterprise, although the deals with his family-owned corporations were also quite profitable to Herrig. Worse, in spite of the profits that inured to Cookies, no money had been paid out in dividends to other shareholders because of restrictions in the financing agreement Cookies had with the Small Business Administration. The shareholder plaintiffs sought to argue in their derivative suit that Herrig's large personal profits were "unfair," that they breached his fiduciary duty to the corporation, and that the difference between the fair market value of his and his family corporations' services and what the Cookies Food Products Corporation actually paid to Herrig and his corporations ought to be recovered by the Corporation, presumably for eventual distribution to all the shareholders. The relevant rule was that specified by the Iowa Corporate Code Section 496A.34, quoted by the Court in pertinent part:

> No contract or other transaction between a corporation and one or more of its directors or any other corporation, firm, association or entity in which one or more of its directors are directors or officers or are financially interested, shall be either void or voidable because of such relationship or interest … if any of the following occur:

> 1.   The fact of such relationship or interest is disclosed or known to the board of directors or committee which authorizes, approves, or ratifies the contract or transaction … without counting the votes … of such interested director.

> 2.   The fact of such relationship or interest is disclosed or known to the shareholders entitled to vote [on the transaction] and they authorize … such contract or transaction by vote or written consent.

3. The contract or transaction is fair and reasonable to the corporation.

Applying this statute, the court in *Cookies Food Products* decided that there had been full disclosure as required by paragraph (1) of 496A.34 (even though the precise amount of the profits to Herrig were not revealed), but that since Herrig controlled the Board and was the majority shareholder, though he might avoid the statutory possibility of having the transaction made voidable, he still had the burden of proving the transaction fair to the corporation. As the court put it, indicating that the statute was not intended to change the common law fiduciary duty of directors, "We * * * require directors who engage in self-dealing to establish the additional element that they have acted in good faith, honesty and fairness." Id., at 452–453. The majority of the court affirmed the trial court's determination that because of Herrig's nearly superhuman efforts to render the corporation profitable he had demonstrated that his self-dealing was fair to the corporation. The dissent, evaluating the same evidence, thought that the trial court had improperly discounted testimony which suggested that Herrig and his corporations had charged more than was fair. There seemed also to be an implication in the dissenting opinion that Herrig had failed to meet his burden of proof by demonstrating that any profits he had received were not unreasonable. Is *Cookies Food Products* an easier or harder case than *Holden v. Construction Machinery Co.*?

3. You may have discerned, by now, that there are essentially four aspects, requirements, or tests to be employed in the determination of whether the duty of loyalty has been violated, and a transaction should therefore be set aside or damages should be collected. They are:

(1) The duty fully to disclose the fact of a conflict of interest, as well as the material facts regarding the transaction that may be known to the person with the conflict of interest, but may not be known to the corporation.

(2) The requirement that the transaction be approved by a disinterested corporate decision-maker, such as a disinterested majority of the board, or a disinterested majority of the shareholders, or perhaps a corporate official or outside advisors specifically designated for the purpose.

(3) The requirement that the transaction be fair to the corporation.

(4) That if the requirements of (1) and (2) are met, the burden of proving that the transaction does not meet the requirement of (3) is on any party challenging the transaction, while if the requirement of (2) is not met, the burden is on the party with the conflict of interest to prove the transaction fair. It is fairly common for courts reviewing transactions involving a conflict of interest to find that if the requirements of (1) are not met, this means that the transaction should be deemed not to meet the requirements of (3). In other words, it is inherently unfair if there is a failure to disclose.

If you were drafting a statute to cover matters of director or officer conflict of interest, what additional requirements would you impose, or what additional determinations would you suggest?

No doubt you have also realized that the interested director or officer transaction (the problem in *Cookies Food Products*, and to some extent, at least, the problem in *Holden v. Construction Machinery Co.*) is not the only factual situation that may give rise to conflict of interest problems. The most notable other such situations are the taking of a "corporate opportunity" by an officer or director (see, e.g., Klinicki v. Lundren, 298 Or. 662, 695 P.2d 906 (Or. 1985)), the setting of executive compensation (see, e.g., Lewis v. Vogelstein, 699 A.2d 327 (Del. Ch. 1997)), and the sale of a controlling interest in the corporation (see, e.g., Perlman v. Feldmann, 219 F.2d 173 (2nd Cir. 1955), cert. den. 349 U.S. 952, 75 S.Ct. 880, 99 L.Ed. 1277 (1955)). Perhaps because of the difficulty of proving a violation of the duty of loyalty pursuant to state corporate law, there has been a felt need to supplement the state law rules of self-dealing with federal ones, to which we will soon turn.

E.   A NOTE ON "THE DUTY TO ACT IN GOOD FAITH": THE DISNEY CASE

The nature and scope of the fiduciary duties of directors and officers of Delaware corporations was somewhat amplified and clarified by the Delaware Supreme Court's important opinion, *In re The Walt Disney Company Derivative Litigation*, 906 A.2d 27 (2006). The case arose out of the hiring and relatively rapid firing of Disney President Michael Ovitz. Ovitz, one of the top talent agents in Hollywood, was brought in by Disney Chairman Michael Eisner, a friend of Ovitz. Ovitz had been earning around $20 million per year in his position at the agency he headed before assuming the Disney job. When Ovitz was hired, the stock of Disney, which had formerly been passing through a troubled period, shot up approximately $1 billion in value.

Ovitz's employment agreement with Disney stipulated that if he were fired by Disney without cause he was entitled to a substantial severance payment. Unfortunately, Ovitz seems to have had some difficulty adapting to the "Disney Culture," and he eventually fell out with his former friend Eisner, and Eisner eventually terminated Ovitz's employment fourteen months after he had been hired. Disney's lawyers could find no legal cause to support this termination, which triggered the severance pay provisions of Ovitz's employment agreement, resulting in an eventual payout to him of more than $130 million. This was, at the time, the highest such payment ever recorded in the corporate world, and a number of Disney's stockholders sued the directors and officers, alleging that they had breached their fiduciary duties both in acquiescing in such a lucrative severance arrangement for Ovitz, and in failing to determine a "cause" to fire Ovitz and avoid this payment. The Supreme Court of Delaware, affirming an earlier decision by the Delaware Chancellor, rejected the stockholders' argument and held that there was no breach of fiduciary duty.

The Court began by noting the "presumptions that cloak director action" under the business judgment rule. Said the Court, "Our law presumes that 'in making a business decision the directors of a corporation acted on an informed basis, in good faith, and in the honest belief that the action taken was in the best interests of the company.' " 906 A.2d, at 52. The Court went on to observe that "Those presumptions can be rebutted if the plaintiff shows that the directors breached their fiduciary duty of care or of loyalty or acted in bad faith. If that is shown, the burden then shifts to the director defendants to demonstrate that the challenged act or transaction was entirely fair to the corporation and its shareholders." Ibid. Quoting from its earlier decision in *Brehm v. Eisner,* 746 A.2d 244, 264, n. 66 (Del. 2000) the Court remarked in a footnote that "Thus, directors' decisions will be respected by courts unless the directors are interested or lack independence relative to the decision, do not act in good faith, act in a manner that cannot be attributed to a rational business purpose or reach their decision by a grossly negligent process that includes the failure to consider all material facts reasonably available." Ibid. Note 62.

The Court took special note of the provisions of Section 102 (b) (7) of the Delaware Corporate Code, which, as indicated earlier, was passed in the wake of the *Smith v. Van Gorkom* decision. To reiterate, that Section provides, in pertinent part, that Delaware corporations may place in their charter "A provision eliminating or limiting the personal liability of a director to the corporation or its stockholders for monetary damages for breach of fiduciary duty as a director, provided that such provision shall not eliminate or limit the liability of a director: (i) For any breach of the director's duty of loyalty to the corporation or its stockholders; (ii) *for acts or omissions not in good faith* or which involve intentional misconduct or a knowing violation of law ... or (iv) for any transaction from which the director derived an improper personal benefit.... " (emphasis supplied).

Disney had placed a provision of the type authorized by 102(b)(7) in its charter, and the real question in the case was whether the directors or officers had forfeited the liability shield of 102(b)(7) because they had failed to act with "good faith," in their transactions with Eisner. Ovitz's compensation arrangement had been approved by a committee of the Board, to which the other members of the Board deferred. This was fine, said the Delaware Supreme court, as the committee or at least some of its members spent a significant amount of time discussing the question of appropriate compensation and even retained an expert to help in that determination. Furthermore, the Compensation Committee was well aware that Ovitz had left "a very lucrative and secure position" at his talent agency, where he had been a controlling partner, "to join a publicly held corporation to which Ovitz was a stranger, and that had a very different culture and an environment which prevented him from completely controlling his destiny." Id., at 57–58. The Court further observed that "The committee members knew that by leaving [his talent agency] and coming to Disney, Ovitz would be sacrificing 'booked' [agency] commissions of $150 to $200 million—an amount that Ovitz demanded as protection against the risk that his employment relationship with Disney might not work out." Id., at 58. This suggested that the financial arrangement the Board had approved for Ovitz was reasonable under the circumstances, and this appeared to be, to the Delaware Supreme Court, evidence of the "good faith" of the Board.

The Supreme Court, for the first time in Delaware Jurisprudence, appeared to make clear that the duty to act in "good faith" of the Officers and Board could be viewed as a third obligation in addition to the two other fiduciary duties of Care and Loyalty. The Court proceeded to define "good faith," quoting a definition previously offered by the Chancellor for the *absence* of good faith. This was "the concept of intentional dereliction of duty, a conscious disregard for one's responsibilities.... Deliberate indifference and inaction in the face of a duty to act is, in my mind, conduct that is clearly disloyal to the corporation. It is the epitome of faithless conduct." Id., at 62. (Is there a clear difference between the duty of good faith and the duty of loyalty?). The Court indicated that there was a wealth of scholarship recently published on the purported duty of "good faith," citing, in its footnote 99, Id., at 64, "See, e.g., Hillary A. Sale, *Delaware's Good Faith*, 89 CORNELL L. REV. 456 (2004); Matthew R. Berry, *Does Delaware's Section 102(b)(7) Protect Reckless Directors From Personal Liability? Only if Delaware Courts Act in Good Faith*, 79 WASH. L. REV. 1125 (2004); John L. Reed and Matt Neiderman, *Good Faith and the Ability of Directors to Assert § 102(b)(7) of the Delaware Corporation Law as a Defense to Claims Alleging Abdication, Lack of Oversight, and Similar Breaches of Fiduciary Duty*, 29 DEL. J. CORP. L. 111 (2004); David Rosenberg, *Making Sense of Good Faith in Delaware Corporate Fiduciary Law: A Contractarian Approach*, 29 DEL. J. CORP. L. 491 (2004); Sean J. Griffith, *Good Faith Business Judgment: A Theory of Rhetoric in Corporate Law Jurisprudence*, 55 DUKE L. J. 1 (2005) ... Melvin A. Eisenberg, *The Duty of Good Faith in Corporate Law*, 31 DEL. J. CORP. L. 1 (2005); Filippo Rossi, *Making Sense of the Delaware Supreme Court's Triad of Fiduciary Duties* (June 22, 2005), available at http://ssrn.com/abstract=755784; Christopher M. Bruner, *"Good Faith," State of Mind, and the Outer Boundaries of Director Liability in Corporate Law* (Boston Univ. Sch. of Law Working Paper No. 05–19), available at http://ssrn.com/abstract=832944; Sean J. Griffith & Myron T. Steele, *On Corporate Law Federalism Threatening the Thaumatrope*, 61 Bus. LAW. 1 (2005)," all of which might be consulted by anyone wishing further to research the topic.

Still, the Court recognized that "to date" the duty of good faith "is not a well-developed area of our corporate fiduciary law," and "the duty to act in good faith is, up to this point relatively uncharted." Id., at 64. Indeed, the Court stated that the Chancellor, in the opinion below, "observed, after surveying the sparse case law on the subject, that both the meaning and the contours of the duty to act in good faith were 'shrouded in the fog of ...

hazy jurisprudence." Id., at 64, note 98. Trying to remove the fog, the Delaware Supreme Court declared that there were actually three different categories that had been discerned in Delaware jurisprudence on the duty of good faith.

"The first category," said the Court, "involves so-called 'subjective bad faith,' that is, fiduciary conduct motivated by an actual intent to do harm. That such conduct constitutes classic, quintessential bad faith is a proposition so well accepted in the liturgy of fiduciary law that it borders on axiomatic." Id., at 64. (But does this actually sound more like the Duty of Loyalty, rather than the Duty to Act in Good Faith?) Continuing, the Court stated that "The second category of conduct, which is at the opposite end of the spectrum, involves lack of due care—that is, fiduciary action taken solely by reason of gross negligence and without any malevolent intent." Ibid. (But is this, then, strictly speaking, a matter of "good faith," or really a question of whether the requisite Duty of Care has been met?). In any event, the Delaware Supreme Court seemed to reject this purported Second category as actually relevant to the inquiry into good faith. Commenting on what the Chancellor below had found, the Court stated: "Although the Chancellor found, and we agree, that the appellants failed to establish gross negligence, to afford guidance we address the issue of whether gross negligence (including a failure to inform one's self of available material facts), without more, can also constitute bad faith. The answer is clearly no." Id., at 64–65.

Having then rejected the second category, the Court observed that "That leaves the third category of fiduciary conduct, which falls in between the first two categories of (1) conduct motivated by subjective bad intent and (2) conduct resulting from gross negligence. This third category is what the Chancellor's definition of bad faith—intentional dereliction of duty, a conscious disregard for one's responsibilities—is intended to capture." Id., at 66. (Is it now clear to you what is required by the Duty to Act in Good Faith?) Surely this is something less than a model of clarity, and perhaps that explains why the Supreme Court went on once again to quote the Chancellor below, "The good faith required of a corporate fiduciary includes not simply the duties of care and loyalty … but all actions required by a true faithfulness and devotion to the interests of the corporation and its shareholders." Id., at 67. (Do you recall anything written by Benjamin Cardozo on fiduciary duty that sounds similar?) Further quoting from the Chancellor, the Delaware Supreme Court observed that "A failure to act in good faith may be shown, for instance, [1] where the fiduciary intentionally acts with a purpose other than that of advancing the best interests of the corporation, [2] where the fiduciary acts with the intent to violate applicable positive law, or [3] where the fiduciary intentionally fails to act in the face of a known duty to act, demonstrating a conscious disregard for his duties. There may be other examples of bad faith yet to be proven or alleged, but these three are the most salient."

Ibid. (Now can you distinguish the Duty to Act in Good Faith from the Duty of Loyalty and the Duty of Care?).

The plaintiffs in the Disney case had also argued that the Directors and Officers who approved the generous severance package for Mr. Ovitz had engaged in "waste" of corporate assets. The Delaware Supreme Court rather summarily rejected that claim. Said the Court, "To recover on a claim of corporate waste, the plaintiffs must shoulder the burden of proving that the exchange was 'so one sided that no business person of ordinary, sound judgment could conclude that the corporation has received adequate consideration.' " Id., at 74. The Court continued by stating that "A claim of waste will arise only in the rare, 'unconscionable case where directors irrationally squander or give away corporate assets.' " Ibid. (You have seen unconscionability before, in a contracts context. Is this like that?) The Court concluded by stating that "This onerous standard for waste is a corollary of the proposition that where business judgment presumptions are applicable, the board's decision will be upheld unless it cannot be 'attributed to any rational business purpose.' " Ibid. Since it was rational to believe that Ovitz could not have been persuaded to leave his talent agency without a substantial severance package, the Court decided, there was no "waste" and the plaintiffs were entitled to no relief.

Smith v. Van Gorkom was clearly a case where the Supreme Court of Delaware imposed a rigid requirement that the Board be fully informed before it acted, and many believed that the Court had substituted its business judgment for that of the Board. What do you suppose the Court was doing in *Disney*?

CHAPTER 6

FEDERAL LAW REGARDING
DUTIES TO SHAREHOLDERS

■ ■ ■

A. INSIDER TRADING

UNITED STATES v. O'HAGAN

Supreme Court of the United States.
521 U.S. 642, 117 S.Ct. 2199, 138 L.Ed.2d 724 (1997).

JUDGES: GINSBURG, J., delivered the opinion of the Court, in which STEVENS, O'CONNOR, KENNEDY, SOUTER, and BREYER, JJ., joined, and in Parts I, III, and IV of which SCALIA, J., joined. SCALIA, J., filed an opinion concurring in part and dissenting in part. THOMAS, J., filed an opinion concurring in the judgment in part and dissenting in part, in which REHNQUIST, C.J., joined.

OPINION BY: GINSBURG

* * *

I

Respondent James Herman O'Hagan was a partner in the law firm of Dorsey & Whitney in Minneapolis, Minnesota. In July 1988, Grand Metropolitan PLC (Grand Met), a company based in London, England, retained Dorsey & Whitney as local counsel to represent Grand Met regarding a potential tender offer for the common stock of the Pillsbury Company, headquartered in Minneapolis. Both Grand Met and Dorsey & Whitney took precautions to protect the confidentiality of Grand Met's tender offer plans. O'Hagan did no work on the Grand Met representation. Dorsey & Whitney withdrew from representing Grand Met on September 9, 1988. Less than a month later, on October 4, 1988, Grand Met publicly announced its tender offer for Pillsbury stock.

On August 18, 1988, while Dorsey & Whitney was still representing Grand Met, O'Hagan began purchasing call options for Pillsbury stock. * * * Later in August and in September, O'Hagan made additional purchases of Pillsbury call options. By the end of September, he owned 2,500 unexpired Pillsbury options, apparently more than any other individual investor.... O'Hagan also purchased, in September 1988, some 5,000 shares of Pillsbury common stock, at a price just under $39 per share. When Grand Met announced its tender offer in October, the price of Pillsbury stock rose to nearly $60 per share. O'Hagan then sold his Pillsbury call options and common stock, making a profit of more than $4.3 million.

The Securities and Exchange Commission (SEC or Commission) initiated an investigation into O'Hagan's transactions, culminating in a 57-count indictment. The indictment alleged that O'Hagan defrauded his law firm and its client, Grand Met, by using for his own trading purposes material, nonpublic information regarding Grand Met's planned tender offer * * *. According to the indictment, O'Hagan used the profits he gained through this trading to conceal his previous embezzlement and conversion of unrelated client trust funds * * *. O'Hagan was charged with * * * 17 counts of securities fraud, in violation of § 10(b) of the Securities Exchange Act of 1934 (Exchange Act) * * * and SEC Rule 10b–5, [and] 17 counts of fraudulent trading in connection with a tender offer, in violation of § 14(e) of the Exchange Act, * * * and SEC Rule 14e–3(a) * * * A jury convicted O'Hagan on all * * * counts, and he was sentenced to a 41–month term of imprisonment.

*   *   *

A divided panel of the Court of Appeals for the Eighth Circuit reversed all of O'Hagan's convictions. ... Liability under § 10(b) and Rule 10b–5, the Eighth Circuit held, may not be grounded on the "misappropriation theory" of securities fraud on which the prosecution relied.* * * The Court of Appeals also held that Rule 14e–3(a)—which prohibits trading while in possession of material, nonpublic information relating to a tender offer—exceeds the SEC's § 14(e) rulemaking authority because the rule contains no breach of fiduciary duty requirement. * * * Judge Fagg, dissenting, stated that he would recognize and enforce the misappropriation theory, and would hold that the SEC did not exceed its rulemaking authority when it adopted Rule 14e–3(a) without requiring proof of a breach of fiduciary duty. ...

*   *   *

II

We address first the Court of Appeals' reversal of O'Hagan's convictions under § 10(b) and Rule 10b–5. Following the Fourth Circuit's lead, see *United States v. Bryan, 58 F.3d 933, 943–959 (1995),* the Eighth Circuit rejected the misappropriation theory as a basis for § 10(b) liability. We hold, in accord with several other Courts of Appeals, that criminal liability under § 10(b) may be predicated on the misappropriation theory.

A

In pertinent part, § 10(b) of the Exchange Act provides:

"It shall be unlawful for any person, directly or indirectly, by the use of any means or instrumentality of interstate commerce or of the mails, or of any facility of any national securities exchange—

.....

"(b) To use or employ, in connection with the purchase or sale of any security registered on a national securities exchange or any security not so registered, any manipulative or deceptive device or contrivance in contravention of such rules and regulations as the [Securities and Exchange] Commission may prescribe as necessary or appropriate in the public interest or for the protection of investors."

The statute thus proscribes (1) using any deceptive device (2) in connection with the purchase or sale of securities, in contravention of rules prescribed by the Commission. The provision, as written, does not confine its coverage to deception of a purchaser or seller of securities * * * rather, the statute reaches any deceptive device used "in connection with the purchase or sale of any security."

Pursuant to its § 10(b) rulemaking authority, the Commission has adopted Rule 10b–5, which, as relevant here, provides:

"It shall be unlawful for any person, directly or indirectly, by the use of any means or instrumentality of interstate commerce, or of the mails or of any facility of any national securities exchange,

"(a) To employ any device, scheme, or artifice to defraud, [or]

* * *

"(c) To engage in any act, practice, or course of business which operates or would operate as a fraud or deceit upon any person,

"in connection with the purchase or sale of any security."

* * *

Under the "traditional" or "classical theory" of insider trading liability, § 10(b) and Rule 10b–5 are violated when a corporate insider trades in the securities of his corporation on the basis of material, nonpublic information. Trading on such information qualifies as a "deceptive device" under § 10(b), we have affirmed, because "a relationship of trust and confidence [exists] between the shareholders of a corporation and those insiders who have obtained confidential information by reason of their position with that corporation." * * * That relationship, we recognized, "gives rise to a duty to disclose [or to abstain from trading] because of the 'necessity of preventing a corporate insider from ... taking unfair advantage of * * * uninformed ... stockholders.' " * * * The classical theory applies not only to officers, directors, and other permanent insiders of a corporation, but also to attorneys, accountants, consultants, and others who temporarily become fiduciaries of a corporation. * * *

The "misappropriation theory" holds that a person commits fraud "in connection with" a securities transaction, and thereby violates § 10(b) and Rule 10b–5, when he misappropriates confidential information for securities trading purposes, in breach of a duty owed to the source of the information. * * * Under this theory, a fiduciary's undisclosed, self-serving use of a principal's information to purchase or sell securities, in breach of a duty of loyalty and confidentiality, defrauds the principal of the exclusive use of that information. In lieu of premising liability on a fiduciary relationship between company insider and purchaser or seller of the company's stock, the misappropriation theory premises liability on a fiduciary-turned-trader's deception of those who entrusted him with access to confidential information.

* * *

In this case, the indictment alleged that O'Hagan, in breach of a duty of trust and confidence he owed to his law firm, Dorsey & Whitney, and to its client, Grand Met, traded on the basis of nonpublic information regarding Grand Met's planned tender offer for Pillsbury common stock. * * * This conduct, the Government charged, constituted a fraudulent device in connection with the purchase and sale of securities. * * *

B

We agree with the Government that misappropriation, as just defined, satisfies § 10(b)'s requirement that chargeable conduct involve a "deceptive device or contrivance" used "in connection with" the purchase or sale of securities. We observe, first, that misappropriators, as the Government describes them, deal in deception. * * * A fiduciary who "[pretends] loyalty to the principal while secretly converting the principal's information for personal gain," * * * "dupes" or defrauds the principal....

We addressed fraud of the same species in *Carpenter v. United States, 484 U.S.* 19 *(1987),* which involved the mail fraud statute's proscription of "any scheme or artifice to defraud," * * * Affirming convictions under that statute, we said in *Carpenter* that an employee's undertaking not to reveal his employer's confidential information "became a sham" when the employee provided the information to his co-conspirators in a scheme to obtain trading profits.* * * A company's confidential information, we recognized in *Carpenter,* qualifies as property to which the company has a right of exclusive use. * * * The undisclosed misappropriation of such information, in violation of a fiduciary duty, the Court said in *Carpenter,* constitutes fraud akin to embezzlement—" 'the fraudulent appropriation to one's own use of the money or goods entrusted to one's care by another.' " * * * *Carpenter*'s discussion of the fraudulent misuse of confidential information, the Government notes, "is a particularly apt source of guidance here, because [the mail fraud statute] (like Section 10(b)) has long been held to require deception, not merely the breach of a fiduciary duty." ...

Deception through nondisclosure is central to the theory of liability for which the Government seeks recognition. As counsel for the Government stated in explanation of the theory at oral argument: "To satisfy the common law rule that a trustee may not use the property that [has] been entrusted [to] him, there would have to be consent. To satisfy the requirement of the Securities Act that there be no deception, there would only have to be disclosure." * * *

We turn next to the § 10(b) requirement that the misappropriator's deceptive use of information be "in connection with the purchase or sale of [a] security." This element is satisfied because the fiduciary's fraud is consummated, not when the fiduciary gains the confidential information, but when, without disclosure to his principal, he uses the information to purchase or sell securities. The securities transaction and the breach of duty thus coincide. This is so even though the person or entity defrauded is not the other party to the trade, but is, instead, the source of the nonpublic information. * * * A misappropriator who trades on the basis of material, nonpublic information, in short, gains his advantageous market position through deception; he deceives the source of the information and simultaneously harms members of the investing public. * * *

The misappropriation theory targets information of a sort that misappropriators ordinarily capitalize upon to gain no-risk profits through the purchase or sale of securities. Should a misappropriator put such information to other use, the statute's prohibition would not be implicated. The theory does not catch all conceivable forms of fraud involving confidential information; rather, it catches fraudulent means of capitalizing on such information through securities transactions.

* * *

The misappropriation theory comports with § 10(b)'s language, which requires deception "in connection with the purchase or sale of any security," not deception of an identifiable purchaser or seller. The theory is also well-tuned to an animating purpose of the Exchange Act: to insure honest securities markets and thereby promote investor confidence. * * * Although informational disparity is inevitable in the securities markets, investors likely would hesitate to venture their capital in a market where trading based on misappropriated nonpublic information is unchecked by law. * * *

* * *

III

We consider next the ground on which the Court of Appeals reversed O'Hagan's convictions for fraudulent trading in connection with a tender offer, in violation of § 14(e) of the Exchange Act and SEC Rule 14e–3(a). A sole question is before us as to these convictions: Did the Commission, as the Court of Appeals held, exceed its rulemaking authority under

§ 14(e) when it adopted Rule 14e–3(a) without requiring a showing that the trading at issue entailed a breach of fiduciary duty? We hold that the Commission, in this regard and to the extent relevant to this case, did not exceed its authority.

The governing statutory provision, § 14(e) of the Exchange Act, reads in relevant part:

> "It shall be unlawful for any person ... to engage in any fraudulent, deceptive, or manipulative acts or practices, in connection with any tender offer * * *. The [SEC] shall, for the purposes of this subsection, by rules and regulations define, and prescribe means reasonably designed to prevent, such acts and practices as are fraudulent, deceptive, or manipulative." * * *

Section 14(e)'s first sentence prohibits fraudulent acts in connection with a tender offer. * * * The section's second sentence delegates definitional and prophylactic rulemaking authority to the Commission. * * *

Through § 14(e) and other provisions on disclosure in the [securities laws], Congress sought to ensure that shareholders "confronted by a cash tender offer for their stock [would] not be required to respond without adequate information." * * * As we recognized in *Schreiber v. Burlington Northern, Inc., 472 U.S. 1 (1985),* Congress designed the Williams Act [a revision of the securities laws of which 14(e) was a part] to make "disclosure, rather than court-imposed principles of 'fairness' or 'artificiality,' * * * the preferred method of market regulation."* * * Section 14(e), we explained, "supplements the more precise disclosure provisions found elsewhere in the Williams Act, while requiring disclosure more explicitly addressed to the tender offer context than that required by § 10(b)." * * *

Relying on § 14(e)'s rulemaking authorization, the Commission, in 1980, promulgated Rule 14e–3(a). That measure provides:

> "(a) If any person has taken a substantial step or steps to commence, or has commenced, a tender offer (the 'offering person'), it shall constitute a fraudulent, deceptive or manipulative act or practice within the meaning of section 14(e) of the [Exchange] Act for any other person who is in possession of material information relating to such tender offer which information he knows or has reason to know is nonpublic and which he knows or has reason to know has been acquired directly or indirectly from:
>
> "(1) The offering person,
>
> "(2) The issuer of the securities sought or to be sought by such tender offer, or
>
> "(3) Any officer, director, partner or employee or any other person acting on behalf of the offering person or such issuer, to purchase or sell or cause to be purchased or sold any of such securities or any securities convertible into or exchangeable for any such securities or any option or right to obtain or to dispose of any of the

foregoing securities, unless within a reasonable time prior to any purchase or sale such information and its source are publicly disclosed by press release or otherwise." ...

As characterized by the Commission, Rule 14e–3(a) is a "disclose or abstain from trading" requirement.... The Second Circuit concisely described the rule's thrust:

> "One violates Rule 14e–3(a) if he trades on the basis of material nonpublic information concerning a pending tender offer that he knows or has reason to know has been acquired 'directly or indirectly' from an insider of the offeror or issuer, or someone working on their behalf. Rule 14e–3(a) is a disclosure provision. It creates a duty in those traders who fall within its ambit to abstain or disclose, *without regard to whether the trader owes a pre-existing fiduciary duty* to respect the confidentiality of the information." *United States v. Chestman, 947 F.2d 551, 557 (1991)* * * * (emphasis added) * * *.

* * *

In the Eighth Circuit's view, because Rule 14e–3(a) applies whether or not the trading in question breaches a fiduciary duty, the regulation exceeds the SEC's § 14(e) rulemaking authority....

The Eighth Circuit homed in on the essence of § 14(e)'s rulemaking authorization: "The statute empowers the SEC to 'define' and 'prescribe means reasonably designed to prevent' 'acts and practices' which are 'fraudulent.'" * * * All that means, the Eighth Circuit found plain, is that the SEC may "identify and regulate," in the tender offer context, "acts and practices" the law already defines as "fraudulent"; but, the Eighth Circuit maintained, the SEC may not "create its own definition of fraud." * * *

This Court, the Eighth Circuit pointed out, held in *Schreiber* that the word "manipulative" in the § 14(e) phrase "fraudulent, deceptive, or manipulative acts or practices" means just what the word means in § 10(b): Absent misrepresentation or nondisclosure, an act cannot be indicted as manipulative. * * * Section 10(b) interpretations guide construction of § 14(e), the Eighth Circuit added * * * citing this Court's acknowledgment in *Schreiber* that § 14(e)'s "'broad antifraud prohibition' ... [is] modeled on the antifraud provisions of § 10(b) ... and Rule 10b–5," * * *.

For the meaning of "fraudulent" under § 10(b), the Eighth Circuit looked to [an earlier Supreme Court case, *Chiarella v. United States*, 445 US 222 (1980)]. In that case, the Eighth Circuit recounted, this Court held that a failure to disclose information could be "fraudulent" under § 10(b) only when there was a duty to speak arising out of " 'a fiduciary or other similar relationship of trust and confidence.'" * * * Just as § 10(b) demands a showing of a breach of fiduciary duty, so such a breach is necessary to make out a § 14(e) violation, the Eighth Circuit concluded.

As to the Commission's § 14(e) authority to "prescribe means reasonably designed to prevent" fraudulent acts, the Eighth Circuit stated: "Properly read, this provision means simply that the SEC has broad regulatory powers in the field of tender offers, but the statutory terms have a fixed meaning which the SEC cannot alter by way of an administrative rule." * * *

The United States urges that the Eighth Circuit's reading of § 14(e) misapprehends both the Commission's authority to define fraudulent acts and the Commission's power to prevent them. "The 'defining' power," the United States submits, "would be a virtual nullity were the SEC not permitted to go beyond common law fraud (which is separately prohibited in the first [self-operative] sentence of Section 14(e))." * * *

In maintaining that the Commission's power to define fraudulent acts under § 14(e) is broader than its rulemaking power under § 10(b), the United States questions the Court of Appeals' reading of *Schreiber*. * * * Parenthetically, the United States notes that the word before the *Schreiber* Court was "manipulative"; unlike "fraudulent," the United States observes, " 'manipulative' * * * is 'virtually a term of art when used in connection with the securities markets.' " * * * Most tellingly, the United States submits, *Schreiber* involved acts alleged to violate the self-operative provision in § 14(e)'s first sentence, a sentence containing language similar to § 10(b). But § 14(e)'s second sentence, containing the rulemaking authorization, the United States points out, does not track § 10(b), which simply authorizes the SEC to proscribe "manipulative or deceptive devices or contrivances." * * * Instead, § 14(e)'s rulemaking prescription tracks § 15(c)(2)(D) of the Exchange Act * * * which concerns the conduct of broker-dealers in over-the-counter markets. * * * Since 1938, § 15(c)(2) has given the Commission authority to "define, and prescribe means reasonably designed to prevent, such [broker-dealer] acts and practices as are fraudulent, deceptive, or manipulative." * * * When Congress added this same rulemaking language to § 14(e) in 1970, the Government states, the Commission had already used its § 15(c)(2) authority to reach beyond common law fraud. * * *

We need not resolve in this case whether the Commission's authority under § 14(e) to "define ... such acts and practices as are fraudulent" is broader than the Commission's fraud-defining authority under § 10(b), for we agree with the United States that Rule 14e–3(a), as applied to cases of this genre, qualifies under § 14(e) as a "means reasonably designed to prevent" fraudulent trading on material, nonpublic information in the tender offer context. A prophylactic measure, because its mission is to prevent, typically encompasses more than the core activity prohibited. As we noted in *Schreiber*, § 14(e)'s rulemaking authorization gives the Commission "latitude," even in the context of a term of art like "manipulative," "to regulate nondeceptive activities as a 'reasonably designed' means of preventing manipulative acts, without suggesting any change in the meaning of the term 'manipulative' itself." * * * We hold, accordingly, that under § 14(e), the Commission may prohibit acts, not themselves fraudulent under the common law or § 10(b), if the prohibition is "reasonably designed to prevent * * * acts and practices [that] are fraudulent." * * *

Because Congress has authorized the Commission, in § 14(e), to prescribe legislative rules, we owe the Commission's judgment "more than mere deference or weight."* * * Therefore, in determining whether Rule 14e–3(a)'s "disclose or abstain from trading" requirement is reasonably designed to prevent fraudulent acts, we must accord the Commission's assessment "controlling weight unless [it is] arbitrary, capricious, or manifestly contrary to the statute." * * * In this case, we conclude, the Commission's assessment is none of these.

In adopting the "disclose or abstain" rule, the SEC explained:

"The Commission has previously expressed and continues to have serious concerns about trading by persons in possession of material, nonpublic information relating to a tender offer. This practice results in unfair disparities in market information and market disruption. Security holders who purchase from or sell to such persons are effectively denied the benefits of disclosure and the substantive protections of the Williams Act. If furnished with the information, these security holders would be able to make an informed investment decision, which could involve deferring the purchase or sale of the securities until the material information had been disseminated or until the tender offer has been commenced or terminated." * * *

The Commission thus justified Rule 14e–3(a) as a means necessary and proper to assure the efficacy of Williams Act protections.

The United States emphasizes that Rule 14e–3(a) reaches trading in which "a breach of duty is likely but difficult to prove." * * * "Particularly in the context of a tender offer," as the Tenth Circuit recognized, "there is a fairly wide circle of people with confidential information," * * *, notably, the attorneys, investment bankers, and accountants involved in structuring the transaction. The availability of that information may lead to abuse, for "even a hint of an upcoming tender offer may send the price of the target company's stock soaring." * * * Individuals entrusted with nonpublic information, particularly if they have no long-term loyalty to the issuer, may find the temptation to trade on that information hard to resist in view of "the very large short-term profits potentially available [to them]." * * *

It may be possible to prove circumstantially that a person [traded on the basis of material, nonpublic information], but almost impossible to prove that the trader obtained such information in breach of a fiduciary duty owed either by the trader or by the ultimate insider source of the information. * * * The example of a "tippee" who trades on information received from an insider illustrates the problem. Under Rule 10b–5, "a tippee assumes a fiduciary duty to the shareholders of a corporation not to trade on material nonpublic information only when the insider has breached his fiduciary duty to the shareholders by disclosing the information to the tippee and the tippee knows or should know that there has been a breach." [*Dirks v. SEC*, 463 US 646, 660 (1983)] To show that a tippee who traded on nonpublic information about a tender offer had breached a fiduciary duty would require proof not only that the insider source breached a fiduciary duty, but that the tippee knew or should have known of that breach. "Yet, in most cases, the only parties to the [information transfer] will be the insider and the alleged tippee." * * *

In sum, it is a fair assumption that trading on the basis of material, nonpublic information will often involve a breach of a duty of confidentiality to the bidder or target company or their representatives. The SEC, cognizant of the proof problem that could enable sophisticated traders to escape responsibility, placed in Rule 14e–3(a) a "disclose or abstain from trading" command that does not require specific proof of a breach of fiduciary duty. That prescription, we are satisfied, applied to this case, is a "means reasonably designed to prevent" fraudulent trading on material, nonpublic information in the tender offer context.* * * Therefore, insofar as it serves to prevent the type of misappropriation charged against O'Hagan, Rule 14e–3(a) is a proper exercise of the Commission's prophylactic power under § 14(e).

* * *

The judgment of the Court of Appeals for the Eighth Circuit is reversed, and the case is remanded for further proceedings consistent with this opinion.

It is so ordered.

JUSTICE SCALIA, concurring in part and dissenting in part.

I do not agree, ... with Part II of the Court's opinion, containing its analysis of respondent's convictions under § 10(b) and Rule 10b–5.

* * *

While the Court's explanation of the scope of § 10(b) and Rule 10b–5 would be entirely reasonable in some other context, it does not seem to accord with the principle of lenity we apply to criminal statutes * * * In light of that principle, it seems to me that the unelaborated statutory language: "to use or employ in connection with the purchase or sale of any security * * * any manipulative or deceptive device or contrivance," § 10(b), must be construed to require the manipulation or deception of a party to a securities transaction.

JUSTICE THOMAS, with whom THE CHIEF JUSTICE joins, concurring in the judgment in part and dissenting in part.

* * * Central to the majority's holding is the need to interpret § 10(b)'s requirement that a deceptive device be "used or employed, in connection with the purchase or sale of any security." * * * Because the Commission's misappropriation theory fails to provide a coherent and con-

sistent interpretation of this essential requirement for liability under § 10(b), I dissent.

The majority also sustains respondent's convictions under § 14(e) of the Securities Exchange Act, and Rule 14e–3(a) promulgated thereunder, regardless of whether respondent violated a fiduciary duty to anybody. I dissent too from that holding because, while § 14(e) does allow regulations prohibiting nonfraudulent acts as a prophylactic against certain fraudulent acts, neither the majority nor the Commission identifies any relevant underlying fraud against which Rule 14e–3(a) reasonably provides prophylaxis ...

* * *

II

* * *

As the majority acknowledges, Rule 14e–3(a) prohibits a broad range of behavior regardless of whether such behavior is fraudulent under our precedents. * * *

The Commission offers two grounds in defense of Rule 14e–3(a). First, it argues that § 14(e) delegates to the Commission the authority to "define" fraud differently than that concept has been defined by this Court, and that Rule 14e–3(a) is a valid exercise of that "defining" power. Second, it argues that § 14(e) authorizes the Commission to "prescribe means reasonably designed to prevent" fraudulent acts, and that Rule 14e–3(a) is a prophylactic rule that may prohibit nonfraudulent acts as a means of preventing fraudulent acts that are difficult to detect or prove.

The majority declines to reach the Commission's first justification, instead sustaining Rule 14e–3(a) on the ground that

> "under § 14(e), the Commission may prohibit acts, not themselves fraudulent under the common law or § 10(b), if the prohibition is 'reasonably designed to prevent ... acts and practices [that] are fraudulent.' " * * *

According to the majority, prohibiting trading on nonpublic information is necessary to prevent such supposedly hard-to-prove fraudulent acts and practices as trading on information obtained from the buyer in breach of a fiduciary duty.* * *

* * * With regard to the Commission's claim of authority to redefine the concept of fraud, I agree with the Eighth Circuit that the Commission misreads the relevant provision of § 14(e).

> "Simply put, the enabling provision of § 14(e) permits the SEC to identify and regulate those 'acts and practices' which fall within the § 14(e) legal definition of 'fraudulent,' but it does not grant the SEC a license to redefine the term." * * *

This conclusion follows easily from our similar statement in *Schreiber v. Burlington Northern, Inc., 472 U.S. 1, 11, n.11 (1985),* that § 14(e) gives the "Commission latitude to regulate nondeceptive activities as a 'reasonably designed' means of preventing manipulative acts, without suggesting any change in the meaning of the term 'manipulative' itself."

Insofar as the Rule 14e–3(a) purports to "define" acts and practices that "are fraudulent," it must be measured against our precedents interpreting the scope of fraud. The majority concedes, however, that Rule 14e–3(a) does not prohibit merely trading in connection with fraudulent nondisclosure, but rather it prohibits trading in connection with *any* nondisclosure, regardless of the presence of a pre-existing duty to disclose. * * * The Rule thus exceeds the scope of the Commission's authority to define such acts and practices as "are fraudulent." * * *

Turning to the Commission's second justification for Rule 14e–3(a), although I can agree with the majority that § 14(e) authorizes the Commission to prohibit non-fraudulent acts as a means reasonably designed to prevent fraudulent ones, I cannot agree that Rule 14e–3(a) satisfies this standard. As an initial matter, the Rule, on its face, does not purport to be an exercise of the Commission's prophylactic power, but rather a redefinition of what "constitutes a fraudulent, deceptive, or manipulative act or practice within the meaning of § 14(e)." That Rule 14e–3(a) *could have been* "conceived and defended, alternatively, as definitional or preventive," * * * misses the point. We evaluate regulations not based on the myriad of explanations that could have been given by the relevant agency, but on those explanations and justifications that were, in fact, given. * * * Rule 14e–3(a) may not be "sensibly read" as an exercise of "preventive" authority * * * it can only be *differently* so read, contrary to its own terms.

Having already concluded that the Commission lacks the power to redefine fraud, the regulation cannot be sustained on its own reasoning. This would seem a complete answer to whether the Rule is valid because, while we might give deference to the Commission's regulatory constructions of § 14(e), the reasoning used by the regulation itself is in this instance contrary to law and we need give no deference to the Commission's *post hoc* litigating justifications not reflected in the regulation.

Even on its own merits, the Commission's prophylactic justification fails. In order to be a valid prophylactic regulation, Rule 14e–3(a) must be reasonably designed not merely to prevent *any* fraud, but to prevent persons from engaging in "fraudulent, deceptive, or manipulative acts or practices, *in connection with* any tender offer." * * * (emphasis added). Insofar as Rule 14e–3(a) is designed to prevent the type of misappropriation at issue in this case, such acts are not legitimate objects of prevention because the Commission's misappropriation theory does not represent a coherent interpretation of the statutory "in connection with" requirement. * * * Even assuming that a person misappropriating information from the bidder commits fraud on the bidder, the Commission has provided no coherent or consistent explanation as to why such fraud is "in connection with" a tender offer, and thus the Commission may not seek to prevent indirectly conduct which it could not, under its current theory, prohibit directly. * * *

Finally, even further assuming that the Commission's misappropriation theory is a valid basis for direct liability, I fail to see how Rule 14e–3(a)'s elimination of the requirement of a breach of fiduciary duty is "reasonably designed" to prevent the underlying "fraudulent" acts. The majority's primary argument on this score is that in many cases " 'a breach of duty is likely but difficult to prove.' " * * * Although the majority's hypothetical difficulties involved in a tipper-tippee situation might have some merit in the context of "classical" insider trading, there is no reason to suspect similar difficulties in "misappropriation" cases. In such cases, Rule 14e–3(a) requires the Commission to prove that the defendant "knows or has reason to know" that the nonpublic information upon which trading occurred came from the bidder or an agent of the bidder. Once the source of the information has been identified, it should be a simple task to obtain proof of any breach of duty. After all, it is the bidder itself that was defrauded in misappropriation cases, and there is no reason to suspect that the victim of the fraud would be reluctant to provide evidence against the perpetrator of the fraud. * * * There being no particular difficulties in proving a breach of duty in such circumstances, a rule removing the requirement of such a breach cannot be said to be "reasonably designed" to prevent underlying violations of the misappropriation theory.

What Rule 14e–3(a) was in fact "designed" to do can be seen from the remainder of the majority's discussion of the Rule. Quoting at length from the Commission's explanation of the Rule in the Federal Register, the majority notes the Commission's concern with " 'unfair disparities in market information and market disruption.' " * * * In the Commission's further explanation of Rule 14e–3(a)'s purpose—continuing the paragraph partially quoted by the majority—an example of the problem to be addressed is the so-called "stampede effect" based on leaks and rumors that may result from trading on material, nonpublic information.* * *.

Although this reasoning no doubt accurately reflects the Commission's purposes in adopting Rule 14e–3(a), it does little to support the validity of that Rule as a means designed to prevent such behavior: None of the above-described acts involve breaches of fiduciary duties, hence a Rule designed to prevent them does not satisfy § 14(e)'s requirement that the Commission's Rules promulgated under that section be "reasonably designed to prevent" acts and practices that "are fraudulent, deceptive, or manipulative." As the majority itself recognizes, there is no " 'general duty between all participants in market transactions to forgo actions based on material, nonpublic information,' " and such duty only " 'arises from a specific relationship between two parties.' " * * * Unfair disparities in market information, and the potential "stampede effect" of leaks, do not necessarily involve a breach of any duty to anyone, and thus are not proper objects for regulation in the name of "fraud" under § 14(e). * * *

While enhancing the overall efficacy of the Williams Act may be a reasonable goal, it is not one that may be pursued through § 14(e), which limits its grant of rulemaking authority to the prevention of fraud, deceit, and manipulation. As we have held in the context of § 10(b), "not every instance of financial unfairness constitutes fraudulent activity." * * * Because, in the context of misappropriation cases, Rule 14e–3(a) is not a means "reasonably designed" to prevent persons from engaging in fraud "in connection with" a tender offer, it exceeds the Commission's authority under § 14(e), and respondent's conviction for violation of that Rule cannot be sustained.

*   *   *

NOTES AND QUESTIONS

1. There is always pressure on the federal government to act when state law seems inadequately to be performing its regulatory function, particularly when that regulatory function is perceived as the protection of investors. There are at least five main areas in which the federal government has acted to protect investors in publicly traded corporations 1) insider trading, 2) proxy voting, 3) new issues, 4) tender offers and takeovers, and 5) executive misconduct. The *O'Hagan* case is our introduction to insider trading, which will be more fully discussed in the following notes. We will treat proxy voting in the following case, *J.I. Case v. Borak*, and you have already caught a glimpse of the problems in that area through your study of *Campbell v. Loew's* in Chapter Three. The topic of the federal regulation of new issues we leave for another course, usually the one in "Securities Regulation." For our purposes we need only observe that the regulation of new issues, covered by the Securities Act of 1933, and the regulations promulgated thereunder, goes principally to ensuring that potential buyers of securities are given sufficient information to evaluate their possible purchase, both by requiring particular disclosures from issuers (in registration statements filed with the SEC and in "Prospectuses" furnished to investors) and by punishing misstatements or omissions in those materials. These two goals—disclosure and the prevention of fraud—are also those of the other areas of federal regulation of corporate affairs. We will briefly treat federal regulation of tender offers and takeovers in Chapter Eight. Federal regulation of executive misconduct will be examined in a note on the Sarbanes/Oxley Act, the new and controversial federal statute which deals with such matters, which concludes this Chapter.

2. *United States v. O'Hagan*, which you have just read, was the culmination of a long line of securities fraud cases, and it clearly established the viability of three different theories of liability under the 1934 Securities Exchange Act, and, in particular, Sections 10(b) and 14(e) of that act, as amended, and two important regulations thereunder, Rule 10b–5 and Rule 14e–3. The relevant portions of the text of these measures is given in *O'Hagan*. Were you able to glean an understanding of the misconduct against which they were targeted? Would you be surprised to learn that of all the areas of federal law this one is probably the one that encourages the most litigation? Much of it has been in the form of civil actions brought by individu-

als who claim to have been damaged by corporate insiders or corporate management acting in violation of Section 10(b) and Rule 10b–5. Section 10(b) does not expressly permit private persons to bring actions based on violations of the section, but that has been the practice since at least the 1940's, and Congress has made clear that such actions will be permitted to continue, although it has sought, in such measures as the Private Securities Litigation Reform Acts of 1995 and 1997 to diminish somewhat the overabundance of such lawsuits by eliminating so-called "professional plaintiffs" and by specifying stricter pleading standards. It is perhaps significant that the 1995 Act is the only measure ever successfully passed by the requisite two-thirds majority of both houses of Congress over the veto of President Clinton. Can you understand why President Clinton might choose to veto such a measure, and why Congress might pass it over his veto? Are you comfortable with providing a private remedy through litigation for those injured by violations of the securities law? Consider the explanation provided for the practice in *J.I. Case v. Borak*, which appears in the next section. * * *

3. The Private Securities Litigation Reform Act of 1995 (PSLRA) was passed one year after an important Supreme Court decision, *Central Bank of Denver, N. A. v. First Interstate Bank Of Denver, N. A.*, 511 U.S. 164, 114 S.Ct. 1439, 128 L.Ed.2d 119 (1994), in which the Court ruled that private actions could not be brought under 10(b) and 10b–5 against persons who "aided and abetted" securities fraud, but only against those who directly engaged in such fraudulent conduct. In Section 104 of the PSLRA, however, the SEC, was directed to prosecute persons guilty of such secondary liability. In 2008, in *Stoneridge Investment Partners v. Scientific–Atlanta, Inc.*, 552 U.S. 148, 128 S.Ct. 761, 169 L.Ed.2d 627 (2008) the Court reaffirmed its holding in *Central Bank of Denver*, and made clear that it would not permit "scheme liability," whereby a plaintiff seeks to impose liability on parties doing business with parties guilty of securities fraud. "Scheme liability" would have created a bonanza for trial lawyers bringing securities-fraud class actions, particularly since the pressure to settle such cases and avoid expensive discovery and other proceedings would have been difficult to resist even for innocent parties who were contractually involved with violators of Rule 10b–5. Writing for the Court, in a 5 to 3 decision (Justice Breyer had recused himself because he had investments in the parent corporation of one of the parties to the case), Justices Stevens, Ginsberg, and Souter dissenting, Justice Kennedy observed in *Stoneridge* that to have ruled for the plaintiffs would have been to authorize "a private cause of action against the entire marketplace in which the issuing company [that allegedly making a false or misleading statement] operates," 552 U.S., at 162, and, further, that if Congress had wanted to open the floodgates to such private actions, it could have done so instead of just directing the SEC to bring actions against "aiders and abetters" in the PSLRA. The trial lawyers and their friends in Congress, in November 2009, however, had drafted legislation as part of a broader effort to impose greater financial regulation on the market, expressly to permit private actions against those who "aided and abetted" securities law violators, thus reversing *Central Bank of Denver*. It is possible that by the time you read this, it will have been enacted into law. See generally "Dodd's Lawsuit Makeover," The Wall Street Journal,

Friday, November 13, at A22 (Editorial opposing the return of private actions for "aiding and abetting" securities fraud).

4. What then, were the three theories of liability examined (or at least mentioned) in *O'Hagan*? The first is the "classical" theory of liability under Section 10(b). This applies only to corporate fiduciaries, such as officers or directors, and suggests, simply, that such officials may not trade in their corporation's securities without disclosing any material facts that a shareholder with whom they might deal would want to know. It is the most basic form of the "disclose or abstain from trading" rule.

The second is the "misappropriation" theory, which applies to persons who are entrusted with information to be used for a particular purpose and then misuse that information in order to take advantage by trading in the market with shareholders who are unaware of the information. In *O'Hagan* the information was the fact that a tender offer for Pillsbury stock was forthcoming. There was an important earlier case where the theory might have supported prosecution of the defendant, *Chiarella v. United States*, 445 U.S. 222, 100 S.Ct. 1108, 63 L.Ed.2d 348 (1980). Chiarella was a financial printer who misappropriated information about a forthcoming tender offer, but the misappropriation theory was not clearly presented to the jury, and the Supreme Court in *Chiarella* did not pass on the validity of the theory, leaving that to the *O'Hagan* court. A "misappropriator" has a fiduciary duty to his or her employer not to misuse the information, although the duty does not actually run to the stockholder with whom the misappropriator trades. Do you understand why the dissenters in *O'Hagan* had trouble with finding liability under the misappropriation theory when no duties ran to shareholders? Nevertheless, *O'Hagan* makes clear that the misappropriation theory is now a permissible basis for finding a violation of the securities laws has taken place.

The third theory is occasionally referred to as the "equal playing field" theory. Its notion is that *any* person who trades in the securities market should not be able to take advantage of inside information whether or not that person has a fiduciary duty or whether or not that person has a duty not to misappropriate information. If you consult the language of Section 10(b) and Rule 10b–5 which refer to "any person" using any "manipulative device or contrivance," you will be tempted to believe that the "equal playing field" theory has a firm statutory basis, and this was the position both the Justice Department and the SEC had argued for. At least one Supreme Court Justice, HARRY BLACKMUN, was sympathetic to the theory, but a majority of the Supreme Court rejected it in the *Chiarella* case, holding that 10(b) and Rule 10b–5 were limited to cases in which persons were under a duty to shareholders to disclose or abstain from trading, as was true, for example in the case of corporate fiduciaries. Foiled in their use of the "equal playing field" theory under Section 10(b) and Rule 10b–5, the SEC tried again by promulgating Rule 14e–3, pursuant to the authority granted it by Section 14(e) of the Securities Exchange Act. This time, in *O'Hagan*, the "equal playing field" theory was accepted, but limited only to the problem of inside information regarding tender offers. You will have noticed that there were dissenters on this holding as well. What was the basis for that dissent, and do you agree?

5. Two other bases for liability for insider trading need our attention before we move on. The first of these is the so-called "tippee" liability, dis-

cussed in *Dirks v. SEC*, 463 U.S. 646, 103 S.Ct. 3255, 77 L.Ed.2d 911 (1983), also cited in *United States v. O'Hagan*. "Tippee liability" is imposed on persons who receive inside information from corporate fiduciaries and then proceed to trade on the basis of that information without disclosing it. Where the corporate fiduciary breaches his or her own duty of loyalty to the corporation, the tippee is said to "inherit the breach," and is liable in the same manner the fiduciary would be for failing to follow the "disclose or abstain from trading rule." The *Dirks* court made clear that the corporate fiduciary breaches his or her duty, and the tippee inherits the breach, whenever the corporate fiduciary receives some consideration in exchange for the information, or whenever the corporate fiduciary wishes to confer a gift or benefit on the tippee. * * *

6. The other form of liability for insider trading does not involve any of these subtle distinctions, and simply imposes a penalty of possible disgorgement of profits on any officer, director, or 10% beneficial shareholder who buys and sells his or her corporation's stock within a six month (called a "short swing") period. This is pursuant to Section 16(b) of the Securities Exchange Act of 1934, which provides that:

> For the purpose of preventing the unfair use of information which may have been obtained by such beneficial owner, director, or officer by reason of his relationship to the issuer, any profit realized by him from any purchase and sale, or any sale and purchase, of any equity security of such issuer * * * within any period of less than six months * * * shall inure to and be recoverable by the issuer, irrespective of any intention on the part of such beneficial owner, director, or officer in entering into such transaction of holding the security * * * for a period exceeding six months. Suit to recover such profit may be instituted at law or in equity in any court of competent jurisdiction by the issuer, or by the owner of any security of the issuer in the name and in behalf of the issuer if the issuer shall fail or refuse to bring such suit within sixty days after request or shall fail diligently to prosecute the same thereafter; but no such suit shall be brought more than two years after the date such profit was realized. This subsection shall not be construed to cover any transaction where such beneficial owner was not such both at the time of the purchase and sale, or the sale and purchase, of the security * * *.

Would you have voted for Section 16(b) if you were a member of Congress? Does it represent a different sort of theory of legislation than does Section 10(b)?

7. Consider the following hypothetical. Domestic Diva has a thriving business which provides household management and decorating tips to American women. Ms. Diva has made millions and has invested much of her cash in other corporations. One of these is a drug company, which has an application before the FDA seeking approval for a cancer drug. Ms. Diva is also a personal friend of the CEO of the drug company, and the CEO and Diva share a Broker at Merrill Lynch. The CEO receives advance word that in two days the FDA is going formally to deny the application to approve the cancer drug. The CEO knows that when this information becomes public the drug company's stock will plummet in price. CEO proceeds to alert his family members to sell their holdings in the drug company, and seeks to sell some of his own shares, but Broker advises him that to do so would violate the federal

securities laws. The family members, through Broker, sell their drug company shares. One day before the public FDA announcement of disapproval of the cancer drug Broker calls up Diva and tells her that CEO's family has been selling their shares in the drug company. Diva tells Broker to sell her shares in the drug company. Has anyone violated Section 10(b) and Rule 10b–5? On what theories?

B.   THE FEDERAL PROXY RULES

GAUDIOSI v. MELLON

United States Court of Appeals Third Circuit.
269 F.2d 873(1959), cert. den., 361 U.S. 902, 80 S.Ct. 211, 4 L.Ed.2d 157 (1959).

[Kalodner, J., for the court.] [After dismissing several of the shareholder plaintiffs' claims regarding procedural irregularities as "specious,"] we will consider together the remaining appeals—No. 12,618 from dismissal of plaintiffs' first action on May 6, 1958 and Nos. 12,744–45 from entry of judgment for defendants on August 18, 1958, in plaintiffs' second action.

Both actions sought equitable relief in the proxy contest for the office of director of Railroad, in which plaintiffs [holders of a very small minority of shares] sought to break Railroad management's slate of six nominees by electing [one of the plaintiffs, Randolph] Phillips. * * * Broadly stated, in each, plaintiffs assailed as illegal and inequitable defendants' conduct in the proxy contest and sought to invalidate management proxies received and later cast in support of its six nominees at the May 13, 1958 annual meeting. Further, in both actions, plaintiffs complained that defendants had unlawfully denied rights which allegedly inured to them in the proxy contest, and sought injunctions to enforce them.

The District Court's opinion in the second action * * * contains a detailed recital, in its Findings of Fact, of the complex sequence of events in the proxy contest on which plaintiffs sought to premise both of their actions.

In its Findings of Fact * * * the District Court found that the defendants had not, in any respect, in their conduct of the proxy contest, either committed the unlawful and inequitable acts alleged by the plaintiffs or denied to them their legal and equitable rights, and that, on the other hand, Phillips had 'deliberately and maliciously' in violation of the applicable rules of the Securities and Exchange Commission, in the course of the proxy contest, sought to 'intimidate' registered owners of some 800,000 shares of Pennsylvania Railroad Company stock to the end that they would not execute management proxies or vote their stock for management nominees. * * * Based on these factfindings, the District Court, in paragraph 26 of its Conclusions of Law, ruled that 'In this action Phillips came into equity with unclean hands', and in paragraph 27, that

'Phillips' unclean hands bar the grant to Phillips of any equitable relief.'

On review of the record we are of the opinion that it amply sustains the District Court's fact-findings and Conclusions of Law with respect to Phillips' 'unclean hands' and that its Order of August 18, 1958, entering judgment for defendants, except as to the representative claim in the class action embodied in Count IV of their second action, should be affirmed.

It appears that during the proxy contest the New York Times published a news account stating, in substance, that the Swiss Bankers Association had urged its member banks to vote in favor of management whenever they voted proxies on behalf of stockholders in American corporations and that Phillips had knowledge of this account prior to April 30, 1958.

It further appears that on April 30, 1958, Credit Suisse, a Swiss bank, was the registered owner of 362,156 shares of Railroad stock and that the Swiss Bank Corporation, another Swiss bank, was the registered owner of 444,657 shares of the same stock. At the time mentioned Phillips was of the belief that the two Swiss banks were each the registered or beneficial owners of approximately 361,000 shares of Railroad stock, and that they had executed and intended to deliver to Railroad proxies to vote in favor of the six management nominees for director.

On April 30, 1958, without prior submission to the Securities and Exchange Commission for 'clearance', as required by Rule X–14-A–1, et seq. of the Securities and Exchange Act, Phillips sent to the two Swiss banks identical telegrams as follows:

'I understand that your Bank which is the nominee for 360,918 shares of Pennsylvania Railroad Co. capital stock intends to vote said stock for the 6 management nominees for director at the Railroad's annual election to be held on May 13, 1958, without informing the owners of said stock of the contest for directors now existing and without giving them an opportunity to determine for themselves whether or not their stock should be voted and without giving them an opportunity to vote for myself as the 1 non-management nominee for director, or for the 6 management nominees, or for 5 or less of the management nominees and the 1 non-management nominee. Such arbitrary and undemocratic action by your Bank not only violates American equitable and common law principles applicable to banks when they act as fiduciaries but also violates the rules of the Securities and Exchange Commission and New York Stock Exchange as well as American banking practices applicable to all stock exchange brokers and banks in this country. It is a violation of the concept of a free and fair election on a fully informed basis, it constitutes a fraud upon the stockholders, and can only be of comfort to dictators and totalitarians in or out of corporation management.

'Such action by your Bank also constitutes a combination with the Pennsylvania Railroad management and other company managements that is prohibited under the antitrust laws of this country and which are applicable to your Bank since it is doing business in the United States.

'Such improper practices which already have been criticized in the United States Senate threaten to damage immeasurably myself and many thousands of associated stockholders. Unless you give me prompt assurance of the immediate termination of these practices I will reluctantly be compelled to take prompt and appropriate legal action in the courts. Kindly advise me by return wire of your answer to this telegram.'

When authorized officials of the Securities and Exchange Commission discovered the transmission of the foregoing telegrams without prior submission to the Commission, they directed Phillips to file copies of them as 'soliciting material'. Upon his submission of the copies, under protest, on May 9, 1958, the Commission's staff expressed its disapproval and Phillips, either in anticipation of or as a result of it, sent the following telegram to each of the banks:

"I hereby withdraw all statements in my telegram to you dated April 30, 1958 except the first sentence, and I hereby substitute in place of said withdrawn statement the statement that If said stock is voted by your Bank I reserve all rights in law and equity to take legal and other appropriate action against you for just and equitable relief".

For eight years preceding 1958 the two Swiss banks had sent in their proxies to management for virtually the entire number of shares held by them. However, at the election on May 13, 1958 they together voted approximately only 100,000 shares as to which they had specific instructions from the beneficial owners. They withheld the remaining 700,000 shares, as found by the District Court, as the direct result of the receipt of Phillips' telegram of April 30, 1958.

That that is so is made manifest by these circumstances: the so-called 'withdrawal' telegrams of May 9th specifically contained the threat that if the stock of the Swiss banks was voted for management nominees Phillips reserved 'all rights in law and equity to take legal and other appropriate action' against the banks; Phillips the very day that the telegrams were sent filed an amendment to his second complaint by adding the Swiss banks as defendants and copies of the amended complaint were served on the Swiss banks on May 12, 1958; and May 9th, the day the telegrams were sent, was Friday and the week-end intervened between that day and Tuesday, May 13th when the annual meeting took place.

The foregoing negatives Phillips' contention that the telegrams of May 9th had 'righted' any wrongs committed by him in his April 30th telegrams.

We do not need to dwell further on the District Court's findings of 'unclean hands' on Phillips' part except to say that his dire threats to the Swiss banks in his April 30th telegrams of possible anti-trust action, and his invocation of the spectres of 'fraud', 'violation of American equitable and common law principles applicable to banks', violation of 'the rules of the Securities and Exchange Commission and New York Stock Exchange as well as American banking practices applicable to all stock exchange brokers and banks in this country' amply supported the District Court's fact-finding of 'deliberate and malicious' wrongdoing with intent to 'intimidate' in violation of the Rules of the Securities and Exchange Commission in proxy contests.

Clearly Phillips' conduct constituted the 'unclean hands' which barred his prayers for equitable relief.

The bar of 'unclean hands' extends to plaintiffs' first action although it was not there considered in the District Court's disposition of it, and was not raised by defendants.

It will be recalled that plaintiffs' first action was dismissed on May 6, 1958. Phillips' telegrams to the Swiss banks on April 30, 1958 preceded that dismissal. Plaintiffs appeal from that dismissal is before us in Appeal No. 12,618.

These principles are well-settled:

One who comes into equity must come with clean hands and keep those hands clean throughout the pendency of the litigation even to the time of ultimate disposition by an appellate court. * * *

Courts are concerned primarily with their own integrity in the application of the clean hands maxim and even though not raised by the parties the court will of its own motion apply it. * * *

The clean hands maxim gives wide sweep to the equity court's exercise of discretion 'in refusing to aid the unclean litigant.' * * *

The equity court 'is not bound by formula or restrained by any limitation that tends to trammel the free and just exercise of discretion.' * * *

The principles stated are dispositive with respect to plaintiff's first and second actions, although, as previously stated, the issue of 'unclean hands' was not raised by defendants or considered by the District Court in the first action as it was in the second action. The April 30, 1958 telegrams to the Swiss banks tainted the first action to the same extent that it did the second. The District Court properly exercised its discretion in applying the 'unclean hands' maxim in denying relief to plaintiffs in the second action. The fact that it did not invoke maxim in its disposition of the first action is immaterial. We can and must do so here under the cases cited.

As we stated in *Root Refining Co. v. Universal Oil Products Co., 3 Cir., 1948, 169 F.2d 514, 534, 535,* Universal Oil Products Co. v. William Whitman Co., 335 U.S. 912, 69 S.Ct. 481, 93 L.Ed. 444, 336 U.S. 915, 69 S.Ct. 601, 93 L.Ed. 1079:

> '* * * No principle is better settled than the maxim that he who comes into equity must come with clean hands and keep them clean

throughout the course of the litigation, and that if he violates this rule, he must be denied all relief whatever may have been the merits of his claim. * * *'

Plaintiffs' contention that defendants were not 'injured' by reason of the sending of the April 30, 1958 telegrams is irrelevant to the issue. As Judge Learned Hand in his dissenting opinion in *Art Metal Works v. Abraham & Straus, 2 Cir., 1934, 70 F.2d 641, at page 646,* certiorari denied *293 U.S. 596, 55 S.Ct. 110, 79 L.Ed. 689,* so aptly stated:

'The doctrine (of unclean hands) is confessedly derived from the unwillingness of a court, originally and still nominally one of conscience, to give its peculiar relief to a suitor who in the very controversy has so conducted himself as to shock the moral sensibilities of the judge. It has nothing to do with the rights or liabilities of the parties; indeed the defendant who invokes it need not be damaged, and the court may even raise it *sua sponte* [on its own]. * * *' (Emphasis supplied.)

There remains for disposition Phillips' contention that 'the maxim of 'unclean hands' does not dispose of the rights of others', and that 'neither plaintiffs Gaudiosi or Schwartz participated in these acts of Phillips, thus the defense is totally inapplicable to them, as well as to the 23,000, or less, stockholders upon whose behalf all three plaintiffs sued.'

The contention is utterly without merit. It ignores the earlier cited principle that courts are concerned primarily with their own integrity in the application of the clean hands maxim. Courts in such situations act for their own protection and not as a matter of 'defense' to the defendant.* * * Public policy not only makes it obligatory for courts to deny a plaintiff relief once his 'unclean hands' are established but to refuse to even hear a case under such circumstances. Thus it has been held that even in a stockholders' derivative action 'unclean hands' on the part of a plaintiff will require dismissal of the action. * * *

Apart from the foregoing, to subscribe to this last contention would require us to ignore the fact that plaintiffs' two actions (apart from the derivative claim in Count IV) were specifically instituted to further Phillips' candidacy for director. The startling result would be to permit Phillips to eat his apple with 'unclean hands'. Justice may be blind but it isn't 'dumb'.

For the reasons earlier stated the appeals in Nos. 12,742 and 12,743 will be dismissed and the Orders in appeals Nos. 12,618, 12,744, 12,745 and 12,759 will be affirmed.

J.I. CASE CO. ET AL. v. BORAK

Supreme Court of the United States.
377 U.S. 426, 84 S.Ct. 1555, 12 L.Ed.2d 423 (1964).

MR. JUSTICE CLARK delivered the opinion of the Court.

This is a civil action brought by respondent, a stockholder of petitioner J. I. Case Company, charging deprivation of the pre-emptive rights of respondent and other shareholders by reason of a merger between Case and the American Tractor Corporation. It is alleged that the merger was effected through the circulation of a false and misleading proxy statement by those proposing the merger. The complaint was in two counts, the first based on diversity and claiming a breach of the directors' fiduciary duty to the stockholders. The second count alleged a violation of § 14 (a)[1] of the Securities Exchange Act of 1934 with reference to the proxy solicitation material. The trial court held that as to this count it had no power to redress the alleged violations of the Act but was limited solely to the granting of declaratory relief thereon under § 27 of the Act.[2] The court held Wis. Stat., 1961, § 180.405 (4), which requires posting security for expenses in derivative actions, applicable to both counts, except that portion of Count 2 requesting declaratory relief. It ordered the respondent to furnish a bond in the amount of $75,000 thereunder and, upon his failure to do so, dismissed the complaint, save that part of Count 2 seeking a declaratory judgment. On interlocutory appeal the Court of Appeals reversed on both counts, holding that the District Court had the power to grant remedial relief and that the Wisconsin statute was not applicable. * * * We consider only the question of whether § 27 of the Act authorizes a federal cause of action for rescission or damages to a corporate stockholder with respect to a consummated merger which was authorized pursuant to the use of a proxy statement alleged to contain false and misleading statements violative of § 14(a) of the Act. * * *

I.

Respondent, the owner of 2,000 shares of common stock of Case acquired prior to the merger, brought this suit based on diversity jurisdiction seeking to enjoin a proposed merger between Case and the American Tractor Corporation (ATC) on various grounds, including breach of the fiduciary duties of the Case directors, self-dealing among the management

---

1. Section 14 (a) of the Securities Exchange Act of 1934, 48 Stat. 895, 15 U. S. C. § 78n (a), provides: "It shall be unlawful for any person, by the use of the mails or by any means or instrumentality of interstate commerce or of any facility of any national securities exchange or otherwise to solicit or to permit the use of his name to solicit any proxy or consent or authorization in respect of any security (other than an exempted security) registered on any national securities exchange in contravention of such rules and regulations as the [Securities and Exchange] Commission may prescribe as necessary or appropriate in the public interest or for the protection of investors."

2. Section 27 of the Act, 48 Stat. 902–903, 15 U. S. C. § 78aa, provides in part: "The district courts of the United States, the Supreme Court of the District of Columbia, and the United States courts of any Territory or other place subject to the jurisdiction of the United States shall have exclusive jurisdiction of violations of this title or the rules and regulations thereunder, and of all suits in equity and actions at law brought to enforce any liability or duty created by this title or the rules and regulations thereunder. Any criminal proceeding may be brought in the district wherein any act or transaction constituting the violation occurred. Any suit or action to enforce any liability or duty created by this title or rules and regulations thereunder, or to enjoin any violation of such title or rules and regulations, may be brought in any such district or in the district wherein the defendant is found or is an inhabitant or transacts business, and process in such cases may be served in any other district of which the defendant is an inhabitant or wherever the defendant may be found."

of Case and ATC and misrepresentations contained in the material circulated to obtain proxies. The injunction was denied and the merger was thereafter consummated. Subsequently successive amended complaints were filed and the case was heard on the aforesaid two-count complaint. The claims pertinent to the asserted violation of the Securities Exchange Act were predicated on diversity jurisdiction as well as on § 27 of the Act. They alleged: that petitioners, or their predecessors, solicited or permitted their names to be used in the solicitation of proxies of Case stockholders for use at a special stockholders' meeting at which the proposed merger with ATC was to be voted upon; that the proxy solicitation material so circulated was false and misleading in violation of § 14(a) of the Act and Rule 14a–9[3] which the Commission had promulgated thereunder; that the merger was approved at the meeting by a small margin of votes and was thereafter consummated; that the merger would not have been approved but for the false and misleading statements in the proxy solicitation material; and that Case stockholders were damaged thereby. The respondent sought judgment holding the merger void and damages for himself and all other stockholders similarly situated, as well as such further relief "as equity shall require." The District Court ruled that the Wisconsin security for expenses statute did not apply to Count 2 since it arose under federal law. However, the court found that its jurisdiction was limited to declaratory relief in a private, as opposed to a government, suit alleging violation of § 14(a) of the Act. Since the additional equitable relief and damages prayed for by the respondent would, therefore, be available only under state law, it ruled those claims subject to the security for expenses statute. After setting the amount of security at $75,000 and upon the representation of counsel that the security would not be posted, the court dismissed the complaint, save that portion of Count 2 seeking a declaration that the proxy solicitation material was false and misleading and that the proxies and, hence, the merger were void.

II.

It appears clear that private parties have a right under § 27 to bring suit for violation of § 14(a) of the Act. Indeed, this section specifically grants the appropriate District Courts jurisdiction over "all suits in equity and actions at law brought to enforce any liability or duty created" under the Act. The petitioners make no concessions, however, emphasizing that Congress made no specific reference to a private right of action in § 14(a) * * *.

---

3. 17 CFR § 240.14a–9 provides: "False or misleading statements. No solicitation subject to § § 240.14a–1 to 240.14a–10 shall be made by means of any proxy statement, form of proxy, notice of meeting, or other communication written or oral containing any statement which at the time and in the light of the circumstances under which it is made, is false or misleading with respect to any material fact, or which omits to state any material fact necessary in order to make the statements therein not false or misleading or necessary to correct any statement in any earlier communication with respect to the solicitation of a proxy for the same meeting or subject matter which has become false or misleading."

III.

The purpose of § 14 (a) is to prevent management or others from obtaining authorization for corporate action by means of deceptive or inadequate disclosure in proxy solicitation. The section stemmed from the congressional belief that "fair corporate suffrage is an important right that should attach to every equity security bought on a public exchange." H. R. Rep. No. 1383, 73d Cong., 2d Sess., 13. It was intended to "control the conditions under which proxies may be solicited with a view to preventing the recurrence of abuses which ... [had] frustrated the free exercise of the voting rights of stockholders." *Id.*, at 14. "Too often proxies are solicited without explanation to the stockholder of the real nature of the questions for which authority to cast his vote is sought." S. Rep. No. 792, 73d Cong., 2d Sess., 12. These broad remedial purposes are evidenced in the language of the section which makes it "unlawful for any person ... to solicit or to permit the use of his name to solicit any proxy or consent or authorization in respect of any security ... registered on any national securities exchange in contravention of such rules and regulations as the Commission may prescribe as necessary or appropriate in the public interest *or for the protection of investors.*" (Italics supplied.) While this language makes no specific reference to a private right of action, among its chief purposes is "the protection of investors," which certainly implies the availability of judicial relief where necessary to achieve that result.

The injury which a stockholder suffers from corporate action pursuant to a deceptive proxy solicitation ordinarily flows from the damage done the corporation, rather than from the damage inflicted directly upon the stockholder. The damage suffered results not from the deceit practiced on him alone but rather from the deceit practiced on the stockholders as a group. To hold that derivative actions are not within the sweep of the section would therefore be tantamount to a denial of private relief. Private enforcement of the proxy rules provides a necessary supplement to Commission action. As in antitrust treble damage litigation, the possibility of civil damages or injunctive relief serves as a most effective weapon in the enforcement of the proxy requirements. The Commission advises that it examines over 2,000 proxy statements annually and each of them must necessarily be expedited. Time does not permit an independent examination of the facts set out in the proxy material and this results in the Commission's acceptance of the representations contained therein at their face value, unless contrary to other material on file with it. Indeed, on the allegations of respondent's complaint, the proxy material failed to disclose alleged unlawful market manipulation of the stock of ATC, and this unlawful manipulation would not have been apparent to the Commission until after the merger.

We, therefore, believe that under the circumstances here it is the duty of the courts to be alert to provide such remedies as are necessary to make effective the congressional purpose. As was said in *Sola Electric Co.* v. *Jefferson Electric Co., 317 U.S. 173, 176 (1942):*

"When a federal statute condemns an act as unlawful, the extent and nature of the legal consequences of the condemnation, though left by the statute to judicial determination, are nevertheless federal questions, the answers to which are to be derived from the statute and the federal policy which it has adopted."

* * * It is for the federal courts "to adjust their remedies so as to grant the necessary relief" where federally secured rights are invaded. "And it is also well settled that where legal rights have been invaded, and a federal statute provides for a general right to sue for such invasion, federal courts may use any available remedy to make good the wrong done." *Bell v. Hood, 327 U.S. 678, 684 (1946)*. Section 27 grants the District Courts jurisdiction "of all suits in equity and actions at law brought to enforce any liability or duty created by this title...." In passing on almost identical language found in the Securities Act of 1933, the Court found the words entirely sufficient to fashion a remedy to rescind a fraudulent sale, secure restitution and even to enforce the right to restitution against a third party holding assets of the vendor. *Deckert v. Independence Shares Corp., 311 U.S. 282 (1940)*. This significant language was used:

"The power *to enforce* implies the power to make effective the right of recovery afforded by the Act. And the power to make the right of recovery effective implies the power to utilize any of the procedures or actions normally available to the litigant according to the exigencies of the particular case." At 288. * * *

Nor do we find merit in the contention that such remedies are limited to prospective relief. This was the position taken in *Dann v. Studebaker-Packard Corp., 288 F.2d 201,* where it was held that the "preponderance of questions of state law which would have to be interpreted and applied in order to grant the relief sought ... is so great that the federal question involved ... is really negligible in comparison." At 214. But we believe that the overriding federal law applicable here would, where the facts required, control the appropriateness of redress despite the provisions of state corporation law, for it "is not uncommon for federal courts to fashion federal law where federal rights are concerned." *Textile Workers v. Lincoln Mills, 353 U.S. 448, 457 (1957)*. In addition, the fact that questions of state law must be decided does not change the character of the right; it remains federal. As Chief Justice Marshall said in *Osborn v. Bank of the United States, 9 Wheat. 738 (1824):*

"If this were sufficient to withdraw a case from the jurisdiction of the federal Courts, almost every case, although involving the construction of a law, would be withdrawn...." At 819–820.

Moreover, if federal jurisdiction were limited to the granting of declaratory relief, victims of deceptive proxy statements would be obliged to go into state courts for remedial relief. And if the law of the State happened to attach no responsibility to the use of misleading proxy statements, the whole purpose of the section might be frustrated. Furthermore, the hurdles that the victim might face (such as separate suits, as contemplated by *Dann v. Studebaker–Packard Corp., supra,* security for expenses statutes, bringing in all parties necessary for complete relief, etc.) might well prove insuperable to effective relief.

IV.

Our finding that federal courts have the power to grant all necessary remedial relief is not to be construed as any indication of what we believe to be the necessary and appropriate relief in this case. We are concerned here only with a determination that federal jurisdiction for this purpose does exist. Whatever remedy is necessary must await the trial on the merits. * * *

* * *

NOTES AND QUESTIONS

1. These two cases are offered to give you some sort of a sense of the manner in which federal regulation under the proxy rules works. In particular, does *J.I. Case v. Borak* help you understand why the United States Court of Appeals for the Third Circuit held that Randolph Phillips, one of the plaintiffs in *Gaudiosi v. Mellon* had "unclean hands?" Phillips and some of his fellow shareholders sought relief in the federal trial court, acting as a court of equity, which they asked to issue an injunction to prevent the management nominees of the Pennsylvania Railroad from being seated as directors, alleging that the proxies which management obtained and voted for those seats were somehow obtained in a manner that violated the securities law. Note that the Court doesn't reach the merits of this issue because of the securities violations of Phillips himself. Do you understand what those violations were, and do you approve of the "unclean hands" doctrine?

2. Consider the nature of the federal proxy regulations, and how they operate. As indicated earlier, the aims of federal regulation of securities transactions are the promotion of disclosure and the prevention of fraud. To that end, the SEC is authorized to require that certain information be provided shareholders when they are asked to authorize that their votes be cast by "proxy." Because in large publicly-held corporations there may be millions of shareholders it is impossible that they all cast their votes at shareholder meetings in person, and so whenever shareholder meetings are necessary (as they are, for example, to elect directors—as in *Gaudiosi v. Mellon,* to remove directors for cause—as we saw in *Campbell v. Loew's*—or for other major changes in the corporation, such as Amendments of the Charter, mergers, dissolution, or sale of substantially all of the assets) the method that has evolved is for shareholders to grant a "proxy" allowing someone else, usually a member of corporate management, to cast their votes at the shareholder meeting for them. Management or others may solicit proxies from shareholders, but the SEC requires that such solicitations not be misleading, and that shareholders are supplied with information at the time proxies are solicited, or on an ongoing basis by the corporation (in Annual Reports, quarterly reports and supplemental reports when major economic changes occur to the corporation)

so that they can authorize proxies in an informed manner. When management solicits proxies it will usually recommend a course of action for the shareholder, indicating that management recommends that the proxies be cast to authorize a vote in the manner approved by management, but shareholders are free to vote against management proposals when they cast proxy votes, and this is always clearly indicated in the proxy solicitations. These days one can cast proxies (that is, authorize the manner in which one's shares are to be voted at shareholder meetings) by mail, by phone, or even over the internet. You may not be surprised to learn that the vast majority of proxy votes cast favor management, but it is not uncommon for large institutional shareholders to contest recommendations of management, and occasionally management proposals are defeated. *   *   *

3.   What sort of information must be supplied when proxies are solicited, what is involved in the solicitation of proxies, and when is a statement by management or others to be construed as a solicitation? Some of the answers to these questions are suggested by *J.I. Case v. Borak.* It observes that Section 14(a) of the Securities Exchange Act of 1934 authorizes the SEC to promulgate rules regarding proxy solicitation "for the protection of investors," and that solicitation of proxies in violation of those rules is "unlawful," and, because unlawful conduct under the securities act can virtually always be the subject of criminal prosecution by the Justice Department or a civil proceeding brought by the SEC, the consequences of non-compliance with the proxy rules can be severe. You will have noticed that *J.I. Case v. Borak* holds that violations of the proxy rules can also lead to civil actions being brought by individuals who allege injury as a result of such non-compliance. Do you agree with the court's reasoning on this point? Is the reasoning weakened by the suggestion, made by the defendant in the case, and often repeated since then, that other sections of the Securities Laws expressly permit private actions, and if none is expressly permitted in Section 14(a) then the courts should not grant such permission? You will remember that similar issues were raised by the courts' permitting private actions grounded on violations of Section 10(b), though such actions are now expressly acknowledged as valid by Congressional statute.

A brief review of some of the provisions of the proxy rules may help clarify the issues in this area. These are collected in the SEC's Regulation 14A, and can be found on the web, at http://www.sec.gov/divisions/corpfin/forms/14a.htm. We ought to begin with the definition of a proxy "solicitation," from Regulation 14a–1(l):

(l) Solicitation.

(1) The terms "solicit" and "solicitation" include:

(i) Any request for a proxy whether or not accompanied by or included in a form of proxy;

(ii) Any request to execute or not to execute, or to revoke, a proxy; or

(ii) The furnishing of a form of proxy or other communication to security holders under circumstances reasonably calculated to result in the procurement, withholding or revocation of a proxy.

Does this definition strike you as too broad? Would it conflict, for example, with the First Amendment? Would a corporation's press release, extolling the performance of the company, or of particular director who might be standing for reelection come within the definition? Consider what is required if a given communication is deemed to be a "solicitation." This is covered by Rule 14a–3, which provides, in pertinent part:

(a) No solicitation subject to this regulation shall be made unless each person solicited is concurrently furnished or has previously been furnished with a publicly-filed preliminary or definitive written proxy statement containing the information specified in Schedule 14A * * * or with a publicly-filed preliminary or definitive written proxy statement included in a registration statement filed under the Securities Act of 1933 * * *

(b) If the solicitation is made on behalf of the registrant other than an investment company registered under the Investment Company Act of 1940, and relates to an annual (or special meeting in lieu of the annual) meeting of security holders, or written consent in lieu of such meeting, at which directors are to be elected, each proxy statement furnished pursuant to paragraph (a) of this section shall be accompanied or preceded by an annual report to security holders as follows:

* * *

(1) The report shall include, for the registrant and its subsidiaries consolidated, audited balance sheets as of the end of each of the two most recent fiscal years and audited statements of income and cash flows for each of the three most recent fiscal years * * *

(2) (i) Financial statements and notes thereto shall be presented in roman type at least as large and as legible as 10–point modern type. If necessary for convenient presentation, the financial statements may be in roman type as large and as legible as 8-point modern type. All type shall be leaded at least 2 points.

(ii) Where the annual report to security holders is delivered through an electronic medium, issuers may satisfy legibility requirements applicable to printed documents, such as type size and font, by presenting all required information in a format readily communicated to investors.

(3) The report shall contain the supplementary financial information required by Item 302 of Regulation S–K (§ 229.302 of this chapter).

(4) The report shall contain information concerning changes in and disagreements with accountants on accounting and financial disclosure required by Item 304 of Regulation S–K (§ 229.304 of this chapter).

(5) (i) The report shall contain the selected financial data required by Item 301 of Regulation S–K (§ 229.301 of this chapter).

(ii) The report shall contain management's discussion and analysis of financial condition and results of operations required by Item 303 of Regulation S–K (§ 229.303 of this chapter) or, if applicable, a plan of operation required by Item 303(a) of Regulation S–B (§ 228.303(a) of this chapter).

(iii) The report shall contain the quantitative and qualitative disclosures about market risk required by Item 305 of Regulation S–K (§ 229.305 of this chapter).

(6) The report shall contain a brief description of the business done by the registrant and its subsidiaries during the most recent fiscal year which will, in the opinion of management, indicate the general nature and scope of the business of the registrant and its subsidiaries.

(7) The report shall contain information relating to the registrant's industry segments, classes of similar products or services, foreign and domestic operations and exports sales required by paragraphs (b), (c)(1)(i) and (d) of Item 101 of Regulation S–K (§ 229.101 of this chapter).

(8) The report shall identify each of the registrant's directors and executive officers, and shall indicate the principal occupation or employment of each such person and the name and principal business of any organization by which such person is employed.

(9) The report shall contain the market price of and dividends on the registrant's common equity and related security holder matters required by Item 201(a), (b) and (c) of Regulation S–K (§ 229.201 of this chapter).

(10) The registrant's proxy statement, or the report, shall contain an undertaking in bold face or otherwise reasonably prominent type to provide without charge to each person solicited upon the written request of any such person, a copy of the registrant's annual report on Form 10–K and Form 10–KSB, including the financial statements and the financial statement schedules, required to be filed with the Commission pursuant to Rule 13a–1 under the Act for the registrant's most recent fiscal year, and shall indicate the name and address (including title or department) of the person to whom such a written request is to be directed. * * *

You will not, of course, be aware of the precise requirements of disclosure here required without consulting the other SEC forms or federal law referenced, but have you seen enough to determine the quality and quantity of information likely to be supplied in a proxy statement?

You can get some sense of the information required, by considering what must be in a Schedule 14A, which must be supplied for proxies not solicited at the time of the annual meeting (when an annual report must accompany proxies). Among the directions for filling out Schedule 14A are:

(1) Describe briefly any substantial interest, direct or indirect, by security holdings or otherwise, of each participant as defined in paragraphs (a)(ii), (iii), (iv), (v) and (vi) of Instruction 3 to Item 4 of this Schedule 14A, in any matter to be acted upon at the meeting, and include with respect to each participant the following information, or a fair and adequate summary thereof:

(i) Name and business address of the participant.

(ii) The participant's present principal occupation or employment and the name, principal business and address of any corporation or other organization in which such employment is carried on.

(iii) State whether or not, during the past ten years, the participant has been convicted in a criminal proceeding (excluding traffic violations or similar misdemeanors) and, if so, give dates, nature of conviction, name and location of court, and penalty imposed or other disposition of the case. A negative answer need not be included in the proxy statement or other soliciting material.

(iv) State the amount of each class of securities of the registrant which the participant owns beneficially, directly or indirectly.

(v) State the amount of each class of securities of the registrant which the participant owns of record but not beneficially.

(vi) State with respect to all securities of the registrant purchased or sold within the past two years, the dates on which they were purchased or sold and the amount purchased or sold on each such date.

(vii) If any part of the purchase price or market value of any of the shares specified in paragraph (b)(1)(vi) of this Item is represented by funds borrowed or otherwise obtained for the purpose of acquiring or holding such securities, so state and indicate the amount of the indebtedness as of the latest practicable date. If such funds were borrowed or obtained otherwise than pursuant to a margin account or bank loan in the regular course of business of a bank, broker or dealer, briefly describe the transaction, and state the names of the parties.

(viii) State whether or not the participant is, or was within the past year, a party to any contract, arrangements or understandings with any person with respect to any securities of the registrant, including, but not limited to, joint ventures, loan or option arrangements, puts or calls, guarantees against loss or guarantees of profit, division of losses or profits, or the giving or withholding of proxies. If so, name the parties to such contracts, arrangements or understandings and give the details thereof.

(ix) State the amount of securities of the registrant owned beneficially, directly or indirectly, by each of the participant's associates and the name and address of each such associate.

(x) State the amount of each class of securities of any parent or subsidiary of the registrant which the participant owns beneficially, directly or indirectly.

(xi) Furnish for the participant and associates of the participant the information required by Item 404(a) of Regulation S–K (§ 229.404(a) of this chapter).

(xii) State whether or not the participant or any associates of the participant have any arrangement or understanding with any person—

(A) with respect to any future employment by the registrant or its affiliates; or

(B) with respect to any future transactions to which the registrant or any of its affiliates will or may be a party. If so, describe such arrangement or understanding and state the names of the parties thereto.

Would this information help you in deciding whether or not to grant a proxy? Compliance with the proxy rules is required of corporations which are publicly traded and registered pursuant to the 1933 Securities Act, and not those close corporations which are privately held. Still, many publicly-held businesses are relatively small businesses. Can you understand how the costs of compliance might be substantial, and also how compliance is unlikely to be accomplished without the aid of professionals, at least lawyers and accountants? In general, forms for solicitation of proxies and proxy statements must be filed with the SEC before they are distributed to shareholders, and the SEC will review these documents, not necessarily for the truth contained therein, but the SEC may ask for explanations of particular statements, may suggest revisions, and may indicate where materials do not comply with SEC requirements. You will remember that this happened in *Gaudiosi v. Mellon*, and you will have probably inferred that proxy solicitors are well-advised to revise in line with SEC staff suggestions, or to decline to send out materials which the SEC has indicated are problematic. The SEC reviews many thousands of such documents, and whether or not the SEC comments on the materials the person or firm soliciting proxies remains responsible for their accuracy. As you have seen, Rule 14a–9 creates liability for false or misleading statements, and, as you have seen from *J.I. Case v. Borak*, violations of 14a–9 can lead to private actions by those purportedly injured by such false or misleading statements. One solicits proxies, then, at one's peril.

4. So far we have been examining the Regulations which relate to the solicitation of proxies, but we should also note one other means of shareholder communication and control, also covered in Regulation 14A. This is the federally-provided-for right of shareholders to put items on the agenda for the annual shareholder meeting, to be voted on by their fellow shareholders. The SEC regards this as a very important matter, and note that the language of this Rule, which is provided below, is carefully drafted in a form that shareholders can purportedly understand. Why do you suppose that the SEC has not done this for all of its Regulations?

Shareholder Proposals

§ 240.14a–8.

This section addresses when a company must include a shareholder's proposal in its proxy statement and identify the proposal in its form of proxy when the company holds an annual or special meeting of shareholders. In summary, in order to have your shareholder proposal included on a company's proxy card, and included along with any supporting statement in its proxy statement, you must be eligible and follow certain procedures. Under a few specific circumstances, the company is permitted to exclude your proposal, but only after submitting its reasons to the Commission. We structured this section in a question-and-answer format so that it is easier to understand. The references to "you" are to a shareholder seeking to submit the proposal.

(a) Question 1: What is a proposal?

A shareholder proposal is your recommendation or requirement that the company and/or its board of directors take action, which you intend to present at a meeting of the company's shareholders. Your proposal should state as clearly as possible the course of action that you believe the company should follow. If your proposal is placed on the company's proxy card, the company must also provide in the form of proxy means for shareholders to specify by boxes a choice between approval or disapproval, or abstention. Unless otherwise indicated, the word "proposal" as used in this section refers both to your proposal, and to your corresponding statement in support of your proposal (if any).

(b) Question 2: Who is eligible to submit a proposal, and how do I demonstrate to the company that I am eligible?

(1) In order to be eligible to submit a proposal, you must have continuously held at least $2,000 in market value, or 1%, of the company's securities entitled to be voted on the proposal at the meeting for at least one year by the date you submit the proposal. You must continue to hold those securities through the date of the meeting.

*   *   *

(c) Question 3: How many proposals may I submit?

Each shareholder may submit no more than one proposal to a company for a particular shareholders' meeting.

(d) Question 4: How long can my proposal be?

The proposal, including any accompanying supporting statement, may not exceed 500 words.

*   *   *

(f) Question 6: What if I fail to follow one of the eligibility or procedural requirements explained in answers to Questions 1 through 4 of this section?

(1) The company may exclude your proposal, but only after it has notified you of the problem, and you have failed adequately to correct it. Within 14 calendar days of receiving your proposal, the company must notify you in writing of any procedural or eligibility deficiencies, as well as of the time frame for your response. Your response must be postmarked, or transmitted electronically, no later than 14 days from the date you received the company's notification. A company need not provide you such notice of a deficiency if the deficiency cannot be remedied, such as if you fail to submit a proposal by the company's properly determined deadline. If the company intends to exclude the proposal, it will later have to make a submission under § 240.14a–8 and provide you with a copy under Question 10 below, § 240.14a–8(j).

(2) If you fail in your promise to hold the required number of securities through the date of the meeting of shareholders, then the company will be permitted to exclude all of your proposals from its proxy materials for any meeting held in the following two calendar years.

(g) Question 7: Who has the burden of persuading the Commission or its staff that my proposal can be excluded?

Except as otherwise noted, the burden is on the company to demonstrate that it is entitled to exclude a proposal.

(h) Question 8: Must I appear personally at the shareholders' meeting to present the proposal?

(1) Either you, or your representative who is qualified under state law to present the proposal on your behalf, must attend the meeting to present the proposal. * * *

                   *   *   *

(3) If you or your qualified representative fail to appear and present the proposal, without good cause, the company will be permitted to exclude all of your proposals from its proxy materials for any meetings held in the following two calendar years.

(i) Question 9: If I have complied with the procedural requirements, on what other bases may a company rely to exclude my proposal?

(1) Improper under state law: If the proposal is not a proper subject for action by shareholders under the laws of the jurisdiction of the company's organization;

* * * In our experience, most proposals that are cast as recommendations or requests that the board of directors take specified action are proper under state law. Accordingly, we will assume that a proposal drafted as a recommendation or suggestion is proper unless the company demonstrates otherwise.

(2) Violation of law: If the proposal would, if implemented, cause the company to violate any state, federal, or foreign law to which it is subject; * * *

(3) Violation of proxy rules: If the proposal or supporting statement is contrary to any of the Commission's proxy rules, including § 240.14a–9, which prohibits materially false or misleading statements in proxy soliciting materials;

(4) Personal grievance; special interest: If the proposal relates to the redress of a personal claim or grievance against the company or any other person, or if it is designed to result in a benefit to you, or to further a personal interest, which is not shared by the other shareholders at large;

(5) Relevance: If the proposal relates to operations which account for less than 5 percent of the company's total assets at the end of its most recent fiscal year, and for less than 5 percent of its net earnings and gross sales for its most recent fiscal year, and is not otherwise significantly related to the company's business;

(6) Absence of power/authority: If the company would lack the power or authority to implement the proposal;

(7) Management functions: If the proposal deals with a matter relating to the company's ordinary business operations;

(8) Relates to election: If the proposal relates to an election for membership on the company's board of directors or analogous governing body;

(9) Conflicts with company's proposal: If the proposal directly conflicts with one of the company's own proposals to be submitted to shareholders at the same meeting; * * *

(10) Substantially implemented: If the company has already substantially implemented the proposal;

(11) Duplication: If the proposal substantially duplicates another proposal previously submitted to the company by another proponent that will be included in the company's proxy materials for the same meeting;

(12) Resubmissions: If the proposal deals with substantially the same subject matter as another proposal or proposals that has or have been previously included in the company's proxy materials within the preceding 5 calendar years, a company may exclude it from its proxy materials for any meeting held within 3 calendar years of the last time it was included if the proposal received:

(i) Less than 3% of the vote if proposed once within the preceding 5 calendar years;

(ii) Less than 6% of the vote on its last submission to shareholders if proposed twice previously within the preceding 5 calendar years; or

(iii) Less than 10% of the vote on its last submission to shareholders if proposed three times or more previously within the preceding 5 calendar years; and

(13) Specific amount of dividends: If the proposal relates to specific amounts of cash or stock dividends.

(j) Question 10: What procedures must the company follow if it intends to exclude my proposal?

(1) If the company intends to exclude a proposal from its proxy materials, it must file its reasons with the Commission no later than 80 calendar days before it files its definitive proxy statement and form of proxy with the Commission. The company must simultaneously provide you with a copy of its submission. The Commission staff may permit the company to make its submission later than 80 days before the company files its definitive proxy statement and form of proxy, if the company demonstrates good cause for missing the deadline.

(2) The company must file six paper copies of the following:

(i) The proposal;

(ii) An explanation of why the company believes that it may exclude the proposal, which should, if possible, refer to the most recent applicable authority, such as prior Division letters issued under the rule; and

(iii) A supporting opinion of counsel when such reasons are based on matters of state or foreign law.

(k) Question 11: May I submit my own statement to the Commission responding to the company's arguments?

Yes, you may submit a response, but it is not required. * * *

(l) Question 12: If the company includes my shareholder proposal in its proxy materials, what information about me must it include along with the proposal itself?

(1) The company's proxy statement must include your name and address, as well as the number of the company's voting securities that you hold. However, instead of providing that information, the company may instead include a statement that it will provide the information to shareholders promptly upon receiving an oral or written request. * * *

(m) Question 13: What can I do if the company includes in its proxy statement reasons why it believes shareholders should not vote in favor of my proposal, and I disagree with some of its statements?

(1) The company may elect to include in its proxy statement reasons why it believes shareholders should vote against your proposal. The company is allowed to make arguments reflecting its own point of view, just as you may express your own point of view in your proposal's supporting statement.

(2) However, if you believe that the company's opposition to your proposal contains materially false or misleading statements that may violate our anti-fraud rule, § 240.14a–9, you should promptly send to the Commission staff and the company a letter explaining the reasons for your view, along with a copy of the company's statements opposing your proposal. To the extent possible, your letter should include specific factual information demonstrating the inaccuracy of the company's claims. Time permitting, you may wish to try to work out your differences with the company by yourself before contacting the Commission staff.

(3) We require the company to send you a copy of its statements opposing your proposal before it mails its proxy materials, so that you may bring to our attention any materially false or misleading statements, under the following timeframes:

(i) If our no-action response requires that you make revisions to your proposal or supporting statement as a condition to requiring the company to include it in its proxy materials, then the company must provide you with a copy of its opposition statements no later than 5 calendar days after the company receives a copy of your revised proposal; or

(ii) In all other cases, the company must provide you with a copy of its opposition statements no later than 30 calendar days before it files definitive copies of its proxy statement and form of proxy under § 240.14a–6.

Are shareholder proposals a beneficial means of furthering corporate goals, or are they, more often than not, a frivolous exercise, and an opportunity for imposing costs of compliance on the corporation? Like many other points involving the proxy rules this one is subject to some debate, although as institutional investors are coming to play more and more of a role at making shareholder proposals pursuant to Rule 14a–8, the passage of such proposals does become somewhat more likely, particularly if they have to do with ensuring transparency about the conduct of the corporation. Consider a number of possible proposals pursuant to Rule 14a–8, and determine whether you think they are appropriate for inclusion on the annual meeting agenda or not:

(1) a proposal that the corporation cease manufacturing napalm

(2) a proposal that the corporation increase the number of outside directors

(3) a proposal that the corporation speed up its already-existing plans to cease manufacturing which produces chlorofluorocarbons

(4) a proposal that the corporation cease the manufacturing of *fois gras*

(5) a proposal that the directors take action against a CEO who has a practice of showing up at the office inebriated

(6) a proposal that the corporation cease trade with nations known to be harboring terrorists

(7) a proposal that the corporation condemn the practice of the United States making war on other countries without UN Security Council authorization.

5.   The proxy rules that we have been considering in this section, as we have seen, were conceived as a means of making it easier for shareholders to cast their votes in an informed manner, and, in the case of the rules regarding shareholder proposals we have just reviewed, of giving them an enhanced ability to communicate with their fellow shareholders. There is no doubt that the law still conceives of the shareholders as the owners of corporations, and that the basic understanding of corporate law is that corporations are to be run primarily if not exclusively for the benefit of their shareholders (so long as corporations comply with applicable laws and regulations). Still, to what extent ought efforts be undertaken to encourage and expand "shareholder democracy?" In a provocative and perceptive Op-ed in the Wall Street Journal on September 27, 2007 entitled "Corporations Shouldn't Be Democracies," UCLA Law Professor Lynn Stout argued against a change to the proxy rules, proposed by the SEC's Democratic Commissioners (there are five SEC Commissioners, who are appointed by the President to serve for staggered five-year terms, and no more than three Commissioners may belong to the same political party) which would have required publicly-traded corporations to "pay the expenses of dissident shareholders seeking to replace the company's board of directors," in particular by requiring corporations to place on the annual ballots shareholder nominees for directors.

Ms. Stout suggested that this proposed rule "is driven by the emotional claim, unsupported by evidence, that American corporations benefit from 'shareholder democracy.'" Ms. Stout argued that "Successful corporations are not, and never have been, democratic institutions. Since the public corporation first evolved over a century ago, U.S. law has discouraged shareholders from taking an active role in corporate governance, and this 'hands off' approach has proven a recipe for tremendous success." "Companies seem to succeed best when they are controlled by boards of directors, not by shareholders," Ms. Stout explained, because "board control is more informed and efficient decision making. An even more important factor," she continued, "is that board control 'locks in' and protects corporate assets and investment capital." Because of the huge amount of sunk costs required for the kind of complex software and electronics, new drugs and medical treatments, valuable trademarks and brand names in which today's corporations traffic, said Ms. Stout, Board control over these assets is necessary because it "protects those assets and gives them time to work, allowing shareholders collectively to recoup the value of their initial investment (and then some) over the long haul."

Such long term-investment would be impossible, Ms. Stout believes, "if shareholders have the power to drain cash out of the firm at any time—say, by threatening to remove directors who refuse to cut expenses or sell assets in order to pay shareholders a special dividend or fund a massive share repurchase program." And these are not idle worries, according to Ms. Stout because "Whether out of ignorance, greed, or short-sightedness, these are exactly the sorts of threats that today's activist shareholders, usually at hedge funds, typically make." "By giving activists even greater leverage over boards," Ms. Stout concluded, the SEC's Democratic commissioners' proposed proxy access rule would "undermine American corporations' ability to do exactly what investors, and the larger society, want them to do: pursue big, long-term, innovative business projects."

In early December, 2007, the SEC, by a three to one vote (the lone Democrat then on the SEC was the dissenter) rejected the so-called "shareholder access" proposal against which Ms. Stout had argued. On December 7, 2007, the Wall Street Journal, in an editorial that could fairly be described as exulting in the rejection, wrote that "In the case of proxy challenges, the main agitators are unions and their political allies who run public pension funds." "These groups," said the Journal "have their own political agendas that they want companies to pursue, and those agendas may or may not serve the larger interest of increasing shareholder value. In the worst case, such agitation could empower special-interests on boards that reduce a company's value." A recent study by University of Chicago researcher Ashwini Agrawal, the Journal reported, suggested that "the dominant concern of ... pension fund holders is union representation, not overall corporate performance."

The December 7, 2007, Wall Street Journal Editorial concluded by observing that "under current law, nothing stops a company from adopting by-laws that would provide for easier proxy access by shareholders. If there were an advantage in doing so—if a company received a stock-price premium—more companies would do it because more investors would insist on it. That no such premium exists explains why investors at large aren't clamoring for this kind of proxy 'reform.'" Is this persuasive? For further argument along the lines suggested by Ms. Stout, see the seminal article by her UCLA colleague, Stephen Bainbridge, Director Primacy and Shareholder Disempowerment, 119 Harv.L.Rev. 1735 (2006), which maintains that other academics' proposals for increased shareholder participation in corporate governance are misguided given that the marketplace does not seem to favor them. Is this the right reference for corporate governance policy? Would Randolph Phillips have favored the proposal to require publicly-held corporations to list shareholder-nominated contestants for the Board of Directors?

6.   What is the state law regarding shareholder participation in corporate governance, and, in particular, what measures might states take to ensure

that shareholders have the requisite information intelligently to participate—assuming, that is, that participation in corporate governance is something appropriate for shareholders (it might not be if most investors wish passively to invest and sell their shares instead of seeking to change the corporation if they are unsatisfied with its performance)? Consider the next case, dealing with Delaware's law regarding shareholder examination of books and records. After you read the case ask yourself if you believe federal action in this area, such as Rule 14a–8, the other proxy rules, or shareholder access for director elections is warranted.

C. STATE LAW REGARDING INSPECTION OF BOOKS AND RECORDS (DELAWARE)

THOMAS & BETTS CORP. v. LEVITON MFG. CO., INC.

Supreme Court of Delaware.
681 A.2d 1026 (1996).

VEASEY, Chief Justice:

*   *   *

I. FACTS

Plaintiff below-appellant, Thomas & Betts Corporation ("Thomas & Betts" or "plaintiff"), appeals from a decision of the Court of Chancery granting in part and denying in part its request for inspection of certain books and records of defendant below-appellee, Leviton Manufacturing Co., Inc. ("Leviton" or "defendant"). * * *

Leviton is a closely held Delaware corporation engaged in the business of manufacturing electronic components and residential wiring devices. Thomas & Betts is a publicly traded New Jersey corporation engaged in the electronics business. Thomas & Betts and Leviton are not considered to be in competition with one another. This is due, in large part, to Leviton's focus on the residential market. For a number of years, Thomas & Betts has expressed an interest either in acquiring Leviton or engaging in some form of joint venture. During the summer of 1993, Thomas & Betts and Leviton engaged in preliminary negotiations concerning a possible union of the two companies, but no agreement was ever reached. To date, Leviton has not expressed any interest in participating in a change-of-control or joint venture transaction with Thomas & Betts.

Leviton's President and CEO, Harold Leviton, is also the company's majority stockholder. Harold Leviton and his wife control a voting trust which represents 76.45 percent of Leviton's Class A voting stock. He and the other Leviton insiders are members of the Leviton family and most bear some relationship to the company's founder. By all accounts, Harold

Leviton is the dominant figure in the corporation, deciding the company's strategy, operations and future goals.

Thomas & Betts decided to seek a minority position in Leviton in order to force a sale of the company to Thomas & Betts. In April of 1994, without the knowledge of Harold Leviton, Thomas & Betts began negotiations with Leviton's former Group Vice President, Thomas Blumberg ("Blumberg"). Blumberg and his wife, who is Harold Leviton's niece, owned approximately 29.1 percent of Leviton's outstanding shares. Negotiations for the sale of the Blumberg stock to Thomas & Betts were clandestine. In furtherance of the transaction, Blumberg provided Thomas & Betts with confidential internal Leviton documents and disclosed various facets of Leviton's internal strategies and accounting figures. Ultimately, Thomas & Betts paid Blumberg $50 million for his Leviton stake, with a promise of up to an additional $20 million if Thomas & Betts were to accomplish its desired acquisition of Leviton. Thomas & Betts indemnified Blumberg against, *inter alia,* litigation by Leviton, and also agreed to pay up to $7.5 million to Blumberg, in equal quarterly installments, if the sale of his shares were enjoined. At the time of sale, Thomas & Betts was fully aware that Leviton did not pay dividends and that Leviton's accounting practices did not follow Generally Accepted Accounting Principles ("GAAP").

The sale of the Blumberg shares was consummated on July 12, 1994, and Harold Leviton was informed of the sale the following day. Harold Leviton immediately fired Blumberg, only to hire him back and fire him again days later, along with his children and their secretaries. Harold Leviton rebuffed overtures from Thomas & Betts to establish an amicable relationship. Instead, Harold Leviton sought to buy out the interest of Thomas & Betts. From July 1994 to February of 1995, various representatives of Thomas & Betts met with Leviton insiders in an attempt to cultivate a working relationship. On October 6, 1994, Kevin Dunnigan ("Dunnigan"), the CEO of Thomas & Betts, reported to the board of Thomas & Betts on his strategy:

> On the Leviton front, we are moving to the next phase. I will write to Harold Leviton next week to give him a rationale on why it is in everyone's best interests to start a dialogue. We will follow this up with a legal request to review all the books and records of Leviton which will start either a dialogue or a lawsuit.

Harold Leviton, however, remained obstinate in his opposition to Thomas & Betts' ownership position. Although some concessions were made and Thomas & Betts was allowed limited access to Leviton's books and records, by February 1995 it was abundantly clear that Harold Leviton intended to thwart any acquisition of Leviton by Thomas & Betts.

On February 8, 1995, Thomas & Betts served Leviton with a formal demand seeking inspection of the following documents:

1. Leviton's stockholder list,

2. Minutes of Leviton shareholder and directors meetings as well as written consents,

3. Audited financial statements for Leviton and its subsidiaries,

4. Internal financial statements for the current fiscal year provided on a monthly basis,

5. Tax returns filed for Leviton and its subsidiaries,

6. Organizational charts for Leviton and its subsidiaries,

7. Documents relating to interested party transactions between Leviton or its subsidiaries and its shareholders, directors or officers,

8. Documents relating to "key man" life insurance policies taken out by Leviton,

9. Material contracts between Leviton and its subsidiaries,

10. Documents relating to Leviton leases for real estate or equipment.

On February 16, 1995, Dunnigan wrote to Harold Leviton and offered to purchase the balance of Leviton's stock for $250 million, net of expenses. Dunnigan's letter threatened litigation if this final offer were rebuffed:

> You are forcing us down a road where given a choice, I am sure neither of us wants to go. Often, once this process gets started, it ends up with consequences that were never intended. Watch!-It won't be long before the lawyers, the government and the courts are completely in charge, and in the end neither you nor I will have much say in the outcome. There will be only victims, but it won't be the lawyers.

On February 17, 1995, Leviton formally refused both Thomas & Betts' acquisition offer and its inspection demand.

On February 27, 1995, Thomas & Betts filed this action in the Court of Chancery seeking to compel inspection of Leviton's books and records pursuant to *8 Del. C. § 220.*[4] After a four-day trial, the Court of Chancery

---

4. [Editor's note]. As recently revised the relevant Delaware law now provides in pertinent part:

§ 220. Inspection of books and records.

* * *

(b) Any stockholder, in person or by attorney or other agent, shall, upon written demand under oath stating the purpose thereof, have the right during the usual hours for business to inspect for any proper purpose, and to make copies and extracts from:

(1) The corporation's stock ledger, a list of its stockholders, and its other books and records; and

(2) A subsidiary's books and records, to the extent that:

a. The corporation has actual possession and control of such records of such subsidiary; or

b. The corporation could obtain such records through the exercise of control over such subsidiary, provided that as of the date of the making of the demand:

1. The stockholder inspection of such books and records of the subsidiary would not constitute a breach of an agreement between the corporation or the subsidiary and a person or persons not affiliated with the corporation; and

2. The subsidiary would not have the right under the law applicable to it to deny the corporation access to such books and records upon demand by the corporation.

determined that: (1) plaintiff's demand was not motivated by its stated purposes of investigating waste and mismanagement, facilitation of the equity method of accounting for its Leviton shares and valuation of those shares; (2) plaintiff's actual motivation was to gain leverage in its efforts to acquire Leviton; (3) this motive was antithetical to the interests of Leviton; (4) despite the initially improper purpose of its demand, Thomas & Betts was entitled to limited inspection so it could value its Leviton shares since a fundamental change of circumstances had occurred; and (5) this inspection should be narrowly circumscribed. From this decision, Thomas & Betts appeals. * * *

In every instance where the stockholder is other than a record holder of stock in a stock corporation or a member of a nonstock corporation, the demand under oath shall state the person's status as a stockholder, be accompanied by documentary evidence of beneficial ownership of the stock, and state that such documentary evidence is a true and correct copy of what it purports to be. A proper purpose shall mean a purpose reasonably related to such person's interest as a stockholder. In every instance where an attorney or other agent shall be the person who seeks the right to inspection, the demand under oath shall be accompanied by a power of attorney or such other writing which authorizes the attorney or other agent to so act on behalf of the stockholder. * * *

(c) If the corporation, or an officer or agent thereof, refuses to permit an inspection sought by a stockholder or attorney or other agent acting for the stockholder pursuant to subsection (b) of this section or does not reply to the demand within 5 business days after the demand has been made, the stockholder may apply to the Court of Chancery for an order to compel such inspection. The Court of Chancery is hereby vested with exclusive jurisdiction to determine whether or not the person seeking inspection is entitled to the inspection sought. The Court may summarily order the corporation to permit the stockholder to inspect the corporation's stock ledger, an existing list of stockholders, and its other books and records, and to make copies or extracts therefrom; or the Court may order the corporation to furnish to the stockholder a list of its stockholders as of a specific date on condition that the stockholder first pay to the corporation the reasonable cost of obtaining and furnishing such list and on such other conditions as the Court deems appropriate. Where the stockholder seeks to inspect the corporation's books and records, other than its stock ledger or list of stockholders, such stockholder shall first establish that:

(1) Such stockholder is a stockholder;

(2) Such stockholder has complied with this section respecting the form and manner of making demand for inspection of such documents; and

(3) The inspection such stockholder seeks is for a proper purpose.

Where the stockholder seeks to inspect the corporation's stock ledger or list of stockholders and establishes that such stockholder is a stockholder and has complied with this section respecting the form and manner of making demand for inspection of such documents, the burden of proof shall be upon the corporation to establish that the inspection such stockholder seeks is for an improper purpose. The Court may, in its discretion, prescribe any limitations or conditions with reference to the inspection, or award such other or further relief as the Court may deem just and proper. The Court may order books, documents and records, pertinent extracts therefrom, or duly authenticated copies thereof, to be brought within this State and kept in this State upon such terms and conditions as the order may prescribe.

(d) Any director (including a member of the governing body of a nonstock corporation) shall have the right to examine the corporation's stock ledger, a list of its stockholders and its other books and records for a purpose reasonably related to the director's position as a director. The Court of Chancery is hereby vested with the exclusive jurisdiction to determine whether a director is entitled to the inspection sought. The Court may summarily order the corporation to permit the director to inspect any and all books and records, the stock ledger and the list of stockholder's and to make copies or extracts therefrom. The burden of proof shall be upon the corporation to establish that the inspection such director seeks is for an improper purpose. The Court may, in its discretion, prescribe any limitations or conditions with reference to the inspection, or award such other and further relief as the Court may deem just and proper. * * *

II. PROPER PURPOSE

Thomas & Betts' Demand Letter purported to state three separate purposes for its requested inspection of Leviton's books and records. Specifically, plaintiff asserted that the books and records were necessary: (1) to investigate possible waste and mismanagement; (2) to facilitate its use of the equity method of accounting for its Leviton investment; and (3) to assist in the valuation of Thomas & Betts' Leviton shares. After trial, the Court of Chancery concluded that plaintiff's articulated purposes were not its actual purposes and that plaintiff's actual purpose was improper. * * * Specifically, the trial court held that Thomas & Betts was attempting to use the Section 220 proceeding as leverage in its efforts to acquire Leviton. The trial court concluded, however, that Thomas & Betts should be allowed to inspect those books and records necessary to value its investment in Leviton in view of the fact that there had been a change in circumstances.

Thomas & Betts now asserts that the two purposes for inspection not credited by the trial court—investigation of waste and mismanagement and facilitation of the equity method of accounting—constituted proper purposes under Section 220 and that the trial court erred in refusing inspection of books and records relevant to these purposes. These contentions are addressed *seriatim* below.

"The question of a 'proper purpose' under Section 220(b) of our General Corporation Law is an issue of law and equity which this Court reviews *de novo.*" * * * "The determination of whether [plaintiff's] ... stated purpose for the inspection was its primary purpose, is a question of fact warranting deference to the trial court's credibility assessments." * * *

III. PLAINTIFF'S CLAIMS OF WASTE AND MISMANAGEMENT

As found by the Court of Chancery, plaintiff's claims of waste and mismanagement are grounded on Leviton's purportedly substandard financial performance, the company's failure to pay dividends, Leviton's poor cash flow and the company's higher than average expenses. As specific instances of misconduct, plaintiff asserted that: "(a) Leviton has paid for the Leviton family's personal expenses, including use of the company's accounting firm for tax and estate planning purposes; (b) Leviton has been overcompensating its officers and directors at the shareholders' expense; and (c) Leviton's lease agreements with members of the Leviton family are self-dealing transactions." * * * The trial court found, however, that these claims "are so lacking in record support" that inspection could not be justified.

Plaintiff contends that the Court of Chancery applied an incorrect legal standard in determining that plaintiff's stated purpose lacked adequate record support. Specifically, Thomas & Betts points to portions of the trial court's holding which appear to impose on plaintiff "a greater-than-normal evidentiary burden," to "adduce evidence from which a credible possibility of mismanagement and waste may be inferred" and to "adduce specific evidence of waste and mismanagement." * * *

The Court of Chancery incorrectly articulated the governing legal standard. It is well established that investigation of waste and mismanagement is a proper purpose for a Section 220 books and records inspection. * * * When a stockholder seeks inspection of books and records, the burden of proof is on the stockholder to demonstrate that his purpose is proper. * * *[5] In order to meet that burden of proof, a stockholder must present some credible basis from which the court can infer that waste or mismanagement may have occurred. *Skouras v. Admiralty Enters., Inc., Del. Ch., 386 A.2d 674, 678 (1978)* ("more than a general statement is required in order for the Court to determine the propriety of a demand"); *Helnsman Management Servs., Inc. v. A & S Consultants, Inc., Del. Ch., 525 A.2d 160, 166 (1987)* ("A mere statement of a purpose to investigate possible general mismanagement, without more, will not entitle a shareholder to broad § 220 inspection relief. There must be some evidence of possible mismanagement as would warrant further investigation of the matter."); * * * While stockholders have the burden of coming forward with specific and credible allegations sufficient to warrant a suspicion of waste and mismanagement, they are not required to prove by a preponderance of the evidence that waste and management are actually occurring. * * *

A general standard that a stockholder seeking inspection of books and records bears "a greater-than-normal evidentiary burden" is unclear and could be interpreted as placing an unduly difficult obstacle in the path of stockholders seeking to investigate waste and mismanagement. Viewed in context, however, the articulation in dispute here accurately describes a stockholder's position in cases such as the one at bar, where substantial evidence supports a finding that plaintiff's primary motives for the inspection are improper.

In the final analysis, the decision of the trial court did not turn solely on a legal conclusion that Thomas & Betts had failed to meet an elevated evidentiary burden. As discussed further, *infra,* the trial court's determination turned, in large part, on the Vice Chancellor's determination that plaintiff's witnesses were not credible. According appropriate deference to the factual findings of the Court of Chancery, we conclude that plaintiff failed to satisfy the appropriate standard for inspection of the books and records with regard to the claim of waste and mismanagement. *Levitt v. Bouvier, Del. Supr., 287 A.2d 671, 673 (1972)* ("When the determination of facts turns on a question of credibility and the acceptance or rejection of

---

5. While a stockholder has the burden to show a proper purpose for an inspection of books and records, the corporation has the burden of showing an improper purpose when a stockholder seeks only to inspect the stockholder list. 8 Del. C. § 220(c). The trial court held that plaintiff "has established a proper purpose for seeking inspection of Leviton's shareholder list," and the corporation failed to meet its burden that plaintiff's purpose was improper. * * *

'live' testimony by the trial judge, his findings will be approved upon review."). * * *

Thomas & Betts argues that the trial court erroneously characterized as hearsay certain witness statements concerning Blumberg's discussions with Thomas & Betts. Where an in-court witness testifies to the substance of statements made by an out-of-court declarant and the testimony is offered to prove the truth of the matter asserted, a hearsay problem arises. This is precisely the situation faced by the trial court. Plaintiffs did not call Blumberg to the witness stand. Rather, various Thomas & Betts insiders sought to prove that waste and mismanagement had occurred at Leviton by testifying to the substance of statements made by Blumberg during his negotiations with Thomas & Betts.

Plaintiff contends, however, that the statements were not offered to prove the truth of the matter asserted, but were intended to show that Thomas & Betts believed that waste and mismanagement were occurring at Leviton (*i.e.,* to show Thomas & Betts' state of mind). This argument is unavailing in light of the discussion above. Thomas & Betts' subjective belief that wrongdoing has occurred is insufficient to meet the evidentiary burden required to compel inspection. Plaintiff's contention that testimony concerning Blumberg's statements falls within the hearsay exception of *D.R.E.* 801(d)(2)(D) is similarly unavailing. *D.R.E.* 801(d)(2)(D) allows hearsay testimony of an agent or servant concerning matters within the scope of his agency or employment. Here, Blumberg was acting in his capacity as a stockholder of Leviton when the statements were made. Moreover, as the trial court found, Blumberg was actively engaged in the process of defecting to the Thomas & Betts camp. Statements made in this context lack independent guarantees of trustworthiness and are inherently unreliable. The trial court was correct in so concluding.

More significantly, the trial court did not exclude this testimony. Rather, the Vice Chancellor heard the testimony and found it unworthy of belief. In this posture, plaintiff's evidentiary objections carry little weight. * * *

Finally, plaintiff's arguments ignore the underlying posture of this case. Unlike the cases relied on by plaintiff, this case does not involve a typical uninformed stockholder seeking to protect his or her investment. Thomas & Betts acquired its shares in Leviton with the acknowledged purpose of acquiring the company. Moreover, Thomas & Betts did so with full knowledge that Leviton's CEO would likely oppose any such transaction. Thomas & Betts first praised Harold Leviton for his expert management of the company, seeking an amicable union of the two corporations. When Thomas & Betts' friendly overtures proved unavailing, it filed an inspection demand to create leverage. Its self-avowed acquisition motives cast serious doubt on the genuineness of its claim that it seeks the books and records to investigate waste and mismanagement.

These facts were properly before the Court of Chancery. *See, e.g., Helmsman Management Servs., 525 A.2d at 164* [HN6] ("The propriety of a demanding shareholder's purpose must be determined from the facts in each case, and the burden of proving a proper purpose is upon the shareholder."). The Court of Chancery concluded that "Thomas & Betts' initial primary purpose in seeking a books and records inspection was ... to exert pressure on Harold Leviton to negotiate a sale of his controlling interest or, alternatively, the entire company." * * * Ultimately, the Court of Chancery found Thomas & Betts' articulated purpose to be "highly opportunistic" and unworthy of belief. Thomas & Betts has provided no reason for this Court to revisit those factual determinations and credibility assessments.

IV. FACILITATING THE EQUITY METHOD OF ACCOUNTING

At trial, plaintiff contended that it needed access to certain Leviton records to facilitate use of the equity method of accounting for its Leviton investment. The trial court concluded that: (1) plaintiff's stated accounting purpose is not a proper purpose as contemplated by Section 220 because it is not related to Thomas & Betts' status as a stockholder of Leviton; (2) Thomas & Betts' inability to use the equity accounting method was "a problem of its own making"; and (3) the "factual *bona fides* of Thomas & Betts' contention ... are highly suspect." * * * Plaintiff now argues that: (1) the trial court erred in holding that facilitation of equity accounting is not a proper purpose; and (2) it has met the evidentiary burden required to compel inspection. Accordingly, Thomas & Betts contends that it should be allowed access to a broad array of Leviton internal documents.

Plaintiff's first contention—that the Court of Chancery erred in holding that Thomas & Betts' accounting purpose was improper—is without merit. As the trial court properly recognized, Section 220, by its express language, entitles a stockholder of a corporation to: "inspect for any proper purpose the corporation's stock-ledger, a list of its stockholders, and its other books and records, and to make copies or extracts therefrom. *A proper purpose shall mean a purpose reasonably related to such person's interest as a stockholder....*" *8 Del. C. § 220(b)* (emphasis supplied).

The need to account for the Leviton investment by a particular method stems from Thomas & Betts' relationship with *its own* stockholders and bears no relationship to Thomas & Betts' status as a Leviton stockholder. As the Court of Chancery held in *Lynn v. Envirosource, Inc., Del. Ch., C.A. No. 11770, 1991 WL 80242, *1 (Del.Ch.), Chandler, V.C. (May 13, 1991), "what is required by ... section [220] is that the purpose for the demand be reasonably related 'to such person's interest as a stockholder.' That is, the purpose must be something that stockholders would be interested in because of their position as stockholders." Conversely, "[a] purely individual purpose in no way germane to the relationship of stockholder to the corporation is not a proper purpose within the meaning of the statute." * * * The Court of Chancery here correctly concluded that facili-*

tation of equity accounting was not a proper purpose under Section 220. The need for equity accounting stems from Thomas & Betts' position as a publicly held corporation. Thus, it is the relationship of Thomas & Betts to its stockholders that created this need and not the relationship of Thomas & Betts to Leviton.

Thomas & Betts contends that the trial court overlooked a number of cases where the stockholder's purpose for inspection was unique to the individual stockholder. The purpose advanced in each of these cases, however, was valuation of shares, the only purpose advanced by Thomas & Betts which the trial court accepted.[6]

Assuming *arguendo* that Thomas & Betts' accounting purpose is deemed proper, it nevertheless failed to meet its evidentiary burden. Despite Thomas & Betts' insistence on the use of equity accounting and KPMG Peat Marwick's purported concurrence in that view, Thomas & Betts has failed to demonstrate that this is the actual purpose for the information sought. As the trial court found, equity accounting may be used only in instances where the accounting stockholder exercises a degree of control over the company in which it holds an equity stake. GAAP provides that a stockholder with a 20 percent or greater stake enjoys a rebuttable presumption that such influence is exercised.

This presumption has been rebutted in the case of Thomas & Betts' stake in Leviton. Thomas & Betts now owns a 29.1 percent interest in Leviton. * * * Harold Leviton, however, controls a voting trust representing 76.45 percent of the company's voting stock. Thomas & Betts has no representation on the Leviton board. Moreover, Harold Leviton has made it abundantly clear that he will thwart any effort by Thomas & Betts to exercise control, or a lesser measure of influence, over Leviton. On these facts, it is * * * questionable whether Thomas & Betts can even justify use of equity accounting under GAAP.[7] Thomas & Betts' stated purpose is questionable at best and lacks record support sufficient to warrant granting the requested relief. * * *

---

6. For example, in Ostrow, inspection was granted on the basis of two purposes advanced by the plaintiffs, viz., "the valuation of their shares, especially in connection with a possible exercise of a contractual right to put those shares to the Company; and secondly, the investigation of possible fraud or breach of duty on the part of [the CEO]...." Ostrow v. Bonney Forge, Del. Ch., C.A. No. 13270, 1994 WL 114807, Allen, C. (April 6, 1994). In State ex rel. Nat'l Bank v. Jessup & Moore Paper Co., Del. Super., 27 Del. 248, 88 A. 449 (1913), the stockholder sought inspection for the purpose of valuing shares held in a non-publicly traded company. The fact that the stockholder was a bank and needed to account to a regulatory agency for the value of these shares was of no moment. Valuation is a proper purpose for inspection. Finally, the related case of State ex rel. Brumley v. Jessup & Moore Paper Co., Del. Super., 26 Del. 329, 83 A. 30 (1912), involved an inspection request by a stockholder who had received her shares by devise from her deceased husband. As in National Bank, supra, the Brumley plaintiff simply wanted to value her shares.

7. When Leviton's Chief Financial Officer reviewed a draft of Thomas & Betts' press release announcing the purchase of Blumberg's shares, he suggested that Thomas & Betts delete the reference to its intention to account for the investment using the equity method of accounting. He informed Thomas & Betts that Leviton would not provide the information he believed was necessary to use this method of accounting. Thomas & Betts publicly committed, nevertheless, to use the equity method with full knowledge of the difficulties it could face.

V. THE SCOPE OF THE INSPECTION

After trial, the Court of Chancery found that Thomas & Betts had failed to meet its burden of establishing that it sought inspection in furtherance of its concerns regarding accounting and mismanagement. The trial court found that Thomas & Betts' primary purpose for inspection was to further its plans for acquiring Leviton and that this interest was antithetical to the interests of the corporation. Despite Thomas & Betts' initially improper motives, the Court acknowledged that Thomas & Betts had experienced a fundamental change of circumstances. The court reasoned that, owing to Harold Leviton's unwillingness to negotiate a change-of-control transaction, Thomas & Betts was now in the unenviable position of a "locked-in" minority stockholder. Based on this fact, the trial court allowed inspection of certain Leviton books and records, but limited the scope of that inspection to those documents which are "essential and sufficient" to Thomas & Betts' valuation purpose. Thomas & Betts now contends that the Court of Chancery abused its discretion in limiting the scope of its inspection of Leviton's books and records.

Absent any apparent error of law, this Court reviews for abuse of discretion the decision of the trial court regarding the scope of a stockholder's inspection of books and records. *8 Del. C. § 220(c) * * *.* The plaintiff bears the burden of proving that each category of books and records is essential to accomplishment of the stockholder's articulated purpose for the inspection. * * *

The plain language of *8 Del. C. § 220(c)* provides that "the Court may, *in its discretion,* prescribe any limitations or conditions with reference to the inspection." (emphasis supplied). The responsibility of the trial court to narrowly tailor the inspection right to a stockholder's stated purpose is well established. * * * In discharging this responsibility, the trial court has wide latitude in determining the proper scope of inspection. Undergirding this discretion is a recognition that the interests of the corporation must be harmonized with those of the inspecting stockholder.

Here, the trial court has found that Thomas & Betts' primary purpose for inspection is at odds with the interests of the corporation. In this posture, it was entirely appropriate for the Court of Chancery to limit plaintiff's inspection to those documents which are essential and sufficient to its valuation purpose.

Moreover, even in a case where no improper purpose has been attributed to the inspecting stockholder, the burden of proof is always on the party seeking inspection to establish that each category of the books and records requested is essential and sufficient to the stockholder's stated purpose. * * * The trial court specifically found that Thomas & Betts had not met its burden of proof as to certain of the books and records of Leviton. This finding is supported by the record and is the product of an orderly and logical deductive process. * * * Accordingly, the finding of the Court of Chancery and its concomitant decision to limit inspection will not be disturbed on appeal.

VI. CONCLUSION

We AFFIRM the order of the Court of Chancery.

NOTES AND QUESTIONS

1. What is meant by the terms "proper purpose" in Delaware Section 220, and why was Thomas & Betts's desire to enable itself to comply with the "equity method" of accounting for its shares not a proper purpose? The equity method of accounting, according to one authority, is

> A method of accounting for investments in common stock where the investor owns more than 20% of the outstanding voting stock of another company and can exercise significant influence. When an investor corporation can exercise significant influence over the operations and financial policies of an investee corporation, generally accepted accounting principles require that the investment in the investee be reported using the equity method. Significant influence can be determined by such factors as representation on the board of directors, participation in policy-making processes, material intercompany transactions, interchange of managerial personnel, and technological dependency. It is presumed that an investor can exercise significant influence if he or she owns 20% to 25% of the outstanding common stock of the investee, unless evidence to the contrary is available.
>
> The equity method of accounting for common stock investments reflects the economic substance rather than the legal form that underlies the investment in common stock of another company. When the equity method of accounting is used, the investor initially records the investment in the stock of an investee at cost. The investment account is then adjusted to recognize the investor's share of the income or losses of the investee after the date of acquisition when it is earned by the investee.
>
> * * *

"Equity Method of Accounting," from Encyclopedia of Banking & Finance (9th Edition) by Charles J Woelfel, quoted on the internet at http://www.eagletraders.com/advice/securities/equity_method_of_accounting.htm. Was the court correct or incorrect that properly adhering to the equity method of accounting was not related to Thomas & Betts's status as a shareholder in Leviton?

2. Note that Section 220 now provides for inspection of corporate books and records by directors. Would this have helped Tomlinson in Campbell v. Loew's?

3. Would contacting other shareholders in order to get further participation in a class action lawsuit against the corporation accusing management of misconduct be a proper purpose for seeking a shareholder list? It is quite clear that investigating possible management misconduct is a proper purpose for a shareholder to examine the books and records of the corporation, and that such examination of records might properly serve as the foundation for a derivative lawsuit. *Security First Corp. v. U.S. Die Casting and Development Co.*, 687 A.2d 563 (Del. 1997). Although the Delaware Court did make clear

that a "proper purpose" could not be one inimical to the interests of the corporation, the court did hold in Compaq Computer Corp. v. Horton, 631 A.2d 1 (Del. 1993), that "a shareholder states a proper purpose for inspection under our statute in seeking to solicit the participation of other shareholders in legitimate non-derivative litigation against the defendant corporation." The Delaware court seems prepared to encourage shareholder litigation, both derivative and individual, in order to prevent mismanagement by corporate fiduciaries, but is this an effective remedy? Given the apparent explosion in corporate wrongdoing by purported corporate miscreants and their advisors such as those running Enron, WorldCom, and the accounting firm Arthur A. Anderson, the United States Congress apparently thought not, and passed legislation known as Sarbanes/Oxley, to which we now turn. * * *

D. SARBANES/OXLEY

A Note on Sarbanes/Oxley[8]

In the wake of the early twenty-first century scandals involving WorldCom, Enron, and the Arthur Anderson firm which had served as accountants to both corporations, pressure built on Congress to come up with some federal legislation to prevent further such misadventures. Conventional wisdom had it that the accountants did not do an adequate job policing expenditures at these and other corporations, and that had stricter internal controls been in place, the possible looting of these corporations by senior management, and the questionable business practices in which they engaged, might not have occurred, and thus the bankruptcies that eventually resulted might have been avoided. Congress appears to have believed that state law—the primary regulator of conduct among shareholders, officers, and directors—was failing to put in place sufficient safeguards against accounting and officer/director misconduct, and thus, for the first time, Congress was emboldened to try to dictate in more detail than it ever had before (1) how accounting ought to be done, (2) how corporate oversight ought to be conducted, and (3) how relations between corporations and their officers ought to be adjusted. Reminiscent of the time more than a century earlier when Congress felt it ought to come up with some bill "to punish the trusts," and the result was the Sherman Antitrust Act (1890), the Sarbanes/Oxley Act of 2002, P.L. 107–204 (hereafter "the Act"), might be described as a broad brush attempt to protect against or punish corporate miscreants and rogue accountants. At this point there has been little litigation challenging the provisions or the Constitutionality of Sarbanes/Oxley, but there have already been small fortunes spent by corporations in complying with its provisions. Only time will tell whether this act, like so many other provisions of federal law regulating securities, may have to be changed in light of realities in the

---

8. A principal source for this Note is the "Executive Summary of the Sarbanes-Oxley Act of 2002 P.L. 107–204," prepared for the Conference of State Bank Supervisors, and available at http://www.csbs.org/government/legislative/misc/2002_sarbanes-oxley_summary.htm. Materials in quotes are taken from that Executive Summary unless otherwise indicated.

corporate world, especially if its costs exceed its benefits, but for now it is necessary to review its main provisions, since they will, for the foreseeable future, have considerable impact on publicly-traded corporations.

Creation of the Public Company Accounting Oversight Board. Title I of the act establishes a five-member "Public Company Accounting Oversight Board" ("the Board"), which is subject to general oversight by the SEC, and which is given the responsibility of establishing audit report standards and rules. The Board is authorized to inspect and oversee the auditing of publicly-traded companies, and is given the power to enforce compliance with its standards and rules by registered public accounting firms, which are all of those conducting audits of any publicly-traded company. As well as being tasked with the establishment of general auditing standards, including quality control and ethics standards, there are several substantive regulations mandated by the statute, including a seven-year retention period for audit work papers (reflecting the fact that Anderson was accused of shredding documents involved in its audit of Enron), a requirement that a second accounting-firm partner review and approve audits (to prevent accountants from becoming too chummy with the clients, as again was perceived as the situation between Anderson and Enron), and assorted provisions requiring the evaluation of internal control structures regarding receipts and expenditures (presumably to prevent the kind of lavish lifestyle WorldCom enabled its top executive to enjoy). The activities of the Board are funded through fees to be collected from issuers (thus imposing an indirect cost on their shareholders—who are thus required to pay for what the federal government believes is their own protection). The Board is given the power to impose disciplinary or remedial sanctions upon accountants for intentional misconduct or for repeated instances of negligent conduct. Title I of the Act contemplates the creation of a "principles-based accounting system" under the auspices of the SEC, and a report on such a system to the Congress which is to be used in the preparation of federally-mandated financial reports such as corporations' annual reports to shareholders. It might be said, in summary, that Title I federalizes accounting for publicly-traded corporations. Given the somewhat wonderful departures from generally accepted accounting principles in some parts of the federal government (for example Social Security) one might be forgiven for lifting an eyebrow at the notion that we ought to have that government regulate accounting.

Ensuring Auditor Independence. Whether or not it was accurate, there was a widespread perception that one reason that accounting firms auditing publicly-traded companies may have failed to be sufficiently objective or independent was that the firms also had vigorous and lucrative consulting practices, and that maintaining consulting contracts may have led them to fail vigorously to question corporations' accounting or other practices. Accordingly, Title II of the Act prohibits firms conducting audits from simultaneously performing some specified consulting services. Other services are permitted by the Act, if they are approved by the corporation's audit committee, a body which is given other particular tasks by the Act. These include, for example, the receiving of reports on the accounting policies and practices used in the accountants' audits, the consideration of alternative accounting treatments of various matters, and a review of written communications between the auditors and senior management of the issuer (again, to avoid overly friendly or compromising arrangements, as was thought to have occurred in Enron and WorldCom). Accounting firms are prohibited from rendering audit services if any of the corporation's senior executives had been employed by the accounting firm and had participated in an audit in the prior year. Auditor rotation, the requirement that a partner in the accounting firm may not be the lead or reviewing auditor for more than five consecutive years, is now mandated.

Mandating Corporate Compliance Structures. Never before has the federal government sought so extensively to dictate the internal organization of publicly-traded corporations, but Title III of the Act now dictates the composition of a mandatory audit committee, composed of outside members of the board of directors who are not permitted to have any other affiliation with or compensation from the corporation. The audit committee is charged with ensuring that the auditors do their job, and is given the responsibility for hiring, paying for, and conducting oversight of the audit. The Act gives the audit committee the express authority to hire independent counsel or other advisors, and requires the corporation to pay for those consultants to the audit committee. This could, of course, involve substantial expenditures by the Corporation, over which the corporation's Board of Directors as a whole will have no control. It is a nice question, then, whether or not this substantially modifies the omnipresent state corporate law provisions that the entire Board of Directors is charged with monitoring the affairs of the corporation. Title III also directs the SEC to promulgate new rules which will require the CEO and CFO personally to certify matters in periodic financial reports. These include certifying that the reports contain no untrue statements or material omissions, that the reports fairly present the financial conditions of corporations, and that the officers have supervised internal controls so that the officers receive material information regarding the corporation and its consolidated subsidiaries, that the officers have reviewed the internal controls within 90 days prior to the report in question, and that the officers have reported any significant changes to the internal controls. Once again there is federal mandating of particular executive tasks, in an unprecedented manner.

Other provisions of Title III (1) forbid corporate personnel from attempting improperly to influence an audit, (2) require that CEO's and CFO's must forfeit specified bonuses and compensation received if the corporation must make an accounting restatement due to prior material noncompliance with the federally-mandated standards, (3) authorize the prohibiting of those who violate particular SEC rules from continuing to serve as officers or directors, and (4) ban trading by directors and executives in a public company's stock during pension fund blackout periods (conduct that purportedly took place during some of the contemporary scandals). Finally, and most controversially for the legal profession, Section 307 of the Act requires lawyers appearing before the SEC to report violations of securities laws or other corporation or officer misconduct to the chief legal counsel or to the CEO of the corporation. Further regulations to be issued by the SEC may specify that if a lawyer's advice in this regard is not acted upon by the corporation, the lawyer must make a "noisy withdrawal" and give public notice that he or she will no longer represent the corporation. Because such regulations raise questions about compromising the traditional lawyer-client privilege, formulating these regulations has not been easy, and it is unclear whether a compromise between those seeking such disclosure and those wishing to protect lawyer-client confidentiality can be achieved.

Further Financial Disclosures. Title IV of the Act includes new requirements for financial disclosures for listed corporations. One facet of the Enron imbroglio was that many of the company's projects which turned out to be massive money-losers were conducted through partnerships that were not carried on Enron's balance sheets. Accordingly, this Title of the Act now requires disclosure of all off-balance sheet transactions and relationships that may have a material effect on the corporation's financial status. Attempting to correct an abuse at WorldCom and other corporations this title also prohibits most personal loans extended by the corporation to executives and directors. Another new provision requires that within 2 business days following the transaction, officers, directors, and 10% beneficial shareholders must report changes in their stock ownership. The former requirement had been that such reports need not be made until ten days after the close of the month in which such transactions occurred. In other provisions of this Title corporations are required to include an "internal control report" in their annual reports stating that corporate management is responsible for oversight procedures, and assessing the effectiveness of the internal controls for the previous fiscal year. This section, 404, appears to have spawned a variety of new software programs, and a plethora of new consulting opportunities, and will probably require many millions, if not billions of dollars for effective compliance. "According to a survey of 321 companies by Financial Executives International, companies with more than $5 billion in revenue expect to spend on average $4.7 million implementing Section 404 controls and about $1.5 million annually to maintain this level of compliance."[9] Put slightly differently, this means that roughly for every billion dollars in revenues, compliance costs generated by Sarbanes/Oxley will be more than a million dollars. Finally, Title IV requires each registered corporation to indicate whether it has adopted a code of ethics for its senior financial officers and to indicate whether its audit committee includes at

---

9. Paul Volker [former Chairman of the Board of Governors of the Federal Reserve System], and Arthur Levitt, Jr. [former Chairman of the SEC] "In Defense of Sarbanes-Oxley," Wall Street Journal, June 14, 2004, page A16.

least one member who is a financial expert. While neither of these appears actually to be required by the law, it is a safe bet that virtually all publicly-traded corporations will adopt such codes and place such a person on their audit committees.

Expanding the Budget of the SEC. Given its new supervisory responsibilities, which practically amount to the SEC becoming something of a super-Board of Directors for all corporations, it is not surprising that Title VI of the act mandates a 77.21% increase over the appropriations for FY 2002, including amounts for "pay parity, information and technology, security enhancements, and recovery and mitigation activities related to the September 11th terrorist attacks." There is a $98 million authorization for the hiring of no fewer than 200 additional "qualified professionals to provide improved oversight of auditors and audit services."

Ratcheting Up the Penalties for Corporate and Criminal Fraud. Title VIII of the act imposes new penalties "for knowingly destroying, altering, concealing, or falsifying records with intent to obstruct or influence either a Federal investigation or a matter in bankruptcy and for failure of an auditor to maintain for a five year period all audit or review work papers" of a corporate audit. These penalties include up to ten years in federal prison. Title VIII also extends the statute of limitation for a private right of action for securities fraud violations to "not later than two years [after the discovery of such fraud] or five years after the date of the violation," (prior limits were 1 year and 3 years respectively) thus enhancing the ability of "private attorneys general" to litigate in the manner permitted by *J.I. Case v. Borak.* Another provision of Title VIII prohibits retaliatory action against "whistleblower" employees of listed corporations in connection with the investigation of fraud or other misconduct by "Federal regulators, Congress or supervisors," or in connection with the bringing of proceedings (presumably civil or criminal litigation) "relating to fraud against shareholders." Title VIII also increases the penalties formerly prevailing for securities fraud, to up to 25 years imprisonment. Provisions of Title IX increase penalties for mail and wire fraud from five to twenty years in prison, increase penalties for violations of the federal pension law (ERISA) up to $500,000 and ten years imprisonment, and "[E]stablishes criminal liability for failure of corporate officers to certify financial reports," including maximum imprisonment of twenty years for "willfully certifying a statement knowing it does not comply" with the Act. Title XI establishes a maximum 20 year sentence for "tampering with a record or otherwise impeding an official proceeding, and also authorizes the SEC to prohibit a corporate official who violates Section 10(b) from serving as an officer or director of a publicly traded corporation if the person's conduct demonstrates unfitness to serve." Finally, not only does Title XI increase penalties for violations of the Securities Exchange Act of 1934 up to $25 million dollars, it also provides for imprisonment for up to twenty years for violations of that Act.

If possible fines and imprisonments are the test of government seriousness about corporate misconduct, the federal government is now very serious indeed. A former Chairman of the Federal Reserve and a former Chairman of the SEC have written that Sarbanes/Oxley is "the most far-reaching corporate reform legislation in 60 years," and have observed that it was passed "with the support of all but three members of Congress who voted." They conclude that

> $5 million down and $1.5 million a year is not too much to pay for a multibillion-dollar international company when compared to how much investors have lost—and stand to lose—if internal controls are not improved. Put it in the context of the tens of millions of dollars paid to investment bankers to advise on a deal, or on legal fees when things go wrong—or think of the $90 billion investors lost just on the collapse of Enron alone. By that calculus, Sarbanes-Oxley clearly meets the cost-benefit test, and is worth every penny.[10]

Are you pleased with what appears to be an increasing federalization of corporate law? Would you have voted for Sarbanes/Oxley if you were a member of Congress? Some critics have suggested that the result of Sarbanes/Oxley will be to reduce the number of publicly-traded corporations as many giant firms become closely held, among just a few stockholders. Would this be a felicific development? We consider the closely-held corporation in the next chapter.

---

10. Volker and Leavitt, supra.

CHAPTER 7

THE CLOSE CORPORATION

■ ■ ■

A. FIDUCIARY RESPONSIBILITY IN THE CLOSELY–HELD CORPORATION

EUPHEMIA DONAHUE v. RODD ELECTROTYPE COMPANY OF NEW ENGLAND, INC.

Supreme Judicial Court of Massachusetts.
367 Mass. 578, 328 N.E.2d 505 (1975).

[TAURO, C.J.] The plaintiff, Euphemia Donahue, a minority stockholder in the Rodd Electrotype Company of New England, Inc. (Rodd Electrotype), a Massachusetts corporation, brings this suit against the directors of Rodd Electrotype, Charles H. Rodd, Frederick I. Rodd and Mr. Harold E. Magnuson, against Harry C. Rodd, a former director, officer, and controlling stockholder of Rodd Electrotype and against Rodd Electrotype (hereinafter called defendants). The plaintiff seeks to rescind Rodd Electrotype's purchase of Harry Rodd's shares in Rodd Electrotype * * * and to compel Harry Rodd "to repay to the corporation the purchase price of said shares, $36,000, together with interest from the date of purchase." * * * The plaintiff alleges that the defendants caused the corporation to purchase the shares in violation of their fiduciary duty to her, a minority stockholder of Rodd Electrotype. * * *

The trial judge, after hearing oral testimony, dismissed the plaintiff's bill on the merits. He found that the purchase was without prejudice to the plaintiff and implicitly * * * found that the transaction had been carried out in good faith and with inherent fairness. The Appeals Court affirmed with costs. * * * The case is before us on the plaintiff's application for further appellate review.

*   *   *

* * * In 1935, the defendant, Harry C. Rodd, began his employment with Rodd Electrotype, then styled the Royal Electrotype Company of New England, Inc. (Royal of New England). At that time, the company was a wholly-owned subsidiary of a Pennsylvania corporation, the Royal

308

Electrotype Company (Royal Electrotype). Mr. Rodd's advancement within the company was rapid. The following year he was elected a director, and, in 1946, he succeeded to the position of general manager and treasurer.

In 1936, the plaintiff's husband, Joseph Donahue (now deceased), was hired by Royal of New England as a "finisher" of electrotype plates. His duties were confined to operational matters within the plant. Although he ultimately achieved the positions of plant superintendent (1946) and corporate vice president (1955), Donahue never participated in the "management" aspect of the business.

In the years preceding 1955, the parent company, Royal Electrotype, made available to Harry Rodd and Joseph Donahue shares of the common stock in its subsidiary, Royal of New England. Harry Rodd took advantage of the opportunities offered to him and acquired 200 shares for $20 a share. Joseph Donahue, at the suggestion of Harry Rodd, who hoped to interest Donahue in the business, eventually obtained fifty shares in two twenty-five share lots priced at $20 a share. The parent company at all times retained 725 of the 1,000 outstanding shares. One Lawrence W. Kelley owned the remaining twenty-five shares.

In June of 1955, Royal of New England purchased all 725 of its shares owned by its parent company. The total price amounted to $135,000. Royal of New England remitted $75,000 of this total in cash and executed five promissory notes of $12,000 each, due in each of the succeeding five years. Lawrence W. Kelley's twenty-five shares were also purchased at this time for $1,000. A substantial portion of Royal of New England's cash expenditures was loaned to the company by Harry Rodd, who mortgaged his house to obtain some of the necessary funds.

The stock purchases left Harry Rodd in control of Royal of New England. Early in 1955, before the purchases, he had assumed the presidency of the company. His 200 shares gave him a dominant eighty per cent interest. Joseph Donahue, at this time, was the only minority stockholder.

Subsequent events reflected Harry Rodd's dominant influence. In June, 1960, more than a year after the last obligation to Royal Electrotype had been discharged, the company was renamed the Rodd Electrotype Company of New England, Inc. In 1962, Charles H. Rodd, Harry Rodd's son (a defendant here), who had long been a company employee working in the plant, became corporate vice president. In 1963, he joined his father on the board of directors. In 1964, another son, Frederick I. Rodd (also a defendant), replaced Joseph Donahue as plant superintendent. By 1965, Harry Rodd had evidently decided to reduce his participation in corporate management. That year, Charles Rodd succeeded him as president and general manager of Rodd Electrotype.

From 1959 to 1967, Harry Rodd pursued what may fairly be termed a gift program by which he distributed the majority of his shares equally among his two sons and his daughter, Phyllis E. Mason. Each child received thirty-nine shares. * * * Two shares were returned to the corporate treasury in 1966.

* * * In May of 1970, Harry Rodd was seventy-seven years old. The record indicates that for some time he had not enjoyed the best of health and that he had undergone a number of operations. His sons wished him to retire. Mr. Rodd was not averse to this suggestion. However, he insisted that some financial arrangements be made with respect to his remaining eighty-one shares of stock. A number of conferences ensued. Harry Rodd and Charles Rodd (representing the company) negotiated terms of purchase for forty-five shares which, Charles Rodd testified, would reflect the book value and liquidating value of the shares.

A special board meeting convened on July 13, 1970. As the first order of business, Harry Rodd resigned his directorship of Rodd Electrotype. The remaining incumbent directors, Charles Rodd and Mr. Harold E. Magnuson (clerk of the company and a defendant and defense attorney in the instant suit), elected Frederick Rodd to replace his father. The three directors then authorized Rodd Electrotype's president (Charles Rodd) to execute an agreement between Harry Rodd and the company in which the company would purchase forty-five shares for $800 a share ($36,000).

The stock purchase agreement was formalized between the parties on July 13, 1970. Two days later, a sale pursuant to the July 13 agreement was consummated. At approximately the same time, Harry Rodd resigned his last corporate office, that of treasurer.

Harry Rodd completed divestiture of his Rodd Electrotype stock in the following year. As was true of his previous gifts, his later divestments gave equal representation to his children. Two shares were sold to each child on July 15, 1970, for $800 a share. Each was given ten shares in March, 1971. * * * Thus, in March, 1971, the shareholdings in Rodd Electrotype were apportioned as follows: Charles Rodd, Frederick Rodd and Phyllis Mason each held fifty-one shares; the Donahues[1] held fifty shares.

A special meeting of the stockholders of the company was held on March 30, 1971. At the meeting, Charles Rodd, company president and general manager, reported the tentative results of an audit conducted by the company auditors and reported generally on the company events of the year. For the first time, the Donahues learned that the corporation had purchased Harry Rodd's shares. According to the minutes of the meeting, following Charles Rodd's report, the Donahues raised questions about the purchase. They then voted against a resolution, ultimately adopted by the remaining stockholders, to approve Charles Rodd's report. * * * [T]he trial judge found * * * that the Donahues did not ratify the purchase of Harry Rodd's shares. * * *

---

1. Joseph Donahue gave his wife, the plaintiff, joint ownership of his fifty shares in 1962. In 1968, they transferred five shares to their son, Dr. Robert Donahue. On Joseph Donahue's death, the plaintiff became outright owner of the forty-five share block. This was the ownership pattern which obtained in March, 1971.

A few weeks after the meeting, the Donahues, acting through their attorney, offered their shares to the corporation on the same terms given to Harry Rodd. Mr. Harold E. Magnuson replied by letter that the corporation would not purchase the shares and was not in a financial position to do so. * * * This suit followed.

In her argument before this court, the plaintiff has characterized the corporate purchase of Harry Rodd's shares as an unlawful distribution of corporate assets to controlling stockholders. She urges that the distribution constitutes a breach of the fiduciary duty owed by the Rodds, as controlling stockholders, to her, a minority stockholder in the enterprise, because the Rodds failed to accord her an equal opportunity to sell her shares to the corporation. The defendants reply that the stock purchase was within the powers of the corporation and met the requirements of good faith and inherent fairness imposed on a fiduciary in his dealings with the corporation. They assert that there is no right to equal opportunity in corporate stock purchases for the corporate treasury. For the reasons hereinafter noted, we agree with the plaintiff and reverse the decree of the Superior Court. However, we limit the applicability of our holding to "close corporations," as hereinafter defined. Whether the holding should apply to other corporations is left for decision in another case, on a proper record.

A. *Close Corporations.* In previous opinions, we have alluded to the distinctive nature of the close corporation * * * but have never defined precisely what is meant by a close corporation. There is no single, generally accepted definition. Some commentators emphasize an "integration of ownership and management" (Note, Statutory Assistance for Closely Held Corporations, *71 Harv. L. Rev. 1498* [1958]), in which the stockholders occupy most management positions. *Kruger v. Gerth, 16 N. Y. 2d 802, 806 (1965)* (Fuld, J., dissenting) * * * Others focus on the number of stockholders and the nature of the market for the stock. In this view, close corporations have few stockholders; there is little market for corporate stock. The Supreme Court of Illinois adopted this latter view in *Galler v. Galler, 32 Ill. 2d 16 (1965):* "For our purposes, a close corporation is one in which the stock is held in a few hands, or in a few families, and wherein it is not at all, or only rarely, dealt in by buying or selling." * * * We accept aspects of both definitions. We deem a close corporation to be typified by: (1) a small number of stockholders; (2) no ready market for the corporate stock; and (3) substantial majority stockholder participation in the management, direction and operations of the corporation.

As thus defined, the close corporation bears striking resemblance to a partnership. Commentators and courts have noted that the close corporation is often little more than an "incorporated" or "chartered" partnership.[2] * * * The stockholders "clothe" their partnership "with the benefits

---

2. The United States Internal Revenue Code gives substantial recognition to the fact that close corporations are often merely incorporated partnerships. The so called Subchapter S, 26 U. S. C. §§ 1371–1379 (1970), enables "small business corporations," defined by the statute (26 U.

peculiar to a corporation, limited liability, perpetuity and the like." * * * In essence, though, the enterprise remains one in which ownership is limited to the original parties or transferees of their stock to whom the other stockholders have agreed,[3] in which ownership and management are in the same hands, and in which the owners are quite dependent on one another for the success of the enterprise. * * * Just as in a partnership, the relationship among the stockholders must be one of trust, confidence and absolute loyalty if the enterprise is to succeed. Close corporations with substantial assets and with more numerous stockholders are no different from smaller close corporations in this regard. All participants rely on the fidelity and abilities of those stockholders who hold office. Disloyalty and self-seeking conduct on the part of any stockholder will engender bickering, corporate stalemates, and, perhaps, efforts to achieve dissolution. * * *

In *Helms v. Duckworth, 249 F. 2d 482 (D. C. Cir. 1957),* the United States Court of Appeals for the District of Columbia Circuit had before it a stockholders' agreement providing for the purchase of the shares of a deceased stockholder by the surviving stockholder in a small "two-man" close corporation. The court held the surviving stockholder to a duty "to deal fairly, honestly, and openly with … [his] fellow stockholders." *Id. at 487.* Judge Burger, now Chief Justice Burger, writing for the court, emphasized the resemblance of the two-man close corporation to a partnership: "In an intimate business venture such as this, stockholders of a close corporation occupy a position similar to that of joint adventurers and partners. While courts have sometimes declared stockholders 'do not bear toward each other that same relation of trust and confidence which prevails in partnerships,' this view ignores the practical realities of the organization and functioning of a small 'two-man' corporation organized to carry on a small business enterprise in which the stockholders, directors, and managers are the same persons" (footnotes omitted). *Id. at 486.*

Although the corporate form provides the above-mentioned advantages for the stockholders (limited liability, perpetuity, and so forth), it also supplies an opportunity for the majority stockholders to oppress or disadvantage minority stockholders. The minority is vulnerable to a variety of oppressive devices, termed "freeze-outs," which the majority may

---

S. C. § 1371 [a] [1970]), to make an election which generally exempts the corporation from taxation (26 U. S. C. § 1372 [b] [1] [1970]) and causes inclusion of the corporation's undistributed, as well as distributed, taxable income in the gross income of the stockholders for the year (26 U. S. C. § 1373 [a] [1970]). This is essentially the manner in which partnership earnings are taxed. See 26 U. S. C. § 701 (1970).

3. The original owners commonly impose restrictions on transfers of stock designed to prevent outsiders who are unacceptable to the other stockholders from acquiring an interest in the close corporation. These restrictions often take the form of agreements among the stockholders and the corporation or by-laws which give the corporation or the other stockholders a right of "first refusal" when any stockholder desires to sell his shares. See Albert E. Touchet, Inc. v. Touchet, 264 Mass. 499, 502 (1928); Hornstein, Stockholders' Agreements in the Closely Held Corporation, 59 Yale L. J. 1040, 1048–1049 (1950). In a partnership, of course, a partner cannot transfer his interest in the partnership so as to give his assignee a right to participate in the management or business affairs of the continuing partnership without the agreement of the other partners. G. L. c. 108A, § 27. See Hazen v. Warwick, 256 Mass. 302, 308 (1926).

employ. See, generally, Note, Freezing Out Minority Shareholders, *74 Harv. L. Rev. 1630 (1961)*. An authoritative study of such "freeze-outs" enumerates some of the possibilities: "The squeezers [those who employ the freeze-out techniques] may refuse to declare dividends; they may drain off the corporation's earnings in the form of exorbitant salaries and bonuses to the majority shareholder-officers and perhaps to their relatives, or in the form of high rent by the corporation for property leased from majority shareholders ... ; they may deprive minority shareholders of corporate offices and of employment by the company; they may cause the corporation to sell its assets at an inadequate price to the majority shareholders ...." F. H. O'Neal and J. Derwin, Expulsion or Oppression of Business Associates, 42 (1961). In particular, the power of the board of directors, controlled by the majority, to declare or withhold dividends and to deny the minority employment is easily converted to a device to disadvantage minority stockholders. * * *

The minority can, of course, initiate suit against the majority and their directors. Self-serving conduct by directors is proscribed by the director's fiduciary obligation to the corporation. * * * However, in practice, the plaintiff will find difficulty in challenging dividend or employment policies. * * * Such policies are considered to be within the judgment of the directors. This court has said: "The courts prefer not to interfere ... with the sound financial management of the corporation by its directors, but declare as a general rule that the declaration of dividends rests within the sound discretion of the directors, refusing to interfere with their determination unless a plain abuse of discretion is made to appear." *Crocker v. Waltham Watch Co. 315 Mass. 397, 402 (1944)*. * * * Judicial reluctance to interfere combines with the difficulty of proof when the standard is "plain abuse of discretion" or bad faith, * * * to limit the possibilities for relief. Although contractual provisions in an "agreement of association and articles of organization" (*Crocker v. Waltham Watch Co., supra, at 401)* or in by-laws * * * have justified decrees in this jurisdiction ordering dividend declarations, generally, plaintiffs who seek judicial assistance against corporate dividend or employment policies[4] do not prevail. * * *

Thus, when these types of "freeze-outs" are attempted by the majority stockholders, the minority stockholders, cut off from all corporation-related revenues, must either suffer their losses or seek a buyer for their shares. Many minority stockholders will be unwilling or unable to wait for an alteration in majority policy. Typically, the minority stockholder in a close corporation has a substantial percentage of his personal assets invested in the corporation. * * * The stockholder may have anticipated

---

4. Attacks on allegedly excessive salaries voted for officers and directors fare better in the courts. See Stratis v. Andreson, 254 Mass. 536 (1926); Sagalyn v. Meekins, Packard & Wheat, Inc. 290 Mass. 434 (1935). What is "reasonable compensation" is a question of fact. Black v. Parker Mfg. Co. 329 Mass. 105, 116 (1952). The proof which establishes an excess over such "reasonable compensation" appears easier than the proof which would establish bad faith or plain abuse of discretion.

that his salary from his position with the corporation would be his liveli-
hood. Thus, he cannot afford to wait passively. He must liquidate his
investment in the close corporation in order to reinvest the funds in
income-producing enterprises.

At this point, the true plight of the minority stockholder in a close
corporation becomes manifest. He cannot easily reclaim his capital. In a
large public corporation, the oppressed or dissident minority stockholder
could sell his stock in order to extricate some of his invested capital. By
definition, this market is not available for shares in the close corporation.
In a partnership, a partner who feels abused by his fellow partners may
cause dissolution by his "express will ... at any time" (*G. L. c. 108A, § 31*
[1] [b] and [2]) and recover his share of partnership assets and accumulated profits. * * * If dissolution results in a breach of the partnership
articles, the culpable partner will be liable in damages. *G. L. c. 108A, § 38*
(2) (a) II. By contrast, the stockholder in the close corporation or "incorporated partnership" may achieve dissolution and recovery of his share of
the enterprise assets only by compliance with the rigorous terms of the
applicable chapter of the General Laws. * * * "The dissolution of a corporation which is a creature of the Legislature is primarily a legislative
function, and the only authority courts have to deal with this subject is
the power conferred upon them by the Legislature." *Leventhal v. Atlantic
Fin. Corp., 316 Mass. 194, 205 (1944).* To secure dissolution of the ordinary close corporation subject to G. L. c. 156B, the stockholder, in the
absence of corporate deadlock, must own at least fifty per cent of the
shares (*G. L. c. 156B, § 99* [a]) or have the advantage of a favorable provision in the articles of organization (*G. L. c. 156B, § 100* [a] [2]). The
minority stockholder, by definition lacking fifty per cent of the corporate
shares, can never "authorize" the corporation to file a petition for dissolution under *G. L. c. 156B, § 99* (a), by his own vote. He will seldom have at
his disposal the requisite favorable provision in the articles of organization.

Thus, in a close corporation, the minority stockholders may be
trapped in a disadvantageous situation. No outsider would knowingly
assume the position of the disadvantaged minority. The outsider would
have the same difficulties. To cut losses, the minority stockholder may be
compelled to deal with the majority. This is the capstone of the majority
plan. Majority "freeze-out" schemes which withhold dividends are
designed to compel the minority to relinquish stock at inadequate prices.
* * * When the minority stockholder agrees to sell out at less than fair
value, the majority has won.

Because of the fundamental resemblance of the close corporation to
the partnership, the trust and confidence which are essential to this scale
and manner of enterprise, and the inherent danger to minority interests
in the close corporation, we hold that stockholders[5] in the close corpora-

---

5. We do not limit our holding to majority stockholders. In the close corporation, the minority
may do equal damage through unscrupulous and improper "sharp dealings" with an unsuspect-
ing majority. See Helms v. Duckworth, 249 F. 2d 482 (D. C. Cir. 1957).

tion owe one another substantially the same fiduciary duty in the operation of the enterprise[6] that partners owe to one another. In our previous decisions, we have defined the standard of duty owed by partners to one another as the "utmost good faith and loyalty." *Cardullo v. Landau, 329 Mass. 5, 8 (1952). DeCotis v. D'Antona, 350 Mass. 165, 168 (1966).* Stockholders in close corporations must discharge their management and stockholder responsibilities in conformity with this strict good faith standard. They may not act out of avarice, expediency or self-interest in derogation of their duty of loyalty to the other stockholders and to the corporation.

We contrast * * * this strict good faith standard with the somewhat less stringent standard of fiduciary duty to which directors and stockholders[7] of all corporations must adhere in the discharge of their corporate responsibilities. Corporate directors are held to a good faith and inherent fairness standard of conduct * * * and are not "permitted to serve two masters whose interests are antagonistic." *Spiegel v. Beacon Participations, Inc. 297 Mass. 398, 411 (1937).* "Their paramount duty is to the corporation, and their personal pecuniary interests are subordinate to that duty." *Durfee v. Durfee & Canning, Inc. 323 Mass. 187, 196 (1948).*

The more rigorous duty of partners and participants in a joint adventure * * * here extended to stockholders in a close corporation, was described by then Chief Judge Cardozo of the New York Court of Appeals in *Meinhard v. Salmon, 249 N. Y. 458 (1928):* "Joint adventurers, like copartners, owe to one another, while the enterprise continues, the duty of the finest loyalty. Many forms of conduct permissible in a workaday world for those acting at arm's length, are forbidden to those bound by fiduciary duties.... Not honesty alone, but the punctilio of an honor the most sensitive, is then the standard of behavior." *Id. at 463–464.* * * *

Application of this strict standard of duty to stockholders in close corporations is a natural outgrowth of the prior case law. In a number of cases involving close corporations, we have held stockholders participating in management to a standard of fiduciary duty more exacting than the traditional good faith and inherent fairness standard because of the trust and confidence reposed in them by the other stockholders. In *Silversmith v. Sydeman, 305 Mass. 65 (1940),* the plaintiff brought suit for an accounting of the liquidation of a close corporation which he and the defendant

---

6. We stress that the strict fiduciary duty which we apply to stockholders in a close corporation in this opinion governs only their actions relative to the operations of the enterprise and the effects of that operation on the rights and investments of other stockholders. We express no opinion as to the standard of duty applicable to transactions in the shares of the close corporation when the corporation is not a party to the transaction. Cf. Andrews, The Stockholder's Right to Equal Opportunity in the Sale of Shares, 78 Harv. L. Rev. 505 (1965). Compare Perlman v. Feldmann, 219 F. 2d 173 (2d Cir.), 349 U.S. 952 (1955), with Zahn v. Transamerica Corp. 162 F. 2d 36 (3d Cir. 1947).

7. The rule set out in many jurisdictions is: "The majority has the right to control; but when it does so, it occupies a fiduciary relation toward the minority, as much so as the corporation itself or its officers and directors." Southern Pac. Co. v. Bogert, 250 U.S. 483, 487–488 (1919). * * * See generally Berle, "Control" in Corporate Law, 58 Col. L. Rev. 1212, 1222 (1958).

had owned. In assessing their relative rights in the discount of a note, we had occasion to consider the defendant's fiduciary duty with respect to the financial affairs of the company. We implied that, in addition to the fiduciary duty owed by an officer to the corporation, a more rigorous standard of fiduciary duty applied to the defendant by virtue of the relationship between the stockholders: "... it could be found that the plaintiff and the defendant were acting as partners in the conduct of the company's business and in the liquidation of its property even though they had adopted a corporate form as the instrumentality by which they should associate in furtherance of their joint venture." *Id. at 68.*

In *Samia v. Central Oil Co. of Worcester, 339 Mass. 101 (1959),* sisters alleged that their brothers had systematically excluded them from management, income and partial ownership of a close corporation formed from a family partnership. In rejecting arguments that the plaintiffs' suit was barred by the statute of limitations or laches, we stressed the familial relationship among the parties, which should have given rise to a particularly scrupulous fidelity in serving the interests of all of the stockholders * * *.

* * * In the instant case, we extend this strict duty of loyalty to all stockholders in close corporations. The circumstances which justified findings of relationships of trust and confidence in these particular cases exist universally in modified form in all close corporations. * * *

B. *Equal Opportunity in a Close Corporation*. Under settled Massachusetts law, a domestic corporation, unless forbidden by statute, has the power to purchase its own shares. * * * An agreement to reacquire stock "is enforceable, subject, at least, to the limitations that the purchase must be made in good faith and without prejudice to creditors and stockholders." * * * When the corporation reacquiring its own stock is a close corporation, the purchase is subject to the additional requirement, in the light of our holding in this opinion, that the stockholders, who, as directors or controlling stockholders, caused the corporation to enter into the stock purchase agreement, must have acted with the utmost good faith and loyalty to the other stockholders.

To meet this test, if the stockholder whose shares were purchased was a member of the controlling group, the controlling stockholders must cause the corporation to offer each stockholder an equal opportunity to sell a ratable number of his shares to the corporation at an identical price.[8] Purchase by the corporation confers substantial benefits on the members of the controlling group whose shares were purchased. These benefits are not available to the minority stockholders if the corporation does not also offer them an opportunity to sell their shares. The control-

---

8. Of course, a close corporation may purchase shares from one stockholder without offering the others an equal opportunity if all other stockholders give advance consent to the stock purchase arrangements through acceptance of an appropriate provision in the articles of organization, the corporate by-laws * * * or a stockholder's agreement. Similarly, all other stockholders may ratify the purchase. * * *

ling group may not, consistent with its strict duty to the minority, utilize its control of the corporation to obtain special advantages and disproportionate benefit from its share ownership. * * *

The benefits conferred by the purchase are twofold: (1) provision of a market for shares; (2) access to corporate assets for personal use. By definition, there is no ready market for shares of a close corporation. The purchase creates a market for shares which previously had been unmarketable. It transforms a previously illiquid investment into a liquid one. If the close corporation purchases shares only from a member of the controlling group, the controlling stockholder can convert his shares into cash at a time when none of the other stockholders can. Consistent with its strict fiduciary duty, the controlling group may not utilize its control of the corporation to establish an exclusive market in previously unmarketable shares from which the minority stockholders are excluded. * * *

The purchase also distributes corporate assets to the stockholder whose shares were purchased. Unless an equal opportunity is given to all stockholders, the purchase of shares from a member of the controlling group operates as a *preferential* distribution of assets. In exchange for his shares, he receives a percentage of the contributed capital and accumulated profits of the enterprise. The funds he so receives are available for his personal use. The other stockholders benefit from no such access to corporate property and cannot withdraw their shares of the corporate profits and capital in this manner unless the controlling group acquiesces. Although the purchase price for the controlling stockholder's shares may seem fair to the corporation and other stockholders under the tests established in the prior case law * * * the controlling stockholder whose stock has been purchased has still received a relative advantage over his fellow stockholders, inconsistent with his strict fiduciary duty—an opportunity to turn corporate funds to personal use.

The rule of equal opportunity in stock purchases by close corporations provides equal access to these benefits for all stockholders. We hold that, in any case in which the controlling stockholders have exercised their power over the corporation to deny the minority such equal opportunity, the minority shall be entitled to appropriate relief. * * *

C. *Application of the Law to this Case.* * * *

The strict standard of duty is plainly applicable to the stockholders in Rodd Electrotype. Rodd Electrotype is a close corporation. Members of the Rodd and Donahue families are the sole owners of the corporation's stock. In actual numbers, the corporation, immediately prior to the corporate purchase of Harry Rodd's shares, had six stockholders. The shares have not been traded, and no market for them seems to exist. Harry Rodd, Charles Rodd, Frederick Rodd, William G. Mason (Phyllis Mason's husband), and the plaintiff's husband all worked for the corporation. The Rodds have retained the paramount management positions.

Through their control of these management positions and of the majority of the Rodd Electrotype stock, the Rodds effectively controlled the corporation. In testing the stock purchase from Harry Rodd against the applicable strict fiduciary standard, we treat the Rodd family as a single controlling group. * * * From the evidence, it is clear that the Rodd family was a close-knit one with strong community of interest. * * * Harry Rodd had hired his sons to work in the family business, Rodd Electrotype. As he aged, he transferred portions of his stock holdings to his children. * * * Charles Rodd and Frederick Rodd were given positions of responsibility in the business as he withdrew from active management. In these circumstances, it is realistic to assume that appreciation, gratitude, and filial devotion would prevent the younger Rodds from opposing a plan which would provide funds for their father's retirement.

Moreover, a strong motive of interest requires that the Rodds be considered a controlling group. When Charles Rodd and Frederick Rodd were called on to represent the corporation in its dealings with their father, they must have known that further advancement within the corporation and benefits would follow their father's retirement and the purchase of his stock. The corporate purchase would take only forty-five of Harry Rodd's eighty-one shares. The remaining thirty-six shares * * * were to be divided among Harry Rodd's children in equal amounts by gift and sale.* * * Receipt of their portion of the thirty-six shares and purchase by the corporation of forty-five shares would effectively transfer full control of the corporation to Frederick Rodd and Charles Rodd, if they chose to act in concert with each other or if one of them chose to ally with his sister.[9] Moreover, Frederick Rodd was the obvious successor to his father as director and corporate treasurer when those posts became vacant after his father's retirement. Failure to complete the corporate purchase (in other words, impeding their father's retirement plan) would have delayed, and perhaps have suspended indefinitely, the transfer of these benefits to the younger Rodds. They could not be expected to oppose their father's wishes in this matter. Although the defendants are correct when they assert that no express agreement involving a quid pro quo—subsequent stock gifts for votes from the directors—was proved, no express agreement is necessary to demonstrate the identity of interest which disciplines a controlling group acting in unison. * * *

On its face, then, the purchase of Harry Rodd's shares by the corporation is a breach of the duty which the controlling stockholders, the Rodds, owed to the minority stockholders, the plaintiff and her son. The purchase distributed a portion of the corporate assets to Harry Rodd, a member of the controlling group, in exchange for his shares. The plaintiff and her son were not offered an equal opportunity to sell their shares to the corpora-

---

9. Charles Rodd admitted in his trial testimony that the parties to the negotiations which led to the stock purchase agreement structured subsequent transactions so that each of the Rodd children would eventually own fifty-one shares of corporate stock. * * * [T]his was precisely the number of shares which would permit any two of Harry Rodd's children to outvote the third child and the remaining stockholders.

tion. In fact, their efforts to obtain an equal opportunity were rebuffed by the corporate representative. * * *

Because of the foregoing, we hold that the plaintiff is entitled to relief. Two forms of suitable relief are set out hereinafter. The judge below is to enter an appropriate judgment. The judgment may require Harry Rodd to remit $36,000 with interest at the legal rate from July 15, 1970, to Rodd Electrotype in exchange for forty-five shares of Rodd Electrotype treasury stock. This, in substance, is the specific relief requested in the plaintiff's bill of complaint. * * * In the alternative, the judgment may require Rodd Electrotype to purchase all of the plaintiff's shares for $36,000 * * *. In the circumstances of this case, we view this as the equal opportunity which the plaintiff should have received. Harry Rodd's retention of thirty-six shares, which were to be sold and given to his children within a year of the Rodd Electrotype purchase, cannot disguise the fact that the corporation acquired one hundred per cent of that portion of his holdings (forty-five shares) which he did not intend his children to own. The plaintiff is entitled to have one hundred per cent of her forty-five shares similarly purchased. * * *

* * *

WILKINS, J. (concurring).

I agree with much of what the Chief Justice says in support of granting relief to the plaintiff. However, I do not join in any implication * * * that the rule concerning a close corporation's purchase of a controlling stockholder's shares applies to all operations of the corporation as they affect minority stockholders. That broader issue, which is apt to arise in connection with salaries and dividend policy, is not involved in this case. The analogy to partnerships may not be a complete one.

NOTES AND QUESTIONS

1. This case is our introduction to the problems of the close corporation. It is concerned with the duty that those in control of a close corporation owe to the minority shareholders. What was the purported breach of fiduciary duty here? Given that the company would not be what it was but for Harry Rodd's efforts, did the court reach the appropriate conclusion in the case? For a different approach to the question of selective purchases by the corporation of some but not all of shareholders' stock, see, e.g., Toner v. Baltimore Envelope Co., 304 Md. 256, 498 A.2d 642 (1985) and Delahoussaye v. Newhard, 785 S.W.2d 609 (Mo.App. 1990). Delaware appears to permit selective redemption of shares in an appropriate situation, such as resistance to a coercive tender-offer, see e.g., Unocal Corp. v. Mesa Petroleum Co., 493 A.2d 946 (Del. Supr.1985). But see the so-called "all holders rule" of federal law, a regulation of the Securities and Exchange Commission, which requires that when a tender offer is made for shares in a publicly-held corporation all shareholders holding the same class of shares must be treated equally. SEC Rule13e–4(f)(8)(i). Still, should that rule broadly apply in the case of privately-held corporations?

2. *Donahue* provides a concise definition of a close corporation: "We deem a close corporation to be typified by: (1) a small number of stockholders; (2) no ready market for the corporate stock; and (3) substantial majority stockholder participation in the management, direction and operations of the corporation." Do you understand how these characteristics of the close corporation pose the risk of breaches of fiduciary duties? Does it make sense, as did the court, to conclude that "stockholders in the close corporation owe one another substantially the same fiduciary duty in the operation of the enterprise that partners owe to one another?" Why do you suppose Justice Wilkins expressed some reservations on this point? Can you understand how the fiduciary duty imposed in *Donahue* is different from that owed to the publicly-held corporation by directors and officers? Should there be a difference? Where they have the potential to obstruct the business of the close corporation, do minority shareholders owe others the same fiduciary duty a majority shareholder has to the minority in a close corporation? For an affirmative answer see, e.g., Wilkes v. Springside Nursing Home, Inc. 370 Mass. 842, 353 N.E.2d 657 (Mass. 1976). For a superb discussion of the *Donahue* case, including some treatment of *Wilkes v. Springside Nursing Home*, see Douglas K. Moll, "Protection of Minority Shareholders in Closely–Held Corporations: *Donahue v. Rodd Electrotype Co.*," Chapter 6 in Jonathan R. Macey, ed., The Iconic Cases in Corporate Law 98 (2008). In his analysis, Professor Moll, one of the country's leading experts in the law of the close corporation, praises the *Donahue* case in general, but does offer some critical comments on the decision. He indicates that "Although the validity of the equal opportunity rule and the usefulness of the partnership analogy can be questioned, the significance of the *Donahue* decision lies less in its detail and more in its overall push for enhanced minority shareholder rights." Id., at 105. Do you agree?

3. It is probably difficult to overstate the importance (or the recent importance) of the closely-held corporation. As late as 1990 it could be said that "close corporations account for most of American business." Steven C. Bahls, Resolving Shareholder Dissension: Selection of the Appropriate Equitable Remedy, 15 J. Corp. L. 285, 287 (1990) (observing that "family-owned businesses alone represent 95% of all United States businesses")(cited in Douglas Moll, Shareholder Oppression in Close Corporations: The Unanswered Question of Perspective, 53 Vand. L. Rev. 749, 754 (2000)). Some of these businesses may be shifting to the Limited Liability Company (LLC) form, but it is likely the questions of fiduciary duty will be similarly analyzed whatever the small business vehicle chosen. Is it important to keep much of American business in the hands of small groups of entrepreneurs? Do you sympathize with the plight of the Donahues? Clearly the Rodds were getting some remuneration from their position as officials of the corporation, and, indeed, as you may have discerned from the *Holden v. Construction Company* case we considered in Chapter Five, shareholders in a close corporation often cannot count on dividends, and may only expect to receive remuneration from salaries they receive as officials of the corporation. As nicely put in a recent article on the close corporation:

> A characteristic of close corporations that has been central to many oppression cases is that distribution of business income to the owners is

commonly in the form of salary and employment benefits rather than dividends. Federal income tax advantages are one major reason. For "C corporations" (all corporations except those that qualify for and elect pass-through "S" status), salary payments are taxable income to the recipient. These payments, however, are a business deduction to the corporation, so are effectively taxed just once. Dividend payments, in sharp contrast, are income to the recipient but not deductible by the corporation. Therefore, the dividend payments are double taxed.

Experts describe salary and other employment benefits, which may be at the high end of a reasonable range of compensation for services, as "de facto dividends." Moreover, some characterize employment by closely held corporations of their shareholders as an investment interest of the shareholders, not a separate relationship as in other situations. A shareholder of a close corporation who is terminated from employment with the company may lose not only the job but also all income and all return on investment. Though the person may continue to own shares, they produce no income in the absence of employment and are not salable at fair value. The minority's investment is locked in, producing no return to the minority, and serving only to promote the interests of the controlling shareholders.

Robert C. Art, Shareholder Rights and Remedies in Close Corporations: Oppression, Fiduciary Duties, and Reasonable Expectations, 28 Iowa J. Corp. L. 371, 383–384 (2003) (footnotes omitted). Does this give you a better sense of the plight faced by the Donahues? How might one seek to plan around this possible problem of oppression of the minority by the majority in a close corporation (or in an LLC)? Consider the next case.

B. SHAREHOLDER AGREEMENTS IN THE CLOSE CORPORATION

GALLER v. GALLER

Supreme Court of Illinois.
32 Ill.2d 16, 203 N.E.2d 577 (1964).

[UNDERWOOD, J.] Plaintiff, Emma Galler, sued in equity for an accounting and for specific performance of an agreement made in July, 1955, between plaintiff and her husband, of one part, and defendants, Isadore A. Galler and his wife, Rose, of the other. Defendants appealed from a decree of the superior court of Cook County granting the relief prayed. The First District Appellate Court reversed the decree and denied specific performance * * *. That decision is appealed here * * *.

* * * From 1919 to 1924, Benjamin and Isadore Galler, brothers, were equal partners in the Galler Drug Company, a wholesale drug concern. In 1924 the business was incorporated under the Illinois Business Corporation Act, each owning one half of the outstanding 220 shares of stock. In 1945 each contracted to sell 6 shares to an employee, Rosenberg,

at a price of $10,500 for each block of 6 shares, payable within 10 years. They guaranteed to repurchase the shares if Rosenberg's employment were terminated, and further agreed that if they sold their shares, Rosenberg would receive the same price per share as that paid for the brothers' shares. Rosenberg was still indebted for the 12 shares in July, 1955, and continued to make payments on account even after Benjamin Galler died in 1957 and after the institution of this action by Emma Galler in 1959. Rosenberg was not involved in this litigation either as a party or as a witness, and in July of 1961, prior to the time that the master in chancery hearings were concluded, defendants Isadore and Rose Galler purchased the 12 shares from Rosenberg. A supplemental complaint was filed by the plaintiff, Emma Galler, asserting an equitable right to have 6 of the 12 shares transferred to her and offering to pay the defendants one half of the amount that the defendants paid Rosenberg. The parties have stipulated that pending disposition of the instant case, these shares will not be voted or transferred. For approximately one year prior to the entry of the decree by the chancellor in July of 1962, there were no outstanding minority shareholder interests.

In March, 1954, Benjamin and Isadore, on the advice of their accountant, decided to enter into an agreement for the financial protection of their immediate families and to assure their families, after the death of either brother, equal control of the corporation. In June, 1954, while the agreement was in the process of preparation by an attorney-associate of the accountant, Benjamin suffered a heart attack. Although he resumed his business duties some months later, he was again stricken in February, 1955, and thereafter was unable to return to work. During his brother's illness, Isadore asked the accountant to have the shareholders' agreement put in final form in order to protect Benjamin's wife, and this was done by another attorney employed in the accountant's office. On a Saturday night in July, 1955, the accountant brought the agreement to Benjamin's home, and 6 copies of it were executed there by the two brothers and their wives. The accountant then collected all signed copies of the agreement and informed the parties that he was taking them for safe keeping. Between the execution of the agreement in July, 1955, and Benjamin's death in December, 1957, the agreement was not modified. Benjamin suffered a stroke late in July, 1955, and on August 2, 1955, Isadore and the accountant and a notary public brought to Benjamin for signature two powers of attorney which were retained by the accountant after Benjamin executed them with Isadore as a witness. The plaintiff did not read the powers and she never had them. One of the powers authorized the transfer of Benjamin's bank account to Emma and the other power enabled Emma to vote Benjamin's 104 shares. Because of the state of Benjamin's health, nothing further was said to him by any of the parties concerning the agreement. It appears from the evidence that some months after the agreement was signed, the defendants Isadore and Rose Galler and their son, the defendant, Aaron Galler, sought to have the agreements destroyed. The evidence is undisputed that defendants had decided prior to Benjamin's death they would not honor the agreement, but never disclosed their intention to plaintiff or her husband.

On July 21, 1956, Benjamin executed an instrument creating a trust naming his wife as trustee. The trust covered, among other things, the 104 shares of Galler Drug Company stock and the stock certificates were endorsed by Benjamin and delivered to Emma. When Emma presented the certificates to defendants for transfer into her name as trustee, they sought to have Emma abandon the 1955 agreement or enter into some kind of a noninterference agreement as a price for the transfer of the shares. Finally, in September, 1956, after Emma had refused to abandon the shareholders' agreement, she did agree to permit defendant Aaron to become president for one year and agreed that she would not interfere with the business during that year. The stock was then reissued in her name as trustee. During the year 1957 while Benjamin was still alive, Emma tried many times to arrange a meeting with Isadore to discuss business matters but he refused to see her.

Shortly after Benjamin's death, Emma went to the office and demanded the terms of the 1955 agreement be carried out. Isadore told her that anything she had to say could be said to Aaron, who then told her that his father would not abide by the agreement. He offered a modification of the agreement by proposing the salary continuation payment but without her becoming a director. When Emma refused to modify the agreement and sought enforcement of its terms, defendants refused and this suit followed.

During the last few years of Benjamin's life both brothers drew an annual salary of $42,000. Aaron, whose salary was $15,000 as manager of the warehouse prior to September, 1956, has since the time that Emma agreed to his acting as president drawn an annual salary of $20,000. In 1957, 1958, and 1959 a $40,000 annual dividend was paid. Plaintiff has received her proportionate share of the dividend.

The July, 1955, agreement in question here, entered into between Benjamin, Emma, Isadore and Rose, recites that Benjamin and Isadore each own 47 1/2% of the issued and outstanding shares of the Galler Drug Company, an Illinois corporation, and that Benjamin and Isadore desired to provide income for the support and maintenance of their immediate families. No reference is made to the shares then being purchased by Rosenberg. The essential features of the contested portions of the agreement are substantially as set forth in the opinion of the Appellate Court: (2) that the bylaws of the corporation will be amended to provide for a board of four directors; that the necessary quorum shall be three directors; and that no directors' meeting shall be held without giving ten days notice to all directors. (3) The shareholders will cast their votes for the above named persons (Isadore, Rose, Benjamin and Emma) as directors at said special meeting and at any other meeting held for the purpose of electing directors. (4, 5) In the event of the death of either brother his wife shall have the right to nominate a director in place of the decedent. (6) Certain annual dividends will be declared by the corporation. The dividend shall be $50,000 payable out of the accumulated earned surplus in excess of $500,000. If 50% of the annual net profits after taxes exceeds the minimum $50,000, then the directors shall have discretion to declare a dividend up to 50% of the annual net profits. If the net profits are less than $50,000, nevertheless the minimum $50,000 annual dividend shall be declared, providing the $500,000 surplus is maintained. * * * (9) The certificates evidencing the said shares of Benjamin Galler and Isadore Galler shall bear a legend that the shares are subject to the terms of this agreement. (10) A salary continuation agreement shall be entered into by the corporation which shall authorize the corporation upon the death of Benjamin Galler or Isadore Galler, or both, to pay a sum equal to twice the salary of such officer, payable monthly over a five-year period. Said sum shall be paid to the widow during her widowhood, but should be paid to such widow's children if the widow remarries within the five-year period. (11, 12) The parties to this agreement further agree and hereby grant to the corporation the authority to purchase, in the event of the death of either Benjamin or Isadore, so much of the stock of Galler Drug Company held by the estate as is necessary to provide sufficient funds to pay the federal estate tax, the Illinois inheritance tax and other administrative expenses of the estate. If as a result of such purchase from the estate of the decendent the amount of dividends to be received by the heirs is reduced, the parties shall nevertheless vote for directors so as to give the estate and heirs the same representation as before (2 directors out of 4, even though they own less stock), and also that the corporation pay an additional benefit payment equal to the diminution of the dividends. In the event either Benjamin or Isadore decides to sell his shares he is required to offer them first to the remaining shareholders and then to the corporation at book value, according each six months to accept the offer.

The Appellate Court found the 1955 agreement void because "the undue duration, stated purpose and substantial disregard of the provisions of the Corporation Act outweigh any considerations which might call for divisibility" and held that "the public policy of this state demands voiding this entire agreement".

While the conduct of defendants towards plaintiff was clearly inequitable, the basically controlling factor is the absence of an adverse effect upon a minority interest, together with the absence of public detriment. Since the issues here presented must be resolved in accordance with the public policy of this State as exemplified in prior decisions or pertinent statutes, it will be helpful to review the applicable case law.

Faulds v. Yates, 57 Ill. 416, decided by this court in 1870, established the general rule that the owners of the majority of the stock of a corporation have the right to select the agents for the management of the corporation. This court observed *(57 Ill. 416, 421):* "It is strange that a man can not, for honest purposes, unite with others in the protection and security of his property and rights without liability to the charge of fraud and inequity".

In *Higgins v. Lansingh, 154 Ill. 301, 357,* this court again recognized the right of majority owners of stock to combine to secure the board of directors in the management of the corporation. There, the court went further and denied the corporation and some of its stockholders the right to question the validity of an issue of preferred stock not provided for in the corporate charter, where the stockholders authorized the issue, the corporation paid dividends on it and all treated it as valid for 22 years.

In *Kantzler v. Bensinger, 214 Ill. 589,* decided in 1905, the issue of statutory violation was raised, and this court again followed *Faulds v. Yates*, emphasizing and quoting the following (p. 598):

> "In *Faulds v. Yates, 57 Ill. 416,* it was objected that an agreement between certain persons owning a majority of the stock of a corporation that they would elect the directors and manage the business was against public policy. There were other stockholders, but they made no objection. The court upheld the agreement, and on page 420 said: 'There was no fraud in the agreement which has been so bitterly assailed in the argument. There was nothing unlawful in it. There was nothing which necessarily affected the rights and interests of the minority. Three persons owning a majority of the stock had the unquestioned right to combine, and thus secure the board of directors and the management of the property. Corporations are governed by the republican principle that the whole are bound by the acts of the majority, when the acts conform to the law of their creation. The co-operation, then, of these parties in the election of the officers of the company, and their agreement not to buy or sell stock except for their joint benefit, cannot properly be characterized as dishonest and violative of the rights of others and in contravention of public policy. * * * The agreement complained of was entered into by Faulds and his partners. The shareholders whom he is so solicitous to defend and protect have not complained. He cannot invoke their shield to fight imaginary wrongs. The transaction which he, through his counsel, denounces as fraudulent and nefarious was conceived and consummated by him as much as by his partners. Every motive which could influence a man for good should have prompted him to silence. If this combination was fraudulent and intended for bad purposes, the stockholders who are in a minority and who may have suffered have ample redress. We prefer to listen to them before any decision as to their wrongs.' * * *."

Again, in 1913, this court in *Venner v. Chicago City Railway Co. 258 Ill. 523, 539,* followed the *Faulds* case and said:

> "There is no statute of this State which prohibits a trust of the stock of a corporation for the purpose of controlling its management. There is no rule of public policy in this State which prohibits the com-

bination of the owners of the majority of the stock of a corporation for the purpose of controlling the corporation. On the contrary, it has been expressly held that a contract by the owners of more than one-half of the shares of stock of a corporation to elect the directors of the corporation so as to secure the management of its property, to ballot among themselves for directors and officers if they could not agree, to cast their vote as a unit as the majority should decide so as to control the election, and not to buy or sell stock except for their joint benefit is not dishonest, violative of the rights of others or in contravention of public policy * * *."

In *Thompson v. Thompson Carnation Co. 279 Ill. 54, 58,* we again approved a contract by which the owners of a majority of stock agreed to vote for certain persons for directors so as to secure to themselves the control and management of the corporation and held such an agreement not to be illegal or void so long as no fraud is committed on the corporation or wrong done to the other stockholders. In this case, as in the others, this court found that no fraud was practiced or intended to be practiced by the contract in question, and insofar as its validity was assailed on those grounds it was sustained as a valid exercise of the right of contract.

In *Schumann–Heink v. Folsom, 328 Ill. 321, 330,* we said:

"In considering whether any contract is against public policy it should be remembered that it is to the interests of the public that persons should not be unnecessarily restricted in their freedom to make their own contracts. Agreements are not held to be void, as being contrary to public policy, unless they be clearly contrary to what the constitution, the statutes or the decisions of the courts have declared to be the public policy or unless they be manifestly injurious to the public welfare. Courts must act with care in extending those rules which say that a given contract is void because against public policy, since if there be one thing more than any other which public policy requires, it is that men of full age and competent understanding shall have the utmost liberty of contract, and that their contracts, when entered into fairly and voluntarily, shall be held sacred and shall be enforced by the courts."

Later, we said in *Electrical Contractors' Ass'n v. Schulman Electric Co. 391 Ill. 333, 339:*

"The power by which courts may declare a contract void as against public policy is far-reaching and it is to be exercised only when it clearly appears that it is contrary to a constitutional mandate, a statute, judicial decisions, or that it manifestly tends to injure the public in some way. * * * The question must be determined from the terms of the contract itself and, in considering the ends to which it leads, the courts are not privileged to ascribe illegal purposes where there is nothing in the contract from which such a conclusion may be reasonably drawn. * * *"

The power to invalidate the agreements on the grounds of public policy is so far reaching and so easily abused that it should be called into action to set aside or annul the solemn engagement of parties dealing on equal terms only in cases where the corrupt or dangerous tendency clearly and unequivocally appears upon the face of the agreement itself or is the necessary inference from the matters which are expressed, and the only apparent exception to this general rule is to be found in those cases where the agreement, though fair and unobjectionable on its face, is a part of a corrupt scheme and is made to disguise the real nature of the transaction. * * *

Defendants have referred us to cases in other jurisdictions and the Appellate Courts of this State, particularly *Odman v. Oleson, 319 Mass. 24, 64 N.E.2d 439,* and *Teich v. Kaufman, 174 Ill. App. 306.* Neither is persuasive, for *Odman* exemplifies the public policy of Massachusetts whose courts, while not holding agreements such as we have here invalid *per se*, have not relaxed their requirements of strict statutory compliance when dealing with close corporations, at least where all the stockholders have not signed the agreement in question. * * * In any event, decisions setting forth the public policies of other jurisdictions will not be followed if not harmonious with the judicially declared public policy of Illinois. * * * *Teich* held the majority agreement void as benefitting the individual interests of the major shareholders at corporate expense and to the detriment of the minority who had no knowledge of the agreement.

At this juncture it should be emphasized that we deal here with a so-called close corporation. Various attempts at definition of the close corporation have been made. * * * For our purposes, a close corporation is one in which the stock is held in a few hands, or in a few families, and wherein it is not at all, or only rarely, dealt in by buying or selling. * * * Moreover, it should be recognized that shareholder agreements similar to that in question here are often, as a practical consideration, quite necessary for the protection of those financially interested in the close corporation. While the shareholder of a public-issue corporation may readily sell his shares on the open market should management fail to use, in his opinion, sound business judgment, his counterpart of the close corporation often has a large total of his entire capital invested in the business and has no ready market for his shares should he desire to sell. He feels, understandably, that he is more than a mere investor and that his voice should be heard concerning all corporate activity. Without a shareholder agreement, specifically enforceable by the courts, insuring him a modicum of control, a large minority shareholder might find himself at the mercy of an oppressive or unknowledgeable majority. Moreover, as in the case at bar, the shareholders of a close corporation are often also the directors and officers thereof. With substantial shareholding interests abiding in each member of the board of directors, it is often quite impossible to secure, as in the large public-issue corporation, independent board judgment free from personal motivations concerning corporate policy. For these and other reasons too voluminous to enumerate here, often the only sound basis for protection is afforded by a lengthy, detailed shareholder agreement securing the rights and obligations of all concerned. * * *

* * * [T]here has been a definite * * * trend toward eventual judicial treatment of the close corporation as *sui generis*. Several shareholder-director agreements that have technically "violated" the letter of the Business Corporation Act have nevertheless been upheld in the light of the existing practical circumstances, *i.e.*, no apparent public injury, no apparent injury to a minority interest, and no apparent prejudice to creditors. However, we have thus far not attempted to limit these decisions as applicable only to close corporations and have seemingly implied that general considerations regarding judicial supervision of all corporate behavior apply.

The practical result of this series of cases, while liberally giving legal efficacy to particular agreements in special circumstances notwithstanding literal "violations" of statutory corporate law, has been to inject much doubt and uncertainty into the thinking of the bench and corporate bar of Illinois concerning shareholder agreements. * * *

It is therefore necessary, we feel, to discuss the instant case with the problems peculiar to the close corporation particularly in mind.

It would admittedly facilitate judicial supervision of corporate behavior if a strict adherence to the provisions of the Business Corporation Act were required in all cases without regard to the practical exigencies peculiar to the close corporation. * * * However, courts have long ago quite realistically, we feel, relaxed their attitudes concerning statutory compliance when dealing with close corporate behavior, permitting "slight deviations" from corporate "norms" in order to give legal efficacy to common business practice. See, *e.g., Clark v. Dodge, 269 N.Y. 410, 199 N.E. 641; Benintendi v. Kenton Hotel, 294 N.Y. 112, 60 N.E.2d 829* (dissenting opinion subsequently legislatively approved.) This attitude is illustrated by the following language in *Clark* v. *Dodge*:

> "Public policy, the intention of the Legislature, detriment to the corporation, are phrases which in this connection [the court was discussing a shareholder-director agreement whereby the directors pledged themselves to vote for certain people as officers of the corporation] mean little. Possible harm to bona fide purchasers of stock or to creditors or to stockholding minorities have more substance; but such harms are absent in many instances. If the enforcement of a particular contract damages nobody—not even, in any perceptible degree, the public—one sees no reason for holding it illegal, even though it impinges slightly on the broad provisions of [the relevant statute providing that the business of a corporation shall be managed by its board of directors.]. Damage suffered or threatened is a logical and practical test, and has come to be the one generally adopted by the courts. * * * "

Clark v. Dodge, 199 N.E. 641, 642.

Again,

"As the parties to the action are the complete owners of the corporation, there is no reason why the exercise of the power and discretion of the directors cannot be controlled by valid agreement between themselves, provided that the interests of creditors are not affected."

Clark v. Dodge, 119 N.E. 641, 643 * * *.

* * * One [law review] article [on this subject] concludes with the following:

"New needs compel fresh formulation of corporate 'norms'. There is no reason why mature men should not be able to adapt the statutory form to the structure they want, so long as they do not endanger other stockholders, creditors, or the public, or violate a clearly mandatory provision of the corporation laws. In a typical close corporation the stockholders' agreement is usually the result of careful deliberation among all initial investors. In the large public-issue corporation, on the other hand, the 'agreement' represented by the corporate charter is not consciously agreed to by the investors; they have no voice in its formulation, and very few ever read the certificate of incorporation. Preservation of the corporate norms may there be necessary for the protection of the public investors."

Hornstein, "Stockholders' Agreements in the Closely Held Corporation", *59 Yale L. Journal, 1040, 1056.*

This court has recognized * * * the significant conceptual differences between the close corporation and its public-issue counterpart in, among other cases, *Kantzler v. Benzinger, 214 Ill. 589,* where an agreement quite similar to the one under attack here was upheld. Where, as in *Kantzler* and here, no injury to a minority interest appears, no fraud or apparent injury to the public or creditors is present, and no clearly prohibitory statutory language is violated, we can see no valid reason for precluding the parties from reaching any arrangements concerning the management of the corporation which are agreeable to all.

Perhaps, as has been vociferously advanced, a separate comprehensive statutory scheme governing the close corporation would best serve here. * * * Some states have enacted legislation dealing specifically with the close corporation. * * *

At any rate, however, the courts can no longer fail to expressly distinguish between the close and public-issue corporation when confronted with problems relating to either. What we do here is to illuminate this problem—before the bench, corporate bar, and the legislature, in the context of a particular fact situation. To do less would be to shirk our responsibility, to do more would, perhaps be to invade the province of the legislative branch.

We now, in the light of the foregoing, turn to specific provisions of the 1955 agreement.

The Appellate Court correctly found many of the contractual provisions free from serious objection, and we need not prolong this opinion with a discussion of them here. That court did, however, find difficulties in the stated purpose of the agreement as it relates to its duration, the election of certain persons to specific offices for a number of years, the requirement for the mandatory declaration of stated dividends (which the Appellate Court held invalid), and the salary continuation agreement.

Since the question as to the duration of the agreement is a principal source of controversy, we shall consider it first. The parties provided no specific termination date, and while the agreement concludes with a paragraph that its terms "shall be binding upon and shall inure to the benefits of" the legal representatives, heirs and assigns of the parties, this clause is, we believe, intended to be operative only as long as one of the parties is living. It further provides that it shall be so construed as to carry out its purposes, and we believe these must be determined from a consideration of the agreement as a whole. Thus viewed, a fair construction is that its purposes were accomplished at the death of the survivor of the parties. While these life spans are not precisely ascertainable, and the Appellate Court noted Emma Galler's life expectancy at her husband's death was 26.9 years, we are aware of no statutory or public policy provision against stockholder's agreements which would invalidate this agreement on that ground. * * * While defendants argue that the public policy evinced by the legislative restrictions upon the duration of voting trust agreements (Ill. Rev. Stat. 1963, chap. 32, par. 157.30a) should be applied here, this agreement is not a voting trust, but as pointed out by the dissenting justice in the Appellate Court, is a straight contractual voting control agreement which does not divorce voting rights from stock ownership. That the policy against agreements in which stock ownership and voting rights are separated, indicated in *Luthy v. Ream, 270 Ill. 170,* is inapplicable to voting control agreements was emphasized in [a prior case] wherein a control agreement was upheld as not attempting to separate ownership and voting power. While limiting voting trusts in 1947 to a maximum duration of 10 years, the legislature has indicated no similar policy regarding straight voting agreements although these have been common since prior to 1870. In view of the history of decisions of this court generally upholding, in the absence of fraud or prejudice to minority interests or public policy, the right of stockholders to agree among themselves as to the manner in which their stock will be voted, we do not regard the period of time within which this agreement may remain effective as rendering the agreement unenforceable.

The clause that provides for the election of certain persons to specified offices for a period of years likewise does not require invalidation. In *Kantzler v. Benzinger, 214 Ill. 589,* this court upheld an agreement entered into by all the stockholders providing that certain parties would be elected to the offices of the corporation for a fixed period. In *Faulds v. Yates, 57 Ill. 416,* we upheld a similar agreement among the majority stockholders of a corporation, notwithstanding the existence of a minority which was not before the court complaining thereof. * * *

We turn next to a consideration of the effect of the stated purpose of the agreement upon its validity. The pertinent provision is: "The said Benjamin A. Galler and Isadore A. Galler desire to provide income for the support and maintenance of their immediate families." Obviously, there is no evil inherent in a contract entered into for the reason that the persons originating the terms desired to so arrange their property as to provide post-death support for those dependent upon them. Nor does the fact that the subject property is corporate stock alter the situation so long as there exists no detriment to minority stock interests, creditors or other public injury. It is, however, contended by defendants that the methods provided by the agreement for implementation of the stated purpose are, as a whole, violative of the Business Corporation Act (Ill. Rev. Stat. 1963, chap. 32, pars. 157.28, 157.30a, 157.33, 157.34, 157.41) to such an extent as to render it void *in toto.*

The terms of the dividend agreement require a minimum annual dividend of $50,000, but this duty is limited by the subsequent provision that it shall be operative only so long as an earned surplus of $500,000 is maintained. It may be noted that in 1958, the year prior to commencement of this litigation, the corporation's net earnings after taxes amounted to $202,759 while its earned surplus was $1,543,270, and this was increased in 1958 to $1,680,079 while earnings were $172,964. The minimum earned surplus requirement is designed for the protection of the corporation and its creditors, and we take no exception to the contractual dividend requirements as thus restricted. * * *

The salary continuation agreement is a common feature, in one form or another, of corporate executive employment. It requires that the widow should receive a total benefit, payable monthly over a five-year period, aggregating twice the amount paid her deceased husband in one year. This requirement was likewise limited for the protection of the corporation by being contingent upon the payments being income tax-deductible by the corporation. The charge made in those cases which have considered the validity of payments to the widow of an officer and shareholder in a corporation is that a gift of its property by a noncharitable corporation is in violation of the rights of its shareholders and *ultra vires.* Since there are no shareholders here other than the parties to the contract, this objection is not here applicable, and its effect, as limited, upon the corporation is not so prejudicial as to require its invalidation.

* * *

* * * The cause is remanded to the circuit court of Cook County with directions to proceed in accordance herewith.

* * *

NOTES AND QUESTIONS

1. What do you make of the "shareholder agreement" entered into by the Gallers? Note that the appellate court voided the agreement. Do you understand why it did so? Why did the Supreme Court disagree? Do you understand how the shareholder agreement is a device that can alleviate the potential problems of the close corporation? An analogue to the shareholder agreement is the "operating agreement" now often employed for LLC's. See, e.g., Sandra K. Miller, "The Role of the Court in Balancing Contractual Freedom with the Need for Mandatory Constraints on Opportunistic and Abusive Conduct in the LLC," 152 U.Pa. L. Rev. 1609 (2004).

2. The key provision of the shareholder agreement in this case was probably the one that fixed the selection of the directors of the corporation. Why might this be against public policy? There is a line of close corporation cases in New York that suggests that the shareholders may not enter into an agreement that they will manage the corporation, or certain aspects of its operation, in a manner that "sterilizes" the board of directors, see, e.g. McQuade v. Stoneham, 263 N.Y. 323, 189 N.E. 234 (1934), Clark v. Dodge, 269 N.Y. 410, 199 N.E. 641 (1936). Why do you suppose that is? Compare § 350 and § 351 of the Delaware corporations code, *infra*, which permit shareholders of a close corporation to enter into agreements restricting the operation of the Board of Directors, or even to dispense with the Board altogether and manage the corporation themselves. Is this wise? Does Homer's story (told in Book XII of the Odyssey) of Odysseus and the Sirens help suggest the role directors might play even in a close corporation?

3. Note that the *Galler v. Galler* Court indicates that the agreement before it is not a "voting trust," and thus does not conflict with the Illinois statutory policy limiting voting trusts to ten years. What is a "voting trust," and why might one be concerned with voting trusts that are not limited in duration?

> A voting trust generally is a voluntary arrangement in which several stockholders of a corporation pool their stock into a trust for a specified period of time in order to control a corporation. All of the stock in the trust is voted by a third party trustee. Sometimes, the voting instructions for the trustee are spelled out in the trust document; other times, the trustee is given discretion concerning how to vote. Additionally, the trust beneficiaries may give voting instructions to the trustee. The primary purpose of the trust is to promote continuity of ownership and corporate direction for a period of time.

Richard L. Epling, Fun With Non-Voting Stock, 10 Bank. Dev. J. 17, n.6 (1993). A "voting trust" can also be created by a sole shareholder either to satisfy creditors (who may take stock as collateral and wish to vote it the better to secure their debt) or "to vest control of his business in managers." Melvin Aron Eisenberg, Corporations and Other Business Organizations: Cases and Materials 265 (Concise 8th ed., 2000). Can you discern a difference in the *Galler* court's attitude toward voting trusts and shareholder agreements? Is there a difference in your attitude toward the two?

4.   You will have noticed that the court in *Galler* suggested it might be a good thing for the Illinois legislature to pass special provisions for dealing with the close corporation. "In 1977, Illinois adopted The Close Corporation Act [ILL. REV. STAT. ch. 32, PP1201–1216 (1983)] which authorizes share-holders' agreements for the conduct of the affairs of corporations qualifying as close corporations under that Act. That statutory provision is consistent with *Galler* in that the statutorily-authorized agreement must be between all shareholders of the close corporation and the statutory grant of validity applies only 'as between the parties' to the agreement, without purporting to deal with the question of validity when third-party rights are involved." James M. Van Vliet, Jr., The New Illinois Business Corporation Act Needs More Work, 61 Chi.-Kent. L. Rev. 1, 30 (1985). There seems to be a trend for state legislatures to treat the special problems of the close corporation by spe-cial statutory provisions. For an evaluation of these efforts, see, e.g. George J. Seidel, Close Corporation Law: Michigan, Delaware, and the Model Act, 11 Del. J. Corp. L. 383 (1987). For some criticism of the Illinois statutory approach, especially insofar as it permits dissolution of the close corporation to prevent minority shareholder oppression, see Timothy J. Storm, "Remedies for Oppression of Non-Controlling Shareholders in Illinois Closely-Held Cor-porations: An Idea Whose Time Has Gone," 33 Loy. U. Chi. L.J. 379 (2002). For a more favorable evaluation of Illinois Law regarding close corporations, see, e.g., William R. Quinlan & John F. Kennedy, FAMILY BUSINESS LEGAL & FINANCIAL ADVISOR CONFERENCE: The Rights and Remedies of Shareholders in Closely Held Corporations Under Illinois Law, 29 Loy. U. Chi. L.J. 585 (1998).

It is to the problem of oppression in the close corporation context, and appropriate remedies, that we next turn.

C.   OPPRESSION IN THE CLOSE CORPORATION

BAKER v. COMMERCIAL BODY BUILDERS, INC.

Supreme Court of Oregon.
264 Ore. 614, 507 P.2d 387 (1973).

[Tongue, J.] This is a suit under *ORS 57.595* by the owners of 49% of the stock in a "close corporation" to compel a dissolution of the corporation for alleged "illegal, oppressive and fraudulent" conduct by defendants ... as directors of the corporation and for "misapplication and waste" of its assets.[10]

---

10.   ORS 57.595 provides, in part, as follows:

"(1) The circuit courts shall have full power to liquidate the assets and business of a corpora-tion:

"(a) In an action by a shareholder when it is established:

" * * *

"(B) That the acts of the directors or those in control of the corporation are illegal, oppressive or fraudulent; or

Plaintiffs appeal from a decree dismissing their complaint, based on findings by the trial court that "[p]laintiffs have not established by the required quantum of evidence, that any acts of the defendants ... as directors, have been or now are illegal, oppressive or fraudulent" or "any showing of circumstances which would justify the equitable relief prayed for." We affirm.

* * *

1. SUMMARY OF EVIDENCE.

a. *Organization of corporation. Subsequent purchase of stock by Baker. Original agreement between parties.*

Defendant Commercial Body Builders, Inc., ("Commercial") was originally organized in August 1966 by defendants Charles Siler and his wife as a family corporation. Its purpose was to engage in the construction of truck bodies, lift gates, and related truck equipment—a business with which Siler was thoroughly familiar and experienced.

About a year later, in 1967, at the suggestion of defendant Siler, plaintiff Baker invested $14,210 in the corporation. Baker was not familiar with the business, but was engaged in the insurance and real estate business. At that time an additional 100 shares of stock were issued and Baker and his wife became owners of 98 shares of the corporation's stock, while Siler and his wife retained ownership of 102 shares. * * * Baker also signed a promissory note for $5,000, payable to Siler, with no time specified for payment, but with payment to be made from the "proceeds" of future bonuses to be paid to employees, including Baker.[11]

At the same time, Siler was elected president and his wife treasurer of the corporation, while Baker was elected vice-president and his wife secretary. Monthly salaries were also established, including a salary of $800 to Siler, $200 to his wife, and $100 to Baker. Siler, however, spent full time in the business and his wife worked approximately six hours each business day as bookkeeper, while it was agreed that Baker would spend one day each week at the office. At that time, however, he apparently devoted at least part of that day to the transaction of his insurance and real estate business. As stated by Baker, there was no "formal understanding" what he was to do for Commercial, but the monthly salary of

---

"* * *

"(D) That the corporate assets are being misapplied or wasted."

ORS 57.600 provides, in part, as follows:

"(1) In proceedings to liquidate the assets and business of a corporation the court shall have power to issue injunctions, to appoint a receiver or receivers * * * with such powers and duties as the court, from time to time, may direct, and to take such other proceedings as may be requisite to preserve the corporate assets wherever situated, and carry on the business of the corporation until a full hearing can be had."

11. The reason for this note, according to Siler, was that because he and his wife had started the business he was not willing to let Baker come in on the basis under which he would "match dollar for dollar" what Siler and his wife had "put in."

$100 was used by him to pay off the mortgage loan by which he raised the money to purchase the stock.

Shortly afterwards, a "buy-sell" agreement was prepared by Baker's attorney and was signed by the parties. By its terms, if either party desired to sell his stock he was required to first offer it to the other party "at the same price as offered on the market or at the book value of said shares as computed by the accounting methods regularly recognized for the computation of book value of corporate stock, whichever is less."

b. *Two profitable years of operation. Increase in salaries and bonuses.*

At the end of the following fiscal year on June 30, 1968, the corporation showed a profit of $9,743.90. At that time the following bonuses were paid: Siler, $1,750; Baker, $1,000, and Mrs. Siler, $500. As of the same date salaries were increased as follows: Siler to $1,000 per month, his wife to $350 per month, and Baker to $250 per month.

Similarly, at the end of the next fiscal year on June 30, 1969, the corporation showed a further profit of $19,712.16. According to Siler, however, as of that date Baker, although "doing a satisfactory job," was not making any contacts or sales. Nevertheless, the following additional bonuses were then paid: Siler, $2,625; Baker, $1,500, and Mrs. Siler, $750. On October 6, 1969, Siler's salary was also increased to $1,500, as of July 1, 1969, with no corresponding increase to Baker or to Mrs. Siler. To provide for future expansion, the corporation also loaned $1,370.58 each to Siler and to Baker to provide funds for use as a down payment for the purchase of adjacent property. That property was then apparently purchased by them as partners, under the name of Dorpat Investment Co., and was leased to the corporation.

c. *Termination of Baker and negotiations for purchase of his stock.*

During the fiscal year 1969–1970, according to Siler, business was "terrible" and although sales increased by $50,000, labor costs increased even more. During that same year, as a result of the organization of Dorpat and the leasing of larger quarters from it, payments for rent, insurance, taxes, "moving in" expenses, and other items were increased. The profit for the fiscal year ending June 30, 1970, dropped to $269.52.

Also, according to both Siler and Baker, the relationship between them deteriorated in early 1970. Siler testified that Baker made only one small sale while he was with the company and that he was not "getting out and calling on the trade" or spending as much time as he should for the company.[12] Baker testified, however, that Siler told him not to contact large companies, such as the telephone company, because any resulting orders would be too large for the small business to handle and that rela-

---

12. Siler also testified that he was upset at Baker because Baker twice purchased new sets of tires for the company car which he rented from the company, at a somewhat nominal rental, and that he paid more for the tires than Siler could get them for and charged them to the corporation, contrary to instructions that such purchases were to be "cleared" through Siler.

tions deteriorated because Siler wanted him to sell out and because Siler thought that a Mr. Ahern could do more for the business than Baker could.

In early May 1970, Mr. Ahern tried to talk to Baker about purchasing his stock, but Baker refused to talk to him about a price for the sale of his stock. According to Baker, he was then offered $20,000 for his stock by Siler, who "intimated" that if Baker didn't sell he would get no profits from the business.

Siler denied that statement and denied making an offer to Baker for his stock, but said that Ahern also wanted to buy Siler's stock and had offered to pay $45,000 for it, because 51% was worth much more than 49%, and that Siler told Baker that if he sold out the purchaser might operate the business in such a way that it would show no profits. Siler also testified that he told Baker, apparently on another occasion, that Ahern would pay Baker $22,500 for his stock; that he talked to Baker about that offer; that Baker said he didn't know what to do, and that he told Baker that if Baker didn't sell to Ahern, Siler was going to do so. In addition, Siler testified that he tried to get Baker to buy him out, but that Baker would not do so and would not tell Ahern whether or not he would sell out to him.

On June 25, 1970, after these negotiations failed, Baker was terminated as a salesman "because of unsatisfactory work performance." According to Siler, this was done because Baker had made no sales and because Siler decided that Baker "was not doing the company any good." On July 10, 1970, Baker and his wife were "voted out" as directors and officers. After that date no notices were sent to Baker of any further stockholders' meetings and he was not consulted by Siler thereafter about the business. Baker also testified that he was also not permitted to see the company books and that he had to get "legal redress" in order to do so. This was denied by Siler.

Also, at the meeting on July 10, 1970, Siler's salary was increased to $1,800 per month and his wife's salary was increased to $500. There were no subsequent salary increases and no bonuses were paid to Siler or to his wife, however, either at the end of the 1969–70 fiscal year or at any later date.[13]

During the period of the years from 1967 to 1970, prior to Baker's "termination," he was paid $7,975 in salary for his services for one day each week, plus $2,500 in bonuses, for a total of $10,475, not including the value of medical insurance and the use of a company car at a somewhat

---

13.   Payment of a salary to Siler of $1,800 per month had previously been recommended by the CPA engaged by the company at the time when Siler's salary was increased to $1,500. In addition, Siler justified these salary increases by the savings resulting from the elimination of Baker's salary and automobile expenses. Siler and his wife continued, as in the past, to use a company owned pickup truck and car. Baker also complained that Siler employed his own son. Siler, however, justified this by saying that he paid his son less than previously paid to the employee who was replaced by his son.

nominal rental. As previously stated, he was offered $22,500 for the stock, for which he had paid $14,210. As also previously noted, Baker also had given Siler a $5,000 note payable from the "proceeds" of the corporation, on which he subsequently paid $1,000 to Siler.

d. *Funds and services provided by corporation to Advance Hydro Wreckers, Mfg., Inc.*

In late 1970, a new corporation was organized named Advance Hydro Wreckers, Mfg., Inc. ("Hydro"). Siler was its president and was issued 30% of its stock, in return for his "ability to set the operation in motion." The remaining stock was apparently issued to Ahern, who was "to furnish the money," and to a man named Mr. Nowell, who claimed to own patents for certain wrecker equipment.

According to Siler, this corporation was organized because Commercial could not otherwise build such equipment in view of these patents. Siler did not consult Baker about the Hydro venture.

Hydro leased a portion of Commercial's unused shop space and also used Commercial's office. Prior to December 1, 1970 (when Hydro apparently acquired its own crew), the Commercial crew did work for Hydro. Commercial also furnished bookkeeping services to Hydro. As of May 1971, Hydro owed $10,700 to Commercial. Nevertheless, the Commercial financial statements for the fiscal year ending June 30, 1971, as prepared by a CPA, show a net profit of $15,772.53 and a net worth in the sum of $74,498.11, after including that profit as "retained earnings."

Hydro apparently ceased active operations after a few months and Commercial advanced $2,510 to pay a debt owed by Hydro for the purchase of a wrecker chassis. Commercial also billed $6,700 to Hydro for labor made available by the Commercial crew to build the wrecker on that chassis, which Commercial then took over in payment for these advances and was holding for sale at the time of trial. Commercial also billed Hydro for $1,500 for bookkeeping and managerial services. Hydro was also delinquent in some rental payments and at the time of trial owed a balance of approximately $5,000 to Commercial.

Although the Commercial accounts receivable increased substantially after the advent of Hydro and apparently included substantial amounts owed by Hydro, at least at one time, and although, as a result, Commercial had to borrow $7,000, and was Hydro's largest creditor, there was no direct proof that, as a result, Commercial had suffered any actual loss as of the time of trial in January 1972. As of that date it appears that Hydro had ceased active operations and that Commercial had ceased making any further "advances" to it. It also appears that Hydro then still owned some completed "wreckers," which it had for sale. In addition, Siler was apparently negotiating with Nowell to take over the assets of Hydro, including the alleged patent rights, for enough money to pay the balance owed by Hydro to Commercial.

Neither was there evidence whether Commercial made a profit or suffered a loss during the period between the end of the fiscal year on June 30, 1971, and at the time of trial in January 1972. According to Siler, Hydro did not compete with Commercial and the Commercial crew worked for Hydro during "slack periods," so as to keep the crew busy, rather than lay off men and risk losing them. Also, Baker testified on trial that he presumed that the last financial statements, which were prepared by a CPA and showed a net worth of $74,498, were accurate and that the corporation was worth more at the time of trial than when he was "terminated" in June 1970.

Indeed, at the conclusion of the trial plaintiffs' attorney stated that his "calculation [based upon that same amount] is that at the present time the book value of 49% is worth $36,504.07" and that was the amount for which plaintiffs demanded judgment in the trial court as the "value of their stock," and as an alternative to a forced dissolution of the corporation.

2. *Plaintiffs' contentions—Browning v. C & C Plywood Corp.*

Plaintiffs' primary contentions are: (1) that the trial court erred when it failed to find that the conduct of defendants Siler was "oppressive" within the meaning of *ORS 57.595*, as construed by this court in *Browning v. C & C Plywood Corp., 248 Or. 574, 434 P.2d 339 (1967),* and (2) that the trial court should have used its equitable powers to provide a remedy even if it felt that those provided in *ORS 57.595* and *57.600* were inappropriate.

Plaintiffs say that this court formerly subscribed to the "robber baron" theory of corporation law to the effect that the majority stockholders who control the operation of a corporation can do "anything," including a "squeeze out" of minority stockholders, so long as they break no specific laws and commit no actual fraud and that they owe no fiduciary duty to minority stockholders, citing *McMunn v. ML & H Lumber, 247 Or. 319, 429 P.2d 798 (1967),* and *Jackson v. Nicolai–Neppach Co., 219 Or. 560, 348 P.2d 9 (1959),* as our most recent decisions "reiterating the old 'robber baron' theory."

Plaintiffs also say that in *Browning v. C & C Plywood Corp., supra,* this court "modified" that "line of cases in Oregon" and "adopted the modern rule expressed in O'Neal," citing 2 O'Neal, Close Corporations (1971 ed) 43–45, § 8.07, to the effect that court decisions are "outmoded" which allow a "squeeze out" or "freeze out," including one accomplished by the following "form of conduct":

> " * * * The shareholder, director, officers refuse to declare dividends but provide high compensation for themselves and otherwise enjoy to the fullest the 'patronage' which corporate control entails, leaving minority shareholders who do not hold corporate office with the choice of getting little or no return on their investments for an indefinite period of time or selling out to the majority shareholders at whatever price they will offer * * *."

In *Browning* the "squeeze out" was accomplished by what is recognized in O'Neal, *supra* (at 43), as an entirely different "form of conduct." Thus, in that case the majority increased the amount of corporate stock, with pre-emptive rights to existing stockholders to participate in the purchase of such stock in an amount proportionate to the percentage of their previous stock ownership in the corporation. This court found, however, that this was done with knowledge that plaintiff, who then owned a 32% stock interest, would be financially unable to purchase that percentage of the newly issued stock and was done with the purpose of eliminating his interest in the corporation and in such a manner as to reduce that interest from 32% to 1%.

Although the majority opinion in *Browning* (at p. 581) cited O'Neal, *supra*, as providing "the best analysis of the few cases that are relevant to the question at hand," it did not embrace the proposals by O'Neal to the extent implied by the plaintiffs in this case. Indeed, the only further reference to O'Neal was as follows (at p 581):

> " * * * [t]he authors examine the reluctance of the courts to interfere in intra-corporate disputes but also find that courts have given relief when the purpose of the increased stock issue is only for the benefit of the majority and serves no corporate purpose. * * * "

It is true that in *Browning* this court, instead of decreeing a dissolution of the corporation, remanded the case to the trial court with instructions to determine the feasibility of alternative relief under which plaintiff would be permitted to purchase additional stock in an amount sufficient to retain his 32% interest, to be paid for, in part, by credit for unpaid salary or by an award of damages.

In so holding, however, this court in *Browning* neither cited nor overruled previous decisions * * * in which the court, after reviewing the history of *ORS 57.595*, rejected the view that "would permit dissolution whenever the jurisdictional facts are proven" * * * and held (at p. 587) that in a suit under *ORS 57.595* (as in this case) the court is not required to dissolve a corporation upon proof of a deadlock between its stockholders * * * but that in such a suit the court may consider the equities of the individual case, recognizing that dissolution is a harsh remedy, and that in such cases courts of equity retain the discretion whether to grant or refuse equitable relief. * * *

We still subscribe to these views. In doing so, however, we do not mean to approve what plaintiff refers to as the "robber baron" theory of corporate operation, much less to give approval to "squeeze out" or "freeze out" tactics in "close" corporations.

3. *What is "oppressive" conduct for the purposes of ORS 57.595.*

In considering the meaning and application of the term "oppressive" conduct it is first to be noted that by the very terms of *ORS 57.595* conduct need not be fraudulent or illegal to be "oppressive" within the meaning of that statute. * * *

* * * [P]erhaps the most widely quoted definitions are that "oppressive conduct" for the purposes of such a statute is:

" 'burdensome, harsh and wrongful conduct; a lack of probity and fair dealing in the affairs of a company to the prejudice of some of its members; or a visual departure from the standards of fair dealing, and a violation of fair play on which every shareholder who entrusts his money to a company is entitled to rely.' " * * *[14]

We agree, however, that the question of what is "oppressive" conduct by those in control of a "close" corporation as its majority stockholders is closely related to what we agree to be the fiduciary duty of a good faith and fair dealing owed by them to its minority stockholders. * * *

Thus, an abuse of corporate position for private gain at the expense of the stockholders is "oppressive" conduct. * * * Or the plundering of a "close" corporation by the siphoning off of profits by excessive salaries or bonus payments and the operation of the business for the sole benefit of the majority of the stockholders, to the detriment of the minority stockholders, would constitute such "oppressive" conduct as to authorize a dissolution of the corporation under the terms of *ORS 57.595.* * * *

On the other hand, it has been said that a single act in breach of such a fiduciary duty may not constitute such "oppressive" conduct as to authorize the dissolution of a corporation unless extremely serious in nature * * * and that even a continuing course of "oppressive" conduct may not be sufficient for that purpose unless it appears that, as a result, there has been a disproportionate loss to the minority * * * or that those in control of the corporation are so incorrigible that they can no longer be trusted to manage it fairly in the interests of its stockholders. * * *

In other words, although a showing of "imminent disaster" is not required, liquidation is not available upon a showing of mere vague apprehensions of possible future mischief or injury or to extricate minority stockholders from an investment that turns out to be a bad bargain. * * * We also reject the concept that a "close corporation" is like a partnership to the extent that a minority stockholder should have the same right as a partner to demand a dissolution of the business upon substantially the same showing as may be sufficient for the dissolution of a partnership. * * * After all, the remedy of a forced dissolution of a corporation may equally be "oppressive" * * * to the majority stockholders.

It has also been said that the decision by a court whether or not to require dissolution of a corporation for "oppressive" conduct requires an "appraisal of the future" of the corporation and that if the future appears to hold "no hope" or if the majority is "incorrigible" dissolution may be an appropriate remedy. * * *

---

14. Comment, 1965 Duke LJ 128, 134, quoting from Scottish Co-op. Wholesale Soc'y, Ltd. v. Meyer, [1958] 3 All ER 66, 71, 86 (HL) and Elder v. Elder & Watson, Ltd., [1952] Sess Cas 49, 55. * * *

In any event * * * while a showing of "oppressive" conduct may be sufficient to confer jurisdiction upon the court under *ORS 57.595*, such a showing does not require the court to exercise the power conferred upon it by that statute to require either the dissolution of a corporation or any other alternative equitable remedy. * * * We thus come to the question of what, if any, other remedies may be appropriate in such a case as an alternative to the forced dissolution of a corporation.

4. *Remedies available for "oppressive" conduct as an alternative to dissolution.*

We have already held in *Browning, supra* (at p 582), that in a suit under *ORS 57.595* for "oppressive" conduct consisting of a "squeeze out" or "freeze out" in a "close" corporation the courts are not limited to the remedy of dissolution, but may, as an alternative, consider other appropriate equitable relief. Depending upon the facts of the case and the nature of the problem involved, various alternative remedies may be appropriate. Among those suggested are the following:

(a) The entry of an order requiring dissolution of the corporation at a specified future date, to become effective only in the event that the stockholders fail to resolve their differences prior to that date; * * *

(b) The appointment of a receiver, not for the purposes of dissolution, but to continue the operation of the corporation for the benefit of all of the stockholders, both majority and minority, until differences are resolved or "oppressive" conduct ceases; * * *

(c) The appointment of a "special fiscal agent" to report to the court relating to the continued operation of the corporation, as a protection to its minority stockholders, and the retention of jurisdiction of the case by the court for that purpose; * * *

(d) The retention of jurisdiction of the case by the court for the protection of the minority stockholders without appointment of a receiver or "special fiscal agent"; * * *

(e) The ordering of an accounting by the majority in control of the corporation for funds alleged to have been misappropriated; * * *

(f) The issuance of an injunction to prohibit continuing acts of "oppressive" conduct and which may include the reduction of salaries or bonus payments found to be unjustified or excessive; * * *

(g) The ordering of affirmative relief by the required declaration of a dividend or a reduction and distribution of capital; * * *

(h) The ordering of affirmative relief by the entry of an order requiring the corporation or a majority of its stockholders to purchase the stock of the minority stockholders at a price to be determined according to a specified formula or at a price determined by the court to be a fair and reasonable price; * * *

(i) The ordering of affirmative relief by the entry of an order permitting minority stockholders to purchase additional stock under conditions specified by the court; * * *

(j) An award of damages to minority stockholders as compensation for any injury suffered by them as the result of "oppressive" conduct by the majority in control of the corporation.* * *

5. *Analysis of plaintiffs' charges of "specific acts of wrongdoing."*

As "specific acts of wrongdoing" upon which plaintiffs rely in support of its contention that Silers' conduct amount to "oppressive" conduct, plaintiffs list the following:

> "Defendants continued to pay themselves ever increasing salaries and fringe benefits while excluding the Bakers from corporate participation. They have paid money to a debtor corporation in which they own a 1/3 interest during the time that corporation owes Defendant corporation money. They have permitted the other corporation, Advanced Hydro Wreckers, to compete with the Defendant corporation and to use the facilities of the defendant corporation without just compensation * * *. Although the business is still profitable, Defendants have siphoned all profits off into their own pockets and have excluded the Plaintiffs from any corporate benefits and have openly and flagrantly applied the 'squeeze out-freeze out'. Defendants have failed to notify the Plaintiffs of corporate meetings on occasion and have falsified the records concerning those meetings. They have at all times treated the corporation as if it were the Silers' private property with which they can do as they see fit, to the exclusion of the Bakers."

Before undertaking to reach any conclusions whether the foregoing charges constitute "oppressive" conduct within the meaning of *ORS 57.595* so serious as to require the intervention of a court of equity and, if so, what would be an appropriate remedy, reference should also be made to the following facts as they appear from the record in this case:

(a) It is true that Siler and his wife excluded Baker and his wife from "corporate participation." It must be remembered, however, that Siler had started the business before Baker came in; that Siler was probably the only one with the knowledge and experience required for the successful operation, and that his wife had also worked some six hours per day, five days a week, as bookkeeper for the business, whereas it appears that Baker only purported to spend one day per week with the business and apparently contributed little, if anything, to its successful operation other than his monetary investment. Accordingly, while he could not be properly excluded from "corporate participation" as a stockholder, it is an entirely different question whether it was "oppressive" to terminate his salary as an employee, together with his use of a company car and his medical insurance as an employee, despite the fact that Siler and his wife retained such benefits as full time employees of the corporation.

(b) While this would not justify the Silers in "siphoning all profits into their own pocket" by the payment of "ever increasing salaries and fringe benefits," to the detriment of plaintiffs, as stockholders, the evidence in this case does not support that charge. During the two-year period of Baker's active "participation," Siler's monthly salary had been increased from $800 to $1,500 and his wife's salary from $200 to $350. In addition, Siler was paid bonuses of $1,750 and $2,625 and his wife received $500 and $750 in bonuses. During the period after Baker's termination on May 31, 1970, and continuing to the date of trial in January 1972, no further bonuses were paid, although Siler's salary was increased from $1,500 to $1,800 and his wife's salary from $350 to $500 per month. There was no evidence, however, that such salaries were excessive, whether on a comparative basis, considering salaries paid to others in the same business for similar work, or on any other objective basis. * * * In addition, the financial statement for the year ending June 30, 1971, as prepared by a CPA and conceded by plaintiffs to be accurate, showed a profit of $15,772.53 during that period. Plaintiffs also concede that the net worth of the business at the time of trial was at least as much as on that date.

(c) It is also true that the Bakers, as stockholders, had a legitimate interest in the participation in profits earned by the corporation. Plaintiffs do not, however, request the court in this proceeding to require the declaration of a dividend so as to distribute profits improperly withheld by the corporation. The question whether profits must be distributed as dividends, rather than "plowed back" into a business, is by no means a simple problem. No attempt was made by plaintiffs to litigate that problem on the trial of this case and it is one that is normally litigated by a stockholder's derivative suit, rather than in a suit of this kind. * * *

(d) It may have been improvident for Siler to advance corporate funds to Hydro, in which he owned an interest. However, there was no evidence that Hydro's production of "wreckers," for which it apparently held some patents, improperly "competed" with Commercial or that Hydro was not charged "just compensation" for using corporate "facilities." It appears, however, that defendants have provided plaintiffs with the accounting demanded by them and that there is no evidence that as a result of any such conduct the corporation suffered financial loss in any ascertainable amount. On the contrary, the corporation apparently made a substantial profit during that same year. Moreover, the Hydro venture is now being liquidated and there was no evidence to indicate that it may be revived in the future.

(e) It was highly improper for defendants to prevent plaintiffs from examining the corporate records, to fail to notify plaintiffs of certain corporate meetings and to "falsify" records of such meetings so as to indicate that plaintiffs had been notified or were present. It appears, however, that plaintiffs have since been permitted to examine the records and that the meetings in question occurred in 1969 and 1970. There was also no evidence that there is any reason to believe that proper notice will not be given to them of future meetings.

(f) In evaluating plaintiffs' further charge that defendants' conduct has not only been "inequitable," but "will result in a severe financial loss" to plaintiffs, it must also be remembered that plaintiffs were offered $22,500 for their stock and that they apparently were not interested in any sale of their stock at that time. It is true this was less than what plaintiffs considered to be its book value of $36,504.07, which they demanded on trial as an alternative to a forced corporate dissolution. On the other hand, it is common knowledge that, as a practical matter, the stock acquired by one who purchases a 49% interest in a "close" family corporation, as in this case, is worth considerably less than 49% of the book value of such stock. Furthermore, considering the expenses of a receiver, as well as other expenses incurred in dissolution proceedings, as well as the fact that on such a dissolution the value of the assets of the corporation as a going concern might be destroyed, the result of a forced dissolution, as originally demanded by plaintiffs, might well result in a return to the stockholders, including plaintiffs, of considerably less than the book value of their stock.

Upon considering plaintiffs' charges of "specific acts of wrongdoing," in the light of the foregoing additional facts, we conclude that although some of the conduct of defendants Siler in 1970 was "oppressive" conduct within the meaning of *ORS 57.595*, we cannot say that the trial judge, who heard the witnesses and observed their demeanor, was in error in finding, in effect, that such conduct was not so serious as to require the relief prayed for by plaintiffs in this case and after examination of the entire record we agree with his finding to that effect. For the same reasons, we also conclude that none of the alternative equitable remedies listed above would be appropriate in this case. In that connection, it should again be noted that most of the conduct complained of by plaintiffs occurred in 1970 and did not continue after that year.

Affirmed, without costs to either party.

NOTES AND QUESTIONS

1.   Do you subscribe to the "robber baron" theory of corporation law? In your opinion was Baker "oppressed" by the Silers? What does constitute "oppression" in a close corporation context? If you were an Oregon legislator, would you have voted for the passage of *ORS 57.595*? Is dissolution of the corporation an appropriate remedy for majority shareholder misconduct, in your view? When dissolution of the corporation takes place, its official existence comes to an end, and its assets are sold (usually at an auction) to the highest bidder. After the debts of the corporation are paid, the proceeds (if any) are distributed to the shareholders in proportion to their share ownership. Do you agree with the Court's assertion that "the remedy of a forced dissolution of a corporation may equally be 'oppressive' * * * to the majority stockholders." When would this be the case? Who is likely to be the buyer of the corporate

assets? If you were advising the Bakers, would you have suggested they ask for different relief (for example, a declaration of dividends)? Note that the court does conclude that some conduct of Siler's was "highly improper." Where is the line to be drawn between conduct that is "highly improper" and that which is so "oppressive" that dissolution is called for? Does the attitude of this court seem similar to, or different from, the attitude of the Massachusetts Court in the *Donahue* case, *supra*?

2.   Note that, as we saw earlier, the failure to pay dividends in the close corporation context can be a tactic to squeeze or freeze out a minority share-holder. When is it appropriate for a court to intervene and declare the pay-ment of dividends? This is something courts are reluctant to do, but for some suggestions on when it is appropriate, see, e.g., Douglas K. Moll, "Shareholder Oppression & Dividend Policy in the Close Corporation," 60 Wash & Lee L. Rev. 841 (2003). As indicated earlier, Professor Moll observes that those in control of a close corporation are in a position to pay themselves "de facto dividends" such as high salary payments or other arrangements that favor them at the expense of the minority shareholders. Moll concludes that:

> With respect to disputes involving de facto dividends, a minority share-holder's expectation of dividends should be considered reasonable, and thus enforceable [by the courts], whenever the majority shareholder receives a disproportionate amount of the company's profits. Regardless of whether such disputes arise from the fault of the majority, the fault of the minority, or from no fault at all, such a position mirrors the understand-ings that the shareholders themselves likely would have reached had they contemplated the possibility of an exclusion from de facto dividends.

Id., at 923. For further reading on the close corporation and the problem of oppression of minority shareholders see generally the leading treatises in the field, cited by the Baker court in an earlier edition, F. Hodge O'Neal & Robert B. Thompson, O'Neal's Close Corporations (3d ed. 2003) and F. Hodge O'Neal & Robert B. Thompson, O'Neal's Oppression of Minority Shareholders (2d ed. 1999) and for O'Neal's co-author's take on oppression, see Robert B. Thomp-son, The Shareholder's Cause of Action for Oppression, 48 Bus. Law. 699 (1993). See also Robert B. Thompson, Corporate Dissolution and Sharehold-ers' Reasonable Expectations, 66 Wash. U. L.Q. 193 (1988).

3.   Should officers in a close corporation have the same business judg-ment rule protection that is available to managers in a publicly held corpora-tion? Professor Moll, exploring this question in the article cited in the last note, observes that several distinguished commentators have argued that this should not be the case. Moll, supra at n.88, citing, *inter alia*, Frank H. East-erbrook & Daniel R. Fischel, Close Corporations and Agency Costs, 38 Stan. L. Rev. 271 (1986), F. Hodge O'Neal, Close Corporations: Existing Legislation and Recommended Reform, 33 Bus. Law. 873 (1978), and Henry G. Manne, Our Two Corporation Systems: Law and Economics, 53 Va. L. Rev. 259 (1967). Why not?

4.   The *Baker* Court gives a list of things that it might be appropriate for a court to do in remedying an oppressive situation. Can a statutory scheme alleviate the problem? Consider that of Delaware, which follows. Statutes are

not exactly light reading, but see if, as you read through, you can discern responses to the particular needs of shareholders in close corporations.

D. SPECIAL STATUTORY TREATMENT OF THE CLOSE CORPORATION

TITLE 8

Corporations

CHAPTER 1. [Delaware] GENERAL CORPORATION LAW
Subchapter XIV. Close Corporations; Special Provisions

* * *

§ 342. *Close corporation defined; contents of certificate of incorporation.*

(a) A close corporation is a corporation organized under this chapter whose certificate of incorporation contains the provisions required by § 102 of this title[15] and, in addition, provides that:

(1) All of the corporation's issued stock of all classes, exclusive of treasury shares, shall be represented by certificates and shall be held of record by not more than a specified number of persons, not exceeding 30; and

(2) All of the issued stock of all classes shall be subject to 1 or more of the restrictions on transfer permitted by § 202 of this title;[16] and

---

15. Section 102 requires that the charter of each corporation set forth its name, include the word "corporation," "association," "ltd.," or something similar in its title, set forth the address, the nature of the business, the types of stock it may issue, and a variety of optional provisions.

16. § 202. Restrictions on transfer and ownership of securities.

(a) A written restriction or restrictions on the transfer or registration of transfer of a security of a corporation, or on the amount of the corporation's securities that may be owned by any person or group of persons, if permitted by this section and noted conspicuously on the certificate or certificates representing the security or securities so restricted * * *may be enforced against the holder of the restricted security or securities or any successor or transferee of the holder * * *. Unless noted conspicuously on the certificate or certificates representing the security or securities so restricted * * * a restriction, even though permitted by this section, is ineffective except against a person with actual knowledge of the restriction.

(b) A restriction on the transfer or registration of transfer of securities of a corporation, or on the amount of a corporation's securities that may be owned by any person or group of persons, may be imposed by the certificate of incorporation or by the bylaws or by an agreement among any number of security holders or among such holders and the corporation. * * *

(c) A restriction on the transfer * * * of securities of a corporation or on the amount of such securities that may be owned by any person or group of persons is permitted by this section if it:

(1) Obligates the holder of the restricted securities to offer to the corporation or to any other holders of securities of the corporation or to any other person or to any combination of the foregoing, a prior opportunity, to be exercised within a reasonable time, to acquire the restricted securities; or

(2) Obligates the corporation or any holder of securities of the corporation or any other person or any combination of the foregoing, to purchase the securities which are the subject of an agreement respecting the purchase and sale of the restricted securities; or

(3) Requires the corporation or the holders of any class or series of securities of the corporation to consent to any proposed transfer of the restricted securities or to approve the proposed transferee of the restricted securities, or to approve the amount of securities of the corporation that may be owned by any person or group of persons; or

(3) The corporation shall make no offering of any of its stock of any class which would constitute a "public offering" within the meaning of the United States Securities Act of 1933, 15 U.S.C. § 77a et seq. as it may be amended from time to time.

(b) The certificate of incorporation of a close corporation may set forth the qualifications of stockholders, either by specifying classes of persons who shall be entitled to be holders of record of stock of any class, or by specifying classes of persons who shall not be entitled to be holders of stock of any class or both.

* * *

§ 343. *Formation of a close corporation.*

A close corporation shall be formed in accordance with §§ 101,[17] 102[18] and 103[19] of this title, except that:

(1) Its certificate of incorporation shall contain a heading stating the name of the corporation and that it is a close corporation; and

(2) Its certificate of incorporation shall contain the provisions required by § 342 of this title. * * *

---

(4) Obligates the holder of the restricted securities to sell or transfer an amount of restricted securities to the corporation or to any other holders of securities of the corporation or to any other person or to any combination of the foregoing, or causes or results in the automatic sale or transfer of an amount of restricted securities to the corporation or to any other holders of securities of the corporation or to any other person or to any combination of the foregoing; or

(5) Prohibits or restricts the transfer of the restricted securities to, or the ownership of restricted securities by, designated persons or classes of persons or groups of persons, and such designation is not manifestly unreasonable.

(d) Any restriction on the transfer or the registration of transfer of the securities of a corporation, or on the amount of securities of a corporation that may be owned by a person or group of persons, for any of the following purposes shall be conclusively presumed to be for a reasonable purpose:

(1) Maintaining any local, state, federal or foreign tax advantage to the corporation or its stockholders * * *.

(2) Maintaining any statutory or regulatory advantage or complying with any statutory or regulatory requirements under applicable local, state, federal or foreign law.

(e) Any other lawful restriction on transfer or registration of transfer of securities, or on the amount of securities that may be owned by any person or group of persons, is permitted by this section. * * *

17. § 101. Incorporators; how corporation formed; purposes.

(a) Any person, partnership, association or corporation, singly or jointly with others, and without regard to such person's or entity's residence, domicile or state of incorporation, may incorporate or organize a corporation under this chapter by filing with the Division of Corporations in the Department of State a certificate of incorporation which shall be executed, acknowledged and filed in accordance with § 103 of this title.

(b) A corporation may be incorporated or organized under this chapter to conduct or promote any lawful business or purposes, except as may otherwise be provided by the Constitution or other law of this State.

* * *

18. See note 15, supra.

19. Section 103 specifies directions for filing articles of incorporation with the Delaware Secretary of State.

§ 344. Election *of existing corporation to become a close corporation.*

Any corporation organized under this chapter may become a close corporation under this subchapter by executing, acknowledging and filing, in accordance with § 103 of this title, a certificate of amendment of its certificate of incorporation which shall contain a statement that it elects to become a close corporation, the provisions required by § 342 of this title to appear in the certificate of incorporation of a close corporation, and a heading stating the name of the corporation and that it is a close corporation. Such amendment shall be adopted in accordance with the requirements of § 241[20] or 242[21] of this title, except that it must be approved by a vote of the holders of record of at least two thirds of the shares of each class of stock of the corporation which are outstanding. * * *

§ 345. *Limitations on continuation of close corporation status.*

A close corporation continues to be such and to be subject to this subchapter until:

(1) It files with the Secretary of State a certificate of amendment deleting from its certificate of incorporation the provisions required or permitted by § 342 of this title to be stated in the certificate of incorporation to qualify it as a close corporation; or

(2) Any 1 of the provisions or conditions required or permitted by § 342 of this title to be stated in a certificate of incorporation to qualify a corporation as a close corporation has in fact been breached and neither the corporation nor any of its stockholders takes the steps required by § 348 of this title to prevent such loss of status or to remedy such breach. * * *

§ 346. *Voluntary termination of close corporation status by amendment of certificate of incorporation; vote required.*

(a) A corporation may voluntarily terminate its status as a close corporation and cease to be subject to this subchapter by amending its certificate of incorporation to delete therefrom the additional provisions required or permitted by § 342 of this title to be stated in the certificate of incorporation of a close corporation. Any such amendment shall be adopted and shall become effective in accordance with § 242 of this title, except that it must be approved by a vote of the holders of record of at least two-thirds of the shares of each class of stock of the corporation which are outstanding.

(b) The certificate of incorporation of a close corporation may provide that on any amendment to terminate its status as a close corporation, a vote greater than two-thirds or a vote of all shares of any class shall be required; and if the certificate of incorporation contains such a provision,

---

20. Section 241 provides for amendment of the certificate before any stock is sold by a vote of a majority of the incorporators.

21. Section 242 provides procedures for amending the certificate after stock has been issued, principally by requiring an affirmative vote of a majority of the board of directors, followed by an affirmative vote of a majority of the shareholders.

that provision shall not be amended, repealed or modified by any vote less than that required to terminate the corporation's status as a close corporation. * * *

§ 347. *Issuance or transfer of stock of a close corporation in breach of qualifying conditions.*

(a) If stock of a close corporation is issued or transferred to any person who is not entitled under any provision of the certificate of incorporation permitted by subsection (b) of § 342 of this title to be a holder of record of stock of such corporation, and if the certificate for such stock conspicuously notes the qualifications of the persons entitled to be holders of record thereof, such person is conclusively presumed to have notice of the fact of such person's ineligibility to be a stockholder.

(b) If the certificate of incorporation of a close corporation states the number of persons, not in excess of 30, who are entitled to be holders of record of its stock, and if the certificate for such stock conspicuously states such number, and if the issuance or transfer of stock to any person would cause the stock to be held by more than such number of persons, the person to whom such stock is issued or transferred is conclusively presumed to have notice of this fact.

(c) If a stock certificate of any close corporation conspicuously notes the fact of a restriction on transfer of stock of the corporation, and the restriction is one which is permitted by § 202 of this title, the transferee of the stock is conclusively presumed to have notice of the fact that such person has acquired stock in violation of the restriction, if such acquisition violates the restriction.

(d) Whenever any person to whom stock of a close corporation has been issued or transferred has, or is conclusively presumed under this section to have, notice either (1) that such person is a person not eligible to be a holder of stock of the corporation, or (2) that transfer of stock to such person would cause the stock of the corporation to be held by more than the number of persons permitted by its certificate of incorporation to hold stock of the corporation, or (3) that the transfer of stock is in violation of a restriction on transfer of stock, the corporation may, at its option, refuse to register transfer of the stock into the name of the transferee.

(e) Subsection (d) of this section shall not be applicable if the transfer of stock, even though otherwise contrary to subsection (a), (b) or (c), of this section has been consented to by all the stockholders of the close corporation, or if the close corporation has amended its certificate of incorporation in accordance with § 346 of this title.

(f) The term "transfer," as used in this section, is not limited to a transfer for value.

(g) The provisions of this section do not in any way impair any rights of a transferee regarding any right to rescind the transaction or to recover under any applicable warranty express or implied. * * *

§ 348. *Involuntary termination of close corporation status; proceeding to prevent loss of status.*

(a) If any event occurs as a result of which 1 or more of the provisions or conditions included in a close corporation's certificate of incorporation pursuant to § 342 of this title to qualify it as a close corporation has been breached, the corporation's status as a close corporation under this subchapter shall terminate unless:

(1) Within 30 days after the occurrence of the event, or within 30 days after the event has been discovered, whichever is later, the corporation files with the Secretary of State a certificate, executed and acknowledged in accordance with § 103 of this title, stating that a specified provision or condition included in its certificate of incorporation pursuant to § 342 of this title to qualify it as a close corporation has ceased to be applicable, and furnishes a copy of such certificate to each stockholder; and

(2) The corporation concurrently with the filing of such certificate takes such steps as are necessary to correct the situation which threatens its status as a close corporation, including, without limitation, the refusal to register the transfer of stock which has been wrongfully transferred as provided by § 347 of this title, or a proceeding under subsection (b) of this section.

(b) The Court of Chancery, upon the suit of the corporation or any stockholder, shall have jurisdiction to issue all orders necessary to prevent the corporation from losing its status as a close corporation, or to restore its status as a close corporation by enjoining or setting aside any act or threatened act on the part of the corporation or a stockholder which would be inconsistent with any of the provisions or conditions required or permitted by § 342 of this title to be stated in the certificate of incorporation of a close corporation, unless it is an act approved in accordance with § 346 of this title. The Court of Chancery may enjoin or set aside any transfer or threatened transfer of stock of a close corporation which is contrary to the terms of its certificate of incorporation or of any transfer restriction permitted by § 202 of this title, and may enjoin any public offering, as defined in § 342 of this title, or threatened public offering of stock of the close corporation. * * *

§ 349. *Corporate option where a restriction on transfer of a security is held invalid.*

If a restriction on transfer of a security of a close corporation is held not to be authorized by § 202 of this title, the corporation shall nevertheless have an option, for a period of 30 days after the judgment setting aside the restriction becomes final, to acquire the restricted security at a price which is agreed upon by the parties, or if no agreement is reached as to price, then at the fair value as determined by the Court of Chancery. In order to determine fair value, the Court may appoint an appraiser to receive evidence and report to the Court such appraiser's findings and recommendation as to fair value. * * *

§ 350. *Agreements restricting discretion of directors.*

A written agreement among the stockholders of a close corporation hold-ing a majority of the outstanding stock entitled to vote, whether solely among themselves or with a party not a stockholder, is not invalid, as between the parties to the agreement, on the ground that it so relates to the conduct of the business and affairs of the corporation as to restrict or interfere with the discretion or powers of the board of directors. The effect of any such agreement shall be to relieve the directors and impose upon the stockholders who are parties to the agreement the liability for mana-gerial acts or omissions which is imposed on directors to the extent and so long as the discretion or powers of the board in its management of corpo-rate affairs is controlled by such agreement. * * *

§ 351. *Management by stockholders.*

The certificate of incorporation of a close corporation may provide that the business of the corporation shall be managed by the stockholders of the corporation rather than by a board of directors. So long as this provision continues in effect:

(1) No meeting of stockholders need be called to elect directors;

(2) Unless the context clearly requires otherwise, the stockholders of the corporation shall be deemed to be directors for purposes of apply-ing provisions of this chapter; and

(3) The stockholders of the corporation shall be subject to all liabili-ties of directors.

Such a provision may be inserted in the certificate of incorporation by amendment if all incorporators and subscribers or all holders of record of all of the outstanding stock, whether or not having voting power, autho-rize such a provision. An amendment to the certificate of incorporation to delete such a provision shall be adopted by a vote of the holders of a majority of all outstanding stock of the corporation, whether or not other-wise entitled to vote. If the certificate of incorporation contains a provision authorized by this section, the existence of such provision shall be noted conspicuously on the face or back of every stock certificate issued by such corporation. * * *

§ 352. *Appointment of custodian for close corporation.*

(a) In addition to § 226[22] of this title respecting the appointment of a cus-todian for any corporation, the Court of Chancery, upon application of any

---

22. § 226. Appointment of custodian or receiver of corporation on deadlock or for other cause.

(a) The Court of Chancery, upon application of any stockholder, may appoint 1 or more persons to be custodians, and, if the corporation is insolvent, to be receivers, of and for any corporation when:

(1) At any meeting held for the election of directors the stockholders are so divided that they have failed to elect successors to directors whose terms have expired or would have expired upon qualification of their successors; or

(2) The business of the corporation is suffering or is threatened with irreparable injury because the directors are so divided respecting the management of the affairs of the corpora-tion that the required vote for action by the board of directors cannot be obtained and the

stockholder, may appoint 1 or more persons to be custodians, and, if the corporation is insolvent, to be receivers, of any close corporation when:

(1) Pursuant to § 351 of this title the business and affairs of the corporation are managed by the stockholders and they are so divided that the business of the corporation is suffering or is threatened with irreparable injury and any remedy with respect to such deadlock provided in the certificate of incorporation or bylaws or in any written agreement of the stockholders has failed; or

(2) The petitioning stockholder has the right to the dissolution of the corporation under a provision of the certificate of incorporation permitted by § 355 of this title.

(b) In lieu of appointing a custodian for a close corporation under this section or § 226 of this title the Court of Chancery may appoint a provisional director, whose powers and status shall be as provided in § 353 of this title if the Court determines that it would be in the best interest of the corporation. Such appointment shall not preclude any subsequent order of the Court appointing a custodian for such corporation. * * *

§ 353.   Appointment of a provisional director in certain cases.

(a) Notwithstanding any contrary provision of the certificate of incorporation or the bylaws or agreement of the stockholders, the Court of Chancery may appoint a provisional director for a close corporation if the directors are so divided respecting the management of the corporation's business and affairs that the votes required for action by the board of directors cannot be obtained with the consequence that the business and affairs of the corporation can no longer be conducted to the advantage of the stockholders generally.

(b) An application for relief under this section must be filed

(1) by at least one half of the number of directors then in office,

(2) by the holders of at least one third of all stock then entitled to elect directors, or,

---

stockholders are unable to terminate this division; or

(3) The corporation has abandoned its business and has failed within a reasonable time to take steps to dissolve, liquidate or distribute its assets.

(b) A custodian appointed under this section shall have all the powers and title of a receiver appointed under § 291 of this title, but the authority of the custodian is to continue the business of the corporation and not to liquidate its affairs and distribute its assets, except when the Court shall otherwise order and except in cases arising under paragraph (3) of subsection (a) of this section or paragraph (2) of subsection (a) of § 352 of this title. * * *

§ 291.   Receivers for insolvent corporations; appointment and powers.

Whenever a corporation shall be insolvent, the Court of Chancery, on the application of any creditor or stockholder thereof, may, at any time, appoint 1 or more persons to be receivers of and for the corporation, to take charge of its assets, estate, effects, business and affairs, and to collect the outstanding debts, claims, and property due and belonging to the corporation, with power to prosecute and defend, in the name of the corporation or otherwise, all claims or suits, to appoint an agent or agents under them, and to do all other acts which might be done by the corporation and which may be necessary or proper. The powers of the receivers shall be such and shall continue so long as the Court shall deem necessary. * * *

(3) if there be more than 1 class of stock then entitled to elect 1 or more directors, by the holders of two thirds of the stock of any such class;

but the certificate of incorporation of a close corporation may provide that a lesser proportion of the directors or of the stockholders or of a class of stockholders may apply for relief under this section.

(c) A provisional director shall be an impartial person who is neither a stockholder nor a creditor of the corporation or of any subsidiary or affiliate of the corporation, and whose further qualifications, if any, may be determined by the Court of Chancery. A provisional director is not a receiver of the corporation and does not have the title and powers of a custodian or receiver appointed under §§ 226 and 291[23] of this title. A provisional director shall have all the rights and powers of a duly elected director of the corporation, including the right to notice of and to vote at meetings of directors, until such time as such person shall be removed by order of the Court of Chancery or by the holders of a majority of all shares then entitled to vote to elect directors or by the holders of two thirds of the shares of that class of voting shares which filed the application for appointment of a provisional director. A provisional director's compensation shall be determined by agreement between such person and the corporation subject to approval of the Court of Chancery, which may fix such person's compensation in the absence of agreement or in the event of disagreement between the provisional director and the corporation.

(d) Even though the requirements of subsection (b) of this section relating to the number of directors or stockholders who may petition for appointment of a provisional director are not satisfied, the Court of Chancery may nevertheless appoint a provisional director if permitted by subsection (b) of § 352 of this title. * * *

§ 354. *Operating corporation as partnership.*

No written agreement among stockholders of a close corporation, nor any provision of the certificate of incorporation or of the bylaws of the corporation, which agreement or provision relates to any phase of the affairs of such corporation, including but not limited to the management of its business or declaration and payment of dividends or other division of profits or the election of directors or officers or the employment of stockholders by the corporation or the arbitration of disputes, shall be invalid on the ground that it is an attempt by the parties to the agreement or by the stockholders of the corporation to treat the corporation as if it were a partnership or to arrange relations among the stockholders or between the stockholders and the corporation in a manner that would be appropriate only among partners. * * *

§ 355. *Stockholders' option to dissolve corporation.*

(a) The certificate of incorporation of any close corporation may include a provision granting to any stockholder, or to the holders of any specified

---

23. See note 22, supra.

number or percentage of shares of any class of stock, an option to have the corporation dissolved at will or upon the occurrence of any specified event or contingency. Whenever any such option to dissolve is exercised, the stockholders exercising such option shall give written notice thereof to all other stockholders. After the expiration of 30 days following the sending of such notice, the dissolution of the corporation shall proceed as if the required number of stockholders having voting power had consented in writing to dissolution of the corporation as provided by § 228[24] of this title.

(b) If the certificate of incorporation as originally filed does not contain a provision authorized by subsection (a) of this section, the certificate may be amended to include such provision if adopted by the affirmative vote of the holders of all the outstanding stock, whether or not entitled to vote, unless the certificate of incorporation specifically authorizes such an amendment by a vote which shall be not less than two thirds of all the outstanding stock whether or not entitled to vote.

(c) Each stock certificate in any corporation whose certificate of incorporation authorizes dissolution as permitted by this section shall conspicuously note on the face thereof the existence of the provision. Unless noted conspicuously on the face of the stock certificate, the provision is ineffective. * * *

§ 356.   *Effect of this subchapter on other laws.*

This subchapter shall not be deemed to repeal any statute or rule of law which is or would be applicable to any corporation which is organized under this chapter but is not a close corporation.* * *

NOTES AND QUESTIONS

1.   If you were a Delaware legislator, would you have voted for this special subchapter of the Delaware Corporations law, which sets out special rules for the close corporation?

2.   Can you explain any of these provisions with reference to the cases you have studied?

3.   What do you make, in particular, of the remedy of a "provisional director" provided for in Section 353? One recent commentator on the concept suggested that:

---

24.   § 228. *Consent of stockholders or members in lieu of meeting.*

(a) Unless otherwise provided in the certificate of incorporation, any action required by this chapter to be taken at any annual or special meeting of stockholders of a corporation, or any action which may be taken at any annual or special meeting of such stockholders, may be taken without a meeting, without prior notice and without a vote, if a consent or consents in writing, setting forth the action so taken, shall be signed by the holders of outstanding stock having not less than the minimum number of votes that would be necessary to authorize or take such action at a meeting at which all shares entitled to vote thereon were present and voted and shall be delivered to the corporation by delivery to its registered office in this State, its principal place of business or an officer or agent of the corporation having custody of the book in which proceedings of meetings of stockholders are recorded. Delivery made to a corporation's registered office shall be by hand or by certified or registered mail, return receipt requested.

The appointment of a provisional director is not the answer for all forms of deadlock within corporations. However, it can be an important and effective first step in resolving certain impasses in corporate enterprises. Perhaps courts should be more willing to grant the provisional director remedy as a first line of attack in corporate deadlock cases, even in situations in which the differences seem irreconcilable upon first glance.

Susanna M. Kim, "The Provisional Director Remedy for Corporate Deadlock: A Proposed Model Statute," 60 Wash & Lee L. Rev. 111, 181 (2003). Would you agree with Professor Kim?

4. Note the possibility of allowing stockholders in a Delaware close corporation to decide to dissolve the corporation, provided by section 355. We've touched on this before, but do you believe that dissolution is a good remedy for deadlock or oppression in a close corporation? See generally Harvey Gelb, "Fiduciary Duties and Dissolution in the Closely Held Business," 3 Wyo. L. Rev. 547 (2003).

5. By now it should be clear that careful planning on the part of counsel can avoid at least some possible close corporation problems, and that, in particular, a shareholder agreement might be a useful tool in preventing shareholder oppression or deadlock. Note that the Delaware statute seems to encourage such agreements, even if they restrict the traditional role of directors. On the usefulness of such agreements see, e.g., Manuel A. Utset, "A Theory of Self-Control Problems and Incomplete Contracting: The Case of Shareholder Contracts," 2003 Utah L. Rev. 1329. There is much more that might be said about the close corporation, and even more about the emerging issues involving Limited Liability Companies (LLC's) which bid fair to replace the close corporation vehicle. In an introductory course of this nature, though, we can stop here and return to the general problems of corporations, specifically organic change that ends one phase of corporate life, and perhaps begins another.

CHAPTER 8

ASPECTS OF THE ENDGAME

■ ■ ■

A. THE DISCRETION OF THE BOARD IN AN ENDGAME SITUATION

PARAMOUNT COMMUNICATIONS, INC. v. TIME, INC.

Supreme Court of Delaware.
571 A.2d 1140 (Del. 1990).

* * *

JUDGES: HORSEY, MOORE, AND HOLLAND, JUSTICES.

OPINION BY: HORSEY

OPINION

Paramount Communications, Inc. ("Paramount") and two other groups of plaintiffs * * * ("Shareholder Plaintiffs"), shareholders of Time Incorporated ("Time"), a Delaware corporation, separately filed suits in the Delaware Court of Chancery seeking a preliminary injunction to halt Time's tender offer for 51% of Warner Communication, Inc.'s ("Warner") outstanding shares at $70 cash per share. The court below * * * denied plaintiffs' motion. * * * [On] July 14, 1989, the Chancellor refused to enjoin Time's consummation of its tender offer, concluding that the plaintiffs were unlikely to prevail on the merits.* * *

On the same day, plaintiffs filed in this Court an interlocutory appeal, which we accepted on an expedited basis. Pending the appeal, a stay of execution of Time's tender offer was entered for ten days * * * Following briefing and oral argument, on July 24 we concluded that the decision below should be affirmed. * * *

The principal ground for reversal, asserted by all plaintiffs, is that Paramount's June 7, 1989 uninvited all-cash, all-shares, "fully negotiable" (though conditional) tender offer for Time triggered duties under *Unocal Corp. v. Mesa Petroleum Co.,* Del. Supr., 493 A.2d 946 (1985), and that Time's board of directors, in responding to Paramount's offer, breached those duties. As a consequence, plaintiffs argue that in our review of the Time board's decision of June 16, 1989 to enter into a revised merger agreement with Warner, Time is not entitled to the benefit and protection of the business judgment rule.

Shareholder Plaintiffs also assert a claim based on *Revlon v. MacAndrews & Forbes Holdings, Inc.,* Del. Supr. 506 A.2d 173 (1986). They argue that the original Time–Warner merger agreement of March 4, 1989 resulted in a change of control which effectively put Time up for sale, thereby triggering *Revlon* duties. Those plaintiffs argue that Time's board breached its *Revlon* duties by failing, in the face of the change of control, to maximize shareholder value in the immediate term.

* * * [W]e affirm the Chancellor's ultimate finding and conclusion under *Unocal.* We find that Paramount's tender offer was reasonably perceived by Time's board to pose a threat to Time and that the Time board's "response" to that threat was, under the circumstances, reasonable and proportionate. Applying *Unocal,* we reject the argument that the only corporate threat posed by an all-shares, all-cash tender offer is the possibility of inadequate value.

We also find that Time's board did not by entering into its initial merger agreement with Warner come under a *Revlon* duty either to auction the company or to maximize short-term shareholder value, notwithstanding the unequal share exchange. Therefore, the Time board's original plan of merger with Warner was subject only to a business judgment rule analysis. * * *

I

Time is a Delaware corporation with its principal offices in New York City. Time's traditional business is publication of magazines and books; however, Time also provides pay television programming through its Home Box Office, Inc. and Cinemax subsidiaries. In addition, Time owns and operates cable television franchises through its subsidiary, American Television and Communication Corporation. During the relevant time period, Time's board consisted of sixteen directors. Twelve of the directors were "outside," nonemployee directors. Four of the directors were also officers of the company. The outside directors included: James F. Bere, chairman of the board and CEO of Borg–Warner Corporation (Time director since 1979); Clifford J. Grum, president and CEO of Temple–Inland, Inc. (Time director since 1980); Henry C. Goodrich, former chairman of Sonat, Inc. (Time director since 1978); Matina S. Horner, then president of Radcliffe College (Time director since 1975); David T. Kearns, chairman and CEO of Xerox Corporation (Time director since 1978); Donald S. Perkins, former chairman of Jewel Companies, Inc. (Time director since 1979); Michael D. Dingman, chairman and CEO of The Henley Group, Inc. (Time director since 1978); Edward S. Finkelstein, chairman and CEO of R.H. Macy & Co. (Time director since 1984); John R. Opel, former chairman and CEO of IBM Corporation (Time director since 1984); Arthur Temple, chairman of Temple–Inland, Inc. (Time director since 1983); Clifton R. Wharton, Jr., chairman and CEO of Teachers Insurance and Annuity Association—College Retirement Equities Fund (Time director since 1982); and Henry R. Luce III, president of The Henry Luce Foundation Inc. (Time director since 1967). Mr. Luce, the son of the founder of Time, individually and in a representative capacity controlled 4.2% of the outstanding Time stock. The inside officer directors were: J. Richard Munro, Time's chairman and CEO since 1980: N.J. Nicholas, Jr., president and chief operating officer of the company since 1986; Gerald M. Levin, vice chairman of the board; and Jason D. McManus, editor-in-chief of *Time* magazine and a board member since 1988. * * *

As early as 1983 and 1984, Time's executive board began considering expanding Time's operations into the entertainment industry. In 1987, Time established a special committee of executives to consider and propose corporate strategies for the 1990s. The consensus of the committee was that Time should move ahead in the area of ownership and creation of video programming. This expansion, as the Chancellor noted, was predicated upon two considerations: first, Time's desire to have greater control, in terms of quality and price, over the film products delivered by way of its cable network and franchises; and second, Time's concern over the increasing globalization of the world economy. Some of Time's outside directors, especially Luce and Temple, had opposed this move as a threat to the editorial integrity and journalistic focus of Time.[1] Despite this concern, the board recognized that a vertically integrated video enterprise to complement Time's existing HBO and cable networks would better enable it to compete on a global basis.

In late spring of 1987, a meeting took place between Steve Ross, CEO of Warner Brothers, and Nicholas of Time. Ross and Nicholas discussed the possibility of a joint venture between the two companies through the creation of a jointly-owned cable company. Time would contribute its cable system and HBO. Warner would contribute its cable system and provide access to Warner Brothers Studio. The resulting venture would be a larger, more efficient cable network, able to produce and distribute its own movies on a worldwide basis. Ultimately the parties abandoned this plan, determining that it was impractical for several reasons, chief among them being tax considerations.

On August 11, 1987, Gerald M. Levin, Time's vice chairman and chief strategist, wrote J. Richard Munro a confidential memorandum in which he strongly recommended a strategic consolidation with Warner. In June 1988, Nicholas and Munro sent to each outside director a copy of the "comprehensive long-term planning document" prepared by the committee of Time executives that had been examining strategies for the 1990s. The

---

1. The primary concern of Time's outside directors was the preservation of the "Time Culture." They believed that Time had become recognized in this country as an institution built upon a foundation of journalistic integrity. Time's management made a studious effort to refrain from involvement in Time's editorial policy. Several of Time's outside directors feared that a merger with an entertainment company would divert Time's focus from news journalism and threaten the Time Culture. [footnotes are from the original opinion, though some have been omitted, and the remaining footnotes have been renumbered here]

memo included reference to and a description of Warner as a potential acquisition candidate.

Thereafter, Munro and Nicholas held meetings with Time's outside directors to discuss, generally, long-term strategies for Time, and specifically, a combination with Warner. Nearly a year later, Time's board reached the point of serious discussion of the "nuts and bolts" of a consolidation with an entertainment company. On July 21, 1988, Time's board met, with all outside directors present. The meeting's purpose was to consider Time's expansion into the entertainment industry on a global scale. Management presented the board with a profile of various entertainment companies in addition to Warner, including Disney, 20th Century Fox, Universal, and Paramount.

Without any definitive decision on choice of a company, the board approved in principle a strategic plan for Time's expansion. The board gave management the "go-ahead" to continue discussions with Warner concerning the possibility of a merger. With the exception of Temple and Luce, most of the outside directors agreed that a merger involving expansion into the entertainment field promised great growth opportunity for Time. Temple and Luce remained unenthusiastic about Time's entry into the entertainment field. * * *

The board's consensus was that a merger of Time and Warner was feasible, but only if Time controlled the board of the resulting corporation and thereby preserved a management committed to Time's journalistic integrity. To accomplish this goal, the board stressed the importance of carefully defining in advance the corporate governance provisions that would control the resulting entity. Some board members expressed concern over whether such a business combination would place Time *"in play."* The board discussed the wisdom of adopting further defensive measures to lessen such a possibility.[2]

Of a wide range of companies considered by Time's board as possible merger candidates, Warner Brothers, Paramount, Columbia, M.C.A., Fox, MGM, Disney, and Orion, the board, in July 1988, concluded that Warner was the superior candidate for a consolidation. Warner stood out on a number of counts. Warner had just acquired Lorimar and its film studios. Time–Warner could make movies and television shows for use of HBO. Warner had an international distribution system, which Time could use to sell films, videos, books and magazines. Warner was a giant in the music and recording business, an area into which Time wanted to expand. None of the other companies considered had the musical clout of Warner. Time and Warner's cable systems were compatible and could be easily integrated; none of the other companies considered presented such a compatible cable partner. Together, Time and Warner would control half of New

---

2.   Time had in place a panoply of defensive devices, including a staggered board, a "poison pill" preferred stock rights plan triggered by an acquisition of 15% of the company, a fifty-day notice period for shareholder motions, and restrictions on shareholders' ability to call a meeting or act by consent.

York City's cable system; Warner had cable systems in Brooklyn and Queens; and Time controlled cable systems in Manhattan and Queens. Warner's publishing company would integrate well with Time's established publishing company. Time sells hardcover books and magazines, and Warner sells softcover books and comics. Time–Warner could sell all of these publications and Warner's videos by using Time's direct mailing network and Warner's international distribution system. Time's network could be used to promote and merchandise Warner's movies.

In August 1988, Levin, Nicholas, and Munro, acting on instructions from Time's board, continued to explore a business combination with Warner. By letter dated August 4, 1988, management informed the outside directors of proposed corporate governance provision to be discussed with Warner. The provisions incorporated the recommendations of several of Time's outside directors.

From the outset, Time's board favored an all-cash or cash and securities acquisition of Warner as the basis for consolidation. Bruce Wasserstein, Time's financial advisor, also favored an outright purchase of Warner. However, Steve Ross, Warner's CEO, was adamant that a business combination was only practicable on a stock-for-stock basis. Warner insisted on a stock swap in order to preserve its shareholders' equity in the resulting corporation. Time's officers, on the other hand, made it abundantly clear that Time would be the acquiring corporation and that Time would control the resulting board. Time refused to permit itself to be cast as the "acquired" company.

Eventually Time acquiesced in Warner's insistence on a stock-for-stock deal, but talks broke down over corporate governance issues. Time wanted Ross' position as a co-CEO to be temporary and wanted Ross to retire in five years. Ross, however, refused to set a time for his retirement and viewed Time's proposal as indicating a lack of confidence in his leadership. Warner considered it vital that their executives and creative staff not perceive Warner as selling out to Time. Time's request of a guarantee that Time would dominate the CEO succession was objected to as inconsistent with the concept of a Time–Warner merger "of equals." Negotiations ended when the parties reached an impasse. Time's board refused to compromise on its position on corporate governance. Time, and particularly its outside directors, viewed the corporate governance provisions as critical for preserving the "Time Culture" through a pro-Time management at the top. *See supra* note 1.

Throughout the fall of 1988, Time pursued its plan of expansion into the entertainment field; Time held informal discussions with several companies, including Paramount. Capital Cities/ABC approached Time to propose a merger. Talks terminated, however, when Capital Cities/ABC suggested that it was interested in purchasing Time or in controlling the resulting board. Time steadfastly maintained it was not placing itself up for sale.

Warner and Time resumed negotiations in January 1989. The catalyst for the resumption of talks was a private dinner between Steve Ross and

Time outside director, Michael Dingman. Dingman was able to convince Ross that the transitional nature of the proposed co-CEO arrangement did not reflect a lack of confidence in Ross. Ross agreed that this course was best for the company and a meeting between Ross and Munro resulted. Ross agreed to retire in five years and let Nicholas succeed him. Negotiations resumed and many of the details of the original stock-for-stock exchange agreement remained intact. In addition, Time's senior management agreed to long-term contracts.

Time insider directors Levin and Nicholas met with Warner's financial advisors to decide upon a stock exchange ratio. Time's board had recognized the potential need to pay a premium in the stock ratio in exchange for dictating the governing arrangement of the new Time–Warner. Levin and outside director Finkelstein were the primary proponents of paying a premium to protect the "Time Culture." The board discussed premium rates of 10%, 15% and 20%. Wasserstein also suggested paying a premium for Warner due to Warner's rapid growth rate. The market exchange ratio of Time stock for Warner stock was .38 in favor of Warner. Warner's financial advisors informed its board that any exchange rate over .400 was a fair deal and any exchange rate over .450 was "one hell of a deal." The parties ultimately agreed upon an exchange rate favoring Warner of .465. On that basis, Warner stockholders would have owned approximately 62% of the common stock of Time–Warner.

On March 3, 1989, Time's board, with all but one director in attendance, met and unanimously approved the stock-for-stock merger with Warner. Warner's board likewise approved the merger. The agreement called for Warner to be merged into a wholly-owned Time subsidiary with Warner becoming the surviving corporation. The common stock of Warner would then be converted into common stock of Time at the agreed upon ratio. Thereafter, the name of Time would be changed to Time–Warner, Inc.

The rules of the New York Stock Exchange required that Time's issuance of shares to effectuate the merger be approved by a vote of Time's stockholders. The Delaware General Corporation Law required approval of the merger by a majority of the Warner stockholders. Delaware law did not require any vote by Time stockholders. The Chancellor concluded that the agreement was the product of "an arms-length negotiation between two parties seeking individual advantage through mutual action."

The resulting company would have a 24–member board, with 12 members representing each corporation. The company would have co-CEO's, at first Ross and Munro, then Ross and Nicholas, and finally, after Ross' retirement, by Nicholas alone. The board would create an editorial committee with a majority of members representing Time. A similar entertainment committee would be controlled by Warner board members. A two-thirds supermajority vote was required to alter CEO successions but an earlier proposal to have supermajority protection for the editorial committee was abandoned. Warner's board suggested raising the compensation levels for Time's senior management under the new corporation. Warner's management, as with most entertainment executives, received higher salaries than comparable executives in news journalism. Time's board, however, rejected Warner's proposal to equalize the salaries of the two management teams.

At its March 3, 1989 meeting, Time's board adopted several defensive tactics. Time entered an automatic share exchange agreement with Warner. Time would receive 17,292,747 shares of Warner's outstanding common stock (9.4%) and Warner would receive 7,080,016 shares of Time's outstanding common stock (11.1%). Either party could trigger the exchange. Time sought out and paid for "confidence" letters from various banks with which it did business. In these letters, the banks promised not to finance any third-party attempt to acquire Time. Time argues these agreements served only to preserve the confidential relationship between itself and the banks. The Chancellor found these agreements to be inconsequential and futile attempts to "dry up" money for a hostile takeover. Time also agreed to a "no-shop" clause, preventing Time from considering any other consolidation proposal, thus relinquishing its power to consider other proposals, regardless of their merits. Time did so at Warner's insistence. Warner did not want to be left "on the auction block" for an unfriendly suitor, if Time were to withdraw from the deal.

Time's board simultaneously established a special committee of outside directors, Finkelstein, Kearns, and Opel, to oversee the merger. The committee's assignment was to resolve any impediments that might arise in the course of working out the details of the merger and its consummation.

Time representatives lauded the lack of debt [financing involved in the transaction] to the United States Senate and to the President of the United States. Public reaction to the announcement of the merger was positive. Time–Warner would be a media colossus with international scope. The board scheduled the stockholder vote for June 23. * * * On May 24, 1989, Time sent out extensive proxy statements to the stockholders regarding the approval vote on the merger. In the meantime, with the merger proceeding without impediment, the special committee had concluded, shortly after its creation, that it was not necessary either to retain independent consultants, legal or financial, or even to meet. Time's board was unanimously in favor of the proposed merger with Warner; and, by the end of May, the Time–Warner merger appeared to an accomplished fact.

On June 7, 1989, these wishful assumptions were shattered by Paramount's surprising announcement of its all-cash offer to purchase all outstanding shares of Time for $175 per share. The following day, June 8, the trading price of Time's stock rose from $126 to $170 per share. Paramount's offer was said to be "fully negotiable." * * *

Time found Paramount's "fully negotiable" offer to be in fact subject to at least three conditions. First, Time had to terminate its merger agreement and stock exchange agreement with Warner, and remove certain other of its defensive devices, including the redemption of Time's shareholder rights [that is, Time had to agree to cancel its "poison pill"]. Second, Paramount had to obtain the required cable franchise transfers from Time in a fashion acceptable to Paramount in its sole discretion. Finally, the offer depended upon a judicial determination that section 203 of the General Corporate Law of Delaware (The Delaware Anti–Takeover Statute) was inapplicable to any Time–Paramount merger. While Paramount's board had been privately advised that it could take months, perhaps over a year, to forge and consummate the deal, Paramount's board publicly proclaimed its ability to close the offer by July 5, 1989. Paramount executives later conceded that none of its directors believed that July 5th was a realistic date to close the transaction.

On June 8, 1989, Time formally responded to Paramount's offer. Time's chairman and CEO, J. Richard Munro, sent an aggressively worded letter to Parmount's CEO, Martin Davis. Munro's letter attacked Davis' personal integrity and called Paramount's offer "smoke and mirrors." Time's nonmanagement directors were not shown the letter before it was sent. However, at a board meeting that same day, all members endorsed management's response as well as the letter's content.

Over the following eight days, Time's board met three times to discuss Paramount's $175 offer. The board viewed Paramount's offer as inadequate and concluded that its proposed merger with Warner was the better course of action. Therefore, the board declined to open any negotiations with Paramount and held steady its course toward a merger with Warner.

In June, Time's board of directors met several times. During the course of their June meetings, Time's outside directors met frequently without management, officers or directors being present. At the request of the outside directors, corporate counsel was present during the board meetings and, from time to time, the management directors were asked to leave the board sessions. During the course of these meetings, Time's financial advisors informed the board that, on an auction basis, Time's per share value was materially higher than Warner's $175 per share offer. * * * After this advice, the board concluded that Paramount's $175 offer was inadequate.

At these June meetings, certain Time directors expressed their concern that Time stockholders would not comprehend the long-term benefits of the Warner merger. Large quantities of Time shares were held by institutional investors. The board feared that even though there appeared to be wide support for the Warner transaction, Paramount's cash premium would be a tempting prospect to these investors. In mid-June, Time sought permission from the New York Stock Exchange to alter its rules and allow the Time–Warner merger to proceed without stockholder approval. Time did so at Warner's insistence. The New York Stock

Exchange rejected Time's request on June 15; and, on that day, the value of Time stock reached $182 per share.

The following day, June 16, Time's board met to take up Paramount's offer. The board's prevailing belief was that Paramount's bid posed a threat to Time's control of its own destiny and retention of the "Time Culture." Even after Time's financial advisors made another presentation of Paramount and its business attributes, Time's board maintained its position that a combination with Warner offered greater potential for Time. Warner provided Time a much desired production capability and an established international marketing chain. Time's advisors suggested various options, including defensive measures. The board considered and rejected the idea of purchasing Paramount in a "Pac Man" defense. * * * The board considered other defenses, including a recapitalization, the acquisition of another company, and a material change in the present capitalization structure or dividend policy. The board determined to retain its same advisors even in light of the changed circumstances. The board rescinded its agreement to pay its advisors a bonus based on the consummation of the Time–Warner merger and agreed to pay a flat fee for any advice rendered. Finally, Time's board formally rejected Paramount's offer. * * *

At the same meeting, Time's board decided to recast its consolidation with Warner into an outright cash and securities acquisition of Warner by Time; and Time so informed Warner. Time accordingly restructured its proposal to acquire Warner as follows: Time would make an immediate all-cash offer for 51% of Warner's outstanding stock at $70 per share. The remaining 49% would be purchased at some later date for a mixture of cash and securities worth $70 per share. To provide the funds required for its outright acquisition of Warner, Time would assume 7–10 billion dollars worth of debt, thus eliminating one of the principal transaction-related benefits of the original merger agreement. Nine billion dollars of the total purchase price would be allocated to the purchase of Warner's goodwill.

Warner agreed but insisted on certain terms. Warner sought a control premium and guarantees that the governance provisions found in the original merger agreement would remain intact. Warner further sought agreements that Time would not employ its poison pill against Warner and that, unless enjoined, Time would be legally bound to complete the transaction. Time's board agreed to these last measures only at the insistence of Warner. For its part, Time was assured of its ability to extend its efforts into production areas and international markets, all the while maintaining the Time identity and culture. The Chancellor found the initial Time–Warner transaction to have been negotiated at arms' length and the restructured Time–Warner transaction to have resulted from Paramount's offer and its expected effect on a Time shareholder vote.

On June 23, 1989, Paramount raised its all-cash offer to buy Time's outstanding stock to $200 per share. Paramount still professed that all aspects of the offer were negotiable. Time's board met on June 26, 1989 and formally rejected Paramount's $200 per share second offer. The board reiterated its belief that, despite the $25 increase, the offer was still inadequate. The Time board maintained that the Warner transaction offered a greater long-term value for the stockholders and, unlike Paramount's offer, did not pose a threat to Time's survival and its "culture." Paramount then filed this action in the Court of Chancery.

II

The Shareholder Plaintiffs first assert a *Revlon* claim. They contend that the March 4 Time–Warner agreement effectively put Time up for sale, triggering *Revlon* duties, requiring Time's board to enhance short-term shareholder value and to treat all other interested acquirors on an equal basis. The Shareholder Plaintiffs base this argument on two facts: (i) the ultimate Time–Warner exchange ratio of .465 favoring Warner, resulting in Warner shareholders' receipt of 62% of the combined company; and (ii) the subjective intent of Time's directors as evidenced in their statements that the market might perceive the Time–Warner merger as putting Time up "for sale" and their adoption of various defensive measures.

The Shareholder Plaintiffs further contend that Time's directors, in structuring the original merger transaction to be "takeover-proof," triggered *Revlon* duties by foreclosing their shareholders from any prospect of obtaining a control premium. In short, plaintiffs argue that Time's board's decision to merge with Warner imposed a fiduciary duty to maximize immediate share value and not erect unreasonable barriers to further bids. Therefore, they argue, the Chancellor erred in finding: that Paramount's bid for Time did not place Time "for sale"; that Time's transaction with Warner did not result in any transfer of control; and that the combined Time–Warner was not so large as to preclude the possibility of the stockholders of Time–Warner receiving a future control premium.

Paramount asserts only a *Unocal* claim in which the shareholder plaintiffs join. Paramount contends that the Chancellor, in applying the first part of the *Unocal* test, erred in finding that Time's board had reasonable grounds to believe that Paramount posed both a legally cognizable threat to Time shareholders and a danger to Time's corporate policy and effectiveness. Paramount also contests the court's finding that Time's board made a reasonable and objective investigation of Paramount's offer so as to be informed before rejecting it. Paramount further claims that the court erred in applying *Unocal's* second part in finding Time's response to be "reasonable." Paramount points primarily to the preclusive effect of the revised agreement which denied Time shareholders the opportunity both to vote on the agreement and to respond to Paramount's tender offer. Paramount argues that the underlying motivation of Time's board in adopting these defensive measures was management's desire to perpetuate itself in office.

The Court of Chancery posed the pivotal question presented by this case to be: Under what circumstances must a board of directors abandon an in-place plan of corporate development in order to provide its share-holders with the option to elect and realize an immediate control pre-mium? As applied to this case, the question becomes: Did Time's Board, having developed a strategic plan of global expansion to be launched through a business combination with Warner, come under a fiduciary duty to jettison its plan and put the corporation's future in the hands of its shareholders?

While we affirm the result reached by the Chancellor, we think it unwise to place undue emphasis upon long-term versus short-term corpo-rate strategy. Two key predicates underpin our analysis. First, Delaware law imposes on a board of directors the duty to manage the business and affairs of the corporation. 8 *Del. C.* § 141(a). This broad mandate includes a conferred authority to set a corporate course of action, including time frame, designed to enhance corporate profitability.[3] Thus, the question of "long-term" versus "short-term" values is largely irrelevant because direc-tors, generally, are obliged to chart a course for a corporation which is in its best interest without regard to a fixed investment horizon. Second, absent a limited set of circumstances as defined under *Revlon*, a board of directors, while always required to act in an informed manner, is not under any *per se* duty to maximize shareholder value in the short term, even in the context of a takeover. In our view, the pivotal question pre-sented by this case is: "Did Time, by entering into the proposed merger with Warner, put itself up for sale?" A resolution of that issue through application of *Revlon* has a significant bearing upon the resolution of the derivative *Unocal* issue.

A.

We first take up plaintiffs' principal *Revlon* argument, summarized above. In rejecting this argument, the Chancellor found the original Time–Warner merger agreement not to constitute a "change of control" and concluded that the transaction did not trigger *Revlon* duties. The Chancellor's conclusion is premised on a finding that "[b]efore the merger agreement was signed, control of the corporation existed in a fluid aggre-gation of unaffiliated shareholders representing a voting majority—in other words, in the market." The Chancellor's findings of fact are sup-ported by the record and his conclusion is correct as a matter of law. How-ever, we premise our rejection of plaintiffs' *Revlon* claim on different grounds, namely, the absence of any substantial evidence to conclude that Time's board, in negotiating with Warner, made the dissolution or breakup of the corporate entity inevitable, as was the case in *Revlon*.

Under Delaware law there are, generally speaking and without excluding other possibilities, two circumstances which may implicate *Rev-lon* duties. The first, and clearer one, is when a corporation initiates an

---

3. Thus, we endorse the Chancellor's conclusion that it is not breach of faith for directors to determine that the present stock market price of shares is not representative of true value or that there may indeed be several market values for any corporation's stock.

active bidding process seeking to sell itself or to effect a business reorganization involving a clear break-up of the company.[4] * * * However, *Revlon* duties may also be triggered where, in response to a bidder's offer, a target abandons its long-term strategy and seeks an alternative transaction also involving the breakup of the company. Thus, in *Revlon*, when the board responded to Pantry Pride's offer by contemplating a "bust-up" sale of assets in a leveraged acquisition, we imposed upon the board a duty to maximize immediate shareholder value and an obligation to auction the company fairly. If, however, the board's reaction to a hostile tender offer is found to constitute only a defensive response and not an abandonment of the corporation's continued existence, *Revlon* duties are not triggered, though *Unocal* duties attach. * * *

The plaintiffs insist that even though the original Time–Warner agreement may not have worked "an objective change of control," the transaction made a "sale" of Time inevitable. Plaintiffs rely on the subjective intent of Time's board of directors and principally upon certain board members' expressions of concern that the Warner transaction *might* be viewed as effectively putting Time up for sale. Plaintiffs argue that the use of a lock-up agreement, a no-shop clause, and so-called "dry-up" agreements prevented shareholders from obtaining a control premium in the immediate future and thus violated *Revlon*.

We agree with the Chancellor that such evidence is entirely insufficient to invoke *Revlon* duties; and we decline to extend *Revlon's* application to corporate transactions simply because they might be construed as putting a corporation either "in play" or "up for sale." * * * The adoption of structural safety devices alone does not trigger *Revlon*. * * * Rather, as the Chancellor stated, such devices are properly subject to a *Unocal* analysis.

Finally, we do not find in Time's recasting of its merger agreement with Warner from a share exchange to a share purchase a basis to conclude that Time had either abandoned its strategic plan or made a sale of Time inevitable. * * * The Chancellor found that although the merged Time–Warner company would be large (with a value approaching approximately $30 billion), recent takeover cases have proven that acquisition of the combined company might nonetheless be possible. * * * The legal consequence is that *Unocal* alone applies to determine whether the business judgment rule attaches to the revised agreement. * * *

B.

We turn now to plaintiffs' *Unocal* claim. We begin by noting, as did the Chancellor, that our decision does not require us to pass on the wisdom of

---

4. As we stated in Revlon, in both such cases, "[t]he duty of the board [has] changed from the preservation of ... [the] corporate entity to the maximization of the company's value at a sale for the stockholder's benefit.... [The board] no longer face[s] threats to corporate policy and effectiveness, or to the stockholders' interests, from a grossly inadequate bid." Revlon v. MacAndrews & Forbes Holdings, Inc., Del. Supr., 506 A.2d 173, 182 (1986).

the board's decision to enter into the original Time–Warner agreement. That is not a court's task. Our task is simply to review the record to determine whether there is sufficient evidence to support the Chancellor's conclusion that the initial Time–Warner agreement was the product of a proper exercise of business judgment. * * *

We have purposely detailed the evidence of the Time board's deliberative approach, beginning in 1983–84, to expand itself. Time's decision in 1988 to combine with Warner was made only after what could be fairly characterized as an exhaustive appraisal of Time's future as a corporation. After concluding in 1983–84 that the corporation must expand to survive, and beyond journalism into entertainment, the board combed the field of available entertainment companies. By 1987 Time had focused upon Warner; by late July 1988 Time's board was convinced that Warner would provide the best "fit" for Time to achieve its strategic objectives. The record attests to the zealousness of Time's executives, fully supported by their directors, in seeing to the preservation of Time's "culture," i.e., its perceived editorial integrity in journalism. We find ample evidence in the record to support the Chancellor's conclusion that the Time board's decision to expand the business of the company through its March 3 merger with Warner was entitled to the protection of the business judgment rule. * * *

The Chancellor reached a different conclusion in addressing the Time–Warner transaction as revised three months later. He found that the revised agreement was defense-motivated and designed to avoid the potentially disruptive effect that Paramount's offer would have had on consummation of the proposed merger were it put to a shareholder vote. Thus, the court declined to apply the traditional business judgment rule to the revised transaction and instead analyzed the Time board's June 16 decision under *Unocal*. The court ruled that *Unocal* applied to all director actions taken, following receipt of Paramount's hostile tender offer, that were reasonably determined to be defensive. Clearly that was a correct ruling and no party disputes that ruling.

In *Unocal*, we held that before the business judgment rule is applied to a board's adoption of a defensive measure, the burden will lie with the board to prove (a) reasonable grounds for believing that a danger to corporate policy and effectiveness existed; and (b) that the defensive measure adopted was reasonable in relation to the threat posed. *Unocal*, 493 A.2d 946. Directors satisfy the first part of the *Unocal* test by demonstrating good faith and reasonable investigation. We have repeatedly stated that the refusal to entertain an offer may comport with a valid exercise of a board's business judgment. * * *

Unocal involved a two-tier, highly coercive [front-end loaded] tender offer. In such a case, the threat is obvious: shareholders may be compelled to tender to avoid being treated adversely in the second stage of the transaction.[5] * * * In subsequent cases the Court of Chancery has suggested that an all-cash, all-shares offer, falling within a range of values that a shareholder might reasonably prefer, cannot constitute a legally recognized "threat" to shareholder interests sufficient to withstand a *Unocal* analysis. *AC Acquisitions Corp. v. Anderson, Clayton Co.,* Del. Ch., 519 A.2d 103 (1986); *See Grand Metropolitan, PLC v. Pillsbury Co.,* Del. Ch., 558 A.2d 1049 (1988); *City Capital Associates v. Interco, Inc.,* Del. Ch., 551 A.2d 787 (1988). In those cases, the Court of Chancery determined that whatever threat existed related only to the shareholders and only to price and not to the corporation.

From those decisions by our Court of Chancery, Paramount and the individual plaintiffs extrapolate a rule of law that an all-cash, all-shares offer with values reasonably in the range of acceptable price cannot pose any objective threat to a corporation or its shareholders. Thus, Paramount would have us hold that only if the value of Paramount's offer were determined to be clearly inferior to the value created by management's plan to merge with Warner could the offer be viewed—objectively—as a threat.

Implicit in the plaintiffs' argument is the view that a hostile tender offer can pose only two types of threats: the threat of coercion that results from a two-tier offer promising unequal treatment for nontendering shareholders [those left at the back end]; and the threat of inadequate value from an all-shares, all-cash offer at a price below what a target board in good faith deems to be the present value of its shares. * * * Since Paramount's offer was all-cash, the only conceivable "threat," plaintiffs argue, was inadequate value. * * * We disapprove of such a narrow and rigid construction of *Unocal,* for the reasons which follow.

Plaintiffs' position represents a fundamental misconception of our standard of review under *Unocal* principally because it would involve the court in substituting its judgment as to what is a "better" deal for that of a corporation's board of directors. To the extent that the Court of Chancery has recently done so in certain of its opinions, we hereby reject such approach as not in keeping with a proper *Unocal* analysis. * * *

The usefulness of *Unocal* as an analytical tool is precisely its flexibility in the face of a variety of fact *scenarios. Unocal* is not intended as an abstract standard; neither is it a structured and mechanistic procedure of appraisal. Thus, we have said that directors may consider, when evaluating the threat posed by a takeover bid, the "inadequacy of the price offered, nature and timing of the offer, questions of illegality, the impact on 'constituencies' other than shareholders, the risk of nonconsummation and the quality of securities being offered in the exchange." [*Unocal* ,] 493 A.2d at 955. The open-ended analysis mandated by *Unocal* is not intended

---

5. In a front-end loaded two-tiered tender offer, such as the one threatened in the *Unocal* case, a bidder acquires a majority of the shares for cash (in the first stage, or "front end" of the transaction) and then uses its majority control to freeze-out the remaining shareholders (those left at the "back end") usually giving them, instead of cash, high-risk debt instruments, or as they are also known, "junk bonds."—Ed.

to lead to a simple mathematical exercise: that is, of comparing the discounted value of Time–Warner's expected trading price at some future date with Paramount's offer and determining which is the higher. Indeed, in our view, precepts underlying the business judgment rule militate against a court's engaging in the process of attempting to appraise and evaluate the relative merits of a long-term versus a short-term investment goal for shareholders. To engage in such an exercise is a distortion of the *Unocal* process and, in particular, the application of the second part of *Unocal's* test, discussed below.

In this case, the Time board reasonably determined that inadequate value was not the only legally cognizable threat that Paramount's all-cash, all-shares offer could present. Time's board concluded that Paramount's eleventh hour offer posed other threats. One concern was that Time shareholders might elect to tender into Paramount's cash offer in ignorance or a mistaken belief of the strategic benefit which a business combination with Warner might produce. Moreover, Time viewed the conditions attached to Paramount's offer as introducing a degree of uncertainty that skewed a comparative analysis. Further, the timing of Paramount's offer to follow issuance of Time's proxy notice was viewed as arguably designed to upset, if not confuse, the Time stockholders' vote. Given this record evidence, we cannot conclude that the Time board's decision of June 6 that Paramount's offer posed a threat to corporate policy and effectiveness was lacking in good faith or dominated by motives of either entrenchment or self-interest.

Paramount also contends that the Time board had not duly investigated Paramount's offer. Therefore, Paramount argues, Time was unable to make an informed decision that the offer posed a threat to Time's corporate policy. Although the Chancellor did not address this issue directly, his findings of fact do detail Time's exploration of the available entertainment companies, including Paramount, before determining that Warner provided the best strategic "fit." In addition, the court found that Time's board rejected Paramount's offer because Paramount did not serve Time's objectives or meet Time's needs. Thus, the record does, in our judgment, demonstrate that Time's board was adequately informed of the potential benefits of a transaction with Paramount. We agree with the Chancellor that the Time board's lengthy pre-June investigation of potential merger candidates, including Paramount, mooted any obligation on Time's part to halt its merger process with Warner to reconsider Paramount. Time's board was under no obligation to negotiate with Paramount. * * * Time's failure to negotiate cannot be fairly found to have been uninformed. The evidence supporting this finding is materially enhanced by the fact that twelve of Time's sixteen board members were outside independent directors. * * *

We turn to the second part of the *Unocal* analysis. The obvious requisite to determining the reasonableness of a defensive action is a clear identification of the nature of the threat. As the Chancellor correctly noted, this "requires an evaluation of the importance of the corporate objective threatened; alternative methods of protecting that objective; impacts of the 'defensive' action, and other relevant factors." * * * It is not until both parts of the *Unocal* inquiry have been satisfied that the business judgment rule attaches to defensive actions of a board of directors. *Unocal,* 493 A.2d at 954. * * * As applied to the facts of this case, the question is whether the record evidence supports the Court of Chancery's conclusion that the restructuring of the Time–Warner transaction, including the adoption of several preclusive defensive measures, was a *reasonable response* in relation to a perceived threat.

Paramount argues that, assuming its tender offer posed a threat, Time's response was unreasonable in precluding Time's shareholders from accepting the tender offer or receiving a control premium in the immediately foreseeable future. Once again, the contention stems, we believe, from a fundamental misunderstanding of where the power of corporate governance lies. Delaware law confers the management of the corporate enterprise to the stockholders' duly elected board representatives. 8 *Del. C.* § 141(a). The fiduciary duty to manage a corporate enterprise includes the selection of a time frame for achievement of corporate goals. That duty may not be delegated to the stockholders. * * * Directors are not obliged to abandon a deliberately conceived corporate plan for a short-term shareholder profit unless there is clearly no basis to sustain the corporate strategy. * * *

Although the Chancellor blurred somewhat the discrete analyses required under *Unocal,* he did conclude that Time's board reasonably perceived Paramount's offer to be a significant threat to the planned Time–Warner merger and that Time's response was not "overly broad." We have found that even in light of a valid threat, management actions that are coercive in nature or force upon shareholders a management-sponsored alternative to a hostile offer may be struck down as unreasonable and nonproportionate responses. * * *

Here, on the record facts, the Chancellor found that Time's responsive action to Paramount's tender offer was not aimed at "cramming down" on its shareholders a management-sponsored alternative, but rather had as its goal the carrying forward of a pre-existing transaction in an altered form. * * * Thus, the response was reasonably related to the threat. The Chancellor noted that the revised agreement and its accompanying safety devices did not preclude Paramount from making an offer for the combined Time–Warner company or from changing the conditions of its offer so as not to make the offer dependent upon the nullification of the Time–Warner agreement. Thus, the response was proportionate. We affirm the Chancellor's rulings as clearly supported by the record. Finally, we note that although Time was required, as a result of Paramount's hostile offer, to incur a heavy debt to finance its acquisition of Warner, that fact alone does not render the board's decision unreasonable so long as the directors could reasonably perceive the debt load not to be so injurious to the corporation as to jeopardize its well being.

B.

Conclusion

Applying the test for grant or denial of preliminary injunctive relief, we find plaintiffs failed to establish a reasonable likelihood of ultimate success on the merits. Therefore, we affirm.

PARAMOUNT COMMUNICATIONS INC. v. QVC NETWORK, INC.

Supreme Court of Delaware.
637 A.2d 34 (Del. 1994).

JUDGES: Veasey, Chief Justice, Moore and Holland, Justices.

OPINION BY: VEASEY

Veasey, Chief Justice

In this appeal we review an order of the Court of Chancery dated November 24, 1993 (the "November 24 Order"), preliminarily enjoining certain defensive measures designed to facilitate a so-called strategic alliance between Viacom Inc. ("Viacom") and Paramount Communications Inc. ("Paramount") approved by the board of directors of Paramount (the "Paramount Board" or the "Paramount directors") and to thwart an unsolicited, more valuable, tender offer by QVC Network Inc. ("QVC"). In affirming, we hold that the sale of control in this case, which is at the heart of the proposed strategic alliance, implicates enhanced judicial scrutiny of the conduct of the Paramount Board under *Unocal Corp. v. Mesa Petroleum Co.,* Del. Supr. 493 A.2d 946 (1985), and *Revlon, Inc. v. MacAndrews & Forbes Holdings, Inc.,* Del. Supr., 506 A.2d 173 (1986). We further hold that the conduct of the Paramount Board was not reasonable as to process or result.

QVC and certain stockholders of Paramount commenced separate actions (later consolidated) in the Court of Chancery seeking preliminary and permanent injunctive relief against Paramount, certain members of the Paramount Board, and Viacom. This action arises out of a proposed acquisition of Paramount by Viacom through a tender offer followed by a second-step merger (the "Paramount–Viacom transaction"), and a competing unsolicited tender offer by QVC. The Court of Chancery granted a preliminary injunction * * * We affirmed by order dated December 9, 1993 * * * (the "December 9 Order"). * * *

The Court of Chancery found that the Paramount directors violated their fiduciary duties by favoring the Paramount–Viacom transaction over the more valuable unsolicited offer of QVC. The Court of Chancery preliminarily enjoined Paramount and the individual defendants (the "Paramount defendants") from amending or modifying Paramount's stockholder rights agreement (the "Rights Agreement"), including the redemption of the Rights, or taking other action to facilitate the consummation of the pending tender offer by Viacom or any proposed second-step merger, including the Merger Agreement between Paramount and Viacom dated September 12, 1993 (the "Original Merger Agreement"), as amended on October 24, 1993 (the "Amended Merger Agreement"). Viacom and the Paramount defendants were enjoined from taking any action to exercise any provision of the Stock Option Agreement between Paramount and Viacom dated September 12, 1993 (the "Stock Option Agreement"), as amended on October 24, 1993. The Court of Chancery did not grant preliminary injunctive relief as to the termination fee provided for the benefit of Viacom in Section 8.05 of the Original Merger Agreement and the Amended Merger Agreement (the "Termination Fee").

Under the circumstances of this case, the pending sale of control implicated in the Paramount–Viacom transaction required the Paramount Board to act on an informed basis to secure the best value reasonably available to the stockholders. Since we agree with the Court of Chancery that the Paramount directors violated their fiduciary duties, we have AFFIRMED the entry of the order of the Vice Chancellor granting the preliminary injunction and have REMANDED these proceedings to the Court of Chancery for proceedings consistent herewith. * * *

I. FACTS

* * *

Paramount is a Delaware corporation with its principal offices in New York City. Approximately 118 million shares of Paramount's common stock are outstanding and traded on the New York Stock Exchange. The majority of Paramount's stock is publicly held by numerous unaffiliated investors. Paramount owns and operates a diverse group of entertainment businesses, including motion picture and television studios, book publishers, professional sports teams and amusement parks.

There are 15 persons serving on the Paramount Board. Four directors are officer-employees of Paramount: Martin S. Davis ("Davis"), Paramount's Chairman and Chief Executive Officer since 1983; Donald Oresman ("Oresman"), Executive Vice–President, Chief Administrative Officer, and General Counsel; Stanley R. Jaffe, President and Chief Operating Officer; and Ronald L. Nelson, Executive Vice President and Chief Financial Officer. Paramount's 11 outside directors are distinguished and experienced business persons who are present or former senior executives of public corporations or financial institutions. * * *

Viacom is a Delaware corporation with its headquarters in Massachusetts. Viacom is controlled by Sumner M. Redstone ("Redstone"), its Chairman and Chief Executive Officer, who owns indirectly approximately 85.2 percent of Viacom's voting Class A stock and approximately 69.2 percent of Viacom's nonvoting Class B stock * * *. Viacom has a wide range of entertainment operations, including a number of well-known cable television channels such as MTV, Nickelodeon, Showtime, and The Movie Channel. Viacom's equity co-investors in the Paramount–Viacom transaction include NYNEX Corporation and Blockbuster Entertainment Corporation.

QVC is a Delaware corporation with its headquarters in West Chester, Pennsylvania. QVC has several large stockholders, including Liberty Media Corporation, Comcast Corporation, Advance Publications, Inc., and Cox Enterprises Inc. Barry Diller ("Diller"), the Chairman and Chief Executive Officer of QVC, is also a substantial stockholder. QVC sells a variety of merchandise through a televised shopping channel. QVC has several equity co-investors in its proposed combination with Paramount, including BellSouth Corporation and Comcast Corporation.

Beginning in the late 1980s, Paramount investigated the possibility of acquiring or merging with other companies in the entertainment, media, or communications industry. Paramount considered such transactions to be desirable, and perhaps necessary, in order to keep pace with competitors in the rapidly evolving field of entertainment and communications. Consistent with its goal of strategic expansion, Paramount made a tender offer for Time Inc. in 1989, but was ultimately unsuccessful. * * *

Although Paramount had considered a possible combination of Paramount and Viacom as early as 1990, recent efforts to explore such a transaction began at a dinner meeting between Redstone and Davis on April 20, 1993. Robert Greenhill ("Greenhill"), Chairman of Smith Barney Shearson Inc. ("Smith Barney"), attended and helped facilitate this meeting. After several more meetings between Redstone and Davis, serious negotiations began taking place in early July.

It was tentatively agreed that Davis would be the chief executive officer and Redstone would be the controlling stockholder of the combined company, but the parties could not reach agreement on the merger price and the terms of a stock option to be granted to Viacom. With respect to price, Viacom offered a package of cash and stock (primarily Viacom Class B nonvoting stock) with a market value of approximately $61 per share, but Paramount wanted at least $70 per share.

Shortly after negotiations broke down in July 1993, two notable events occurred. First, Davis apparently learned of QVC's potential interest in Paramount, and told Diller over lunch on July 21, 1993, that Paramount was not for sale. Second, the market value of Viacom's Class B nonvoting stock increased from $46.875 on July 6 to $57.25 on August 20. QVC claims (and Viacom disputes) that this price increase was caused by open market purchases of such stock by Redstone or entities controlled by him.

On August 20, 1993, discussions between Paramount and Viacom resumed when Greenhill arranged another meeting between Davis and Redstone. After a short hiatus, the parties negotiated in earnest in early September, and performed due diligence with the assistance of their financial advisors, Lazard Freres & Co. ("Lazard") for Paramount and Smith Barney for Viacom. On September 9, 1993, the Paramount Board was informed about the status of the negotiations and was provided information by Lazard, including an analysis of the proposed transaction.

On September 12, 1993, the Paramount Board met again and unanimously approved the Original Merger Agreement whereby Paramount would merge with and into Viacom. The terms of the merger provided that each share of Paramount common stock would be converted into 0.10 shares of Viacom Class A voting stock, 0.90 shares of Viacom Class B non-voting stock, and $9.10 in cash. In addition, the Paramount Board agreed to amend its "poison pill" Rights Agreement to exempt the proposed merger with Viacom. The Original Merger Agreement also contained several provisions designed to make it more difficult for a potential competing bid to succeed. We focus, as did the Court of Chancery, on three of these defensive provisions: a "no-shop" provision (the "No–Shop Provision"), the Termination Fee, and the Stock Option Agreement.

First, under the No–Shop Provision, the Paramount Board agreed that Paramount would not solicit, encourage, discuss, negotiate, or endorse any competing transaction unless: (a) a third party "makes an unsolicited written, bona fide proposal, which is not subject to any material contingencies relating to financing"; and (b) the Paramount Board determines that discussions or negotiations with the third party are necessary for the Paramount Board to comply with its fiduciary duties.

Second, under the Termination Fee provision, Viacom would receive a $100 million termination fee if: (a) Paramount terminated the Original Merger Agreement because of a competing transaction; (b) Paramount's stockholders did not approve the merger; or (c) the Paramount Board recommended a competing transaction.

The third and most significant deterrent device was the Stock Option Agreement, which granted to Viacom an option to purchase approximately 19.9 percent (23,699,000 shares) of Paramount's outstanding common stock at $69.14 per share if any of the triggering events for the Termination Fee occurred. In addition to the customary terms that are normally associated with a stock option, the Stock Option Agreement contained two provisions that were both unusual and highly beneficial to Viacom: (a) Viacom was permitted to pay for the shares with a senior subordinated note of questionable marketability instead of cash, thereby avoiding the need to raise the $1.6 billion purchase price (the "Note Feature"); and (b) Viacom could elect to require Paramount to pay Viacom in cash a sum equal to the difference between the purchase price and the market price of Paramount's stock (the "Put Feature"). Because the Stock Option Agreement was not "capped" to limit its maximum dollar value, it had the potential to reach (and in this case did reach) unreasonable levels.

After the execution of the Original Merger Agreement and the Stock Option Agreement on September 12, 1993, Paramount and Viacom announced their proposed merger. In a number of public statements, the parties indicated that the pending transaction was a virtual certainty. Redstone described it as a "marriage" that would "never be torn asunder" and stated that only a "nuclear attack" could break the deal. Redstone also called Diller and John Malone of Tele–Communications Inc., a major stockholder of QVC, to dissuade them from making a competing bid.

Despite these attempts to discourage a competing bid, Diller sent a letter to Davis on September 20, 1993, proposing a merger in which QVC would acquire Paramount for approximately $80 per share, consisting of 0.893 shares of QVC common stock and $30 in cash. QVC also expressed its eagerness to meet with Paramount to negotiate the details of a transaction. When the Paramount Board met on September 27, it was advised by Davis that the Original Merger Agreement prohibited Paramount from having discussions with QVC (or anyone else) unless certain conditions were satisfied. In particular, QVC had to supply evidence that its proposal was not subject to financing contingencies. The Paramount Board was also provided information from Lazard describing QVC and its proposal.

On October 5, 1993, QVC provided Paramount with evidence of QVC's financing. The Paramount Board then held another meeting on October 11, and decided to authorize management to meet with QVC. Davis also informed the Paramount Board that Booz–Allen & Hamilton ("Booz–Allen"), a management consulting firm, had been retained to assess, *inter alia,* the incremental earnings potential from a Paramount–Viacom merger and a Paramount–QVC merger. Discussions proceeded slowly, however, due to a delay in Paramount signing a confidentiality agreement. In response to Paramount's request for information, QVC provided two binders of documents to Paramount on October 20.

On October 21, 1993, QVC filed this action and publicly announced an $80 cash tender offer for 51 percent of Paramount's outstanding shares (the "QVC tender offer"). Each remaining share of Paramount common stock would be converted into 1.42857 shares of QVC common stock in a second-step merger. The tender offer was conditioned on, among other things, the invalidation of the Stock Option Agreement, which was worth over $200 million by that point. [By November 15, 1993, the value of the Stock Option Agreement had increased to nearly $500 million based on the $90 QVC bid.] QVC contends that it had to commence a tender offer because of the slow pace of the merger discussions and the need to begin seeking clearance under federal antitrust laws.

Confronted by QVC's hostile bid, which on its face offered over $10 per share more than the consideration provided by the Original Merger Agreement, Viacom realized that it would need to raise its bid in order to remain competitive. Within hours after QVC's tender offer was announced, Viacom entered into discussions with Paramount concerning a revised transaction. These discussions led to serious negotiations concerning a comprehensive amendment to the original Paramount–Viacom transaction. In effect, the opportunity for a "new deal" with Viacom was at hand for the Paramount Board. With the QVC hostile bid offering greater value to the Paramount stockholders, the Paramount Board had considerable leverage with Viacom.

At a special meeting on October 24, 1993, the Paramount Board approved the Amended Merger Agreement and an amendment to the Stock Option Agreement. The Amended Merger Agreement was, however, essentially the same as the Original Merger Agreement, except that it included a few new provisions. One provision related to an $80 per share cash tender offer by Viacom for 51 percent of Paramount's stock, and another changed the merger consideration so that each share of Paramount would be converted into 0.20408 shares of Viacom Class A voting stock, 1.08317 shares of Viacom Class B nonvoting stock, and 0.20408 shares of a new series of Viacom convertible preferred stock. The Amended Merger Agreement also added a provision giving Paramount the right not to amend its Rights Agreement to exempt Viacom if the Paramount Board determined that such an amendment would be inconsistent with its fiduciary duties because another offer constituted a "better alternative." Finally, the Paramount Board was given the power to terminate the Amended Merger Agreement if it withdrew its recommendation of the Viacom transaction or recommended a competing transaction.

Although the Amended Merger Agreement offered more consideration to the Paramount stockholders and somewhat more flexibility to the Paramount Board than did the Original Merger Agreement, the defensive measures designed to make a competing bid more difficult were not removed or modified. In particular, there is no evidence in the record that Paramount sought to use its newly-acquired leverage to eliminate or modify the No–Shop Provision, the Termination Fee, or the Stock Option Agreement when the subject of amending the Original Merger Agreement was on the table.

Viacom's tender offer commenced on October 25, 1993, and QVC's tender offer was formally launched on October 27, 1993. Diller sent a letter to the Paramount Board on October 28 requesting an opportunity to negotiate with Paramount, and Oresman responded the following day by agreeing to meet. The meeting, held on November 1, was not very fruitful, however, after QVC's proposed guidelines for a "fair bidding process" were rejected by Paramount on the ground that "auction procedures" were inappropriate and contrary to Paramount's contractual obligations to Viacom.

On November 6, 1993, Viacom unilaterally raised its tender offer price to $85 per share in cash and offered a comparable increase in the value of the securities being proposed in the second-step merger. At a telephonic meeting held later that day, the Paramount Board agreed to recommend Viacom's higher bid to Paramount's stockholders.

QVC responded to Viacom's higher bid on November 12 by increasing its tender offer to $90 per share and by increasing the securities for its second-step merger by a similar amount. In response to QVC's latest offer, the Paramount Board scheduled a meeting for November 15, 1993. Prior to the meeting, Oresman sent the members of the Paramount Board a document summarizing the "conditions and uncertainties" of QVC's offer. One director testified that this document gave him a very negative impression of the QVC bid.

At its meeting on November 15, 1993, the Paramount Board determined that the new QVC offer was not in the best interests of the stockholders. The purported basis for this conclusion was that QVC's bid was excessively conditional. The Paramount Board did not communicate with QVC regarding the status of the conditions because it believed that the No–Shop Provision prevented such communication in the absence of firm financing. Several Paramount directors also testified that they believed the Viacom transaction would be more advantageous to Paramount's future business prospects than a QVC transaction.[1] Although a number of materials were distributed to the Paramount Board describing the Viacom and QVC transactions, the only quantitative analysis of the consideration to be received by the stockholders under each proposal was based on then-current market prices of the securities involved, not on the anticipated value of such securities at the time when the stockholders would receive them. * * *

The preliminary injunction hearing in this case took place on November 16, 1993. On November 19, Diller wrote to the Paramount Board to inform it that QVC had obtained financing commitments for its tender offer and that there was no antitrust obstacle to the offer. On November 24, 1993, the Court of Chancery issued its decision granting a preliminary injunction in favor of QVC and the plaintiff stockholders. This appeal followed.

II. APPLICABLE PRINCIPLES OF ESTABLISHED DELAWARE LAW

The General Corporation Law of the State of Delaware (the "General Corporation Law") and the decisions of this Court have repeatedly recognized the fundamental principle that the management of the business and affairs of a Delaware corporation is entrusted to its directors, who are the duly elected and authorized representatives of the stockholders. 8 *Del. C.* § 141(a) * * * Under normal circumstances, neither the courts nor the stockholders should interfere with the managerial decisions of the directors. The business judgment rule embodies the deference to which such decisions are entitled. * * *

Nevertheless, there are rare situations which mandate that a court take a more direct and active role in overseeing the decisions made and

---

1. [Most footnotes have been omitted. Those that remain have been renumbered] This belief may have been based on a report prepared by Booz–Allen and distributed to the Paramount Board at its October 24 meeting. The report, which relied on public information regarding QVC, concluded that the synergies of a Paramount–Viacom merger were significantly superior to those of a Paramount–QVC merger. QVC has labelled the Booz–Allen report as a "joke."

actions taken by directors. In these situations, a court subjects the directors' conduct to enhanced scrutiny to ensure that it is reasonable.[2] The decisions of this Court have clearly established the circumstances where such enhanced scrutiny will be applied. * * * The case at bar implicates two such circumstances: (1) the approval of a transaction resulting in a sale of control, and (2) the adoption of defensive measures in response to a threat to corporate control.

A.   The Significance of a Sale or Change * * * of Control

When a majority of a corporation's voting shares are acquired by a single person or entity, or by a cohesive group acting together, there is a significant diminution in the voting power of those who thereby become minority stockholders. Under the statutory framework of the General Corporation Law, many of the most fundamental corporate changes can be implemented only if they are approved by a majority vote of the stockholders. Such actions include elections of directors, amendments to the certificate of incorporation, mergers, consolidations, sales of all or substantially all of the assets of the corporation, and dissolution. * * * Because of the overriding importance of voting rights, this Court and the Court of Chancery have consistently acted to protect stockholders from unwarranted interference with such rights. * * *

In the absence of devices protecting the minority stockholders, * * * stockholder votes are likely to become mere formalities where there is a majority stockholder. For example, minority stockholders can be deprived of a continuing equity interest in their corporation by means of a cash-out merger. *Weinberger,* 457 A.2d at 703. Absent effective protective provisions, minority stockholders must rely for protection solely on the fiduciary duties owed to them by the directors and the majority stockholder, since the minority stockholders have lost the power to influence corporate direction through the ballot. The acquisition of majority status and the consequent privilege of exerting the powers of majority ownership come at a price. That price is usually a control premium which recognizes not only the value of a control block of shares, but also compensates the minority stockholders for their resulting loss of voting power.

In the case before us, the public stockholders (in the aggregate) currently own a majority of Paramount's voting stock. Control of the corporation is not vested in a single person, entity, or group, but vested in the fluid aggregation of unaffiliated stockholders. In the event the Paramount–Viacom transaction is consummated, the public stockholders will receive cash and a minority equity voting position in the surviving corporation. Following such consummation, there will be a controlling

---

2. Where actual self-interest is present and affects a majority of the directors approving a transaction, a court will apply even more exacting scrutiny to determine whether the transaction is entirely fair to the stockholders. *E.g., Weinberger v. UOP, Inc.,* Del. Supr., 457 A.2d 701, 710–11 (1983) * * *.

stockholder who will have the voting power to: (a) elect directors; (b) cause a break-up of the corporation: (c) merge it with another company; (d) cash-out the public stockholders: (e) amend the certificate of incorporation; (f) sell all or substantially all of the corporate assets; or (g) otherwise alter materially the nature of the corporation and the public stockholders' interests. Irrespective of the present Paramount Board's vision of a long-term strategic alliance with Viacom, the proposed sale of control would provide the new controlling stockholder with the power to alter that vision.

Because of the intended sale of control, the Paramount–Viacom transaction has economic consequences of considerable significance to the Paramount stockholders. Once control has shifted, the current Paramount stockholders will have no leverage in the future to demand another control premium. As a result, the Paramount stockholders are entitled to receive, and should receive, a control premium and/or protective devices of significant value. There being no such protective provisions in the Viacom–Paramount transaction, the Paramount directors had an obligation to take the maximum advantage of the current opportunity to realize for the stockholders the best value reasonably available.

B. The Obligations of Directors in a Sale or Change of Control Transaction

The consequences of a sale of control impose special obligations on the directors of a corporation. * * * In particular, they have the obligation of acting reasonably to seek the transaction offering the best value reasonably available to the stockholders. The courts will apply enhanced scrutiny to ensure that the directors have acted reasonably. * * * The directors' fiduciary duties in a sale of control context are those which generally attach. In short, "the directors must act in accordance with their fundamental duties of care and loyalty." *Barkan v. Amsted Indus., Inc.,* Del. Supr., 567 A.2d 1279, 1286 (1989). As we held in [*Mills Acquisition Co. v.*] *Macmillan, Inc.* [559 A.2d 1261 (1989)]:

> It is basic to our law that the board of directors has the ultimate responsibility for managing the business and affairs of a corporation. In discharging this function, the directors owe fiduciary duties of care and loyalty to the corporation and its shareholders. **This unremitting obligation extends equally to board conduct in a sale of corporate control.**

559 A.2d at 1280 (emphasis supplied) (citations omitted).

In the sale of control context, the directors must focus on one primary objective—to secure the transaction offering the best value reasonably available for the stockholders—and they must exercise their fiduciary duties to further that end. The decisions of this Court have consistently emphasized this goal. *Revlon,* 506 A.2d at 182 ("The duty of the board ... [is] the maximization of the company's value at a sale for the stockholders' benefit."); *Macmillan,* 559 A.2d at 1288 ("In a sale of corporate control the responsibility of the directors is to get the highest value reasonably attainable for the shareholders."); *Barkan,* 567 A.2d at 1286 ("The board must act in a neutral manner to encourage the highest possible price for shareholders."). * * *

In pursuing this objective, the directors must be especially diligent. * * * In particular, this Court has stressed the importance of the board being adequately informed in negotiating a sale of control: "The need for adequate information is central to the enlightened evaluation of a transaction that a board must make." *Barkan,* 567 A.2d at 1287. This requirement is consistent with the general principle that "directors have a duty to inform themselves, prior to making a business decision, of all material information reasonably available to them." *Aronson [v. Lewis],* 473 A.2d [805 (1984)] at 812. *See also* * * * *Smith v. Van Gorkom,* Del. Supr., 488 A.2d 858, 872 (1985). Moreover, the role of outside, independent directors becomes particularly important because of the magnitude of a sale of control transaction and the possibility, in certain cases, that management may not necessarily be impartial. * * *

Barkan teaches some of the methods by which a board can fulfill its obligation to seek the best value reasonably available to the stockholders. 567 A.2d at 1286–87. These methods are designed to determine the existence and viability of possible alternatives. They include conducting an auction, canvassing the market, etc. Delaware law recognizes that there is "no single blueprint" that directors must follow. * * *

In determining which alternative provides the best value for the stockholders, a board of directors is not limited to considering only the amount of cash involved, and is not required to ignore totally its view of the future value of a strategic alliance. * * * Instead, the directors should analyze the entire situation and evaluate in a disciplined manner the consideration being offered. Where stock or other non-cash consideration is involved, the board should try to quantify its value, if feasible, to achieve an objective comparison of the alternatives. * * * In addition, the board may assess a variety of practical considerations relating to each alternative including:

> [an offer's] fairness and feasibility; the proposed or actual financing for the offer, and the consequences of that financing; questions of illegality; ... the risk of non-consummation; ... the bidder's identity, prior background and other business venture experiences; and the bidder's business plans for the corporation and their effects on stockholder interests.

Macmillan, 559 A.2d at 1282 n. 29. These considerations are important because the selection of one alternative may permanently foreclose other opportunities. While the assessment of these factors may be complex, the board's goal is straightforward: Having informed themselves of all material information reasonably available, the directors must decide which alternative is most likely to offer the best value reasonably available to the stockholders.

C. Enhanced Judicial Scrutiny of a Sale or Change of Control Transaction

Board action in the circumstances presented here is subject to enhanced scrutiny. Such scrutiny is mandated by: (a) the threatened diminution of the current stockholders' voting power; (b) the fact that an asset belonging to public stockholders (a control premium) is being sold and may never be available again: and (c) the traditional concern of Delaware courts for actions which impair or impede stockholder voting rights * * * In *Macmillan,* this Court held:

> When *Revlon* duties devolve upon directors, this Court will continue to exact an enhanced judicial scrutiny at the threshold, as in *Unocal,* before the normal presumptions of the business judgment rule will apply. * * *

559 A.2d at 1288. The *Macmillan* decision articulates a specific two-part test for analyzing board action where competing bidders are not treated equally: * * *

> In the face of disparate treatment, the trial court must first examine whether the directors properly perceived that shareholder interests were enhanced. In any event the board's action must be reasonable in relation to the advantage sought to be achieved, or conversely, to the threat which a particular bid allegedly poses to stockholder interests.

Id. * * *

The key features of an enhanced scrutiny test are: (a) a judicial determination regarding the adequacy of the decisionmaking process employed by the directors, including the information on which the directors based their decision; and (b) a judicial examination of the reasonableness of the directors' action in light of the circumstances then existing. The directors have the burden of proving that they were adequately informed and acted reasonably.

Although an enhanced scrutiny test involves a review of the reasonableness of the substantive merits of a board's actions,[3] a court should not ignore the complexity of the directors' task in a sale of control. There are many business and financial considerations implicated in investigating and selecting the best value reasonably available. The board of directors

---

3. It is to be remembered that, in cases where the traditional business judgment rule is applicable and the board acted with due care, in good faith, and in the honest belief that they are acting in the best interests of the stockholders (which is not this case), the Court gives great deference to the substance of the directors' decision and will not invalidate the decision, will not examine its reasonableness, and "will not substitute our views for those of the board if the latter's decision can be 'attributed to any rational business purpose.'" *Unocal,* 493 A.2d at 949 *(quoting Sinclair Oil Corp. v. Levien,* Del. Supr., 280 A.2d 717, 720 (1971)). * * *

is the corporate decisionmaking body best equipped to make these judgments. Accordingly, a court applying enhanced judicial scrutiny should be deciding whether the directors made **a reasonable** decision, not **a perfect** decision. If a board selected one of several reasonable alternatives, a court should not second-guess that choice even though it might have decided otherwise or subsequent events may have cast doubt on the board's determination. Thus, courts will not substitute their business judgment for that of the directors, but will determine if the directors' decision was, on balance, within a range of reasonableness. * * *

D. *Revlon* and *Time–Warner* Distinguished

The Paramount defendants and Viacom assert that the fiduciary obligations and the enhanced judicial scrutiny discussed above are not implicated in this case in the absence of a "break-up" of the corporation, and that the order granting the preliminary injunction should be reversed. This argument is based on their erroneous interpretation of our decisions in *Revlon* and *Time-Warner.*

In *Revlon,* we reviewed the actions of the board of directors of Revlon, Inc. ("Revlon"), which had rebuffed the overtures of Pantry Pride, Inc. and had instead entered into an agreement with Forstmann Little & Co. ("Forstmann") providing for the acquisition of 100 percent of Revlon's outstanding stock by Forstmann and the subsequent break-up of Revlon. Based on the facts and circumstances present in *Revlon,* we held that "the directors' role changed from defenders of the corporate bastion to auctioneers charged with getting the best price for the stockholders at a sale of the company." 506 A.2d at 182. We further held that "when a board ends an intense bidding contest on an insubstantial basis, ... [that] action cannot withstand the enhanced scrutiny which *Unocal* requires of director conduct." 506 A.2d at 184.

It is true that one of the circumstances bearing on these holdings was the fact that "the break-up of the company ... had become a reality which even the directors embraced." 506 A.2d at 182. It does not follow, however, that a "break-up" must be present and "inevitable" before directors are subject to enhanced judicial scrutiny and are required to pursue a transaction that is calculated to produce the best value reasonably available to the stockholders. In fact, we stated in *Revlon* that "when bidders make relatively similar offers, **or** dissolution of the company becomes inevitable, the directors cannot fulfill their enhanced *Unocal* duties by playing favorites with the contending factions." 506 A.2d at 184 (emphasis added). *Revlon* thus does not hold that an inevitable dissolution or "break-up" is necessary.

The decisions of this Court following *Revlon* reinforced the applicability of enhanced scrutiny and the directors' obligation to seek the best value reasonably available for the stockholders where there is a pending sale of control, regardless of whether or not there is to be a break-up of the corporation. In *Macmillan,* this Court held:

We stated in *Revlon,* and again here, that **in a sale of corporate control** the responsibility of the directors is to get the highest value reasonably attainable for the shareholders.

559 A.2d at 1288 (emphasis added). In *Barkan,* we observed further:

We believe that the general principles announced in *Revlon,* in *Unocal Corp. v. Mesa Petroleum Co.,* Del. Supr., 493 A.2d 946 (1985), and in *Moran v. Household International, Inc.,* Del. Supr., 500 A.2d 1346 (1985) govern this case and every case in which a **fundamental change of corporate control** occurs or is contemplated.

567 A.2d at 1286 (emphasis added).

Although *Macmillan* and *Barkan* are clear in holding that a change of control imposes on directors the obligation to obtain the best value reasonably available to the stockholders, the Paramount defendants have interpreted our decision in *Time-Warner* as requiring a corporate break-up in order for that obligation to apply. The facts in *Time-Warner,* however, were quite different from the facts of this case, and refute Paramount's position here. In *Time-Warner,* the Chancellor held that there was no change of control in the original stock-for-stock merger between Time and Warner because Time would be owned by a fluid aggregation of unaffiliated stockholders both before and after the merger:

If the appropriate inquiry is whether a change in control is contemplated, the answer must be sought in the specific circumstances surrounding the transaction. Surely under some circumstances a stock for stock merger could reflect a transfer of corporate control. That would, for example, plainly be the case here if Warner were a private company. But where, as here, the shares of both constituent corporations are widely held, corporate control can be expected to remain unaffected by a stock for stock merger. This in my judgment was the situation with respect to the original merger agreement. When the specifics of that situation are reviewed, it is seen that, aside from legal technicalities and aside from arrangements thought to enhance the prospect for the ultimate succession of [Nicholas J. Nicholas, Jr., president of Time], neither corporation could be said to be acquiring the other. **Control of both remained in a large, fluid, changeable and changing market.**

The existence of a control block of stock in the hands of a single shareholder or a group with loyalty to each other does have real consequences to the financial value of "minority" stock. The law offers some protection to such shares through the imposition of a fiduciary duty upon controlling shareholders. **But here, effectuation of the merger would not have subjected Time shareholders to the risks and consequences of holders of minority shares. This is a reflection of the fact that no control passed to anyone in the transaction contemplated.** The shareholders of Time would have "suffered" dilution, of course, but they would suffer the same type of dilution upon the public distribution of new stock.

Paramount Communications Inc. v. Time Inc., Del. Ch., No. 10866, Allen, C. (July 17, 1989), reprinted at 15 Del. J. Corp. L. 700, 739 (emphasis added). Moreover, the transaction actually consummated in *Time-Warner* was not a merger, as originally planned, but a sale of Warner's stock to Time.

In our affirmance of the Court of Chancery's well-reasoned decision, this Court held that "The Chancellor's findings of fact are supported by the record and **his conclusion is correct as a matter of law.**" 571 A.2d at 1150 (emphasis added). Nevertheless, the Paramount defendants here have argued that a break-up is a requirement and have focused on the following language in our *Time-Warner* decision:

> However, we premise our rejection of plaintiffs' *Revlon* claim on different grounds, namely, the absence of any substantial evidence to conclude that Time's board, in negotiating with Warner, made the dissolution or break-up of the corporate entity inevitable, as was the case in *Revlon.*
>
> Under Delaware law there are, generally speaking and **without excluding other possibilities,** two circumstances which may implicate *Revlon* duties. The first, and clearer one, is when a corporation **initiates an active bidding process seeking to sell itself** or to effect a business reorganization involving a clear breakup of the company. However, *Revlon* duties may also be triggered where, in response to a bidder's offer, a target abandons its long-term strategy and seeks an alternative transaction involving the breakup of the company.

Id. at 1150 (emphasis added) (citation and footnote omitted).

The Paramount defendants have misread the holding of *Time-Warner.* Contrary to their argument, our decision in *Time-Warner* expressly states that the two general scenarios discussed in the above-quoted paragraph are not the **only** instances where "*Revlon* duties" may be implicated. The Paramount defendants' argument totally ignores the phrase "without excluding other possibilities." Moreover, the instant case is clearly within the first general scenario set forth in *Time-Warner.* The Paramount Board, albeit unintentionally, had "initiated an active bidding process seeking to sell itself" by agreeing to sell control of the corporation to Viacom in circumstances where another potential acquiror (QVC) was equally interested in being a bidder.

The Paramount defendants' position that **both** a change of control **and** a break-up are **required** must be rejected. Such a holding would unduly restrict the application of *Revlon,* is inconsistent with this Court's decisions in *Barkan* and *Macmillan,* and has no basis in policy. There are few events that have a more significant impact on the stockholders than a sale of control or a corporate break-up. Each event represents a fundamental and perhaps irrevocable) change in the nature of the corporate enterprise from a practical standpoint. It is the significance of **each** of these events that justifies: (a) focusing on the directors' obligation to seek the best value reasonably available to the stockholders; and (b) requiring a close scrutiny of board action which could be contrary to the stockholders' interests.

Accordingly, when a corporation undertakes a transaction which will cause: (a) a change in corporate control; **or** (b) a break-up of the corporate entity, the directors' obligation is to seek the best value reasonably available to the stockholders. This obligation arises because the effect of the Viacom–Paramount transaction, if consummated, is to shift control of Paramount from the public stockholders to a controlling stockholder, Viacom. Neither *Time-Warner* nor any other decision of this Court holds that a "break-up" of the company is essential to give rise to this obligation where there is a sale of control.

III. BREACH OF FIDUCIARY DUTIES BY PARAMOUNT BOARD

We now turn to duties of the Paramount Board under the facts of this case and our conclusions as to the breaches of those duties which warrant injunctive relief.

A. The Specific Obligations of the Paramount Board

Under the facts of this case, the Paramount directors had the obligation: (a) to be diligent and vigilant in examining critically the Paramount–Viacom transaction and the QVC tender offers; (b) to act in good faith; (c) to obtain, and act with due care on, all material information reasonably available, including information necessary to compare the two offers to determine which of these transactions, or an alternative course of action, would provide the best value reasonably available to the stockholders; and (d) to negotiate actively and in good faith with both Viacom and QVC to that end.

Having decided to sell control of the corporation, the Paramount directors were required to evaluate critically whether or not all material aspects of the Paramount–Viacom transaction (separately and in the aggregate) were reasonable and in the best interests of the Paramount stockholders in light of current circumstances, including: the change of control premium, the Stock Option Agreement, the Termination Fee, the coercive nature of both the Viacom and QVC tender offers,[4] the No–Shop Provision, and the proposed disparate use of the Rights Agreement as to the Viacom and QVC tender offers, respectively.

These obligations necessarily implicated various issues, including the questions of whether or not those provisions and other aspects of the

---

4. Both the Viacom and the QVC tender offers were for 51 percent cash and a "back-end" of various securities, the value of each of which depended on the fluctuating value of Viacom and QVC stock at any given time. Thus, both tender offers were two-tiered, front-end loaded, and coercive. Such coercive offers are inherently problematic and should be expected to receive particularly careful analysis by a target board. *See Unocal,* 493 A.2d at 956.

Paramount–Viacom transaction (separately and in the aggregate): (a) adversely affected the value provided to the Paramount stockholders; (b) inhibited or encouraged alternative bids; (c) were enforceable contractual obligations in light of the directors' fiduciary duties; and (d) in the end would advance or retard the Paramount directors' obligation to secure for the Paramount stockholders the best value reasonably available under the circumstances.

The Paramount defendants contend that they were precluded by certain contractual provisions including the No–Shop Provision, from negotiating with QVC or seeking alternatives. Such provisions, whether or not they are presumptively valid in the abstract, may not validly define or limit the directors' fiduciary duties under Delaware law or prevent the Paramount directors from carrying out their fiduciary duties under Delaware law. To the extent such provisions are inconsistent with those duties, they are invalid and unenforceable. *See Revlon,* 506 A.2d at 184–85.

Since the Paramount directors had already decided to sell control, they had an obligation to continue their search for the best value reasonably available to the stockholders. This continuing obligation included the responsibility, at the October 24 board meeting and thereafter, to evaluate critically both the QVC tender offers and the Paramount–Viacom transaction to determine if: (a) the QVC tender offer was, or would continue to be, conditional; (b) the QVC tender offer could be improved; (c) the Viacom tender offer or other aspects of the Paramount–Viacom transaction could be improved; (d) each of the respective offers would be reasonably likely to come to closure, and under what circumstances; (e) other material information was reasonably available for consideration by the Paramount directors; (f) there were viable and realistic alternative courses of action; and (g) the timing constraints could be managed so the directors could consider these matters carefully and deliberately.

B. The Breaches of Fiduciary Duty by the Paramount Board

The Paramount directors made the decision on September 12, 1993, that, in their judgment, a strategic merger with Viacom on the economic terms of the Original Merger Agreement was in the best interests of Paramount and its stockholders. Those terms provided a modest change of control premium to the stockholders. The directors also decided at that time that it was appropriate to agree to certain defensive measures (the Stock Option Agreement, the Termination Fee, and the No–Shop Provision) insisted upon by Viacom as part of that economic transaction. Those defensive measures, coupled with the sale of control and subsequent disparate treatment of competing bidders, implicated the judicial scrutiny of *Unocal, Revlon* * * * and their progeny. We conclude that the Paramount directors' process was not reasonable, and the result achieved for the stockholders was not reasonable under the circumstances.

When entering into the Original Merger Agreement, and thereafter, the Paramount Board clearly gave insufficient attention to the potential consequences of the defensive measures demanded by Viacom. The Stock Option Agreement had a number of unusual and potentially "draconian" * * * provisions, including the Note Feature and the Put Feature. Furthermore, the Termination Fee, whether or not unreasonable by itself, clearly made Paramount less attractive to other bidders, when coupled with the Stock Option Agreement. Finally, the No–Shop Provision inhibited the Paramount Board's ability to negotiate with other potential bidders, particularly QVC which had already expressed an interest in Paramount. * * *

Throughout the applicable time period, and especially from the first QVC merger proposal on September 20 through the Paramount Board meeting on November 15, QVC's interest in Paramount provided the **opportunity** for the Paramount Board to seek significantly higher value for the Paramount stockholders than that being offered by Viacom. QVC persistently demonstrated its intention to meet and exceed the Viacom offers, and frequently expressed its willingness to negotiate possible further increases.

The Paramount directors had the opportunity in the October 23–24 time frame, when the Original Merger Agreement was renegotiated, to take appropriate action to modify the improper defensive measures as well as to improve the economic terms of the Paramount–Viacom transaction. Under the circumstances existing at that time, it should have been clear to the Paramount Board that the Stock Option Agreement, coupled with the Termination Fee and the No–Shop Clause, were impeding the realization of the best value reasonably available to the Paramount stockholders. Nevertheless, the Paramount Board made no effort to eliminate or modify these counterproductive devices, and instead continued to cling to its vision of a strategic alliance with Viacom. Moreover, based on advice from the Paramount management, the Paramount directors considered the QVC offer to be "conditional" and asserted that they were precluded by the No–Shop Provision from seeking more information from, or negotiating with, QVC.

By November 12, 1993, the value of the revised QVC offer on its face exceeded that of the Viacom offer by over $1 billion at then current values. This significant disparity of value cannot be justified on the basis of the directors' vision of future strategy, primarily because the change of control would supplant the authority of the current Paramount Board to continue to hold and implement their strategic vision in any meaningful way. Moreover, their uninformed process had deprived their strategic vision of much of its credibility. *See Van Gorkom,* 488 A.2d at 872 * * *.

When the Paramount directors met on November 15 to consider QVC's increased tender offer, they remained prisoners of their own misconceptions and missed opportunities to eliminate the restrictions they had imposed on themselves. Yet, it was not "too late" to reconsider negotiating with QVC. The circumstances existing on November 15 made it clear that the defensive measures, taken as a whole, were problematic: (a) the No–Shop Provision could not define or limit their fiduciary duties; (b) the Stock Option Agreement had become "draconian"; and (c) the Termination Fee, in context with all the circumstances, was similarly deterring the realization of possibly higher bids. Nevertheless, the Paramount directors remained paralyzed by their uninformed belief that the QVC offer was "illusory." This final opportunity to negotiate on the stockholders' behalf and to fulfill their obligation to seek the best value reasonably available was thereby squandered. * * *

IV. VIACOM'S CLAIM OF VESTED CONTRACT RIGHTS

Viacom argues that it had certain "vested" contract rights with respect to the No–Shop Provision and the Stock Option Agreement. * * * In effect, Viacom's argument is that the Paramount directors could enter into an agreement in violation of their fiduciary duties and then render Paramount, and ultimately its stockholders, liable for failing to carry out an agreement in violation of those duties. Viacom's protestations about vested rights are without merit. This Court has found that those defensive measures were improperly designed to deter potential bidders, and that such measures do not meet the reasonableness test to which they must be subjected. They are consequently invalid and unenforceable under the facts of this case.

The No–Shop Provision could not validly define or limit the fiduciary duties of the Paramount directors. To the extent that a contract, or a provision thereof, purports to require a board to act or not act in such a fashion as to limit the exercise of fiduciary duties, it is invalid and unenforceable. * * * Despite the arguments of Paramount and Viacom to the contrary, the Paramount directors could not contract away their fiduciary obligations. Since the No–Shop Provision was invalid, Viacom never had any vested contract rights in the provision.

As discussed previously, the Stock Option Agreement contained several "draconian" aspects, including the Note Feature and the Put Feature. While we have held that lock-up options are not *per se* illegal, *see Revlon,* 506 A.2d at 183, no options with similar features have ever been upheld by this Court. Under the circumstances of this case, the Stock Option Agreement clearly is invalid. Accordingly, Viacom never had any vested contract rights in that Agreement.

Viacom, a sophisticated party with experienced legal and financial advisors, knew of (and in fact demanded) the unreasonable features of the Stock Option Agreement. It cannot be now heard to argue that it obtained vested contract rights by negotiating and obtaining contractual provisions from a board acting in violation of its fiduciary duties. As the Nebraska Supreme Court said in rejecting a similar argument in *ConAgra, Inc. v. Cargill, Inc.,* Neb. Supr., 222 Neb. 136, 382 N.W.2d 576, 587–88 (1986), "To so hold, it would seem, would be to get the shareholders coming and going." * * *

V. CONCLUSION

The realization of the best value reasonably available to the stockholders became the Paramount directors' primary obligation under these facts in light of the change of control. That obligation was not satisfied, and the Paramount Board's process was deficient. The directors' initial hope and expectation for a strategic alliance with Viacom was allowed to dominate their decisionmaking process to the point where the arsenal of defensive measures established at the outset was perpetuated (not modified or eliminated) when the situation was dramatically altered. QVC's unsolicited bid presented the opportunity for significantly greater value for the stockholders and enhanced negotiating leverage for the directors. Rather than seizing those opportunities, the Paramount directors chose to wall themselves off from material information which was reasonably available and to hide behind the defensive measures as a rationalization for refusing to negotiate with QVC or seeking other alternatives. Their view of the strategic alliance likewise became an empty rationalization as the opportunities for higher value for the stockholders continued to develop.

It is the nature of the judicial process that we decide only the case before us—a case which, on its facts, is clearly controlled by established Delaware law. Here, the proposed change of control and the implications thereof were crystal clear. In other cases they may be less clear. The holding of this case on its facts, coupled with the holdings of the principal cases discussed herein where the issue of sale of control is implicated, should provide a workable precedent against which to measure future cases. * * *

NOTES AND QUESTIONS

1. How much discretion does a board of directors have to wrap up a deal for the sale of a corporation? To answer this question requires coming to grips with what the former Chief Justice of the Delaware Supreme Court, Justice Veasey, who wrote the opinion in *Paramount v. QVC*, has called the "defining tension" in corporate governance today. For Justice Veazey this is "the tension between deference to directors' decisions and the scope of judicial review." E. Norman Veasey, The Defining Tension in Corporate Governance in America, 52 Bus. Law. 393, 403 (1997). Do you agree or disagree with the Delaware Supreme Court's resolution of these issues in *Time v. Paramount* and *Paramount v. QVC*? Can you explain why the discretion of the board is affirmed in the first case and overruled in the second?

Both of these cases were controversial, although, among scholars, there has probably been greater approval of what the Delaware Supreme Court did in *Paramount v. QVC*. Can you understand why this might be true? For an entertaining review of *Paramount v. QVC*, with some pointed criticisms of *Time v. Paramount*, see Ehud Kamar, "The Story of *Paramount Communications v. QVC Network*: Everything is Personal," Chapter 10 of J. Mark Ramseyer, ed. Corporate Law Stories 293 (2009).

2. Following these two cases the Delaware Supreme Court was confronted with another interesting endgame situation in *Omnicare, Inc. v. NCS Healthcare, Inc.*, 818 A.2d 914 (Del. 2003). NCS Healthcare ("NCS") was an insolvent pharmacy services provider, which for many months had been seeking a merger partner to bail it out of its financial difficulties. NCS had retained two different investment banks as advisors in its search for a merger partner, and it considered about fifty different entities. At one point it sought to sell itself to Omnicare, another corporation in the same line of business, but Omnicare indicated that it was not interested in anything but a purchase of NCS's assets in a bankruptcy proceeding. This meant that while there might be some relief for NCS's creditors through a deal with Omnicare, NCS's shareholders would receive no consideration for their stock. Still another corporation in the same line of business, Genesis Health Ventures ("Genesis"), however, did offer a transaction which appeared more advantageous to NCS's board, because it indicated it was willing not only to enter into a deal which would have provided full relief to the debt holders, but also would have provided $1.00 per share to the common shareholders. By this time NCS's fortunes had improved somewhat, and Omnicare abruptly changed its views, and proposed to acquire NCS and pay a higher rate, $3.00, for the NCS shares. In the words of the Court, however, "Omnicare's proposal ... was expressly conditioned on negotiating a merger agreement, obtaining certain third party consents, and [Omnicare's] completing its due diligence." NCS was wary of Omnicare, however, and while NCS was able to use Omnicare's new interest as leverage to get Genesis to offer a higher price than the $3.00 for the common shareholders, Genesis insisted that if it was going to go forward with any deal with NCS, NCS had to agree to submit the NCS merger deal to a vote by its shareholders even if there were a competing offer which was more attractive to the Board, and Genesis also managed to get the two majority shareholders in NCS contractually to agree to vote their shares in support of the deal with Genesis. Finally, Genesis insisted that the NCS Board not have a "fiduciary out" clause in the merger agreement with Genesis. (Such a clause would have permitted the NCS Board to back out of the merger agreement if it determined that its fiduciary obligations required such a move.) Omnicare then launched a tender offer for NCS shares at a price slightly higher than that Genesis was offering, and asked the Delaware courts to invalidate the NCS/Genesis deal and the majority shareholder agreements.

NCS argued that its decision to go with the Genesis deal was a proper exercise of the directors' business judgment, especially in light of the fact that Genesis, at the time negotiations first began with NCS, was the only firm that was offering relief to NCS's shareholders, and Genesis had insisted on "lock-up" arrangements because Genesis had had a prior unpleasant experience where Omnicare bested it in a struggle to acquire another entity by coming in at the last moment, and offering a higher price. The Delaware Supreme Court, in a rare 3–2 decision, ruled for Omnicare, and declared that NCS's attempt to "lock-up" the deal with Genesis impermissibly violated the NCS board's fiduciary duties to its shareholders, and was impermissibly "draconian" and "preclusive."

Two very powerful dissents were filed in the Omnicare case. One was by then Chief Justice Veasey, himself, who stated that:

> The process by which this merger agreement came about involved a joint decision by the controlling stockholders and the board of directors to secure what appeared to be the only value-enhancing transaction available for a company on the brink of bankruptcy. The Majority adopts a new rule of law that imposes a prohibition on the NCS board's ability to act in concert with controlling stockholders to lock up this merger. The Majority reaches this conclusion by analyzing the challenged deal protection measures as isolated board actions. The Majority concludes that the board owed a duty to the NCS minority stockholders to refrain from acceding to the Genesis demand for an irrevocable lock-up notwithstanding the compelling circumstances confronting the board and the board's disinterested, informed, good faith exercise of its business judgment. Because we believe this Court must respect the reasoned judgment of the board of directors and give effect to the wishes of the controlling stockholders, we respectfully disagree with the Majority's reasoning that results in a holding that the confluence of board and stockholder action constitutes a breach of fiduciary duty. The essential fact that must always be remembered is that this agreement and the voting commitments of [the two majority shareholders] concluded a lengthy search and intense negotiation process in the context of insolvency and creditor pressure where no other viable bid had emerged.

The other dissent was by Justice Steele (who, as this third edition is written, is now the Chief Justice), who observed that

> Delaware corporate citizens now face the prospect that in *every* circumstance, boards must obtain the highest price, even if that requires breaching a contract entered into at a time when no one could have reasonably foreseen a truly "Superior Proposal." The majority's proscriptive rule limits the scope of a board's cost benefit analysis by taking the bargaining chip of foregoing a fiduciary out "off the table" in all circumstances. For that new principle to arise from the context of this case, when Omnicare, after striving to buy NCS on the cheap by buying off its creditors, slinked back into the fray, reversed its historic antagonistic strategy and offered a conditional "Superior Proposal" seems entirely counterintuitive.

Who gets it right, in light of *Time v. Paramount* and *Paramount v. QVC*—the majority in *Omnicare*, who held that the Board's duty was to get the highest price for the shareholders, or the dissent, who believed that the Board ought to have the discretion to favor a bird in hand over a bird in the bush?

3.   *Omnicare* created quite a stir:

> "When the Delaware Supreme Court issued its opinion in *Omnicare Inc. v. NCS Healthcare Inc.* * * * some observers called the decision the court's most important in a generation [because by] holding that a target company couldn't irrevocably lock up an agreement to sell itself, *Omnicare* turned its back on Delaware's strong preference for vesting boards of directors with broad discretionary powers."

David Marcus, Disney's Dudley Do-Wrong, Daily Deal, June 16, 2003, available at 2003 WL 4169554, quoted in Wayne O. Hanewicz, Director Primacy, Omnicare, and the Function of Corporate Law, 71 Tenn. L. Rev. 511, 512 n.6 (2004). Mr. Marcus concluded that "The ruling may have a very short shelf life." As the third edition of this book went to press, however, in December, 2009, *Omnicare* was still good law. Intriguingly, *Omnicare* has its defenders. For subtle appreciation of the majority's opinion, see Hanewicz, *supra.* Given the majority's decision in *Omnicare*, do you suppose those in corporate boardrooms will be more comfortable? Is there any similarity between the 3 to 2 *Omnicare* ruling and the 3 to 2 decision in *Smith v. Van Gorkom*?

In an informative piece posted on the web in August of 2005, "*Omnicare v. NCS Healthcare*—More Bark than Bite?", three lawyers from Morrison and Foerster, Michael G. O'Bryan, Lawrence T. Yanowitch, and Jacob D. Bernstein argue that *Omnicare* "has ended up having relatively little impact on the M & A landscape, in part because parties to M & A transactions have discovered ways to work within its constraints." See http://www.mofo.com/news/updates/files/update02057.html (accessed 12 November 2009). Thus, these authors point out, it is possible to avoid the difficulties of *Omnicare* if, for example, stockholder approval follows immediately following execution of the merger agreement, although they imply that it might still be a wise move to insert a "fiduciary out" provision in the merger agreement. Such a fiduciary out provision could, however, be limited in time, say to 30 days. The authors also note that it might be wise to include in any merger agreement "deal protections that terminate or become less restrictive if a competing bid materializes." (But would such a strategy have killed the deal in the *Omnicare* case itself?)

The authors also note that the only post-*Omnicare* "deal protection" case from the Delaware court, *Orman v. Cullman*, 2004 Del. Ch. LEXIS 150, upheld a majority shareholder agreement similar to the one in the *Omnicare* case where the board was still free to consider other unsolicited acquisition proposals, where the board reserved the right to withdraw their recommendation of the acquisition proposal in question, and where approval was still needed from a majority of the minority public shareholders. Thus, as the dissenters in *Omnicare* suggested, *Omnicare* may be limited to its facts, a situation where it is "mathematically certain" that a transaction that is the subject of a "lock-up" will occur. Finally, as Messrs. O'Bryan, Yanowitch, and Bernstein observed in passing, "Justice Joseph Walsh, whose vote was one of three comprising the Omnicare majority, has since retired. The swing vote now rests in the hands of the recently sworn-in Justice and former Vice–Chancellor Jack Jacobs. Nobody knows whether Justice Jacobs would support the *Omnicare* majority decision, but clearly the *Omnicare* majority is not as secure today as it was before Justice Walsh retired." Note, then, how important the identity of the particular five members of the Delaware Supreme Court is, just as is true for the nine members of the United States Supreme Court. See also, for an argument that the impact of *Omnicare* may be limited, Daniel C. Davis, "*Omnicare v. NCS Healthcare*: A Critical Appraisal," 4 Berkeley Business Law Journal 177, 203 (2007) which asserts that "If *Omnicare* is applied broadly, it would be reasonable to expect some level of legislative intervention, much like the addition of Section 102(b)(7) to the DGCL following the *Van Gorkom* decision."

What, exactly, are the fiduciary duties of officers and directors when the corporate existence, in effect, comes to an end, or transforms into something else? We will not explore each of these areas, but similar problems present themselves when the corporation is dissolved, when there is sale of substantially all of the assets of the corporation, or when the corporation merges with another. There is a simple procedure that must be followed in such cases; first the Board of Directors must vote on the transaction, and, second, the transaction must be ratified by vote of the shareholders. Still, because of the potential conflict of interest posed by the fact that officers, directors, or majority shareholders may have interests adverse to those of other corporate stakeholders, courts, and particularly the Delaware Supreme Court, have applied close scrutiny to sale of control situations, particularly in the takeover context.

4.   What should be the standard of law to guide directors and officers faced with a hostile takeover bid? Such bids are often made because the target's share prices are depressed, and there is one school of academic thought which holds that share prices of such companies are depressed because incumbent management is doing a poor job. A bidder for such a company believes, so the argument goes, that it can do a better job managing the company and thus is in a position to increase value not only for itself, as a new majority owner, but also for the remaining shareholders. If one accepts this theory, then incumbent management should not be able to resist a tender offer, and such resistance, in fact, would probably be an act manifesting a conflict of interest between those of the incumbent managers (who want to hold on to their jobs) and shareholders (who would theoretically see their shares increase in value if a new management team were in place). Following this theory, in a brilliant article, Frank Easterbrook (now Chief Judge of the United States Court of Appeals for the Seventh Circuit, in Chicago) and Daniel Fischel (now a Professor at Northwestern University School of Law) argued that the only proper position of incumbent managers when faced with a hostile tender offer was supine. See generally Frank Easterbook and Daniel Fischel, The Proper Role of a Target's Management In Responding to a Tender Offer, 94 Harv. L. Rev. 1161 (1981). Do you agree?

5.   Though the Delaware Supreme Court noted Fischel and Easterbook's argument in its first opinion on the proper response of target management, Unocal Corp. v. Mesa Petroleum Co. 493 A.2d 946 (Del.1985), it chose not to accept it. Basing its opinion in part on empirical data that since has been more-or-less discredited, the Court took the position that resisting a tender offer could increase shareholder value, and gave target management some discretion to combat such an offer. Realizing, however, that such a situation could present a conflict of interest for incumbent management, the Court said that it would subject the board's decision to resist to "enhanced scrutiny." This meant that the normal manner of applying the business judgment rule was not enough, and that, instead, the Court would require incumbent managers, if challenged, to demonstrate that they reasonably perceived a threat to the corporation or its constituencies (employees, creditors, consumers, even the

community), and that the action they took to resist the takeover was reasonable in light of the threat posed. In the next major takeover case, Moran v. Household Int'l, Inc., 500 A.2d 1346, 1356 (Del.1985), the Supreme Court indicated that incumbent managers could put defensive tactics, such as "poison pills" or "shareholder rights plans" (as they are also known) in place even if there is no immediate takeover threat to the corporation, so long as it was reasonable to perceive such a threat, and the response chosen was reasonable in light of the threat perceived.

The third major takeover case, Revlon, Inc. v. MacAndrews & Forbes Holdings, Inc., 506 A.2d 173, 182 (Del.1985), spun Delaware anti-takeover law in a new direction, when it indicated that there were certain situations where incumbent managers would no longer be free to erect or employ defensive measures, and when, in fact, their role would shift from protecting the integrity of the corporation against hostile bids to simply making sure that the shareholders received the highest possible price for their shares. In *Revlon* the court indicated that two such situations were when a corporate "bust-up" was inevitable (in *Revlon* this was the case since it was clear that some divisions of the company were inevitably going to be sold), or when the corporation was on the auction block (that is, when there were multiple bidders, as there were for *Revlon*). The Court further made clear in *Revlon* that when a corporation was in "*Revlon mode*," as it came to be called, the Board could not take steps to protect other corporate constituencies, and could only look to the welfare of the shareholders, by securing the highest price for their shares. The *Revlon* court also made clear that its earlier comments in *Unocal* about permitting Boards to take defensive tactics to protect corporate constituencies other than the shareholders should be limited to situations in which the long-term shareholder wealth was enhanced by such actions.

Following *Revlon*, the crucial determination was whether the corporation which was the target of a hostile bid was in "*Unocal Mode*," in which situation the Board could decide that resistance was appropriate, or in "*Revlon Mode*," when it could not. You have just read the two important cases attempting to elucidate this point. In the first, Paramount Communications, Inc. v. Time Inc., 571 A.2d 1140 (Del.1989), Time shareholders challenged Time's decision to form an alliance with Warner Brothers, rather than to accept a tender offer from Paramount, since Paramount was offering a price for Time shares much higher than market, and the deal with Warner, as it worked out, simply involved a purchase of Warner, putting time 10 billion dollars in debt. There was, as you saw, some question whether Time was in "*Unocal*" or "*Revlon*" mode. Time had been courting strategic partners for a possible merger, and some Time shareholders argued that Time was, in fact, putting itself up for sale, thus triggering *Revlon Mode* duties to garner the best price for shareholders. Paramount argued that even if Time was simply in *Unocal Mode*, Paramount's all-cash all-shares offer could not be perceived as presenting a threat to the corporation, and Time should not be permitted to consummate its deal with Warner, which would have precluded Paramount's purchase of Time.

The Delaware Court rejected the contention that Time was in *Revlon Mode*, ostensibly because it had never actually put itself on the auction block and because not only was no breakup of Time inevitable, it actually was following a strategy which enhanced rather than diminished its ongoing business. Considering that Time was in *Unocal Mode*, then, the Court declared that resisting Paramount's bid, and deciding to acquire Warner was a valid defensive strategy, and deferred to the Time Board's decision that an alliance with Warner was in Time's long-term best interests, and thus in the long term best interests of the shareholders. The Time Board, said the Delaware Court, could reasonably decide that a combination with Warner would result in the long term prospects for shareholder value being greater than the price Paramount was offering now. Do you agree?

In Paramount Communications Inc. v. QVC Network Inc., 637 A.2d 34 (Del.1994), as you remember, the Delaware Supreme Court distinguished the situation from *Time v. Paramount*. Following its unsuccessful courtship of Time, Paramount sought a "strategic alliance" with Viacom, a corporation whose cable interests and other pursuits, in the opinion of Paramount management, maximized Paramount's prospects. This was to be accomplished through a tender offer by Viacom for Paramount. QVC then made a competing tender offer for Paramount, which Paramount rebuffed, on the grounds that even though QVC was offering a nominally higher price, a long-term alliance with Viacom would result in the most value for shareholders. Paramount pointed to the *Time v. Paramount* case, where the court had enthusiastically endorsed Time's similar strategic plan. The Delaware Supreme Court held, however, that since a new entity was to gain majority control of Paramount, this meant that Paramount was in *"Revlon Mode"* and its duty was to get the highest price for shareholders. Paramount had argued that no bust-up was contemplated, and that it had not put Paramount up for sale, and that, in prior cases, these two things seemed to have been required before *Revlon Mode* could exist. The Court rejected this argument, and held, that any time majority control changes it is a *"Revlon"* rather than a *"Unocal"* situation. Does that make sense?

If you're having a little trouble grasping just when *"Revlon Mode"* or *"Unocal Mode"* occurs, you're not alone. When there is no certainty that there will be competing bidders, how does one measure value, and when should a court upset the calculation made by incumbent management? We next take a brief detour from analyzing proper procedures for officers and directors, and consider this matter of substance, the value of shares in a corporation. How should courts figure value? We'll look first at a traditional means of performing such a calculation, still in use in some states, although, significantly, that traditional means no longer has preferred status in the state whose name it bears. We will then look at one more Delaware Supreme Court case, for more learning both on evaluating substance and procedure in endgame situations.

You have probably also observed that a major issue in these takeover defensive cases, an issue that we've touched on in earlier chapters, is for whom the directors and officers should act as trustees, or, if you like, what should be the social responsibility of corporations. For further thoughts on these matters, and for further evaluation of how contemporary theories of corporate responsibilities can be integrated with governance implications, see Timothy L. Fort, Ethics and Governance: Business as Mediating Institution

(Oxford University Press, 2001). For a provocative analysis of how consensus notions of ethical business behavior might contribute to general conditions of social harmony, see Timothy L. Fort & Cindy A. Schipani, The Role of Business in Fostering Peaceful Societies (Cambridge University Press, 2004).

B. VALUATION

PIEMONTE v. NEW BOSTON GARDEN CORPORATION
Supreme Judicial Court of Massachusetts.
377 Mass. 719, 387 N.E.2d 1145 (1979).

[WILKINS, J.] The plaintiffs were stockholders in Boston Garden Arena Corporation (Garden Arena), a Massachusetts corporation whose stockholders voted on July 19, 1973, to merge with the defendant corporation in circumstances which entitled each plaintiff to "demand payment for his stock from the resulting or surviving corporation and an appraisal in accordance with the provisions of [*G. L. c. 156B, § § 86–98*]." * * * The plaintiffs commenced this action * * * seeking a judicial determination of the "fair value" of their shares "as of the day preceding the date of the vote approving the proposed corporate action." * * * Each party has appealed from a judgment determining the fair value of the plaintiffs' stock. * * *

On July 18, 1973, Garden Arena owned all the stock in a subsidiary corporation that owned both a franchise in the National Hockey League (NHL), known as the Boston Bruins, and a corporation that held a franchise in the American Hockey League (AHL), known as the Boston Braves. Garden Arena also owned and operated Boston Garden Sports Arena (Boston Garden), an indoor auditorium with facilities for the exhibition of sporting and other entertainment events, and a corporation that operated the food and beverage concession at the Boston Garden. A considerable volume of documentary material was introduced in evidence concerning the value of the stock of Garden Arena on July 18, 1973, the day before Garden Arena's stockholders approved the merger. Each side presented expert testimony. The judge gave consideration to the market value of the Garden Arena stock, to the value of its stock based on its earnings, and to the net asset value of Garden Arena's assets. Weighting these factors, the judge arrived at a total, per share value of $75.27.[29]

In this appeal, the parties raise objections to certain of the judge's conclusions. * * * We conclude that the judge followed acceptable proce-

---

29. The judge determined the market value, earnings value, and net asset value of the stock and then weighted these values as follows:

	Value	Weight		Result
Market Value:	$ 26.50	× 10%	=	$ 2.65
Earnings Value:	$ 52.60	× 40%	=	$21.04
Net Asset Value:	$103.16	× 50%	=	$51.58
Total Value Per Share:				$75.27

dures in valuing the Garden Arena stock; that his determinations were generally within the range of discretion accorded a fact finder; but that, in three instances, the judge's treatment of the evidence was or may have been in error and, accordingly, the case should be remanded to him for further consideration of those three points.

GENERAL PRINCIPLES OF LAW

The statutory provisions applicable to this case were enacted in 1964 as part of the Massachusetts Business Corporation Law. St. 1964, c. 723, § 1. The appraisal provisions (*G. L. c. 156B, § § 86–98*) were based on a similar, but not identical, Delaware statute (*Del. Code tit. 8, § 262*). * * * In these circumstances, consideration of the Delaware law, including judicial decisions, is appropriate, but in no sense should we feel compelled to adhere without question to that law, which has been in the process of development since our enactment of G. L. c. 156B in 1964. We do not perceive a legislative intent to adopt judicial determinations of Delaware law made prior to the enactment of G. L. c. 156B and certainly no such intent as to judicial interpretations made since that date. * * *

The Delaware courts have adopted a general approach to the appraisal of stock which a Massachusetts judge might appropriately follow, as did the judge in this case. The Delaware procedure, known as the "Delaware block approach," calls for a determination of the market value, the earnings value, and the net asset value of the stock, followed by the assignment of a percentage weight to each of the elements of value. See generally, Note, Valuation of Dissenters' Stock under Appraisal Statutes, *79 Harv. L. Rev. 1453, 1456–1471 (1966)*.

* * * In the *Martignette* case,[30] the court held that even where stock had an established market, market price was not determinative and that "it is for the appraisers in the particular case to determine the weight of the relevant factors." * * * If the corporation is solvent or has significant earnings prospects, "the earnings and worth of the corporation as a going concern are important."[31] * * *

With these considerations in mind, we turn to the specific issues that have been argued on appeal, considering, in order, the judge's determination of market value, earnings value and net asset value of the stock; his decision concerning the weighting of these components; the defendant's objection to the consideration of certain evidence; and, finally, the judge's decision on the rate of interest to be allowed to the plaintiffs.

MARKET VALUE

The judge was acting within reasonable limits when he determined that the market value of Garden Arena stock on July 18, 1973, was $26.50 a share. Each party challenges this determination. The plaintiffs' conten-

---

30. Martignette v. Sagamore Mfg. Co., 340 Mass. 136 (1959)

31. Id. at 142–143.

tion is that market value should be disregarded because it was not ascertainable due to the limited trading in Garden Arena stock.[32] The defendant argues that the judge was obliged to reconstruct market value based on comparable companies, and, in doing so, should have arrived at a market value of $22 a share.

Market value may be a significant factor, even the dominant factor, in determining the "fair value" of shares of a particular corporation under *G. L. c. 156B, § 92.* Shares regularly traded on a recognized stock exchange are particularly susceptible to valuation on the basis of their market price, although even in such cases the market value may well not be conclusive. * * * On the other hand, where there is no established market for a particular stock, actual market value cannot be used. In such cases, a judge might undertake to "reconstruct" market value, but he is not obliged to do so. * * * Indeed, the process of the reconstruction of market value may actually be no more than a variation on the valuation of corporate assets and corporate earnings.

In this case, Garden Arena stock was traded on the Boston Stock Exchange, but rarely. Approximately ninety per cent of the company's stock was held by the controlling interests and not traded. Between January 1, 1968, and December 4, 1972, 16,741 shares were traded. During this period, an annual average of approximately 1.5% of the outstanding stock changed hands. In 1972, 4,372 shares were traded at prices ranging from $20.50 a share to $29 a share. The public announcement of the proposed merger was made on December 7, 1972. The last prior sale of 200 shares on December 4, 1972, was made at $26.50 a share. The judge accepted that sale price as the market price to be used in his determination of value.

The judge concluded that the volume of trading was sufficient to permit a determination of market value and expressed a preference for the actual sale price over any reconstruction of a market value, which he concluded would place "undue reliance on corporations, factors, and circumstances not applicable to Garden Arena stock." The decision to consider market value and the market value selected were within the judge's discretion.

VALUATION BASED ON EARNINGS

The judge determined that the average per share earnings of Garden Arena for the five-fiscal-year period which ended June 30, 1973, was $5.26. To this amount he applied a factor, or multiplier, of 10 to arrive at $52.60 as the per share value based on earnings.

Each party objects to certain aspects of this process. We reject the plaintiffs' argument that the judge could not properly use any value based

---

32. This argument also bears on the relative weight to be assigned to market value as against net asset value and earnings value, a subject we shall consider subsequently.

on earnings and also reject the parties' various challenges to the judge's method of determining value based on earnings.

Delaware case law, which, as we have said, we regard as instructive but not binding, has established a method of computing value based on corporate earnings. The appraiser [or the judge] generally starts by computing the average earnings of the corporation for the past five years. * * * Extraordinary gains and losses are excluded from the average earnings calculation. The appraiser then selects a multiplier (to be applied to the average earnings) which reflects the prospective financial condition of the corporation and the risk factor inherent in the corporation and the industry. * * * In selecting a multiplier, the appraiser generally looks to other comparable corporations. *Universal City Studios, Inc. v. Francis I. duPont & Co., 334 A.2d 216, 219–221(Del. 1975).* (averaging price-earnings ratios of nine other motion picture companies as of date of merger); *Gibbons v. Schenley Indus., Inc., 339 A.2d 460, 471 (Del. Ch. 1975)* (using Standard & Poor's Distiller's Index as of date of merger); *Felder v. Anderson, Clayton & Co., 39 Del. Ch. 76, 87 (1960)* (averaging price-earnings ratios of representative stocks over previous five-year period because of recent boom in industry). The appraiser's choice of a multiplier is largely discretionary and will be upheld if it is "within the range of reason." *Universal City Studios, Inc. v. Francis I. duPont & Co., supra at 219* (approving multiplier of 16.1). *Application of Del. Racing Ass'n, 213 A.2d 203, 213 (Del. 1965)* (Swanton v. State Guar. Corp., 42 Del. Ch. 477, 483 (1965) (approving multiplier of 14). * * *

The judge chose not to place "singular reliance on comparative data preferring to choose a multiplier based on the specific situation and prospects of the Garden Arena." He weighed the favorable financial prospects of the Bruins: the popularity and success of the team, the relatively low average age of its players, the popularity of Bobby Orr and Phil Esposito, the high attendance record at home games (each home team retained all gate receipts), and the advantageous radio and television contracts. On the other hand, he recognized certain risks, the negative prospects: the existence of the World Hockey Association with its potential, favorable impact on players' bargaining positions, and legal threats to the players' reserve clause. He concluded that a multiplier of 10 was appropriate. There was ample evidentiary support for his conclusion. He might have looked to and relied on price-earnings ratios of other corporations, but he was not obliged to.

The judge did not have to consider the dividend record of Garden Arena, as the defendant urges. Dividends tend to reflect the same factors as earnings and, therefore, need not be valued separately. * * * And since dividend policy is usually reflected in market value, the use of market value as a factor in the valuation process permitted the low and sporadic dividend rate to be given some weight in the process. Beyond that, the value of the plaintiffs' stock should not be depreciated because the controlling interests often chose to declare low dividends or none at all.

The judge did not abuse his discretion in including expansion income (payments from teams newly admitted to the NHL) received during two of the five recent fiscal years. His conclusion was well within the guidelines of decided cases. See *Gibbons v. Schenley Indus., Inc., 339 A.2d 460, 470 (Del. Ch. 1975)* (gain from sale of real estate not extraordinary where corporation often sold such assets); *Felder v. Anderson, Clayton & Co., 39 Del. Ch. 76, 86–87 (1960)* (loss attributable to a drought not extraordinary). The Bruins first received expansion income ($2,000,000) during the fiscal year which ended on June 30, 1967, a year not included in the five-year average. The franchise received almost $1,000,000 more in 1970 and approximately $860,000 in 1972. This 1970 and 1972 income was reflected in the computation of earnings. Expansion income did not have to be treated as extraordinary income. The judge concluded that it did not distort "an accurate projection of the earnings value of Garden Arena" and noted, as of July 18, 1973, an NHL expansion plan for the admission of two more teams in 1974–1975 and for expansion thereafter.

VALUATION BASED ON NET ASSET VALUE

The judge determined total net asset value by first valuing the net assets of Garden Arena apart from the Bruins franchise and the concession operations at Boston Garden. He selected $9,400,000 (the June 30, 1973, book value of Garden Arena) as representing that net asset value. Then, he added his valuations of the Bruins franchise ($9,600,000) and the concession operation ($4,200,000) to arrive at a total asset value of $23,200,000, or $103.16 a share.[33]

The parties raise various objections to these determinations. The defendant argues that the judge included certain items twice in his valuation of the net assets of Garden Arena and that he should have given no separate value to the concession operation. The plaintiff argues that the judge undervalued both the Boston Garden and the value of the Bruins franchise.

The defendant objects to the judge's refusal to deduct $1,116,000 from the $9,400,000 that represented the net asset value of Garden Arena (exclusive of the net asset value of the Bruins franchise and the concession operation). The defendant's expert testified that the $9,400,000 figure included $1,116,000 attributable to the good will of the Bruins, net player investment, and the value of the AHL franchise. The judge recognized that the items included in the $1,116,000 should not be valued twice and seemingly agreed that they would be more appropriately included in the value of the Bruins franchise than in the $9,400,000. He was not plainly wrong, however, in declining to deduct them from the $9,400,000, because, as is fully warranted from the testimony of the defendant's expert, the judge concluded that the defendant's expert did not include these items in his determination of the value of the Bruins franchise. * * * The defendant's expert, whose determination the judge accepted, arrived at his

---

33. $23,200,000 / 224,892 (the number of outstanding shares).

value of the Bruins franchise by adding certain items to the cost of a new NHL franchise, but none of those items included good will, net player investment, or the value of an AHL franchise. Acceptance of the defendant's argument would have resulted in these items being entirely omitted from the net asset valuation of Garden Arena. * * *

The plaintiffs object that the judge did not explicitly determine the value of the Boston Garden and implicitly undervalued it. Garden Arena had purchased the Boston Garden on May 25, 1973, for $4,000,000, and accounted for it on the June 30, 1973, balance sheet as a $4,000,000 asset with a corresponding mortgage liability of $3,437,065. Prior to the purchase, Garden Arena had held a long-term lease which was unfavorable to the owner of the Boston Garden.[34] The existence of the lease would tend to depress the purchase price.

The judge stated that the $9,400,000 book value "*includes* a reasonable value for Boston Garden" (emphasis supplied). He did not indicate whether, if he had meant to value the Boston Garden at its purchase price (with an adjustment for the mortgage liabilities), he had considered the effect the lease would have had on that price. While we recognize that the fact-finding role of the judge permits him to reject the opinions of the various experts, * * * we conclude, in the absence of an explanation of his reasons, that it is possible that the judge did not give adequate consideration to the value of the Garden property. The judge should consider this subject further on remand.

A major area of dispute was the value of the Bruins franchise. The judge rejected the value advanced by the plaintiffs' expert ($18,000,000), stating that "[a]lthough the defendant's figure of [$9,600,000] seems somewhat low in comparison with the cost of expansion team franchises, *the Court is constrained* to accept defendant's value as it is the more creditable and legally appropriate expert opinion in the record" (emphasis supplied). Although the choice of the word "constrained" may have been inadvertent, it connotes a sense of obligation.* * *As the trier of fact, the judge was not bound to accept the valuation of either one expert or the other. He was entitled to reach his own conclusion as to value. * * *

Because the judge may have felt bound to accept the value placed on the Bruins franchise by the defendant's expert, we shall remand this case for him to arrive at his own determination of the value of the Bruins franchise. He would be warranted in arriving at the same valuation as that advanced on behalf of the defendant, but he is not obliged to do so.

The defendant argues that, in arriving at the value of the assets of Garden Arena, the judge improperly placed a separate value on the right to operate concessions at the Boston Garden. We agree with the judge.

---

34. The lease, which ran until June 1, 1986, contained a fixed maximum rent and an obligation on the lessee to pay only two-thirds of any increase in local real estate taxes. In a period of inflation and rising local real estate taxes, the value of the lease to the lessor was decreasing annually.

The fact that earnings from concessions were included in the computation of earnings value, one component in the formula, does not mean that the value of the concessions should have been excluded from the computation of net asset value, another such component.

The value of the concession operation was not reflected in the value of the real estate. Real estate may be valued on the basis of rental income, but it is not valued on the basis of the profitability of business operations within the premises. * * * Moreover, it is manifest that the value of the concession operation was not included in the value placed on the Boston Garden. The record indicates that Garden Arena already owned the concession rights when it purchased the Boston Garden. The conclusion that the value of the concession operation was not reflected in the value of the Boston Garden is particularly warranted because the determined value of the right to operate the concessions ($4,200,000) was higher than the May 25, 1973, purchase price ($4,000,000) of the Boston Garden.

We do conclude, however, that the judge may have felt unnecessarily bound to accept the plaintiffs' evidence of the value of the concession operation. He stated that "since the defendant did not submit evidence on this issue, the Court will accept plaintiffs' expert appraisal of the value of the concession operation." Although the judge did not express the view that he was "constrained" to accept the plaintiffs' valuation, as he did concerning the defendant's valuation of the Bruins franchise, he may have misconstrued his authority on this issue. The judge was not obliged to accept the plaintiffs' evidence at face value merely because no other evidence was offered. * * *

On remand, the judge should reconsider his determination of the value of the concession operation and exercise his own judgment concerning the bases for the conclusion arrived at by the plaintiffs' expert. However, the evidence did warrant the value selected by the judge, and no reduction in that value is required on this record.

WEIGHTING OF VALUATIONS

The judge weighted the three valuations as follows:

Market Value	—	10%
Earnings Value	—	40%
Net Asset Value	—	50%

We accept these allocations as reasonable and within the range of the judge's discretion.

Any determination of the weight to be given the various elements involved in the valuation of a stock must be based on the circumstances. * * * The decision to weight market value at only 10% was appropriate, considering the thin trading in the stock of Garden Arena. The decision to attribute 50% weight to net asset value was reasonably founded. The judge concluded that, because of tax reasons, the value of a sports franchise, unlike many corporate activities, depends more on its assets than on its earnings; that Garden Arena had been largely a family corporation in which earnings were of little significance; that Garden Arena had approximately $5,000,000 in excess liquid assets; and that the Garden property was a substantial real estate holding in an excellent location.

The judge might have reached different conclusions on this record. He was not obliged, however, to reconstruct market value and, as the defendant urges, attribute 50% weight to it. Nor was he obliged, as the plaintiffs argue, to consider only net asset value. * * * Market value and earnings value properly could be considered in these circumstances.

Although we would have found no fault with a determination to give even greater weight to the price per share based on the net asset value of Garden Arena, the judge was acting within an acceptable range of discretion in selecting the weights he gave to the various factors.

*   *   *

CONCLUSION

We have concluded that the judge's method of valuing the Garden Arena stock was essentially correct. In this opinion, we have indicated, however, that the case should be remanded to him for clarification and further consideration on the record of three matters: his valuation of the Boston Garden, the Bruins franchise, and the concession operation.

So ordered.

NOTES AND QUESTIONS

1. As you may have already discerned, lawyers and judges are leery of numbers. Valuation presents a particular problem for them. You have encountered the valuation problem before, in *Smith v. Van Gorkom*. There, you may remember, the Board members of Trans Union, most notably the CEO, Jerome Van Gorkom, believed that the only manner in which value could really be discerned was a "market test." In other words, there may really be no such thing as "intrinsic value," contrary to the belief of the three-person majority of the Delaware Supreme Court in its opinion in the *Smith* case. Is believing in "intrinsic value" like believing in Santa Claus or the Easter Bunny? Do you believe in "intrinsic value?" How might you discern it? As you have seen, the problem often comes up in the case of thinly-traded stock in closely-held corporations, especially in merger situations, when dissenters (those who don't want to remain after the merger) seek valuation of their stock and a buy-out of their shares.

2. The Delaware Block Method, as you will soon learn, is no longer the exclusive or favored method in Delaware, but it does have a certain appeal. It is an attempt to capture three temporal dimensions of value—asset value (which looks toward the past), earnings value (which looks toward the future), and market value (which purportedly looks at the present). As you may have

been able to discern, however, the method gives judges (or referees) an extraordinary amount of discretion. What do you see as its weak and its strong points? Given any business experience you may have, is the Delaware Block Method sufficiently anchored in business reality?

3. A particularly acute need for valuation comes for those practicing mergers and acquisitions law, when they may need to defend a client's behavior in resisting a tender offer, or, perhaps, defend a client's bid for a target. In a splendidly sophisticated study of such valuation techniques Dean Samuel Thompson, of the University of Miami School of Law, reports that:

> There are many techniques for determining the value of the assets or shares of a target corporation. These include: (1) valuation based on comparable target corporations—similar to the traditional technique for valuing real estate; (2) valuation based on comparable transactions—looking to transactions that are similar to the one in which the stock or assets of the target are being acquired; (3) valuation based on the liquidation value of the assets of the target corporation; (4) valuation based on the replacement value of the target's assets; (5) valuation based on a leveraged buyout (LBO) analysis by a financial buyer; and (6) valuation based on the discounting to present value of the target's expected future cash flows through the use of the discounted cash flow (DCF) technique, with the discount rate determined by the use of (a) the capital asset pricing model (CAPM), (b) arbitrage pricing theory (APT), or (c) the weighted average cost of capital (WACC). * * *

Samuel C. Thompson, Jr., A Lawyer's Guide to Modern Valuation Techniques in Mergers and Acquisitions, 21 Iowa J. Corp. L. 457, 460–461 (1996). For explanations of CAPM, APT, or WACC, you'll need to consult a financial analyst or Thompson's article, but can you understand from the brief excerpt from Thompson's piece why a court might cling to the Delaware Block Method? DCF may now be the preferred method for sophisticated financial analysts, but do you see merit in any of the other techniques Thompson lists? Considering the difficulty of figuring out substantive value, is it any surprise that lawyers are more comfortable evaluating procedure? Is it this preference that helps explain the outcome of the following case?

C. FREEZEOUTS AND THE ENTIRE FAIRNESS TEST

WEINBERGER v. UOP

Supreme Court of Delaware.
457 A.2d 701 (1983).

* * *

[MOORE, J.] This post-trial appeal was reheard en banc from a decision of the Court of Chancery. It was brought by the class action plaintiff below, a former shareholder of UOP, Inc., who challenged the elimination of UOP's minority shareholders by a cash-out merger between UOP and its majority owner, The Signal Companies, Inc. The present Chancellor held that the terms of the merger were fair to the plaintiff and the other minority shareholders of UOP. * * *

* * * [W]e address only the following questions presented by the trial court's opinion:

> 1) The plaintiff's duty to plead sufficient facts demonstrating the unfairness of the challenged merger;

> 2) The burden of proof upon the parties where the merger has been approved by the purportedly informed vote of a majority of the minority shareholders;

> 3) The fairness of the merger in terms of adequacy of the defendants' disclosures to the minority shareholders;

> 4) The fairness of the merger in terms of adequacy of the price paid for the minority shares and the remedy appropriate to that issue; and

> 5) The continued force and effect of *Singer v. Magnavox Co., Del. Supr., 380 A.2d 969, 980 (1977),* and its progeny.

In ruling for the defendants, the Chancellor re-stated his earlier conclusion that the plaintiff in a suit challenging a cash-out merger must allege specific acts of fraud, misrepresentation, or other items of misconduct to demonstrate the unfairness of the merger terms to the minority. We approve this rule and affirm it.

The Chancellor also held that even though the ultimate burden of proof is on the majority shareholder to show by a preponderance of the evidence that the transaction is fair, it is first the burden of the plaintiff attacking the merger to demonstrate some basis for invoking the fairness obligation. We agree with that principle. However, where corporate action has been approved by an informed vote of a majority of the minority shareholders, we conclude that the burden entirely shifts to the plaintiff to show that the transaction was unfair to the minority. * * * But in all this, the burden clearly remains on those relying on the vote to show that they completely disclosed all material facts relevant to the transaction.

Here, the record does not support a conclusion that the minority stockholder vote was an informed one. Material information, necessary to acquaint those shareholders with the bargaining positions of Signal and UOP, was withheld under circumstances amounting to a breach of fiduciary duty. We therefore conclude that this merger does not meet the test of fairness * * * and no burden thus shifted to the plaintiff by reason of the minority shareholder vote. * * *

* * *

Our treatment of these matters has necessarily led us to a reconsideration of the business purpose rule announced in the trilogy of *Singer v.*

Magnavox Co., supra; Tanzer v. International General Industries, Inc., Del. Supr., 379 A.2d 1121 (1977); and *Roland International Corp. v. Najjar, Del. Supr., 407 A.2d 1032 (1979).* For the reasons hereafter set forth we consider that the business purpose requirement of these cases is no longer the law of Delaware.

I.

* * *

Signal is a diversified, technically based company operating through various subsidiaries. Its stock is publicly traded on the New York, Philadelphia and Pacific Stock Exchanges. UOP, formerly known as Universal Oil Products Company, was a diversified industrial company engaged in various lines of business, including petroleum and petro-chemical services and related products, construction, fabricated metal products, transportation equipment products, chemicals and plastics, and other products and services including land development, lumber products and waste disposal. Its stock was publicly held and listed on the New York Stock Exchange.

In 1974 Signal sold one of its wholly-owned subsidiaries for $420,000,000 in cash. * * * While looking to invest this cash surplus, Signal became interested in UOP as a possible acquisition. Friendly negotiations ensued, and Signal proposed to acquire a controlling interest in UOP at a price of $19 per share. UOP's representatives sought $25 per share. In the arm's length bargaining that followed, an understanding was reached whereby Signal agreed to purchase from UOP 1,500,000 shares of UOP's authorized but unissued stock at $21 per share.

This purchase was contingent upon Signal making a successful cash tender offer for 4,300,000 publicly held shares of UOP, also at a price of $21 per share. This combined method of acquisition permitted Signal to acquire 5,800,000 shares of stock, representing 50.5% of UOP's outstanding shares. The UOP board of directors advised the company's shareholders that it had no objection to Signal's tender offer at that price. Immediately before the announcement of the tender offer, UOP's common stock had been trading on the New York Stock Exchange at a fraction under $14 per share.

The negotiations between Signal and UOP occurred during April 1975, and the resulting tender offer was greatly oversubscribed. However, Signal limited its total purchase of the tendered shares so that, when coupled with the stock bought from UOP, it had achieved its goal of becoming a 50.5% shareholder of UOP.

Although UOP's board consisted of thirteen directors, Signal nominated and elected only six. Of these, five were either directors or employees of Signal. The sixth, a partner in the banking firm of Lazard Freres & Co., had been one of Signal's representatives in the negotiations and bargaining with UOP concerning the tender offer and purchase price of the UOP shares.

However, the president and chief executive officer of UOP retired during 1975, and Signal caused him to be replaced by James V. Crawford, a long-time employee and senior executive vice president of one of Signal's wholly-owned subsidiaries. Crawford succeeded his predecessor on UOP's board of directors and also was made a director of Signal.

By the end of 1977 Signal basically was unsuccessful in finding other suitable investment candidates for its excess cash, and by February 1978 considered that it had no other realistic acquisitions available to it on a friendly basis. Once again its attention turned to UOP.

The trial court found that at the instigation of certain Signal management personnel, including William W. Walkup, its board chairman, and Forrest N. Shumway, its president, a feasibility study was made concerning the possible acquisition of the balance of UOP's outstanding shares. This study was performed by two Signal officers, Charles S. Arledge, vice president (director of planning), and Andrew J. Chitiea, senior vice president (chief financial officer). Messrs. Walkup, Shumway, Arledge and Chitiea were all directors of UOP in addition to their membership on the Signal board.

Arledge and Chitiea concluded that it would be a good investment for Signal to acquire the remaining 49.5% of UOP shares at any price up to $24 each. Their report was discussed between Walkup and Shumway who, along with Arledge, Chitiea and Brewster L. Arms, internal counsel for Signal, constituted Signal's senior management. In particular, they talked about the proper price to be paid if the acquisition was pursued, purportedly keeping in mind that as UOP's majority shareholder, Signal owed a fiduciary responsibility to both its own stockholders as well as to UOP's minority. It was ultimately agreed that a meeting of Signal's Executive Committee would be called to propose that Signal acquire the remaining outstanding stock of UOP through a cash-out merger in the range of $20 to $21 per share.

The Executive Committee meeting was set for February 28, 1978. As a courtesy, UOP's president, Crawford, was invited to attend, although he was not a member of Signal's executive committee. On his arrival, and prior to the meeting, Crawford was asked to meet privately with Walkup and Shumway. He was then told of Signal's plan to acquire full ownership of UOP and was asked for his reaction to the proposed price range of $20 to $21 per share. Crawford said he thought such a price would be "generous", and that it was certainly one which should be submitted to UOP's minority shareholders for their ultimate consideration. He stated, however, that Signal's 100% ownership could cause internal problems at UOP. He believed that employees would have to be given some assurance of their future place in a fully-owned Signal subsidiary. Otherwise, he feared the departure of essential personnel. Also, many of UOP's key employees had stock option incentive programs which would be wiped out by a merger. Crawford therefore urged that some adjustment would have to be made, such as providing a comparable incentive in Signal's shares, if after the merger he was to maintain his quality of personnel and efficiency at UOP.

Thus, Crawford voiced no objection to the $20 to $21 price range, nor did he suggest that Signal should consider paying more than $21 per share for the minority interests. Later, at the Executive Committee meeting the same factors were discussed, with Crawford repeating the position he earlier took with Walkup and Shumway. Also considered was the 1975 tender offer and the fact that it had been greatly oversubscribed at $21 per share. For many reasons, Signal's management concluded that the acquisition of UOP's minority shares provided the solution to a number of its business problems.

Thus, it was the consensus that a price of $20 to $21 per share would be fair to both Signal and the minority shareholders of UOP. Signal's executive committee authorized its management "to negotiate" with UOP "for a cash acquisition of the minority ownership in UOP, Inc., with the intention of presenting a proposal to [Signal's] board of directors ... on March 6, 1978". Immediately after this February 28, 1978 meeting, Signal issued a press release stating:

> The Signal Companies, Inc. and UOP, Inc. are conducting negotiations for the acquisition for cash by Signal of the 49.5 per cent of UOP which it does not presently own, announced Forrest N. Shumway, president and chief executive officer of Signal, and James V. Crawford, UOP president.

> Price and other terms of the proposed transaction have not yet been finalized and would be subject to approval of the boards of directors of Signal and UOP, scheduled to meet early next week, the stockholders of UOP and certain federal agencies.

The announcement also referred to the fact that the closing price of UOP's common stock on that day was $14.50 per share.

Two days later, on March 2, 1978, Signal issued a second press release stating that its management would recommend a price in the range of $20 to $21 per share for UOP's 49.5% minority interest. This announcement referred to Signal's earlier statement that "negotiations" were being conducted for the acquisition of the minority shares.

Between Tuesday, February 28, 1978 and Monday, March 6, 1978, a total of four business days, Crawford spoke by telephone with all of UOP's non-Signal, i.e., outside, directors. Also during that period, Crawford retained Lehman Brothers to render a fairness opinion as to the price offered the minority for its stock. He gave two reasons for this choice. First, the time schedule between the announcement and the board meetings was short (by then only three business days) and since Lehman Brothers had been acting as UOP's investment banker for many years, Crawford felt that it would be in the best position to respond on such brief notice. Second, James W. Glanville, a long-time director of UOP and a partner in Lehman Brothers, had acted as a financial advisor to UOP for many years. Crawford believed that Glanville's familiarity with UOP, as a member of its board, would also be of assistance in enabling Lehman Brothers to render a fairness opinion within the existing time constraints.

Crawford telephoned Glanville, who gave his assurance that Lehman Brothers had no conflicts that would prevent it from accepting the task. Glanville's immediate personal reaction was that a price of $20 to $21 would certainly be fair, since it represented almost a 50% premium over UOP's market price. Glanville sought a $250,000 fee for Lehman Brothers' services, but Crawford thought this too much. After further discussions Glanville finally agreed that Lehman Brothers would render its fairness opinion for $150,000.

During this period Crawford also had several telephone contacts with Signal officials. In only one of them, however, was the price of the shares discussed. In a conversation with Walkup, Crawford advised that as a result of his communications with UOP's non-Signal directors, it was his feeling that the price would have to be the top of the proposed range, or $21 per share, if the approval of UOP's outside directors was to be obtained. But again, he did not seek any price higher than $21.

Glanville assembled a three-man Lehman Brothers team to do the work on the fairness opinion. These persons examined relevant documents and information concerning UOP, including its annual reports and its Securities and Exchange Commission filings from 1973 through 1976, as well as its audited financial statements for 1977, its interim reports to shareholders, and its recent and historical market prices and trading volumes. In addition, on Friday, March 3, 1978, two members of the Lehman Brothers team flew to UOP's headquarters in Des Plaines, Illinois, to perform a "due diligence" visit, during the course of which they interviewed Crawford as well as UOP's general counsel, its chief financial officer, and other key executives and personnel.

As a result, the Lehman Brothers team concluded that "the price of either $20 or $21 would be a fair price for the remaining shares of UOP". They telephoned this impression to Glanville, who was spending the weekend in Vermont.

On Monday morning, March 6, 1978, Glanville and the senior member of the Lehman Brothers team flew to Des Plaines to attend the scheduled UOP directors meeting. Glanville looked over the assembled information during the flight. The two had with them the draft of a "fairness opinion letter" in which the price had been left blank. Either during or immediately prior to the directors' meeting, the two-page "fairness opinion letter" was typed in final form and the price of $21 per share was inserted.

On March 6, 1978, both the Signal and UOP boards were convened to consider the proposed merger. Telephone communications were maintained between the two meetings. Walkup, Signal's board chairman, and also a UOP director, attended UOP's meeting with Crawford in order to present Signal's position and answer any questions that UOP's non-Signal directors might have. Arledge and Chitiea, along with Signal's other designees on UOP's board, participated by conference telephone. All of UOP's outside directors attended the meeting either in person or by conference telephone.

First, Signal's board unanimously adopted a resolution authorizing Signal to propose to UOP a cash merger of $21 per share as outlined in a certain merger agreement and other supporting documents. This proposal required that the merger be approved by a majority of UOP's outstanding minority shares voting at the stockholders meeting at which the merger would be considered, and that the minority shares voting in favor of the merger, when coupled with Signal's 50.5% interest would have to comprise at least two-thirds of all UOP shares. Otherwise the proposed merger would be deemed disapproved.

UOP's board then considered the proposal. Copies of the agreement were delivered to the directors in attendance, and other copies had been forwarded earlier to the directors participating by telephone. They also had before them UOP financial data for 1974–1977, UOP's most recent financial statements, market price information, and budget projections for 1978. In addition they had Lehman Brothers' hurriedly prepared fairness opinion letter finding the price of $21 to be fair. Glanville, the Lehman Brothers partner, and UOP director, commented on the information that had gone into preparation of the letter.

Signal also suggests that the Arledge–Chitiea feasibility study, indicating that a price of up to $24 per share would be a "good investment" for Signal, was discussed at the UOP directors' meeting. The Chancellor made no such finding, and our independent review of the record, detailed *infra*, satisfies us by a preponderance of the evidence that there was no discussion of this document at UOP's board meeting. Furthermore, it is clear beyond peradventure that nothing in that report was ever disclosed to UOP's minority shareholders prior to their approval of the merger.

After consideration of Signal's proposal, Walkup and Crawford left the meeting to permit a free and uninhibited exchange between UOP's non-Signal directors. Upon their return a resolution to accept Signal's offer was then proposed and adopted. While Signal's men on UOP's board participated in various aspects of the meeting, they abstained from voting. However, the minutes show that each of them "if voting would have voted yes".

On March 7, 1978, UOP sent a letter to its shareholders advising them of the action taken by UOP's board with respect to Signal's offer. This document pointed out, among other things, that on February 28, 1978 "both companies had announced negotiations were being conducted".

Despite the swift board action of the two companies, the merger was not submitted to UOP's shareholders until their annual meeting on May 26, 1978. In the notice of that meeting and proxy statement sent to shareholders in May, UOP's management and board urged that the merger be approved. The proxy statement also advised:

> The price was determined after *discussions* between James V. Crawford, a director of Signal and Chief Executive Officer of UOP, and officers of Signal which took place during meetings on February 28, 1978, and in the course of several subsequent telephone conversations. (Emphasis added.)

In the original draft of the proxy statement the word "negotiations" had been used rather than "discussions". However, when the Securities and Exchange Commission sought details of the "negotiations" as part of its review of these materials, the term was deleted and the word "discussions" was substituted. The proxy statement indicated that the vote of UOP's board in approving the merger had been unanimous. It also advised the shareholders that Lehman Brothers had given its opinion that the merger price of $21 per share was fair to UOP's minority. However, it did not disclose the hurried method by which this conclusion was reached.

As of the record date of UOP's annual meeting, there were 11,488,302 shares of UOP common stock outstanding, 5,688,302 of which were owned by the minority. At the meeting only 56%, or 3,208,652, of the minority shares were voted. Of these, 2,953,812, or 51.9% of the total minority, voted for the merger, and 254,840 voted against it. When Signal's stock was added to the minority shares voting in favor, a total of 76.2% of UOP's outstanding shares approved the merger while only 2.2% opposed it.

By its terms the merger became effective on May 26, 1978, and each share of UOP's stock held by the minority was automatically converted into a right to receive $21 cash.

II.

A.

A primary issue mandating reversal is the preparation by two UOP directors, Arledge and Chitiea, of their feasibility study for the exclusive use and benefit of Signal. This document was of obvious significance to both Signal and UOP. Using UOP data, it described the advantages to Signal of ousting the minority at a price range of $21–$24 per share. Mr. Arledge, one of the authors, outlined the benefits to Signal:

Purpose Of The Merger

    1) Provides an outstanding investment opportunity for Signal— (Better than any recent acquisition we have seen.)

    2) Increases Signal's earnings.

    3) Facilitates the flow of resources between Signal and its subsidiaries—(Big factor—works both ways.)

    4) Provides cost savings potential for Signal and UOP.

    5) Improves the percentage of Signal's 'operating earnings' as opposed to 'holding company earnings'.

6) Simplifies the understanding of Signal.

7) Facilitates technological exchange among Signal's subsidiaries.

8) Eliminates potential conflicts of interest.

Having written those words, solely for the use of Signal, it is clear from the record that neither Arledge nor Chitiea shared this report with their fellow directors of UOP. We are satisfied that no one else did either. This conduct hardly meets the fiduciary standards applicable to such a transaction. While Mr. Walkup, Signal's chairman of the board and a UOP director, attended the March 6, 1978 UOP board meeting and testified at trial that he had discussed the Arledge–Chitiea report with the UOP directors at this meeting, the record does not support this assertion. Perhaps it is the result of some confusion on Mr. Walkup's part. In any event Mr. Shumway, Signal's president, testified that he made sure the Signal outside directors had this report prior to the March 6, 1978 Signal board meeting, but he did not testify that the Arledge-Chitiea report was also sent to UOP's outside directors.

Mr. Crawford, UOP's president, could not recall that any documents, other than a draft of the merger agreement, were sent to UOP's directors before the March 6, 1978 UOP meeting. Mr. Chitiea, an author of the report, testified that it was made available to Signal's directors, but to his knowledge it was not circulated to the outside directors of UOP. He specifically testified that he "didn't share" that information with the outside directors of UOP with whom he served.

None of UOP's outside directors who testified stated that they had seen this document. The minutes of the UOP board meeting do not identify the Arledge–Chitiea report as having been delivered to UOP's outside directors. This is particularly significant since the minutes describe in considerable detail the materials that actually were distributed. While these minutes recite Mr. Walkup's presentation of the Signal offer, they do not mention the Arledge–Chitiea report or any disclosure that Signal considered a price of up to $24 to be a good investment. If Mr. Walkup had in fact provided such important information to UOP's outside directors, it is logical to assume that these carefully drafted minutes would disclose it. The post-trial briefs of Signal and UOP contain a thorough description of the documents purportedly available to their boards at the March 6, 1978, meetings. Although the Arledge-Chitiea report is specifically identified as being available to the Signal directors, there is no mention of it being among the documents submitted to the UOP board. Even when queried at a prior oral argument before this Court, counsel for Signal did not claim that the Arledge–Chitiea report had been disclosed to UOP's outside directors. Instead, he chose to belittle its contents. This was the same approach taken before us at the last oral argument.

Actually, it appears that a three-page summary of figures was given to all UOP directors. Its first page is identical to one page of the Arledge–

Chitiea report, but this dealt with nothing more than a justification of the $21 price. Significantly, the contents of this three-page summary are what the minutes reflect Mr. Walkup told the UOP board. However, nothing contained in either the minutes or this three-page summary reflects Signal's study regarding the $24 price.

The Arledge–Chitiea report speaks for itself in supporting the Chancellor's finding that a price of up to $24 was a "good investment" for Signal. It shows that a return on the investment at $21 would be 15.7% versus 15.5% at $24 per share. This was a difference of only two-tenths of one percent, while it meant over $17,000,000 to the minority. Under such circumstances, paying UOP's minority shareholders $24 would have had relatively little long-term effect on Signal, and the Chancellor's findings concerning the benefit to Signal, even at a price of $24, were obviously correct. * * *

Certainly, this was a matter of material significance to UOP and its shareholders. Since the study was prepared by two UOP directors, using UOP information for the exclusive benefit of Signal, and nothing whatever was done to disclose it to the outside UOP directors or the minority shareholders, a question of breach of fiduciary duty arises. This problem occurs because there were common Signal-UOP directors participating, at least to some extent, in the UOP board's decision-making processes without full disclosure of the conflicts they faced.[35]

B.

In assessing this situation, the Court of Chancery was required to:

examine what information defendants had and to measure it against what they gave to the minority stockholders, in a context in which 'complete candor' is required. In other words, the limited function of the Court was to determine whether defendants had disclosed all information in their possession germane to the transaction in issue. And by 'germane' we mean, for present purposes, information such as a reasonable shareholder would consider important in deciding whether to sell or retain stock.

* * *

… Completeness, not adequacy, is both the norm and the mandate under present circumstances.

* * * This is merely stating in another way the long-existing principle of Delaware law that these Signal designated directors on UOP's board

---

35. Although perfection is not possible, or expected, the result here could have been entirely different if UOP had appointed an independent negotiating committee of its outside directors to deal with Signal at arm's length. * * * Since fairness in this context can be equated to conduct by a theoretical, wholly independent, board of directors acting upon the matter before them, it is unfortunate that this course apparently was neither considered nor pursued. * * * Particularly in a parent-subsidiary context, a showing that the action taken was as though each of the contending parties had in fact exerted its bargaining power against the other at arm's length is strong evidence that the transaction meets the test of fairness.* * *

still owed UOP and its shareholders an uncompromising duty of loyalty. The classic language of *Guth v. Loft, Inc., Del. Supr., 23 Del. Ch. 255, 5 A.2d 503, 510 (1939),* requires no embellishment:

> A public policy, existing through the years, and derived from a profound knowledge of human characteristics and motives, has established a rule that demands of a corporate officer or director, peremptorily and inexorably, the most scrupulous observance of his duty, not only affirmatively to protect the interests of the corporation committed to his charge, but also to refrain from doing anything that would work injury to the corporation, or to deprive it of profit or advantage which his skill and ability might properly bring to it, or to enable it to make in the reasonable and lawful exercise of its powers. The rule that requires an undivided and unselfish loyalty to the corporation demands that there shall be no conflict between duty and self-interest.

Given the absence of any attempt to structure this transaction on an arm's length basis, Signal cannot escape the effects of the conflicts it faced, particularly when its designees on UOP's board did not totally abstain from participation in the matter. There is no "safe harbor" for such divided loyalties in Delaware. When directors of a Delaware corporation are on both sides of a transaction, they are required to demonstrate their utmost good faith and the most scrupulous inherent fairness of the bargain. * * * The requirement of fairness is unflinching in its demand that where one stands on both sides of a transaction, he has the burden of establishing its entire fairness, sufficient to pass the test of careful scrutiny by the courts. * * *

There is no dilution of this obligation where one holds dual or multiple directorships, as in a parent-subsidiary context. * * * Thus, individuals who act in a dual capacity as directors of two corporations, one of whom is parent and the other subsidiary, owe the same duty of good management to both corporations, and in the absence of an independent negotiating structure (see note [35] *supra*), or the directors' total abstention from any participation in the matter, this duty is to be exercised in light of what is best for both companies. * * * The record demonstrates that Signal has not met this obligation.

C.

The concept of fairness has two basic aspects: fair dealing and fair price. The former embraces questions of when the transaction was timed, how it was initiated, structured, negotiated, disclosed to the directors, and how the approvals of the directors and the stockholders were obtained. The latter aspect of fairness relates to the economic and financial considerations of the proposed merger, including all relevant factors: assets, market value, earnings, future prospects, and any other elements that affect the intrinsic or inherent value of a company's stock. * * * However, the test for fairness is not a bifurcated one as between fair dealing and price. All aspects of the issue must be examined as a whole since the question is one of entire fairness. However, in a non-fraudulent transaction we recognize that price may be the preponderant consideration outweighing other features of the merger. Here, we address the two basic aspects of fairness separately because we find reversible error as to both.

D.

Part of fair dealing is the obvious duty of candor * * * Moreover, one possessing superior knowledge may not mislead any stockholder by use of corporate information to which the latter is not privy. * * * Delaware has long imposed this duty even upon persons who are not corporate officers or directors, but who nonetheless are privy to matters of interest or significance to their company. * * * With the well-established Delaware law on the subject, and the Court of Chancery's findings of fact here, it is inevitable that the obvious conflicts posed by Arledge and Chitiea's preparation of their "feasibility study", derived from UOP information, for the sole use and benefit of Signal, cannot pass muster.

The Arledge–Chitiea report is but one aspect of the element of fair dealing. How did this merger evolve? It is clear that it was entirely initiated by Signal. The serious time constraints under which the principals acted were all set by Signal. It had not found a suitable outlet for its excess cash and considered UOP a desirable investment, particularly since it was now in a position to acquire the whole company for itself. For whatever reasons, and they were only Signal's, the entire transaction was presented to and approved by UOP's board within four business days. Standing alone, this is not necessarily indicative of any lack of fairness by a majority shareholder. It was what occurred, or more properly, what did not occur, during this brief period that makes the time constraints imposed by Signal relevant to the issue of fairness.

The structure of the transaction, again, was Signal's doing. So far as negotiations were concerned, it is clear that they were modest at best. Crawford, Signal's man at UOP, never really talked price with Signal, except to accede to its management's statements on the subject, and to convey to Signal the UOP outside directors' view that as between the $20–$21 range under consideration, it would have to be $21. The latter is not a surprising outcome, but hardly arm's length negotiations. Only the protection of benefits for UOP's key employees and the issue of Lehman Brothers' fee approached any concept of bargaining.

As we have noted, the matter of disclosure to the UOP directors was wholly flawed by the conflicts of interest raised by the Arledge–Chitiea report. All of those conflicts were resolved by Signal in its own favor without divulging any aspect of them to UOP.

This cannot but undermine a conclusion that this merger meets any reasonable test of fairness. The outside UOP directors lacked one material piece of information generated by two of their colleagues, but shared only with Signal. True, the UOP board had the Lehman Brothers' fairness opinion, but that firm has been blamed by the plaintiff for the hurried task it performed, when more properly the responsibility for this lies with Signal. There was no disclosure of the circumstances surrounding the rather cursory preparation of the Lehman Brothers' fairness opinion. Instead, the impression was given UOP's minority that a careful study had been made, when in fact speed was the hallmark, and Mr. Glanville, Lehman's partner in charge of the matter, and also a UOP director, having spent the weekend in Vermont, brought a draft of the "fairness opinion letter" to the UOP directors' meeting on March 6, 1978 with the price left blank. We can only conclude from the record that the rush imposed on Lehman Brothers by Signal's timetable contributed to the difficulties under which this investment banking firm attempted to perform its responsibilities. Yet, none of this was disclosed to UOP's minority.

Finally, the minority stockholders were denied the critical information that Signal considered a price of $24 to be a good investment. Since this would have meant over $17,000,000 more to the minority, we cannot conclude that the shareholder vote was an informed one. Under the circumstances, an approval by a majority of the minority was meaningless. * * *

Given these particulars and the Delaware law on the subject, the record does not establish that this transaction satisfies any reasonable concept of fair dealing, and the Chancellor's findings in that regard must be reversed.

E.

Turning to the matter of price, plaintiff also challenges its fairness. His evidence was that on the date the merger was approved the stock was worth at least $26 per share. In support, he offered the testimony of a chartered investment analyst who used two basic approaches to valuation: a comparative analysis of the premium paid over market in ten other tender offer-merger combinations, and a discounted cash flow analysis.

In this breach of fiduciary duty case, the Chancellor perceived that the approach to valuation was the same as that in an appraisal proceeding. Consistent with precedent, he rejected plaintiff's method of proof and accepted defendants' evidence of value as being in accord with practice under prior case law. This means that the so-called "Delaware block" or weighted average method was employed wherein the elements of value, i.e., assets, market price, earnings, etc., were assigned a particular weight and the resulting amounts added to determine the value per share. This procedure has been in use for decades. * * * However, to the extent it excludes other generally accepted techniques used in the financial community and the courts, it is now clearly outmoded. It is time we recognize this in appraisal and other stock valuation proceedings and bring our law current on the subject.

While the Chancellor rejected plaintiff's discounted cash flow method of valuing UOP's stock, as not corresponding with "either logic or the existing law" * * * it is significant that this was essentially the focus, i.e., earnings potential of UOP, of Messrs. Arledge and Chitiea in their evaluation of the merger. Accordingly, the standard "Delaware block" or weighted average method of valuation, formerly employed in appraisal and other stock valuation cases, shall no longer exclusively control such proceedings. We believe that a more liberal approach must include proof of value by any techniques or methods which are generally considered acceptable in the financial community and otherwise admissible in court * * *. This will obviate the very structured and mechanistic procedure that has heretofore governed such matters. * * *

Fair price obviously requires consideration of all relevant factors involving the value of a company. This has long been the law of Delaware as stated in *Tri-Continental Corp. [v. Battye], 74 A.2d[71,] 72 [Del.1950]:*

> The basic concept of value under the appraisal statute is that the stockholder is entitled to be paid for that which has been taken from him, viz., his proportionate interest in a going concern. By value of the stockholder's proportionate interest in the corporate enterprise is meant the true or intrinsic value of his stock which has been taken by the merger. In determining what figure represents this true or intrinsic value, the appraiser and the courts must take into consideration all factors and elements which reasonably might enter into the fixing of value. Thus, market value, asset value, dividends, earning prospects, the nature of the enterprise and any other facts which were known or which could be ascertained as of the date of merger and which throw any light on *future prospects* of the merged corporation are not only pertinent to an inquiry as to the value of the dissenting stockholders' interest, but *must be considered* by the agency fixing the value. (Emphasis added.)

This is not only in accord with the realities of present day affairs, but it is thoroughly consonant with the purpose and intent of our statutory law. Under *8 Del. C. § 262(h)*, the Court of Chancery:

> shall appraise the shares, determining their *fair* value exclusive of any element of value arising from the accomplishment or expectation of the merger, together with a fair rate of interest, if any, to be paid upon the amount determined to be the *fair* value. In determining such *fair* value, the Court shall take into account *all relevant factors* … (Emphasis added)

* * *

It is significant that section 262 now mandates the determination of "fair" value based upon "all relevant factors". Only the speculative elements of value that may arise from the "accomplishment or expectation" of the merger are excluded. We take this to be a very narrow exception to the appraisal process, designed to eliminate use of *pro forma* data and projections of a speculative variety relating to the completion of a merger.

But elements of future value, including the nature of the enterprise, which are known or susceptible of proof as of the date of the merger and not the product of speculation, may be considered. When the trial court deems it appropriate, fair value also includes any damages, resulting from the taking, which the stockholders sustain as a class. If that was not the case, then the obligation to consider "all relevant factors" in the valuation process would be eroded. * * *

* * *

* * * Clearly, there is a legislative intent to fully compensate shareholders for whatever their loss may be, subject only to the narrow limitation that one can not take speculative effects of the merger into account.

Although the Chancellor received the plaintiff's evidence, his opinion indicates that the use of it was precluded because of past Delaware practice. While we do not suggest a monetary result one way or the other, we do think the plaintiff's evidence should be part of the factual mix and weighed as such. Until the $21 price is measured on remand by the valuation standards mandated by Delaware law, there can be no finding at the present stage of these proceedings that the price is fair. Given the lack of any candid disclosure of the material facts surrounding establishment of the $21 price, the majority of the minority vote, approving the merger, is meaningless.

* * *

While a plaintiff's monetary remedy ordinarily should be confined to the more liberalized appraisal proceeding herein established, we do not intend any limitation on the historic powers of the Chancellor to grant such other relief as the facts of a particular case may dictate. The appraisal remedy we approve may not be adequate in certain cases, particularly where fraud, misrepresentation, self-dealing, deliberate waste of corporate assets, or gross and palpable overreaching are involved. * * * Under such circumstances, the Chancellor's powers are complete to fashion any form of equitable and monetary relief as may be appropriate, including rescissory damages. Since it is apparent that this long completed transaction is too involved to undo, and in view of the Chancellor's discretion, the award, if any, should be in the form of monetary damages based upon entire fairness standards, i.e., fair dealing and fair price.

* * *

III.

Finally, we address the matter of business purpose. The defendants contend that the purpose of this merger was not a proper subject of inquiry by the trial court. The plaintiff says that no valid purpose existed—the entire transaction was a mere subterfuge designed to eliminate the minority. The Chancellor ruled otherwise, but in so doing he clearly circumscribed the thrust and effect of *Singer. Weinberger v. UOP,*

426 A.2d at 1342–43, 1348–50. This has led to the thoroughly sound observation that the business purpose test "may be … virtually interpreted out of existence, as it was in *Weinberger*".[36]

The requirement of a business purpose is new to our law of mergers and was a departure from prior case law. * * *

In view of the fairness test which has long been applicable to parent-subsidiary mergers, * * * the expanded appraisal remedy now available to shareholders, and the broad discretion of the Chancellor to fashion such relief as the facts of a given case may dictate, we do not believe that any additional meaningful protection is afforded minority shareholders by the business purpose requirement of the trilogy of *Singer, Tanzer,* * * * *Najjar,* * * * and their progeny. Accordingly, such requirement shall no longer be of any force or effect.

The judgment of the Court of Chancery, finding both the circumstances of the merger and the price paid the minority shareholders to be fair, is reversed. The matter is remanded for further proceedings consistent herewith. * * *

NOTES AND QUESTIONS

1.   Taking into consideration the result in this case, and also the result in such cases as *Omnicare* and *Smith v. Van Gorkom,* can it really truthfully be said that the law of Delaware waters down the rights of shareholders to a "thin gruel?" Did the UOP shareholders really need protection in this case? Given the fact that the original tender offer made by Signal for its minority stake in UOP was significantly oversubscribed, and given the further fact that UOP had been trading at $14.50 per share before Signal's attempt to acquire the remaining shares at that same $21 price, is it as clear as the Delaware Supreme Court makes out that the conduct of Signal's officials was unfair to the UOP minority shareholders? Note that the court does suggest a means by which Signal might have been able to buy the remaining shares of UOP and avoid having the transaction attacked by disgruntled shareholders. What was that means, and are you satisfied that it would adequately protect the interests of UOP minority shareholders?

2.   As indicated earlier, this case moves on from the Delaware Block method to suggest that other means of valuation might appropriately be employed in Delaware courts. Note that Discounted Cash Flow (DCF) and Comparative Premium Studies seem implicitly to be approved. Do you have more confidence in those means than in the Delaware Block method? Why? Note further that the Delaware Supreme Court reiterates its belief, expressed in *Smith v. Van Gorkom,* that there is such a thing as "intrinsic" or "fair" value that can be demonstrated or at least suggested by appropriate financial analysis. Do you share the court's confidence on this point? What do you make of the Court's intriguing suggestion, implicitly criticizing the conduct of Signal, when it stated that:

---

36.   Weiss, The Law of Take Out Mergers: A Historical Perspective, 56 N.Y.U. L. Rev. 624, 671, n. 300 (1981).

The Arledge–Chitiea report speaks for itself in supporting the Chancellor's finding that a price of up to $24 was a "good investment" for Signal. It shows that a return on the investment at $21 would be 15.7% versus 15.5% at $24 per share. This was a difference of only two-tenths of one percent, while it meant over $17,000,000 to the minority. Under such circumstances, paying UOP's minority shareholders $24 would have had relatively little long-term effect on Signal, and the Chancellor's findings concerning the benefit to Signal, even at a price of $24, were obviously correct.

Is there any kind of slip in the Court's reasoning on this point?

3. *Weinberger v. UOP*, insofar as it rejects the "business purpose" test for "freezeout" mergers, makes such transactions easier to accomplish. Other states have not rejected the "business purpose," test and do not permit such "freezeouts," whereby the minority interest is terminated, usually through purchase of the minority's shares by the majority, unless there is a purpose for the merger apart from the simple desire to appropriate the entire enterprise for the majority holder. Such a "business purpose" might include such matters as taking the corporation "private," so as to avoid particular regulatory consequences, including adverse tax treatment or compliance with disclosure requirements of the Securities Exchange Commission. Why abandon the "business purpose" requirement? Does the "entire fairness" test, as explained in *Weinberger*, do an adequate job of protecting shareholders potentially subject to a "freezeout?" As a policy matter, should reducing the number of owners, or eliminating minority ownership in large-scale businesses be something we should encourage or discourage? Given what you now know about Delaware law and tender offers, would you believe that there is a need for the federal government to step in to protect minority (or even majority) shareholders who might be faced with a tender offer, particularly one made by a bidder hostile to incumbent management? What do you make of the "Williams Act," considered next, in which the Congress did respond to what it believed to be inadequacies in state law?

Why do we continue to rely on a corporate structure that gives primacy to director/officer decision making? In the last chapter, there was an off-hand suggestion that the tale of Ulysses and the Sirens had something to teach us about close corporations. For the suggestion that this is true for the publicly-held corporation as well see Lynn A. Stout, The Shareholder as Ulysses: Some Empirical Evidence on Why Investors in Public Corporations Tolerate Board Governance, 152 U. Pa. L. Rev. 667, 689 (2003). For a panoramic view of developments at the Delaware Supreme Court and at the federal level see the recent after-dinner speech of the Chief Justice of the Delaware Supreme Court, E. Norman Veasey, Views from the Bench: Musings on the Dynamics of Corporate Governance Issues, Director Liability Concerns, Corporate Control Transactions, Ethics and Federalism, 152 U. Pa. L. Rev. 1007 (2003).

D. A NOTE ON THE WILLIAMS ACT
AND STATE STATUTES

"In recent years we have seen proud old companies reduced to corpo-rate shells after white-collar pirates have seized control with funds from sources which are unknown in many cases, then sold or traded away the best assets, later to split up most of the loot among themselves...."[37] So said Senator Harrison Williams, when he introduced the federal legisla-tion designed to regulate tender offers, soon to be called the "Williams Act."[38] You will note that Senator Williams does not appear to be a great friend to takeovers, and while some legislative history of the Williams Act says it was designed to be neutral, neither favoring or discouraging hos-tile bids for companies, it is very difficult to read it as anything but rais-ing the costs of such bids. The act regulates "tender offers," the procedure whereby a bidder indicates that he is willing, if a specified number of shareholders "tender" their shares to the bidder at a specified price, to purchase those shares. The bidder is free to decline to purchase any of the shares if an insufficient number of them are tendered to meet the bidder's stated requirements. Do you understand why a tender offer is a much more effective takeover strategy than open-market purchases? Do you favor or oppose tender offers? There are many provisions of the Williams Act, and many regulations authorized by it, but for our purposes we need only highlight some of the major provisions.

Disclosure. For example, the Williams Act provides that when one either acquires 5% or more of a corporation listed on a national stock exchange (a "toehold interest") or makes a tender offer for 5% or more of such a company, one is required to file with the issuer and the SEC a statement indicating, among other things, one's identity, the source of one's funding, and one's future plans with regard to acquisition of addi-tional interests in the target and whether a bust-up of the target is con-templated. See generally § 14(d)(1) of the Securities Exchange Act of 1934, as amended, 15 U.S.C. § 78n(d)(1) (1988), and the regulations thereunder. Would you be in favor of such a provision?

Duration. There was a time, in the early days of regulation of tender offers and takeovers, when one could make an offer that would be open for only eight days (the so-called "Saturday Night Special,") but under the Williams Act Rule 14e–1(a), 17 C.F.R. § 240.14e–1(a) (1990), and other federal legislation, such as the Hart-Scott-Rodino Antitrust Improvements Act, Pub. L. 94–435 (1976), a tender offer must remain open for at least 20, and sometimes as long as 50 days, while the FTC examines whether there are anti-competitive implications and thus whether or not it should permit a tender offer and associated merger to be accomplished. Who ben-

---

37. 111 CONG. REC. 28,257 (1965).

38. Pub. L. No. 90–439, 82 Stat. 454 (1968) (codified as amended at 15 U.S.C. §§ 78m(d)–(e), 78n(d)–(f) (1988)). The Williams Act provisions became § 13(d)–(e) and § 14(d)–(f) of the Exchange Act, 15 U.S.C. §§ 78a–78ll (1988).

efits when a tender offer must be kept open for a substantial period of time? Who bears the cost?

Pro-Rating. In the early days of employment of tender offers, a bidder had the freedom to make such an offer for a specified percentage of the shares of a target corporation, and offer cash for those shares, and then freeze-out the remaining shareholders in a shares for debt swap. Such a transaction is known in the trade as a "Front-End-Loaded Two-Tiered Tender Offer," and it is a fearsome device, indeed. At the "back-end," the hapless minority shareholders often receive "junk-bonds" (non-investment grade securities, debt instruments that carry a high rate of interest, but that are often highly subordinated (their interest will not be paid until other creditors of the corporation are paid), and bear a high risk of declining in value). Fear of being at the back end of such a transaction often stampeded shareholders into accepting the tender offer, even if the price might not have been as high as such shareholders would have expected or desired. In order to alleviate the problem, under the current Williams Act regulations, a bidder is required, instead of being able to accept tendered shares on a first-come first-served basis, to purchase an aliquot portion of all shares tendered during the period the offer is required to remain open. Rule 14d–8, 17 C.F.R. § 240.14d–8 (1990). Do you understand why this, combined with the duration provisions mentioned above, reduces the threat of the Front-End-Loaded Two-Tiered Tender Offer? For a case involving a Front-End-Loaded Two-Tiered Tender Offer, explaining why it is a coercive device, and approving tactics to defeat it, see, e.g., Unocal Corp. v. Mesa Petroleum Co., 493 A.2d 946 (Del. 1985).

Upping the Ante. There was a time when one could make a tender offer for a specified number of shares, say $50 for 51% of the shares, and if, for example, only 40% of the shares were tendered, the bidder was free to lock in those shares at $50, and then issue an additional tender offer for 11% of the shares, at a higher price, perhaps $55. This is no longer possible, as the Williams Act now provides that if the price of a tender offer is raised, all shares (even those previously tendered) must be purchased at the higher price. § 14(d)(7) of the Securities Exchange Act of 1937, as amended, 15 U.S.C. § 78n(d)(7) (1988). Can this be interpreted as anything but an attempt to discourage tender offers?

Withdrawal. At one time it was possible for the bidder to exert control over shares tendered for a set period of time before the bidder made the decision (as a bidder may do) to accept the tender of those shares and purchase them. The period in which the bidder could lock up such tendered shares was at first fourteen days, and then it was reduced to seven days. At the present time, however, Williams Act regulations provide that a shareholder who has tendered shares may withdraw them at any time before they have been accepted for purchase by the bidder. Rule 14d–7, 17 C.F.R. § 240.14d–7 (1990). Such a non-withdrawal provision gave the bidder the opportunity to keep shares off the market, and thus made it more difficult for competing tender offers. Do you favor the ending of this lock-up period?

All-Holders Rule. Before the passage of this recent revision of the Williams Act, it was possible for a tender offeror to make a selective bid targeted only at some shareholders, but not others. Such a bid might be made, for example, to shareholders at the back end of a Front-End-Loaded Two-Tiered Tender Offer by the target itself (a "self-tender") in order to raise the cost and thereby defeat that coercive tactic. Do you understand how this might work? See, e.g., Unocal Corp. v. Mesa Petroleum Co., 493 A.2d 946 (Del. 1985), where the Delaware Supreme Court approved of such a selective tender, as a defensive strategy. Now the "all-holders rule" provides that a tender offer must be open to all holders of a given class of stock. Rule 14d–10, 17 C.F.R. § 240.14d–10 (1990). Was this federal non-discrimination rule wise?

Advice from the Target to its Shareholders. Whether or not academic theorists believe that the position of target management should be supine, a relatively new regulation under the Williams Act, Rule 14e–2, 17 C.F.R. § 240.14e–2 (1990), provides that within ten business days of the commencement of a tender offer, a target must publish or send to its shareholders a statement indicating that it recommends acceptance or rejection of the tender offer, has chosen to remain neutral, or is unable to take a position on the tender offer. The statements of the corporation are subject to the general and broad anti-fraud provisions of the Williams Act, which provide penalties for untrue or misleading statements made in connection with a tender offer. For further application of the anti-fraud rules under the Williams Act, see, e.g., *United States v. O'Hagan, supra.*

As well as the Williams Act, there are now state statutory provisions which have the effect of delaying or making takeovers more difficult. There was some doubt about whether such statutes could be permitted, or whether the area (at least that of large publicly-held corporations) ought to be left for federal law. This was settled by the United States Supreme Court, allowing some regulatory freedom for the states in this area. See generally, CTS Corp. v. Dynamics Corp. of America, 481 U.S. 69, 107 S.Ct. 1637, 95 L.Ed.2d 67 (1987), which permitted states to make rules regarding "control share acquisitions." Subsequent state legislation which seeks to protect shareholders at the back end of a front-end-loaded two-tiered tender offer, state legislation which imposes a waiting period for the exercise of control by a bidder, and state legislation which gives discretion to board members to consider the effects of a takeover on corporate constituencies other than shareholders in deciding what action to take in response to a hostile offer appear to have met constitutional muster. For a useful brief note on this state legislation, see Melvin Eisenberg, Corporations and Other Business Organizations: Cases and Materials 874–877 (Concise 8th ed., 2000).

This completes our brief introduction to the law of business organizations. The next and final chapter briefly considers some related areas of law of particular concern to practicing managers.

CHAPTER 9

RELATED ISSUES OF CONCERN

■ ■ ■

In most of the chapters of this casebook we have been concerned with issues of business organization, and, in particular, the relationships and duties among shareholders, directors, and officers. There are other legal problems, of course, that affect anyone involved in the running of a business. In several decades of teaching managers in Northwestern's Kellogg School of Management, I've discovered that the four such matters about which managers remain the most curious are employment discrimination, intellectual property, contracts, and antitrust. Each of these is usually accorded separate treatment as at least one law school course, but some of the main principles and issues can still be suggested by a brief look at three cases, the first dealing with employment discrimination, the second with intellectual property and contracts, and the third with antitrust.

A. EMPLOYMENT DISCRIMINATION

MCDONELL DOUGLAS CORP. v. GREEN
Supreme Court of the United States.
411 U.S. 792, 93 S.Ct. 1817, 36 L.Ed.2d 668 (1973).

MR. JUSTICE POWELL delivered the opinion of [a unanimous] Court.

The case before us raises significant questions as to the proper order and nature of proof in actions under Title VII of the Civil Rights Act of 1964, 78 Stat. 253, *42 U. S. C. § 2000c et seq.*

Petitioner, McDonnell Douglas Corp., is an aerospace and aircraft manufacturer headquartered in St. Louis, Missouri, where it employs over 30,000 people. Respondent, a black citizen of St. Louis, worked for petitioner as a mechanic and laboratory technician from 1956 until August 28, 1964 * * * when he was laid off in the course of a general reduction in petitioner's work force.

Respondent, a long-time activist in the civil rights movement, protested vigorously that his discharge and the general hiring practices of petitioner were racially motivated.[1] As part of this protest, respondent

---

1. The Court of Appeals noted that respondent then "filed formal complaints of discrimination with the President's Commission on Civil Rights, the Justice Department, the Department of the

and other members of the Congress on Racial Equality illegally stalled their cars on the main roads leading to petitioner's plant for the purpose of blocking access to it at the time of the morning shift change. The District Judge described the plan for, and respondent's participation in, the "stall-in" as follows:

> "Five teams, each consisting of four cars would 'tie up' five main access roads into McDonnell at the time of the morning rush hour. The drivers of the cars were instructed to line up next to each other completely blocking the intersections or roads. The drivers were also instructed to stop their cars, turn off the engines, pull the emergency brake, raise all windows, lock the doors, and remain in their cars until the police arrived. The plan was to have the cars remain in position for one hour. Acting under the 'stall in' plan, plaintiff [respondent in the present action] drove his car onto Brown Road, a McDonnell access road, at approximately 7:00 a.m., at the start of the morning rush hour. Plaintiff was aware of the traffic problems that would result. He stopped his car with the intent to block traffic. The police arrived shortly and requested plaintiff to move his car. He refused to move his car voluntarily. Plaintiff's car was towed away by the police, and he was arrested for obstructing traffic. Plaintiff pleaded guilty to the charge of obstructing traffic and was fined." * * *

On July 2, 1965, a "lock-in" took place wherein a chain and padlock were placed on the front door of a building to prevent the occupants, certain of petitioner's employees, from leaving. Though respondent apparently knew beforehand of the "lock-in," the full extent of his involvement remains uncertain.[2]

Some three weeks following the "lock-in," on July 25, 1965, petitioner publicly advertised for qualified mechanics, respondent's trade, and respondent promptly applied for re-employment. Petitioner turned down respondent, basing its rejection on respondent's participation in the "stall-in" and "lock-in." Shortly thereafter, respondent filed a formal complaint

---

Navy, the Defense Department, and the Missouri Commission on Human Rights." 463 F.2d 337, 339 (1972).

2. The "lock-in" occurred during a picketing demonstration by ACTION, a civil rights organization, at the entrance to a downtown office building which housed a part of petitioner's offices and in which certain of petitioner's employees were working at the time. A chain and padlock were placed on the front door of the building to prevent ingress and egress. Although respondent acknowledges that he was chairman of ACTION at the time, that the demonstration was planned and staged by his group, that he participated in and indeed was in charge of the picket line in front of the building, that he was told in advance by a member of ACTION "that he was planning to chain the front door," and that he "approved of" chaining the door, there is no evidence that respondent personally took part in the actual "lock-in," and he was not arrested. * * *

The Court of Appeals majority, however, found that the record did "not support the trial court's conclusion that Green 'actively cooperated' in chaining the doors of the downtown St. Louis building during the 'lock-in' demonstration." * * * Judge Johnsen, in dissent, agreed with the District Court that the "chaining and padlocking [were] carried out as planned, [and that] Green had in fact given it … approval and authorization." * * * In view of respondent's admitted participation in the unlawful "stall-in," we find it unnecessary to resolve the contradictory contentions surrounding this "lock-in."

with the Equal Employment Opportunity Commission, claiming that petitioner had refused to rehire him because of his race and persistent involvement in the civil rights movement, in violation of §§ 703 (a)(1) and 704 (a) of the Civil Rights Act of 1964, *42 U. S. C. §§ 2000e–2* (a)(1) and 2000e–3 (a).[3] The former section generally prohibits racial discrimination in any employment decision while the latter forbids discrimination against applicants or employees for attempting to protest or correct allegedly discriminatory conditions of employment.

The Commission made no finding on respondent's allegation of racial bias under § 703 (a)(1), but it did find reasonable cause to believe petitioner had violated § 704 (a) by refusing to rehire respondent because of his civil rights activity. After the Commission unsuccessfully attempted to conciliate the dispute, it advised respondent in March 1968, of his right to institute a civil action in federal court within 30 days.

On April 15, 1968, respondent brought the present action, claiming initially a violation of § 704 (a) and, in an amended complaint, a violation of § 703 (a)(1) as well. * * * The District Court dismissed the latter claim of racial discrimination in petitioner's hiring procedures on the ground that the Commission had failed to make a determination of reasonable cause to believe that a violation of that section had been committed. The District Court also found that petitioner's refusal to rehire respondent was based solely on his participation in the illegal demonstrations and not on his legitimate civil rights activities. The court concluded that nothing in Title VII or § 704 protected "such activity as employed by the plaintiff in the 'stall in' and 'lock in' demonstrations." * * *

On appeal, the Eighth Circuit affirmed that unlawful protests were not protected activities under § 704 (a), * * * but reversed the dismissal of respondent's § 703 (a)(1) claim relating to racially discriminatory hiring practices, holding that a prior Commission determination of reasonable cause was not a jurisdictional prerequisite to raising a claim under that section in federal court. The court ordered the case remanded for trial of respondent's claim under § 703 (a)(1).

In remanding, the Court of Appeals attempted to set forth standards to govern the consideration of respondent's claim. The majority noted that respondent had established a prima facie case of racial discrimination; that petitioner's refusal to rehire respondent rested on "subjective" criteria which carried little weight in rebutting charges of discrimination; that,

---

3. Section 703 (a)(1) of the Civil Rights Act of 1964, 42 U. S. C. § 2000e–2 (a)(1), in pertinent part provides:

* * * "It shall be an unlawful employment practice for an employer ... to fail or refuse to hire or to discharge any individual, or otherwise to discriminate against any individual with respect to his compensation, terms, conditions, or privileges of employment, because of such individual's race, color, religion, sex, or national origin...."

Section 704 (a) of the Civil Rights Act of 1964, 42 U. S. C. § 2000e–3 (a), in pertinent part provides:

* * * "It shall be an unlawful employment practice for an employer to discriminate against any of his employees or applicants for employment ... because he has opposed any practice made an unlawful employment practice by this subchapter...."

though respondent's participation in the unlawful demonstrations might indicate a lack of a responsible attitude toward performing work for that employer, respondent should be given the opportunity to demonstrate that petitioner's reasons for refusing to rehire him were mere pretext. * * * In order to clarify the standards governing the disposition of an action challenging employment discrimination, we granted certiorari * * *.

We agree with the Court of Appeals that absence of a Commission finding of reasonable cause cannot bar suit under an appropriate section of Title VII and that the District Judge erred in dismissing respondent's claim of racial discrimination under § 703 (a)(1). Respondent satisfied the jurisdictional prerequisites to a federal action (i) by filing timely charges of employment discrimination with the Commission and (ii) by receiving and acting upon the Commission's statutory notice of the right to sue * * *. The Act does not restrict a complainant's right to sue to those charges as to which the Commission has made findings of reasonable cause, and we will not engraft on the statute a requirement which may inhibit the review of claims of employment discrimination in the federal courts. The Commission itself does not consider the absence of a "reasonable cause" determination as providing employer immunity from similar charges in a federal court, *29 CFR § 1601.30*, and the courts of appeal have held that, in view of the large volume of complaints before the Commission and the nonadversary character of many of its proceedings, "court actions under Title VII are de novo proceedings and … a Commission 'no reasonable cause' finding does not bar a lawsuit in the case." * * *

Petitioner argues, as it did below, that respondent sustained no prejudice from the trial court's erroneous ruling because in fact the issue of racial discrimination in the refusal to re-employ "was tried thoroughly" in a trial lasting four days with "at least 80%" of the questions relating to the issue of "race." * * * Petitioner, therefore, requests that the judgment below be vacated and the cause remanded with instructions that the judgment of the District Court be affirmed.* * * We cannot agree that the dismissal of respondent's § 703 (a)(1) claim was harmless error. It is not clear that the District Court's findings as to respondent's § 704 (a) contentions involved the identical issues raised by his claim under § 703 (a)(1). The former section relates solely to discrimination against an applicant or employee on account of his participation in legitimate civil rights activities or protests, while the latter section deals with the broader and centrally important question under the Act of whether, for any reason, a racially discriminatory employment decision has been made. Moreover, respondent should have been accorded the right to prepare his case and plan the strategy of trial with the knowledge that the § 703 (a)(1) cause of action was properly before the District Court.[4] Accordingly, we remand the case for trial of respondent's claim of racial discrimination consistent with the views set forth below.

---

4. The trial court did not discuss respondent's § 703 (a)(1) claim in its opinion and denied requests for discovery of statistical materials which may have been relevant to that claim.

II

The critical issue before us concerns the order and allocation of proof in a private, non-class action challenging employment discrimination. The language of Title VII makes plain the purpose of Congress to assure equality of employment opportunities and to eliminate those discriminatory practices and devices which have fostered racially stratified job environments to the disadvantage of minority citizens. *Griggs v. Duke Power Co., 401 U.S. 424, 429 (1971)* * * *. As noted in *Griggs* * * *:

> "Congress did not intend by Title VII, however, to guarantee a job to every person regardless of qualifications. In short, the Act does not command that any person be hired simply because he was formerly the subject of discrimination, or because he is a member of a minority group. Discriminatory preference for any group, minority or majority, is precisely and only what Congress has proscribed. What is required by Congress is the removal of artificial, arbitrary, and unnecessary barriers to employment when the barriers operate invidiously to discriminate on the basis of racial or other impermissible classification."
> *Id., at 430–431.*

There are societal as well as personal interests on both sides of this equation. The broad, overriding interest, shared by employer, employee, and consumer, is efficient and trustworthy workmanship assured through fair and racially neutral employment and personnel decisions. In the implementation of such decisions, it is abundantly clear that Title VII tolerates no racial discrimination, subtle or otherwise.

In this case respondent, the complainant below, charges that he was denied employment "because of his involvement in civil rights activities" and "because of his race and color." * * * Petitioner denied discrimination of any kind, asserting that its failure to re-employ respondent was based upon and justified by his participation in the unlawful conduct against it. Thus, the issue at the trial on remand is framed by those opposing factual contentions. The two opinions of the Court of Appeals and the several opinions of the three judges of that court attempted, with a notable lack of harmony, to state the applicable rules as to burden of proof and how this shifts upon the making of a prima facie case. * * * We now address this problem.

The complainant in a Title VII trial must carry the initial burden under the statute of establishing a prima facie case of racial discrimination. This may be done by showing (i) that he belongs to a racial minority; (ii) that he applied and was qualified for a job for which the employer was seeking applicants; (iii) that, despite his qualifications, he was rejected; and (iv) that, after his rejection, the position remained open and the employer continued to seek applicants from persons of complainant's qualifications. * * * In the instant case, we agree with the Court of Appeals that respondent proved a prima facie case. * * * Petitioner sought mechanics, respondent's trade, and continued to do so after respondent's rejection. Petitioner, moreover, does not dispute respondent's qualifications[5] and acknowledges that his past work performance in petitioner's employ was "satisfactory." * * *

The burden then must shift to the employer to articulate some legitimate, nondiscriminatory reason for the employee's rejection. We need not attempt in the instant case to detail every matter which fairly could be recognized as a reasonable basis for a refusal to hire. Here petitioner has assigned respondent's participation in unlawful conduct against it as the cause for his rejection. We think that this suffices to discharge petitioner's burden of proof at this stage and to meet respondent's prima facie case of discrimination.

The Court of Appeals intimated, however, that petitioner's stated reason for refusing to rehire respondent was a "subjective" rather than objective criterion which "carr[ies] little weight in rebutting charges of discrimination,"* * *. This was among the statements which caused the dissenting judge to read the opinion as taking "the position that such unlawful acts as Green committed against McDonnell would not legally entitle McDonnell to refuse to hire him, even though no racial motivation was involved...." * * * Regardless of whether this was the intended import of the opinion, we think the court below seriously underestimated the rebuttal weight to which petitioner's reasons were entitled. Respondent admittedly had taken part in a carefully planned "stall-in," designed to tie up access to and egress from petitioner's plant at a peak traffic hour.[6] Nothing in Title VII compels an employer to absolve and rehire one who has engaged in such deliberate, unlawful activity against it.[7] In upholding, under the National Labor Relations Act, the discharge of employees who had seized and forcibly retained an employer's factory buildings in an illegal sit-down strike, the Court noted pertinently:

> "We are unable to conclude that Congress intended to compel employers to retain persons in their employ regardless of their unlawful conduct,—to invest those who go on strike with an immunity from discharge for acts of trespass or violence against the employer's property.... Apart from the question of the constitutional validity of an enactment of that sort, it is enough to say that such a legislative intention should be found in some definite and unmistakable expression." *NLRB v. Fansteel Corp., 306 U.S. 240, 255 (1939).*

---

5. We note that the issue of what may properly be used to test qualifications for employment is not present in this case. Where employers have instituted employment tests and qualifications with an exclusionary effect on minority applicants, such requirements must be "shown to bear a demonstrable relationship to successful performance of the jobs" for which they were used, Griggs v. Duke Power Co., 401 U.S. 424, 431 (1971). * * *

6. The trial judge noted that no personal injury or property damage resulted from the "stall-in" due "solely to the fact that law enforcement officials had obtained notice in advance of plaintiff's [here respondent's] demonstration and were at the scene to remove plaintiff's car from the highway." * * *

7. The unlawful activity in this case was directed specifically against petitioner. We need not consider or decide here whether, or under what circumstances, unlawful activity not directed against the particular employer may be a legitimate justification for refusing to hire.

Petitioner's reason for rejection thus suffices to meet the prima facie case, but the inquiry must not end here. * * * While Title VII does not, without more, compel rehiring of respondent, neither does it permit petitioner to use respondent's conduct as a pretext for the sort of discrimination prohibited by § 703 (a)(1). On remand, respondent must, as the Court of Appeals recognized, be afforded a fair opportunity to show that petitioner's stated reason for respondent's rejection was in fact pretext. Especially relevant to such a showing would be evidence that white employees involved in acts against petitioner of comparable seriousness to the "stall-in" were nevertheless retained or rehired. Petitioner may justifiably refuse to rehire one who was engaged in unlawful, disruptive acts against it, but only if this criterion is applied alike to members of all races.

Other evidence that may be relevant to any showing of pretext includes facts as to the petitioner's treatment of respondent during his prior term of employment; petitioner's reaction, if any, to respondent's legitimate civil rights activities; and petitioner's general policy and practice with respect to minority employment.[8] On the latter point, statistics as to petitioner's employment policy and practice may be helpful to a determination of whether petitioner's refusal to rehire respondent in this case conformed to a general pattern of discrimination against blacks. * * * Blumrosen, Strangers in Paradise: *Griggs* v. *Duke Power Co.*, and the Concept of Employment Discrimination, *71 Mich. L. Rev. 59, 91–94 (1972).*[9] In short, on the retrial respondent must be given a full and fair opportunity to demonstrate by competent evidence that the presumptively valid reasons for his rejection were in fact a coverup for a racially discriminatory decision.

The court below appeared to rely upon *Griggs v. Duke Power Co., supra,* in which the Court stated: "If an employment practice which operates to exclude Negroes cannot be shown to be related to job performance, the practice is prohibited." *401 U.S., at 431.* * * * But *Griggs* differs from the instant case in important respects. It dealt with standardized testing devices which, however neutral on their face, operated to exclude many blacks who were capable of performing effectively in the desired positions. *Griggs* was rightly concerned that childhood deficiencies in the education and background of minority citizens, resulting from forces beyond their control, not be allowed to work a cumulative and invidious burden on such

---

8. We are aware that some of the above factors were, indeed, considered by the District Judge in finding under § 704 (a), that "defendant's [here petitioner's] reasons for refusing to rehire the plaintiff were motivated solely and simply by the plaintiff's participation in the 'stall in' and 'lock in' demonstrations." * * * We do not intimate that this finding must be overturned after consideration on remand of respondent's § 703 (a)(1) claim. We do, however, insist that respondent under § 703 (a)(1) must be given a full and fair opportunity to demonstrate by competent evidence that whatever the stated reasons for his rejection, the decision was in reality racially premised.

9. The District Court may, for example, determine, after reasonable discovery that "the [racial] composition of defendant's labor force is itself reflective of restrictive or exclusionary practices." See Blumrosen, supra, at 92. We caution that such general determinations, while helpful, may not be in and of themselves controlling as to an individualized hiring decision, particularly in the presence of an otherwise justifiable reason for refusing to rehire. * * *

citizens for the remainder of their lives. *Id., at 430.* Respondent, however, appears in different clothing. He had engaged in a seriously disruptive act against the very one from whom he now seeks employment. And petitioner does not seek his exclusion on the basis of a testing device which overstates what is necessary for competent performance, or through some sweeping disqualification of all those with any past record of unlawful behavior, however remote, insubstantial, or unrelated to applicant's personal qualifications as an employee. Petitioner assertedly rejected respondent for unlawful conduct against it and, in the absence of proof of pretext or discriminatory application of such a reason, this cannot be thought the kind of "artificial, arbitrary, and unnecessary barriers to employment" which the Court found to be the intention of Congress to remove. *Id., at 431.*[10]

III

In sum, respondent should have been allowed to pursue his claim under § 703 (a)(1). If the evidence on retrial is substantially in accord with that before us in this case, we think that respondent carried his burden of establishing a prima facie case of racial discrimination and that petitioner successfully rebutted that case. But this does not end the matter. On retrial, respondent must be afforded a fair opportunity to demonstrate that petitioner's assigned reason for refusing to re-employ was a pretext or discriminatory in its application. If the District Judge so finds, he must order a prompt and appropriate remedy. In the absence of such a finding, petitioner's refusal to rehire must stand. * * *

NOTES AND QUESTIONS

1. Now that you have read this case, can you understand whether it was or was not appropriate for the corporation to have terminated Mr. Green's employment? What do you understand to be the thrust of Title VII, the Civil Rights statute in question, and do you suppose its framers would have been pleased or displeased with the opinion in this case?

2. What do you make of *Griggs v. Duke Power Co.*, probably the leading case on employment discrimination? As an employer, would you say that *Griggs* was correctly decided? Would you say the same if you were a member of a minority group adversely affected by a history of discrimination? Which is more important, giving discretion to employers to hire whom they please, or ensuring that the nation adheres to its statutorily-stated goals of freedom from employment discrimination? In *Griggs*, the United States Supreme

---

10. It is, of course, a predictive evaluation, resistant to empirical proof, whether "an applicant's past participation in unlawful conduct directed at his prospective employer might indicate the applicant's lack of a responsible attitude toward performing work for that employer." * * * But in this case, given the seriousness and harmful potential of respondent's participation in the "stall-in" and the accompanying inconvenience to other employees, it cannot be said that petitioner's refusal to employ lacked a rational and neutral business justification. As the Court has noted elsewhere:

> "Past conduct may well relate to present fitness; past loyalty may have a reasonable relationship to present and future trust." Garner v. Los Angeles Board, 341 U.S. 716, 720 (1951).

Court held that "Ostensibly neutral practices are unlawful ... if they operate to maintain the effects of past discrimination.... that intent or discriminatory purpose is irrelevant; it is consequences that matter. Tests used for hiring and promotion must be job related.... [and, also] practices, however neutral in intent, that caused a disparate impact upon a group protected by [Title VII] [are impermissible]." Herbert Hill, "Griggs v. Duke Power Co.," The Oxford Companion to the Supreme Court of the United States 351 (K.Hall, ed., 1992).

3.   You may have been able to discern that the question of burden of proof of matters such as "disparate impact," "discriminatory intent," or the "job related" character of employment tests might be crucial in resolving disputes over whether there has been impermissible discrimination. Who should have the burden of proof in such cases? For example, if a given workforce has among it a percentage of minority workers far less than their percentage in the local population, should the burden of proving non-discriminatory intent be on the employer or the employee? The answer to the question of how to allocate burden of proof in employment discrimination cases has varied over time, although it is now clear that Under Title VII, the employee has the burden of demonstrating that a particular employment requirement has a legally significant disparate impact, and then the employer is required to prove that the use of that requirement is dictated by "business necessity." 42 U.S.C., Section 2000e–2(k)(1)(A)(i) (1991). Does this statutory allocation seem satisfactory? For further reading on employment and employment discrimination law see, e.g., Robert N. Covington and Kurt H. Decker, Employment Law in a Nutshell (2nd ed. 2002), Harold S. Lewis, Hornbook on Employment Discrimination Law and Practice (2nd ed. 2004), and Mack A. Player, Federal Law of Employment Discrimination in a Nutshell (5th ed. 2004).

B.   CONTRACTS AND INTELLECTUAL PROPERTY

PROCD, INC. v. ZEIDENBERG

United States Court of Appeals for the Seventh Circuit.
86 F.3d 1447 (1996).

EASTERBROOK, *Circuit Judge.* Must buyers of computer software obey the terms of shrinkwrap licenses? The district court held not, for two reasons: first, they are not contracts because the licenses are inside the box rather than printed on the outside; second, federal law forbids enforcement even if the licenses are contracts. *908 F. Supp. 640 (W.D. Wis. 1996).* The parties and numerous *amici curiae* have briefed many other issues, but these are the only two that matter—and we disagree with the district judge's conclusion on each. Shrinkwrap licenses are enforceable unless their terms are objectionable on grounds applicable to contracts in general (for example, if they violate a rule of positive law, or if they are unconscionable). * * *

I

ProCD, the plaintiff, has compiled information from more than 3,000 telephone directories into a computer database. We may assume that this database cannot be copyrighted, although it is more complex, contains more information (nine-digit zip codes and census industrial codes), is organized differently, and therefore is more original than the single alphabetical directory at issue in *Feist Publications, Inc. v. Rural Telephone Service Co., 499 U.S. 340 * * * (1991). * * ** ProCD sells a version of the database, called SelectPhone (trademark), on CD-ROM discs. (* * * The "shrinkwrap license" gets its name from the fact that retail software packages are covered in plastic or cellophane "shrinkwrap," and some vendors, though not ProCD, have written licenses that become effective as soon as the customer tears the wrapping from the package. Vendors prefer "end user license," but we use the more common term.) A proprietary method of compressing the data serves as effective encryption too. Customers decrypt and use the data with the aid of an application program that ProCD has written. This program, which is copyrighted, searches the database in response to users' criteria (such as "find all people named Tatum in Tennessee, plus all firms with 'Door Systems' in the corporate name"). The resulting lists (or, as ProCD prefers, "listings") can be read and manipulated by other software, such as word processing programs.

The database in SelectPhone (trademark) cost more than $10 million to compile and is expensive to keep current. It is much more valuable to some users than to others. The combination of names, addresses, and SIC codes[11] enables manufacturers to compile lists of potential customers. Manufacturers and retailers pay high prices to specialized information intermediaries for such mailing lists; ProCD offers a potentially cheaper alternative. People with nothing to sell could use the database as a substitute for calling long distance information, or as a way to look up old friends who have moved to unknown towns, or just as a electronic substitute for the local phone book. ProCD decided to engage in price discrimination, selling its database to the general public for personal use at a low price (approximately $150 for the set of five discs) while selling information to the trade for a higher price. It has adopted some intermediate strategies too: access to the SelectPhone (trademark) database is available via the America Online service for the price America Online charges to its clients (approximately $3 per hour), but this service has been tailored to be useful only to the general public.

If ProCD had to recover all of its costs and make a profit by charging a single price—that is, if it could not charge more to commercial users than to the general public—it would have to raise the price substantially over $150. The ensuing reduction in sales would harm consumers who value the information at, say, $200. They get consumer surplus of $50 under the current arrangement but would cease to buy if the price rose substantially. If because of high elasticity of demand in the consumer segment of the market the only way to make a profit turned out to be a price attractive to commercial users alone, then all consumers would lose out-

---

11. The Standard Industrial Classification (SIC) Codes indicate the type of business carried on by a particular concern.—Ed.

and so would the commercial clients, who would have to pay more for the listings because ProCD could not obtain any contribution toward costs from the consumer market.

To make price discrimination work, however, the seller must be able to control arbitrage. An air carrier sells tickets for less to vacationers than to business travelers, using advance purchase and Saturday-night-stay requirements to distinguish the categories. A producer of movies segments the market by time, releasing first to theaters, then to pay-per-view services, next to the videotape and laserdisc market, and finally to cable and commercial TV. Vendors of computer software have a harder task. Anyone can walk into a retail store and buy a box. Customers do not wear tags saying "commercial user" or "consumer user." Anyway, even a commercial-user-detector at the door would not work, because a consumer could buy the software and resell to a commercial user. That arbitrage would break down the price discrimination and drive up the minimum price at which ProCD would sell to anyone.

Instead of tinkering with the product and letting users sort themselves—for example, furnishing current data at a high price that would be attractive only to commercial customers, and two-year-old data at a low price-ProCD turned to the institution of contract. Every box containing its consumer product declares that the software comes with restrictions stated in an enclosed license. This license, which is encoded on the CD-ROM disks as well as printed in the manual, and which appears on a user's screen every time the software runs, limits use of the application program and listings to non-commercial purposes.

Matthew Zeidenberg bought a consumer package of SelectPhone (trademark) in 1994 from a retail outlet in Madison, Wisconsin, but decided to ignore the license. He formed Silken Mountain Web Services, Inc., to resell the information in the SelectPhone (trademark) database. The corporation makes the database available on the Internet to anyone willing to pay its price—which, needless to say, is less than ProCD charges its commercial customers. Zeidenberg has purchased two additional SelectPhone (trademark) packages, each with an updated version of the database, and made the latest information available over the World Wide Web, for a price, through his corporation. ProCD filed this suit seeking an injunction against further dissemination that exceeds the rights specified in the licenses (identical in each of the three packages Zeidenberg purchased). The district court held the licenses ineffectual because their terms do not appear on the outside of the packages * * * and a purchaser does not agree to—and cannot be bound by—terms that were secret at the time of purchase. * * *

II

Following the district court, we treat the licenses as ordinary contracts accompanying the sale of products, and therefore as governed by the common law of contracts and the Uniform Commercial Code. * * *

Zeidenberg [argues], and the district court held, that placing the package of software on the shelf is an "offer," which the customer "accepts" by paying the asking price and leaving the store with the goods. * * * In Wisconsin, as elsewhere, a contract includes only the terms on which the parties have agreed. One cannot agree to hidden terms, the judge concluded. So far, so good—but one of the terms to which Zeidenberg agreed by purchasing the software is that the transaction was subject to a license. Zeidenberg's position therefore must be that the printed terms on the outside of a box are the parties' contract—except for printed terms that refer to or incorporate other terms. But why would Wisconsin fetter the parties' choice in this way? Vendors can put the entire terms of a contract on the outside of a box only by using microscopic type, removing other information that buyers might find more useful (such as what the software does, and on which computers it works), or both. The "Read Me" file included with most software, describing system requirements and potential incompatibilities, may be equivalent to ten pages of type; warranties and license restrictions take still more space. Notice on the outside, terms on the inside, and a right to return the software for a refund if the terms are unacceptable (a right that the license expressly extends), may be a means of doing business valuable to buyers and sellers alike. See E. Allan Farnsworth, 1 *Farnsworth on Contracts* § 4.26 (1990); *Restatement (2d) of Contracts* § 211 comment a (1981) ("Standardization of agreements serves many of the same functions as standardization of goods and services; both are essential to a system of mass production and distribution. Scarce and costly time and skill can be devoted to a class of transactions rather than the details of individual transactions."). Doubtless a state could forbid the use of standard contracts in the software business, but we do not think that Wisconsin has done so.

Transactions in which the exchange of money precedes the communication of detailed terms are common. Consider the purchase of insurance. The buyer goes to an agent, who explains the essentials (amount of coverage, number of years) and remits the premium to the home office, which sends back a policy. On the district judge's understanding, the terms of the policy are irrelevant because the insured paid before receiving them. Yet the device of payment, often with a "binder" (so that the insurance takes effect immediately even though the home office reserves the right to withdraw coverage later), in advance of the policy, serves buyers' interests by accelerating effectiveness and reducing transactions costs. Or consider the purchase of an airline ticket. The traveler calls the carrier or an agent, is quoted a price, reserves a seat, pays, and gets a ticket, in that order. The ticket contains elaborate terms, which the traveler can reject by canceling the reservation. To use the ticket is to accept the terms, even terms that in retrospect are disadvantageous. See *Carnival Cruise Lines, Inc. v. Shute, 499 U.S. 585 * * * (1991).* * * * Just so with a ticket to a concert. The back of the ticket states that the patron promises not to record the concert; to attend is to agree. A theater that detects a violation will confiscate the tape and escort the violator to the exit. One *could* arrange things so that every concertgoer signs this promise before forking over the money, but that cumbersome way of doing things not only would lengthen queues and raise prices but also would scotch the sale of tickets by phone or electronic data service.

Consumer goods work the same way. Someone who wants to buy a radio set visits a store, pays, and walks out with a box. Inside the box is a leaflet containing some terms, the most important of which usually is the warranty, read for the first time in the comfort of home. By Zeidenberg's lights, the warranty in the box is irrelevant; every consumer gets the standard warranty implied by the UCC in the event the contract is silent; yet so far as we are aware no state disregards warranties furnished with consumer products. Drugs come with a list of ingredients on the outside and an elaborate package insert on the inside. The package insert describes drug interactions, contraindications, and other vital information—but, if Zeidenberg is right, the purchaser need not read the package insert, because it is not part of the contract.

Next consider the software industry itself. Only a minority of sales take place over the counter, where there are boxes to peruse. A customer may place an order by phone in response to a line item in a catalog or a review in a magazine. Much software is ordered over the Internet by purchasers who have never seen a box. Increasingly software arrives by wire. There is no box; there is only a stream of electrons, a collection of information that includes data, an application program, instructions, many limitations ("MegaPixel 3.14159 cannot be used with Byte-Pusher 2.718"), and the terms of sale. The user purchases a serial number, which activates the software's features. On Zeidenberg's arguments, these unboxed sales are unfettered by terms—so the seller has made a broad warranty and must pay consequential damages for any shortfalls in performance, two "promises" that if taken seriously would drive prices through the ceiling or return transactions to the horse-and-buggy age.

According to the district court, the UCC[12] does not countenance the sequence of money now, terms later. * * * One of the court's reasons—that by proposing as part of the draft Article 2B a new *UCC § 2–2203* that would explicitly validate standard-form user licenses, the American Law Institute and the National Conference of Commissioners on Uniform Laws [associations who have the responsibility for promulgating the text of the UCC that may be accepted for legislative passage] have conceded the invalidity of shrinkwrap licenses under current law * * *—depends on a faulty inference. To propose a change in a law's *text* is not necessarily to propose a change in the law's *effect*. New words may be designed to fortify the current rule with a more precise text that curtails uncertainty. To

---

12. The Uniform Commercial Code (UCC), in force in all the states as a result of acts by the fifty state legislatures, sets forth the basic laws that govern contracts involving the sale of individual goods, bulk sales, bills and notes, security interests, and a variety of other matters. (Because Louisiana has a legal system based on the Napoleonic Code rather than the common law, it has not enacted all of the provisions of the UCC, and there are slight variations among different state versions of the UCC. None are relevant to this opinion).—Ed.

judge by the flux of law review articles discussing shrinkwrap licenses, uncertainty is much in need of reduction—although businesses seem to feel less uncertainty than do scholars, for only three cases (other than ours) touch on the subject, and none directly addresses it. See *Step-Saver Data Systems, Inc. v. Wyse Technology, 939 F.2d 91 (3d Cir. 1991); Vault Corp. v. Quaid Software Ltd., 847 F.2d 255, 268–70 (5th Cir. 1988); Arizona Retail Systems, Inc. v. Software Link, Inc., 831 F. Supp. 759 (D. Ariz. 1993).* As their titles suggest, these are not consumer transactions. *Step-Saver* is a battle-of-the-forms case, in which the parties exchange incompatible forms and a court must decide which prevails. * * * Our case has only one form; *UCC § 2–207*[13] is irrelevant. *Vault* holds that Louisiana's special shrinkwrap-license statute is preempted by federal law, a question to which we return. And *Arizona Retail Systems* did not reach the question, because the court found that the buyer knew the terms of the license before purchasing the software.

What then does the current version of the UCC have to say? We think that the place to start is § 2–204(1): "A contract for sale of goods may be made in any manner sufficient to show agreement, including conduct by both parties which recognizes the existence of such a contract." A vendor, as master of the offer, may invite acceptance by conduct, and may propose limitations on the kind of conduct that constitutes acceptance. A buyer may accept by performing the acts the vendor proposes to treat as acceptance. And that is what happened. ProCD proposed a contract that a buyer would accept by *using* the software after having an opportunity to read the license at leisure. This Zeidenberg did. He had no choice, because the software splashed the license on the screen and would not let him proceed without indicating acceptance. So although the district judge was right to say that a contract can be, and often is, formed simply by paying the price and walking out of the store, the UCC permits contracts to be formed in other ways. ProCD proposed such a different way, and without protest Zeidenberg agreed. Ours is not a case in which a consumer opens a package to find an insert saying "you owe us an extra $10,000" and the

---

13. UCC 2–207 is the marvelously elusive "battle of the forms" provision. It states:

(1) A definite and seasonable expression of acceptance or a written confirmation which is sent within a reasonable time operates as an acceptance even though it states terms additional to or different from those offered or agreed upon, unless acceptance is expressly made conditional on assent to the additional or different terms.

(2) The additional terms are to be construed as proposals for addition to the contract. Between merchants such terms become part of the contract unless:

(a) the offer expressly limits acceptance to the terms of the offer;

(b) they materially alter it; or

(c) notification of objection to them has already been given or is given within a reasonable time after notice of them is received.

(3) Conduct by both parties which recognizes the existence of a contract is sufficient to establish a contract for sale although the writings of the parties do not otherwise establish a contract. In such case the terms of the particular contract consist of those terms on which the writings of the parties agree, together with any supplementary terms incorporated under any other provisions of this Act.

Can you explain the meaning of 2–207?—Ed.

seller files suit to collect. Any buyer finding such a demand can prevent formation of the contract by returning the package, as can any consumer who concludes that the terms of the license make the software worth less than the purchase price. Nothing in the UCC requires a seller to maximize the buyer's net gains.

Section 2–606, which defines "acceptance of goods", reinforces this understanding. A buyer accepts goods under § 2–606(1)(b) when, after an opportunity to inspect, he fails to make an effective rejection under § 2–602(1). ProCD extended an opportunity to reject if a buyer should find the license terms unsatisfactory; Zeidenberg inspected the package, tried out the software, learned of the license, and did not reject the goods. We refer to § 2–606 only to show that the opportunity to return goods can be important; acceptance of an offer differs from acceptance of goods after delivery * * * ; but the UCC consistently permits the parties to structure their relations so that the buyer has a chance to make a final decision after a detailed review.

Some portions of the UCC impose additional requirements on the way parties agree on terms. A disclaimer of the implied warranty of merchantability must be "conspicuous." *UCC § 2–316(2)*, incorporating *UCC § 1–201(10)*. Promises to make firm offers, or to negate oral modifications, must be "separately signed." *UCC § § 2–205*, 2–209(2). These special provisos reinforce the impression that, so far as the UCC is concerned, other terms may be as inconspicuous as the forum-selection clause on the back of the cruise ship ticket in *Carnival Lines*. Zeidenberg has not located any Wisconsin case—for that matter, any case in any state—holding that under the UCC the ordinary terms found in shrinkwrap licenses require any special prominence, or otherwise are to be undercut rather than enforced. In the end, the terms of the license are conceptually identical to the contents of the package. Just as no court would dream of saying that SelectPhone (trademark) must contain 3,100 phone books rather than 3,000, or must have data no more than 30 days old, or must sell for $100 rather than $150—although any of these changes would be welcomed by the customer, if all other things were held constant—so, we believe, Wisconsin would not let the buyer pick and choose among terms. Terms of use are no less a part of "the product" than are the size of the database and the speed with which the software compiles listings. Competition among vendors, not judicial revision of a package's contents, is how consumers are protected in a market economy. * * * ProCD has rivals, which may elect to compete by offering superior software, monthly updates, improved terms of use, lower price, or a better compromise among these elements. As we stressed above, adjusting terms in buyers' favor might help Matthew Zeidenberg today (he already has the software) but would lead to a response, such as a higher price, that might make consumers as a whole worse off.

III

The district court held that, even if Wisconsin treats shrinkwrap licenses as contracts, § 301(a) of the Copyright Act, *17 U.S.C. § 301*(a), prevents their enforcement. * * * The relevant part of § 301(a) preempts any "legal or equitable rights [under state law] that are equivalent to any of the exclusive rights within the general scope of copyright as specified by section 106 in works of authorship that are fixed in a tangible medium of expression and come within the subject matter of copyright as specified by sections 102 and 103". ProCD's software and data are "fixed in a tangible medium of expression", and the district judge held that they are "within the subject matter of copyright". The latter conclusion is plainly right for the copyrighted application program, and the judge thought that the data likewise are "within the subject matter of copyright" even if, after Feist, they are not sufficiently original to be copyrighted. * * * *Baltimore Orioles, Inc. v. Major League Baseball Players Ass'n, 805 F.2d 663, 676 (7th Cir. 1986),* supports that conclusion, with which commentators agree. E.g., Paul Goldstein, III *Copyright* § 15.2.3 (2d ed. 1996) * * *. One function of § 301(a) is to prevent states from giving special protection to works of authorship that Congress has decided should be in the public domain, which it can accomplish only if "subject matter of copyright" includes all works of a *type* covered by sections 102 and 103, even if federal law does not afford protection to them. * * *

But are rights created by contract "equivalent to any of the exclusive rights within the general scope of copyright"? Three courts of appeals have answered "no." *National Car Rental Systems, Inc. v. Computer Associates International, Inc., 991 F.2d 426, 433 (8th Cir. 1993); Taquino v. Teledyne Monarch Rubber, 893 F.2d 1488, 1501 (5th Cir. 1990); Acorn Structures, Inc. v. Swantz, 846 F.2d 923, 926 (4th Cir. 1988).* The district court disagreed with these decisions, * * * but we think them sound. Rights "equivalent to any of the exclusive rights within the general scope of copyright" are rights established *by law*—rights that restrict the options of persons who are strangers to the author. Copyright law forbids duplication, public performance, and so on, unless the person wishing to copy or perform the work gets permission; silence means a ban on copying. A copyright is a right against the world. Contracts, by contrast, generally affect only their parties; strangers may do as they please, so contracts do not create "exclusive rights." Someone who found a copy of SelectPhone (trademark) on the street would not be affected by the shrinkwrap license—though the federal copyright laws of their own force would limit the finder's ability to copy or transmit the application program.

Think for a moment about trade secrets. One common trade secret is a customer list. After *Feist*, a simple alphabetical list of a firm's customers, with address and telephone numbers, could not be protected by copyright. Yet *Kewanee Oil Co. v. Bicron Corp., 416 U.S. 470 * * * (1974)*, holds that contracts about trade secrets may be enforced—precisely because they do not affect strangers' ability to discover and use the information independently. * * * Think, too, about everyday transactions in intellectual property. A customer visits a video store and rents a copy of *Night of the Lepus.* The customer's contract with the store limits use of the tape to home viewing and requires its return in two days. May the customer keep the tape, on the ground that § 301(a) makes the promise unenforceable?

A law student uses the LEXIS [or WESTLAW] database, containing public-domain documents, under a contract limiting the results to educational endeavors; may the student resell his access to this database to a law firm from which LEXIS [or WESTLAW] seeks to collect a much higher hourly rate? Suppose ProCD hires a firm to scour the nation for telephone directories, promising to pay $100 for each that ProCD does not already have. The firm locates 100 new directories, which it sends to ProCD with an invoice for $10,000. ProCD incorporates the directories into its database; does it have to pay the bill? Surely yes; *Aronson v. Quick Point Pencil Co., 440 U.S. 257, 59 L. Ed. 2d 296, 99 S. Ct. 1096 (1979),* holds that promises to pay for intellectual property may be enforced even though federal law (in Aronson, the patent law) offers no protection against third-party uses of that property. * * * But these illustrations are what our case is about. ProCD offers software and data for two prices: one for personal use, a higher price for commercial use. Zeidenberg wants to use the data without paying the seller's price; if the law student and Quick Point Pencil Co. could not do that, neither can Zeidenberg.

Although Congress possesses power to preempt even the enforcement of contracts about intellectual property * * * courts usually read preemption clauses to leave private contracts unaffected. *American Airlines, Inc. v. Wolens, 130 L. Ed. 2d 715, 115 S. Ct. 817 (1995),* provides a nice illustration. A federal statute preempts any state "law, rule, regulation, standard, or other provision ... relating to rates, routes, or services of any air carrier." *49 U.S.C. App. § 1305*(a)(1). Does such a law preempt the law of contracts—so that, for example, an air carrier need not honor a quoted price (or a contract to reduce the price by the value of frequent flyer miles)? The Court allowed that it is possible to read the statute that broadly but thought such an interpretation would make little sense. Terms and conditions offered by contract reflect private ordering, essential to the efficient functioning of markets. *115 S. Ct. at 824–25.* Although some principles that carry the name of contract law are designed to defeat rather than implement consensual transactions, *id.* at 826 n.8, the rules that respect private choice are not preempted by a clause such as § 1305(a)(1). Section 301(a) plays a role similar to § 1301(a)(1): it prevents states from substituting their own regulatory systems for those of the national government. Just as § 301(a) does not itself interfere with private transactions in intellectual property, so it does not prevent states from respecting those transactions. Like the Supreme Court in *Wolens,* we think it prudent to refrain from adopting a rule that anything with the label "contract" is necessarily outside the preemption clause: the variations and possibilities are too numerous to foresee. *National Car Rental* likewise recognizes the possibility that some applications of the law of contract could interfere with the attainment of national objectives and therefore come within the domain of § 301(a). But general enforcement of shrinkwrap licenses of the kind before us does not create such interference.

Aronson emphasized that enforcement of the contract between Aronson and Quick Point Pencil Company would not withdraw any information from the public domain. That is equally true of the contract between ProCD and Zeidenberg. Everyone remains free to copy and disseminate all 3,000 telephone books that have been incorporated into ProCD's database. Anyone can add SIC codes and zip codes. ProCD's rivals have done so. Enforcement of the shrinkwrap license may even make information more readily available, by reducing the price ProCD charges to consumer buyers. To the extent licenses facilitate distribution of object code while concealing the source code (the point of a clause forbidding disassembly), they serve the same procompetitive functions as does the law of trade secrets. *Rockwell Graphic Systems, Inc. v. DEV Industries, Inc., 925 F.2d 174, 180 (7th Cir. 1991)*. Licenses may have other benefits for consumers: many licenses permit users to make extra copies, to use the software on multiple computers, even to incorporate the software into the user's products. But whether a particular license is generous or restrictive, a simple two-party contract is not "equivalent to any of the exclusive rights within the general scope of copyright" and therefore may be enforced.

REVERSED AND REMANDED.

NOTES AND QUESTIONS

1.   In terms of pure candlepower, now Chief Judge Frank Easterbrook, the author of this opinion, is one of the most brilliant judges sitting on the federal court bench. Is that evident from this opinion? Why does Judge Easterbrook use "Night of the Lepus" as his example for a video rental?

2.   Do you understand why Easterbrook rules that a "shrinkwrap" license is a binding contract? Does it strike you as the right result? Note Easterbrook's economic analysis of ProCD's differential pricing scheme. Does it persuade you that this scheme should be something upheld by the courts? What principles of the law of contracts do you discern from this opinion? Do you have any problem with the application of those principles? For some basic reading on the law of contracts, consult the now-classic treatise, Arthur L. Corbin, Corbin on Contracts: One Volume Edition (1952), and for an appreciation of that book and the suggestion that it is "the greatest law book ever written," see the delightful Grant Gilmore, The Death of Contract (Ronald K.L. Collins, ed. 2nd ed. 1995). For two other celebrated (and somewhat more modern) treatments see E. Allen Farnsworth, Contracts (4th ed. 2004), and Joseph M. Perillo and John D.Calamari, Calamari and Perillo on Contracts (5th ed. 2003).

3.   This case is also offered as a way to begin to appreciate the law of intellectual property. The issue in the case involves copyright protection for

ProCD's computer program, and also whether the directory listings themselves should be subject to copyright. Should they? Why or why not? Do you understand the intriguing issue of whether federal law on copyright should pre-empt state law on contract? Should it? What does Easterbrook think, and why? For the suggestion that Judge Easterbrook should have held that federal copyright law did pre-empt state law under the circumstances before him, and, further, that federal copyright law should have been construed to protect the directory listings on ProCD's discs, see Brett L. Tolman, NOTE: ProCD, Inc. v. Zeidenberg: The End Does Not Justify the Means in Federal Copyright Analysis, 1998 B.Y.U.L. Rev. 303. Tolman notes the United States Supreme Court's 1991 reaffirmation that the "most fundamental axiom of copyright law is that '[n]o author may copyright his ideas or the facts he narrates.'" Id., at n.1, citing Feist Publications, Inc. v. Rural Tel. Serv. Co., 499 U.S. 340, 344–45, 111 S.Ct. 1282, 113 L.Ed.2d 358 (1991) (quoting Harper & Row, Publishers, Inc. v. Nation Enters., 471 U.S. 539, 556, 105 S.Ct. 2218, 85 L.Ed.2d 588 (1985)), but that the Court also indicated that "compilations of facts *are* within the subject matter of copyright." Tolman, supra at 303, quoting Feist, 499 U.S. at 345 (emphasis added). How does one discern when one has before one "facts" as opposed to "compilations of facts?"

Intellectual property is a field in substantial flux, but the beginnings of an understanding of the issues can be gained by consulting a little gem, Benjamin Kaplan, An Unhurried View of Copyright (1967), and, for a quick survey, see Arthur R. Miller and Michael H. Davis, Intellectual Property: Patents, Trademarks and Copyrights (3rd ed. 2000).

C. ANTITRUST

THE STANDARD OIL CO. OF NEW JERSEY, ET AL. v. THE UNITED STATES

Supreme Court of the United States.
221 U.S. 1, 31 S.Ct. 502, 55 L.Ed. 619 (1911).

MR. CHIEF JUSTICE WHITE delivered the opinion of the court.

The Standard Oil Company of New Jersey and 33 other corporations, John D. Rockefeller, William Rockefeller and five other individual defendants prosecute this appeal to reverse a decree of the court below. Such decree was entered upon a bill filed by the United States under authority of § 4, of the act of July 2, 1890, c. 647, p. 209, known as the Anti-trust Act * * *

* * * The bill was divided into thirty numbered sections, and sought relief upon the theory that the various defendants were engaged in conspiring "to restrain the trade and commerce in petroleum, commonly called 'crude oil,' in refined oil, and in the other products of petroleum, among the several States and Territories of the United States and the District of Columbia and with foreign nations, and to monopolize the said

commerce." The conspiracy was alleged to have been formed in or about the year 1870 * * *.

The general charge concerning the period from 1870 to 1882 was as follows:

> "That during said first period the said individual defendants, in connection with the Standard Oil Company of Ohio, purchased and obtained interests through stock ownership and otherwise in, and entered into agreements with, various persons, firms, corporations, and limited partnerships engaged in purchasing, shipping, refining, and selling petroleum and its products among the various States for the purpose of fixing the price of crude and refined oil and the products thereof, limiting the production thereof, and controlling the transportation therein, and thereby restraining trade and commerce among the several States, and monopolizing the said commerce."

To establish this charge it was averred that John D. and William Rockefeller and several other named individuals, * * * organized in the year 1870, a corporation known as the Standard Oil Company of Ohio and transferred to that company the business [partnerships in which the individuals had previously been engaged], the members thereof becoming, in proportion to their prior ownership, stockholders in the corporation. It was averred that the other individual defendants soon afterwards became participants in the illegal combination and either transferred property to the corporation or to individuals to be held for the benefit of all parties in interest in proportion to their respective interests in the combination; that is, in proportion to their stock ownership in the Standard Oil Company of Ohio. By the means thus stated, it was charged that by the year 1872, the combination had acquired substantially all but three or four of the thirty-five or forty oil refineries located in Cleveland, Ohio. By reason of the power thus obtained and in further execution of the intent and purpose to restrain trade and to monopolize the commerce, interstate as well as intrastate, in petroleum and its products, the bill alleged that the combination and its members obtained large preferential rates and rebates in many and devious ways over their competitors from various railroad companies, and that by means of the advantage thus obtained many, if not virtually all, competitors were forced either to become members of the combination or were driven out of business; and thus, it was alleged, during the period in question the following results were brought about: a. That the combination, in addition to the refineries in Cleveland which it had acquired as previously stated, and which it had either dismantled to limit production or continued to operate, also from time to time acquired a large number of refineries of crude petroleum, situated in New York, Pennsylvania, Ohio and elsewhere. * * *. b. That the combination had obtained control of the pipe lines available for transporting oil from the oil fields to the refineries in Cleveland, Pittsburg, Titusville, Philadelphia, New York and New Jersey. c. That the combination during the period named had obtained a complete mastery over the oil industry, controlling 90 per cent of the business of producing, shipping, refining and selling petroleum and its products, and thus was able to fix the price of crude and refined petroleum and to restrain and monopolize all interstate commerce in those products.

The averments bearing upon the second period (1882 to 1899) had relation to the claim:

"That during the said second period of conspiracy the defendants entered into a contract and trust agreement, by which various independent firms, corporations, limited partnerships and individuals engaged in purchasing, transporting, refining, shipping and selling oil and the products thereof among the various States turned over the management of their said business, corporations and limited partnerships to nine trustees, composed chiefly of certain individuals defendant herein, which said trust agreement was in restraint of trade and commerce and in violation of law, as hereinafter more particularly alleged."

The trust agreement thus referred to was set out in the bill. It was made in January, 1882. By its terms the stock of forty corporations, including the Standard Oil Company of Ohio, and a large quantity of various properties which had been previously acquired by the alleged combination and which was held in diverse forms, as we have previously indicated, for the benefit of the members of the combination, was vested in the trustees and their successors, "to be held for all parties in interest jointly." * * * The agreement provided for the issue of Standard Oil Trust certificates to represent the interest arising under the trust in the properties affected by the trust, which of course in view of the provisions of the agreement and the subject to which it related caused the interest in the certificates to be coincident with and the exact representative of the interest in the combination, that is, in the Standard Oil Company of Ohio. Soon afterwards it was alleged the trustees organized the Standard Oil Company of New Jersey and the Standard Oil Company of New York * * * The bill alleged "that pursuant to said trust agreement the said trustees caused to be transferred to themselves the stocks of all corporations and limited partnerships named in said trust agreement, and caused various of the individuals and copartnerships, who owned apparently independent refineries and other properties employed in the business of refining and transporting and selling oil in and among said various States and Territories of the United States as aforesaid, to transfer their property situated in said several States to the respective Standard Oil Companies of said States of New York, New Jersey, Pennsylvania and Ohio, and other corporations organized or acquired by said trustees from time to time.... " * * * It was alleged that in 1888 the trustees "unlawfully controlled the stock and ownership of various corporations and limited partnerships engaged in such purchase and transportation, refining, selling, and shipping of oil," * * *.

The bill charged that during the second period *quo warranto*[14] pro-

___

14. Literally "by what warrant," a proceeding by which the charter of a corporation may be

ceedings were commenced against the Standard Oil Company of Ohio, which resulted in the entry by the Supreme Court of Ohio, on March 2, 1892, of a decree adjudging the trust agreement to be void, not only because the Standard Oil Company of Ohio was a party to the same, but also because the agreement in and of itself was in restraint of trade and amounted to the creation of an unlawful monopoly. It was alleged that shortly after this decision, seemingly for the purpose of complying therewith, voluntary proceedings were had apparently to dissolve the trust, but that these proceedings were a subterfuge and a sham because they simply amounted to a transfer of the stock held by the trust in 64 of the companies which it controlled to some of the remaining 20 companies, it having controlled before the decree 84 in all, thereby, while seemingly in part giving up its dominion, yet in reality preserving the same by means of the control of the companies as to which it had retained complete authority. * * * The bill further alleged that in 1897 the Attorney-General of Ohio instituted contempt proceedings in the *quo warranto* case based upon the claim that the trust had not been dissolved as required by the decree in that case. About the same time also proceedings in *quo warranto* were commenced to forfeit the charter of a pipe line known as the Buckeye Pipe Line Company, an Ohio corporation, whose stock, it was alleged, was owned by the members of the combination, on the ground of its connection with the trust which had been held to be illegal.

The result of these proceedings, the bill charged, caused a resort to the alleged wrongful acts asserted to have been committed during the third period, as follows:

> "That during the third period of said conspiracy and in pursuance thereof the said individual defendants operated through the Standard Oil Company of New Jersey, as a holding corporation, which corporation obtained and acquired the majority of the stocks of the various corporations engaged in purchasing, transporting, refining, shipping, and selling oil into and among the various States and Territories of the United States and the District of Columbia and with foreign nations, and thereby managed and controlled the same, in violation of the laws of the United States, as hereinafter more particularly alleged."

It was alleged that in or about the month of January, 1899, the individual defendants caused the charter of the Standard Oil Company of New Jersey to be amended; "so that the business and objects of said company were stated as follows, to wit: 'To do all kinds of mining, manufacturing, and trading business; transporting goods and merchandise by land or water in any manner; to buy, sell, lease, and improve land; build houses, structures, vessels, cars, wharves, docks, and piers; to lay and operate pipe lines; to erect lines for conducting electricity; to enter into and carry out contracts of every kind pertaining to its business; to acquire,

---

taken away by the state granting it, when the corporation is operating in a manner inconsistent with the charter granted, and failing to operate in the public interest.—Ed.

use, sell, and grant licenses under patent rights; to purchase or otherwise acquire, hold, sell, assign, and transfer shares of capital stock and bonds or other evidences of indebtedness of corporations, and to exercise all the privileges of ownership, including voting upon the stock so held; to carry on its business and have offices and agencies therefor in all parts of the world, and to hold, purchase, mortgage, and convey real estate and personal property outside the State of New Jersey.' "

The capital stock of the company—which since March 19, 1892, had been $10,000,000—was increased to $110,000,000; and the individual defendants, as theretofore, continued to be a majority of the board of directors.

Without going into detail it suffices to say that it was alleged in the bill that shortly after these proceedings the trust came to an end, the stock of the various corporations which had been controlled by it being transferred by its holders to the Standard Oil Company of New Jersey, which corporation issued therefor certificates of its common stock to the amount of $97,250,000. The bill contained allegations referring to the development of new oil fields, for example, in California, southeastern Kansas, northern Indian Territory, and northern Oklahoma, and made reference to the building or otherwise acquiring by the combination of refineries and pipe lines in the new fields for the purpose of restraining and monopolizing the interstate trade in petroleum and its products.

* * *[T]he bill at great length additionally set forth various means by which during the second and third periods * * * the monopoly and restraint complained of was continued. * * * [S]uch averments may properly be grouped under the following heads: Rebates, preferences and other discriminatory practices in favor of the combination by railroad companies; restraint and monopolization by control of pipe lines, and unfair practices against competing pipe lines; contracts with competitors in restraint of trade; unfair methods of competition, such as local price cutting at the points where necessary to suppress competition; espionage of the business of competitors, the operation of bogus independent companies, and payment of rebates on oil, with the like intent; the division of the United States into districts and the limiting of the operations of the various subsidiary corporations as to such districts so that competition in the sale of petroleum products between such corporations had been entirely eliminated and destroyed; and finally reference was made to what was alleged to be the "enormous and unreasonable profits" earned by the Standard Oil Trust and the Standard Oil Company as a result of the alleged monopoly * * *.

* * *[I]n general terms the substantial relief asked was, first, that the combination in restraint of interstate trade and commerce and which had monopolized the same, as alleged in the bill, be found to have existence and that the parties thereto be perpetually enjoined from doing any further act to give effect to it; second, that the transfer of the stocks of the various corporations to the Standard Oil Company of New Jersey, as

alleged in the bill, be held to be in violation of the first and second sections of the Anti-trust Act, and that the Standard Oil Company of New Jersey be enjoined and restrained from in any manner continuing to exert control over the subsidiary corporations by means of ownership of said stock or otherwise; third, that specific relief by injunction be awarded against further violation of the statute by any of the acts specifically complained of in the bill. * * *

* * *

Certain of the defendants filed separate answers, and a joint answer was filed on behalf of the Standard Oil Company of New Jersey and numerous of the other defendants. * * *

"It is sufficient to say that * * * they deny all the allegations respecting combinations or conspiracies to restrain or monopolize the oil trade; and particularly that the so-called trust of 1882, or the acquisition of the shares of the defendant companies by the Standard Oil Company of New Jersey in 1899, was a combination of independent or competing concerns or corporations. The averments of the petition respecting the means adopted to monopolize the oil trade are traversed either by a denial of the acts alleged or of their purpose, intent or effect."

On June 24, 1907 * * * a special examiner was appointed to take the evidence, and his report was filed March 22, 1909. It was heard on April 5 to 10, 1909, * * * before a Circuit Court consisting of four judges.

The court decided in favor of the United States. * * *

By the decree which was entered it was adjudged that the combining of the stocks of various companies in the hands of the Standard Oil Company of New Jersey in 1899 constituted a combination in restraint of trade and also an attempt to monopolize and a monopolization under § 2 of the Anti-trust Act. * * *

The Standard Oil Company of New Jersey was enjoined from voting the stocks or exerting any control over the * * * 37 subsidiary companies, and the subsidiary companies were enjoined from paying any dividends as to the Standard Oil Company or permitting it to exercise any control over them by virtue of the stock ownership or power acquired by means of the combination. The individuals and corporations were also enjoined from entering into or carrying into effect any like combination which would evade the decree. Further, the individual defendants, the Standard Oil Company, and the 37 subsidiary corporations were enjoined from engaging or continuing in interstate commerce in petroleum or its products during the continuance of the illegal combination.

* * *

* * * While both sides agree that the determination of the controversy rests upon the correct construction and application of the first and

second sections of the Anti-trust Act, yet the views as to the meaning of the act are as wide apart as the poles. * * *

So also is it as to the facts. Thus, on the one hand, with relentless pertinacity and minuteness of analysis, it is insisted that the facts establish that the assailed combination took its birth in a purpose to unlawfully acquire wealth by oppressing the public and destroying the just rights of others, and that its entire career exemplifies an inexorable carrying out of such wrongful intents, since, it is asserted, the pathway of the combination from the beginning to the time of the filing of the bill is marked with constant proofs of wrong inflicted upon the public and is strewn with the wrecks resulting from crushing out, without regard to law, the individual rights of others. Indeed, so conclusive, it is urged, is the proof on these subjects that it is asserted that the existence of the principal corporate defendant—the Standard Oil Company of New Jersey—with the vast accumulation of property which it owns or controls, because of its infinite potency for harm and the dangerous example which its continued existence affords, is an open and enduring menace to all freedom of trade and is a byword and reproach to modern economic methods. On the other hand, in a powerful analysis of the facts, it is insisted that they demonstrate that the origin and development of the vast business which the defendants control was but the result of lawful competitive methods, guided by economic genius of the highest order, sustained by courage, by a keen insight into commercial situations, resulting in the acquisition of great wealth, but at the same time serving to stimulate and increase production, to widely extend the distribution of the products of petroleum at a cost largely below that which would have otherwise prevailed, thus proving to be at one and the same time a benefaction to the general public as well as of enormous advantage to individuals. It is not denied that in the enormous volume of proof contained in the record in the period of almost a lifetime to which that proof is addressed, there may be found acts of wrongdoing, but the insistence is that they were rather the exception than the rule, and in most cases were either the result of too great individual zeal in the keen rivalries of business or of the methods and habits of dealing which, even if wrong, were commonly practiced at the time. * * *

* * * [W]e shall first come to consider the meaning of the first and second sections of the Anti-trust Act by the text, and after discerning what by that process appears to be its true meaning we shall proceed to consider the respective contentions of the parties * * * as well as the accuracy of the meaning of the act as deduced from the text in the light of the prior decisions of this court concerning it. * * *

First. The text of the act and its meaning.

* * *

"SECTION 1. Every contract, combination in the form of trust or otherwise, or conspiracy, in restraint of trade or commerce, among the several States, or with foreign nations, is hereby declared to be illegal.

Every person who shall make any such contract, or engage in any such combination or conspiracy, shall be deemed guilty of a misdemeanor, and, on conviction thereof, shall be punished by fine not exceeding five thousand dollars, or by imprisonment not exceeding one year, or by both said punishments, in the discretion of the court.

"SEC. 2. Every person who shall monopolize, or attempt to monopolize, or combine or conspire with any other person or persons, to monopolize any part of the trade or commerce among the several States, or with foreign nations, shall be deemed guilty of a misdemeanor, and, on conviction thereof, shall be punished by fine not exceeding five thousand dollars, or by imprisonment not exceeding one year, or by both said punishments, in the discretion of the court."

The debates show that doubt as to whether there was a common law of the United States which governed the subject in the absence of legislation was among the influences leading to the passage of the act. They conclusively show, however, that the main cause which led to the legislation was the thought that it was required by the economic condition of the times, that is, the vast accumulation of wealth in the hands of corporations and individuals, the enormous development of corporate organization, the facility for combination which such organizations afforded, the fact that the facility was being used, and that combinations known as trusts were being multiplied, and the widespread impression that their power had been and would be exerted to oppress individuals and injure the public generally. * * *

There can be no doubt that the sole subject with which the first section deals is restraint of trade as therein contemplated, and that the attempt to monopolize and monopolization is the subject with which the second section is concerned. It is certain that those terms, at least in their rudimentary meaning, took their origin in the common law, and were also familiar in the law of this country prior to and at the time of the adoption of the act in question.

We shall endeavor then, first to seek their meaning * * * by making a very brief reference to the elementary and indisputable conceptions of both the English and American law on the subject prior to the passage of the Anti-trust Act.

a. It is certain that at a very remote period the words "contract in restraint of trade" in England came to refer to some voluntary restraint put by contract by an individual on his right to carry on his trade or calling. Originally all such contracts were considered to be illegal, because it was deemed they were injurious to the public as well as to the individuals who made them. In the interest of the freedom of individuals to contract this doctrine was modified so that it was only when a restraint by contract was so general as to be coterminous with the kingdom that it was treated as void. That is to say, if the restraint was partial in its operation and was otherwise reasonable the contract was held to be valid:

b.   Monopolies were defined by Lord Coke as follows:

> " 'A monopoly is an institution, or allowance by the king by his grant, commission, or otherwise to any person or persons, bodies politic or corporate, of or for the sole buying, selling, making, working or using of anything, whereby any person or persons, bodies politic or corporate, are sought to be restrained of any freedom or liberty that they had before, or hindered in their lawful trade.' (3 Inst. 181, c. 85.)"

Hawkins thus defined them:

> " 'A monopoly is an allowance by the king to a particular person or persons of the sole buying, selling, making, working, or using of anything whereby the subject in general is restrained from the freedom of manufacturing or trading which he had before.' (Hawk. P.C. bk. 1, c. 29.)"

The frequent granting of monopolies and the struggle which led to a denial of the power to create them, that is to say, to the establishment that they were incompatible with the English constitution is known to all and need not be reviewed. The evils which led to the public outcry against monopolies and to the final denial of the power to make them may be thus summarily stated: 1. The power which the monopoly gave to the one who enjoyed it to fix the price and thereby injure the public; 2. The power which it engendered of enabling a limitation on production; and, 3. The danger of deterioration in quality of the monopolized article which it was deemed was the inevitable resultant of the monopolistic control over its production and sale. As monopoly as thus conceived embraced only a consequence arising from an exertion of sovereign power, no express restrictions or prohibitions obtained against the creation by an individual of a monopoly as such. But as it was considered, at least so far as the necessaries of life were concerned, that individuals by the abuse of their right to contract might be able to usurp the power arbitrarily to enhance prices, one of the wrongs arising from monopoly, it came to be that laws were passed relating to offenses such as forestalling * * * and engrossing by which prohibitions were placed upon the power of individuals to deal under such circumstances and conditions as, according to the conception of the times, created a presumption that the dealings were not simply the honest exertion of one's right to contract for his own benefit unaccompanied by a wrongful motive to injure others, but were the consequence of a contract or course of dealing of such a character as to give rise to the presumption of an intent to injure others through the means, for instance, of a monopolistic increase of prices. This is illustrated by the definition of engrossing found in the statute, 5 and 6 Edw. VI, ch. 14, as follows:

> "Whatsoever person or persons ... shall engross or get into his or their hands by buying, contracting, or promise-taking, other than by demise, grant, or lease of land, or tithe, any corn growing in the fields, or any other corn or grain, butter, cheese, fish, or other dead victual, whatsoever, within the realm of England, to the intent to sell the

same again, shall be accepted, reputed, and taken an unlawful engrosser or engrossers."

As by the statutes providing against engrossing the quantity engrossed was not required to be the whole or a proximate part of the whole of an article, it is clear that there was a wide difference between monopoly and engrossing, etc. But as the principal wrong which it was deemed would result from monopoly, that is, an enhancement of the price, was the same wrong to which it was thought the prohibited engrossment would give rise, it came to pass that monopoly and engrossing were regarded as virtually one and the same thing. In other words, the prohibited act of engrossing because of its inevitable accomplishment of one of the evils deemed to be engendered by monopoly, came to be referred to as being a monopoly or constituting an attempt to monopolize. * * *

And by operation of the mental process which led to considering as a monopoly acts which although they did not constitute a monopoly were thought to produce some of its baneful effects, so also because of the impediment or burden to the due course of trade which they produced, such acts came to be referred to as in restraint of trade. This is shown by my Lord Coke's definition of monopoly as being "an institution or allowance ... whereby any person or persons, bodies politic or corporate, are sought to be restrained of any freedom or liberty that they had before or hindered in their lawful trade." It is illustrated also by the definition which Hawkins gives of monopoly wherein it is said that the effect of monopoly is to restrain the citizen "from the freedom of manufacturing or trading which he had before." * * *

* * *

From the development of more accurate economic conceptions and the changes in conditions of society it came to be recognized that the acts prohibited by the engrossing, forestalling, etc., statutes did not have the harmful tendency which they were presumed to have when the legislation concerning them was enacted, and therefore did not justify the presumption which had previously been deduced from them, but, on the contrary, such acts tended to fructify and develop trade. See the statutes of 12th George III, ch. 71, enacted in 1772, and statute of 7 and 8 Victoria, ch. 24, enacted in 1844, repealing the prohibitions against engrossing, forestalling, etc., upon the express ground that the prohibited acts had come to be considered as favorable to the development of and not in restraint of trade. It is remarkable that nowhere at common law can there be found a prohibition against the creation of monopoly by an individual. This would seem to manifest, either consciously or intuitively, a profound conception as to the inevitable operation of economic forces and the equipoise or balance in favor of the protection of the rights of individuals which resulted. * * * After all, this was but an instinctive recognition of the truisms that the course of trade could not be made free by obstructing it, and that an individual's right to trade could not be protected by destroying such right.

From the review just made it clearly results that outside of the restrictions resulting from the want of power in an individual to voluntarily and unreasonably restrain his right to carry on his trade or business and outside of the want of right to restrain the free course of trade by contracts or acts which implied a wrongful purpose, freedom to contract and to abstain from contracting and to exercise every reasonable right incident thereto became the rule in the English law. * * *

In this country also the acts from which it was deemed there resulted a part if not all of the injurious consequences ascribed to monopoly, came to be referred to as a monopoly itself. * * *

It is also true that while the principles concerning contracts in restraint of trade, that is, voluntary restraint put by a person on his right to pursue his calling, hence only operating subjectively, came generally to be recognized in accordance with the English rule, it came moreover to pass that contracts or acts which it was considered had a monopolistic tendency, especially those which were thought to unduly diminish competition and hence to enhance prices—in other words, to monopolize—came also in a generic sense to be spoken of and treated as they had been in England, as restricting the due course of trade, and therefore as being in restraint of trade. The dread of monopoly as an emanation of governmental power, while it passed at an early date out of mind in this country, as a result of the structure of our Government, did not serve to assuage the fear as to the evil consequences which might arise from the acts of individuals producing or tending to produce the consequences of monopoly. It resulted that treating such acts as we have said as amounting to monopoly, sometimes constitutional restrictions, again legislative enactments or judicial decisions, served to enforce and illustrate the purpose to prevent the occurrence of the evils recognized in the mother country as consequent upon monopoly, by providing against contracts or acts of individuals or combinations of individuals or corporations deemed to be conducive to such results. * * *

It will be found that as modern conditions arose the trend of legislation and judicial decision came more and more to adapt the recognized restrictions to new manifestations of conduct or of dealing which it was thought justified the inference of intent to do the wrongs which it had been the purpose to prevent from the beginning. * * *

* * * [I]t may be with accuracy said that the dread of enhancement of prices and of other wrongs which it was thought would flow from the undue limitation on competitive conditions caused by contracts or other acts of individuals or corporations, led, as a matter of public policy, to the prohibition or treating as illegal all contracts or acts which were unreasonably restrictive of competitive conditions * * *. * * *

Let us consider the language of the first and second sections, guided by the principle that where words are employed in a statute which had at the time a well-known meaning at common law or in the law of this country they are presumed to have been used in that sense unless the context compels to the contrary. * * *

As to the first section, the words to be interpreted are: "Every contract, combination in the form of trust or otherwise, or conspiracy in restraint of trade or commerce … is hereby declared to be illegal." As there is no room for dispute that the statute was intended to formulate a rule for the regulation of interstate and foreign commerce, the question is what was the rule which it adopted?

In view of the common law and the law in this country as to restraint of trade, which we have reviewed, and the illuminating effect which that history must have under the rule to which we have referred, we think it results:

a.   That the context manifests that the statute was drawn in the light of the existing practical conception of the law of restraint of trade, because it groups as within that class, not only contracts which were in restraint of trade in the subjective sense, but all contracts or acts which theoretically were attempts to monopolize, yet which in practice had come to be considered as in restraint of trade in a broad sense.

b.   That in view of the many new forms of contracts and combinations which were being evolved from existing economic conditions, it was deemed essential by an all-embracing enumeration to make sure that no form of contract or combination by which an undue restraint of interstate or foreign commerce was brought about could save such restraint from condemnation. The statute under this view evidenced the intent not to restrain the right to make and enforce contracts, whether resulting from combination or otherwise, which did not unduly restrain interstate or foreign commerce, but to protect that commerce from being restrained by methods, whether old or new, which would constitute an interference that is an undue restraint.

c.   And as the contracts or acts embraced in the provision were not expressly defined, since the enumeration addressed itself simply to classes of acts, those classes being broad enough to embrace every conceivable contract or combination which could be made concerning trade or commerce or the subjects of such commerce, and thus caused any act done by any of the enumerated methods anywhere in the whole field of human activity to be illegal if in restraint of trade, it inevitably follows that the provision necessarily called for the exercise of judgment which required that some standard should be resorted to for the purpose of determining whether the prohibitions contained in the statute had or had not in any given case been violated. Thus not specifying but indubitably contemplating and requiring a standard, it follows that it was intended that the standard of reason which had been applied at the common law and in this country in dealing with subjects of the character embraced by the statute, was intended to be the measure used for the purpose of determining whether in a given case a particular act had or had not brought about the wrong against which the statute provided.

* * *

Undoubtedly, the words "to monopolize" and "monopolize" as used in the [second] section reach every act bringing about the prohibited results. The ambiguity, if any, is involved in determining what is intended by monopolize. But this ambiguity is readily dispelled in the light of the previous history of the law of restraint of trade to which we have referred and the indication which it gives of the practical evolution by which monopoly and the acts which produce the same result as monopoly, that is, an undue restraint of the course of trade, all came to be spoken of as, and to be indeed synonymous with, restraint of trade. In other words, having by the first section forbidden all means of monopolizing trade, that is, unduly restraining it by means of every contract, combination, etc., the second section seeks, if possible, to make the prohibitions of the act all the more complete and perfect by embracing all attempts to reach the end prohibited by the first section, that is, restraints of trade, by any attempt to monopolize, or monopolization thereof, even although the acts by which such results are attempted to be brought about or are brought about be not embraced within the general enumeration of the first section. And, of course, when the second section is thus harmonized with and made as it was intended to be the complement of the first, it becomes obvious that the criteria to be resorted to in any given case for the purpose of ascertaining whether violations of the section have been committed, is the rule of reason guided by the established law and by the plain duty to enforce the prohibitions of the act and thus the public policy which its restrictions were obviously enacted to subserve. And it is worthy of observation, as we have previously remarked concerning the common law, that although the statute by the comprehensiveness of the enumerations embodied in both the first and second sections makes it certain that its purpose was to prevent undue restraints of every kind or nature, nevertheless by the omission of any direct prohibition against monopoly in the concrete it indicates a consciousness that the freedom of the individual right to contract when not unduly or improperly exercised was the most efficient means for the prevention of monopoly, since the operation of the centrifugal and centripetal forces resulting from the right to freely contract was the means by which monopoly would be inevitably prevented if no extraneous or sovereign power imposed it and no right to make unlawful contracts having a monopolistic tendency were permitted. In other words that freedom to contract was the essence of freedom from undue restraint on the right to contract.

* * *

[We next consider the] contentions of the parties as to the meaning of the statute and the decisions of this court relied upon concerning those contentions.

[The Government argues that] the language of the statute embraces every contract, combination, etc., in restraint of trade, and hence its text leaves no room for the exercise of judgment, but simply imposes the plain duty of applying its prohibitions to every case within its literal language. The error involved lies in assuming the matter to be decided. This is true because as the acts which may come under the classes stated in the first section and the restraint of trade to which that section applies are not specifically enumerated or defined, it is obvious that judgment must in every case be called into play in order to determine whether a particular act is embraced within the statutory classes, and whether if the act is within such classes its nature or effect causes it to be a restraint of trade within the intendment of the act. To hold to the contrary would require the conclusion either that every contract, act or combination of any kind or nature, whether it operated a restraint on trade or not, was within the statute, and thus the statute would be destructive of all right to contract or agree or combine in any respect whatever as to subjects embraced in interstate trade or commerce, or if this conclusion were not reached, then the contention would require it to be held that as the statute did not define the things to which it related and excluded resort to the only means by which the acts to which it relates could be ascertained—the light of reason—the enforcement of the statute was impossible because of its uncertainty. The merely generic enumeration which the statute makes of the acts to which it refers and the absence of any definition of restraint of trade as used in the statute leaves room for but one conclusion, which is, that it was expressly designed not to unduly limit the application of the act by precise definition, but while clearly fixing a standard, that is, by defining the ulterior boundaries which could not be transgressed with impunity, to leave it to be determined by the light of reason, guided by the principles of law and the duty to apply and enforce the public policy embodied in the statute, in every given case whether any particular act or contract was within the contemplation of the statute.

But, it is said, persuasive as these views may be, they may not be here applied, because the previous decisions of this court have given to the statute a meaning which expressly excludes the construction which must result from the reasoning stated. The cases are *United States v. [Trans-Missouri] Freight Association, 166 U.S. 290,* and *United States v. Joint Traffic Association, 171 U.S. 505.* Both the cases involved the legality of combinations or associations of railroads engaged in interstate commerce for the purpose of controlling the conduct of the parties to the association or combination in many particulars. The association or combination was assailed in each case as being in violation of the statute. It was held that they were. It is undoubted that in the opinion in each case general language was made use of, which, when separated from its context, would justify the conclusion that it was decided that reason could not be resorted to for the purpose of determining whether the acts complained of were within the statute. It is, however, also true that the nature and character of the contract or agreement in each case was fully referred to and suggestions as to their unreasonableness pointed out in order to indicate that they were within the prohibitions of the statute. * * *

[Further, in all of our previous anti-trust cases] reason was the guide by which the provisions of the act were in every case interpreted. Indeed intermediate the decision of the two cases, that is, after the decision in the Freight Association Case and before the decision in the Joint Traffic Case, the case of *Hopkins v. United States, 171 U.S. 578,* was decided, the opinion being delivered by Mr. Justice Peckham, who wrote both the opinions in the Freight Association and the Joint Traffic cases. And, referring in the Hopkins Case to the broad claim made as to the rule of interpretation announced in the Freight Association Case, it was said (p. 592): "To treat as condemned by the act all agreements under which, as a result, the cost of conducting an interstate commercial business may be increased would enlarge the application of the act far beyond the fair meaning of the language used. There must be some direct and immediate effect upon interstate commerce in order to come within the act." And in the Joint Traffic Case this statement was expressly reiterated and approved and illustrated by example * * *.

If the criterion by which it is to be determined in all cases whether every contract, combination, etc., is a restraint of trade within the intendment of the law, is the direct or indirect effect of the acts involved, then of course the rule of reason becomes the guide, and the construction which we have given the statute, instead of being refuted by the cases relied upon, is by those cases demonstrated to be correct. This is true, because as the construction which we have deduced from the history of the act and the analysis of its text is simply that in every case where it is claimed that an act or acts are in violation of the statute the rule of reason, in the light of the principles of law and the public policy which the act embodies, must be applied. * * *

If it be true that there is this identity of result between the rule intended to be applied in the Freight Association Case, that is, the rule of direct and indirect, and the rule of reason which under the statute as we construe it should be here applied, it may be asked how was it that in the opinion in the Freight Association Case much consideration was given to the subject of whether the agreement or combination which was involved in that case could be taken out of the prohibitions of the statute upon the theory of its reasonableness. The question is pertinent and must be fully and frankly met, for if it be now deemed that the Freight Association Case was mistakenly decided or too broadly stated, the doctrine which it announced should be either expressly overruled or limited.

* * *

And in order not in the slightest degree to be wanting in frankness, we say that in so far, however, as by separating the general language used in the opinions in the Freight Association and Joint Traffic cases from the context and the subject and parties with which the cases were concerned, it may be conceived that the language referred to conflicts with the construction which we give the statute, they are necessarily now limited and qualified. * * *

So far as the objections of the defendants are concerned they are all embraced under two headings:-

a.   That the act, even if the averments of the bill be true, cannot be constitutionally applied, because to do so would extend the power of Congress to subjects dehors the reach of its authority to regulate commerce, by enabling that body to deal with mere questions of production of commodities within the States. But all the structure upon which this argument proceeds is based upon the decision in *United States v. E.C. Knight Co., 156 U.S. 1.* The view, however, which the argument takes of that case and the arguments based upon that view have been so repeatedly pressed upon this court in connection with the interpretation and enforcement of the Anti-trust Act, and have been so necessarily and expressly decided to be unsound as to cause the contentions to be plainly foreclosed and to require no express notice. * * *

b.   [Defendants argue] that the statute cannot be applied under the facts of this case without impairing rights of property and destroying the freedom of contract or trade, which is essentially necessary to the well-being of society and which it is insisted is protected by the constitutional guaranty of due process of law. But the ultimate foundation of all these arguments is the assumption that reason may not be resorted to in interpreting and applying the statute, and therefore that the statute unreasonably restricts the right to contract and unreasonably operates upon the right to acquire and hold property. As the premise is demonstrated to be unsound by the construction we have given the statute, of course the propositions which rest upon that premise need not be further noticed.

[Defendants' argument is essentially] that, consistently with the fundamental principles of due process of law, it never can be left to the judiciary to decide whether in a given case particular acts come within a generic statutory provision. But to reduce the propositions, however, to this their final meaning makes it clear that in substance they deny the existence of essential legislative authority and challenge the right of the judiciary to perform duties which that department of the government has exerted from the beginning. * * * Yet, let us demonstrate that which needs no demonstration, by a few obvious examples. Take for instance the familiar cases where the judiciary is called upon to determine whether a particular act or acts are within a given prohibition, depending upon wrongful intent. Take questions of fraud. Consider the power which must be exercised in every case where the courts are called upon to determine whether particular acts are invalid which are, abstractly speaking, in and of themselves valid, but which are asserted to be invalid because of their direct effect upon interstate commerce.

We come then to the third proposition requiring consideration, viz:

Third. The facts and the application of the statute to them.

Beyond dispute the proofs establish substantially as alleged in the bill the following facts:

1. The creation of the Standard Oil Company of Ohio;

2. The organization of the Standard Oil Trust of 1882, and also a previous one of 1879, not referred to in the bill, and the proceedings in the Supreme Court of Ohio, culminating in a decree based upon the finding that the company was unlawfully a party to that trust; the transfer by the trustees of stocks in certain of the companies; the contempt proceedings; and, finally, the increase of the capital of the Standard Oil Company of New Jersey and the acquisition by that company of the shares of the stock of the other corporations in exchange for its certificates.

The vast amount of property and the possibilities of far-reaching control which resulted from the facts last stated are shown by the statement * * * concerning the parties to the trust agreement of 1882, and the corporations whose stock was held by the trustees under the trust and which came therefore to be held by the New Jersey corporation. * * * [T]he proof, we think, establishes that the result of enlarging the capital stock of the New Jersey company and giving it the vast power to which we have referred produced its normal consequence, that is, it gave to the corporation, despite enormous dividends and despite the dropping out of certain corporations enumerated in the decree of the court below, an enlarged and more perfect sway and control over the trade and commerce in petroleum and its products. * * *

Giving to the facts just stated, the weight which it was deemed they were entitled to * * * the court below held that the acts and dealings established by the proof operated to destroy the "potentiality of competition" which otherwise would have existed to such an extent as to cause the transfers of stock which were made to the New Jersey corporation and the control which resulted over the many and various subsidiary corporations to be a combination or conspiracy in restraint of trade in violation of the first section of the act, but also to be an attempt to monopolize and a monopolization bringing about a perennial violation of the second section.

We see no cause to doubt the correctness of these conclusions * * *.

* * *

Recurring to the acts done by the individuals or corporations who were mainly instrumental in bringing about the expansion of the New Jersey corporation during the period prior to the formation of the trust agreements of 1879 and 1882, including those agreements, not for the purpose of weighing the substantial merit of the numerous charges of wrongdoing made during such period, but solely as an aid for discovering intent and purpose, we think no disinterested mind can survey the period in question without being irresistibly driven to the conclusion that the very genius for commercial development and organization which it would seem was manifested from the beginning soon begot an intent and purpose to exclude others which was frequently manifested by acts and dealings wholly inconsistent with the theory that they were made with the single conception of advancing the development of business power by usual methods, but which on the contrary necessarily involved the intent to drive others from the field and to exclude them from their right to trade and thus accomplish the mastery which was the end in view. And, considering the period from the date of the trust agreements of 1879 and 1882, up to the time of the expansion of the New Jersey corporation, the gradual extension of the power over the commerce in oil which ensued, the decision of the Supreme Court of Ohio, the tardiness or reluctance in conforming to the commands of that decision, the method first adopted and that which finally culminated in the plan of the New Jersey corporation, all additionally serve to make manifest the continued existence of the intent which we have previously indicated and which among other things impelled the expansion of the New Jersey corporation. The exercise of the power which resulted from that organization fortifies the foregoing conclusions, since the development which came, the acquisition here and there which ensued of every efficient means by which competition could have been asserted, the slow but resistless methods which followed by which means of transportation were absorbed and brought under control, the system of marketing which was adopted by which the country was divided into districts and the trade in each district in oil was turned over to a designated corporation within the combination and all others were excluded, all lead the mind up to a conviction of a purpose and intent which we think is so certain as practically to cause the subject not to be within the domain of reasonable contention.

The inference that no attempt to monopolize could have been intended, and that no monopolization resulted from the acts complained of, since it is established that a very small percentage of the crude oil produced was controlled by the combination, is unwarranted. As substantial power over the crude product was the inevitable result of the absolute control which existed over the refined product, the monopolization of the one carried with it the power to control the other * * *.

We are thus brought to the last subject which we are called upon to consider, viz:

Fourth. The remedy to be administered.

It may be conceded that ordinarily where it was found that acts had been done in violation of the statute, adequate measure of relief would result from restraining the doing of such acts in the future. * * * But in a case like this, where the condition which has been brought about in violation of the statute, in and of itself, is not only a continued attempt to monopolize, but also a monopolization, the duty to enforce the statute requires the application of broader and more controlling remedies. * * * [T]he application of remedies two-fold in character becomes essential: 1st. To forbid the doing in the future of acts like those which we have found to have been done in the past which would be violative of the statute. 2d.

The exertion of such measure of relief as will effectually dissolve the combination found to exist in violation of the statute * * *.

In applying remedies for this purpose, however, the fact must not be overlooked that injury to the public by the prevention of an undue restraint on, or the monopolization of trade or commerce is the foundation upon which the prohibitions of the statute rest, and moreover that one of the fundamental purposes of the statute is to protect, not to destroy, rights of property.

Let us then, as a means of accurately determining what relief we are to afford, first come to consider what relief was afforded by the court below, in order to fix how far it is necessary to take from or add to that relief, to the end that the prohibitions of the statute may have complete and operative force.

The court below by virtue of §§ 1, 2, and 4 of its decree * * * adjudged that the New Jersey corporation in so far as it held the stock of the various corporations * * * or controlled the same was a combination in violation of the first section of the act, and an attempt to monopolize or a monopolization contrary to the second section of the act. It commanded the dissolution of the combination, and therefore in effect, directed the transfer by the New Jersey corporation back to the stockholders of the various subsidiary corporations entitled to the same of the stock which had been turned over to the New Jersey company in exchange for its stock. To make this command effective § 5 of the decree forbade the New Jersey corporation from in any form or manner exercising any ownership or exerting any power directly or indirectly in virtue of its apparent title to the stocks of the subsidiary corporations, and prohibited those subsidiary corporations from paying any dividends to the New Jersey corporation or doing any act which would recognize further power in that company, except to the extent that it was necessary to enable that company to transfer the stock. So far as the owners of the stock of the subsidiary corporations and the corporations themselves were concerned after the stock had been transferred, § 6 of the decree enjoined them from in any way conspiring or combining to violate the act or to monopolize or attempt to monopolize in virtue of their ownership of the stock transferred to them, and prohibited all agreements between the subsidiary corporations or other stockholders in the future, tending to produce or bring about further violations of the act.

By § 7, pending the accomplishment of the dissolution of the combination by the transfer of stock and until it was consummated, the defendants named in § 2, constituting all the corporations to which we have referred, were enjoined from engaging in or carrying on interstate commerce. And by § 9, among other things a delay of thirty days was granted for the carrying into effect of the directions of the decree.

So far as the decree held that the ownership of the stock of the New Jersey corporation constituted a combination in violation of the first section and an attempt to create a monopoly or to monopolize under the second section and commanded the dissolution of the combination, the decree was clearly appropriate. And this also is true of § 5 of the decree which restrained both the New Jersey corporation and the subsidiary corporations from doing anything which would recognize or give effect to further ownership in the New Jersey corporation of the stocks which were ordered to be retransferred.

But the contention is that, in so far as the relief by way of injunction which was awarded by § 6 against the stockholders of the subsidiary corporations or the subsidiary corporations themselves after the transfer of stock by the New Jersey corporation was completed in conformity to the decree, the relief awarded was too broad: a. Because it was not sufficiently specific and tended to cause those who were within the embrace of the order to cease to be under the protection of the law of the land and required them to thereafter conduct their business under the jeopardy of punishments for contempt for violating a general injunction. * * *. Besides it is said that the restraint imposed by § 6 * * * was moreover calculated to do injury to the public and it may be in and of itself to produce the very restraint on the due course of trade which it was intended to prevent. We say this since it does not necessarily follow because an illegal restraint of trade or an attempt to monopolize or a monopolization resulted from the combination and the transfer of the stocks of the subsidiary corporations to the New Jersey corporation that a like restraint or attempt to monopolize or monopolization would necessarily arise from agreements between one or more of the subsidiary corporations after the transfer of the stock by the New Jersey corporation. For illustration, take the pipe lines. By the effect of the transfer of the stock the pipe lines would come under the control of various corporations instead of being subjected to a uniform control. If various corporations owning the lines determined in the public interests to so combine as to make a continuous line, such agreement or combination would not be repugnant to the act, and yet it might be restrained by the decree. As another example, take the Union Tank Line Company, one of the subsidiary corporations, the owner practically of all the tank cars in use by the combination. If no possibility existed of agreements for the distribution of these cars among the subsidiary corporations, the most serious detriment to the public interest might result. Conceding the merit, abstractly considered, of these contentions they are irrelevant. We so think, since we construe the sixth paragraph of the decree, not as depriving the stockholders or the corporations, after the dissolution of the combination, of the power to make normal and lawful contracts or agreements, but as restraining them from, by any device whatever, recreating directly or indirectly the illegal combination which the decree dissolved. In other words we construe the sixth paragraph of the decree, not as depriving the stockholders or corporations of the right to live under the law of the land, but as compelling obedience to that law. As therefore the sixth paragraph as thus construed is not amenable to the criticism directed against it and cannot produce the harmful results which the arguments suggest it was obviously right. We think that in view of the magnitude of the interests involved and their complexity that the delay of thirty days allowed for executing the decree was too short and should be extended so as to embrace a period of at least six months. So also, in view of the possible serious injury to result to the public from an absolute cessation of interstate commerce in petroleum and its products by such vast agencies as are embraced in the combination, a result which might arise from that portion of the decree which enjoined carrying on of interstate commerce not only by the New Jersey corporation but by all the subsidiary companies until the dissolution of the combination by the transfer of the stocks in accordance with the decree, the injunction provided for in § 7 thereof should not have been awarded.

Our conclusion is that the decree below was right and should be affirmed, except as to the minor matters concerning which we have indicated the decree should be modified. * * *

MR. JUSTICE HARLAN concurring in part, and dissenting in part.

* * *

I concur in holding that the Standard Oil Company of New Jersey and its subsidiary companies constitute a combination in restraint of interstate commerce, and that they have attempted to monopolize and have monopolized parts of such commerce * * *.

In my judgment, the decree below should have been affirmed without qualification. But the court, while affirming the decree, directs some modifications in respect of what it characterizes as "minor matters." It is to be apprehended that those modifications may prove to be mischievous. In saying this, I have particularly in view the statement in the opinion that "it does not necessarily follow that because an illegal restraint of trade or an attempt to monopolize or a monopolization resulted from the combination and the transfer of the stocks of the subsidiary corporations to the New Jersey corporation, that a like restraint of trade or attempt to monopolize or monopolization would necessarily arise from agreements between one or more of the subsidiary corporations after the transfer of the stock by the New Jersey corporation." Taking this language, in connection with other parts of the opinion, the subsidiary companies are thus, in effect, informed—unwisely, I think—that although the New Jersey corporation, being an illegal combination, must go out of existence, they may join in an agreement to restrain commerce among the States if such restraint be not "undue."

In order that my objections to certain parts of the court's opinion may distinctly appear, I must state the circumstances under which Congress passed the Antitrust Act, and trace the course of judicial decisions as to its meaning and scope. This is the more necessary because the court by its decision, when interpreted by the language of its opinion, has not only upset the long settled interpretation of the act, but has usurped the constitutional functions of the legislative branch of the Government. With all due respect for the opinions of others, I feel bound to say that what the court has said may well cause some alarm for the integrity of our institutions. Let us see how the matter stands.

All who recall the condition of the country in 1890 will remember that there was everywhere, among the people generally, a deep feeling of unrest. The Nation had been rid of human slavery—fortunately, as all now feel—but the conviction was universal that the country was in real danger from another kind of slavery sought to be fastened on the American people, namely, the slavery that would result from aggregations of capital in the hands of a few individuals and corporations controlling, for their own profit and advantage exclusively, the entire business of the country, including the production and sale of the necessaries of life. Such a danger was thought to be then imminent, and all felt that it must be met firmly and by such statutory regulations as would adequately protect the people against oppression and wrong. Congress therefore took up the matter and gave the whole subject the fullest consideration. All agreed that the National Government could not, by legislation, regulate the domestic trade carried on wholly within the several States; for, power to regulate such trade remained with, because never surrendered by, the States. But, under authority expressly granted to it by the Constitution, Congress could regulate commerce among the several States and with foreign states. * * *

Guided by these considerations, and to the end that the people, so far as interstate commerce was concerned, might not be dominated by vast combinations and monopolies, having power to advance their own selfish ends, regardless of the general interests and welfare, Congress passed the Anti-trust Act of 1890 in these words * * *.

"[The text of sections 1 and 2, which appear earlier in the Court's opinion are repeated] § 3. Every contract, combination in form of trust or otherwise, or conspiracy, in restraint of trade or commerce in any Territory of the United States or in the District of Columbia, or in restraint of trade or commerce between any such Territory and another, or between any such Territory or Territories and any State or States or the District of Columbia, or with foreign nations, or between the District of Columbia and any State or States or foreign nations, is hereby declared illegal. Every person who shall make any such contract or engage in any such combination or conspiracy, shall be deemed guilty of a misdemeanor, and, on conviction thereof, shall be punished by fine not exceeding five thousand dollars, or by imprisonment not exceeding one year, or by both said punishments, in the discretion of the court." 26 Stat. 209, c. 647.

The important inquiry in the present case is as to the meaning and scope of that act in its application to interstate commerce.

In 1896 this court had occasion to determine the meaning and scope of the act in an important case known as the *Trans–Missouri Freight Case. 166 U.S. 290.* The question there was as to the validity under the Anti-trust Act of a certain agreement between numerous railroad companies, whereby they formed an association for the purpose of establishing and maintaining rates, rules and regulations in respect of freight traffic over specified routes. Two questions were involved: first, whether the act applied to railroad carriers; second, whether the agreement the annulment of which as illegal was the basis of the suit which the United States brought. The court held that railroad carriers were embraced by the act. In determining that question, the court, among other things, said:

> "The language of the act includes every contract, combination in the form of trust or otherwise, or conspiracy, in restraint of trade or commerce among the several States or with foreign nations. So far as the very terms of the statute go, they apply to any contract of the nature described. A contract therefore that is in restraint of trade or commerce is, by the strict language of the act prohibited, even though such contract is entered into between competing common carriers by railroad, and only for the purposes of thereby affecting traffic rates for the transportation of persons and property. If such an agreement restrains trade or commerce, it is prohibited by the statute, unless it can be said that an agreement, no matter what its terms, relating only to transportation cannot restrain trade or commerce. We see no escape from the conclusion that if an agreement of such a nature does restrain it, the agreement is condemned by this act.... Nor is it for the substantial interests of the country that any one commodity should be within the sole power and subject to the sole will of one powerful combination of capital. Congress has, so far as its jurisdiction extends, prohibited all contracts or combinations in the form of trusts entered into for the purpose of restraining trade and commerce.... While the statute prohibits all combinations in the form of trusts or otherwise, the limitation is not confined to that form alone. All combinations which are in restraint of trade or commerce are prohibited, whether in the form of trusts or in any other form whatever." *United States v. Freight Assn., 166 U.S. 290, 312, 324, 326.*

The court then proceeded to consider the second of the above questions, saying:

> "The next question to be discussed is as to what is the true construction of the statute, assuming that it applies to common carriers by railroad. What is the meaning of the language as used in the statute, that 'every contract, combination in the form of trust or otherwise, or conspiracy in restraint of trade or commerce among the several States or with foreign nations, is hereby declared to be illegal?' Is it confined to a contract or combination which is only in unreasonable restraint of trade or commerce, or does it include what the language of the act plainly and in terms covers, all contracts of that nature? It is now with much amplification of argument urged that the statute, in declaring illegal every combination in the form of trust or otherwise, or conspiracy in restraint of trade or commerce, does not mean what

the language used therein plainly imports, but that it only means to declare illegal any such contract which is in unreasonable restraint of trade, while leaving all others unaffected by the provisions of the act; that the common law meaning of the term 'contract in restraint of trade' includes only such contracts as are in unreasonable restraint of trade, and when that term is used in the Federal statute it is not intended to include all contracts in restraint of trade, but only those which are in unreasonable restraint thereof.... By the simple use of the term 'contract in restraint of trade,' all contracts of that nature, whether valid or otherwise, would be included, and not alone that kind of contract which was invalid and unenforceable as being in unreasonable restraint of trade. When, therefore, the body of an act pronounces as illegal every contract or combination in restraint of trade or commerce among the several States, etc., the plain and ordinary meaning of such language is not limited to that kind of contract alone which is in unreasonable restraint of trade, but all contracts are included in such language, and no exception or limitation can be added without placing in the act that which has been omitted by Congress.... If only that kind of contract which is in unreasonable restraint of trade be within the meaning of the statute, and declared therein to be illegal, it is at once apparent that the subject of what is a reasonable rate is attended with great uncertainty.... To say, therefore, that the act excludes agreements which are not in unreasonable restraint of trade, and which tend simply to keep up reasonable rates for transportation, is substantially to leave the question of unreasonableness to the companies themselves.... But assuming that agreements of this nature are not void at common law and that the various cases cited by the learned courts below show it, the answer to the statement of their validity now is to be found in the terms of the statute under consideration.... The arguments which have been addressed to us against the inclusion of all contracts in restraint of trade, as provided for by the language of the act, have been based upon the alleged presumption that Congress, notwithstanding the language of the act, could not have intended to embrace all contracts, but only such contracts as were in unreasonable restraint of trade. Under these circumstances we are, therefore, asked to hold that the act of Congress excepts contracts which are not in unreasonable restraint of trade, and which only keep rates up to a reasonable price, notwithstanding the language of the act makes no such exception. In other words, we are asked to read into the act by way of judicial legislation an exception that is not placed there by the lawmaking branch of the Government, and this is to be done upon the theory that the impolicy of such legislation is so clear that it cannot be supposed Congress intended the natural import of the language it used. This we cannot and ought not to do....

"If the act ought to read, as contended for by defendants, Congress is the body to amend it and not this court, by a process of judicial legislation wholly unjustifiable. Large numbers do not agree that the view taken by defendants is sound or true in substance, and Congress may and very probably did share in that belief in passing the act. The public policy of the Government is to be found in its statutes, and when they have not directly spoken, then in the decisions of the courts and the constant practice of the government officials; but when the lawmaking power speaks upon a particular subject, over which it has constitutional power to legislate, public policy in such a case is what the statute enacts. If the law prohibit any contract or combination in restraint of trade or commerce, a contract or combination made in violation of such law is void, whatever may have been theretofore decided by the courts to have been the public policy of the country on that subject. The conclusion which we have drawn from the examination above made into the question before us is that the Anti-trust Act applies to railroads, and that it renders illegal all agreements which are in restraint of trade or commerce as we have above defined that expression, and the question then arises whether the agreement before us is of that nature."

I have made these extended extracts from the opinion of the court in the Trans–Missouri Freight Case in order to show beyond question, that the point was there urged by counsel that the Anti-trust Act condemned only contracts, combinations, trusts and conspiracies that were in unreasonable restraint of interstate commerce, and that the court in clear and decisive language met that point. It adjudged that Congress had in unequivocal words declared that "every contract, combination, in the form of trust or otherwise, or conspiracy, in restraint of commerce among the several States" shall be illegal, and that no distinction, so far as interstate commerce was concerned, was to be tolerated between restraints of such commerce as were undue or unreasonable, and restraints that were due or reasonable. With full knowledge of the then condition of the country and of its business, Congress determined to meet, and did meet, the situation by an absolute, statutory prohibition of "every contract, combination in the form of trust or otherwise, in restraint of trade or commerce." Still more; in response to the suggestion by able counsel that Congress intended only to strike down such contracts, combinations and monopolies as unreasonably restrained interstate commerce, this court, in words too clear to be misunderstood, said that to so hold was "to read into the act by way of judicial legislation, an exception not placed there by the lawmaking branch of the Government." "This," the court said, as we have seen, "we cannot and ought not to do."

It thus appears that fifteen years ago, when the purpose of Congress in passing the Anti-trust Act was fresh in the minds of courts, lawyers, statesmen and the general public, this court expressly declined to indulge in judicial legislation, by inserting in the act the word "unreasonable" or any other word of like import. It may be stated here that the country at large accepted this view of the act, and the Federal courts throughout the

entire country enforced its provisions according to the interpretation
given in the Freight Association Case. What, then, was to be done by those
who questioned the soundness of the interpretation placed on the act by
this court in that case? As the court had decided that to insert the word
"unreasonable" in the act would be "judicial legislation" on its part, the
only alternative left to those who opposed the decision in that case was to
induce Congress to so amend the act as to recognize the right to restrain
interstate commerce to a reasonable extent. The public press, magazines
and law journals, the debates in Congress, speeches and addresses by
public men and jurists, all contain abundant evidence of the general
understanding that the meaning, extent and scope of the Anti-trust Act
had been judicially determined by this court, and that the only question
remaining open for discussion was the wisdom of the policy declared by
the act—a matter that was exclusively within the cognizance of Congress.
But at every session of Congress since the decision of 1896, the lawmaking branch of the Government, with full knowledge of that decision, has
refused to change the policy it had declared or to so amend the act of 1890
as to except from its operation contracts, combinations and trusts that
reasonably restrain interstate commerce.

But those who were in combinations that were illegal did not despair.
They at once set up the baseless claim that the decision of 1896 disturbed
the "business interests of the country," and let it be known that they
would never be content until the rule was established that would permit
interstate commerce to be subjected to reasonable restraints. Finally, an
opportunity came again to raise the same question which this court had,
upon full consideration, determined in 1896. I now allude to the case of
United States v. Joint–Traffic Association, 171 U.S. 505, decided in 1898.
What was that case?

It was a suit by the United States against more than thirty railroad
companies to have the court declare illegal, under the Anti-trust Act, a
certain agreement between these companies. The relief asked was denied
in the subordinate Federal courts and the Government brought the case
here.

It is important to state the points urged in that case by the defendant
companies charged with violating the Anti-trust Act, and to show that the
court promptly met them. To that end I make a copious extract from the
opinion in the Joint Traffic Case. Among other thing, the court said: "Upon
comparing that agreement [the one in the Joint Traffic Case, then under
consideration, *171 U.S. 505]* with the one set forth in the case of *United
States v. Trans–Missouri Freight Association, 166 U.S. 290,* the great similarity between them suggests that a similar result should be reached in
the two cases" (p. 558). Learned counsel in the Joint Traffic Case urged a
reconsideration of the question decided in the Trans–Missouri Case contending that "the decision in that case [the Trans–Missouri Freight Case]
is quite plainly erroneous, and the consequences of such error are far
reaching and disastrous, and clearly at war with justice and sound policy,

and the construction placed upon the Anti-trust statute has been received by the public with surprise and alarm." They suggested that the point made in the Joint Traffic Case as to the meaning and scope of the act might have been but was not made in the previous case. The court said *(171 U.S. 559)* that "the report of the Trans–Missouri Case clearly shows not only that the point now taken was there urged upon the attention of the court, but it was then intentionally and necessarily decided."

The question whether the court should again consider the point decided in the *Trans–Missouri Case, 171 U.S. 573,* was disposed of in the most decisive language, as follows:

"Finally, we are asked to reconsider the question decided in the Trans–Missouri Case, and to retrace the steps taken therein, because of the plain error contained in that decision and the widespread alarm with which it was received and the serious consequences which have resulted, or may soon result, from the law as interpreted in that case. It is proper to remark that an application for a reconsideration of a question but lately decided by this court is usually based upon a statement that some of the arguments employed on the original hearing of the question have been overlooked or misunderstood, or that some controlling authority has been either misapplied by the court or passed over without discussion or notice. While this is not strictly an application for a rehearing in the same case, yet in substance it is the same thing. The court is asked to reconsider a question but just decided after a careful investigation of the matter involved. There have heretofore been in effect two arguments of precisely the same questions now before the court, and the same arguments were addressed to us on both those occasions. The report of the Trans–Missouri Case shows a dissenting opinion delivered in that case, and that the opinion was concurred in by three other members of the court. That opinion, it will be seen, gives with great force and ability the arguments against the decision which was finally arrived at by the court. It was after a full discussion of the questions involved and with the knowledge of the views entertained by the minority as expressed in the dissenting opinion, that the majority of the court came to the conclusion it did. Soon after the decision a petition for a rehearing of the case was made, supported by a printed argument in its favor, and pressed with an earnestness and vigor and at a length which were certainly commensurate with the importance of the case. This court, with care and deliberation and also with a full appreciation of their importance, again considered the questions involved in its former decision. A majority of the court once more arrived at the conclusion it had first announced, and accordingly it denied the application. And now for the third time the same arguments are employed, and the court is again asked to recant its former opinion, and to decide the same question in direct opposition to the conclusion arrived at in the Trans–Missouri Case. The learned counsel while making the application frankly confess that the argument in opposition to the decision in the case above named has been so fully, so clearly and so forcibly presented in the dissenting opinion of Mr. Justice White [in the Freight Case] that it is hardly possible to add to it, nor is it necessary to repeat it. The fact that there was so close a division of opinion in this court when the matter was first under advisement, together with the different views taken by some of the judges of the lower courts, led us to the most careful and scrutinizing examination of the arguments advanced by both sides, and it was after such an examination that the majority of the court came to the conclusion it did. It is not now alleged that the court on the former occasion overlooked any argument for the respondents or misapplied any controlling authority. It is simply insisted that the court, notwithstanding the arguments for an opposite view, arrived at an erroneous result, which, for reasons already stated, ought to be reconsidered and reversed. As we have twice already deliberately and earnestly considered the same arguments which are now for a third time pressed upon our attention, it could hardly be expected that our opinion should now change from that already expressed."

These utterances, taken in connection with what was previously said in the Trans–Missouri Freight Case, show so clearly and affirmatively as to admit of no doubt that this court, many years ago, upon the fullest consideration, interpreted the Anti-trust Act as prohibiting and making illegal not only every contract or combination, in whatever form, which was in restraint of interstate commerce, without regard to its reasonableness or unreasonableness, but all monopolies or attempts to monopolize "any part" of such trade or commerce. * * *

* * *

In this connection it may be well to refer to the adverse report made in 1909, by Senator Nelson, on behalf of the Senate Judiciary Committee, in reference to a certain bill offered in the Senate and which proposed to amend the Anti-trust Act in various particulars. That report contains a full, careful and able analysis of judicial decisions relating to combinations and monopolies in restraint of trade and commerce. Among other things said in it which bear on the questions involved in the present case are these:

"The Anti-trust Act makes it a criminal offense to violate the law, and provides a punishment both by fine and imprisonment. To inject into the act the question of whether an agreement or combination is reasonable or unreasonable would render the act as a criminal or penal statute indefinite and uncertain, and hence, to that extent, utterly nugatory and void, and would practically amount to a repeal of that part of the act.... And while the same technical objection does not apply to civil prosecutions, the injection of the rule of reasonableness or unreasonableness would lead to the greatest variability and uncertainty in the enforcement of the law. The defense of reasonable restraint would be made in every case and there would be as many different rules of reasonableness as cases, courts and juries. * * * In the case of *People v. Sheldon, 139 N.Y. 264,* Chief Justice Andrews remarks: 'If agreements and combinations to prevent competition in prices are or may be hurtful to trade, the only sure remedy is to prohibit all agreements of that character. If the validity of such an agreement was made to depend upon actual proof of public prejudice or injury, it would be very difficult in any case to establish the invalidity, although the moral evidence might be very convincing.' ... To amend the Anti-trust Act, as suggested by this bill, would be to entirely emasculate it, and for all practical purposes render it nugatory as a remedial statute. Criminal prosecutions would not lie and civil remedies would labor under the greatest doubt and uncertainty. The act as it exists is clear, comprehensive, certain and highly remedial. It practically covers the field of Federal jurisdiction, and is in every respect a model law. To destroy or undermine it at the present juncture, when combinations are on the increase, and appear to be as oblivious as ever of the rights of the public, would be a calamity."

The result was the indefinite postponement by the Senate of any further consideration of the proposed amendments of the Anti-trust Act.

After what has been adjudged, upon full consideration, as to the meaning and scope of the Anti-trust Act, and in view of the usages of this court when attorneys for litigants have attempted to reopen questions that have been deliberately decided, I confess to no little surprise as to what has occurred in the present case. The court says that the previous cases, above cited, "cannot by any possible conception be treated as authoritative without the certitude that reason was resorted to for the purpose of deciding them." And its opinion is full of intimations that this court proceeded in those cases, so far as the present question is concerned, without being guided by the "rule of reason," or "the light of reason." It is more than once intimated, if not suggested, that if the Anti-trust Act is to be construed as prohibiting every contract or combination, of whatever nature, which is in fact in restraint of commerce, regardless of the reasonableness or unreasonableness of such restraint, that fact would show that the court had not proceeded, in its decision, according to "the light of reason," but had disregarded the "rule of reason." If the court, in those cases, was wrong in its construction of the act, it is certain that it fully apprehended the views advanced by learned counsel in previous cases and pronounced them to be untenable. The published reports place this beyond all question. The opinion of the court was delivered by a Justice of wide experience as a judicial officer, and the court had before it the Attorney General of the United States and lawyers who were recognized, on all sides, as great leaders in their profession. The same eminent jurist who delivered the opinion in the Trans–Missouri Case delivered the opinion in the Joint Traffic Association Case, and the Association in that case was represented by lawyers whose ability was universally recognized. Is it to be supposed that any point escaped notice in those cases when we think of the sagacity of the Justice who expressed the views of the court, or of the ability of the profound, astute lawyers, who sought such an interpretation of the act as would compel the court to insert words in the statute which Congress had not put there, and the insertion of which words, would amount to "judicial legislation"? Now this court is asked to do that which it has distinctly declared it could not and would not do, and has now done what it then said it could not constitutionally do. It has, by mere interpretation, modified the act of Congress, and deprived it of practical value as a defensive measure against the evils to be remedied. On reading the opinion just delivered, the first inquiry will be, that as the court is unanimous in holding that the particular things done by the Standard Oil Company and its subsidiary companies, in this case, were illegal under the Anti-trust Act, whether those things were in reasonable or unreasonable restraint of interstate commerce, why was it necessary to make an elaborate argument, as is done in the opinion, to show that according to the "rule of reason" the act as passed by Congress should be interpreted as if it contained the word "unreasonable" or the word "undue"? The only answer which, in frankness, can be given to this question is, that the court intends to decide that its deliberate judgment, fifteen years ago, to the effect that the act permitted no restraint whatever of interstate commerce, whether reasonable or unreasonable, was not in accordance with the "rule of reason." In effect the court says, that it will now, for the first time, bring the discussion under the "light of reason" and apply the "rule of reason" to the questions to be decided. I have the authority of this court for saying that such a course of proceeding on its part would be "judicial legislation."

Still more, what is now done involves a serious departure from the settled usages of this court. Counsel have not ordinarily been allowed to discuss questions already settled by previous decisions. More than once at the present term, that rule has been applied. In *St. Louis, I.M. & S. Ry. Co. v. Taylor, 210 U.S. 281, 295,* the court had occasion to determine the meaning and scope of the original Safety Appliance Act of Congress passed for the protection of railroad employes and passengers on interstate trains. 27 Stat. 531, § 5, c. 196. A particular construction of that act was insisted upon by the interstate carrier which was sued under the Safety Appliance Act; and the contention was that a different construction, than the one insisted upon by the carrier, would be a harsh one. After quoting the words of the act, Mr. Justice Moody said for the court:

> "There is no escape from the meaning of these words. Explanation cannot clarify them, and ought not to be employed to confuse them or lessen their significance. The obvious purpose of the legislature was to supplant the qualified duty of the common law with an absolute duty deemed by it more just. If the railroad does, in point of fact, use cars which do not comply with the standard, it violates the plain prohibi-

tions of the law, and there arises from that violation the liability to make compensation to one who is injured by it. It is urged that this is a harsh construction. To this we reply that, if it be the true construction, its harshness is no concern of the courts. They have no responsibility for the justice or wisdom of legislation, and no duty except to enforce the law as it is written, unless it is clearly beyond the constitutional power of the lawmaking body.... It is quite conceivable that Congress, contemplating the inevitable hardship of such injuries, and hoping to diminish the economic loss to the community resulting from them, should deem it wise to impose their burdens upon those who could measurably control their causes, instead of upon those who are in the main helpless in that regard. Such a policy would be intelligible, and, to say the least, not so unreasonable as to require us to doubt that it was intended, and to seek some unnatural interpretation of common words. We see no error in this part of the case."

And at the present term of this court we were asked, in a case arising under the Safety Appliance Act, to reconsider the question decided in the Taylor Case. We declined to do so * * *.

When counsel in the present case insisted upon a reversal of the former rulings of this court, and asked such an interpretation of the Antitrust Act as would allow reasonable restraints of interstate commerce, this court, in deference to established practice, should, I submit, have said to them: "That question, according to our practice, is not open for further discussion here. This court long ago deliberately held (1) that the act, interpreting its words in their ordinary acceptation, prohibits all restraints of interstate commerce by combinations in whatever form, and whether reasonable or unreasonable; (2) the question relates to matters of public policy in reference to commerce among the States and with foreign nations, and Congress alone can deal with the subject; (3) this court would encroach upon the authority of Congress if, under the guise of construction, it should assume to determine a matter of public policy; (4) the parties must go to Congress and obtain an amendment of the Anti-trust Act if they think this court was wrong in its former decisions; and (5) this court cannot and will not judicially legislate, since its function is to declare the law, while it belongs to the legislative department to make the law. Such a course, I am sure, would not have offended the rule of reason."

But my brethren, in their wisdom, have deemed it best to pursue a different course. They have now said to those who condemn our former decisions and who object to all legislative prohibitions of contracts, combinations and trusts in restraint of interstate commerce, "You may now restrain such commerce, provided you are reasonable about it; only take care that the restraint is not undue." The disposition of the case under consideration, according to the views of the defendants, will, it is claimed, quiet and give rest to "the business of the country." On the contrary, I have a strong conviction that it will throw the business of the country into confusion and invite widely extended and harassing litigation, the injurious effects of which will be felt for many years to come. When Congress prohibited every contract, combination or monopoly, in restraint of commerce, it prescribed a simple, definite rule that all could understand, and which could be easily applied by everyone wishing to obey the law, and not to conduct their business in violation of law. But now, it is to be feared, we are to have, in cases without number, the constantly recurring inquiry—difficult to solve by proof—whether the particular contract, combination, or trust involved in each case is or is not an "unreasonable" or "undue" restraint of trade. Congress, in effect, said that there should be no restraint of trade, in any form, and this court solemnly adjudged many years ago that Congress meant what it thus said in clear and explicit words, and that it could not add to the words of the act. But those who condemn the action of Congress are now, in effect, informed that the courts will allow such restraints of interstate commerce as are shown not to be unreasonable or undue.

It remains for me to refer, more fully than I have heretofore done, to another, and, in my judgment—if we look to the future—the most important aspect of this case. That aspect concerns the usurpation by the judicial branch of the Government of the functions of the legislative department. The illustrious men who laid the foundations of our institutions, deemed no part of the National Constitution of more consequence or more essential to the permanancy of our form of government than the provisions under which were distributed the powers of Government among three separate, equal and coordinate departments—legislative, executive, and judicial. This was at that time a new feature of governmental regulation among the nations of the earth, and it is deemed by the people of every section of our own country as most vital in the workings of a representative republic whose Constitution was ordained and established in order to accomplish the objects stated in its Preamble by the means, but only by the means, provided either expressly or by necessary implication, by the instrument itself. No department of that government can constitutionally exercise the powers committed strictly to another and separate department.

I said at the outset that the action of the court in this case might well alarm thoughtful men who revered the Constitution. I meant by this that many things are intimated and said in the court's opinion which will not be regarded otherwise than as sanctioning an invasion by the judiciary of the constitutional domain of Congress—an attempt by interpretation to soften or modify what some regard as a harsh public policy. This court, let me repeat, solemnly adjudged many years ago that it could not, except by "judicial legislation," read words into the Antitrust Act not put there by Congress, and which, being inserted, give it a meaning which the words of the Act, as passed, if properly interpreted, would not justify. The court has decided that it could not thus change a public policy formulated and declared by Congress; that Congress has paramount authority to regulate interstate commerce, and that it alone can change a policy once inaugurated by legislation. The courts have nothing to do with the wisdom or policy of an act of Congress. Their duty is to ascertain the will of Congress, and if the statute embodying the expression of that will is constitutional, the courts must respect it. They have no function to declare a public policy, nor to amend legislative enactments. "What is termed the policy of Government with reference to any particular legislation," as this court has said, "is generally a very uncertain thing, upon which all sorts of opinions, each variant from the other, may be formed by different persons. It is a ground much too unstable upon which to rest the judgment of the court in the interpretation of statutes." *Hadden v. Collector, 5 Wall. 107.* Nevertheless, if I do not misapprehend its opinion, the court has now read into the act of Congress words which are not to be found there, and has thereby done that which it adjudged in 1896 and 1898 could not be done without violating the Constitution, namely, by interpretation of a statute, changed a public policy declared by the legislative department.

After many years of public service at the National Capital, and after a somewhat close observation of the conduct of public affairs, I am impelled to say that there is abroad, in our land, a most harmful tendency to bring about the amending of constitutions and legislative enactments by means alone of judicial construction. As a public policy has been declared by the legislative department in respect of interstate commerce, over which Congress has entire control, under the Constitution, all concerned must patiently submit to what has been lawfully done, until the People of the United States—the source of all National power—shall, in their own time, upon reflection and through the legislative department of the Government, require a change of that policy. There are some who say that it is a part of one's liberty to conduct commerce among the States without being subject to governmental authority. But that would not be liberty, regulated by law, and liberty, which cannot be regulated by law, is not to be desired. The Supreme Law of the Land—which is binding alike upon all—upon Presidents, Congresses, the Courts and the People—gives to Congress, and to Congress alone, authority to regulate interstate commerce, and when Congress forbids any restraint of such commerce, in any form, all must obey its mandate. To overreach the action of Congress merely by judicial construction, that is, by indirection, is a blow at the integrity of our governmental system, and in the end will prove most dangerous to all. Mr. Justice Bradley wisely said, when on this Bench, that illegitimate and unconstitutional practices get their first footing by silent approaches and slight deviations from legal modes of legal procedure. *Boyd v. United States, 116 U.S. 616, 635.* We shall do well to heed the warnings of that great jurist. * * *

NOTES AND QUESTIONS

1. Antitrust is one of the most elusive areas of law. There have been subsequent statutes dealing with anti-competitive behavior, most notably *the Clayton Antitrust Act*, enacted in 1914 to prohibit particular practices such as (1) exclusive sales contracts, (2) local price-cutting to drive out competitors,

(3) particular interlocking directorates and intercorporate stock holdings, and (4) the use of the Sherman act as a weapon against organized labor; the *Robinson–Patman Act*, passed in 1936, which amended the Clayton Act in a further effort to prevent predatory pricing; and the *Hart–Scott–Rodino Antitrust Improvements Act,* passed in 1976, which gives the Federal Trade Commission (FTC) power to prevent anticompetitive mergers, and authorizes states to bring proceedings against federal antitrust violators to recover money damages. As far as general principles are concerned, however, the Sherman Antitrust Act remains the leading federal statute. It has something of a checkered history. It is not at all clear that the original statute was designed radically to alter the law, and some members of the federal legislature in 1890 (a Congress that was thought be excessively friendly to business, if not completely corrupt) seem only to have striven to accommodate public opinion by producing something that could be labeled a "bill to punish the trusts," without much concern for what it was they had actually wrought. For a summary of the history of the Sherman Act, see, e.g. William Letwin, Law and Economic Policy in America: The Evolution of the Sherman Antitrust Act (1965). * * *

A close reading of the *Standard Oil* case will suggest the difficulties of interpreting the act, and the difficulties of attempting to regulate economic behavior in a manner that helped rather than hurt the public interest. Perhaps the most difficult problem is how to allow manufacturers and suppliers to take advantage of economies of scale, which might lower prices to consumers, and yet prevent them from achieving a position of market dominance, where they might be able to raise prices in a manner unfairly to gouge consumers. Where does one draw the line? This is an area in which economists have had much to contribute, and, indeed, the field of law and economics had its first successful and pronounced influence in antitrust law.

2. Do you understand what the holding is in *Standard Oil*? Of what importance was the common law regarding restraints of trade? The case affirmed sanctions against the "Oil Trust," the combination of petroleum producers and distributors founded by one of the great nineteenth century "robber barons," John D. Rockefeller, but it may be most notable for its embracing of the "rule of reason," the notion that whatever the text of the Sherman Act provided, it should only be invoked to prevent "unreasonable" restraints of trade. In an earlier case, *United States v. Trans–Missouri Freight Association,* discussed in both the majority and dissenting opinions in *Standard Oil*, the Supreme Court majority (of which the dissenting Justice Harlan was a part) declared that the text of the Sherman Act meant what it said, and that it ought to be interpreted to render illegal *all* combinations, contracts, etc. in restraint of trade. Does this make it easier to understand what was upsetting Justice Harlan? Who gets this one right? Apparently Justice White's majority opinion enraged both the "progressives," who like Harlan, believed that White emasculated the Sherman Act, and businesspersons, who were left uncertain as to which practices were permitted and which prohibited. Is there something to be said for creating an interpretive strategy which alarms both friends and foes of the Act?

3. How should the Sherman Act be construed, pursuant to the "rule of reason," with regard to modern technology? Should one telecommunications company have been permitted to control virtually all of the telephone service in the United States? Should one personal computer operating system creator be permitted to control 90% of the market, and bundle its own internet browser with that operating system? Should electronic firms from the Far East be permitted to sell electronic goods more cheaply in America than they did in their home countries in order to drive competing American firms out of business? All of these questions and more have recently vexed the interpretive powers of our courts. Who does a better job of ensuring economic progress and prosperity, federal judges or the free market? For further reading on modern antitrust law see, e.g., Robert Bork, The Antitrust Paradox: A Policy at War with Itself (1993), Herbert Hovenkamp, Federal Antitrust Policy: The Law of Competition and Its Practice (2nd ed. 1999), and Richard Posner, Antitrust Law (2nd ed. 2001).

In this last chapter, examining areas apart from business organization, we have actually concentrated more on federal than state law, although state law was the principal focus of our efforts in most of the other chapters. Which does a better job of regulating business—state or federal law?

GLOSSARY

Ab initio from the beginning.

Action of trespass on the case a proceeding in a common law court to recover damages for a wrong committed by another person, a kind of "tort" which causes harm to property.

Accounting can refer either to the appropriate procedures for keeping track of the financial state of a business, or a legal proceeding by which one recovers wrongfully converted funds.

Administrator generally a court-appointed official who handles the affairs of a deceased's estate when there is no competent executor or executrix.

Adventure an undertaking to pursue a business opportunity, means the same in some contexts as joint venture. Those who undertake such a pursuit can be referred to as "co-adventurers."

Affirm to decide that the resolution of a dispute in the lower court was correct.

Aided and abetted terms to describe conduct whereby someone has aided the primary perpetrator of a crime. "Aiding and abetting" liability is a species of "secondary" liability.

Aliquot a fractional part equal in proportion to that already possessed.

Alter ego a doctrine applied in cases of piercing the corporate veil, to find a shareholder or a parent liable for the acts of a corporation or subsidiary when that shareholder or parent has so dominated the corporation or subsidiary that it has no mind, will, or existence of its own, and exists only to do the bidding of the shareholder or parent, and when the shareholder or parent's control has been used to abuse the corporation or subsidiary in a manner that unjustly damages a third party.

Amici curiae literally "friends of the court," parties not directly involved in a case, but who would be affected by the outcome and who seek, with the court's permission, to put their views before the court.

Answer a term used to describe the document a defendant files denying the claims made by the plaintiff in his or her complaint.

Antitrust treble damage litigation refers to the express grant in the Sherman Antitrust Act of 1890 to private plaintiffs damaged by violations of that act to bring actions in the courts to recover three times the amount of economic harm caused.

Appellee the party who prevailed, usually in a trial court, who defends an attempt to overturn that decision.

Appellant the party who loses in a trial court and seeks to overturn that decision.

Appellate Division an intermediate court in New York, composed of judges who sit on the New York Supreme Court, from which appeals are taken to the Court of Appeals, the highest court in New York.

Arbitrage among other things, the buying and selling by parties not involved in the original purchase and sale, to take advantage of different prices offered in different markets for the goods involved.

Arbitration a proceeding for settling disputes used instead of litigation. Generally speaking arbitration is less expensive, less formal, and quicker than a trial.

Arbitrator the official charged with rendering a decision in an arbitration proceeding. The arbitrator will generally hear evidence directly from the parties concerned, and decide on the facts and the applicable law.

Arguendo for the sake of argument. Generally proceeds a contested assertion in which the writer indicates that even if the contested assertion were true, it would not result in the granting of the relief sought by a party.

Arm's length terms used to describe two parties who have equal bargaining power, that is to say a situation where one party is not controlled by or subservient to the other.

Articles of Incorporation see "Corporate Charter."

Assign a term describing the transfer of legal rights one possesses to another.

Barbeyrac a French jurist who wrote a commentary on Puffendorf.

Below a word used to describe the proceedings in an inferior (lower) court by a reviewing court; for example the proceedings in the trial court as described by the appellate court.

Bench trial trial which is conducted without a jury, when the fact-finding is done by a judge.

Bill a term sometimes used to refer to the document filed by a plaintiff that begins a proceeding in an equity court. The plaintiff's prayer for relief in a court of equity.

Blackstone the author of a four-volume famous treatise on the common law of England.

Bona fide genuine, true, authentic (literally "good faith")

Bracton the author of the first comprehensive treatise on the laws and customs of England, published in the Thirteenth Century

Brief a document containing the legal arguments of a party.

Burden of proof requirement to prove the existence of particular facts. Generally speaking, where an elusive fact, such as a question of fairness, is involved, where the burden of proof is placed may often determine the outcome of a case. Generally the plaintiff has the burden of proving the truth of the allegations that he or she makes, and the defendant has the burden of proving any affirmative defenses to those allegations. In a civil case the burden of proof is generally by a preponderance of the evidence, and, in a criminal case, the government has the burden of proving the guilt of the defendant beyond a reasonable doubt.

Business purpose test a requirement that no longer exists in Delaware, but which is still to be found in some states that does not permit freezing out minority shareholders without a valid business purpose, such as a saving in taxes or regulatory compliance costs.

"Buy-sell" agreement an agreement by which one party agrees to buy and the other agrees to sell, usually on the happening of a particular contingency, such as when a shareholder in a close corporation wishes to divest him or herself of his or her shares.

Bylaws a document which specifies the rules governing the operation of a corporation. The Corporate Charter specifies the fundamental rules governing the operation of a corporation, and it is something like a "Constitution" for the Corporation. The Bylaws might be thought of as governing the day to day operations of a corporation, and are a bit analogous to legislation for the corporation.

Bynkershoek a treatise on the law of nations (that body of law common to all nations) published in the Eighteenth Century.

Call options rights to acquire shares at a particular price, good for a limited period of time.

Capitalism the economic system which prevails in the Unites States characterized principally by the private ownership of the means of production.

Cause technical term referring to wrongdoing.

Cause of action a claim to be able to recover because of a breach of legal duty committed by another party.

Certiorari process by which an appeal is granted to bring a case before the United States Supreme Court.

Chancellor the presiding judge of a chancery court. In Delaware the most important judge who presides over trials involving corporations.

Chancery the trial court in equity; a court which administers the principles of equity. In Delaware the Chancery is the trial court, which hears cases without a jury, and which is the court before whom are brought disputes involving corporations incorporated in Delaware.

Civil action litigation that is not criminal in nature, and which generally seeks monetary compensation for harm caused to a plaintiff.

Class action a civil action brought by or in the name of a group of persons similarly situated (for example, all the common stock holders of a particular corporation).

Code a collection of statutes.

Collateral a term used to describe goods in which a creditor who has advanced funds assumes a security interest.

Common stock ordinary shares of stock, generally with voting rights and a claim on the corporate assets if any remain after creditors and preferred stockholders are paid.

Common Law a term generally used to refer to the decisions by English courts, setting forth rules to be applied in cases involving property, contracts, torts, corporations, and many other matters. Common law is sometimes also referred to as "unwritten law," to distinguish it from statutes (the acts of legislatures), but, of course, the judicial decisions which comprise the common law are generally to be found in written reports, and referred to in published treatises and other compilations.

Common Shares or **Common Stock** the legal name for typical equity ownership in a corporation. Common stock generally has voting rights, may give its owner the right to collect dividends, and is entitled to a portion of any assets remaining if the corporation is dissolved, after payment to creditors and preferred shareholders.

Common weal the good of all. A "commonwealth" is a government devoted to the good of all, thus the official names, for example, of the Commonwealth of Massachusetts, or the Commonwealth of Virginia.

Complaint a term which describes the document which a plaintiff files to begin litigation.

Concomitant resulting from a prior existing set of facts.

Condition precedent a set of facts which must come into existence before an obligation ripens into a legally binding one.

Conversion theft.

Convertible Subordinated Debentures debt instruments which reflect an obligation of the corporation that is junior to other debts, and which may be converted into shares of stock.

Consideration a term from the law of contracts which refers to what is required to be given in exchange for performance by the other party.

Constitutional a term which generally refers to something in accordance with the requirements of the United States Constitution, but which can also be used (especially in England) to refer to conduct in accordance with the required governmental procedures.

Consolidation a combination of two or more legal entities into one.

Convertible Preferred Stock are shares of preferred stock which may be converted into common stock at the option of the owner.

Corporate Charter (also called "Articles of Incorporation") the basic document which sets forth the fundamental provisions governing the operation of a corporation.

Coterminous equal to, including within its terms the same thing.

Course of treaty fancy way of saying in negotiations with to accomplish a particular legal purpose.

Cumulative voting a method of voting shares required in some states, permitted in others, which makes it easier for minority shareholders to gain representation on the Board of Directors. For further details see Chapter Five, Section E, note 5 following the *Campbell v. Loews* case.

Custodian particularly in Delaware, an official appointed by the court of chancery to take charge of a close corporation when there is a deadlock among the shareholders.

Declaration the document filed in court by the plaintiff which alleges that the defendant caused the plaintiff a particular type of harm.

Declaratory relief or **Declaratory Judgment** a decision by a court clarifying the law applicable to a particular transaction, although not ordering any particular relief.

Deadlocked unable to reach a decision, generally because of a tie vote among those with the power to decide.

Defalcations acts of wrongdoing.

Default a term to describe the legal rule that will be applied in the absence of an agreement between parties that a different rule will be applied.

Defendant the person who defends a lawsuit, either one brought by a private person who alleges that the defendant has damaged him or her, or a criminal proceeding brought by the government.

Defendant in Error a term sometimes used to refer to the appellee, the party who wins in a lower court, and who defends an appeal from that decision.

Dehors outside of, beyond the boundaries of.

Demand note a document reflecting a promise to pay a sum of money when the person to whom it is owed requests it.

De novo as if it had not been done before. (More or less literally "as if it were new.")

Depredation state of operating as a predator or wrongdoer.

Diana the Roman goddess of the hunt.

Dictum a part of a judicial opinion which is not necessary to support the court's holding. A pronouncement which is not necessarily binding.

Digests a term that generally refers to collections of cases or legal rules, especially those of Rome.

Dissent an opinion filed by a judge who disagrees with the conclusions reached by a majority of the court of which he or she is a member. The dissenting judge writes in the belief either that someday a majority of his or her court will change its opinion, or perhaps in the belief that some other court may adopt his or her views.

Dissolution the legal termination of a business, in the course of which creditors are paid, and if any funds remain they are distributed among the owners of the business.

Diversity, or, more properly, **Diversity Jurisdiction** the ability to bring an action in a federal court when the plaintiff and defendant are citizens of different states and when the amount in controversy exceeds a sum set by federal legislation (currently $75,000).

Divisibility said of a document or agreement where some provisions might not be legally enforceable but other provisions are.

Dower a portion of the deceased husband's estate that by law, was provided for the widow.

Draconian excessively and impermissibly harsh.

Due diligence the process by which a tender offeror or other party undertakes to assure him or herself of the true value of a corporation, usually by examining the books and records of the corporation and by interviewing corporate officials.

Election of Remedies choosing under which legal theory one wishes to proceed. Occasionally the choice of one theory will imply the unavailability of others.

Eleemosynary a nearly archaic term meaning "charitable."

En banc involving all the judges of a particular court. A term often used to describe a hearing by all the appellate judges.

English constitution the accepted practices of the English government, the laws and customs of England.

Engrossing is cornering the market in an essential of life (for example, bread) in a manner calculated to raise the price beyond which the market price normally had been in order to make exorbitant profits.

Enterprise Liability the concept that a particular enterprise ought to be responsible for the damages it causes.

Equitable a term used to describe a situation dictated by fairness or equity.

Equity a term with many meanings, including but not limited to 1) a type of court first found in England and adopted in the United States which has special jurisdiction to order persons to do particular things (injunctions), to nullify documents, or, in Delaware, to decide matters having to do with Corporations. Equity courts operate without juries, and the equity judge (called the "Chancellor" in Delaware) both finds the facts and determines the law. 2) the amount invested in a particular enterprise (for a business the owners equity is that amount the owners have put into the business), and 3) the application of a fair solution to a dispute (to do "equity" is to do that which is fair).

Estop, Estopped to have committed an act which results in an "estoppel," or the prevention of a party from acting in a manner inconsistent with representations made or actions taken.

Estoppel an equitable concept invoked in a great variety of legal situations when one party makes representations to another on which that person relies to his or her detriment and the person making such representations is required, in the interest of justice, to make good on his or her representations.

Exclusive having the sole possession of particular jurisdiction or rights.

Exceptions the formal objections that the party who loses in the trial court makes to the proceedings in that court, and which form the basis of an appeal.

Executor, Executrix terms used to refer to a man or woman who administers the estate of a deceased person, and who has been named in a will by that person for that task.

Expectancy a property interest that would revert to an heir or to a tenant at the end of a lease.

Ex post happening after a particular event.

Fairness opinion an assessment rendered usually by outside investment bankers or analysts regarding the value of a business, or of shares of a corporation.

Fait accompli fancy way of saying a "done deal."

Feasibility study a document seeking to determine the value and advantages of a particular acquisition or project.

Fiduciary one who has a legal duty to put someone else's interests ahead of his or her own.

Fiduciary out a provision in a merger agreement which allows the directors of a target company to escape from the agreement when a better offer is made by a different party if the directors' fiduciary duties to the stockholders would require them to accept such a better offer.

Fleta an English law treatise published in the Seventeenth Century.

Forum the federal, state, or local body having jurisdiction to hear a particular dispute.

Fora plural of "forum."

Form of proxy official name for a document that requests a shareholder to grant a proxy.

Forstalling According to Sir William Blackstone, the great commentator on English common law, "Forstalling [is] the buying or contracting for any merchandize or victual coming in the way to market; or dissuading persons from bringing their goods or provisions there; or persuading them to enhance the price ..."

Franchise the legal right to operate a particular business, granted by the owner of that business to the franchisee.

Fraud a term that is deliberately never precisely defined by courts, but which describes the action of someone who knowingly makes wrongful representations to another, generally violating a duty of truthfulness which the law imposes on such a person.

General Sessions one of many names used to refer to a trial court.

Hearsay in evidence law, offering as testimony to prove truth a statement made regarding statements of others. Generally speaking such testimony is rejected as not reliable and not offering the best evidence available.

Holmes Oliver Wendell Holmes, Jr. (1841–1935) the man generally regarded as the most brilliant and influential legal scholar the United States has ever produced. He was an Associate Justice of the United States Supreme Court, and of the Supreme Judicial Court of Massachusetts before that, as well as a Professor at the Harvard Law School. His most famous work was *The Common Law* (1881), in which he argued that common law judges were actually functioning as legislators, fashioning rules that made the law better at meeting the needs of the times.

Hypothecate to offer a particular item (such as negotiable instruments, stocks, or bonds) to a creditor who will advance funds, at the same time assuming a security interest in the items hypothecated.

Impeachment a process by which an official, usually a member of the executive or judicial branch, is removed for misconduct by a legislature.

Illiquid refers to assets for which there is no ready market, so that it is difficult or impossible to sell them.

Indemnify to hold someone harmless from the consequences of his or another's actions; to make sure that the person damaged is made whole in a financial sense.

Indenture a legal document which specifies the duties owed to a creditor who advances funds.

Indictment a proceeding issuing from a grand jury, charging a defendant with the commission of a crime.

In futuro for the future.

Injunction an order from an equity court requiring a party to perform or not to perform a particular act.

Insolvency a situation in which a business does not have the resources to meet its debts as they become due (sometimes called the "equity" test for insolvency) or a situation in which a business's balance sheet reveals that the businesses debts are greater than its assets (sometimes called the "bankruptcy" or "balance sheet" test of insolvency).

Internal Affairs Doctrine a generally accepted principle of the law of corporations that the rules which govern the relationship among shareholders, directors, and officers are those specified by the state of incorporation.

Inter alia among other things.

Interlocutory appeal a situation where one of the parties seeks relief from an appellate court to correct legal errors by a trial court before the resolution of a dispute by that court.

In toto totally.

Ipso facto by that fact, by itself.

Jointly and Severally a situation in which several persons are each responsible for an entire sum owed, but in which such persons may assert rights against each other if they are required to make good such an obligation. Partners are generally jointly and severally responsible for the debts of the partnership.

Judicial notice the practice whereby a court recognizes a factual situation without the necessity of a party having to prove it.

Justinian's Institutes a famous Roman treatise on the law.

Key man life insurance a policy insuring the life of a person who is important in operating a business, with amounts payable to the business, or, in some cases, to particular creditors.

Lawyer-client privilege the traditional doctrine by which anything said to a lawyer by a client (except for advice sought in connection with the anticipated commission of a crime) is to be kept confidential and cannot be discovered by prosecutors.

Legal redress relief from authorities, such as a court order.

License permission to use a particular good in a particular manner.

Lien a claim to property resulting from an unpaid obligation.

Liquid refers to assets for which there is a ready market, so that it is easy to convert them to cash.

Liquidation dissolution, termination of the existence of a business, and distribution of the assets remaining after debts to creditors have been met.

Locke the author of a famous seventeenth-century treatise on government.

Master in chancery an equity court official charged with determining the facts and making a recommendation as to the relief that ought to be granted.

Merger the process by which one corporation combines with another.

Misappropriate to steal; to take possession of or convert to one's own use without legal right.

Misdemeanor a crime less serious than a felony.

Municipal a term sometimes used to refer to the law or regulations of a particular jurisdiction.

Negligence a very general term used to refer to a failure to perform a duty owed to another person. Generally speaking negligence is a concept of the law of torts (harm caused to strangers) and negligence is a failure to act with the care of a reasonably prudent person.

Notice the supplying of information in advance about action that is to be taken in the future.

Obligees persons to whom one owes a duty.

Occupancy an archaic term meaning the acquisition of possession.

Option the right to create a legal relationship in the future.

Outside directors term used to refer to directors who are not otherwise part of corporate management, so, for example, save for their directorships, they are not officers of the corporation.

Pac-Man Defense a tactic to resist a tender offer by making a tender offer for the entity that is seeking to acquire your corporation. Named after the video game which offers the player the opportunity to turn about and attack his attackers.

Pandects a term referring to a collection of fifty books compiled in the 7th century on Roman law.

Panel the group of appellate judges hearing a particular case.

Paralogistic illogical.

Parent a corporation which owns one hundred percent of another corporation. The one hundred percent owned corporation is referred to as the subsidiary.

Par Value somewhat archaic term used to refer to the amount of a share's value which comprised the original subscription price. It now refers to that part of the share's value assigned to stated capital.

Per se meeting all the requirements of a particular legal status, literally "by itself."

Petitioner a term sometimes used to refer to a party who appeals an adverse judgment in a trial court.

Pledgee a creditor to whom collateral has been given to secure a debt.

Plaintiff the person who initiates a lawsuit against a defendant.

Poison Pill also known as a "shareholder rights plan." A defensive tactic to thwart hostile takeover bids by granting shareholders the right to purchase shares of their own company or shares of an acquirer at a deep discount. This makes takeovers more difficult and more expensive, hence the descriptive term "poison pill," indicating that it becomes more difficult for the acquirer to swallow the target. Generally poison pills may be cancelled by the target's Board of Directors.

Post hoc literally after the fact. Something that occurs following an important event.

Pre-emptive having the first opportunity to accept an offer.

Pre-emptive rights the right to acquire an aliquot portion of any new issue of securities in order to preserve the same percentage of ownership interest initially possessed in a corporation's stock.

Preferred Stock shares on which dividends are paid before dividends are paid on the common stock, and which have a preferential claim on the corporate assets upon dissolution of the corporation.

"Pre-packaged" bankruptcy process by which, pursuant to an agreement, the assets of an insolvent business are acquired by a third party, the creditors of the business receive some compensation, and the debts of the insolvent corporation are cancelled.

Pretext not the actual motive or reason for a particular action.

Prima facie literally "on its first appearance," meaning essentially what one first assumes from a given state of facts.

Private right of action a proceeding initiated by a private party for relief from harm caused by the violation of a statute. If a statute specifically grants private parties the right to seek such relief it is known as an express private right of action, if such relief is not mandated by statute, the right to bring such an action may still be implied by the courts, as it was for many years in the case of violations of sections 10(b) and 14(a) of the 1934 Securities and Exchange Act.

Privity the situation where two parties have actually had contact with each other.

Privy to have direct knowledge of.

Pro forma merely going through the motions, not really doing what is actually necessary.

Prophylactic designed to prevent harm.

Prospectus a document which the 1933 Securities Act requires to be given to prospective purchasers of a new issue of stock, setting forth particulars regarding the issuer and its operations.

Provisional director in Delaware, a person who may be appointed by the Court of Chancery to act as a director of a close corporation when the directors are divided and unable to manage the corporation for the benefit of the shareholders generally.

Proxy a legal device by which a shareholder gives another person the power to vote his or her shares.

Proxy Statement a document which is required to accompany a request for the granting of proxies, which contains information required by the Securities and Exchange Commission.

Put the opposite of a call option. A put gives a shareholder the right to sell stock at a particular price.

Puffendorf a treatise on the law of nations (that body of law common to all nations) published in the Seventeenth Century.

Quorum the number of persons who must be present before a particular body may act.

Raison D'etre French term meaning literally "reason to be," colloquially "purpose."

Ratio decidendi reason or reasons that support the conclusion reached by a court.

Receiver an official named by a court to manage a business that has become insolvent, usually with the aim of ending it and distributing remaining assets to creditors, but sometimes simply to care for it until the owners can resolve their differences.

Recission an equitable proceeding to cancel a legal arrangement and return the situation to where it was before the legal arrangement was made. Recission is often available in cases of fraud.

Recissory calculated to put a damaged party back to the position he or she occupied before the legal injury in question.

Recitals a term occasionally used to refer to provisions in a document, particularly introductory provisions.

Registered owners those owning shares of stock whose ownership is reflected on the books of the corporation.

Registration Statement a document required by the 1933 Securities Act to be filed by an issuer of new securities with the Securities and Exchange Commission, setting forth particulars regarding the issuer and its history.

Republican partaking of the character of a republic, a government in which the public good prevails.

Representatives those who act in the place of another, for example the heirs or assigns of a tenant.

Remanded returned to a lower court for further proceedings consistent with the directions of the remanding court.

Remit pay.

Rescind to take back or cancel.

Respondent a name for the party who prevails in the court below who contests an attempt to appeal that result by a petitioner.

Respondeat superior ancient doctrine of the common law which holds the master responsible for the consequences of the acts or a servant, or a principal responsible for the consequences of the acts of an agent.

Restitution putting a damaged party back to the position he or she occupied before the injury.

Reversion the interest in property that remains in the ultimate owner following the expiration of a lease.

Rubric generally a category or heading of a document.

Security for expenses a statutory requirement that before being permitted to proceed to bring a civil action a plaintiff must prove, usually by posting a bond, that he or she can meet any court costs that may be imposed if the plaintiff's law suit proves to be without merit.

Security Interest a conditional right to ownership possessed usually by a vendor in property sold on the installment plan. If the person to whom the property is sold fails to pay for the property the security interest enables the vendor to take possession of the property. Once the purchaser pays the full purchase price for the property the security interest of the vendor ceases.

Seriatim one following after another.

Settled out of court terms describing the situation when parties decide to agree to end the dispute that has been in litigation between them, usually involving the payment of money by one party to another.

Settlement an agreement by the parties to litigation to end their dispute, which often involves the payment of an agreed-upon sum by one party to the other.

Sham a series of falsehoods designed to defraud or deceive others.

Share see "stock."

Special Term a name for a trial court in New York.

Specific performance a remedy granted by an equity court ordering a party actually to perform acts that were promised.

Stakeholders term that refers to the various constituencies of a corporation, including shareholders, employees, creditors, and perhaps also customers and the community.

Standing a status recognized by a court as entitling one to bring a cause of action before the court.

Stock an ownership interest in a corporation, sometimes referred to as a "share" or a "share of stock."

Stock option the right to acquire shares of stock at a particular price (sometimes simply referred to as an "option.")

Sub judice before the court.

Subsidiary a corporation which is one hundred percent owned by another corporation. The owner of the subsidiary is referred to as a parent.

Sui generis unique, of its own particular kind.

Summary judgment a procedure whereby a trial court resolves a dispute without having to find the facts, because even if the plaintiffs factual allegations are taken as true, the law provides no remedy.

Super majority more than a majority.

Supra Latin for "above." Lawyers use the term to refer to something that was cited earlier in a document.

Surplus in corporate accounting a term which generally refers to the amount by which accumulated earnings exceed accumulated debts and liabilities.

Tenant in Common someone who leases property with others similarly situated.

Tender Offer an invitation to shareholders to tender their shares for purchase by a tender offeror who seeks to acquire a particular percentage of share ownership at a particular price.

Tippee in securities fraud cases, one who receives inside information from a corporate fiduciary who breaches his fiduciary duty in conveying the information.

Title ownershop of property.

Traversed contested or denied.

Treaty a reinsurance agreement.

Trust the placing of property in the hands of someone who will hold it for the benefit of another.

Trustee a person who has charge of particular property and who is required to protect it in the interests of another person or persons.

Trustee in bankruptcy the official charged by the court with accumulating and managing the assets of a bankrupt, for eventual distribution to creditors.

Trust funds funds held for the benefit of another.

Unclean hands a doctrine used by equity courts to deny relief to plaintiffs who have themselves committed inequitable or wrongful acts.

Ultra vires literally "outside the power." A legal doctrine which forbids a corporation from operating in a manner which goes beyond the powers or purpose granted to it in its charter. Generally speaking charters are now granted allowing corporations to engage in any lawful activity, so that, for most practical purposes, the *ultra vires* doctrine is dead.

Underletting subletting, what happens when a lessee leases property to a third party.

Vacated set aside.

Verdict the decision reached by a jury in favor of a plaintiff or a defendant.

Vesting a situation in which a legal right has ripened, or a process by which a legislature or parties decide to give jurisdiction over a particular matter to a particular forum or court.

Voting trust an arrangement whereby a third party is put in a position to vote shares of stock owned by another. This might be done to secure a debt, to consolidate power in a block of shares owned by a group of family members or related parties, or in order to avoid conflicts of interest. State statutes generally limit the time in which voting trusts can be in effect.

Warranty a representation by a vendor that the goods sold are fit for a particular purpose, or a representation that the terms of a document are accurate.

World Wide Web a nearly-archaic term for what is now known as the "internet" or simply "the net."

Writ of attachment a proceeding to gain possession of property.

Index

References are to Pages

---

†